# ALEXANDER CRUMMELL

# *Alexander Crummell*

## A Study of
## Civilization & Discontent

Wilson Jeremiah Moses

The University of Massachusetts Press    Amherst

Frontispiece: Alexander Crummell, from an engraving in *Harper's Weekly,*
April 4, 1866. Courtesy of the Rhode Island Historical Society.

Copyright © 1989 by Oxford University Press; © 1992 by Wilson Jeremiah Moses
First paperback edition published in 1992 by the University of Massachusetts Press,
through arrangement with Oxford University Press
This book is published with the support and cooperation of
Boston University and the University of Massachusetts at Boston
Printed in the United States of America
LC 91–41158
ISBN 0–87023–796–9

Library of Congress Cataloging-in-Publication Data

Moses, Wilson Jeremiah, 1942–
    Alexander Crummell: a study of civilization and discontent /
Wilson Jeremiah Moses. — 1st pbk. ed.
        p.   cm.
    Originally published: New York : Oxford University Press, 1989.
    Includes bibliographical references and index.
    ISBN 0–87023–796–9 (pbk.: alk. paper)
    1. Crummell, Alexander, 1819–1898. 2. Black nationalism—United
States—History—19th century. 3. Pan-Africanism—History—19th
century. 4. Afro-Americans—Biography.   I. Title.
[E185.97.C87M67   1992]
973.8'092—dc20
    [B]                                                91–41158
    CIP

British Library Cataloguing in Publication data are available.

In memoriam
William Heard Moses
1910–1983

# Acknowledgments

A project such as this is never brought to completion without the support of numerous other scholars, librarians, archivists, and students, who willingly share the products of their own research, collegially exchange ideas, or perform other tasks requiring diligence and common sense. Thanks are due to Clotilda Barnett, George H. Bass, Nell V. Bellamy, E. E. Bigglestone, Randall Burkett, Todd Cavalier, Jay Coughtry, Adelaide Cromwell, Hadassah Davis, Anani Dzidzienyo, William Ferraro, John Hope Franklin, Kevin Gaines, Henry Louis Gates, Jr., William Gravely, E. S. Leedham Green, Carleton Hayden, Eleanor Hearn, K. Melvin Hendrix, Richard G. Hewlett, Rhett S. Jones, Amalie M. Kass, Edith Lee, Leon Litwack, William G. McLoughlin, Donna Mitchell, John Oldfield, James Patterson, F. Garner Ranney, Natalie Robinson, Louis Rosenfeld, Milton Sernett, Tom Shick, Carl Stockton, John Thompson, and Vernon Williams.

Research for this biography was funded by grants from the National Endowment for the Humanities, Southern Fellowships Fund, American Council of Learned Societies, American Philosophical Society, National Research Council, Ford Foundation, and National Academy of Sciences. I also acknowledge the support of the Brown University Library, Southern Methodist University Library, Library of Congress, New York Public Library, New-York Historical Society, Rhode Island Historical Society, Cambridge University Library, Library of Rhodes House in Oxford University, Archives of Oberlin College, Widener Library of Harvard University, Columbia University Library, Johns Hopkins University Library, Archives of the Diocese of Maryland, Archives of the Episcopal Church, Episcopal Seminary of the Southwest, Howard University Library, Fourah Bay College Library, Archives of the Republic of Liberia, University of Iowa Library, Mugar Library of Boston University, Massachusetts Historical Society, and Dr. Williams Library.

Very special thanks are due to Otey Scruggs, who offered me his advice and encouragement at the earliest stages, and to Richard Blackett, who came up with several suggestions for improvements. My wife, Maureen Connor Moses, assisted me with proofreading and did major editing on the bibliography. She also helped to prepare the index, as she did for my two previous books.

I wish to thank Curtis Church, who originally accepted the manuscript before leaving Oxford University Press. William P. Sisler, who inherited the manuscript as something of an orphan, honorably guided it toward publication. Thanks also are in order to Susan Meigs and Irene Pavitt, for their painstaking efforts with the manuscript.

# Contents

# ALEXANDER CRUMMELL

# 1

# Introduction

Tyranny of the majority was more than an abstract concept to the slender, black youth driving a delivery wagon through the streets of riot-torn New York in the long, hot summer of 1834. The violence he observed that summer, and at other crucial points in his early development, led him to his later obsession with "law and order" and his suspicion of the democratic instincts of the American common man. The incendiary pamphlet *David Walker's Appeal* was well known in the abolitionist circles in which Alexander Crummell spent his youth, and Walker's bitter attacks on the hypocrisy of Jeffersonian democracy anticipated the suspicious attitude towards democratic theory that prevailed in Crummell's writings. He was exposed during adolescence to the drunken bois-terousness and racial chauvinism of American Fourth of July celebrations. In the era of Jacksonian democracy, he had good reason to question the nature of American egalitarianism. He learned, as all black children did, that white peo-ple could be dangerous, not only the slavecatchers, but the ordinary people of the city.

Although his parents were respectable and enterprising people, they were forced to keep their family in the most sordid section of New York, and the people with whom Crummell came into contact as a child, whether white or black, were not always worthy of emulation. To resist the harmful influences by which he was surrounded as a youth, he had to become somewhat morally rigid and isolated. Constant exposure to prejudice and racial insults made the sensitive and bookish lad bitter and resentful. As a result, he developed a prickly disposition and often found it difficult to make or to retain friendships—whether black or white. There was no question of his brilliance as a writer or of his capacity for original thought. He had actual genius when it came to turning clichés back upon themselves. And he formulated a complex ideology of his

3

own that stressed free will and individualism, as well as ethnic responsibility. Unfortunately, all too many black leaders of recent years have found it impossible to bring these three ideas into harmony.

Alexander Crummell's name is hardly a household word. Unlike his more celebrated contemporary Frederick Douglass, Crummell did not leave a legacy of three autobiographies, nor was he given to publicizing himself through the retelling of thrilling autobiographical incidents. Crummell's adventures certainly contained enough colorful material to have made a thrilling and engaging narrative, but he was not the brilliant impresario that Douglass was. Neither did he possess the clever opportunism and spirit of enterprise of William Wells Brown, who referred to him as "punctilious."[1] Crummell's personality is not always easy to bear. The logic of his discourse is often unfamiliar to us, although it is systematic and consistent within the worldview that he espoused. Many of his ideas are offensive to the modern reader. For example, his assumptions about what was natural and normal in the relations between man and wife were conservative even for his own times. The authoritarianism and elitism of his political philosophy are also difficult for us to understand or to accept. Crummell was a stern, unbending, Miltonic figure, darkly brooding, with a sometimes smoldering and sometimes explosive passion.

During the early decades of this century, Crummell was mentioned in some of the better-known accounts of black American history, but around the Second World War he began to fade into relative obscurity as a rising generation of scholars apparently found him uninteresting. Perhaps they were bored by the formal tone of his discourse or by the puritanical ethic he represented. Or it may be that they righteously dropped him from the textbooks, driven by the same impulse that led them to neglect Marcus Garvey. His black chauvinism and racial separatism were no doubt perceived as a dangerous distraction from the civil rights struggle by a generation who were correctly focusing their scholarship on the fight for desegregation. The neglect of Crummell coincided with a tendency to downplay the importance of Garvey, whose still smoldering Back to Africa Movement was an embarrassment. Black nationalist ideas were too easily exploited by the likes of Senator Theodore G. Bilbo, whose politics of "African repatriation" constituted an insult and a threat. But even a generation earlier, only five years after Crummell's death, W. E. B. Du Bois had written in *The Souls of Black Folk*, "His name today, in this broad land, means little . . . And herein lies the tragedy of the age: not that men are poor,—all men know something of poverty; not that men are wicked,—who is good? not that men are ignorant,—what is Truth? Nay but that men know so little of men."[2]

As Du Bois observed, much of Crummell's energy, throughout his life, was consumed in a bitter struggle for recognition from white and black alike. The often unconscious hostility of white Americans to any sort of intellectual pretensions by a black person is readily detectable in the correspondence of Crummell's ecclesiastical superiors, many of them decent, well-meaning individuals, who viewed him as a sinister, sardonic, and disruptive force. Black people took their cues from the whites and reacted accordingly. Most people correctly perceived him as an embittered man, who created many of his own problems by refusing to stay in his place. Admittedly he was hard to get along with and determined to outdo his white associates in exemplifying Victorian bourgeois culture. For this he was criticized by whites and blacks alike, and I have known black scholars literally to hoot with derision on hearing of his efforts to place Longfellow and Coleridge in the hands of nineteenth-century African schoolboys.

The name of Alexander Crummell is still unknown to most Americans, although it has begun, of late, to reappear in scholarly treatments of Afro-American history. Du Bois's lament is just as appropriate today as it was eighty years ago, however, for Crummell, despite his remarkable accomplishments, his powerful will, and his tragic love for his people, failed to impress his name on their consciousness. He offended too often with his absolutely domineering and possessive love, a love that could bruise or even strangle in its embrace. Most people found it difficult to endure such love, although even critics and enemies confessed to admiring him. He was a disconcerting anomaly, a black man of letters before the Civil War, knowledgeable in the classics at a time when the average black American was an illiterate slave. He studied in England, where he was graduated from Queens College, Cambridge in 1853. He was an ordained priest of the orderly, solemn Episcopal church, at a time when the religion of the black masses was characterized by evangelical exuberance and frenzy. He spent nearly twenty years in Liberia as a missionary, an educator, and a public moralist, aspiring to the position of a West African Hamilton or Jay, at a time when many black Americans were struggling for forty acres and a mule.[3] Returning to the United States in 1872, he moved to Washington, D.C., where he spent the remaining twenty-five years of his life. There he finally came to be recognized as one of the more prominent Afro-American intellectuals, and he founded the American Negro Academy shortly before his death. He was the author of three published volumes of political sermons, numerous provocative articles, several hundred unpublished tracts, and a voluminous (often vitriolic) correspondence. And yet, during the late 1960s, when black studies programs were springing up all over the United States, he was largely ignored. While scholars were commenting on "the rediscovery of black nationalism," their studies of the movement often neglected one of its more significant nineteenth-century exponents. Even as late as 1980, historians of the black experience who should have been well-acquainted with his work continued to refer to him as obscure.[4]

There was, there had to be, a ruthlessness in his quest for learning. As a young priest, he experienced the perpetual nightmare of the man of letters—poverty, envy, and ridicule. In his own scant autobiographical accounts we read of how he was jeered at and assaulted by whites, simply for desiring a classical education. Men like Crummell were no better understood by their fellow Afro-Americans. They were held up as examples of the "miseducation of the Negro," even by those who should have known better. They were ridiculed for pursuing impractical goals and accused of mindlessly imitating white people. But Crummell was neither an impractical man, nor a mindless imitator. True, his classical education did not help him much when it came to providing for his wife and children, but in the course of his life he tried his hand at several useful pursuits. He was, by turns, a yeoman farmer, a small business-man, a pioneer, and an explorer. According to all reports, he administered a successful program in agricultural education while at Mt. Vaughan High School in Liberia. Nonetheless, as an old man he lived to hear his ideal misrepresented and parodied by Booker T. Washington, who spoke of ragged ministers, their heads full of Greek and formal theology, and their yards full of weeds.[5]

Crummell's intellectual accomplishments represent an interweaving of sev-eral traditions that are too often studied in isolation from one another. While Crummell may profitably be viewed as a Victorian intellectual, an American evangelical, a Liberian nationalist, or an Afro-American leader, it is better not to reduce him to any one of these identities. He is all of these things and more, just as every human personality is greater than the sum of its parts. His achievements were exceptional, and such achievements under such conditions are beyond the capabilities of most people. But if the fact that he earned a Cambridge degree were the most significant thing one could say about Crum-mell, he would be interesting merely as a freak or a prodigy, or an exception to rules. Crummell did not behave as if he considered Cambridge the most important experience in his life, and it is not the most important element in my interpretation of it.

I have tried to avoid forcing Crummell's ideology into frameworks that have evolved in the field of black studies over the past twenty years. In fact, I hope that I have successfully achieved a critique of these and other contemporary biases from the perspective of Alexander Crummell's values and beliefs. At all times, I have tried to bear in mind the peculiar hostility of the present age to the fundamental assumptions that Crummell held with respect to life and mo-rality. In *The Culture of Narcissism,* Christopher Lasch has described the ban-alization of social thought in contemporary American society.[6] Our age is marked by a great emphasis on personal freedom, a reflexive rejection of authority, and an adolescent hostility to any discussion of sexual restraint. These tendencies are readily visible in the rise of bastardized and trivialized Freudianism, cul-tural relativism, and the often childish iconoclasm of "modern art." Scholarly interest in black Americans has often been associated with the cult of modern-ism that has dominated so much of twentieth-century intellectual life.[7] The cult of primitivism in modern art, symbolized by Gershwin and Picasso, has also been sympathetic to "black culture." Such students of black American life as Melville Herskovitz, Eugene Genovese, Lawrence Levine, and Herbert Gutman have seen black studies as a field from which they might launch attacks on conservative cultural establishments and the remaining vestiges of Victorian sexual morality. Black studies has been dominated by liberal, egalitarian, and antiestablishmentarian modes of thought. Thus Crummell, who was conservative, elitist and establishmentarian, fits neither the academic nor the popular stereotype of black culture.

He condemned what he called "blatant American democracy, the vagaries of socialism, the wild dreams of communism." Even more, he condemned "anarchy" and "antinomianism." Like many thinkers of his generation he believed that humanity was caught in a life and death struggle with powerful forces of nature, capable of reducing mankind to savagery unless kept under strictest control. Crummell was described even by his Victorian contemporaries as "rigid," a charge he did not deny. "I am proud of this criticism" he once wrote. "It is evidence that I tolerated no iniquity, and that I rebuked depravity."[8] We may search for flaws in his character, and inevitably some chinks in the armor will be found. His writings doubtless reveal many of the unconscious and semiconscious thoughts that plague even the most righteous of Puritans. To any Freudian analyst, who might discover signs of libidinous longings beneath his proud exterior, Crummell would have made a ready response. He would have offered his own sinfulness as proof of the infinite evil of which humanity is capable. His lapses would simply have proven the need for iron will and strenuous control over the passions. Although Victorian civilization had its discontents, contemporary society has yet to prove its superiority to that of the supposedly stern and obsessive Victorians.

Since I have made the point elsewhere, I need not belabor in this study the point that Crummell and his black contemporaries—including Blyden, Delany, Africanus Horton, and Frederick Douglass—shared with Americans and Europeans an inflated idea of the triumphs of nineteenth-century civilization. Civilization implied a historical process, whereby mankind progressively learned the laws of physical, moral, and economic science. The laws were universal— they did not belong to any race or culture. They were discovered, not invented, and hence not the creation of any race or nation. The fact that Europeans were farther along in the process of civilization did not mean that they had been more intelligent, inventive, or creative, merely that they had *submitted* earlier to the divine and natural law and were now carried along in the current of inevitable progress.[9]

Crummell's black nationalism reflected the unilinear conception of cultural progress that was shared by influential nineteenth-century social thinkers, from Karl Marx to Matthew Arnold. There was very little room in his philosophy for an appreciation of African attitudes towards family life. African religious customs could be viewed as nothing but the most appalling error. Crummell's "common-sense" view of African culture told him that African technological development was retarded. When he saw that Africans did not share North Atlantic marital, familial, and religious values, he believed them to be "backward." When he observed that the Africans lacked military or technological capacities that Americans and Europeans possessed, he attributed their absence to religious "backwardness" or to sexual abominations. While he realized, correctly, that there is a connection between material technology, social structure, and cultural ideals, he rushed too hastily into an assumption of causality in that interrelationship.

The black separatist conception of national greatness was, in many respects, identical to the ideals of Europeans and white Americans. Like their white counterparts, the nationalists had no way of foreseeing the great shift of cultural values and moral fashion that would come with the First World War. Although they, like most other social theorists, spoke much of "progress" and "changing times," it was vaguely, if at all, that they realized what the slogans meant. It did not occur to them that the very standard according to which progress would be measured in the twentieth century was changing. From the early nineteenth century to the imprisonment of Marcus Garvey, there would be anachronistic attempts to build Christian empires in Africa. There would be unrealistic attempts by various leaders to impose Victorian bourgeois sexual morality on the masses of black peasants. Many black leaders seemed to assume that white people would treat black people more tolerantly if whites could be convinced that blacks were becoming solid, assimilated, English-speaking, Bible-reading Americans.

> Remember Christians Negroes black as Cain,
> May be refined and join the angelic train.[10]

Refinement was not, however, the issue here. Whites, for the most part, ignored the efforts that some blacks were making to become civilized, assimilated Christians and to otherwise meet the cultural demands of American society. Whites simply were not fond of Negroes and there was very little that black people could do about it.

Influenced as he was by American and European cultural ideology, and committed to the myth of civilization as progress, Crummell may seem to be a typical "prisoner of culture." So are we all, and most of us find it difficult to see the wisdom in the values of generations immediately proceeding or following our own. Perhaps the day is not far off when we shall be criticized for having rejected too readily the vision of the Victorian age. Crummell was able to find some peace in his world by bringing his personality into adjustment with it, but at the same time he refused to be intimidated by the forces of racism that constantly threatened to destroy his individuality. His life and writings provide us with an opportunity to judge our own "common-sense" values from a perspective that is no longer fashionable, the perspective of a philosophy that even Crummell found it difficult to practice, a philosophy that he described as "submission to authority, respect for rules, quietness, and order."[11]

Crummell's importance as a spokesman for black nationalism is mentioned more often than his place in the history of American conservatism, but neither can be discussed without some mention of the other. The rhetoric of self-help that Alexander Crummell advocated survives today through two distinct traditions. One was passed down by Crummell's disciples in the Garvey Movement, through the black Muslims, and to Minister Farakhan. The other survived in the writings of such black conservatives as George Schuyler, who first learned of Alexander Crummell at his mother's knee. The emphasis placed on self-help by such black conservatives and moderates as Thomas Sowell and William Raspberry, while not directly traceable to Alexander Crummell, is certainly in the same tradition. Unfortunately, the rhetoric of self-help has often consisted of nothing more than the hypocritical efforts of conservative black leaders to exploit the rhetoric of racial pride and self-help that are important to large numbers of black working people. The typical black American is easily touched by appeals to both individual and racial self-reliance. In Crummell, one can identify the sources of both black nationalism and black conservatism, and his position in the history of black thought illustrates the fact that the mentality of the black nationalist and the black conservative are not necessarily very far apart at all.[12]

The purpose of this book is to broaden the definition of nineteenth-century black culture and to give exposure to the ideas of Alexander Crummell and his peers on the concepts of civilization and racial destiny. I have sought to broaden the conception of what constitutes black culture and black consciousness in the nineteenth century and in the present. A number of recent scholars, including John Blassingame, Eugene Genovese, Lawrence Levine, and Sterling Stuckey, have brilliantly reconstructed the origins of black nationalism and Afro-American culture insofar as their roots are in the consciousness of the mass population.[13] Their contributions have been rightly admired, and the present volume would have been impossible without the insights provided by the new social and cultural history of slavery.

There is no denying the continuity between black intellectual life and black mass culture in the United States. I have alluded to this continuity elsewhere, and Sterling Stuckey has ably demonstrated it in his recent study, *Slave Culture: Nationalist Theory and the Foundations of Black America*. Nonetheless, it was from the English/American literary and intellectual traditions that the literate classes of black Americans derived their conceptions of what black culture ought, ideally, to become. It is, therefore, necessary that we attempt to understand those aspects of nineteenth-century black culture that have their roots in places other than retained African folk traditions and slave culture. Some legitimacy must also be accorded to the perspectives of black men and women who not only experienced nineteenth-century black life, but who enjoyed sufficient knowledge and literacy to develop their own theories of black American culture, civilization, and destiny. Their attempts to construct a theory of history, a philosophy of religion, and an ideology of nationalism must not be misconstrued as unimaginative imitations of what white intellectuals were doing. Ideological patterns among black bourgeois writers and thinkers resembled those of white Americans and Europeans because they arose at the same time and represented intellectual responses to many of the same material and intellectual stimuli.

I have presented elsewhere my argument that classical black nationalism brought together the apparently contradictory ideas of cultural assimilationism and geopolitical separatism. I still maintain that position, and thus find myself in respectful, but nonetheless vigorous, disagreement with the position taken by Eugene Genovese and others that black nationalism originated in slave culture. Black nationalism can just as profitably be viewed as an ideology that Northern blacks created by appropriating and adapting to their own ends the militant racial chauvinism and the strident "Christian soldierism" that were universally typical of nineteenth-century Christianity.[14] My study of the life of Alexander Crummell is, thus, consistent with the position I have developed in earlier works. His life symbolizes the intricacy of the experience of black American intellectuals: their conflicting emotions with respect to the Western world, their discontent with "Civilization," and their dependency on it, as they have labored to impose order on their existence both as racial beings and as individuals.

# 2

# The Early Years
# (1819–1840)

Boston Crummell, an oysterman of New York, is reported to have claimed descent from the Temne chiefs of West Africa in the region that is now Sierra Leone.[1] Alexander Crummell said on more than one occasion that his father was "born in the Kingdom of Timanee" and "was stolen thence at about 12 or 13 years."[2] The story survives that he was kidnapped while playing on the beach."[3] One account says that he came to the United States "about the year 1780, when he was 13 years old," and was "brought up in the Episcopal church."[4] Another informant, George W. Forbes, says that he "had come under the influence of missionaries through whom he had received some schooling" before he was "brought" to America. But Forbes's data are not always verifiable; he also reports that Boston Crummell was "a native of the Vey tribe, whose country was included in what is now Liberia."[5] All other reports of the senior Crummell, including those coming directly from Alexander, identify him as a Temne or Timanee. He married a free-born black woman named Charity Hicks, of whom very little is known except that she was born in Jericho, Long Island, gave birth to a number of children, and survived her husband by a number of years. According to one report, she was brought up in the Hicks family, "the same family that produced the celebrated Quaker, Elias Hicks." Alexander later wrote "my *maternal* ancestors have trod American soil, and therefore have used the English language well nigh as long as any descendants of the early settlers of the Empire State." He took his mother to Liberia with him on November 22, 1865.[6]

"From my earliest childhood, my mind was filled with facts and thoughts about Africa," Crummell later reminisced. He recalled his father's "burning love of home, his vivid remembrance of scenes and travels with his [own] father into the interior, and his wide aquaintance with divers tribes and cus-

11

toms.'' Fond recollections of Africa notwithstanding, Boston Crummell seems to have been opposed to colonization. One of the few contemporary references to him is a statement in *The Liberator* (July 25, 1835) reporting his lack of sympathy with the movement.[7] It would have been almost impossible for Boston Crummell not to have known of the 1817 expedition in which Paul Cuffe, a black sea merchant of Rhode Island, took a company of black settlers to Sierra Leone. A mutual friend, Peter Williams, was a major apologist for the project.[8]

Temne country was, by that time, under the protection of the British. Freetown, a city of refuge for repatriated Africans, was a British naval base at the center of the Temne's coastal territory. It is significant that the remnants of the slave trade at the time of Cuffe's voyage were under the control of the Temne themselves. Freed slaves in Freetown were apparently able to advance themselves both politically and economically, and the Temne were the dominant ethnic group in the area.[9] But the senior Crummell was not sufficiently enchanted by the prospects of repatriation to sign on board with Captain Cuffe. Driven by extreme poverty in old age, he applied to the Rev. Dr. Tyng for assistance in getting to Liberia, but he refused to take advantage of the opportunities for repatriation offered by the New York Colonization Society. Crummell's lack of interest in the increasingly available chances to return to his fatherland indicates the slight popularity black nationalism had in the early nineteenth century. Cuffe himself is said to have declined the opportunity of becoming a settler because of his wife's opposition. Boston Crummell apparently encountered a similar obstinacy on the part of his wife, who refused to go to Liberia, particularly under the auspices of the American Colonization Society.[10]

Boston Crummell was shrewd, assertive, strong-minded, and quick to see the shortest distance between two points. According to Alexander, he ''was never emancipated,'' but simply announced to his owner, Peter Schermerhorn, after ten years' service, that ''he would serve him no longer.'' He took his leave, moving to another section of town and ''notwithstanding all remonstrations and intimidations could not be got back.'' There was apparently some hostility between the families for years afterwards; Alexander wrote that one of the Schermerhorn's had ''shown marked dislike to me personally.''[11] The Crummells apparently took great satisfaction in remembering the conditions of Boston's self-emancipation, and Alexander was happy to be known as ''the boy whose father could not be a slave.''[12]

From 1824 to 1834 Boston Crummell is listed in Longworth's annual New York Directory as an ''oysterman'' working at 6 Broad Street.[13] In the directory of 1834–35 his address is given as 3 Amity Lane, and in the next volume of the directory his residence is listed as 548 Broadway. It is certainly significant that Boston Crummell was able to provide stability for his family during Crummell's formative years. What happened after 1834, forcing Boston Crummell to change his address twice and finally to disappear from the New York Directory, is not yet known. We do know that there were many civil calamities in the area during the early 1830s including fires and mob violence, which may have driven the Crummell's from their home in Leonard Street.[14] During the summer of 1834 there was considerable violence and vandalism in the black section of New York, perpetrated by antiabolition mobs.[15] The Crummell family may have lost their home as a result of this uprising. Whatever led Boston Crummell to move from Leonard Street in the mid-thirties, he apparently enjoyed sufficient prosperity and community standing to encourage his eldest son in the ways of ambition and self-respect, no mean task for a black man in antebellum New York.

At the time of Crummell's birth, the family must have had considerable status among the free Africans of New York. The youngster was exposed from early childhood to some of the livelier minds of the community. It was in the Crummell house at 139 Leonard Street that *Freedom's Journal,* the first black newspaper in the United States, was founded.[16] John Russwurm and Samuel Cornish, the editors, were devoted to the idea that black Americans should plead their own cause and work for self-improvement. They were committed to publicizing "useful knowledge of every kind and every thing that relates to Africa [and] to proving that the natives of it are neither so ignorant nor stupid as they have generally been supposed to be."[17]

Despite this stated interest in Africa, the journal opposed African emigration and the efforts of the American Colonization Society, founded by whites in 1817, to promote the resettlement of free Afro-Americans in Liberia. While some of these whites were sincere philanthropists who advocated emancipation, others were inveterate slaveholders, like Henry Clay. When Richard Allen, the senior bishop of the African Methodist church, began to organize the Philadelphia black community to protest against the society, it fell into disrepute among the majority of black people, regardless of their class or educational status. Even maritime capitalists like Paul Cuffe, the sea captain, and James Forten, the sailmaker, who had supported emigration to Africa, vacillated in their commitment with the founding of the American Colonization Society. When Russwurm began to advocate African colonization in 1829, he was denounced by Cornish but encouraged by Peter Williams, Crummell's pastor, and Charles Andrews, his school principal. Russwurm sailed for Liberia later that year, remarking in a private letter on the "violent persecution" he had received at the hands of "the most influential of our people."[18]

As a bright ten-year-old, Alexander was not oblivious to the political turmoil of the times. One of his early recollections was the arrival in New York of a group of fugitive slaves, who had fled from Southhampton County, Virginia, in an open boat. This he recalled as happening around the time of the Nat Turner insurrection.[19] A black child would have had to be quite stupid to be unaware of what a slavecatcher was. At the age of eleven, a child like Crummell would certainly have heard reports of the death of David Walker, a black small businessman and a Boston correspondent for *Freedom's Journal.* In 1829 Walker had published an incendiary pamphlet, entitled *An Appeal in Four Articles Together with a Preamble, to the Coloured Citizens of the World, But in*

*Particular, and Very Expressly, to Those of the United States of America.* Like his boyhood friend Henry Highland Garnet, Crummell would have been inspired by the legend of David Walker. We know that Garnet was aware of the rumor that Walker's death in 1830 was the result of poisoning, and we may assume that Crummell, although three years younger, would have been acquainted with that rumor as well. Crummell's papers and published writings reveal that he and his schoolmates indulged in much schoolboy braggadocio and boasted of their plans to lead slave revolts.[20] Through his Episcopal pastor, the Reverend Peter Williams, and other politically aware blacks, he soon learned of the voyages of Paul Cuffe, who was taking black Americans back to Africa.

Boston Crummell's circle included many of the free African residents of New York who were interested in abolitionist activities. In 1833, black New Yorkers founded the Phoenix Society of New York, with Boston Crummell serving on its board of directors.[21] The Phoenix Society is believed to have had the widest influence and largest membership among organizations of black New Yorkers. Its objects were twofold: to protect against discrimination in public places and to "promote the improvement of the colored people in morals, literature, and the mechanical arts." The society sponsored numerous cultural, intellectual, and social activities, including a series of scientific lectures. It promoted the founding of "Ward Societies," which compiled a registry of colored persons in the city. Among the society's more impressive undertakings was the establishment of a reading room, which operated from four to nine on Monday, Wednesday, and Friday evenings. The librarian was Samuel Cornish, who was also credited with organizing the scientific lectures. Other members of the society included Arthur Tappan, the white abolitionist, and Reverend Peter Williams, a friend of Paul Cuffe, and sometimes advocate of closer ties with West Africa.[22]

Boston Crummell served on a fund-raising committee of the "First" Annual Convention of the People of Color, held in Philadelphia in 1831. There had been at least one earlier convention of black people which had met in that same city in 1830, primarily to protest against the American Colonization Society. In 1831, however, some members of the group again convened to be joined by others in creating what they hoped would be a more permanent association.[23] Self-help and self-uplift—in addition to anticolonization—were the dominant concerns of the convention, and educational opportunity received considerable attention. At the following year's convention, Boston Crummell served on a committee that investigated the possibilities of establishing a trade school in New Haven, Connecticut. A number of reasons were listed for having preferred that site, among them that "New Haven carries an extensive West India trade, and many of the wealthy colored residents in the Islands, would, no doubt, send their sons there to be educated, and thus a fresh tie of friendship would be formed, which might be productive of much real good in the end." Plans for such a Pan-Afro-American educational center were frustrated, however, when indignant white citizens flew into fits of rage and violence. Public debate of the matter coincided with reports of the Nat Turner rebellion in the summer of

1831, and opposition to the "Negro College" was practically unanimous throughout the white community. Inflammatory articles in the press led to mob violence, stone throwing, and attacks on abolitionists. Boston Crummell and other members of the black convention nonetheless constituted a committee that recommended continuing their efforts to establish the school despite the prevailing hostility.[24] Two years later, Prudence Crandall, a white woman, was subjected to intense persecution when she established an academy for colored girls in the same state. She was convicted of "harboring, boarding, and instructing colored persons who were not inhabitants of Connecticut."[25]

In the city of New York, where the Crummells lived, opportunities for the education of black children may be described as approaching adequacy. The first New York African Free School was instituted in 1787, but in 1814 it was destroyed by fire "originating in a distant building which took in its destructive range, St. George's Chapel, besides many private houses." The building was replaced a year later when the City of New York provided a lot on Williams Street, and the board of trustees was able to erect a new brick building which came to be known as African Free School, No. 1. In May 1820, the African Free School, No. 2 was completed and occupied. It was a two-story building at 137 Mulberry Street, capable of accommodating five hundred pupils, and it was there that Alexander Crummell was enrolled "at an early age."[26]

A number of Crummell's schoolmates were already highly sensitized to the condition of black people in America. One of them, Thomas Sidney, a boy three years older than Crummell and much admired by him, composed the following stanza on freedom in 1828.

> Freedom will break the tyrant's chain
> And shatter all his whole domain;
> From slavery she will always free
> And all her aim is liberty.[27]

Typical schoolboy doggerel, it reveals, nonetheless, its twelve-year-old author's belief that a people who truly understand freedom cannot hold another people in bondage. It shows an identification with the plight of his people in slavery and an appreciation of his own position in the world. An early history of the African Free School, compiled by Charles C. Andrews, one of its teachers, contains several examples of prose and poetry by the pupils. On public occasions, they gave vent to their emotions with impassioned oratory on the subject of slavery and racial oppression. One lad, speaking at the annual examination of scholars in 1824, commenced the proceedings with the following words:

O Africa! the land of my fathers, ancestial of the sable exiles of America! My heart bleeds for thy children, while the clanking of their chains and the voice of their groaning ascend to heaven like the blood of Abel. Who can count thy vasal millions—who can sympathize with thy sore distresses? Methinks I hear thy loud and deep appeal burdening the pinions of the southern breezes. . . .[28]

The young man went on to conclude with the observation that "We live in a wonderful age—an age of action, experiment, and progressive promise. Ethiopia shall soon stretch out her hands to God." Thus it is evident that pupils at the African Free School received not only the usual instruction in grammar, mathematics, and the sciences, but were early made aware of the condition and hoped-for destiny of the African peoples. The younger children's sense of racial duty was not only encouraged by their teachers but fired by the rhetoric of the senior pupils.

Boston Crummell was said to have supplemented his children's education at school by privately hiring white teachers. In 1831, he joined with the Reverend Williams; Thomas Downing, a successful restaurateur; and other prominent colored citizens to establish the Canal Street High School. They employed a white teacher to teach Latin and Greek, but this merely whetted Crummell's appetite for education, at a time when New York had nothing more to offer black youth.[29]

Among Crummell's friends at the Canal Street High School was Henry Highland Garnet, a boy three years older than Alexander, whose family had escaped from slavery and moved to New York in 1825. They took an apartment at 137 Leonard Street, next door to the Crummell house. Crummell remembered the father, George Garnet, as a man of naturally princely mien, and he later wrote, "A grander, nobler, more stately man, both in stature and character than George Garnet, I have rarely met." The senior Garnet claimed to be the son of a Mandingo warrior, taken prisoner in a tribal fight. He seemed, in Crummell's words, "a perfect Apollo, in form and figure; with beautifully moulded limbs and fine and delicate features; just like hundreds of the grand Mandingoes I have seen in Africa, whose full blood he carried in his veins." George Garnet was "sober in his demeanor" and "deeply religious," Crummell later recalled "the self-restraint his appearance always evoked among my playmates, and a certain sense of awe which his majestic presence always impressed us with."[30]

As a child, Henry Highland Garnet seems to have been more influenced by his mother's vivacious character. She was a sprightly and mettlesome woman, as Crummell remembered her, "with lustrous, twinkling, laughing eyes—which she gave as an inheritance to her son; and the very soul of fun, wit, frolic, and laughter." But Garnet underwent a series of harrowing experiences in his early teens, as a result of which he became more sober and contemplative. Crummell was a witness to his trials, and thus he experienced vicariously the sufferings of a fugitive slave family.

A most trying ordeal began in the summer of 1829, while Henry Garnet was away at sea, working as a cabin boy. It was just after sunset and Alexander was playing outside his father's door, when a relative of George Garnet's late master knocked on the door of the Garnets' apartment and asked, "Does a man by the name of George Garnet live here?" Mr. Garnet, who answered the door, replied yes, then under the pretense of going to see if he were at home, passed into a side room and leaped from the second story window. He landed in the Crummell's yard, where they kept a "large ill-tempered dog, the terror of the neighborhood.'' The dog remained quiet ''by wondrous providence,'' and George Garnet made his escape through Orange Street, jumping several fences. When Henry returned to New York from one of his voyages to Washington, D.C., he was ''almost crazed'' to discover that his family had been scattered by slave hunters. He purchased a clasp knife and ''walked Broadway, expecting and prepared for an attack from the slave hunters.'' He was hurried out of the city by friends, however, and hidden on Long Island for a time.

Shortly after these incidents, Henry developed a ''white swelling in his right leg, and thus became a cripple for life.'' Crummell felt that Garnet's suffering led him to a religious renewal. Garnet had attached himself to the Presbyterian church, and, under the tutelage of Reverend Theodore S. Wright, soon began to consider a career in the ministry. Wright, according to Crummell, ''became his patron and friend . . . looked upon Garnet as his own 'son in the gospel'; and always to the day of his death, cared and provided for him in all his efforts to secure a liberal education and to reach the ministry.'' Thus it was that Garnet found himself at the Canal Street High School, in 1831, along with Alexander Crummell.[31]

Garnet and Crummell numbered among their schoolmates in the African Free School Patrick Reason, the engraver, and Charles L. Reason, who would later become professor of French at Central College in New York. Another school-mate, George T. Downing, would follow his father's example, becoming a wealthy restaurateur and using his superior advantages and business contacts for the benefit of blacks and their concerns. Ira Aldridge, who was later to become a celebrated actor, was an extra in New York's all-black acting troop, the African Company, while he was a student at the African Free School. Isaiah De Grasse, like Crummell a black Episcopalian and an unsuccessful candidate for admission to the Episcopal seminary, was enrolled at the school. Another schoolmate was Samuel Ringgold Ward, believed by some to be the greatest black orator of the antebellum years. Rivaling Crummell as the most successful scholar, however, was James McCune Smith, who studied medicine at the University of Glasgow, and during the 1840s became Crummell's phy-sician. In 1824, when Lafayette visited the school and addressed the student body, it was Smith who was chosen to deliver the response.[32]

The black schoolchildren, who were jeered in the streets and pelted with stones, often had to be escorted to and from school by their parents. George T. Downing, according to legend, required no such escort, ''and would boldly lead colored boys into chasing white ones from the street.''[33] But the harass-ment of schoolboys was only a sign of white Americans' deeply rooted atti-tudes toward the Negro intellect. Black people, constantly condemned by whites for their lack of mental fitness, were at the same time brutally frustrated in their attempts to gain basic education. David Walker claimed that even where the laws of the states provided for the education of children, they were not provided with the rudiments of English grammar.[34]

For Crummell and other bright, stubborn black adolescents who were reach-ing puberty around the time of the Nat Turner revolt, bookish activity came to be seen as an act of defiance, and, ironically, avoiding ordinary schoolboy pastimes began to take on the character of rebellion for some black youth. Crummell and a group of his friends resolved that while slavery existed, they would not celebrate the fourth of July.

> For years our society met on that day, and the time was devoted to planning schemes for the freeing and upbuilding of our race. The other resolve which was made was, that when we had educated ourselves we should go South, start an insurrection and free our brethren in bondage.[35]

Crummell's most admired associate was perhaps Thomas S. Sidney, who continued on with him and Garnet to the Canal Street High School, and to later adventures.[36] Crummell recalled how in his youth, "while standing one Sunday by a group of boys wasting their time and dishonoring the day by foolish and wicked jesting—the question was put to [Sidney] why he was so silent? Promptly—yet not presumptuously—did the boy of thirteen reply—'A fool has his tongue in continual motion, but a wise man keeps his silence.' 'Then you consider yourself a wise man,' was the quick and angry retort. 'No, I am trying to be,' was his strong and decided answer." The ten-year-old Crummell was much impressed by Sidney's demeanor and over the next decade seems to have been much impressed by the example of his piety and studiousness. Crummell named his eldest son Sidney Garnet, after his two childhood companions.[37]

There were over 14,000 people of African descent in New York's population of over 200,000 in 1830. The free African community at that time was in lower Manhattan, in the so-called Five Points district—the area behind the present New York State Office Building at 80 Centre Street. The district was not known for its refinement, although many of the city's most educated and enterprising free Africans made their homes there. David Ruggles, secretary of the New York Vigilance Committee, lived on Lispenard Street. He was an active worker on the Underground Railroad, who would "conduct" some six hundred slaves to freedom by the end of the War between the States. The Garnets and Crummells lived on Leonard Street, not far from Mother Zion—the Methodist Episcopal Zion Church, built by black people in 1800. The building was funded by Peter Williams, Sr., the tobacconist, whose son Peter became Alexander Crummell's spiritual advisor. St. Philip's Episcopal Church, presided over by Peter Williams, Jr., was at 24 Collect Street, now called Centre Street.[38] Thomas Downing's famous Oyster House was somewhat further uptown, although his son, George T. Downing, was enrolled in the African Free School at 137 Mulberry Street. An English visitor, traveling through New York in 1825, described "a great procession of Negroes, some of them well-dressed, parading through the streets, two-by-two, preceded by music and a flag."[39] He had witnessed the celebration of the passage of New York's abolition law of 1817, by an African club called the Wilberforce Society. "Officers wore ribbons of several colors, and badges like the officers of free masons; marshalls with long staves walked outside of the procession. During a quarter of an hour, scarcely any but black faces were to be seen on Broadway." Frances Trollope observed in 1831 that many of the black people she had met were "elegantly dressed" and assumed "a superior air of gallantry . . . . when in attendance on their belles."[40]

Of course, there were many unsavory elements in the neighborhood. Charles Dickens described the squalid streets of Five Points, with its "leprous houses" and "wolfish dens," with destitute blacks sleeping in frosty garrets: "Where dogs would howl to lie, women, and men, and boys slink off to sleep, forcing the dislodged rats to move away in quest of better lodgings." Dickens described the "lanes and alleys, paved with mud knee deep; underground chambers, where they dance and game . . . hideous tenements which take their name from robbery and murder; all that is loathsome, drooping, and decayed is here." Pigs roamed the streets of old New York, "with perfect self-possession and self-reliance, and immovable composure." Gangs of toughs patrolled the area of Five Points. An old, abandoned, five-story brewing plant, called the Old Brewery, was converted into a flophouse in 1837, its rooms identified by such names as "Den of Thieves" and "Murderers' Alley."[41]

Rioting broke out in the neighborhood in the summer of 1834. New York newspapers are said to have precipitated the violence by overreacting to speeches William Lloyd Garrison delivered during his 1833 tour of England. Garrison returned to the United States on the very day that the New York City Anti-Slavery Society was organized. By this time Garrison had become a "notorious name, a term of opprobrium, a grotesque of abolition fanatacism." When the Society called for a meeting to be held in early October in Clinton Hall, certain antiabolition agitators called for a demonstration to be held outside the hall at the same time. When the mob assembled to find that the meeting had been canceled, they began to raise a cry against Garrison, but nothing came of this activity until summer.[42]

The forces of law and order could not be relied on to protect the rights of black citizens. On the evening of July 7, 1834, the police broke up a meeting of black men and women and drove them from the Chatham Street Chapel, where they were listening to a sermon by a black minister. The following night a crowd of whites assembled at the chapel to be roused by an incendiary speech. The speaker, William W. Wilder, conjured up the evils of immediate abolitionism, which he illustrated with stories of the revolution in San Domingo, where the slaves had taken over the government of Haiti. The mob first invaded a theater in the Bowery, owned by an Englishman, who was made to bear all the irrational resentment generated by Garrison's English tour. After being driven from the theater by the police, the mob stormed the house of the abolitionist Lewis Tappan, destroying much of its contents and building a bonfire with the furniture. The next day, mobs attacked the Laight Street church, presided over by Dr. Samuel Cox, a white abolitionist. The greatest destruction was in the Five Points area. The mob broke into St. Philip's Church on Centre Street— Peter Williams's church which Crummell attended—and left it a ruin.[43] An adjoining house and three houses opposite were also destroyed. The following summer, there was another outbreak of rioting in Five Points, but by that time Alexander Crummell had left the city.

During these summers of violence, Crummell worked as a delivery boy for Elizur Wright, who was secretary in the Anti-Slavery Office of New York City. The hostility and violence he sometimes encountered while going about his chores may explain an accident he had due to "fast driving."[44] On one occasion, he overheard a conversation in the office between Wright and two distinguished Boston lawyers, who had just come from Washington. They happened to have been dining with John C. Calhoun, who, in the course of conversation at the table, had pronounced that "if he could find a Negro, who knew the Greek syntax, he would then believe that the Negro was a human being and should be treated as a man." To the idealistic youth, this was indeed a challenge. With his father's consent, and thanks to the "little scanty earnings" that the New York abolitionists had helped him to acquire, he departed for the Noyes Academy in Canaan, New Hampshire. But rural New Hampshire, too, harbored a mob spirit and a surprisingly explosive hatred for black people.[45]

In 1835, abolitionists had established the Noyes Academy in New Hampshire which was open to both races. Crummell, Garnet, and Sidney set off together on the first leg of their journey, which was by steamboat from New York to Providence. Garnet's health had deteriorated considerably due to his infected leg. He was, in Crummell's words, "a cripple, weak, sickly, feeble; but he had a wonderful spirit and marvelous energy and perseverance." Black people were not allowed cabin passage, so the three youths were "exposed all night, bedless and foodless to the cold and storm." The remaining four hundred miles of the trip were spent on top of a stagecoach, and, reports Crummell, "rarely would an inn or a hotel give us food and nowhere could we get shelter." The trip was a most unpleasant one for all of them, but especially for Garnet. Physical discomfort and fear for their safety accompanied the burdens of emotional violence and harassment. Crummell relates that "The sight of three black youths, in gentlemanly garb, travelling through New England was, in *those days, a most unusual sight*; started not only surprise, brought out universal sneers and ridicule."[46]

The travelers were cordially received by the forty white students at Canaan, but their stay was a brief one. The academy was soon characterized as a "Nigger school" by the local population, and demagogues began to stir up racial hostilities in the surrounding towns, raising a cry for the dissolution of the school. The hostility of the locals can be attributed to the abolitionist activities of the youths as well as to prejudice. Crummell and his friends had arrived in the spring, and by early summer serious trouble was brewing. Garnet, aged twenty, Sidney, aged nineteen, and Crummell, aged sixteen, were by no means temperate or conciliatory in their approach to abolition. They had been encouraged to give vent to their emotions at the African Free School in New York, and they had been led to believe that their antislavery views would be well received in New Hampshire. Therefore, July 4, 1835, found all three of them scheduled to speak at the parish meetinghouse of Plymouth, New Hampshire. Nathaniel P. Rogers, an eyewitness, described the occasion in *The Liberator* of July 25, 1835. He reported that two older abolitionist speakers had spoken first, followed by Garnet, who acquitted himself well.

> Garnet was followed by young Crummell with a spirited, heroic and generous resolution, summoning the country to the experiment of immediate emancipation from the brilliant examples in the West Indies, South America, and the Cape of Good Hope. He sustained his resolution with manliness and talent, very uncommon among young men and beyond anything I had known from a youth of 16. It was seasoned occasionally with sarcasm and an impatience at the flimsy pretexts of slaveholding and its apologies—quite characteristic of the boy, whose father could not be a slave. His speech was heard with deep attention.[47]

Sidney gave his oration late in the evening but a large number of the audience remained to hear. The performances of Garnet, Sidney, and Crummell brought delight to Rogers and the abolitionist founders of the academy. The local gentry, however, responded somewhat differently. At a special mass meeting called in Canaan on July 13, the people of the region decided to drive the students out of town. On August 10, a mob of some three hundred people from Canaan and the surrounding towns assembled at the school, "seized the building, and with ninety yoke of oxen, carried it off into a swamp." At least that was what Crummell remembered thirty-seven years later in his "Eulogium on Garnet." They dragged it onto the common, wrote Jacob Trussell for the *Colored Patriot* of August 11, 1835, "where it stands, not like the monument on Bunker Heights, erected in memory of those departed spirits which fought and fell struggling for liberty—but as a monument of the folly of those living spirits who are struggling to destroy what our fathers gained."[48]

Some of the students were meanwhile sequestered in a boardinghouse, where, under Garnet's leadership, they were moulding bullets in anticipation of an attack. Around eleven o'clock in the evening the young men could hear the hoofbeats of approaching horses. When one rider, on passing the boardinghouse, fired, Garnet returned his fire from a double-barrelled shotgun. This was, fortunately, enough to frighten off the night riders, but the youths were sent notice to quit the state within a fortnight. Garnet, Crummell, and Sidney thus found themselves passing through the Connecticut Valley, crossing the Green Mountains of Vermont, then traveling down the Hudson back to New York. "All through the route, Garnet was a great sufferer," wrote Crummell, "at Troy we had misgivings for his life, and on the river we had to bed him with our coats and shade him with our umbrellas."[49]

A few months after returning to New York, the three received word that Oneida Institute at Whitesboro, New York, had opened its doors to black youth. Once again they set off, this time with happier results. Beriah Green, the founder, described it as an institute "that combines in its course of instruction, manual with mental labor." Although classical and traditional education were not ignored, every student was expected "to devote three hours a day to muscular exercise in some agricultural or mechanical employment.'' The proceeds of this activity, conducted ''under the direction of an experienced and able Superintendent,'' were ''appropriated, so far as they go, to the payment of the board bill.'' It was noted that in most cases the students' labor was not equal to the expense, although on occasion it might be. Crummell's training at Oneida would be of value to him in later years, as he lived through the experiences of a Liberian pioneer and became a high-school instructor of practical farming skills.[50]

Crummell, who left for Oneida only eight days after returning to New York from New Canaan, apparently arrived at the school in time to demonstrate his fitness to join the sophomore class in February 1836. He was identified as a sophomore in the catalogue of that year. So too was Sidney, but Garnet was listed among the pupils in the preparatory department. We may assume that Crummell and Sidney somehow demonstrated some mastery of algebra, Greek grammar and Testament, Hebrew grammar and Genesis, anatomy, physiology, and bookkeeping. In the following years, students kept up their studies in the biblical languages, being introduced to Chaldee, as well. Latin was not emphasized, although it was taught in the preparatory department. Although Greek history and literature were introduced, it was the Greek testament that was emphasized. ''Natural Theology, and Evidences of Christianity'' were taught, which, to a contemporary educator, might have suggested some reliance on the philosophy of William Paley. Butler's *Analogy* occupied a place of prominence in the sophomore curriculum during Crummell's sophomore year.[51]

Crummell and Sidney took rooms directly opposite one another at Oneida and were ''accustomed to rise before daybreak and aid each other with our lessons.'' On more than one occasion, Crummell entered Sidney's room and found him ''in the dark, not infrequently undressed, sometimes the room cold— in deep and fervent prayer.''[52] Crummell describes his own religious state at that time as ''not entirely indifferent to the claims of God our Father upon us,'' but ''nevertheless in a state of sinful rebellion, without God and without hope in the world.'' He underwent ''the course of conversion'' along with Sidney and, by the summer of 1837, spoke of having made ''a profession of religion.''[53] He wrote to the abolitionist Elizur Wright to confess an old matter that still haunted his conscience. Some three of four years later, while in Wright's employ, he had been sent to deliver a rocking chair to Wright's house and had broken it by driving recklessly. He had invented a story that Wright had not believed, but he had held to it even under questioning. He now regretted that he had not had the courage to admit to his wrongdoing at the time and that he had persisted in the ''palpable falsehood.'' Asking Wright's forgiveness, he confessed that he ''then had no principle, as I am disposed to think, very few if any have who love not God.'' In the future he would endeavor ''to be a man of *Principle* convinced that nothing but principle and honesty in every department of life, will make a man—a man of usefulness.''[54]

In 1838 at Peter Williams's direction, Crummell declared to the bishop of

New York, Benjamin T. Onderdonk, his intention of pursuing holy orders. He had nearly completed the academic course at Oneida Institute and had acquired some knowledge of the original languages of the Bible. His religious and literary qualifications were found satisfactory and he was as John Jay reported, "in due canonical form received as a candidate for Holy Orders."[55] Although he was finally ordained to the priesthood in 1842, he was to be bitterly disappointed in his quest for a seminary education, which only attested to the inferior status of black people in the Episcopal church.

The Afro-American group of the Episcopal church traced its origins to the departure of Richard Allen and Absalom Jones from St. George's Methodist Church in Philadelphia in 1787. Allen and Jones founded the Free African Society in that year, which then, in 1792, resolved itself into a corporation called "The Elders and Deacons of the African Church." Both Allen and Jones at first agreed that the church should maintain its connection with the Methodists; Allen, especially, was "confident that there was no religious sect or denomination that would suit the capacity of the colored people so well as the Methodists." There was, however, "a constantly growing sentiment" among the Free Africans that removed them "further and further from the wild and noisy excitement of the Methodists." When the African church held an election to determine which denomination to unite with, there were, as Allen reported, "two in favor of the Methodists, the Reverend Absalom Jones and myself, and a large majority in favor of the Church of England."[56]

By the time the African church had completed the construction of an edifice on July 17, 1794, the people were determined to affiliate with the Episcopal church, which they did formally on October 12, 1794. Richard Allen went his way to develop the independent African Methodist Episcopal church, but Absalom Jones was petitioned to remain with the congregation as their minister. He was ordained a deacon by the bishop of Philadelphia in 1795 and installed as rector of the congregation known as St. Thomas Episcopal Church. The diocese had dispensed with the requirement that he have a knowledge of Greek and Latin, with the provision that it be understood that the African church would not be entitled "to send a clergyman or deputies to the convention or to interfere with the general government of the Episcopal Church, this condition being made in consideration of the peculiar circumstances at present."[57]

St. Philip's Episcopal Church in New York was the first black congregation of that denomination in the city. It was organized on July 3, 1819, the summer after Crummell's birth, when the building was consecrated. On October 20, 1819, Peter Williams was ordained a deacon and installed as the rector.[58] Williams, like his father, had been born in New York. He thought of himself as an American and expressed his dislike for the aims of the American Colonization Society, which, he said, "held out the idea that a colored man, however he may strive to make himself intelligent, virtuous, and useful, can never enjoy the privileges of a citizen of the United States." Nonetheless, he was an admirer of Captain Paul Cuffe, and he had assisted John Russwurm in getting to

Liberia while many of his closest associates were denouncing Russwurm as a traitor. Williams, indeed, saw it as his "duty" to aid "any man of color [who] though it best to emigrate to Africa."[59]

Many of his contemporaries never forgave Williams for complying with the "advice" of his bishop, Benjamin T. Onderdonk, that he resign from the Anti-Slavery Society. The advice was given on July 12, 1834, and complied with two days later. No doubt the rioting against the abolitionists in New York that week had much to do with both Onderdonk's advice and Williams's compliance. Nonetheless, it symbolized dramatically Williams's conformity to the standards of the Anglo-American bourgeoisie, whose society and manners he relished. He wrote the following in his widely distributed letter of resignation from the Anti-Slavery Society:

> I would have offered my resignation long before this, had I not thought that there might be occasions, when by having the privilege of addressing the Board, I might exercise a restraining influence upon measures calculated to advance our people faster than they were prepared to be advanced, and the public feeling would bear. But I am not disposed to blame the members of the Anti-Slavery Society for their measures. I consider them as good men, and good Christians, and true lovers of their country, and of all mankind. I thought they had not an opportunity of knowing my brethren, nor the state of public prejudice against them, as well as myself, and all I supposed that I could do was to aid them in this particular.[60]

Crummell described Williams as "a timid man," who had "felt all his lifetime the extreme pressure of Episcopal power and . . . had exaggerated opinions concerning it. His explanation for this was that Williams had "lived in the dark and gloomy days of New York slavery. The journals of the church will show that his soul was humbled and crushed beneath it."[61] Crummell remarked on other "gross indignities" suffered by the early black churchmen, recalling that "Peter Williams was always called 'Peter' by the clergy of New York. It would have broken their hearts to have entitled him 'Mr. Williams.' " Crummell, who with all the righteousness of youth had vowed "never to submit to such degrading conditions," still harbored the profoundest respect and affection for his old pastor.[62] Crummell observed that, although Williams had been "deprived of the advantages of a liberal education, he placed high value upon learning . . . No man of the African race ever more devoted himself to this particular labor. To this end he brought forward youth and endeavored to secure them the advantages of learning." Crummell, as a direct beneficiary of Williams's commitment to the education of his "poor benighted people," gratefully acknowledged his debt, recalling also that "He charged me never to allow myself to be abused and insulted, as he has suffered himself to be, and expressed the hope that the rising young men of intelligence among his people, especially those in the ministry, should stand erect in their position, as men and not allow themselves to be cowed by any power or authority."[63]

Peter Williams's complex character allowed him to be an abolitionist with a reputation for indoctrinating black youth, and yet to vacillate in his support for the Anti-Slavery Society. He could oppose colonization and yet support the aims of individual black emigrationists. He could be an institutional separatist and yet place himself under the jurisdiction of an all-white ruling body. He was certainly an influence on Crummell, who would eventually go much further than Williams in support of Liberian emigration. By the 1860s, Crummell was even cooperating with agents of the American Colonization Society. Although he was far more militant and aggressive than his old rector, Crummell, nonetheless, required the sanction of the white Episcopalians. And they, for some curious reason, found it necessary to maintain their connection with him. Strangely, neither the white nor the black Episcopalians were willing to unilaterally dissolve their sense of moral linkage. Neither the whites nor the blacks found the association pleasant, but each felt constrained to continue it out of fidelity to their Christian convictions.

How did Crummell, a man for whom black self-reliance and independence were so important, become so psychologically dependent on the Episcopal church? A racial activist like himself, so youthfully impatient with black servility and white dominance, would seemingly have been happier in one of the independent black denominations, rather than struggling to gain acceptance in a church that had no place for black leadership. The explanation Crummell gave for his vocation was, "I was stimulated by the catechising of my pastor, Rev. Peter Williams, then rector of St. Philip's Church, New York, and kindled, as I well remember, by a sermon of Doctor (afterwards Right Rev., Bishop) Whittingham."[64] For whatever reason, Crummell had his heart set on gaining admission to the Episcopal seminary and being ordained as a priest of that church, and it would seem that he had chosen an impossible means to an almost impossible goal. Even among the white churches, there were those in which his talents would have met with readier recognition. Garnet, who also had decided on a career in the ministry, was following in the footsteps of his mentor Theodore S. Wright, having opted for the Presbyterian church.[65] By the time Crummell had made his decision to enter the ministry, almost every American Protestant denomination had its black counterpart. Indeed the Crummell home on Leonard Street was only a stone's throw from the aggressively independent African Methodist Episcopal Zion mother church on Church Street at Leonard. The Zionists had long ago decided to dispense with white priests and bishops and to ordain their own clergy. James Varick had been elected their first bishop in 1822. He was succeeded in 1828 by Christopher Rush, an educated and reliable man, known as an able preacher and successful organizer.[66] Samuel Cornish, a Presbyterian minister for whom Crummell had much respect, would most certainly have welcomed Crummell as a colleague. Crummell, however, for all his youthful militancy and independence, chose to remain in the Episcopal church, despite the obvious hostility of its bishops to Negro priests, and regardless of the difficulties experienced by Peter Williams, Jr. and other priests. One early biographer felt that the influence of Beriah Green and Crummell's gratitude to the Oneida Institute, a Presbyterian institution, "combined to direct his affections towards that church whose benevolence he had experienced."

But his studies and reflections had convinced him of the apostolic origin and scriptural character of the Protestant Episcopal church, and he determined to minister at her altars and under her authority.[67]

Other reasons besides the apostolic argument led Crummell to his stubborn insistence on becoming an Episcopal priest. Certainly the idea of stable tradition extending back to apostolic times was appealing to him. It is also likely that he was drawn to the stately Episcopalian ritual. Crummell was known for the formality of his demeanor. He emulated gentlemanly educated people, both black and white. Since early childhood, the group with which he had been encouraged to associate represented the most aggressively upward aspiring element of the Afro-American petit bourgeoisie.[68] Sarah Grimké observed of Crummell's acquaintance Samuel Cornish that his household was "like the abode of sanctimonious pride and Pharisaical aristocracy," and Theodore Weld confirmed her opinion as "lamentably right."[69] Crummell, whose manner was often described by contemporaries as "cultured," "dignified," even "punctilious," certainly felt some temperamental affinity to the Presbyterian church of the Reverend Cornish.[70] The Episcopalians, however, not only refined but hierarchical and authoritarian, seemed even more appealing.

Although black Americans with views and values similar to Crummell's were entering the Presbyterian and Methodist churches, neither of these gained a hold on him. In later life he often stated his abhorrence of the evangelical emotionalism of black Methodists and Baptists, but even the staid Presbyterians could not lure him away, although they early opened the doors of their seminaries to Africans, and they maintained a reputation for intellectual elitism.[71] But Presbyterians lacked not only the tradition of Episcopal succession, they were purged of the doctrinal orthodoxy of the Episcopalians, and they did not maintain the venerable rituals of the Book of Common Prayer. More important, however, was the Presbyterians' commitment to a strict Calvinism, which Crummell found difficult to accept. Throughout his life, he attempted to hedge on the doctrine of justification by works. The Presbyterian theology was probably a bit too fatalistic for him. As for the Methodists, they were embroiled indecorously during the early 1800s in internecine battles. The Bethel faction, founded in Philadelphia in 1816, was constantly viewed as a rival of the Zion faction, founded in New York in 1810. Despite the efforts of Richard Allen, the senior Bethel bishop, to de-emphasize differences and treat the churches as de facto one and the same, a connection was never established. Whole congregations sometimes defected from one camp to the other. There were schisms within the Zionist group. While some congregations among the African Methodists were genteel and sedate, others were evangelical, experimental, and exuberant. The Methodists did not have the consistency of ritual and certainly of hierarchical authority that appealed to Crummell's temperament.[72]

It is within this context that one must view the dramatic interaction between Crummell and Bishop B. T. Onderdonk. It has been described as tragic, but it was not without a touch of bizarre comedy. It is difficult to say who appears more awkward in his role—the choleric bishop, losing his temper with a gangly black youth, or the sullen young militant, demanding to be accepted as a brother. By a statute of the General Theological Seminary, it was provided that "every person producing to the faculty satisfactory evidence of his having been admitted a candidate for Holy Orders, with full qualifications according to the customs of the Protestant Episcopal Church in the United States, shall be received as a Student of the Seminary." Having been received as a candidate for orders, Crummell applied at once for admission to the seminary. The dean of the faculty, Dr. William Whittingham, received Crummell with relative politeness, saying to him, "You have just as much right of admission here as any other man. If it were left to me you should have immediate admission to this seminary; but the matter has been taken out of my hands in De Grasse's case; and I am sorry to say that I cannot admit you."[73]

Whittingham referred to the case of Isaiah De Grasse, a man some six years older than Crummell, whose term at the Mulberry Street School had overlapped his, De Grasse had applied to the seminary in 1836 and had been admitted after an examination by the faculty. Shortly thereafter, De Grasse encountered the opposition of Bishop Onderdonk, as he related in his journal:

> *October 11*—I called upon the bishop, and he was dissatisfied with the course I had taken in entering the Seminary. Seems to apprehend difficulty from my joining the Commons, and thinks that the South, from whence they receive much support, will object to my entering.
>
> Thus far I have met with no difficulty from the students, but have been kindly treated. I have thought it judicious, however, to leave the Commons for the present.[74]

Onderdonk advised De Grasse that he might continue to attend lectures and to seek advice with individual professors, but that he must give up his room and give up all formal association with the seminary as a student. De Grasse was unwilling to agree to this, and two days later, when he met with the bishop again, he recorded that he was advised, "from a sober consideration of things, the interest of the Seminary—the comfort of myself—and the ultimate good of my people; I had better silently withdraw, and agreeably to my plan, study privately with a clergyman."[75]

De Grasse was a man of light complexion, practically undistinguishable from a white man, and since he had already occupied a room and been cordially received by the other seminarians it seemed unlikely that De Grasse's presence would have caused any comment.[76] The bishop argued, however, that De Grasse was strongly identified with the black people of New York, and that even if he had not a drop of Negro blood, his identity with the people of color would bar the door of the seminary against him.[77] It seemed likely to many of De Grasse's and Crummell's supporters that the real obstacle to their being admitted was not the ostensible concern for the feelings of Southern Episcopalians, but rather the determination of Bishop Onderdonk to make an issue.[78] It was often pointed out that Princeton Seminary, which was even more dependent upon the South than the General Theological Seminary in New York, had long accepted colored applicants.[79]

After consulting with Dr. Whittingham and appraising the situation concerning De Grasse, Crummell, again at Peter Williams's direction, drew up a petition to the trustees of the seminary. The petition was rejected after heated debate during which Crummell's cause was defended only by the Right Reverend George W. Doane of New Jersey. During the debate, Crummell was sent for by Bishop Onderdonk. When the young man appeared in his study, he set upon him, "with a violence and grossness that I have never since encountered save in one instance in Africa." Years later, Crummell confessed that the bishop's vicious conduct had reduced him to tears.[80]

Burning with rage and humiliation, and unable to accept the terms imposed on De Grasse, he had asked the bishop to remove his name from the list of candidates—a request which he subsequently withdrew.[81] "Utterly bewildered" at Onderdonk's refusal either to admit him to the seminary or to remove him from the list of candidates, he brooded in a garret room in New York's Church Street. His name was now anathema to many Episcopalians, and he felt "completely at sea"; thus he was surprised when it was suddenly announced that "a young Gentleman" wished to see him,

> He climbed the narrow stairway, and entered my little cabin. I myself had not then reached my maturity, and he could not have been more than a year or two older than myself, a recent graduate from college. I was charmed with the grace and elegance of his manners, and that mingled beauty and manliness of person that he carried with him through life, but then, in its early youthful glow. He had heard of the rude and unjust treatment I had received, and came to tender his sympathy and succor.[82]

The visitor was John Jay, grandson of the Honorable John Jay, author of *The Federalist,* and first Chief Justice of the United States Supreme Court. Around that time, Crummell also gained the support of William Jay, the young man's father, who had published some four years earlier *An Inquiry into the Character and Tendency of the American Colonization Society and the American Anti-Slavery Societies.* It was a sober argument in favor of immediate emancipation and a defense of the abolitionists from the charges of "incendiarism and treason."[83] The book, completed in February of 1835, was written at least partially in response to the New York riots of the preceding summer. Jay noted that New York colonizationists themselves had been responsible for a series of inflammatory newspaper articles immediately before the antiabolitionist uprisings. The colonizationists claimed that their aims were entirely benevolent and humanitarian. They claimed that their program of gradual emancipation and expatriation would bring about the eventual uplift of the black race and the dark continent. Repatriated blacks, they argued, would serve as civilizing missionaries to the heathen tribes. Once a single city of free, civilized, and self-governing Africans had been established, it would serve as a beacon to the world, a symbol of the capacities of the black race. When Africans could demonstrate such capacities, the world would become willing to listen to arguments on behalf of black equality, and then the work of universal emancipation might have prospects of success. The Jays and other immediate abolitionists rejected this line of argument. The African race was entitled to freedom on the basis of its obvious humanity; freedom was not a privilege to be earned, but a right to which they were entitled.

William Jay charged the colonizationists with "inconsistency (not to use a harsher term)," for on the one hand they maintained that the slaves and free blacks alike were unfit for freedom, and yet they argued that this population, "when landed on the shores of Africa and immersed in all the darkness of paganism, [would] become on a sudden Christian society, and employed in teaching thousands of barbarians"[84] the arts of Christian civilization. The colonizationists were prompted not by altruism, but by the basest of passions; their racial hatred and ungenerous natures led them to characterize the abolitionists as mongrelizers and amalgamationists. Jay protested that the abolitionists had no black wives or mistresses and that they "countenanced no such absurdity" as compulsive intermarriage; however, he did steadfastly insist that he and his Anti-Slavery Society would "labor for the civil and religious equality of blacks."[85]

With support coming from such respectable sources, Crummell was understandably heartened. He had been advised by several clergymen to carry his petition to Bishop Griswold in Boston but to keep quiet concerning his difficulties with Bishop Onderdonk. Although they had assured him of their support if he followed their prudent advice, Crummell "felt that the entire matter, all the correspondence, should be published—exposed to the public eye, and held up to severe scrutiny; and this too at the risk of blasting every hope and desire I have ever cherished concerning the Gospel Ministry."[86]

The Jays supported Crummell's cause, publicly and privately, over the next several years. When the Board of Trustees of the Episcopal Seminary published Bishop Onderdonk's interpretation of the controversy surrounding Crummell's petition, the younger Jay helped Crummell to publish his correspondence with Onderdonk. John Jay published supportive articles in the *Anti-Slavery Standard* and the *Colored American* newspaper, as well as his pamphlet *Caste and Slavery in the American Church,* issued anonymously by "A Churchman."[87] The latter contained a substantial extract from the diary of Isaiah De Grasse, revealing the pain and humiliation he had experienced in his dealings with Bishop Onderdonk. William Jay also helped to publicize Crummell's cause. In his "Introductory Remarks to the Reproof of the American Church," he outlined the story of Crummell's abuse at the hands of the bishop and commented, "This bold-spoken bishop crouched before a prejudice which his own tongue confessed to be 'unrighteous'; and sacrificed duty and independence, lest the Seminary should lose the support of the South!"[88]

For the next decade, Crummell refused to let the matter drop or to allow Onderdonk to have the last word. His most detailed reply to the bishop was drafted in the form of a pamphlet in 1849.[89] Crummell here took issue with the claims of the bishop that either Isaiah De Grasse or Peter Williams had been happy to submit to the humiliating conditions imposed by him. De Grasse had spoken of the mortification he had suffered, and as for Williams, his "soul had frequently swelled at the indignities heaped upon him." He called upon Samuel Cornish to verify that Williams had supported Crummell's claims upon the Diocese of New York, although he feared to support him openly. He accused Onderdonk of "taking advantage of the mobbish violence against the colored people and the abolitionists in 1834" in order to force Williams to resign his office in the Anti-Slavery Society. Crummell observed, near the close of his essay, that "In the providence of God, Bishop Onderdonk has suffered much affliction, has been called to much trial." Crummell believed, as he wrote to John Jay in 1839, that "besides a future day of retribution, there is always a day of retribution at hand." Indeed, the bishop was to undergo much tribulation, and, by the mid-1840s, both Benjamin Onderdonk and his brother Henry, bishop of Philadelphia, would be disgraced. Henry would be accused of indecent behavior while under the influence of alcohol, and Benjamin would be found guilty by the house of bishops of improper conduct with women.[90]

Although he was much occupied by his debate with Onderdonk, Crummell set himself diligently to the task of continuing his theological studies. He lived and traveled considerably in New England from 1839 to 1842, moving between New Haven, Boston, New Bedford, and Providence, Rhode Island. In some capacity that is as yet unclear Crummell studied at Yale during this period. He informed John Jay of his studies in a letter of September 4, 1840, and Jay wrote back to promise, "It will give me pleasure to allow you six dollars a month, from this date, so long as you reside in New Haven and continue a student in the Seminary."[91] He probably studied at Yale under the same conditions that had been imposed a few years earlier for another black student, J. W. C. Pennington. Although Pennington had been refused admission to the Seminary, he was allowed to sit in on classes but not to participate, nor to withdraw books from the library.[92]

Crummell's papers in the Schomburg Collection contain a series of transcriptions in his youthful handwriting, one of which is identified as "Nathaniel Taylor Lecture." Taylor was responsible for certain reforms in theology as it was taught at Yale during the period of Crummell's "association." He put great stress on free will and on the participation of the Christian in his own salvation. Taylor's lectures may have provided the formal and intellectual basis for the Arminian strain in Crummell's later writing.[93]

It was later reported that while he was in New Haven Crummell led the black members out of Trinity parish to form their own congregation, which was called St. Luke's. He received a specific license from his mentor, Rev. Harry Croswell, and was assigned a room, which belonged to Trinity Parish, as a meeting place. The first treasurer of St. Luke's was Alexander Du Bois, the grandfather of W. E. B. Du Bois, who was to idealize Crummell half a century later. During 1840, Alexander Du Bois kept a record of the contributions collected at a series of lectures given by Crummell. He usually received less than one dollar, although on one occasion he was given six. This, along with the allowance from Jay and whatever he received for his ministerial duties, apparently provided his limited support during the Yale interlude. The New Haven black Episcopalians seem to have adopted the poor student priest as a local charity project.[94] On moving to Providence, he continued his studies with Dr. Alexander H. Vinton.[95]

During 1839, Crummell was a traveling agent for the *Colored American* newspaper. He wrote to John Jay saying that he had taken the position "chiefly for the purpose of getting to Boston in order that I may converse with Bishop Griswold and Dr. Stone, Chairman of the standing Committee."[96] Around this time, he apparently made plans to establish a New York Select Academy, a private school for black pupils, which was to be run entirely by Afro-Americans, with Sidney as its principal and Crummell as his assistant. With Crummell's departure for New England, and Sidney's death in 1840, the school passed out of existence.[97]

Sidney had been ill for some time, so his death was no great surprise to Crummell, but, as can be imagined, the loss of a spiritual and intellectual companion affected him deeply. He eulogized him on July 4, 1840, and, though little of Crummell's own ego is consciously displayed in the oration, a great deal of the writer's personality is revealed. For the qualities that he most admired in Sidney were the very ones he attempted to cultivate in himself. The older youth had impressed him as "the most conscientious man of my acquaintance." He was a friend with whom Crummell could seriously converse on classical literature, on the English poets, on the Bible, but most important, on the politics of race relations. "In his plans and suggestions, he not infrequently met with opposition from those who, from utter inability, could not understand him." Such an experience must already have been familiar to Crummell, who like Sidney had experienced some distancing from other Afro-Americans by virtue of his education. The extreme seriousness of these two young men, who on chance encounters in the street would buttress their arguments with quotations from the Greek testament, must also have isolated them from the ordinary black New Yorker.[98]

Perhaps it was this remembered friendship that led Crummell years later to recall "how in our school-days our hearts have become knit as with hooks of steel" to companions whom we have loved as Jonathan loved David, with a "love passing the love of women." Crummell's feelings for Sidney and for Garnet were deeply rooted in powerful emotional experiences. Their sufferings on the journey to and from New Canaan, and their huddling together for protection in a vicious environment, most certainly had knit them together "with hooks of steel." Crummell's feelings for the two were obviously among the most important affectional relationships of his life.

Strangely enough, there is little affectionate recollection in Crummell's references to his first wife, Sarah, whom he married around the time of Sidney's death.[99] Young and vulnerable, Alexander and Sarah Crummell seem to have been married around 1841, when he was twenty-two and she eighteen. The search for marriage records or for any reference to the young couple in legal documents of the time has so far been fruitless. He spoke often in later years of the duty of marriage, and he considered marriage especially desirable in a priest. Then too, he remembered the "apostolic and inspired command . . . , to avoid fornication let every man have his own wife." Although there is an occasional reference to his wife in Crummell's letters, the woman remains a vague and shadowy figure. Financial problems, with the usual attendant difficulties, began to plague the marriage almost immediately. From time to time, Crummell suggests something of his wife's feelings, such as her desire around 1843 to "go West," which apparently resulted from her unhappiness as the wife of an impoverished, unappreciated urban pastor. In one letter to John Jay he describes her as "a woman of first rate capacity," who had done well in school, "taking off all the prizes in Reading, Arithmetic, and Grammar." This is one of the few instances in which Crummell describes her with anything approaching enthusiasm. For the most part, he would speak of their shared poverty and illness, their increasing mutual coldness, and bitter complaint. It is significant that no document has yet been discovered in which Crummell refers to his wife by name. From what little is revealed in his letters, we may assume that Sarah Crummell found life hard. It could not have been easy to be Alexander Crummell's wife. Beneath the rigid formality of his exterior was an intensely passionate soul. Sarah Crummell was to endure at least seven pregnancies, some of which she endured in a semi-invalid state, and some in the heat and misery of an unfamiliar tropical climate. In the end, she was to see her children become alienated from a father whose friends referred to him as "a perfect Tsar." [100]

With the support of Peter Williams, the Jays, and other eminent churchmen, Crummell continued to pursue his goal of a career in the ministry. At the advice of these men, he traveled to Boston to seek the assistance of R. William Croswell, Rector of the Church of the Advent. He was "not only a Divine, but one of the sweetest poets of our church," Crummell wrote, deeply moved by one of his efforts.

> Joy to thy savage realms, O Africa;
> A sign is on thee, that the Great I Am
> Shall work new wonders in the land of Ham;
> And while He tarries for the glorious day
> To bring again His people, there shall be
> A remnant left from Cushan to the sea.
> And though the Ethiop cannot change his skin,
> Or bleach the outward stain, he yet shall roll
> The darkness off that overshades the soul,
> And wash away the deeper dyes of sin.
> Princes submissive to the gospel's sway,
> Shall come from Egypt; and the Morian's land,
> In holy transport, stretch to God its hand;
> Joy to thy savage realms, O Africa! [101]

Crummell compared the verse to "some of Wordsworth's finest." Rash though this may have been, the sonnet was not lacking in interest. It made imaginative use of biblical allusion and employed the device of "literary Ethiopianism," a tradition of making reference to Psalms 68:31, "Princes shall come out of Egypt; Ethiopia shall soon stretch forth her hands unto God." It was a convention that Crummell was fond of using in his own writings, for he saw the lines as a prophecy of Africa's future regeneration through the collateral agencies of Christianity and civilization.[102]

Crummell's later reconstruction of his reception in New England was rather idealized. He recollected that Croswell had received him most kindly, saying to him, "Mr. Crummell, I will do all that I can for you. It happens, however, that I do not belong to that school in the Church which has the most influence here. Go to Dr. Vinton and to Reverend Mr. Clark. They will help you; and I will use all my influence with them and the Bishop, and you may rely upon me."[103] Clark, who was later to become bishop of Rhode Island, was then a young priest, "in the full flush of a brilliant and most successful ministry." Crummell later referred to him as "a splendid spiritual Knight Errant, glowing with Godly ardor; 'valiant for the truth'; with all the impulses of the Christian here." Vinton he recalled as "Somewhat phlegmatic in temperament, quiet in demeanor and utterance, seemingly emancipated from impulse or passion, full of masterful control in every section of his grand being and regulated by massive intellect." Through the influence of these liberal whites, Vinton, Clark, and Croswell, he was introduced to the venerable Bishop Griswold, who received him "with fatherly interest and cordiality," saying to him, "Mr. Crummell, I wish there were twenty men of your race applying for orders. I should be more than glad to receive them as candidates for the ministry of this Diocese." Crummell was to speak of his removal to Boston as a "transition from the darkness of midnight to the golden light of a summer morning," but unfortunately he was to encounter difficulties of a new and more painful variety in New England.[104]

# 3

# The Struggles of a Young Priest
# (1841–1847)

Crummell left New Haven in 1841, without the Yale degree. The time he spent there was apparently not pleasant to recall, for he mentions neither his months at Yale nor his work for the New Haven congregation in his autobiographical essay *Shades and Lights*. Crummell's situation as lay reader in the St. Luke's Chapel of New Haven was less than satisfactory. He would, perhaps, have been able to remain in New Haven, and even to complete his studies at Yale, if his financial situation had been better.

In March 1841, Crummell received a letter from the vestry of Christ Church, a small black congregation in Providence, Rhode Island, asking him to become their lay reader.[1] The twenty-two-year-old pastor arrived in Providence unbendingly righteous, still seething with rage and humiliation over his ongoing feud with Bishop Onderdonk. He could not let the matter drop, as he wrote to John Jay, "because I love truth and hate injustice . . . It may not be supposed that I can enter into any compromise with injustice."[2] To be sure his cause was just, but this trait that Du Bois called "unbending righteousness," and that others called "rigidity," did not always endear him to his associates.[3] Crummell's years in Christ Church were disappointing; not only did the parish not support him, but he also experienced much personal humiliation, which is only hinted at in his autobiographical essay. Yet the years in Christ Church were not entirely without success. Crummell arrived in Providence during the time of political unrest referred to as the Dorr War. Under the leadership of Thomas Wilson Dorr, the people of Rhode Island were rebelling against the restriction of the franchise to a small body of landholders. Both the landholding party and the suffragists were opposed to granting the franchise to black Rhode Islanders. At a meeting of the Suffragist Convention on October 8, 1841, the following transpired:

34

Mr. T. W. Dorr, one of the most efficient members of the Convention, known to be friendly to the freedom, education and encouragement of the colored race, stated that, just before the hour of meeting, a respectable colored man of this city called at his office and handed him a memorial signed by a Committee of colored men, who requested him to communicate it to the Convention. He then handed the memorial to one of the Secretaries and moved that it be read. This was objected to on the supposition that the paper was probably written by some white person unfriendly to the Suffrage cause.

Mr. Dorr then stated that the colored man informed him that it was written by a Mr. Alexander Cromwell [sic], a colored Instructor of youth and preacher.[4]

Although Thomas Wilson Dorr was known to be sympathetic to black people, most of the suffragists were crude Jacksonian democrats, who did not share his racial egalitarianism. True enough, the suffragists made a weak and tardy concession to the black petitioners by promising an eventual plebiscite to determine whether the franchise would be extended to black people. In the course of the Dorr War, however, it became evident that the black leadership, possibly with Crummell's participation, had struck a deal with the aristocrats. Crummell had, after all, been impressed since early youth that white egalitarianism was not always sympathetic to black interests. During the period of hostility, while forces of the Law and Order Party of the landholders were away doing battle with the suffragists, black militiamen were enlisted to patrol the streets. As a reward for their loyalty during the rebellion, the black community was granted the franchise under a new constitution. The suffragists sneered contemptuously at the blacks, referring to them as servants and dependents of the white aristocracy. But it is certainly likely that Crummell, or someone else in the black community with friendly ties to the white aristocrats, dealt privately and efficiently with the Law and Order forces.[5] Crummell later wrote:

I secured—strong as the assertion may appear yet nevertheless true—I secured their political rights in Rhode Island. During the political agitation in that state the leading colored men communicated their interests to my hand and judgement; and laid upon me the burden of drafting the documents and addresses and of taking the steps which secured in the end their political rights.[6]

Crummell was never one to underestimate the value of his contributions to a parish. He felt that he deserved credit for the erection of what others described as "a very handsome church," and for paying off the best portion of the indebtedness thereon. "I planned that Church with my own pencil," he wrote, "and superintended its erection."[7] The vestry of Christ Church was dissatisfied with Crummell, however. About a fortnight before his ordination to the diaconate in late May, 1842, Crummell called on Bishop Griswold, and, during their conversation, Griswold told him that the congregation was disappointed with his ministry. According to one Dr. Crocker of Providence, the bishop's informant, they had charged him with lacking piety and zeal. They accused him of having become so proud that he would no longer visit them. After consulting with Crocker, who would not name his accusers, Crummell wrote a letter to the vestry expressing his hurt and indignation, taking occasion to remind them of his labors in soliciting funds for an edifice, a task which he said he had never promised to undertake. He also expressed his disappointment that the parishioners had not adequately appreciated nor supported him. He insisted that "neither in the letters sent me nor in the communications I held with the committee was there any decision made or expressed that during the time of my study that I was to busy myself in collecting funds. It was distinctly understood that I should study and prepare myself *well* for the ministry. It was only on such condition I consented to come here." [8]

Perhaps the young pastor was somewhat rash to have written an accusatory rather than an inquiring letter to his vestry. He claimed that he "had no idea [he] had so lost reputation in the church," but the method of his taking the matter up would seem to indicate that communications were not in very good order. Was the tone of Crummell's accusation an indication of some smoldering resentment of which he had long been aware, or was it simply a vindication of the parishioners' charge that he was indeed a bit too proud? Some months earlier, according to the vestry minutes, a letter of support urging the bishop to ordain him had been sent to Boston. It was not a strong letter, to be sure; it stated only "that we require an ordained minister" and petitioned Bishop Griswold "to ordain our pastor, Alexander Crummell, if fit to receive orders." The letter was written on April 11, 1842 at Crummell's request. [9] The situation had deteriorated to such an extent that by autumn of 1842 the vestry was openly expressing its dissatisfaction with Crummell. They continued to pressure him to engage in fund-raising, and he continued to resist.

In September 1842, Crummell was beginning to experience marital difficulties resulting from his precarious financial situation. He was forced to take his wife to her mother's home in New York, and, returning to Providence, felt sufficiently alienated from the congregation that he missed officiating for at least one Sunday service and one meeting of the vestry. Finally, on Sunday, October 27, he is reported to have "invited several persons from other Churches to attend in the afternoon, and then he was going to give the Congregation a lecture concerning the business of the Church and past transactions and then leave them." Under these circumstances, several of the parishioners "informed Mr. Crummell after service that the House would not be opened for service on that day—anymore." Crummell sent a final note to the vestry, but they claimed they "could not understand the meaning of the same." The parish officers were angered that his "bill was paid in full by R. Abram Bignall. Bill for Board of $100.—and the balance was paid and a receipt in full was taken—Mr. Crummell left without any other understanding with his own accord and will." [10]

The sparse vestry minutes of Christ Church do not give a complete record of the reasons for Crummell's failure in Providence. It seems the arrogant and embittered twenty-three-year-old failed more for reasons of personality than for neglect of duty. In *Shades and Lights,* Crummell admits that many of his difficulties with congregations resulted from the rigidity of his personality. This was probably the source of his difficulties in Providence. It does not seem likely that the vestry's only disappointment was in his management of finances, for Crummell certainly seems to have done as much as could be expected. His repeated absences were probably an effect rather than a cause of his dissatisfaction. The vestry had entered the relationship with Crummell well aware of his commitments to study, and they were not, at least initially, opposed to his trips between New Haven and Boston. In *Shades and Lights,* Crummell dismisses the entire episode with one sentence: "My first charge was at Providence, R. I.; but there I could get no support." Du Bois's reconstruction of events, which may have been based on Crummell's later recollections, portrayed this as one of the most painful disappointments in Crummell's life.

> The days sped by and the dark young clergyman labored; he wrote his sermons carefully; he intoned his prayers with a soft earnest voice; he haunted the streets and accosted wayfarers; he visited the sick and knelt beside the dying. He worked and toiled week by week, day by day, month by month. And yet month by month the congregation dwindled, week by week the hollow walls echoed more sharply, day by day, the calls came fewer and fewer and day by day the third temptation sat clearer and still more clearly within the Veil; a temptation as it were, bland and smiling, with just a shade of mockery in its smooth tones. First it came casually in the cadence of a voice: "Oh colored folks? Yes." Or perhaps more definitely "What do you *expect?*" In voice and gesture lay the doubt—the temptation of Doubt. How he hated it and how he stormed at it furiously! "Of course they are capable," he cried; "of course they can learn and strive and achieve—" and "Of course," added the temptation softly, "they do nothing of the sort." Of all the three temptations, this one struck the deepest. Hate? He had outgrown so childish a thing. Despair? He had steeled his right arm against it, and fought it with the vigor of determination. But to doubt the worth of his life-work,—to doubt the destiny and capacity of the race his soul loved because it was his; to find listless squalor instead of eager endeavor; to hear his own lips whispering, "They do not care, they cannot know, they are dumb driven cattle,—why cast your pearls before swine?"—this, this seemed more than man could bear; and he closed the door, and sank upon the steps of the chancel, and cast his robe upon the floor and writhed.[11]

Du Bois's idealized portrait captures the poignancy of Crummell's failure, but it gives the overly sentimental impression of a tender, frail, scholarly young man, failing because of excessive sensitivity. Crummell's problems were more likely due to a chronic insensitivity and intolerance. Furthermore, his later, well-known contentiousness and fractiousness were already beginning to manifest themselves as prominent traits. As for his carefully prepared sermons, they are probably neither too scholarly nor too abstract. More likely, they were exceedingly emotional, even disturbingly so. The list of sermons preserved by Alexander Du Bois from the New Haven years, the titles of Crummell's sermons from the *Colored American* newspaper, and the surviving sermons from the 1840s, all add up to a portrait of a young man who could be priggish and denunciatory in the pulpit. His attitude of moral accusation did not endear him to the parishioners. His sermons were no doubt thrilling, but often unsettling, filled as they were with fire and brimstone. Crummell was contemptuous of what he saw as typical black religious expression. Black folk were inclined to go to church for enjoyment, he observed. They wanted "to be made happy by sermons, singing, and pious talk." All of this was correct, so far as it went, but this was only one side of religion; it was what he called "the piety of self-satisfaction." Black people must learn to seek something more than what he called "a comforting piety." [12]

Crummell's troubles with the Providence congregation did not prevent his being elevated to the diaconate by Bishop Griswold, officiating in St. Paul's Cathedral in Boston, on May 30, 1842. Indeed, he was ordained deacon just around the time that the relationship with the Providence community was going sour. Shortly thereafter he moved to Philadelphia, where he was ordained to the priesthood in St. Paul's Church by Bishop Lee of Delaware in 1844.[13] But this was no day of triumph; he had been admitted to the priesthood on special terms. His dream of entering the seminary had been denied so that, as Du Bois told the story, "even when in old St. Paul's the venerable Bishop raised his white arms above the Negro deacon—even then the burden had not lifted from that heart, for there had passed a glory from the earth." [14]

In Philadelphia, as he later related, he faced some of the same problems he had encountered in Providence. "The clergy would not sustain me," he wrote. "I had been a disturber of the peace, and I must be punished by neglect. Not seldom, reverend divines were rude and insulting, and the result was poverty, want, and in the end, sickness. On one occasion I was in a state of starvation." [15]

On first arriving in the diocese of Philadelphia he presented his credentials to Bishop Henry U. Onderdonk, brother of the Bishop Onderdonk who had refused him admission to the seminary in New York. Crummell approached the bishop, endeavoring to hold himself "as meekly as possible," but Onderdonk received him with as little regard as had his brother in the diocese of New York. Having presented his letter dimissory to the bishop, Crummell was entitled to all the rights of a clergyman in that diocese. Onderdonk faced "an embarrassing dilemma," wrote William Jay. "To disregard a dimissory letter from another diocese, and to send back the bearer, without the slightest objection being made to his character or conduct, might lead to very inconvenient results, and would unquestionably cause much 'agitation.' " On the other hand, the bishop could not open the door of the convention to a Negro. Therefore, he presented Crummell with this demand: "I cannot receive you into this diocese unless you will promise that you will never apply for a seat in my convention for yourself or for any church you may raise in this city." Crummell, of course, replied, "That, sir, I shall never do," but as he left the bishop's study, Onderdonk called and said, "You may wait a few days, and I will communicate with you." [16]

While he was waiting, Crummell traveled to Burlington, New Jersey, where he presented himself to Bishop George Doane. He had never made his acquaintance, but this was the same Bishop Doane who had raised the "energetic protest" against his exclusion from the seminary. Crummell stated to the bishop his "deep perplexities" about the condition that had been set by Onderdonk. Bishop Doane "at once thundered forth these words:—Don't you do it! Don't you give him any such promise! Bishop Onderdonk is a strong personal friend of mine, but he has no right to demand any such promise from you. You have the same rights in the Church of God as any other man, and don't you give way to any such demands." Crummell was immensely elevated and gratified by Doane's advice, which not only gave him the resolve to resist Onderdonk's pressure but also strengthened his faith in the liberal forces within the church.[17]

In the meantime, the bishop of Philadelphia had accepted Crummell's letter dimissory but had taken steps to persuade the convention that no African church should ever be admitted on equal terms. Thus it was that some three weeks after Onderdonk's interview with Crummell, the convention of the diocese assembled to pass the following resolution:

> That the following clause be added to the 8th Revised Regulation adopted in 1829, and hereafter to be taken as part thereof: "No Church in this diocese in like peculiar circumstances with the African Church of St. Thomas, shall be entitled to send a clergyman or deputies to the Convention, or to interfere with the general government of the Church."[18]

By employing the phrase "like peculiar circumstances" churchmen had revealed the depths of their hypocrisy. One wonders why they could not forthrightly state that exclusion was to be based on color. Possibly it was because they felt that they were wrong and were ashamed of their actions. At least the majority of them felt that the exclusion must be justified on some grounds other than blatant color prejudice. Moreover, color alone had never been the legal basis for excluding St. Thomas parish, under Peter Williams, from the convention. The resolution on exclusion had been based, at least ostensibly, on Absalom Jones's lack of scholastic qualifications. The restrictions of 1795 were not openly directed towards people of color but towards a congregation that temporarily lacked a bona fide pastor.[19] A congregation presided over by an educated minister, equipped with letters dimissory from a respected diocese, could not be considered "in like circumstances." Crummell wrote to John Jay on 24 July, 1843, that he had consulted with Dr. S. H. Tyng, Rector of St. George's Church in New York. "He says if we (the colored Episcopalians) will but send in a remonstrance he will do all he can against this meanness, and endeavor to procure its repeal."[20] The efforts of liberal Episcopalians were to prove fruitless, however; they were clearly in the minority and met with such hostility that the sympathetic John Jay had to publish his protests anonymously. Crummell wrote bitterly of the "*unity* existing in the church," which stopped the mouths of those who should have opposed injustice and "closed the channels through which human, hearty sympathy would flow forth to assuage the woes and suffering and oppression of our common humanity."[21]

Crummell must certainly have been tempted to wash his hands of the whole business and to remove himself from the dominion of whites in the Episcopal church. Matters were not so simple, of course. He was receiving support and encouragement from a number of prominent white Episcopalians, and he was also discovering that blacks were capable of inflicting just as much pain. Crummell wrote to Jay, even before he had read the proceedings of the Philadelphia convention, stating that he was prepared to protest, "had I not been restrained and hindered, I quake to say, by a Brother himself oppressed." This fellow Afro-American had attributed Crummell's difficulties to abolitionist excesses and had made him understand that if he were to protest the action of the convention Crummell would have neither his sympathy nor influence. When the young priest asked him what course he ought to follow, the gentleman responded "that he would have nothing to say or do about the matter." Crummell, who was at that time twenty-three, a new member of the diocese, and only recently raised to the diaconate, was understandably diffident about going up against a fellow Afro-American, "a Presbyter of some forty years of age and 9 or 10 years in the ministry," who had never raised any objections to racial distinctions in the church.[22]

Crummell was becoming aware of "the art of the oppressor to turn the oppressed against their own suffering ones."[23] It distressed him to think that he was beginning to be "regarded as a dangerous young man," opposed by black and white alike. He wrote to John Jay of the sufferings of the black clergy:

> the long years of mock regard, the deceptive friendship, the oppressive blandness of ecclesiastical superiors, the heartfelt chagrin and self-contempt and littleness, the obsequiousness and meanness—the feeling of wrong and outrage, unendurable yet not to be opposed—the absence of patriotic feeling, the want of manly sentiment, the lack of Christian freedom which my brethren and fathers have experienced—which have restrained them in their official conduct, made them the contempt of their own people and the slaves of others; cancerrated their own hearts and sent them to untimely graves.[24]

Crummell's correspondence mentions building a church in Philadelphia and also refers to attempts to establish a school, "a permanent attractive institution," from which he could "obtain subsistence." If he could succeed in this, he would remain in the city.[25] But he was not successful. The Crummells often went to bed without food during their tour of duty in Philadelphia, "and one dear child, our first born, perished because we had not the means to secure those comforts and necessaries which tend to maintain both a mother and her offspring."[26]

Crummell's contacts with black people during these years were not totally frustrating. He participated in the Convention Movement and received more than adequate intellectual stimulation in politics and public affairs. During his years at Oneida, Crummell had managed to participate in New York politics. The *Colored American* of August 20, 1838, reports that along with his brother, Henry, he represented Ward 11 in a public meeting that same year, called by the colored people of New York for purposes of self-advancement. He represented this group, the Association for the Political Improvement of the People of Color, at a meeting of the New York State Anti-Slavery Society in Utica two months later. In August 1839, the association met again in New York, with Crummell as the principal speaker. Before and after his speech, petitions were circulated to protest to the state legislature the legal requirement that black people must possess special qualifications to exercise voting rights.[27]

During the early 1840s Crummell developed confidence in himself as a writer, a speaker, and an abolitionist. He became known as an advocate of black self-help institutions and an opponent of the Colonization Movement. His political attitudes reflected the values impressed on him by his father as well as by such associates as Samuel Cornish and Peter Williams. To be certain, the youthful Crummell was given to expressing his attitudes with greater vehemence than his elders usually dared, but he was in agreement with them on the necessity of immediate emancipation and on the right of black people to all the privileges of American citizenship. He also shared their belief that the American Colonization Society with its scheme to expatriate the free blacks to Liberia was a threat to the rights of all black people whether slave or free.

There were in his thinking already some elements of the nationalism that would later become obvious. He had been immersed in doctrines of self-help and black independence as varieties of separatist thinking during his youth. While Cornish opposed and Williams was ambivalent about the territorial separatism represented by the Back to Africa Movement, both believed strongly in institutional separatism. Cornish, for example, had derided the movement of a group of Philadelphia Negroes to replace the black Convention Movement with the American Moral Reform Society, which was opposed to separate black conventions.[28] Williams had eulogized the late repatriationist Paul Cuffe, praising his character and speaking of his voyage with admiration.[29] Crummell had made the acquaintance of some of Cuffe's descendants while passing through New Bedford around this time. He was impressed by the evidence of wealth and thrift among the black sea merchants of New Bedford, and, twenty years later, as he developed his own plans for the redemption of Africa, he recalled his meeting with the descendants of Cuffe.[30] While Crummell was by no means a nationalist in 1840, he definitely believed in separatism as a means to the end of black self-reliance and self-respect. He participated actively in black politics and institutions. In 1840 he and his brother Charles took part in the Convention of Colored Citizens at Albany.[31] Here he began to demonstrate what was to be one of his lifelong commitments, a concern for building independent black institutions, without neglecting the struggle for civil rights. That there was need for such concern was illustrated by the case of the New York African Free School, which had been transferred in 1834 from the control of the Manumission Society to that of the New York Public School Society. Under the latter society, which was less directly concerned with the interests of blacks, the number of students and teachers had declined. Leaders like Samuel Cornish spoke out against a tendency towards weakening black institutions or allowing them to be dominated by whites. Since 1829 he had held that while whites might work with blacks for immediate abolition, blacks should make independent efforts for their own social betterment. He opposed the abandonment of the Negro Convention Movement by the Philadelphia Afro-Americans of the American Moral Reform Society, whose members urged integration into white society whenever possible. The Albany convention of 1840 and its aftermath revealed the increasing concern for independent group efforts by Crummell and others, who believed themselves to be witnessing a self-defeating abandonment of the self-help ethic. Crummell is credited with having drafted the "Address" to the convention, which unequivocally insisted that, as black Americans were among the first settlers of the state, they were nothing other than Americans.[32]

Although the convention was composed of "colored citizens," it was dedicated to integrationist aims and civil rights protest. Its first order of business was to issue a protest against discrimination in voting rights. At that time the franchise in the state of New York was limited to whites and to those blacks who met certain residency and property qualifications. The convention also resolved "that all laws established for human government, and all systems of whatever kind founded in the spirit of complexional caste, are in violation of the fundamental principles of Divine Law, evil in their tendencies, and should therefore be effectively destroyed." Crummell was named to a committee of three to oversee the petition of the state legislature on the right to suffrage without a special property qualification. Crummell drafted a report asserting "the solemn duty of the free colored people . . . earnestly to petition the legislature for an equal and impartial exercise of the elective franchise, until they effect a consummation of their desires." But Crummell also supported a controversial resolution recommending to the colored citizens of New York that they "become possessors of the soil, as that not only elevates them to the rights of freemen, but increases the political power in the state in favor of our politics and social elevation." Thus Crummell, while firmly supporting the right to protest against racial discrimination, came down firmly in support of working to improve one's lot within the existing system through efforts at racial self-help.[33]

Other controversial matters arose at Albany. The first was a resolution passed in support of the black National Convention Movement. It affirmed the delegates' willingness "to cooperate with our friends" in promoting "the cause of human rights," but it also asserted their intention to continue assembling in meetings that would embody "the unbiased sentiments of our people."[34] Thus, without actually mentioning exclusivism, the delegates voiced their opposition to abandoning the black Convention Movement in favor of integrated conventions. They went on to issue a statement disapproving of the "national moral reform convention, which was to be held by call in New Haven on the tenth of September." While it is not recorded that either of these resolutions led to much discussion at the convention, they did lead to an exchange of letters in the *Colored American* the following winter. William Whipper of Philadelphia, who had not been present at the Albany meeting, protested in a series of letters that the tone of the convention had been "based on complexional caste."[35] His arguments were answered by one "Sidney," who wrote, "Whenever a people are oppressed . . . distinctive organization or action, is required on the part of the oppressed, to destroy that oppression." The convention heard "somewhat of a debate" over an indictment of "any system of general emigration offered to our people . . . to urge our removal from the land of our birth."[36] The resolution passed despite the opposition of Charles L. Reason and Alexander Crummell, who argued that it "was introduced in opposition to the object of the convention as set forth in its call." Apparently he was already reaching the point of willingness to listen to the emigrationist argument, but he does not seem to have opposed the declaration that "this country is our country," or the convention's profession of a determination to live and die among the American people, whose language, education, religion, and institutions "we love."

The debates at the Albany convention reveal that the black movement at this time was not uniform in its sentiments, and that the conventions of the 1840s were not purely and simply abolitionist convocations. There was indeed, among free blacks, the occasional sentiment that abolitionist agitation might most properly be undertaken by whites, with blacks assuming the responsibility for preparing themselves for survival and competition in the busy world of free citizens. Although strongly in favor of petitioning for and defending all their prerogatives as native-born Americans, they nonetheless supported independent black efforts for their own self-improvement. The contradiction between separatism and assimilation, not only in institutions but in individual minds, was destined to remain one of the more interesting complexities in Afro-American life and thought during at least the next century and a half.

In 1845, Crummell returned to New York City. He had finally been ordained to the priesthood, by Bishop Lee of Delaware, but he returned to his birthplace with mixed feelings, for he was once again in the diocese of B. T. Onderdonk. He also had conflicting emotions with respect to his work in the black community. He felt, on the one hand, a sense of duty to work for the elevation of his people and, on the other, a humiliating lack of appreciation. On one occasion his senior warden told him "that he was laboring in vain among a people who despised [his] efforts." His parents and relations entreated him to give up and move into another field; his wife's connections were "justly displeased at the poverty and almost wretchedness [his] circumstances brought upon her."[37]

He became rector of the Church of the Messiah, the second Episcopal church for colored people in New York, with a congregation made up mostly of "poor servants." The church had been organized around 1837 by John Peterson, one of its wardens, under the name of St. Matthew's, and had had only one prior minister, Isaiah De Grasse, who soon left for Jamaica. He described his experience at the Church of the Messiah as "a repetition of the misfortunes of Providence and Philadelphia." "It would be useless as well as tiresome to enter into particulars concerning my work in New York," he wrote. His trials were mainly pecuniary, but they were exacerbated when fire destroyed the room at 450½ Broadway, in which the congregation worshiped.[38] There was apparently some interest during this period in having him return to St. Philip's as its rector, but Crummell, for some reason, declined. In general, he was not popular in New York and did not know how to ingratiate himself diplomatically with whites or with blacks. He apparently received financial assistance from John Jay and had difficulty repaying the debts. In 1846, he received the discouraging news that the diocese of New York still had no intention of admitting black people as delegates to its convention. He had the heartening experience of befriending Reverend Evan M. Johnson, a man of "singular eccentricities" but "high Christian character," who despite the prevailing prejudices, invited him into his pulpit and entertained him as a guest at his table. Johnson, along with one John A. King, constituted a two-member committee of the convention of 1846 responsible for a minority report recommending that St. Philip's and other African churches be admitted to the convention. They drafted a statement arguing that "However just and proper distinctions in society may be in other respects, yet as members of one Holy Catholic Church, there ought to be no other distinction than that made by superior self denial, holiness and virtue." They recommended that the church "be admitted into union with the convention."[39]

But the convention was adamant, even using the hypocritical argument of black exclusiveness as a justification for its own separatist policies in the majority report.

> We object not to the color of skin, but we question their possession of those qualities which would render their intercourse with the members of a Church Convention useful, or agreeable, even to themselves . . . The colored people have themselves shown their conviction of this truth, by separating themselves from the whites, and forming distinct congregations where they are not continually humbled by being treated as inferiors. Why should not the principle on which they have separated themselves be carried out in the other branches of our Church organization?[40]

The implication of the statement was that it was not color prejudice but patterns of behavior that kept the races apart, yet, of course, even polished and refined blacks were discriminated against. And it was certainly not true that all blacks would have found association with the convention disagreeable. The majority report was more honest when it admitted that white Episcopalians were determined to continue humiliating blacks by treating them as inferiors.

Crummell's public life up to this time was dominated by the issue that affected him most, the crusade against racism. It was mainly his struggles with the Episcopal church, but also his participation in the civil rights movement, that had won Crummell a reputation among black American leaders during his twenties. But unlike many of his contemporaries—Samuel Ringgold Ward, Henry Highland Garnet, and the spectacular young Frederick Douglass—Crummell was not primarily an abolitionist orator. Perhaps this was because he had never been a slave. His formative experiences had not been on the plantation, but in the vice-infected African Quarter of New York. There he had struggled for an education, dodging the street gangs and avoiding the temptations of Cow Bay Alley. While the abolishment of slavery was an endeavor Alexander Crummell conscientiously pursued, the struggle against castelike discrimination occupied his talents to a greater extent, for it was color prejudice, rather than slavery, that had had the more profound effect on him directly.

Crummell clung obstinately to the idea that self-improvement was the most important tactic in blacks' struggle for their civil rights. If this had been apparent before, it became even more obvious in October 1847, when the National Convention of Colored People and Their Friends assembled in Troy, New York. Here again the issue of support for black institutions surfaced as a matter of consequence. Crummell served on a committee of four which reported that "the best means of abolishing slavery is proclamation of truth, and the best means of destroying caste is the mental, moral, and industrial improvement of our people."[41] Frederick Douglass, the member of the committee who read the report to the convention, seems to have influenced it considerably. It discouraged slave revolts, a point on which Douglass had disagreed with Garnet at the convention of 1843.[42] It also neglected to specifically protest the condition of the free Africans in the North. Some delegates were less than satisfied with the lofty abstractions of the report, which was not, primarily, a militant protest document. The emphasis was definitely on self-help, and there was much sentiment in support of establishing a national black press and an Afro-American college. Those who agreed that the best means of eliminating caste and advancing the interests of black people was self-help were the dominant voice at the convention.[43]

Crummell was one of the strongest advocates of the inconclusive movement to establish a black college, but there seemed to be little understanding of the need for such an institution. Although the convention voted 26 to 17 to establish a college, significant voices in the leadership, including Douglass and Garnet, questioned the need for a black college, since a number of colleges were already opening their doors to Afro-Americans. Of course this did not solve the problem of the black intellectual who wanted to make a living as a teacher. Ironically, Crummell would not be in the United States when the debate on this issue of such importance was resumed. It was he who "moved that the third Wednesday of September 1848 be the time for said convention, which motion prevailed."[44] By the time of the next convention, however, he was not only living in England but contemplating a lengthy stay.

Crummell's early writings reveal a conservative but thoughtful mind, concerned with other matters besides racial problems and refusing to be confined to subjects deemed appropriate for the mind of a Negro. As a youth, he had been relatively isolated from the sort of peer pressure and competition that made for the perfect nineteenth-century man of letters. His playmates and youthful companions included several bright and alert young men and women, but others were given to "idle and wicked jesting." It is clear that he had to generate from within the pressure to learn biblical Greek and Euclidean geometry. He obviously had a natural appetite for letters. Not surprisingly, since for several years his principal intellectual companions were older clergymen who were tutoring him for the ministry, Crummell's reading seems to have taken him in a conservative direction. He does not seem to have gravitated towards the attitudes presented in the writings of American abolitionists and other liberals. He was attracted to conservative points of view such as those expressed by Thomas Arnold, father of the now more famous Matthew.

His most important literary contribution surviving from the years prior to his departure for England is his *Eulogium on the Life and Character of Thomas Clarkson*, delivered in 1846; it was not the typical black abolitionist address. There were no striking firsthand accounts of life on the plantation, no harrowing descriptions of lashings, no titillating depictions of slave women stripped half-naked by prurient overseers, no heartrending stories of aged retainers turned out of their households. The eulogium was a philosophical piece. It contained a theory of history and civilization dominated by the idea of progress. It revealed a belief in the power of ideas and a concept of Christian modernism. "It is but recently," he wrote, "that the holy and the good have been able to command deserved attention. The world has been rolling on six thousand years in its course; and now in these latter days the Philanthropist is just beginning to obtain the regard and honor he so richly deserves."[45]

His conversative opinion that the earth was only six-thousand years old reveals that Crummell's faith was in no way shaken by the well-known geological theories of Charles Lyell. Geological evolutionism was not unknown to the general literate public, and the theory was even making its way into the black press. On February 23, 1839, the *Colored American* carried an article by John Morris, reprinted from *American Museum*, in which the author stated his design "to show that there is a perfect consistency between the facts demonstrated by geological researches and the sacred scriptures." The fact that every schoolboy had heard of dinosaurs did not prevent Crummell and many of his educated contemporaries from stubbornly clinging to the biblical chronology of Archbishop Ussher. Frozen mammoths discovered in Siberia were seen as evidence of Noah's Flood.[46]

Unimpressed though he was at the time by geological evolutionism, Crummell embraced the evolutionary metaphysic when it was applied to society. His religious historicism ran parallel to the secular theories of progressive social change that were found in such continental thinkers as Auguste Comte and François Guizot. When, exactly, Crummell became aware of these authors is unknown, although he did cite them in later works. He was affected by both religious perfectionism and secular theories of social progress. As Sidney Pollard and Jacques Barzun have shown, the idea of progress was "in the air" long before the popularity of Charles Darwin or Karl Marx.[47] Crummell accepted the view that history revealed progress towards progressively higher forms of ethical consciousness. Reflecting on ancient history brought to mind "the murderous exploits of a Sesostris or a Shiskah; and the remains of its high and unequalled art are the obelisks and the urns, commemorative of bloody conquerers—or the frowning pyramids, upon whose walls are the hieroglyphic representations of War, Conquest and Slavery." The relics of ancient literature were likewise dominated by brutality, or, as he put it, "the gorgeous representations of sanguinary deeds.'' Warriors and admirals dominated the records of modern times so that "Marlboro and Gustavus, Napoleon and Nelson, and Wellington have attracted as much notice and admiration as any of their contemporaries in the quieter walks of civil life, however distinguished for talent or for genius.''[48]

But Crummell believed that he perceived a changing tide. "We have advanced to a different era and have reached a more open day . . . Higher and nobler and worthier objects are now receiving human admiration.'' Thomas Clarkson, in Crummell's estimation, represented a new type of hero for the new era that was dawning. Clarkson's genius and sensibilities had combined to guarantee his eternal glory, linking his reputation with the welfare of the African race, who were children of destiny under special protection of providence.

> The Providences of God have placed the Negro race, before Europe and America, in the most commanding position. From the sight of us, no nation, no statesman, no ecclesiastics, and no ecclesiastical institution, can escape. And by us and our cause, the character and greatness of individuals and of nations, in this day and generation of the world, are to be decided, either for good or for evil—and so in all coming times, the memory and the fame of the chief actors now on the stage will be decided, by their relation to our cause. The discoveries of Science, the unfoldings of Literature, the dazzlings of Genius, all fade before the demands of this cause. This is the age of BROTHERHOOD AND HUMANITY and the Negro race is its most distinguished test and criterion.[49]

Crummell delivered the admonition that the nineteenth century would forever be judged on its ability to meet the philanthropic challenges offered by the likes of Clarkson, Dickens, Garrison, and Douglass. Like many of his contemporaries, Crummell was sensitive to the irony that the rhetoric of industrial and economic progressivism sprang up in a world of hereditary privilege and unmerited caste distinction. He was philosophically remote from Marx, and far less committed to fundamental social change, but, like Marx, he had inherited the Enlightenment dislike for traditions of hereditary caste.

Crummell was not a radical egalitarian, however, and his values may profitably be contrasted to those of his fellow abolitionist, Frederick Douglass. Born a year earlier than Crummell on a Maryland plantation, the product of a union between a white master and his black slave woman, this wily and resourceful mulatto was driven by a hatred of unmerited privilege. Every aspect of his life was colored by his experiences as a slave, and the battles against slavery and discrimination were his lifelong obsessions. To the crusade against racial slavery and other forms of discrimination he brought the full power of his massive intellect. Still, he was a child of the Romantic era rather than the Enlightenment; his egalitarian sentiments came from the heart rather than the head. It was at the level of emotion and instinct rather than reason that he formed his pragmatic arguments for human rights and freedom. Even the most ignorant classes should be granted full political rights, he argued, simply because they were human. With rhetoric that was eminently egalitarian, he rejected the natural aristocracy arguments of a Jefferson.[50]

Crummell, too, was more indebted to the school of sensibility than to the cult of reason. He was, however, an intellectual elitist, who fell heir to the ancient concept of a "Great Chain of Being." Douglass fought for the rights of the unwashed—the sunburned and the sweaty. Crummell was fighting for the rights of cultivated and refined African people to ascend the ladder of natural aristocracy. If in his belief in a natural aristocracy he was vaguely Jeffersonian, he was certainly no friend of democratic republicanism. Crummell's abolitionism was in the federalist tradition of Hamilton and Jay. He believed in strong institutions to control the passions of the mob. His vantage point during the New York riots of 1834 and his subsequent experiences with mob frenzy in New Hampshire confirmed his natural inclination to distrust the common yeomanry with their Jacksonian democracy. Perhaps it was his distrust of democracy that drew him towards the aristocratic and authoritarian discipline of the Episcopalians, rather than to the more democratic, but no less racist, Methodists or Presbyterians, whose self-governing black congregations would have seemed more hospitable.[51]

Beyond a doubt, had he been willing to accept the boundaries of caste that the church ruthlessly imposed, Crummell could have lived more comfortably among the Episcopalians. Was it only stubbornness that led him to continue pounding the doors of the chancery, demanding a status that his ecclesiastical superiors were dead set against granting? Was it only a desire to make the dogmatic custodians of racial orthodoxy uncomfortable? Or was it really a commitment to the doctrines of the Episcopal church that made him persist? For the man who believes strongly in the doctrine of apostolic succession, there is no salvation outside the branches of the "one, holy, catholic and apostolic church." Whatever the reasons for Crummell's adherence to the church of his oppressors, he confronted a dilemma resulting from his interpretation of Christianity. He was faced with three choices. He could abandon the church of his faith. He could accept an inferior status within it. Or he could remain faithful to the church whose traditions he accepted and whose rituals he admired, protesting the heretical racial policies that its worldly prelates, in the sinfulness of their hearts, endorsed.

A black man with his "simple dignity and . . . unmistakable air of good breeding," could probably have found a position as a polisher of spittoons, or a bellboy. Of course he would have had to be careful not to let his white employers know that he was trained in the classics. A work place in the trades was as difficult for a black man to come by as a first-class cabin on a steamboat. Farming was a worthy occupation for those who had land or the makings of a pioneer. And there were indeed some black families who had the heroic qualities needed to break the land while enduring the daily grinding brutality of life on the white supremacist midwestern frontier. A natural showman like the handsome, witty Frederick Douglass could make a living on the podium doing impersonations of former slavemasters and mocking the Southern dialect. A trickster like William Wells Brown, despite doubtful credentials, would eventually practice medicine, with a level of competency hardly lower than that of legitimate doctors in those days of leeching and bleeding.[52]

A recurrent theme in the writings of the young Crummell is his quest for employment as an educator. He began to suspect early in his career that he was not cut out for the life of a parish priest. He claimed that he did not enjoy preaching, although he was known to be an excellent preacher, whose sermons were often brilliant. He did not enjoy working with parishioners or visiting their homes and complained constantly that his health did not permit such activities. He seems to have had difficulty with his vestries in every post that he held. At least twice, he attempted to found academies for young people, but it is difficult to believe that Crummell could have been happy with any students who were not exceptionally able and highly motivated. He had developed the individualistic and cranky habits of many intellectuals, and he would clearly have been more at home working with mature students than with young pupils.

Given the practical limitations on career choices, Crummell probably had no clear idea of what sort of career he should follow. All that can be said for certain is that he was ambitious, both intellectually and politically, and that he hoped to make a career for himself as a public man of letters. He saw intellectual excellence as a racial duty, for like most educated blacks he believed that his success or failure as an intellectual would be interpreted as an indication of the abilities of black people as a whole. Inspired in early youth by a father who put great value on education, and by Peter Williams, who also encouraged classical studies, Crummell had developed early a belief in education as a means of elevating the status of black Americans. From childhood he had been exposed to sentiments such as those of the militant David Walker, who had viewed grammar school education as a weapon in the fight against the wretched conditions black Americans faced in the North, as well as in the South.

When Crummell tried to disprove Calhoun's pronouncement on the intellectual powers of black people, he was treated as a freak or a monstrosity. Although anti-intellectualism was a problem that all men of letters encountered in the United States, black people had to confront in addition the charge that literary education for black people was somehow "miseducation." Almost as soon as black people began to master the alphabet, they had to face whites' charges that they were not only presumptuous, but buffoonish. Literacy for black people was a serious issue, but what Crummell encountered, of course, even exceeded the usual opposition to black literacy. Crummell presumed to be a humanist, a man of letters, a student of classics and philology. In nineteenth-century America, where the bookish man was often openly ridiculed, Ichabod Crane was even more laughable in blackface.

Even David Walker's *Appeal* had come close to implying that it was ridiculous for black people to become involved in *belles lettres,* which would not prepare them for earning a livelihood. The theme of "miseducation" made many appearances in black writing throughout the nineteenth century. Crummell was soon at odds with the movement headed by Frederick Douglass, which held that the real educational needs of black people would best be served by trade schools.[53] What Crummell encountered was the inability of either the black or the white American social structure to provide him a place. The life of the mind was not intended for a black man, not even one with Crummell's striving personality, industrious habits, and vitriolic brilliance.

It was the anti-intellectualism of America, combined with the hostility to black education, that first set him thinking about going abroad for an education, at least as early as 1839. Crummell probably could not have said himself exactly when he made his decision to go to England. If, indeed, his decision was made primarily for educational reasons, he was not open with all his friends on this score. One thing is certain, however; he did not stumble suddenly on the idea of studying at Cambridge simply because the occasion presented itself. That was exactly what he later claimed in his letters to John Jay, but there is good evidence that he had brooded quietly on the idea for some time. Eight years earlier, Theodore Dwight Weld, who had somehow learned of Crummell's plan, wrote to Gerrit Smith concerning "Young Crummell, who was bastinadoed out of Episcopal Orders the other day, [and] is about leaving the country to get under a monarchy what the despotism of a republic denies him." Why the actual decision took eight years to mature remains a mystery. Perhaps the stubborn young Crummell required this lengthy period of frustration before taking the plunge.[54]

During the summer of 1845, Thomas Fry, a retired tutor at Oxford's Lincoln College, was already making efforts to bring Crummell to England for a university education. He had discovered two wealthy English women who were prepared to pay his and his family's expenses. But when Crummell finally left for England, the ostensible purpose of his trip was to raise funds for his work at home. The vestry of St. Philip's, the church in which he had been brought up by the now deceased Peter Williams, presented him with a strong endorsement on the eve of his departure, commending his intention to raise funds for an edifice for the Church of the Messiah. They wished him success in this venture, commending him "as a zealous Christian, anxious, and (under God) able to do a great work in behalf of his oppressed brethren in America." But even at this point, Crummell probably was considering an alternative plan.[55]

For years, Crummell had listened to and read with keen interest the stories of abolitionists in England. In 1845, Frederick Douglass made his first trip to Great Britain, which no doubt served as something of a catalyst. Douglass's letters from the British Isles were printed regularly in *The Liberator*. Douglass wrote of a land where a black man could employ a cab, be seated next to white people, enter a hotel, sit in the parlor, and dine in the dining room. More important, it was a society in which a black man could participate in the cultural life, go to libraries and museums, public lectures, concerts, and churches. Douglass told, with obvious relish, of the discomfort of white Americans in Europe when he was admitted to public places on equal terms with them.[56] Crummell was naturally curious to see what life might be like in such a society. If he could get an English university degree in the process, so much the better.

Yet the trip was more than a flight from American racial prejudice; it was to provide him with a psychological tool as well as a physical escape. He knew well the emotions of his oppressors, and he discerned in the American mentality, despite its self-conscious swagger, a desire for recognition by a putatively more civilized Europe. Americans longed for acceptance from England, in particular, and just as he longed for acceptance from the white American Episcopalians, so did they desire validation from the Church of England. American nationalism and the heritage of two Anglo-American wars notwithstanding, the American people still viewed England as the source of their culture and civilization. Even the supposed prophet of American cultural independence and self-reliance, Ralph Waldo Emerson, believed the English to be "some ages ahead of the world in the art of living."[57]

It was the white American's grudging and usually self-contradictory admiration for the British that Crummell, like so many of his black contemporaries, hoped to exploit. He would appeal to a higher court of opinion than American democracy—the court of English taste. He would capture at their source the coveted treasures of Anglo-Saxon character, education, and manners—those very English traits so admired by Americans. He would steal for himself the cultivation of a British gentleman and so become a far superior representative of modern European Civilization than the white Americans who sought to ostracize him. What sweet revenge!

# 4

# Arrival in England
# (1848–1849)

Crummell arrived in England at a time when a number of gifted and imaginative black abolitionists were enjoying celebrity of a sort. England was by no means free of racial hostility, but humiliation and discrimination were not so inescapable as they were in the United States. In contrast to what one daily experienced in American society, life in England must have been relatively painless. American blacks had nothing better, at that time, with which to compare their English experiences. An educated and articulate black man was a novelty, and thus excited curiosity rather than the open hostility that was to be experienced in America. Crummell wrote: "My black complexion is a great advantage and a real possession here, connected with other real qualities I am supposed to possess." [1]

Ever since the 1830s black American lecturers had been traveling in England, soliciting support for a variety of causes. Nathaniel Paul, a minister of the African Baptist church, had left his home in Albany to help establish the community of Wilberforce in Canada. His search for financial support led him to a four-year sojourn in England, during which he was successful enough to be able to lend William Lloyd Garrison the two hundred dollars he needed for his return passage to the United States in 1833—a fact that Garrison did not consistently deny. [2] After two years in England, Paul wrote to Garrison saying that "to contrast the difference in the treatment that a colored man received in this country with that which he received in America, my soul is filled with sorrow and indignation." Paul rhapsodized on the hospitable treatment he had received in the churches, in the inns, and on the public carriers. The only difference that he saw between his reception and that of whites was that "I am generally taken for a stranger, and they therefore seem anxious to pay me the greater respect." [3]

Nathaniel Paul's tour overlapped that of Robert Purvis, a well-off Pennsylvanian, whose appearance was indistinguishable from a white man's. Purvis wrote of the hearty reception he received from statesmen in the British Isles, especially from John Scoble, a leader in the British and Foreign Anti-Slavery Society, who introduced him to Daniel O'Connell, the Irish patriot. O'Connell, on hearing that he was an American, declined to take his hand, "but when he understood that I was not only identified with the abolitionists, but with the proscribed and oppressed colored class in the United States, he grasped my hand and warmly shaking it, remarked—'Sir, I will never take the hand of an American, nor should any honest man in this country do so, without first knowing his principles in reference to American slavery, and its ally, the American Colonization Society.' "[4]

Charles Lennox Remond, who toured the British Isles in 1840, quickly learned to take advantage of opportunities to excoriate American democracy before the court of English opinion. Well-aware that Americans, despite their nationalistic braggadocio, had a deeply rooted sense of inferiority to the English, he often referred to American racial prejudice as proof of that cultural inferiority. In a letter to Garrison he reported on British attitudes not only on slavery, but with respect to prejudice "that acts that part to slavery of second king at arms." He averred that to "rouse the honest indignation of the intelligent Englishman," one had only to tell him "of our school and academy exclusions . . . our Negro pews in the house of worship . . . the Jim Crow car, the top of the stagecoach, the forward deck of the steamboat."[5]

Frederick Douglass, as well, saw the advantages of exposing the hypocrisy of republican democracy in America. He took delight in the discomfort of fellow Americans peremptorily reduced to a status of social equality with himself. He commented often that in England he was "received as kindly as though my skin were white." In a letter published in *The Liberator* in 1846, he remarked, "Instead of a democratic government, I am under a monarchial government . . . I breathe, and lo! the chattel becomes a man."[6]

William Craft, who with his wife, Ellen, had escaped from slavery and fled to England, rejoiced at the birth of his "first free born babe," giving thanks that both mother and child were doing well, for though "her sickness was of the severest nature, yet she bore it all firmly, and without a murmur, because she knew she was not bringing a human being into the world to be brutified, but one whom the blessings of liberty and the pursuits of happiness may ever rest upon . . ." He emphatically denied false reports that his wife had consented to return to her former owners in Georgia. Mrs. Craft spoke for herself, saying "I had much rather starve in England, a free woman, than be a slave for the best man that ever breathed upon the American continent." It gave the Crafts obvious satisfaction to refer to England as a land of freedom, contrasting it to America, "the barbarous land of whips and chains."[7]

William Wells Brown characterized England as more egalitarian than America after his extensive tour of the kingdom, claiming that "Here a man is measured by his moral worth, and not by the color of the skin or the curl of the hair."[8] William G. Allen, a graduate of the Oneida Institute and one-time professor at McGraw College in New York, fled to England after marrying one of his white students. He arrived during the later years of Crummell's stay there, became a lecturer of moderate success, appealing even to working-class audiences, and published his memoirs, in which he attacked American color prejudice. In a letter to William Lloyd Garrison, published in *The Liberator,* he wrote: "That in Englishmen which most favorably impresses the colored man from America is the entire absence of prejudice against color." Allen observed a lack of that "patronizing (and, of course, insulting) spirit, even of hundreds of the American abolitionists." He claimed that "Color claims no precedence over character here . . . Reverend Samuel Ringgold Ward of Canada, than whom it is hardly possible to be blacker; and who is an honor to the race in intellectual ability, has been in London several weeks, and can amply testify to the fact that his skin, though 'deepest dyed,' has been no barrier to the best society in the kingdom."[9]

Ward, however, held a somewhat more realistic view of British society. He devoted a chapter of his autobiography to "Pro-Slavery Men in England." Remembering that his "first experience of English dealing was in being charged treble fare by a Liverpool cab man," he was critical of the view that England was a social paradise. Of course Ward made the ritual observation that he was "in a land of freedom, of true equality." He denied, however, the almost mystical experience that some other black Americans referred to. Perhaps in response to Douglass's, "I breathe, and lo!; the chattel becomes a man," Ward said, "I did not feel, as some blacks say they felt upon landing—that I was, for the first time in my life a man. No, I always felt that; however wronged, maltreated, outraged—still a man."[10]

Douglass, to be certain, waxed a bit too poetic on this as on other occasions. Crummell may be accused of the same fault. It was not that either man possessed "A heart too soon made glad, too easily impressed." They were a bit too eager to draw invidious comparisons to American society and thus they failed to recognize the danger of allowing Europeans to acquire so effortlessly a reputation for racial tolerance. Such statements, while motivated by political strategy, were at the very least injudicious. Black travelers in England were accepted up to a point, but barriers of color, class, and culture prevented them from living lives comparable to those of the English gentry, with whom they identified. The desire to point up the irony that a black man might feel safer and freer in monarchial England than in democratic America was of course irresistible. At the same time it prompted such remarkable statements as that of Douglass, or the following one, which Crummell made in a letter to Jay.

> I do indeed thank God for the providence that has brought me to this land, and allowed me, for once in my life, to be a freeman. Oh the acquisition to one's heart, mind, and soul,—the consciousness in all its fullness that one is a man! I never had it before I came to England. I used to think I had, but now I know it.[11]

The reason that Crummell usually gave for traveling in England, and for eventually spending four and a half years there, is that he went to raise money for his parish, the Church of the Messiah in New York. Only after his arrival was he persuaded by English friends to remain and take a degree at Cambridge. He presented the decision as a sudden and unselfish one, explaining himself in the following manner: "Unsolicited, nay, unthought of by myself, a personal interest sprang up in my behalf; and the request came to me that I should retire for a season from over-work, and become a student in the University of Cambridge."[12] Such changes of direction in the lives of mature people are seldom arrived at so suddenly. Crummell had apparently expressed some idea of studying in England as early as October of 1839. In any case, he had not been in England for very long before he made known his plans to pursue a university degree. While he seems to have pursued his fund-raising on behalf of the Church of the Messiah with diligence, he obviously had other concerns. His ambitions were not solely altruistic, and he made certain that the time spent in England would benefit him, his wife, and his children, as well as his congregation at home.

Crummell went to work lecturing and preaching immediately upon his arrival. British newspapers and antislavery journals report lectures he gave throughout 1848. He cultivated influential friends among British abolitionists through the British and Foreign Anti-Slavery Society and its secretary, Henry Venn, whose good offices eventually made it possible for him to enter Cambridge.[13] Printed circulars and newspaper announcements that chart his progress during his first six months in England reveal that he was immediately successful as a fund-raiser. He was not the first black Episcopalian to succeed there. Eli Stokes, who, two years after Crummell left Rhode Island, had followed him to the rectorship of Christ Church in Providence, made an English tour around 1847. His mission was, in the words of the bishop of Rhode Island, "crowned with entire success, and the liberal contributions which he received in that distant land have enabled the gentlemen holding the property in trust to make a satisfactory settlement with the mortgages."[14] Although Christ Church seemed temporarily to have staved off disaster, the parish dissolved within two years, and Stokes went to Liberia under the Domestic and Foreign Missionary Society of the Episcopal Church. Crummell's efforts on behalf of his New York congregation were to be followed by a curiously parallel sequence of events. Like Stokes, he would have the happy success of sending home substantial funds, but he too would fail to save his parish.

Whatever his original intentions in coming to England, it is evident that by early summer 1848 Crummell had attempted to divide his activities into two discrete categories. He had allowed—perhaps encouraged—his British friends to form two committees on his behalf. One was to collect funds for the Church of the Messiah; the other was to solicit contributions to support his family while he pursued his private ends at the university. He wrote to John Jay on July 14, 1848, to describe his successful preaching in the city of Bath. He reported with some gratification that he expected to administer communion in the church of Reverend Mr. Brooks. He also wrote, however, to inform Jay of the offer he had received from Thomas Fry, "a retired and elderly clergyman" of the city, to prepare him for an education "at either Oxford or Cambridge" and to help him with his expenses. He humbly solicited Jay's advice on the matter, but he had obviously taken definite steps toward carrying the plan forward. It seems, therefore, that it was not really advice he was seeking but support, for he was determined to follow a course that few Americans would approve.[15]

At a meeting held on Friday, May 26, Crummell stated his reasons for coming to England and gave an account of the civil and spiritual condition of the black population of the United States. After delivering the standard abolitionist description of the state of affairs in the South, where black people were whipped and scourged, bought and sold, overworked and denied education, he spoke of the spiritual welfare of the slaves, who were "literally and absolutely heathen." Among the free blacks, even those in the North, the mental and spiritual oppression were immeasurably severe. "Caste as strong as any that ever existed in India, met the colored man in every relation of life." A spirit of perfect exclusion "kept their children from the workshops of mechanics and kept them from learning trades." It barred them from public conveyances and even denied them admission to academies of learning. Although he denied coming to England to "render odious the Christian character of any of the religionists in his country," he righteously denounced the spirit of caste in the church and exposed the exclusionist policies of the seminaries.[16]

He went on to describe in detail the low state of education and religion among the black American population, revealing the illiteracy of "many African ministers in the Southern states [who] could not read a single sentence in the Bible." He spoke of his own congregation in New York, the second of two Episcopal churches in that city, which had had as its first pastor the literate and articulate Isaiah De Grasse, now residing in the West Indies. De Grasse had become disgusted with the American caste system and had departed in 1842. Since then, services had often been suspended for want of a minister. The congregation, mostly "poor servants," were worshiping in hired rooms, since they could not afford to build a church and the white Episcopalians were indifferent to their need. Crummell stated his conviction to a gathering of abolitionists that the African race could furnish a needed element to the religion and civilization of America. Both races would remain "unhealthy and incomplete until the Negro race were raised up and received as brethren." It appeared, Crummell was reported to have said, that the African people would ever be "the criterion of American religion." "They were to rise up and furnish in their own distress, in their amelioration, in their enlightenment, the needed element of humanity to the Christianity of America, and of brotherhood to the civilization thereof." The most absolute need of black people at present was spiritual culture and Christian enlightenment. Thus had he come to England to appeal for the spiritual welfare of his people. The English people could help by erecting for them "a temple in which to worship Almighty God, reclaim the hosts of simple wandering ones around them, and rear up their children in the 'nurture and admonition of the Lord'.''

A circular printed and distributed after the meeting introduced Crummell and his goal, bore witness to his legitimacy, and listed the names of the distinguished churchmen who had consented to act as a committee of management.[17] Around 1853, at the end of his work, Crummell printed a circular describing his labors from 1848 to 1851, listing all the donations received, and naming the total sum as £1934. 6s. 3d. Of this sum, £358. 10s. 4d. was expended for printing, travel, and expenses. The English committee were thus able to invest £1400. 6s. 11d. with the view that it should be paid to the committee in New York, ''as soon as it can be shown that it will be applicable either to the purchase of a building or to assist in erecting one for the object for which it was subscribed.'' The specific goal was announced in another circular which read: ''It is desired to purchase a site and to erect an edifice of the plainest, simplest structure, capable of holding from 300 to 1000 persons. To accomplish this purpose a sum of between 3,000 *l*. and 4,000 *l*. will be requisite.'' The circular mentioned Crummell's endorsements from the bishops of London, Llandaff, and Oxford. But Crummell's friends also printed another circular on his behalf that year,[18] listing the members of a committee of management and stating their intention to send him to Cambridge. It also mentioned that ''Mrs. Crummell has embarked at once for England, and brought her little ones with her.''

Some weeks earlier, Thomas Fry had lent his support to a proposal that Crummell's family should be brought over from America.[19] ''A lady having offered to pay the passage and another lady to educate Mrs. Crummell free of expenses,'' Fry estimated that ''£400 would be wanted for Mr. Crummell and at least £300 for the maintenance of the family.'' To the objection that this would depart from the original plan of Crummell's visit by suspending his ministry to the loss of the congregation in New York, he responded that the advantages of sending back an educated minister and his wife would fully outweigh the disadvantages of a loss of time. At the very least, ''Crummell should be supplied with one or two good commentaries and such other books of divinity as would give him a better acquaintance with divine subjects. . . . And would not a year be well spent with some pious clergyman for better training, while his church was in erection?''[19] Fry was obviously one of Crummell's sincerest patrons. By the end of the year he had taken all of the Crummells under his roof at 36 Bathwick Street, Bath.[20]

During the summer of 1848 Crummell traveled to Cambridge, where he addressed a number of meetings and ''breakfasted with several of the Masters and Fellows at large breakfast parties,'' including the masters of Caius and Trinity Colleges. He was a minor celebrity, managing to meet socially with a variety of lords, ladies, and bishops and people of wealth while passing through London. Whether or not including Cambridge in his summer itinerary bore any relation to his eventual admission, the visit must certainly have had some influence on his ultimate decision to attend.[21]

Crummell's speeches during the summer of 1848 were divided into two categories: direct appeals to English munificence on behalf of his church, and general indictments of slavery and caste before antislavery societies. Speeches of the first sort were delivered in Bath, Cheltenham, and Liverpool, where large crowds packed the churches and hotels, sometimes standing to hear him describe the cruelties of slavery in the United States. He constantly reported "the disdain by which the free colored population are treated by the whites even in those states that do not tolerate slavery." He described his church in New York, whose membership during the ten years of its existence "had been forced to worship in hired rooms, their services being often suspended through poverty or want of a minister." He told of vain pleas to the American Episcopalians for support and expressed the hope that "the inhabitants of England would demonstrate that they disavowed the system of Caste." Although it would later be suggested that Crummell's English tour was self-serving, there is ample evidence that he faithfully carried forward his original intention to raise funds for the Church of the Messiah.[22]

One of Crummell's more celebrated speeches was his address before the British and Foreign Anti-Slavery Society in May 1848. At this meeting he moved a resolution that acknowledged and celebrated the abolition of slavery throughout France and its possessions, and paid tribute to Sweden and Denmark for their "extinction of bondage" in their island possessions. The resolution also commended several other governments, especially that of Germany, for her "abolition of serfage in Hungary, Prussian Poland, and Gallicia." After reading the resolution, Crummell spoke for about half an hour. He thanked God for having placed England in her providential position as "foremost of the nations" and told his receptive audience that," amid the decay of empires, He has kept you firm, steady, and unshaken. . . ." The Christian efforts of the English saints, Sharpe, Wilberforce, and Clarkson, would "ultimately tend to restore Africa to her ancient glory among the nations."[23]

He then proceeded to denounce otherwordly religion, a concern that would reappear in his writing throughout his career. He condemned the American Christians "so deeply engaged in saving the souls of men, that they think it unnecessary to manifest much interest in their temporal condition. . . . I confess, Sir, that I have not much respect for a religion that dwells so much in the clouds that it cannot attend to sublunary affairs." He then presented the view that, "wherever the Gospel of salvation wrought its wonders, there was produced not only the glorious liberty of the sons of God, but the amelioration of man's temporal condition and the freedom of the slave." But even if a spirit of Christianity had not commanded a hatred of slavery, there were purely temporal reasons for opposing the system. Slavery was a "man-destroying institution . . . at war with humanity." Every human being on earth was in jeopardy so long as slavery existed anywhere. "We are none of us safe . . . while such an institution exists in any part of the globe." He then embarked on a lengthy attack on Christian hypocrisy in the United States, which was "the grand offender of the nations, against freedom and civilization and good government."

He expressed regret and shame that America was an enslaver of the minds and souls of men, a regret that was "increased by the consideration that my country is a Protestant country. . . . The very fact of my country being so strongly pro-slavery makes perilous the existence of a true Protestant spirit in the land." In the providence of God, however, wonders were being worked and there was reason to hope that one would see "the mighty pillars and the huge buttresses of this colossal iniquity toppling down to eternal destruction and oblivion." England, by the grace of God, Christianizer and civilizer of the world, was to be the agent for promoting change in the United States and elsewhere and for advancing the temporal and spiritual welfare of Africa and her children.[24]

That same summer he preached in St. George's Church in Liverpool, "crowded to repletion," having as his text the eighth chapter of St. Paul's Epistle to Titus, which enjoins, "that they which have believed in God might be careful to maintain good works." Here he spoke on the obligations and duties of Christians to assume the burdens of life in a scientific age. Despite the many scientific advances of the nineteenth century, sophistry, infidelity, paganism, and Romanism were yet to be obliterated. Slavery and serfdom still survived in many quarters of the globe. Africa still suffered from the effects of the slave trade, which had been so destructive of its civilization and domestic institutions. In the United States, slavery made a mockery of Christianity, and a caste system prevented the free black population from receiving religion or enlightenment. However, he concluded, the English people could change all this by following the biblical command to do all good works, and by "support[ing] the charitable institutions of their country."[25]

Throughout the summer of 1848 Crummell continued to ponder "the many advantages of a university course, [but] not so much as to prevent . . . seeing the partial disadvantages. On the one hand, he appreciated the prestige that a Cambridge education would give, not only to him but to his work in New York. On the other hand, he realized that three years' absence would certainly erode his position. He saw immediately the propaganda value of being able to contrast the treatment he had received from an American seminary to his reception at one of the world's great universities. Achieving a Cambridge degree would certainly justify his indignation during the controversy with Onderdonk. In addition to the obvious ecclesiastical and educational advantages would be the social triumph of "being allowed social intercourse for years with the flower of England's youth." Nor was he reluctant to remind his friends that the English universities were considered "superior to our colleges" and that the English degree was "of great value in America." It seemed reasonable to hope that an English degree would place its possessor in a position to "shame contempt, neutralize caste—yea even command respect and consideration."[26]

By consideration he meant status. Crummell had long hoped to combine his ministry with work as an educator. He dreamed of eventually becoming "a Classical teacher in New York . . . , the head of a Seminary for Colored Youth . . . , training young men for the ministry." The permanent advantages of being able to undertake such a mission would certainly offset the temporary disadvantages of his absence from New York. And, of course, there would be advantages for Mrs. Crummell as well, who would be studying French, English, and music, while Crummell studied at Cambridge. Both of them would prepare to make their future household in New York "the fountainhead, whence with God's blessing might flow knowledge, learning, and intelligent religion to many of the youth of our race for generations to come." Was it wrong, he asked, to see to his own family's comfort and welfare, especially when improving their lot would so obviously be a means of advancing the general lot of all black Americans?[27]

When John Jay asked him if a Cambridge education would not perhaps isolate him and overqualify him for work with an illiterate class of people, undercutting his effectiveness, Crummell responded that "true learning leads to simplicity." Besides, the black people of New York were characterized by "a great deal of mental activity," despite their lack of formal education; they were remarkable for their "intellectual inquisitiveness and questioning." Indeed the latter proclivity had led to "no little infidelity." Crummell claimed that his congregation contained "two thirds of the black and colored schoolteachers—illiterate men and women it is true, but to supply them I have to study, while I have but few materials with which to study."[28]

Crummell nonetheless expressed genuine concern, if not guilt, at the thought of abandoning his congregation. He also felt he had to guard against the temptation to remain in England permanently. His wife had been "begging and entreating [him] for years to leave the U.S., for she saw no hope for [them] as a family and none for [their] children in the future." He saw the "danger that we may get weaned from America, and get attached to the freedom of English life and society," and ultimately be unwilling to return to the United States, but he did not fear this temptation. While he was happy indeed to be in England, he knew that his stay was "not permanent." How real were the possibilities of remaining? It is difficult to say. He was offered a chaplaincy with "a large salary," in 1848, but he had declined it and had not wavered since, although he did have "some fears" for his wife. Perhaps he would work with black people in some other quarter of the globe. Even this early he had begun to entertain the possibility. But he was certain his work was to be among some African people, and, although he acknowledged that he was tempted, he had faith in his power to resist. "I am not intoxicated," he wrote. "I know that [my residency] is not permanent; I would not have it permanent. If I know anything of myself, I am identified with my race in America with all its trials, sufferings, struggles, hopes, aspirations, and endeavors." It might be that Providence would someday call him to labors in some other quarter of the globe, but his heart's desire was "to help upbuild my people."[29]

He wrote to Jay soliciting his "advice." He saw the importance of maintaining the friendship of his strongest ally in New York, but Crummell's reasons for maintaining the tie with Jay were more than political. He felt considerable affection for the young aristocrat and required his mental and emotional support. The conventions of the mid-nineteenth century did much to dictate the deferential tone of Crummell's letters to Jay, all questions of color aside. In fact, he probably wrote things to Jay that he would never have written to a black man. Crummell acknowledged his superior status, his breadth of experience, his educational attainments, and his quality of mind. He also admired him for his humility and accessibility, for "here was a young man, fully equipped by ancestry and name, culture and wealth and position for the highest prizes in life; yet seemingly oblivious of them all."[30] Crummell's letters to Jay, although never really obsequious, were always respectful in tone and definitely acknowledged a difference in rank. On one level, they are the letters of one who is concerned with preserving the friendship of an acknowledged social superior. But at times they also read as if their author wanted to remind his white social superior that there was a world beyond America, a world where Americans were the social inferiors. He reminded Jay, the Harvard graduate and scion of one of America's most distinguished families, "You know the English Universities are superior to our colleges. The English degree is of great value in America."[31]

There is a candor in these letters that one does not find in Crummell's letters to anyone else, white or black. I do not think that it was really advice that Crummell sought, but someone to talk to. Some of the letters seem more like journal entries than letters. In these writings, we see him struggling with his conscience and justifying his decision to attend Cambridge. Then again, he reveals his inner moral struggle as he decides to settle in Liberia. Crummell felt a need to justify himself, not only to himself, but to people whom he respected—people like Jay. For all his arrogance and rigidity, he still required friends and supporters. We do not know what sort of letter he was writing to his black friends at this time. Nor do we know how his wife reacted to his shifting plans. We do know that he turned to John Jay, a white man, and wrote him some letters of exceeding candor. What is more, John Jay seems to have listened and to have responded to him. Unfortunately, Jay's letters to Crummell have not yet been found, but it seems clear that Jay did not always agree with Crummell. But friends are not under an obligation always to be in agreement, and Jay seems to have retained Crummell's lifelong friendship.

At the end of Crummell's first year in England, he was settled temporarily in Bath. He may have been drawn by the supposed healing benefits of the waters, for his health was suffering from his rigorous lecture tour. He had been joined by his family and had begun his studies with the Reverend Thomas Fry, former Master of Lincoln College, Oxford. He was, in his own words, "scrupulous about funds for my own family" not coming out of the money collected for the Church of the Messiah.[32] He was careful to let his English and American supporters know that the fund he was collecting for the church was kept separate from the money he was collecting for his education. He corresponded regularly with his chief vestryman in New York, a Mr. Tyson, who often sent him newspapers and letters with news from America. Tyson helped him to stay abreast of harmful rumors in New York concerning his progress in England. He once informed him of a story that he had made a blanket indictment of all the American clergy. Crummell denied this in a letter to Jay, insisting that he had never "attacked or abused directly or indirectly the church as a body or any class as a class." He informed Jay most emphatically, however, that he made no apology for his statements, and insisted that he "should not, even if I had been somewhat more earnest and more personal." Although the oppression in America, especially the ecclesiastical oppression, was "enough to make a man mad," he wryly commented, "I have not been mad—but merely spoken forth the words of truth." [33]

By early 1849, difficulties were beginning to develop with Mr. Tyson and the vestry of the Church of the Messiah. After repeated solicitations from Tyson, Crummell had forwarded a portion of the monies collected to New York and now felt himself in an "unpleasant position." The vestry had somehow allowed the monies to pass out of their coffers, and he had been instructed by members of the British committee that funds collected for the construction of an edifice in New York should not be appropriated for any other use. The committee organized to finance his education was equally emphatic that its funds should be used solely to support the Crummells in England. Crummell's letter to Tyson, which has been lost, apparently contained some powerful language. Tyson showed the letter to Jay, who felt that although the feelings expressed were natural, the manner of expressing them was perhaps unwise. [34]

That he expressed such impatience and exasperation with his vestry is understandable. Crummell had experienced many disappointments in his work among colored people, and he sometimes complained of their treatment of him, "their extravagant expectations, their lack of sympathy, their almost absolute demand of earnest self-sacrifice without the return of sympathy or self-help." [35] Crummell was developing what is called a "difficult personality," or, as one of his early biographers would put it, he was getting a reputation for "unbending righteousness." To his credit, he never really lost faith in black people. He spoke of their shortcomings in the way that one of his British physicians spoke of his coronary problem, "functional" but not "chronic." As he once put it, "In their native state, there is no people more gentle, kind, generous, sympathizing and grateful. But slavery and caste have marred and spoiled one of the best races of men. Their generous qualities have measurably departed. Their fine and genuine sympathy, their benign affections have been corroded." [36] In eulogizing Crummell, Du Bois knew whereof he spoke in suggesting that the most powerful temptation Crummell ever experienced was "the temptation of Doubt," the temptation to question the innate ability of his people—"to doubt the destiny and capability of the race his soul loved. [37] But despite the pain that came to him again and again, in every church and with each successive vestry, never, he said, "can any act whatever of theirs divorce me from them." [38]

During the spring of 1849 he continued to preach in the churches and to speak at public gatherings. It is interesting to note that speeches delivered during this period often did double duty. While his announced purpose, and the burden of his remarks, was to solicit contributions for the church, meetings were sometimes opened by remarks from a sympathetic clergyman, who would mention Crummell's "secondary" motive. At one public meeting in April he was introduced by Reverend J. C. Miller, who announced that several eminent clergymen and noblemen had decided that he should have the benefit of an English university education before he returned to New York. As the *Midland County Herald* put it, "so that by carrying back to America the degrees if not the honors he might be a standing reproach to that spirit of exclusiveness which kept such men out of American colleges." Following this introduction, reported the *Herald,* he "traced his own personal history, especially in his struggle to obtain education," although he was careful to pay tribute to the bishops who had supported his cause.[39] In line with this, he wrote to Jay, asking for help in publishing a pamphlet which was to describe in painstaking detail the controversy with Onderdonk. Crummell instructed Jay to inform him of the cost of publication, promising to send the sum immediately. He requested a copy of his *Caste in the Church* from Jay, which also discussed the Onderdonk confrontation. He was certainly making no secret of the educational obstacles he had encountered, which undoubtedly served to interest English philanthropists in contributing to his Cambridge fund.[40]

On May 11, he spoke in Birmingham before the Ladies' Negroes' Friends Society at a meeting in Dee's Hotel. His speech was one of "considerable length and ability," describing the effects of the slave trade on Africa and commending the heroic efforts that had brought it to an end. Crummell exhorted his audience to continue their crusade against slavery and the slave trade, which continued unabated in the Western Hemisphere. He praised the British and Foreign Anti-Slavery Society for its use of moral suasion; he commended the Royal Navy for sending a squadron to the West Coast of Africa; and he urged the British people to bring economic pressure to bear. He called for a boycott of all products produced by slave labor, presenting arguments from the *Anti-Slavery Reporter* and other publications to support his view that slavery must be attacked by commercial means, a theme that would figure prominently in his writings over the next decade.[41]

Crummell's campaign against the American Colonization Society resulted in one of his more impressive triumphs on the podium in 1849. It was one of the ironies of his life, in view of his later conversion to emigrationism and his willingness to collaborate with the American Colonization Society. In the spring of 1849, while Crummell was speaking in Liverpool, Rev. John Miller happened incidentally to be visiting the city, promoting the views of the American Colonization Society. Crummell took every occasion to speak vigorously against Miller. He wrote to abolitionists in the United States, who, in response, organized a meeting in New York on April 23, 1849. There, Frederick Douglass expressed his thankfulness that "one Alexander Crummell, whom you all know, is on the ground at this moment doing battle against the . . . subtile foe in the person of this Dr. of Divinity." George T. Downing then introduced a resolution, crediting Crummell as the source of the information that had led to the rally, and expressing the "abhorrence and contempt of our people" for the "American Colonization Society or any other similar wicked scheme."[42]

✳

Although much occupied with his political activities, Crummell found occasions to enjoy life's simple pleasures. "It is extremely pleasant to travel about the country at this season of the year," he wrote in early summer of 1849. "I have myself made two or three visits to quarters of extreme loveliness, far surpassing anything of the kind which I have ever seen." He had made several appointments in the diocese of Lichfield, which had given him "opportunity to traverse the rich valley of the Trent, abounding in beautiful succession of hills and dales." He had walked the paths "where old Isaak Walton whiled away many an hour in his favorite sport." But Crummell, "in no way inclined to be one of his followers," took "more pleasure in wandering amid the scenes which abound in that region, or listening to the echo of my own voice, while treading along the aisles of some of those ancient and magnificent churches, for which the neighborhood of the diocese are famed." He had spent a pleasant interlude touring cathedrals with two African friends, one of them a Hausa, "the other of the Timmanee (my father's tribe)." And after attending an impressive Trinity Sunday service in St. Paul's Cathedral, he had met the bishop of London, who despite his reputation for coldness had greeted the three black men most cordially. "With a broken voice, a subdued manner, and, I think, with tears in his eyes," he had convinced Crummell of his warmth, character, and piety. Henry Venn had also spoken with Crummell at the conclusion of the service and had told him of his African friends' success at the missionary college. Crummell was gratified to hear that both had been outstanding students and that the Hausa had "stood the best examination of all the students." Crummell had come a long way from the squalor of New York's Negro Quarter; he had been introduced into some of the most refined circles of England's progressive elite. He was traveling throughout the realm, relishing not only the beauty of its countryside, but the refinement of its gentry. He was a minor celebrity, received with great courtesy everywhere. At Windsor Castle, which he visited "just at the time of the Ascot Races," he reported somewhat cryptically, "I saw Her Majesty and one of the Princes and had a recognition from royalty."[43]

He addressed the meeting of the British and Foreign Anti-Slavery Society in 1849, as he had done in the preceding year, calling again for a boycott of slavery-produced articles. He commended the British people for their suppression of the slave trade, then urged them on to the next step—general abolition, insisting that "to put down the slave trade you must abolish slavery . . . the whole system must be destroyed." He reminded them that they consumed "two thirds of the whole American cotton crop" if they would close down the Lancashire mills and allow their Manchester factory people to stand still, then the effects on the American cotton growers would be "wonderful." He did not say how he thought such a policy might affect the attitudes of the English working-class towards abolitionism or black people in general.[44]

Throughout the years of his preparation for the Cambridge examinations, he would continue to speak on abolitionism. It kept him in touch with his black peers in England and America and preserved his sense of continuing commitment to the struggle. At the British and Foreign Anti-Slavery Society meetings of 1851 he was reunited with the black American abolitionists Josiah Henson, J. W. C. Pennington, and Henry Highland Garnet, each of whom spoke. Garnet, in particular, "was received with loud cheers on rising." He spoke on the effects of slavery, not only on those who were in Southern bondage, but on those who were nominally free. The slaveholders had united with the American colonizationists to make even the free blacks as unhappy as possible. Garnet denounced the colonizationists as the worst enemies of his race; they urged black people to go to Africa and pointed to the misery created by the Fugitive Slave Law as evidence that they ought to leave. Daniel Webster, who had created the Compromise of 1850, with its provision for returning fugitive slaves to their masters, was as great an enemy of the black population as Henry Clay, the slave-holding president of the American Colonization Society. Webster worked hand in hand with Clay, adding to the burdens of the free blacks. "In the name of the mass of the free American blacks," Garnet warned his English friends, "whoever asserts that the colored people or their true friends entertain any other sentiment towards the Society than the deepest contempt and abhorrence, assert that which is entirely false." The colonizationists wished to rid the Western world of free blacks, only to make the system of slavery more secure.[45]

Garnet insisted that he was loyal to Africa, the land of his fathers, maintaining, "I love the country; I love its interests, and feel grateful to any one and everyone who labours to promote its welfare." He conceded that Liberia, although created by the colonizationists, might possibly do some good for the continent, although he had only contempt for the motives of its founders. But the slaveholders would never succeed in eliminating the free black population, nor would they break the spirit of the black race. They were determined to rise. They had developed churches and schools; they had become professors, physicians, editors, and lawyers. They had the sympathy of heaven on their side, as well as the opinion of the civilized world. The system was doomed, but, of course, more efforts were required before the effects of generations of slavery could be obliterated. The fetters of ignorance and degradation must be removed along with the shackles that bound the hands and feet. Once the work of emancipation had been completed, elevation of the race would be rapidly accomplished. England must do her part and strike the death blow to slavery in the Americas by refusing to consume the products of slave labor. "Mr Garnet resumed his seat," the *Anti-Slavery Reporter* observed, "amid loud and long continued applause."[46]

After a short address by a member of parliament, Mr. S. M. Peto, Crummell rose to speak. He too condemned the Fugitive Slave Law, which he saw as part of a "general rising of the surges of slavery and oppression throughout the world, presaging wrath and destruction to the cherished liberties of mankind." He noted "movements of the crowned heads of Europe during the past two or three years," which constituted a "royal conspiracy" to destroy the gains of the present age with respect to the spirit of freedom and natural rights. He asserted that "the liberties of mankind have as much, if not more, to fear from the democracy of the United States as from the aristocracy of Russia.'' Then he turned to the theme of the convention—what steps should be taken to destroy the system of slavery? His answer did not reiterate the points that Garnet had just made, which he had often enough made himself, stressing the importance of political and economic measures. Instead, raising an issue that was his abiding concern, he said, ''If you wish to free a people from the effects of slavery, you must improve and elevate their character.''[47] With Garnet present, who had so masterfully urged the importance of economic warfare, Crummell could focus his attention on what he believed to be of even greater importance. ''I do not pretend to deny that the people to whom I belong in the United States are as a whole, weak and degraded,'' he said. ''For upwards of two centuries they have for the most part been deprived of all religious institutions; debarred from . . . education; cut off from all participation in civil and political prerogatives. . . . And what could be the result of such a regimen as this but degradation and benightedness?'' He considered it one of the marvels of the world that American blacks still preserved so many of the higher and nobler instincts of mankind. The relationship between the free blacks in the North and the slaves in the South was ''close and intimate,'' he said, and therefore any improvement in the lot of one would necessarily affect the other. Thus he called on the English to turn their attention to the ''elevation of the Negro, his culture and enlightenment.'' He reminded them that the Anglo-Saxons had once been a backward people; that British culture ''did not spring up in the brief period of a year or a century.'' Nor, by implication, did it come about independently of intellectual commerce with more civilized peoples. So too must Africa's children be lifted up through evangelization. This certainly did not imply that the pseudo-evangelizing activities of the American Colonization Society or its Liberian experiment were to be the means of black uplift or African redemption. Where had there ever been a colony whose existence had led to the uplift of an indigenous population? Certainly neither in America, New Zealand, Australia, or the Cape of Good Hope. The means of accomplishing the evangelization and civilization of Africa was to develop a class of educated youth.[48] This was a theme that would persist in his writings for the next fifty years. His departure for Africa would in no way imply a departure from the principles of this 1851 address.

# 5

# Cambridge Influences
# (1849–1853)

Crummell began his Cambridge studies in autumn of 1849. His preparation with Fry had been necessary, for at Cambridge one's studies were largely in Greek and Latin classics, as well as in mathematics. In the last of these, his early training had been particularly weak. To be sure, he had been introduced to classical languages, but Beriah Green had emphasized biblical Greek and Hebrew at the Oneida Academy rather than the profane classics. Crummell informed Jay in 1849 that for the first time, under Dr. Fry's tutelage, he was "privileged . . . to get an acquaintance with the classics."[1] Sarah Crummell gave birth to their first daughter, Frances, during the summer, and as soon as she was well enough to travel, the family moved to Cambridge, where friends had hired "a very neat and convenient cottage on a new square and with a good garden attached."[2] When he arrived in the lecture room, he admitted later, he was "unable to read a simple line in Latin or Greek." His first examination was passed in March 1850. "It was a College Examination," as distinct from a university examination, and as such would have little bearing on his actually taking the degree. "Fourteen went into the examination. In Science I stood with the four lowest. In Classics I stood eighth on the list." At the beginning of his studies he had been "the last man in everything."[3]

Crummell's career at Cambridge was not, nor could it have been, a typical experience. He realized this, of course, from the beginning. He wrote to Jay:

My name is entered at Caius College, Cambridge. By a letter received this morning from Bath I find my friends on the Committee there are informed by Mr. Carus that he has reversed the matter and entered my name at Trinity College, Cambridge. I am disposed to regret it. When I go up to reside I shall be the lamest and weakest man there; and Trinity being the first college in the University and the scholars there more prominent than any where else. I fear I may mortify my friends if not disgrace myself. My desire has been to enter one of the minor colleges or the Halls, but my friends have been determined I should have a prominent position and the largest advantages. However, if steady [?] application, untiring industry and a sincere love of letters and learning with the divine assistance will enable a man to overcome difficulties, then I have no fears for the future."[4]

According to *Alumni Cantabrigiensis,* it was due to Benjamin Brodie's influence that Crummell was entered in Queens' College. Queens' was not considered the most prestigious of the colleges in 1849. Few of its graduates were taking honors and Crummell would be no exception. The college was named for the queens who endowed it. It had been founded in 1448, as part of the second great period of growth in Cambridge, by Margaret of Anjou, wife of Henry VI, who petitioned the king "to yeve and graunte unto your seide humble wif the fondacon and determinacon of the seid collage of sainte Margarete and saint Bernard." In 1465, it had come under the patronage of Elizabeth Widville, wife of Henry IV, and in 1484 it was again endowed through the beneficence of Queen Ann, wife of Richard III. The actual founder was one Andrew Dokkett, vicar of St. Botolph's Church, only a few yards away, who, as keeper of the financial records, "succeeded in inculcating the most convenient view of the case, that the college was not so much the foundation of Queen Margaret, as the special object of patronage *ex officio* of the Queens of England." The sentiment had unfortunately not prevailed, and Queens' was thus not among the wealthiest of Cambridge colleges.[5]

Although it was not as ancient as Peterhouse and did not have a chapel as spectacular as that of King's, Queens' was eminently respectable. It could not claim, as could some of the Cambridge colleges, any special association with a Milton or a Newton, but its members could boast that it had once been the headquarters of the Dutch philosopher Erasmus from 1510 to around' 1512 or 1514. It had pleasant, early Renaissance architecture and a quiet charm. The Crummells did not live within the college proper, but for a short time did maintain their household in Cambridge within a stone's throw of the college and quite close to St. Botolph's Church in an ancient house at 13 Botolph Lane.

Crummell could not manage a full-time commitment to study when he arrived at Cambridge in 1849. He told Jay that he would be employed over the summer, preaching for his mission every Sunday in July and the better part of August, but he hoped to stretch his speaking schedule into September. He would "leave home on Friday or Saturday, reach the place appointed in time to pass over the Sunday, return here Monday."[6]

There was continuing distraction from the vestry in New York, who did not approve of his taking up residence in England, setting up a separate fund for his own maintenance, and turning his attention to matters other than fundraising. He was troubled by poor eyesight, varicose veins, and coronary problems. His encounters with physicians seem bizarre by modern standards. Dr. Thomas Hodgkin found "evidence of a large cavity at the upper part of one lung." Another doctor, who had treated him twice in six months, found him to be "of a very delicate constitution." He had by this time developed an impressive history of "leeching and blistering and taking mercury" to get temporary relief. The range of treatments must certainly have aggravated his discomfort and distracted him from his studies.[7]

Life at Cambridge was not designed for a married man, especially a man whose wife and children were constantly ill. And the style of education in the British university, even under the best of circumstances, was hardly relevant to Crummell's political or economic concerns. To be sure Crummell was interested in languages, and he certainly loved moral philosophy, which he studied with avidity.[8] But he also had other interests; he maintained a rigorous speaking schedule on the antislavery platform, and he was becoming increasingly interested in African nationalism. His was a serious and active life, which necessitated intense involvement in the modern world. Education at Cambridge and Oxford was based on the ideal of collegial social interaction. Much of the education took place in intimate tutorials, much of it in conversations among peers. The extent to which Crummell took part in such social interaction is not known. Certainly he had friends among both the Englishmen and the other black scholars, mostly Africans, whom he encountered there. His family responsibilities, however, as well as his race, would have precluded the usual undergraduate pastimes. He had arrived at Cambridge somewhat too late in life.

Sarah Crummell endured many hardships, many of which were the common lot of nineteenth-century women. When she came to England in 1848, she brought their two boys, Alexander, Jr., and Sidney with her. Her firstborn had died in Philadelphia. During her fourth pregnancy, in 1848–49, she was often separated from her husband, who was traveling on his lecture tours, but on June 18, 1849, she gave birth to "a fine and healthy daughter," Frances. In 1851 they lost a second child, their youngest boy Alexander, Jr., who suffocated after "swallowing" a button. The Crummells were consoled by their doctors, who said that the child had had "incipient consumption" and could not have lived another year. His last months, the medical men judged from the postmortem examination, would have been months of pain and anguish. Soon afterwards, a second daughter, Sophia, was born. In February 1852, the children were down with measles, croup, and lung disease. During her sixth pregnancy, in early 1853, Mrs. Crummell was critically ill for three months, under constant medical care, and, for part of the time, obliged to be away from the children. In April, after a very difficult pregnancy, she gave birth to another daughter, Dillwinna.[9]

Alexander Crummell was ill himself, "unable to read," during the last two years of his studies. He suffered from varicose veins and was laid up with a swelling in his left leg for three months in 1851. He sent a letter to John Jay with physicians' statements attesting to the seriousness of his heart condition. His old friend James McCune Smith had told him arround 1846 that "the outer coat of the heart was partially worked off." A doctor in Philadelphia told him that his heart was enlarged. All his doctors told him to slow down or the condition would worsen. A doctor at Ipswich said that the condition was "functional but that it [would] ere long be organic," unless he was careful of himself. London specialists gave him the same advice. One of the reasons for Crummell's move from Cambridge to Ipswich was his conviction that Cambridge was "very unhealthy." Many of the inhabitants were ill. Several students had "died of the fever which is prevalent here every May." [10] In 1851, he was invited to become curate at St. Stephen's, Ipswich. It was a small parish, he wrote; "a birth or a marriage is a rare thing in it." He accepted the position because he needed the money and the duties were light: reading prayers on Sundays and Wednesdays and occasionally preaching. His sermons before the new congregation the few months of his stay excited some attention, but he observed "no fainting fits, no consternation, no fierce and fretful anger, at the appearance of my sable face." [11]

Crummell's stay in Cambridge was noted in the diaries of at least two Cambridge professors, Charles Clayton of Caius College and Joseph Romilly. [12] Clayton escorted him to services in St. Botolph's Church on his visit in April of 1848 and, after he took up residence in Cambridge, occasionally paid a social call or took him for walks. They often dined together or met at relaxed social gatherings. Romilly was interested to learn of Crummell's matriculation, noting his arrival with "a black wife, and black pickaninnies." He recorded incidents in his diary that give a fuller picture of the treatment of a black man in Victorian England than do Crummell's glowing reports to Jay:

> *May 20, 1850*—Had the occasion to see Mr. Crummell (the black undergr.) walking with his black wife and one of his black pickaninnies.
>
> *Sept. 23, 1850*—I should have mentioned yesterday another of [my sister] Lucy's adventures: She met the wooly haired black undergraduate (who is educating to become a missionary to his own native Africa) walking with one of his children; so she immediately spoke to the little fellow and said she often saw him driving his hoop; he was quite pleased at being noticed and grinned so as to display his beautiful pearly teeth.

Unless there was another black undergraduate in Cambridge with a family at the time, the above reference must have been to Crummell and his son, Sidney. Crummell was, of course, not a native African, nor had he made known any intention of going to Africa. It is possible that Romilly was mistaken in some details and correct in others. Crummell may have been considering going to Liberia as early as September 1850, and there is of course some evidence for such a speculation in his letter to Jay of August 9, 1848, where he entertained the possibility that his future work might be in some quarter of the globe other than the United States. [13]

Another entry in Romilly's diary provides excellent insight into the daily life of a black family in England. It is not the sort of anecdote that Crummell would have told to Jay.

> *Jan. 3, 1851*—Mrs. Leapingwell . . . was very entertaining—She told me of her having recommended an Irishwoman to a place (because Kerrick took interest

in her):—she quitted it in a few days and then went to live with the Crummells (a black undergraduate with black wife and 3 black pickaninnies): the wild Irishwoman was soon dismissed by Mrs. Crummell to whom she addressed the following words, "you are a black devil: you are a slave & the daughter of a slave & your heart is as black as your face!!!"

On the one hand, the Crummells had an Irish servant, a white woman working in a household headed by a black male. On the other hand, even an Irish servant, at the bottom of the class ladder, knew how to insult a black woman.

Education in Cambridge during Crummell's stay resembled the current system, being based on successful performances on examinations at several stages, rather than on participation in courses and seminars. There were college examinations, such as the one Crummell passed and mentioned in a letter to Jay on August 2, 1850. There was the "previous examination" or "little go," a university examination, which he passed in 1851. Finally there were the examinations for degrees taken at the end of one's studies, which were of two sorts, honors and ordinary. Crummell took the examination for the ordinary degree, which he failed, but a few weeks later he wrote the so-called "Additional Examination." There were thirty-seven persons sitting this examination, given in early 1853, and he was among eleven who passed it. Thus, although Crummell's career was not distinguished, he was the legitimate recipient of an earned degree, and the official university publications recorded the fact.[14]

A letter to Jay of April 15, 1853, states that his difficulties were with the mathematical sections, although he "did well in classics and moral subjects." A glance at the topics of the examinations reveals that mathematics were still the sine qua non for a first-rate degree at Cambridge at the time of Crummell's matriculation. The little go of March 31 to April 1, 1851, included Euclid, Books I and II, arithmetic, Paley's *Evidences of Christianity,* Old Testament history, the *Apology* and *Crito* of Plato, the *Ars Poetica* of Horace, and the Gospel of St. Mark. In this examination he took a "second class." The Senate House Examination papers of January 1853 reveal that on Wednesday, January 12 he was examined all morning on Euclid and all afternoon on arithmetic and algebra. The following day it was arithmetic and algebra in the morning and Euclid in the afternoon. Friday, he was examined on mechanics and hydrostatics. The examination of Saturday morning, January 15, which covered Tacitus, required a knowledge of geography and history, as well as Latin. In the afternoon he wrote on Sophocles' *Electra.* The following Saturday morning he was examined on Paley's *Moral Philosophy,* Books II, III, and IV, followed in the afternoon by Acts of the Apostles, Chapters 14–28, and the first Epistle to the Corinthians. These were in Greek, of course, and had to be translated and interpreted within the context of ancient history and geography.

Crummell's classical education had many lasting effects. Around 1895 he visited Boston and spent an evening with a company of younger men, including George W. Forbes, who describes the session in terms reminiscent of Plato's *Symposium.* Crummell rhapsodized on the merits of the ancient writers, who were in his view still preeminent. Not only Forbes, but others who knew him in old age were impressed by his "Platonism." According to Forbes, "he greatly preferred the master idealist to his materialist junior Aristotle, holding that no amount of the latter's minute observations and myriad diligence could compensate one moment with him for the poetic vision and splendid generalizations of Plato." Forbes recorded his reverence for the Platonic doctrine of immortality and noted that Crummell was much affected by the idea that the pagan philosopher had discovered certain noble and universal truths, independently of sacred revelation.[15]

Platonic ideas continued to dominate his thinking long after he had completed his examinations at Cambridge. Throughout his life—and this should not be surprising in a clergyman—Crummell believed that the mind and spirit were more important than the body. Some six years after his arrival in Liberia, he wrote that "the body is but the machinery and instrument of the immaterial essence which inhabits it; and while, indeed, desirous, both by skill and kindness, to adjust and restore this machinery, when fractured, or disarranged, or lacerated, or under decay, yet, by so much as the soul is superior to the body, so do we estimate its superior value, and aim the more, directly and indirectly, to seek its good."[16] These are hardly remarkable thoughts from a minister, but they were inspired by more than a minister's concern for spiritual matters. Crummell's spirituality, and even his mysticism, were not predominantly otherworldly. He believed that the worldly interests of the African race could be advanced only by the triumph of ideas. Accordingly, he opposed any theory of black uplift based primarily on the harnessing of mere economic or political forces.

In his speech before the American Negro Academy, "Civilization, the Primal Need of the Race," delivered in 1897, shortly before his death, the heritage of Cambridge Platonism was still dominant. Here, he condemned those men who were "constantly dogmatizing theories of sense and matter as the salvable hope of the race." The "great difficulty with the black race in this era," he wrote, was that "material ideas in divers forms are made prominent as the master-need of the race." The full import of this address is treated more fully in a later chapter, but it is important to note here that Crummell's antimaterialism was one of the chief reasons he could not make common cause with Booker T. Washington and one of the chief reasons Washington withheld support from the American Negro Academy. The antimaterialism of Crummell's later life may have derived from some source other than his Cambridge education, but it was clearly related to the love of Plato that Forbes observed on the evening of the Boston symposium.[17]

Crummell also read Aristotle at Cambridge and was much impressed with his theory of slavery. In a letter to Jay, written some months after his address to the British and Foreign Anti-Slavery Society in the spring of 1851, he thanked the Jays for their reaction to his remarks, but informed them that "the Society was not so well pleased with them." He had taken the position that "the existance, i.e., the origin of slavery was as much subjective as objective, that is that it arose as much from weakness of a race as from the pro-slavery disposition . . . I was surprised on my return home to Cambridge to find that my principle and argument was substantially the same as Aristotle's upon the same subject centuries ago.''[18]

The displeasure of the society was probably that expressed by John Scoble, Secretary of the British and Foreign Anti-Slavery Society. Scoble's misgivings had been reported to Crummell by Peter Jones Bolton, Assistant Secretary of the Society, and Crummell had responded by sending Bolton a copy of his speech, "fully written out"; apparently he had spoken extemporaneously or only from notes. "You heard it," he reminded Bolton, "and I think you will say I have *reported* it nearly as it was delivered." On the origin of slavery he differed with Scoble, and he was even more confirmed in his opinion, "on finding that I was uttering in my speech, tho ignorant of the fact, the philosophy of 'Aristotle'. The only difference being that he thought the inferiority of the enslaved class was natural, which I know is not the case." [19]

The controversial statement, as it was finally recorded in the *Anti-Slavery Reporter,* was that "the origin of slavery is not perhaps to be found so much in any particular laws as in the weakness, the benightedness, and the degradation of that particular class brought into slavery." As he explained to Jay, he believed that the way to destroy slavery was to "destroy the weakness of a race, i.e., raise them to light and culture and manhood and slavery could not even exist." [20] Aristotle had, of course, intended to say nothing of the sort. He had held it to be self-evident that slaves did not have "deliberative powers," and he did not consider whether or not this might be a result of slavery. Crummell's Christian teleology inclined him toward social and historical determinism, an ideology of which Aristotle was innocent. Thus he believed that inferiority was the effect rather than the cause of slavery. He recoiled from Aristotle's opinion that slavery was the natural state of inferior human beings, while equivocating on the fact that this was what Aristotle had believed.

"The slave," said Aristotle, "has no deliberative faculty at all," describing a type he called the "natural slave," the person "for whom such a condition is expedient and right." He said that "where the relation of master and slave between them is natural, they are friendly and have a common interest, but where it rests solely on law and force, the reverse is true." There is, of course, no record of Aristotle having found any inconvenient instances of this "unnatural slavery." He offered no means of identifying a "natural slave" that would be acceptable to a modern reader, and we interpret Aristotle today using a vocabulary that would have been unintelligible to him and almost as meaningless to Crummell. There was very little, if any, relation between the ideas of Crummell and those of Aristotle. The latter's theories were simply a rationalization of the status quo, because their author's culture made any radical questioning of slavery unthinkable.

Crummell tried to justify his ideas with references to Aristotle, because he did not have the social scientific vocabulary or education required to articulate what were really novel ideas. Like many of his contemporaries, he was inclined to validate social theories with logic and the citation of revered names. References to Aristotle were authoritative in both respects. He agreed with Aristotle that slavery would work best with people whose deliberative faculty was impaired. However, as even Aristotle had tacitly admitted, slavery was not in fact confined to those who lacked deliberative faculties. As Crummell well knew, it was the deliberative powers, of most American slaves that made them discontented with their lot.

Nurturing the intellect was impossible under slavery, or so it was widely believed. Many slaveholders assumed that to educate slaves was to ruin them for slavery. Thus, they did all they could to prevent the slaves from developing their deliberative powers. Crummell, Aristotle, and the slaveholders were all agreed that the principal bulwark of slavery was the slaves' own mental state. The significant difference was that Crummell, unlike the defenders of slavery, saw the slave's mental state as entirely the result of their circumstances.

What made Crummell's position so disturbing to abolitionists was that it suggested the inadequacies of their program. Crummell neither rejected nor deprecated the principal methods of abolitionism in the 1850s—moral suasion and economic pressure. He recognized that it was necessary and proper for conventional abolitionism to arouse pity and fear in the hearts of slaveholders. But, at times, it seemed to treat the slaves as mere objects of external philanthropy, viewing them as victims, supplicant objects of pity, not as people responsible for their own destiny. Crummell felt that it was important to put steel into the backbones of the slaves and the freedmen. Henry Highland Garnet could take Crummell's self-help principle to the extreme, arguing that slave revolts and nationalistic enterprises could speedily destroy the institution of slavery. What Crummell and Garnet shared was the desire to apply self-help principles to emancipation. They did not wish to feel entirely dependent on the goodness of whites. Yet Crummell by no means rejected the assistance of whites, nor did he deny the economic and moral issues. He did insist that slavery existed because the enslaved were forcibly deprived of their virtue, their nobility, and their deliberative faculties and thus became helpless accomplices in their own debasement. Like many of the proponents of self-help and independence, he wanted to encourage black people to accept the burden of their own emancipation. In the tradition of David Walker and Denmark Vesey, he called, perhaps unfairly, for black people themselves to destroy the slavery system.

"No one would say that he who is a slave is unworthy to be a slave," wrote Aristotle,[21] a sentiment Denmark Vesey practically paraphrased in 1820 when he told recalcitrant slaves in Charleston that if they could not join his conspiracy, they deserved to be slaves.[22] A major bulwark of the slavery system was the ignorance of the slaves, themselves, reasoned David Walker in 1829, "Our wretchedness [is largely] in consequence of ignorance," he asserted, for ignorance made us actively cooperate in our own degradation. Crummell was only echoing the argument of David Walker's *Appeal*. But, since slaveholders prohibited education, how was the slaves' ignorance to be corrected? "Cultivate the free blacks where slavery now exists and *that* cultivation will undermine the foundations of slavery."[23] Crummell was really more in agreement with

Henry Highland Garnet, David Walker, and the other insurrectionary pamphlet-eers than with Aristotle in his belief that slavery would be destroyed by en-lightening the slaves. Crummell had forgotten, and Aristotle had not forseen, the ability of the Romans to keep highly educated Greeks as slaves, thus dem-onstrating that adjustment to slavery was not inconsistent with the exercise of deliberative powers.

Aristotle was not the only ancient writer Crummell adapted to modern uses. He had a fondness for Tacitus and listed his histories along with Plato's dia-logues and Homer's epics as works striking for their "freshness and power . . . , great original might . . . , and strong personal force . . . , a force which we could not possibly resist, and which indeed we would be loath to escape, or, in any way to separate from us." His fascination with "the robust-ness of Tacitus" grew out of the "simple but ingenious testimony he bears to the primitive virtue of the German tribes, pagan though they were, and which have proven the historic basis of their eminence and unfailing grandeur." The example of Tacitus' noble Germans provided lessons for us, "that people sim-ple, untrained and unadorned have been robust and virtuous; have bred brave and truthful men and chaste and beauteous women . . . And these excellencies have . . . made them immortal." Later in life, speaking at a Church Congress, he asserted that "the very words in which Cicero and Tacitus describe the homes and families of the Germanic tribes can as truly be ascribed to the peo-ple of the West Coast of Africa." The West African nationalist Edward Wilmot Blyden was equally inclined to make comparisons between the barbarian traits of the ancient Germans and those of West Africans.[24]

The classical elements that remained in Crummell's writings consisted of something more than references and quotations. Although he was sometimes guilty of ostentatious allusions, he generally attempted to give his classical education relevancy to his own immediate experience. He was concerned with interpreting Aristotle, Plato, Tacitus, and Cicero in ways that would be useful to his work of propagandizing the virtues of black people. Moreover, he felt that the best way to improve the fortunes of Africa's scattered children was to give them a grasp of the eternal verities—"the large, majestic, and abiding things" which would, he believed, "lift them up to the skies."

As a candidate for an "ordinary degree," Crummell was required to attend lectures; presumably he chose to attend those of William Whewell, who was Knightbridge Professor of Moral Philosophy. Whewell was celebrated for his *History of the Inductive Sciences,* and he is still considered one of the outstand-ing British scientists of his day. In Whewell's lectures, Crummell was classed as "special," rather than "general," meaning that he paid three guineas rather than five for his lecture tickets and thus could attend only Whewell's lectures. Whewell was a man of considerable genius, whose lectures on moral philoso-phy were devoted mainly to attacks on Hobbes, Locke, Bentham, and any system of philosophy that proposed to found a theory of morality on expe-diency, utility, or materialism. Whewell taught that there could be no system of morality independent of the "one supreme and central Idea of Goodness," which was the basis of conscience. Like many other British religious thinkers of the period, Whewell cultivated the fair field of his own English garden. Although he paid appropriate homage to Fichte and Kant, his work showed little concern for the German neology of Strauss and Schleiermacher. The approach to biblical interpretation known as the "Higher Criticism" had little impact on Cambridge during the first half of the nineteenth century. This did not mean, however, that religious thought was stagnant at Cambridge during Crummell's residency. The two-hundred-year-old tradition of Cambridge Platonism was still a strongly felt influence, as were the legacies of Isaac Newton and William Paley. Theological debate at Cambridge centered around the work of famous British moralists, much of which was scrutinized in Whewell's lectures.[25]

Whewell believed in "Conscience, its divine commission, and its due place as the basis of sound Morality," and he was openly hostile to rationalistic and utilitarian systems of morality. The great villain in British moral philosophy was Hobbes, "a man bold, acute, penetrating, unshrinking in speculation, confident in his own powers, contemptuous of the opinions of others, treating with little tenderness, hardly with affected decency, the common prejudices and feelings of mankind, but able to impress his thoughts upon men with singular vividness and energy." Hobbes's utilitarianism was roundly denounced by Whewell, whose lectures must certainly have found a sympathetic listener in Crummell. Temperamentally predisposed to the tradition of Cambridge Platonism, he would share in Whewell's indignation at the triumphant philosophy of Hobbes, who had "dared to proclaim, to the alarmed ears of his contemporaries, that right and wrong had no independent existence; that moral good and evil were sought and must be sought, not for their own sakes, but on account of extraneous advantages; that the natural condition of man is a state of war; that Might is Right, and that Conscience is only Fear."[26]

A devastating early refutation of the Hobbesian school had been, in Whewell's view, delivered by the Cambridge Platonists. Particularly important were Henry More and Ralph Cudworth, generally acknowledged as the most powerful representatives of their philosophy. More's *Enchiridion* "was written with a view of contradicting the poison of Hobbian doctrines; yet the name of Hobbes is . . . nowhere mentioned in the book." The views of More and Plato were seen as similar in that both viewed the passions as "the ministers of the superior faculty which is the proper guide of human action." Whewell may therefore be interpreted as following the tradition of the Cambridge Platonists, hostile as he was to the Hobbesian doctrines, and dependent as he was on Henry More for moral support in his own attacks on them.[27]

If he found in More the antidote to the Hobbesian materialist doctrine that "all our impulses may be resolved into selfish fear and selfish desire," he found in Cudworth an antidote to the sensationalism of Locke. The latter was, to be sure, hardly so poisonous as Hobbes, although he purveyed a dangerous doctrine. Whewell held that "the Lockian philosophy is always in danger of sinking into skepticism," and yet the real errors of the philosophy were not so much with Locke as with his followers. They ignored certain passages in his work in which Locke had paid homage to the importance of ideas, "The *idea* of a Supreme Being . . . , the *idea* of ourselves, as understanding natural beings." Locke also believed in "self-evident propositions," which in Whewell's estimation placed him in some proximity to the Cambridge Platonists. "No moralist, even of the school of Cudworth, would need to claim more than is here [by the acknowledgment of the existence of self-evident propositions] conceded."[28]

Despite the obvious conservatism of his views, Whewell had been something of an innovator at Cambridge. In 1837, he had led a fight along with his friend Julian Hare against the dogmatic approach to the teaching of ethics according to the system of William Paley. Despite these efforts, Paley's works still dominated the moral philosophy examinations during Crummell's time. Paley had attempted to demonstrate "the existence and attributes of the Deity from . . . the appearances of nature." He had argued that the universe was filled with indications of contrivance and manifestations of design, which implied "the hand of an artificer." Whewell had no objection to Paley's conclusions, but he maintained that there were many dangers in his method of demonstrating them. The basis of Paley's scheme was utilitarianism, a dangerous tendency, for utilitarianism must inevitably lead to the mischievious doctrine that morality consists of nothing more than the pursuit of pleasure. Shortly after coming to Cambridge, Whewell had published a series of essays under the title, *Four Sermons on the Foundations of Morals,* in which he had said "that the evils which arise from the countenance . . . of Paley's system are so great as to make it desirable for us to withdraw our sanction from his doctrines without further delay." He then mentioned Joseph Butler as "the principal representative of a better system than Paley" and introduced the "practice of putting forward Butler as a corrective to Paley."[29]

Paley's *Evidences* and Butler's *Analogy* were both esteemed by Crummell, who placed them on a list of books with which every well-educated young Liberian should become acquainted.[30] Paley and the utilitarians, as we have seen, attempted to argue for a system of rational morality. Butler had argued for the existence of a moral faculty with which one apprehended moral distinctions. There is ample support in Crummell's writings for the view that he believed in an inherent moral sensibility, as, for example, when he spoke of the feminine "instinct of chastity" and other innate human propensities.[31] Crummell responded to the kind of reasoning represented by Butler and the school of sensibility that came into being in the eighteenth century. Following in the tradition of the Cambridge Platonists implied the acceptance of innate ideas, or at least of an inborn sense of conscience, which led to intuitively known and universally recognized moral forces. Crummell was immersed in a cult of sensibility that saw a linkage between taste and virtue. He believed that Beauty and Truth could be learned from observing the beauties of nature, an idea he inherited from poets of sensibility like Cowper and Gray, from Archibald Alison's *Essays on Taste,* and from the Romantic poets, whom he admired.[32]

There was indeed such a thing as natural morality, and utilitarian moral logic, but for Crummell there was also a direct and individual perception of the good, springing from the innate moral faculty of every man.

John Grote, Professor of Moral Philosophy at Trinity College, was another professor of whom Crummell would certainly have been aware. Grote is interesting because in attacking utilitarianism he expressed ideas similar to Crummell's about slavery and race. Grote argued that utilitarians like Bentham and John Stuart Mill had attempted the impossible when they tried to justify social morality on utilitarian grounds. Grote drew his arguments from the recent history of slavery and the history of interracial contacts in the modern world. Slavery was the perfect example of an evil system whose wrongness could not be demonstrated by utilitarian arguments. Indeed there were utilitarian arguments in support of slavery, since its proponents argued that the institution was, in truth, beneficial to the inferior races that it enslaved, and that it promoted their happiness and well-being. On an even more callous level, an extreme utilitarian might argue that an inferior person, like an inferior animal, ought to be exploited for the benefit of the higher civilized races. "Utilitarianism," argued Grote, "hinders the settlement of a question which man's moral feeling would otherwise have settled . . . The real force of the feeling against slavery lies in the idea . . . that even in the lowest races of men, mind and reason are developed to such an extent as to take them out of the category of the brute animals. As did Whewell, Grote believed in a natural sympathy between members of the same species. In the case of mankind this was not only a physical sympathy, but a "reasonable sympathy, or real mutual intelligence and regard, and in social and improved man it exists in a higher form still, as mutual and understood *duty*." [33]

By grounding his antislavery position in the idea of an innate moral feeling and cultivated sense of duty, Grote placed himself in the camp with those who saw the crusade against slavery as a war of ideas. Crummell certainly sympathized with this view, for, while he recognized the essentially economic nature of slavery, he also recognized the implications of economic attempts to undermine it. His speech at the Annual Meeting of the British and Foreign Anti-Slavery Society in 1849 showed such recognition. The utilitarian approach of commercial warfare against slavery-produced commodities would precipitate disaster, not only for Southern planters, but for British industrialists and the British working-class. Even as he counseled his audience to allow their factories to stand idle for a season, he must have allowed himself a slight ironic smile. It would have implied a strange view of human nature to argue that British manufacturers were any less venal than American planters—or any less utilitarian. [34]

Crummell's increasing interest in Africa is revealed in a later essay of the Cambridge period, "Hope for Africa," which was originally a sermon delivered on behalf of the Ladies' Negro Education Society. It began with an allusion to the biblical text "Ethiopia shall soon stretch forth her hands unto God."

The sermon was delivered in support of efforts by the society on behalf of Negro education in the British West Indies. Crummell had chosen his text as "singularly appropriate" to the objects of the society, and he praised the association for its plan to extend its influences to "the benighted father land . . . and thus help to raise up the great African family." Crummell, as we have seen, had a teleological view of history, and he firmly believed that Providence was playing an active part in the destiny of Africa. The allusion to the Ethiopian prophecy indicates the mystical historicism that informed his view of social change. His ideology was balanced precariously on the brink of utopianism, for he entertained a faith that the "prophetic announcement" was on the verge of fulfillment.[35]

The address was an expression of the so-called "Ethiopianism" that led several generations of black preachers to tax their exegetical powers in propounding the meaning of Ethiopia's stretching forth her hands. This was usually interpreted to mean that Africa and the African race would shortly be converted and uplifted, spiritually and materially. To some writers the words of the psalmist were no more than a vaguely inspiring passage and Ethiopia's significance merely symbolic. Africans were referred to as Ethiopians for purely poetic reasons, or to gratify a need for identification with symbols of power and stability. Not every such allusion was true Ethiopianism, however, since essential to the tradition was its view of history, which could sometimes be present without any direct mention of Ethiopia. In its purest form, Ethiopianism implied a view of history in which black Africans would eventually rise to a position of power, glory, and, as Crummell would eventually say, "destined superiority."[36]

Crummell did not advocate idle dependence on supernatural forces to solve the problems of this world, however. His mysticism was hardly extraordinary for the times, and it was decidedly not of the sort that encourages a passive reliance on the hand of God. In any case, he was not alone in his confidence in the rising tide of Africa's destiny. Numerous other writers, white and black alike, had participated in the Ethiopian tradition since the late eighteenth century. Like most people possessed by a sense of national history, Crummell was susceptible to the need for identification with symbols of ancient splendor. Thus, in "Hope for Africa," he plunged into a discussion of biblical ethnology, demonstrating that according to the Scriptures, black Africans were children of Ham, and not the accursed Canaan. Naturally, it was of great importance that the black race be descendants of Cush, rather than his brother, Canaan, since the defenders of slavery often cited Noah's curse as proof of the destiny of the black race to be "servants unto their brethren." In a subsequent essay, "The Negro Race Not Under a Curse," Crummell again made this point. As descendants of Cush, the contemporary Africans could claim kinship with the founders of Ninevah and Ethiopia. The evils that had befallen the black race in recent millennia had nothing to do with any curse; they were part of a long-obscured, but soon to be revealed, Providence of God. Even now there were to be seen certain "secular evidences" of the coming elevation of the Negro race. Africa and her children were already giving proof of remarkable spiritual progress. Soon the forces of history would combine to restore the black race to its rightful place in world civilization.[37]

Themes of the past glories of the African race were popular with black American writers of the mid-nineteenth century. The status of black people in biblical times, the validity of Noah's curse, and the mutability of human affairs were ever present topics with black writers of Crummell's generation. From early youth, he was constantly exposed to the prophecy that Ethiopia would some day stretch out her hand to regain her ancient place in the affairs of men. Not only was he exposed to this rhetoric at the commencement day address of the African Free School, he encountered it in the press. The meaning of the Curse of Canaan and whether it had caused the degradation of the black race was debated in *Freedom's Journal*. Notes on the primitive state in which the Romans had found the inhabitants of the British Isles appeared in the *Colored American,* another article argued that all culture had come out of Egypt and Ethiopia. In short, the concern with the cyclical nature of human history which played such an important role in David Walker's celebrated *Appeal* was common in black publications of the antebellum decades.[38] Several black writers, including J. W. C. Pennington, Samuel Ringgold Ward, and William Wells Brown, approached history with a view to demonstrating that no race had been predestined to enjoy unabated exaltation or degradation. It became commonplace to refer to the fact that the Anglo-Saxons had been crude barbarians when the Romans discovered them. If the English had been able to elevate themselves in nineteen hundred years as a result of continental influences and Christian enlightenment, why should one assume the destiny of Africans to be any less promising. True enough, as Samuel Ringgold Ward observed, "the history of the Negro, at least for the past seven centuries" could be summed up in "one word and its cognate—*slavery, slave trade.*" Ward argued, however, that the history of the Negro race was yet to be written. Scholars were to blame, for they knew what had been "written of the ancient Negro—from which they might, if they chose, infer something concerning the modern Negro." The Egyptians and the Assyrians were sons of Ham. Greeks, Romans, and Jews all derived their civilization from the ancient heritages of Egypt and Ethiopia. Ward, like Crummell, spoke before English audiences to show "that the modern Negro is worthy of his ancient paternity." For if one could show that the children of slavery could lay claim to the heritage of ancient civilization, there was reason to believe that they, along with Ethiopia, would soon stretch forth their hands out of the sinkhole of slavery and oppression.[39]

Perhaps it was a faith in such prophecies that led Crummell to announce on September 12, 1851 his decision not to return to the United States. He revealed in a letter to John Jay that he had made up his mind to seek a home in "some other quarter of the globe." He detailed his reasons, which fell into two broad categories: the failure of his health, and the fear that he would never receive adequate support from any free black community in the United States. The sober advice of his physicians, including his old friend James McCune Smith, was that he must seek a milder climate and a less strenuous life than that of a black preacher in the free states of North America. Even in England, where he had enjoyed "an ease, a comfort, a species of social Christian enjoyment, and an enlarged liberty which [he] never knew at home," the climate was too severe. Suffering from various periodic infirmities that forced him occasionally to "give up all duties and live in quiet for weeks," he had come to believe that he must change his life. He sought relief from the cares he had endured at home and wished for a new livelihood with "duties less exciting and trying than those of constant preaching and the care of a congregation." Preaching, especially, he saw as "always an augment to my distress." Desiring to change his profession from preacher to that of teacher, he hoped to be relieved of anxieties for his "pecuniary support."[40]

The idea of returning to the United States and devoting himself to the education of the free black population in the North, he described as "a darling scheme of my mind for years." Especially since arriving in Cambridge, he had kept before him as a "most cherished object" a conception of himself as a vessel for transporting to black America some of the refinements of scholarship with which to construct a temple of learning for colored youths. His optimism had waned considerably, and he now confessed to Jay that he could not trust the free black community to support himself and his family. For, as he put it, "Dear as my people and their interests are to my heart, I cannot allow them to override the imperative duties of a husband and a Father."[41]

The final reason for Crummell's reluctance to return to the United States revealed a great deal about his most basic values. Crummell was convinced that American culture was a tyranny of the majority. "My hopes," he wrote, "are not bright ones even for white men and their children in America; controlled as you are by an unscrupulous and boistrous Democracy, which neither fears God, nor regards man; and by a demagogic priesthood, who devote their best energies in maintaining the sanctity of slavery, and the infallibility of the state." Naturally, he was not happy to consider bringing up his children in a society so conceived. "I think I have a sign," he confided to Jay, "I hear almost a voice—Get thee out of thy country and from thy kindred, and come into the land which I shall shew thee" (Genesis 12). Although he had not yet decided into which land the Abrahamic injunction must lead him, he was convinced that the patterns of his life were "clearly providential."[42]

On hearing of Crummell's plans, Jay expressed some concern for his reputation in abolitionist circles, saying, "You must expose yourself to the charge of being a renegade and ingrate—of accepting favors on a condition and violating that condition." Crummell reminded his benefactor that it was his English and not his American patrons who had sent him to Cambridge, and that they had never imposed on him the condition that he return to America. On the contrary, some of them had counseled him against returning, and one supporter had even gone so far as to assure him that he could remain in England at public expense. He reminded Jay of his past record of personal sacrifice on behalf of his various congregations in America. To his advisor's admonition that he not allow considerations of personal interest or comfort to diminish his sense of obligation, he responded that a black man's sense of racial duty could be determined only by himself. "Dear sir, If you mean by this," he wrote to Jay, "that I should not allow considerations with respect to the comfort of my wife and children in this world to be influencing my considerations in deciding the question of my resuming my place in New York; then I say, first of all, that I have no such loftiness of character . . . ." Mrs. Crummell had expressed an unwillingness to go back to America; she feared that her husband's health would soon break under the strain of the New York ministry and that she and her children would be left destitute. Crummell told Jay that his parents and relatives, his wife and his connections had all entreated him to give up the active ministry and move to a more promising field. The black minister in the United States was in the position of either resorting to menial employment or becoming a slave "to some wealthy corporation, as the Reverend Peter Williams did."[43]

He relished the idea of becoming a teacher after the manner of Cambridge's priestly dons, but the chances of his being able to make a living as an educator seemed extremely unfavorable. He had discussed the possibility of such a venture with J. W. C. Pennington, William Wells Brown, Henry Highland Garnet, and others. Even when sympathetic, they had not been encouraging. Their advice had been, "If you have a mind to try to build up a school or college you may—but you are a fool if you do, for you will be ruined." Furthermore, he had met with little support from either American or British philanthropists in his attempts to generate interest in the education of the free blacks at the Anti-Slavery Society meeting in 1851. The British were inclined to feel that it was better to spend their money in Africa, which had led him to believe that Africa might offer opportunities for a man of his talents.[44]

On hearing of Crummell's plans, one of Crummell's American supporters, the Reverend Arthur Cleveland Coxe, wrote to a mutual friend expressing his desire that Crummell should return to the States and "do what he [could] do to ameliorate the condition of his colored brethren. To this God [had] evidently *called* him, and he must *take up his cross . . . such* was the purpose for which he [had been] educated." Coxe felt that it would be possible for Crummell to gain support for an academy once he returned to New York. Perhaps there were those who might be willing to assist him in preparing for missionary work in Liberia, or aid him in setting up a college for African youth. But, said Coxe, "we cannot expect to excite any great interest in his case while he is so far away from us, and known to very few. He need have no fear as to the slave law—which is very rarely executed."[45]

Crummell was indignant. He fired off a letter to Coxe, emphatically denying that his decision had anything to do with the Fugitive Slave Law. He restated the reasons he had given to Jay, emphasizing his "incapacity" for reasons of health "to resume the onerous duties of a city Parish."[46] He reminded his wealthy benefactors that he was not a rich man, and that he was not able to keep a horse and carriage but must travel the city streets on foot. For a black minister, it was impossible to seek the quieter life of a country parsonage; the black American population congregated in large cities, and the work of a pastor demanded three services on Sundays, abundant visiting, and a great deal of interaction with an assertive vestry. Crummell, even under the best of circumstances, was not temperamentally suited to such work, and it seems likely that the suspicions of Coxe and Jay were justified. The erstwhile pastor of the Church of the Messiah had been spoiled by his English sojourn. He had come to relish the style of life that he had assumed over the preceding three years. Studying, publishing, and speaking in public were more suited to his temperament than the mundane duties of the ministry. But one must wonder whether Crummell's critics would have found much to enjoy in the sort of life they recommended to him.

Crummell had no hopes of finding intellectual and spiritual sustenance in New York. At the same time, he could not morally accept continuing to live as a ward of British benevolence. The African alternative that he was finally to settle on provided him an opportunity to preserve his independence and self-respect—or so he believed at the time. It would make it possible for him to bring up his family under a dark government. Finally, he hoped to be able to pursue a career for which he felt himself better suited than he was for preaching. Liberia seemed to offer opportunities for a man of superior abilities to create a world unto his own liking. He envisioned a future in which he might play the role of a black federalist, formulating an ideology and forging a moral code as Hamilton, Madison, and Jay had created an ideology of national purpose in America.

Crummell's approach to the black condition has been described as "neo-federalist philanthropy."[47] Indeed, Crummell shared with his American friends and backers an indebtedness to the American federalist tradition. He believed in order, authority, and rule by educated elites as the basis of all progress and civilization; he viewed civilization as an essential element in achieving black liberty. Thus Crummell was among the founders of the movement for "Negro Improvement," an idea that would dominate black nationalist thought during the late nineteenth and early twentieth century, most notably in the case of Marcus Garvey. True freedom for the African race must imply freedom of mind as well as of the body. One could not be achieved without the other. Slavery was undeniably the cause of blacks' present ignorance and degradation, yet if they had not been ignorant, they would never have been enslaved, nor would it have been possible to keep them in slavery. One scholar has even said that one finds in Crummell's writings the consummate expression of the idea that blacks had become accomplices in their own degradation. Perhaps so, but among black nationalists he was not alone.[48]

Crummell did not question that the ignorance of the slaves was due to their oppression by their masters, but he also believed, as David Walker had, and as Garnet still did, that an ignorant free black population could do nothing to help the slaves and that a general enlightenment of the black population would be a telling blow against the slave power. So long as the black race was "weak

. . . , degraded . . , benighted" (Crummell used such words frequently), black people would never be free.[49] As both a cause and an effect of slavery, ignorance was the most immediate obstacle to black advancement. Crummell rejected neither the immediate abolitionism of radical agitators like Frederick Douglass, nor the economic tactics of men like Garnet, who encouraged trade embargos against the Cotton States, but during the 1850s he became steadfastly committed to the idea that to free black people from the effects of slavery he must work "to improve and elevate their character." "The origin of slavery," he wrote, "arose as much from the weakness of a race as from the proslavery disposition" of the enslavers. Therefore, he argued, "destroy the weakness of a race, i.e., raise them to light and culture and manhood, and slavery could not even exist. I would therefore cultivate the free blacks where slavery now exists and *that* cultivation will help undermine the foundations of slavery."[50]

But even as he wrote these lines, Crummell had become convinced that the black community of New York was unreceptive to him. True, he had some supporters, for example his senior warden Mr. Tyson, but generally he felt that black New York would not miss him. "My absence will be a source of great joy to most of them," he wrote. Indeed, Tyson had told him that he was "laboring in vain among a people who despised [his] efforts." Finally, during the summer of 1851, "after anxious brooding care" regarding his health he made the following resolutions:

1. I must leave England.
2. I must go to a warm climate which medical advisors say will be best adapted to my constitution.
3. I must get a situation where preaching may be optional and where I can have the charge of a school or academy.
4. I must be relieved from care as to pecuniary support.[51]

Crummell's decision to emigrate was obviously the result of a number of factors, but it is striking that the first reason on his list was that he "must leave England." Could it be that he was tired of overlooking the English brand of racism in order to illustrate the severity of the American brand? Was it that after being patronized by the British for five years he had become capable of perceiving slights and insults to which he had not been sensitive during the first rush of his enthusiasm? A man with small children and an ailing wife does not leave a comfortable, civilized environment and leap into the uncertainties of discomforts of frontier life simply because of the abstract possibility of improving his condition. Not unless the blessings of civilization are outweighed by some specific discomforts. It seems clear that life in England was not the idyllic existence that he implied in his letters to Jay. Crummell did not enjoy thinking of himself as the beneficiary of English charity.

The second reason Crummell gave for going to Africa is not fully convincing. Crummell and his contemporaries often spoke of the curative powers of a warm climate, but everyone knew that the mortality rate among Liberian settlers was high. Anticolonizationists were well acquainted with horror stories about the Liberian climate and the diseases that it was believed to engender. After moving to Liberia, Crummell and his family were, as might well have been anticipated, frequently afflicted with tropical diseases. Thomas Hodgkin, who was known for his avid support of colonization, and who had, after all, examined Crummell, may have sincerely harbored the unsupportable (and racialist) notion that the Liberian climate would be good for Crummell's health. Even after the Civil War and the emancipation of the slaves, Hodgkin continued to support selective emigration, which he felt must still hold an attraction for superiorly gifted Negroes. A man of Crummell's skeptical temperament would not have uncritically accepted the myth of the salutary effects of the African environment, although a man who suffers from chronic health complaints may be tempted to try fairly drastic remedies. If he really did imagine that the climate would be good for his health, he was rapidly to be disabused of such a notion. He soon discovered that, in reality, West Africa, with its heat, insects, and disease, was a dangerous climate for infants, the aged, and the sickly. Crummell's susceptibility to the preachments of the respected physician were probably due to the personal factors that had already predisposed him to consider emigrating to Liberia.[52]

He claimed that he did not like to preach, but this was indeed a strange complaint for an ordained priest to be making, especially a preacher as good as Alexander Crummell. The sermon (whether religious or political) was his stock in trade. If he hoped to become a schoolmaster (a calling similar to that of the preacher), he certainly must have realized that many of the problems he had known in America would repeat themselves in any black community.

Crummell seemed to feel that by going to Africa he would achieve freedom from financial worries. To be assured of making a living, many black Episcopal priests had accepted appointments with the Domestic and Foreign Missionary Society—one of the few viable employment opportunities for black Episcopalians.[53] Of the twenty-five Episcopal priests and deacons ordained in the United States between 1795 and 1865, seventeen eventually migrated to posts outside the United States.

It was later reported that Crummell's conversion to colonizationism occurred when he became "acquainted with President Roberts and others, from whom he obtained such information of Liberia, as determined him to make that country his permanent residence." Roberts made two visits to England during the years of Crummell's residency, the first in 1848, when Crummell was certainly not converted to colonizationism, since 1849 was the year of his most active opposition to the movement. Roberts did, however, visit England again in 1851, and it may have been then that he was able to bring Crummell over to the pro-Liberian position. The situation is fraught with irony, of course, when one considers that Crummell eventually came to hate Roberts with a seething passion and to blame him for many of his disappointments.[54]

Thus it was a combination of reasons that led Crummell gradually to decide that he would go to Liberia, where he could "place [his] family somewhere amid the political institutions of black men."[55] A rumor that the Episcopal church planned to establish a college in Liberia made the prospect particularly attractive. He had been discouraged by white and black alike from entertaining any hopes of supporting himself as a teacher in the United States. Although he had long opposed the American Colonization Society—and he remained hostile to its mission of total black repatriation—he was now prepared to look upon African missionary work as a field where he might serve the cause of God by training young Africans for the ministry and assisting perhaps, "in sending the Gospel to the very center of my fatherland." "You will see," he wrote to Arthur Cleveland Coxe, "that I am forced into a new course by circumstances over which I have not control."[56] Crummell's rising hopes for Africa, as revealed in his speeches of 1851 to 1852, may indeed have been the most important factor in his decision. The progress of civilization and Christianity in the British West Indies and in England's African Possessions gave signs of hope. And now, perhaps, Liberia would provide the needed example of black enterprise to refute Edward Gibbon's assertion that the African race appeared "incapable of forming an extensive plan of government." Crummell admitted the seriousness of Gibbon's charge and acknowledged that a wise man ought "not be too sanguine." Still, when he noted "the rapidity of God's work" during the preceding half-century his spirits were lifted, and it seemed that opportunities to work for the uplift, progress, and civilization of his race were more available in Liberia than elsewhere.[57]

Crummell had left himself open to charges of apostasy and betrayal by deciding to migrate to Liberia in 1853, given his reputation as an anticolonizationist. His principal concern up to the year of his departure for Liberia had been to support the cause of the free black population in the United States. His speeches before the Anti-Slavery Society had sometimes been upsetting to the leadership of that institution because they had focused primarily on the condition of the free blacks rather than on the more spectacular atrocities inflicted on the slaves. He had argued for the uplift of the free blacks, both as an end in itself and as a means of ultimately achieving general emancipation. His voyage to England was not, as in the case of Frederick Douglass, an ambassadorship from the slave community. Crummell represented the black burghers of New York, and he had worked hard on their behalf. Then, with apparent suddenness, he had decided to enroll at Cambridge, but only the better (he told himself) to prepare for the continuation of his work in New York. Thus his friends who had sent him to England and continued to "advise" him while he pursued his studies were shocked and disappointed when he seemed to be taking up the colonizationist cause. Crummell's letters to Jay on the eve of his departure for Africa—lengthy and defensive—indicate that he found it necessary to convince not only his friends, but himself, that he was doing the right thing.[58]

Abolitionists were almost as hostile towards Liberia as they were towards its founders, although between 1859 and 1861 there was to be some drifting on that issue. Men like Garnet and Delany, who had earlier been intransigent, would now begin to consider that perhaps a Liberian nationalist was something other than a "parrot" of the American Colonization Society. Crummell was thus not the only black spokesman to alter his position, but emotional turmoil seems to have accompanied the change. On the one hand he had been aligned with some of the more vocal anticolonizationists.[59] The Jays must have been embarrassed by the defection of their most prominent protégé. His decision, in effect a statement that life in America was intolerable, did not reflect well on liberal whites. Crummell felt, of course, the deepest gratitude to the Jays for their support, and he appreciated the egalitarian principles stated in William Jay's *Inquiry into the Character and Tendency of the American Colonization Society*. Still he was not naïve. He knew that the veil of color, despite the equalizing effect of his education, would perpetually separate him from the likes of the Jay family, who, despite their courageous advocacy of racial fairness, would never be able to accept a black man as an equal.

When Jay toured England in 1848 with his new bride, Crummell seems to have had difficulty even securing an interview. For the Jays to pay a social call on the Crummells would probably have been out of the question, but Crummell tried to arrange a personal meeting "two or three times" and apparently even traveled to London in hopes of seeing his benefactor.[60] Neither of them even seemed to consider it a possibility that Crummell might be welcome in Jay's home and family life at any time. Thus Crummell was forced to face the fact that, even when dealing with his most beloved associates, America was a white man's country, regardless of whatever hopes might exist for her in principle. When Jay rebuked him for converting to emigrationism, Crummell responded with various justifications, foremost among them his health, but he never mentioned the reason that may have been closest to his heart. It was Jay himself who was the real reason for Crummell's apostasy—Jay and others like him—for unconsciously and despite themselves, they would always treat him with condescension and pity, these kindly yet detached observers, who advised that he return to a world of humiliation.

Crummell therefore was willing to face the hostility of the radical abolitionists with resignation. He left for Liberia no doubt with mixed emotions, probably telling himself that he was not retreating from immediate abolitionism, but advancing towards the goal of a truly independent black republic. He never seems to have questioned the wisdom nor the conscience of those who felt it their duty to stay and fight in America. On the other hand he knew that the "enlightened sons of Africa" would recognize that they were called to a "far higher work."[61] Crummell saw his decision as a personal one, an attempt to meet his own private needs. If most of his peers were concerned with the racial altruism of antislavery, he could justify his selfish behavior with the rhetoric of African redemption. In reality, he went to Africa in hopes of achieving the esteem and status that he deserved. As did most settlers, Crummell's family endured hardship and tragedy in adjusting to the dangers and inconveniences of frontier life because they found the indignities of American life intolerable, and because Crummell was too proud to remain where he could never be more than an oddity, an intellectual curiosity. As did many black nationalists, he adopted the collectivist ideology of emigration and racial duty to serve individualistic ends.

# 6

# Adjustment to Africa
# (1853–1861)

Traveling under the auspices of the Protestant Episcopal church of America, Crummell left England for West Africa in May 1853, accompanied by his wife, their three children, and a servant, and bringing along "a well-stocked theological library." After the dreary English winter, during which Sarah Crummell had suffered through another difficult pregnancy, the voyage resembled a pleasure cruise. He commented in later years on the "grand panorama of sights and incidents . . . the Bay of Biscay, the Park of Tenerife, Madeira, with its varied and cosmopolitan life and its beautiful scenery; and its aristocratic society." They reached the coast of Africa ten days after leaving England and stepped ashore at Goree. "A more sterile, desolate spot I had never seen," he wrote. "Nothing but sand, sand, sand, as far as the eye could stretch, glistening in the sunlight." Although he found the prospect "a discouraging introduction to Africa," his racial romanticism was richly rewarded by his first glimpse of native Africans on the continent of their origin. Impressive people they were, Jollofs from the Senegambia. "Their average height was about 6 feet 3 or 4— but with their remarkable slenderness, they seemed 2 or 3 inches taller." He was fascinated by the "depth and brilliancy of their complexions" and remarked that he had never seen "such utter blackness of color." This was neither the copper nor "the ashy blackness that is so common to the negro of America; but black like Satin; with a smoothness and thinness of skin, that you cd. easily see the blood mounting [?] in their cheeks."[1]

The landscape improved as they progressed southward to the Gambia; here the voyagers were introduced to the "variety, richness, grandeur, and even sublimity of African scenery." Two days later they came to Sierra Leone, where on entering the bay they beheld "rising majestically some 2,500 feet peak after peak of mountains, until the highest were lost in the white fleecy clouds." As they entered the bay, Crummell was impressed by the sight of native fishing canoes with their crews at work, fruit trees and garden plots, and brilliant flowers, the "richness of tropical coloring and exuberance of verdure." He noted in particular the beauty of the people in "this Eden-like spot." Although he consistently lamented the heathenism of the African people, he would always insist on their "points of interest and superiority, which command our attention."[2]

John Payne, the missionary bishop to whom Crummell would be responsible, was stationed in Cape Palmas, a settlement farther down the Liberian coast, and was not in Monrovia when Crummell arrived on July 15, 1853. While waiting for the bishop, Crummell occupied himself reading with "a colored young man (an English man) formerly of Trinity College Cambridge" in the Greek Testament and the works of Paley and Butler. He found him "a good Grecian and possessed of much cleverness" and hoped to prepare him, along with another pupil, for the Episcopal ministry. To this end he loaned them books and instructed them in the art of sermonizing, activities he hoped would not displease the bishop. Payne arrived after two months to install Crummell as pastor of Trinity Church. From the beginning, he was not overjoyed to serve under a white bishop, and it would become increasingly difficult with the passage of years. Throughout the twenty years he spent in Liberia, he would walk a tightrope between African nationalism and his loyalty to the Episcopal church.[3]

At first the Crummell family seemed to be enjoying good health, but the children soon began to have attacks of "the fever," and during the autumn, his youngest died. At the close of 1853, Crummell spent two months in the Maryland Colony at Cape Palmas recovering from his own sickness. The family experienced constant financial problems. Despite his resolution to limit his activities to those befitting his churchly office, Crummell was driven to pursue business ventures and farming, and he would probably have accepted a political appointment in the government of President Stephen Alan Benson if one had been offered. His salary from the parent church was never sufficient to support him and his family, as he often complained. Mrs. Crummell experienced many severe trials, including the loss of their baby shortly after her arrival in Liberia. She went through at least two more pregnancies during her first five years in Africa, and at least one more subsequent to that. References to her ill health abound in the correspondence of Crummell and others. This is not surprising given the deficiencies of nineteenth-century medicine, not only in gynecology, but in the treatment of tropical diseases.[4] The lot of an African missionary's wife was a trying one, and Crummell's wife had the additional burden of being a black woman in a mission whose social life was controlled by white women. To add to her own miseries, she had to live with her husband's increasing sense of frustrated righteousness and thwarted ambition. Her social life with Liberians was limited due to the tendency of her husband to make enemies wherever he went, and as the years passed she would watch her children become resentful of their rigid, uncompromising father. Her husband was a passionate man—

sexually as well as morally. This we may deduce from the number of her pregnancies, two of which occurred after her arrival in Liberia and despite her poor health. Family life in the Crummell household seems to have been dominated by a sense of religious duty and social obligation. Although the comforts of religion were constantly referred to in times of trial, it is difficult to believe that life was anything but hard.[5]

Crummell commenced his pastoral duties with a hopeful sermon, despite his problems, promising to set a good example and to "promote peace . . . , and keep out of all quarrellings and contentions, even should he suffer wrong." Such promises were difficult for a man of his temperament to keep. He soon found himself working in an atmosphere of "unpleasant complication," as Bishop Payne reported, arising from the presence in Monrovia of Rev. Eli Worthington Stokes, "a colored minister, connected with the Diocese of Rhode Island." Stokes had indeed been Crummell's successor as Rector of Christ Church. He had been appointed in 1849 as a missionary to Cape Palmas, but Payne dismissed him the following year for "incompetency." He relocated in Monrovia and began organizing what the bishop called an "independent church," but he does not seem to have demonstrated any desire to sever all ties—neither with the Episcopalians, nor with Payne. He traveled to England where he raised funds for a church but soon dissipated them. The bishop did not feel free to forbid Stokes entirely from officiating at Monrovia, and he continued to count him among the priests of his jurisdiction, but when he organized Trinity Church in Monrovia, it was Crummell who was named rector. This did little to discourage Stokes, who in the meantime had applied to and been rejected by the Presbyterians. He departed once again for England and Scotland, where he gained the support of the bishop of Glasgow, and returned with "large means at his command"—at least enough to erect a frame church building, which he called St. Paul's. For his part, Crummell considered Stokes "very mischievous," accused him of appropriating church property and the communion plate, and called him "the most painstaking deceiver and liar that ever I met with . . . [he] keeps the place in confusion."[6]

Although characterized by Crummell and others as "an illiterate and mischievous fellow," Stokes's letters indicate that he was neither. He was apparently a man of some credibility and resourcefulness, as he demonstrated during fund-raising tours. Stokes attributed his problems with Bishop Payne to the fact that Stokes claimed an affinity to the high church, and the bishop was a low churchman. Stokes asserted that the people of Monrovia would have preferred him to Payne as their bishop and that this had been a further cause of discord. But his chief difficulty had been brought about by "that wicked man, Alexander Crummell." Stokes claimed that he had first met Crummell in England, where

> He ran after me a great deal . . . to learn how the opinion of the people here was relative to having their own Bishop, and appeared uncommonly friendly, the same time he was endeavoring to do me all the injury he possibly could and I in

the simplicity of my nature let him read my papers and at the same time told him all that the people here wished, and hoped for. This, it appears, has filled him with an ambitious spirit to come here and try his chance of being made a Bishop.[7]

Actually, both men wanted to become bishop of Liberia, and both resented having a white superior. Crummell was more qualified in terms of formal education, but Stokes was more the man of the people. Crummell accused Stokes of attempting to draw off members from his congregation, describing him as "ever mischievously at work." He gloomily foresaw that Stokes would have a measure of success with those "whose cupidity he can gratify." Cupidity it may have been that caused congregations to drift away from Crummell. More likely it was his inability to express tenderness and compassion that alienated people from him. We may assume that his style of worship and sermonizing met the needs of few Liberians. His admonishing and moralizing discourse— lengthy, systematic, almost always written out beforehand—offered little consolation or spiritual uplift, interesting though it was as political dogma. His services were far too sedate for the sort of people he was minister to. In a report to Irving, he wrote disparagingly of the indecorous ways of neighboring churches, accusing them of "noise and shouting." On the other hand, as he remarked, visiting sea captains often stopped at his church, "and French and German residents sometimes were in attendance at his services."[8]

At first it seemed obvious to Crummell that his primary work in Liberia would be among the repatriates. "The poor benighted heathen" obviously suffered from their lack of the Gospel, but the colonists themselves, "fresh from the plantations," were a heartbreaking sight, "with rare and individual exceptions, ignorant, benighted, besotted, and filthy, both in the inner and the outer man." It seemed that if immigration were to increase, "the church would have nearly as much as she could do for a half century and more to reclaim and upbuild these colonists." Crummell did not divorce himself from the indigenous population nor from non-American repatriates; indeed he seems to have had some success with both groups. By training and disposition, however, he was well prepared to get on with the work of nation building, and he hoped to make use of his academic training by working among the better-educated class of colonists.[9]

In 1853, when Crummell arrived in Monrovia, the population was around 5000. Liberia as a whole included around 10,000 Americo-Liberians and 225,000 natives, some of whom had adopted American ways. The president, Joseph Jenkins Roberts, at that time well into his third term, represented the mulatto faction and its political force, the True Republican Party, later known as the Republican Party. Roberts was committed to territorial expansion and at one point proposed to the British foreign minister that Sierra Leone be annexed to Liberia. The "proposition was received with some indications of surprise, but with little favor." Roberts was equally unsuccessful in attempts to gain diplomatic recognition from the United States for his republic, despite his cozy relationship to the American Colonization Society, with its lobbying efforts in the United States Congress. During the Roberts administration, the republic strengthened its ties with the Maryland Colony, which had been founded some one hundred miles south by the Maryland Colonization Society. The Maryland Colony declared its independence in 1854 and soon afterward united with Liberia.[10]

There seemed to be grounds for modest optimism concerning Liberia's prospects for growth and consolidation. Although Crummell felt that he could not "write the glowing reports of the nation and of the people and the condition and prospects of the Republic which many people do," he believed that with the right kind of leadership the future might be prosperous. The role of a Christian clergyman among the nation's founding fathers should be able to provide a national ideology that would assure greatness. While he claimed that "political partisanship in a minister is unseemly, distracting and despiritualizing," he was not "one of those in whose mind religion is so far divorced from national and governmental affairs that it becomes wrong for a minister to speak about any thing that is political." He asserted that "Christianity should permeate all the relations and all the institutions of society," and that it was his Christian duty not to allow the national holiday to pass without calling attention to it from the pulpit. Since no issue of government or politics lacked a moral dimension, there could be no social system without a religion. He cited the authority of Burke that "we know, and indeed what is better, we feel inwardly that religion is the basis of all civil society, and the source of all good and of all comfort."[11]

This was a self-evident truth, and one consistent with his personal observations. Nothing could be more obvious than the historic triumph of Christian Europe over all lesser forms of civilization. From the undeniable evidence of Christendom's economic and political might, one must posit some relationship between temporal power and ideological rightness. National greatness was "always correlative with the ideas of God and religion." A nation would become great "just in proportion to the clearness of its idea of God."[12] Was this approach to a theory of social change a manifestation of Crummell's "Cambridge Platonism"? Did it stem from a Christian's bias that spirit was more important than matter? Did it result from the "common-sense" observations of a thoroughly Westernized man? Each of these factors influenced his thinking. Burke's self-evident axiom only provided authority for what could be empirically demonstrated. Africa was obviously backward, and what other possible explanation could there be for this backwardness than her idolatry, which was an observable fact all along the West African coast.

> If a people think that God is a Spirit, that idea raises, or will raise them among the first of nations. If, on the other hand, they think that God is a stone, or a carved image or a reptile, they will assuredly be low and rude. A nation that worships stocks, or ugly idols, can never while maintaining such a style of worship, become a great nation.[13]

There had been, it is true, great nations in ancient times that were idolatrous, but they had in their infancy been religiously simple and correct. It was only as they had increased in power and dominance that they had brought back from their conquests "the hideous idolatries which ruined them." In the strength of their youth these archaic empires had adhered to surviving remnants of the primal natural religion. Idolatry had appeared only as they had become decadent and luxurious, and it had inevitably spelled their downfall. The idealism, the antimaterialism, that was ever at the center of Crummell's ideology led him to assert that if the mighty nations of Europe were suddenly to become worshipers of some material object, they would immediately fall into decline.

As evidence for this argument, he cited the fact that the ancestors of the Europeans and North Americans had once been "barbarians without commerce or enlightenment; and then they worshipped dumb idols, and bowed down in fear and awe to graven images." It was only after Christianity was introduced that they began to realize progress. "Where on the face of the earth," he asked, "can you find a nation that worships birds, and beasts, and creeping things that is great, powerful, and free." The true idea of God, that is of God as a spirit standing over and above the material world, seemed to enlarge the soul of man, so that "the depths of the earth are not deep enough for his penetrating gaze; and the boundless seas not grand and majestic enough for his swelling thought; nor the illimitable spheres above vast and extensive enough for excursive reason." In other words, the true concept of God made the individual like unto a God, leading him to seek "satisfaction in the Infinite and Eternal." [14] A nation that held to a true concept of God would be immortal. It was no necessary law of history that every great nation was doomed to fall into decline. The first great nations, Nineveh, Babylon, and Egypt, as they had arisen in the infancy of the world, were inheritors of the wisdom of Adam, "a most complete and proper man." His descendants who founded the early empires must have carried with them "some of his high enlightenment and rare capability." Although fallen, these early peoples had true ideas of God, "and these ideas made them great . . . led to enterprise, originated large ideas and grand purposes, prompted them to build great cities, and to lay the foundations of magnificent empires." The Liberian people must learn from the civilizations of the past to avoid that "luxury [that] cloys and enervates." They must maintain a rigorous Christian culture, thereby placing themselves under the protection of God's "laws and governance," Thus would the nation gain immortality "and live on forever mindless of decay and fearless of ruin." This was a point on which he placed much stress. Black intellectuals of the nineteenth century were fascinated with the cyclical theory of history with its gloomy predictions of decline and fall. Such theories were heartening when applied to the Church of Rome or to the American slave power, but far from consoling when applied to West African dreams. How could the African empire avoid the seemingly resistless tide of destiny that carried every civilization inevitably to senescence and decay? By attaching itself to that power, "which amid the transitoriness of all temporal things, retains the fixed reality of heaven." [15]

Like Emerson, Carlyle, and Hegel, Crummell found himself uniting theological historicism with liberal ideas of individualism. Although national destiny and national duty were important ideas in Crummell's writing, individual-ism was a necessary ingredient of a free society, and it had somehow to be reconciled with social aims. A nation was more than the mass of individuals whom it comprised. Nationality implied the existence of a national spirit, "SO-CIETY in an organized state, under the influence and control of broad principles and superior ideas." National ideals should have a force of their own, control-ling the activities of the flawed mortals who made up the citizenry of a nation. However, since the nation was "the aggregate of the individuals that lived in that nation," the greatness of the nation would never be any loftier than the countless individual moral decisions that its citizens made every day. Individual morality must be the keystone of any great nation that hoped to assume lead-ership in the unfolding ages of the world. Manly integrity and womanly dignity would lead to a spirit of vigorous enterprise and increase the individual wealth of all. Since individual character and national greatness were interdependent, such statements as "Peter the Great made Russia" or "William Pitt saved England" must be understood as merely figurative. Representative men really did no more than amplify the *Zeitgeist,* embodied in the common folk. Thus Crummell found himself in the company of Hegel and Emerson, rather than that of Carlyle, for like the former he believed that the Great Man was repre-sentative of his age, rather than "ahead of his time." [16]

Crummell was ambivalent about the relative importance of national ideals and individual character as sources of national greatness just as he was ambiv-alent about the relative importance of Providence (embodied in national des-tiny) and free will (embodied in individual responsibility). Providence and so-cial forces played their roles in determining human behavior and the patterns of history. Nonetheless, individuals possessed free will and were obliged to work for their own salvation and for the improvement of the world. Like most Christians, Crummell denied that there was a contradiction between predestin-ation and free will. The fact that historical forces existed did not mean that individuals were passive victims of fate, nor did faith in Providence relieve the citizen of the duty to strive constantly for the greatness of the nation. It was precisely this individual striving that would bring the nation as well as the individual to greatness.

He reminded his countrymen that they and he were "members of a but rising race, whose greatness was as yet to be achieved—a race which has been spoiled and degraded for centuries and in consequence of which has been despised." The citizenry of Liberia must be "stirred to energy and activity" by reflecting on the degraded condition of the African race and their duty to vindicate it by national progress. They must by their accomplishments in Liberia give hope and cheer to the downcast brothers and sisters throughout the world. If the Liberians would cultivate right-mindedness there would be reason for opti-mism, for "God's gracious favor is evidently manifested in our race." During Western Europe's rise and expansion, "Other races have been swept out of existence, but God has preserved *our* life . . . And now, wherever we look, the acknowledged manhood of the race has been won, and the race is going upward and onward to high intelligence and increased power." In the Caribbean, as well, there were signs of providence at work. The Republic of Haiti, despite the "incubus of Romanism" showed evidence of "a growing civilization, refinement, and intellectual culture, and commercial expansion." Liberia, which had the advantage of being Protestant, was in a position to take the lead for the entire black race "and tread with firmness the open pathway of science, letters, religion and civilization."[17]

Despite his hopes for the future development of the African race, Crummell had little good to say about its present state. Like most of his contemporaries among black nationalists, he was in a paradoxical position, wanting to create a black nationality, but conceiving of that nationality in cosmopolitan terms, which led to a number of contradictions. They spoke of the need for a black nationality, and yet they borrowed the very rhetoric of black nationalism from American and European racialistic theories. Thus in their very rejection of assimilationist theories they unintentionally became an example of a sort of cultural assimilation. The political and territorial separatism for which they strove stood in ironic contrast to the cultural imitativeness that they endorsed. The logic of their simultaneous endorsement of territorial separatism and assimilation is easy to understand. They wanted all the things that whites had but that they feared whites would never let them enjoy in an integrated society. Then, too, they needed European technology just as certainly as they desired freedom from European control. They did not conceive of this knowledge and technology as the property of Europe; it was simply universal truth, upon which Europe happened to have stumbled first. The story of civilization was no more than Providence's grand design, which ultimately would be fulfilled through the agency of Christian culture. Since the dawn of history, civilization had been passing from people to people. Nations and customs indeed perished, but civilization was an immortal as truth. It could not be the possession of any one people; it was the common heritage of all humanity. Although it happened at this historical moment to be most perfectly realized in North America and Western Europe, it should not be seen as the peculiar expression of these nations' racial singularities.

Crummell viewed the laws of civilization as "discovered not devised." The evolving African nation would not undermine Victorian manners and morality; it would seek to perfect them, for the black race would learn from the folly of the white and thus avoid its infidelity to the laws of God and nature. Crummell would not question European literary and scientific traditions. It is true that he called for the creation of an African civilization, but it was never clear precisely what he meant by this. If the *Négritude* ideal was prefigured in his writings and those of his mid-century compatriots, it was chiefly in the political sense, for there was precious little of the cultural nationalism that appears in the twentieth-century writings of Césaire, Senghor, or the figures of the Harlem Renaissance. Nineteenth-century black nationalism was formulated in cosmopolitan terms, but it would be many years before it developed a cultural pluralism that could appreciate African religion, music, and dance.[18]

In contrast to German nationalism, which had long been obsessed with re-
acting to French, Mediterranean, and Jewish influences, West African nationalism was not yet culturally chauvinistic. Not till later in the century would it
produce its counterparts of the Grimm brothers—glorifiers of African folklore
and the homely arts of primeval African peoples. The shortcomings of tribal
culture were all too obvious to a generation whose fathers and mothers were
the victims of West African slaving wars. As for Afro-American culture, what
fascination could it hold for the nationalists, when its bearers were slaves,
whose customs were a shameful reminder of the plantation? To glorify slave
culture would be to glorify slavery; to glorify African culture would be to
glorify heathenism. The patterns of thought common to the Liberian patriots of
the nineteenth century did not correspond to any definition of cultural nationalism that we would accept today. They were "civilizationists," as opposed to
"culturalists," and they saw civilization as a process governed by universal
rules which they viewed from the biased perspective of Western Christianity.
They believed that progressively higher forms of civilization could be measured
on one universal scale. French customs, English manners, and American tastes
may indeed have manifested national peculiarities, but the greatness of each
people existed in proportion to its discovery of civilization's universal principles. Thus, if progress was to be achieved by an African state, it would have
to be based on some decidedly and singularly black manifestation of universal
Christian truth.

It was inconceivable that the hoped-for nation might spring up independently
from any indigenous African culture. It would be the product of transplanted
civilization, just as the cultures of Western Europe were perceived to be. Crummell saw Victorian civilization as resulting from the importation of Roman
discipline and Christian morals; it could never have been accomplished through
some grotesque eruption of pre-Christian Druidic paganism. Crummell thus saw
his work in Liberia in relation to a grand conception of the rapid civilization
and enlightenment of a West Africa that could eventually rise to a position of
leadership and even dominance in world affairs. He was, however, forced to
work with people whose hopes were far less ambitious.

The Right Reverend John Payne, his immediate superior, was the Missionary
Bishop of the Protestant Episcopal church in the United States of America at
Cape Palmas and parts adjacent. Bishop Payne remembered a day when the
mission had been concerned primarily with the natives within a fifty-mile radius
of Cape Palmas, but he also had been working among the colonists of the
region since 1846, when he organized St. Mark's Church. He had had little to
do with Monrovia until the arrival of the ambitious, irritable Crummell forced
him to address a series of annoying issues. These he had hoped would disappear with the discharge of Stokes, but Stokes and Crummell apparently had
one thing in common—their annoyance at being under a white superior, here,
in what ought to have been the black man's preserve. The difficulties between
Payne and Crummell grew out of the situation in which they found themselves,
as well as from some inflexibility on the part of each. The bishop accepted the

fact that the work of the mission at Cape Palmas was well enough established that now might be the time to undertake expansion into Liberia proper, but he heard the call of Providence with conflicting emotions. Taking up the work in Monrovia meant working with a different sort of population. It also meant straining financial resources. He hoped that the additional expenses could be defrayed by promised contributions from the church in Virginia.[19]

Crummell and the bishop agreed that a mission at Monrovia should be established as soon as possible, and that it would require raising funds for "a suitable edifice." Crummell obviously placed much importance on an imposing building, for it seemed to him to be "wise and judicious, that . . . in the Capitol, the great place of resort from every part of the republic, our Church should make as strong an impression as possible, both spiritually and also in externals." The bishop supported Crummell's plan to found an institution for higher education, but he believed that he should "accomplish the former object first." There does not seem to have been open conflict over an agenda. Crummell agreed with the bishop that a respectable building had to be constructed in Monrovia as soon as possible. The bishop, for his part, seemed to accept the idea that Crummell would retain charge of the church in Monrovia, only "until a more important department of our operations in that vicinity can be organized . . . a high school or college for the training of teachers and ministers." The bishop seemed quite persuaded that Crummell was extraordinarily well qualified to teach, and he hoped the churches in England and America would soon fund the establishment of a "regular College . . . the institution to be under the care of Rev. Mr. Crummell."[20]

Privately, however, the bishop was taking a different line. He wrote to the Foreign Committee of the Episcopal Board of Missions to express the hope that they would not insist on Crummell's connection with the "proposed institution." He reminded them that the first stone had not yet been laid for any college building. He believed that it would be "far better . . . to have a school only such as we have at Mt. Vaughan." He referred to the mission school at Cape Palmas, where native children were instructed in the basic skills of mathematics and the English language, in addition to the agricultural and industrial arts. His plan for Monrovia was to have Crummell work to establish Trinity Church and its congregation. In a year or two, after Crummell had undergone some seasoning in Africa, he might "commence the educational building."[21]

Crummell in the meantime was organizing his Liberian pastoral work, teaching a Sunday School, assembling a catechism class. He had received five hundred dollars from Payne towards the construction of his church and had received architectural drawings from a friend in England. A year after the gathering of his congregation, he had laid the cornerstone, and work commenced "with drilling and blasting; and the masons laying the foundations as fast as a clearance was made." A visiting clergyman wrote disparagingly that when he inspected the site, "none of the workmen were to be seen, and the blasting consisted of building a small fire on a solid mass of rock, by which fissures are said to be made and the fragments are then taken out." Reports apparently reached Bishop Payne that Crummell's plans were too grandiose, and Crummell had to send him a description of the dimensions. The bishop was "gratified and relieved to learn . . . that the church is not the Cathedral into which invidious rumor had magnified it." The dimensions named were quite acceptable, and although the costs were somewhat in excess of what had been anticipated, they seemed reasonable enough.[22]

In later years Crummell maintained that he had been insulted by the bishop only six months after he had arrived in Liberia. He was seated at the bishop's table, "the only black man in the midst of white American missionaries," when the bishop had made "the bitter vulgar remark—'your race is the lowest, meanest, most lying, thievish, treacherous, back biting race on earth.' " Crummell, accustomed to being humiliated by his bishops, made no response, but the wives of two of the white missionaries were sensitive enough to share his embarrassment and came to him "with tears in their eyes, and expressed cordial sympathy." Around that time the bishop had sent him a reproving letter, urging him to meekness, and advising him that he would have fewer difficulties if he could bring himself to some "modification of manner." Some months later, he wrote again "alluding to the darker features of your ministerial life . . . the indisposition of your people to *give toward missionary objects.*" He made comparisons, not only with the white race, but also with the native converts at Cape Palmas. It was his impression that the Methodists in Monrovia also contributed generously to the church building fund.[23]

It was a rather confused and contradictory letter, beginning as a general indictment of black people, who Payne said were poor supporters of missions. Suddenly, he began making invidious comparisons between Monrovian Episcopalians and other black congregations in Africa and the West Indies who he said did give generously to missions. The letter had drifted from a racial indictment to a criticism of Monrovian Episcopalians, who differed from the other good black people throughout the English-speaking world. The letter had not been carefully thought out before it was set down. Although the bishop's central point is difficult to discern, it is clear that he wanted to hurt Crummell, and the letter gives credence to Crummell's claims. Payne was clearly capable of making a "bitter, vulgar remark," and his letters were not only unkind, but characterized by the emotionalism and inconsistency that are often revealed in the statements of racialists. The bishop was obviously unprepared to deal with a black man whose manner was so supercilious and whose ambitions were so high. Feeling it was his place to rebuke Crummell for his pride, he enclosed a snatch of verse he recalled from Charles Swain.

> 'Tis a truth that I have known
> And a truth that's worth revealing
> More offend from want of thought
> Than from any want of feeling.

One may charitably hope that in jotting down these lines for Crummell's benefit the bishop realized that they might with some justice be applied to himself.

There is, however, nothing to suggest that the bishop was capable of such self-awareness. Neither he nor Crummell seems to have been capable of profiting from this little literary irony, and the burden of understanding should have been more on the bishop's part than on Crummell's.

There were several reasons for the lack of trust between Crummell and his bishop. The small community of white missionaries at Cape Palmas, of which Payne was the head, viewed themselves as saintly apostles to the aboriginal heathen. They supported this self-image quite cozily within the little community, nurturing one another's sense of martyrdom and long-suffering with occasional publications in *Spirit of Missions*. They were concerned mainly with the tribes within a radius of fifty miles from the cape, where they calculated the native population at 100,000. The peoples of the area had suffered greatly from the slave trade, and, in Payne's view, were being "more entirely shattered by subsequent hostile collision with the Liberians." Because the native population was so large in comparison to that of the settlers, Payne maintained that the "plan of operation" ought to be "to establish a church and training school at each of the principal Liberian settlements as the base for extending our influence as rapidly as possible among the heathen."[24]

Crummell believed that the needs of the colonists had to be attended to first. He offended the white missionaries with his belief that an independent, educated elite of Liberian nationals must eventually assume all responsibility for uplifting the masses of heathen and settler alike. He wanted to educate the people for the task of nation building, and he wanted to begin erecting the stately, bourgeois institutions in Monrovia itself as soon as possible. The church and the academy in their buildings and grounds must symbolize the wealth, the power, and the leadership roles that the new nation would assume in world affairs. The white church had much to offer in terms of its wealth, refinement, and wisdom, but the black church, like the black nation, must ultimately govern itself. Crummell was inspired by the dignity and the substance of the Episcopal church in New York and London; he hoped to establish something equally impressive in Liberia. He also intended to see the church play a leading role in the creation of national identity among the settlers. He felt that the education of the heathen must be carried out by an indigenous ministry. The role for a man like himself was to form the civil religion of the Afro-American settlers.[25]

Devoted though he was to Liberian nationalism, Crummell could not bring himself to go the way of Stokes; the latter, it was reported, took up "warmly the cause of African nationality." This made him "popular notwithstanding his various defects." Crummell could no more break with Payne than he could have with the Onderdonks years earlier, despite his personal dislike for the man. Temperamental conservatism, a respect for authority, and a commitment to the apostolic church apparently won out over racial assertiveness. Payne was nonetheless disturbed when he became aware of a convocation of black Episcopalians in which Crummell was involved. The convocation seemed determined to transform the Liberian church into a diocese, independent of Cape Palmas. The bishop claimed to be hurt by Crummell's decision to participate in such a movement without first discussing his feelings with him. "I would have wished," he wrote, "that in conversation, or letter or in any way with the frankness which I had supposed was characteristic of you—you had opened your mind to me on this subject." The bishop knew quite well why Crummell had not opened his mind. Crummell and the other black churchmen felt that the bishop had dealt less than directly with them. They had read in the *Journal of the General Convention of the Church in America* that the bishop had petitioned to have his title changed from Bishop of Cape Palmas and Parts Adjacent to Bishop of Liberia and Parts Adjacent. The national sentiment of Liberians could not easily allow a white man and a non-national to assume such a title. They were in fact "looking steadily forward to the formation of a National Church coextensive with the limits of the Republic, and National in all its leading characteristics." The secretary of the convocation was charged with sending copies of the proceedings, including a resolution that the Liberian church be placed "on a new and Thoroughly National basis," to the Foreign Committee and to Bishop Payne. Thus the convocation could not be described as having hidden its activities from Payne. On the other hand this was clearly a case of "black folks' business" and Payne revealed his awareness of the point by observing that "the *prejudice of caste* is equally opposed to the spirit of Christ in a descendant of Shem, Ham, or Japhet." The bishop viewed Crummell as a radical black nationalist; the Liberians all too often saw him as a creature of the white man because of his desire to maintain ties to white America and the American church.[26]

Payne wrote to the Foreign Committee, conjecturing that Crummell was one of those blacks who in the United States appeared to be the "personification of meekness" but on reaching the African coast "were suddenly transformed into the most imperious and supercilious of men."[27] This was strange, for Crummell's reputation in the United States was hardly one of meekness. Indeed, it was his reputation for haughtiness and irritability that often confirmed the board in its repeated decisions to ignore the possibility of racial bias and to support the bishop's authority. Crummell, for his part was aware of the "imputation of 'oversensitiveness' on the part of black men."[28] In his own view, he had indeed been meek and suffered long for justice's sake, while Payne did all he could to rob him of self-respect and independence. From the bishop's perspective, Crummell had no right to agitate for the establishment of the episcopate in the upper part of Liberia. This was a matter to be considered only with "the consent and confidence of the members there as well as of the church in the United States, by which the mission must be long supported."[29]

A bishop usually has ways of disciplining an upstart clergyman, and Payne, although he often committed himself on paper to the financial support of Crummell's various interests, in practice opposed him. In 1854, while constantly declaring his support for the church and the academy to be constructed in Monrovia, he diverted two thousand dollars to another end. The Virginia church had contributed the funds for educational purposes in Monrovia, but the bishop used them to construct Grace Church at Clay-Ashland, a settlement some ten miles up river. Under the pastorship of Rev. A. F. Russell, formerly a Methodist minister, Grace Church seemed to thrive for a while but eventually dwindled to eleven communicants. Russell, who represented the hated mulatto group that Crummell blamed for many of his disappointments, eventually served for a few months as president of the republic. Crummell, maintaining that Payne favored Russell because he was a mulatto related to the McKliffes of Kentucky, declared him "a bastard child; with the blood of both races in his veins and with the virtues of neither."[30]

Bishops may be able to discipline their subordinates through the power of the purse, but a preacher nursing a sense of injured righteousness also has singular means of retribution at his disposal. On December 17, 1854, Crummell preached on the Last Judgement, the burning wrath of the Savior, who "drove the money changers from the temple . . . , looked at the Pharisees and Sadducees, seeking a sign in the face, and called them hypocrites and an adulterous generation and refused them any sign save the sign of Jonah the prophet." Anyone who opened his eyes could see that the world "is in a distracted state: that wrong and error prevail: that sin maintains an ascendency: and that justice and right are loose and relaxed in their hold upon the conscience of man." Only with the Last Judgement and the Second Coming would the hidden sins of hypocrites be made known. Only on that day would justice be granted to "honest men and innocent women persecuted, belied, and traduced by foul slander."[31]

Fundamental to Crummell's theology was his belief that the question of salvation or damnation would ultimately be decided on the basis of works, not by mere professions of faith. The Last Judgement was to be "that awful event at which God intends to mete out to every man the full rewards for all his deeds and life." On that day Christ would be "no longer the Lord of Mercy, but the Dispenser of Justice." His mildness, tenderness, supplication and tears, would be "turned to rigidity and inflexibility." Every man must then "render an account of the thoughts, deeds and words of his mortal life." Then all would know "the concealed designs of the mind of which the world was not aware; and also of all those deeds; and those shameful passionate words, which have done harm to man and dishonored God."

Two remarkable ideas in Crummell's thinking are revealed here: First, that at the Last Judgement, men and women were to be saved or damned on the basis of their deeds. Second, that the justice of God and the conscience of man responded to laws of the universe, "which his own moral economy has created." The significance of the Last Judgement for Crummell was that it was not only a fulfillment of the divine plan; it was a response to the "groans of nature" and to the "natural desires" of man that the evils of the world be settled and that works and deeds receive their just recompense.

> There is a requirement in our nature—the nature given us by God,—that the evils
> of the world should yet be settled by Divine justice! But the evils of the world
> *are not* settled in the world. And yet still our moral nature makes the requirement
> for justice: and the pale and troubled shades of mighty millions who have gone

down to the grave unredressed; aye the whole creation; and the angels on high, and the Church of Christ Jesus and the broken moral Law and the very attributes of God himself, cry out to the Eternal Throne—Justice! Justice! O. God. And God meets and satisfies the demand and requirement of the universe.

Salvation involved more than the acknowledgment of Christ, for, while it was true that one must be washed in the blood of Jesus, Crummell was clearly far more interested in exhorting his congregation to righteousness than in pleading with them to get to know Jesus. Both concerns were present, but the emphasis was overwhelmingly practical. He placed great emphasis on character-building and the moral responsibilities of life, without which piety would have no meaning. Not everyone who cried Lord! Lord! would enter the kingdom of heaven; only the virtuous would be admitted, and virtue would be measured by deeds.[32]

He spoke almost as if the Christian were attempting to take heaven by storm, saying, "We shall be safe and assured only then, when we plant our feet upon the battlements of heaven." Profession of religion did not automatically bring one into the community of saints, and one could be certain of salvation only after death. His almost explicit rejection of the doctrine of justification by faith alone made him a "strict churchman," placing him on theological terrain that was closer to the Oxford movement than to the Cambridge evangelicals by whom he had been educated. He stressed the belief that there was "no safety this side of heaven" and gravitated towards the borderline Thomism of the most extreme Oxfordians, who seemed almost to believe in justification through works and were sometimes referred to as Anglo-Catholics. On the sermon's second to last page appeared lines from the *Dies Irae,* a twelfth-century hymn from the Roman Catholic Mass for the Dead.[33]

> That day of wrath that dreadful day
> When heaven and earth shall pass away!
> What power shall bid the summons stay
> How shall we meet that dreadful day?
> When shrivelling like a parched scroll
> The flaming heavens together roll:
> When louder yet, and yet more dread
> Swells the high trump that wakes the dead
> O on that day that dreadful wrathful day
> When man to judgement wakes from clay
> Be thou the trembling sinner's stay
> Though heaven and earth shall pass away

The sermon was typical of Crummell. Unlike the radically Calvinistic evangelicals, he believed that God had "thrown personal responsibility upon every man to achieve his own salvation." When Christ came to judgement, he would come to "call men to account for the deeds done in the flesh." He would judge according to works, rendering "to every man according to what he had done, during the period of His earthly test and trial." He would "bring to light the hidden things of darkness and make manifest the counsels of the heart." Worldly tyrants would be stripped of their power. "The deceitful and the lying, the slanderous men and women, whose trade was mischief on this earth, and who dealt in the soul-murder of their neighbors," would be there along with "unfaithful and wicked ministers."[34]

It is tempting to think that the Doomsday Sermon, coming as it did at the end of Crummell's first unsatisfactory year with Payne, was inspired at least partially by a sense of being unjustly treated. Clearly he felt that the bishop was a great hypocrite, and it would have been natural enough for him to give vent to his emotions in a sermon. He raised the question himself, "Does not human nature require *satisfaction* for all this wrong?" He did not speak specifically of wrongs done to him, only of the crimes committed against his people through slavery, and the unredressed wrongs committed by supposedly civil society. And yet he spoke with passion, asking his congregation with a fervor that was perhaps more than rhetorical, "Does not your soul rise up with mine, aye and with every man who has a soul; and does not the fervent utterance go up to Heaven—'How long, O Lord how long!' "

Unfortunately, the Crummells' problems were just beginning. For some months, they had been having trouble with their landlord. The bishop had mentioned their difficulties with housing and had proposed in November of 1854 that the church make some provisions for them, possibly in the form of a mission house, which would later become the center of the proposed educational institution. Of course with all the designated monies being sent to Russell at Clay-Ashland, the building program had been shunted aside. Then, on January 11, 1855, Payne wrote to the Board of Missions to report that Crummell had been driven out of his home by his landlord, adding, "he informs me he is in the same danger of similar treatment again." Crummell wrote to Jay around the same time that on the evening of January 10, 1855, while he had been out walking with his assistant, Rev. H. Greene, he had heard the cry of "Fire!" and "running with the crowd toward my residence, we discovered our house to be on fire." He reported to the board that the town was ill supplied with water, especially during the dry season, and that despite the "generous enthusiasm" of the young men of the town, everything in the house, "save our library and a few articles of furniture," was lost.[35]

After waiting in Monrovia for "some two weeks" unable to find a house, Crummell moved his family into the country. The bishop commented privately on this, observing that the Crummells were eventually able to build a "comfortable house." He came down the river with his assistant Greene to Monrovia only for Sunday services, a situation which the bishop considered "ruinous." He opined that Crummell's housing problems were largely his own fault. He had been ejected from his first house by his landlord and driven from the second by fire. "And about the third some altercation between him and his landlord led to his giving up." Here was more grist for the bishop's mill, and he returned with relish to one of his favorite themes, the defects in Crummell's personality.[36]

It would be some comfort to be able to learn that in all this Mr. C. has been merely unfortunate. But the general—almost universal testimony is that while possessed of undoubted talent, and a fine preacher, he is imperious, self willed, and so *thoroughly* English, that he cannot and will not adapt himself to circumstances.

During the first few weeks in the country, he was forced to accept the charity of a Mr. Richardson, who took the family into his own home for five weeks while he helped them to put up their own house on land donated by the government. Not only was he beset by financial hardship during this period, but the family's health was still poor. Mrs. Crummell was confined to her bed for most of the year. She had already become disillusioned with Liberia, though Crummell wistfully expressed the hope that she might "yet learn to live in Africa" and wondered if perhaps her condition might be improved by a sea cruise to a temperate climate. Although bedridden, she still did the family's sewing and mending, while Crummell learned to use the plough and harrow, donated to him by English friends. He took satisfaction in boasting that he raised his own potatoes, beans, yanyah and rice. Two of his children were now old enough to help him with the farming, and no doubt the experience of practical education at Beriah Green's Oneida Institute now stood him in good stead. Nonetheless, the family often went "for long periods without tasting a piece of meat." As he observed in a letter to the Board of Missions, cattle would not thrive, and stores must be constantly replenished by donations from American friends. The situation was particularly difficult because of a failure of the rice crop that year, which had led to "fearful apprehension of famine," and inflation of the price of food. Crummell stressed that he was asking for provisions rather than money, and he doggedly continued with his farming activities, experimenting with the cultivation of sugar and coffee with the help of native labor.

Hardship did not prevent Crummell from continuing to minister to the congregation in Monrovia, nor from attending to other matters. Payne gave him quite a satisfactory report in *Spirit of Missions,* saying that Trinity Church had attained "a somewhat established character," although they still worshiped in "a small borrowed house." Towards the end of the year they lost even that place, and the new building was not yet completed, but apparently some provisions were made, for Crummell was able to conduct services with "a good deal of regularity," and his mission was found to be in "a satisfactory condition on the whole," though he was "somewhat interrupted by ill-health." Dr. James Hall, an agent of the American Colonization Society who visited the church in January 1856, described the building as "of stone, very roughly built, of one story, and nothing to distinguish the exterior from an ordinary dwelling." The interior was very plain, but comfortable, about twenty by thirty feet, with a few wooden benches.

The room was Episcopalized by a wooden screen, behind which the pastor could do whatever is usually done in church vestrys. . . . Mr. Crummell read, or performed, or conducted, which ever may be the proper term, the Episcopal service *well*. . . . His sermon, too, was one of the best we ever heard, and delivered, as he read the service, well. The number in church was 26, of whom three were passengers by our ship, our own party, so that the inference is, Mr. Crummell's preaching, good as it is, from some cause, is not destined to affect many in Liberia.[37]

Bishop Payne was in absolute agreement with Dr. Hall. In his letters to the Board of Foreign Missions, he described Crummell as *"exceedingly unpopular,"* reporting that his congregation had been reduced to "sometimes . . . about twenty-five." Payne began to unveil his "perplexity" with respect to the "character and influence of Mr. Crummell." He was now certain that Crummell was not the man to be entrusted with the administration of "the proposed educational establishment." Crummell was inflexible, totally unwilling "to adapt himself to the people so far as to make himself acceptable, while his angry altercations have created him many enemies." He did not have the aptitude for training young men. The two young men whom he had taken into his home at the expense of the mission, had been "either sent away or [had] deserted." The bishop had in any case come to recommend strongly that the proposed "educational establishment" (he no longer referred to it as a college) "be placed under the care of a well educated, prudent—if possible *not young,* foreign Missionary." He still professed to believe that Africa must eventually be "evangelized by Africans, but for some time to come, the church must be employed in raising up the instruments." The work could not yet be entrusted to black laborers either native or Liberian, and he suggested that the Foreign Committee send a white man to head up the academy. There was, for example, a Scotsman who had been recommended, though the bishop could not remember his name. That such an appointment would be proper was implied by his observation that "the Presbyterian and the Methodist High Schools in Monrovia are both under the care of white men."[38]

Crummell was hardly so ineffective as the bishop claimed, and his character was having some effect on Monrovian life—poorly attended though his church services were. He had soon established a day school and through friends in the Unites States had been able to raise funds for a public library. The president of Liberia, Stephen A. Benson, thanked him for his efforts at some length during a public address. Crummell thought of the president as "a great man." He wrote to Jay, "My friend President Benson would give me a government office but he has none now vacant which as to stipend would relieve me." But even if such an offer were to be made, he did not believe that he could in conscience "step out from the sphere and duties of a clergyman to those of a statesman or politician, albeit it is too common here."[39] Despite his disavowals of any political aspirations, however, he gave an intensely political sermon on July 26, Independence Day, of 1855. It was entitled "The Duty of a Rising Christian State to Contribute to the World's Well-Being and Civilization, and the Means by Which It May Perform the Same." The tone of this address was markedly different from that of his Independence Day oration the preceding year. The oration of 1854 had treated mainly the importance of ideals in the creation of a modern republic; the oration of 1855 was remarkable for its attention to practical concerns. It was not that Crummell was in any danger of wavering on his philosophical idealism, but two years in Liberia had certainly equipped him to refer to specific problems. Then too, the practical experience he had undergone in developmental economics had enhanced his appreciation of the nation's needs.

The central concern of this year's address was the development of the national economy. Given Crummell's as yet undashed hopes for milling coffee and growing sugar cane, it is not surprising that farming occupied a significant place in his program for national development. For Liberia speedily to take her place in the ranks of civilized nations, her citizens would first have to discover which of the world's wants Liberia was equipped to supply. Agriculture seemed to be a likely area for development, and by cultivating products suited to the currently occupied territories Liberia could meet immediate demands and contribute to her own advancement. Sugar, coffee, flax, hemp, indigo, cinnamon—all of these were important, but by cultivating cotton, Liberia would make an even more important contribution. He hoped some day to see "thousands of bales of [Liberian] cotton, competing with the oppressors of our race in the ports of Liverpool and Glasgow, and beating down their ill-gotten gains!" The Liberian farmers could in this pragmatic way "lessen the needs of distant men, break down the barbarism of unrequited toil, and give cheer by their production to foreign lands."[40]

Recognizing the difficulties of animal husbandry in the West African coastal climate, he stressed the importance of opening roads to the highlands of the Northwest so that the settlers could procure cattle from the interior, rather than sending "some $60,000 to $100,000 out of the Republic for the single article of meats." The development of roads would at the same time civilize distant tribes, who would be enabled "to come unmolested hitherward." Hostile tribes, once subdued, "should be forced, as one of the terms of the treaty, to open a road some thirty or forty miles into the heart of their country. Trade would keep it open, and they cannot fight in an open country." A year later, he wrote to P. P. Irving to report that he had "pressed the opening of roads upon the minds of several enterprising citizens, chiefly churchmen," and that this had resulted in the formation of the "Inland Road Company," which offered special privileges to missionaries and missionary societies. If any special privileges were offered to entrepreneurs, Crummell neglected to mention them.[41]

Despite this emphasis on material development, Crummell stubbornly insisted that "the main modes and measures whereby we may fulfill our national obligation to the human race must be in the cultivation of MEN." It was only men who could make a country great; national wealth was worthless without an enlightened citizenry. "Men cultivate fields; they cultivate cattle, and trees, and birds, and fish; so too can they cultivate men. The old Romans understood something about this; with an iron hand the Spartans tried their skill at it, so too, still more and more wisely, the English in modern times." The skill was however a rare one, and thus real "MEN" were all too rare on earth. The needs of Liberia could be met only by "citizens with large expanded minds, a fine culture with natural or acquired manners, and a constant delicate honor; giving strength and solidarity at home, and fair fame, respect and character abroad."[42]

That Africa should contribute to world civilization was clear, but Crummell's conception of what that distinct contribution might be was vague. His theory of history proclaimed that every race had its distinctive genius and must make its singular contribution. But contributions to civilization did not remain the permanent, exclusive property of any race. The individual nation was "but a section of the great commonwealth of humanity, a phase of the common type of being and no more." This idea was already well known in the traditions of European nationalism. It had appeared in the writings of Herder, whose theories marked him as both a cosmopolite and a father of German nationalism: "Das Menschengeschlecht ist ein Ganzes; wir arbeiten und dulden, säen und ernten für einander." ("The human race is one whole; we work and endure, sow and reap for one another.") Crummell found history to be replete with examples of this truth: "The endless migrations, the strange wanderings, the multitudinous progenitures, and the colonial formations which have originated the nations of earth, eschew the idea of isolation." Among the many illustrations of this truth was the history of the prophet Moses, whose genius had been nurtured by his exposure to the civilization of ancient Egypt.

> The infant boy is carried to the Royal Palace of the Pharaohs; and from that palace comes forth, in time, the superior man, the leader of that immortal race so distinguished in the destinies of man and in the economy of God,—the man Moses; in whose one single name is gathered and included, statesman, lawgiver, general, and prophet. And here we see the rise of that wondrous code of laws, that system of equity, order and justice, that prolific, as well as mysterious ecclesiastical polity, which makes the Jewish race the most singular and prominent; but which has ever since influenced the destinies of man in every way, more than any other cause in human history.[43]

This was a curiously secular interpretation of biblical history, coming from a Protestant clergyman. The message that the Jews gave to humanity did not come to Moses from a voice on Mt. Sinai, but from Moses' knowledge of the fleshpots of Egypt. In any case, the civilization of the ancient Near East had eventually become the common heritage of mankind, spreading first to Greece, "whither flowed the streams, now deep, now shallow, of all the world's high thought." The culture and refinement of Greece now stood forth "in all history the central point of intellectual greatness, taste, and wisdom." But although these contributions were distinctly a product of the Greeks' peculiar racial genius, they "existed not for Greece alone"; "all men of thought throughout the earth seize upon and ponder, and strive to master these fine creations of the Grecian mind."[44]

The contribution of the Romans was equally universal. They had "transmitted the legacy of two valuable principles to man—INVINCIBLE ENERGY, AND

THAT OF LAW AND GOVERNMENT.'' Thus had the Jews, Greeks, and Romans each made a contribution to the world's civilization, which sprang originally from its racial genius, but could no longer be seen as its unique cultural possession. The ancient civilizations had passed away, but their spirit had endured to become the heritage of all nations, serving to "link the present with the past, and clearly show the unity of the race." This progressive view of history, in which "the race in the aggregate [was destined] to go forward and upward," was pervasive in Victorian Christianity. It was a teleology that anticipated the more philanthropic forms of social Darwinism.

> The failure of *this* type or the destruction of *that* form, is no prevention of nature's upward reaching. They are as falling leaves in a foreign autumn, in consequence of which, in spring time, the forest appears, apparelled in beauty, and gorgeously laden with masses of foliage. And to this advancement all the sections of the race are to add their contribution, and to send in their quota of gift and influence.[45]

Of course this was not social Darwinism; it merely showed the influence of theories of social evolutionism then current in British thought. It was a theory of history that defined civilization as inevitable progress and the common destiny of all mankind. The idea that the fruits of civilization belonged rightfully only to Europeans was not acceptable to Crummell, since civilization was simply a continual discovery of certain immutable, universal truths that all mankind was ultimately destined to know. Needless to say, his thinking in no way anticipated that of those twentieth-century writers who use the term "civilization" practically as an expletive.[46]

The process of civilization was one of mutual exchange. Thus the goal of a new nation should not be to create some coveted and closeted national treasure, but to "contribute to the well-being and civilization of man." The history of the world seemed to tell the Liberian nation that they were not to live merely for themselves, and that no other nation had that right. Liberians need feel no shame for their cultural borrowing from Europe, nor should they forever stand in debt to the philanthropic English and Americans who had helped them get their start. They could repay their debt by handing something down to posterity. All the preceding ages had, without regard to nation or race, left a heritage, so every nation was a cultural debtor. Providence had decreed that there should be "no isolation; no absolute disseverance of individual nations; for blood and lineage, and ancient manners, and religion, and letters, and all tend to combine nationalities and link them in indissoluble bonds."[47]

Crummell had no illusions about Liberia's contemporary importance. He did not assume that the great powers of the earth were waiting "with deep concern and breathless expectation, our offerings and our gifts." He believed, nonetheless, that every nation must make a contribution from a sense of moral duty, to say nothing of self-respect. Cosmopolitan attitudes were therefore to be encouraged, for although "nationality [was] to be nurtured as a most precious Jewel . . . the obligations which are connected with it are of equal worth."

The world needed "a higher type of true nationality," which must be built from the lower levels up, for "the moral purity of the masses produces its reflex in their rulers." It was in the "quiet walks of life, in the family, the workshop, and the school" that the effort must begin. And when a sense of national pride and international obligation had grown up, then would be seen the rise of "princely merchants, the merchants of our own town and country, citizens of this Republic!" Then the world would witness "the grateful vision of a manly, noble, and complete African nationality." The realization of this dream seemed "the plain duty and the manifest destiny of LIBERIA."

> And so from this point boldly jutting out into the glad free sea,—this spot, dedicated to nationality, consecrated to freedom, and sacred to religion,—from this spot shall be heard, through all the coming times, the full, clear tones of justice, the grateful symphonies of truth, the silvery voices of piety and virtue, mingling ever harmoniously with the choral echoes of the ocean.[48]

He had clearly mastered the florid style of the black preacher, and yet Crummell could not succeed in his ministerial work. Stokes continued to draw off parishioners, and Crummell was dependent on local white merchants and visiting sea captains to flesh out his Sunday congregations. He informed Irving that he needed German and French prayer books, because "one of the families is that of a German merchant." Crummell claimed that many of the white residents were among the most regular attendants at his services. "They are violently opposed to our neighbors," he wrote, "on account of their noise and shouting. I hope we may do them good: wicked as nearly all foreign residents are on this coast, I am thankful that here we can get them out to church on Sunday, which is a rare thing with them." Financially, the church was far from being a profitable sinecure, and he was forced to continue to press his claims on the Church of the Messiah.[49]

He importuned Jay once again in May 1856, reminding his benefactor of the "sore and grievous trial of fire," which had reduced him "to penury and almost grinding economy." He tried his best to sound independent, expressing great pride in having taken up the vigorous life of a farmer, which he claimed was responsible for the marked improvement in his health. Unfortunately, too many of the colonists were "contemning active industry as low and vulgar," which led him to "great doubts and sad misgivings . . . as to whether Liberia will ever, as an *independent* nation, become a great state, and a beneficient agent. . . ." The missionary societies were partially to blame, contented as they were with "miserably incompetent teachers." And even those who were competent were forced to become traders and legislators, leaving them little time for study. Crummell admitted that the criticism might apply to himself, driven as he was to take up small farming, yet he said the pursuit "pleases me much."

His parents' welfare continued to press on his conscience. A fellow missionary, returning from New York, had delivered a message from Jay, telling of the hardships of Crummell's parents. He wrote back to say that he had received similar news from the Rev. Dr. Bedell of the Church of the Ascension in New York.

> Both of you ask remembrance and provision on my part for these aged, venerable, and honored parents. I am as poor as they are, and a deal more embarrassed in my circumstances. When I arrived here, as soon as I passed the acclimation, I made a small attempt at farming hoping that I might thus be able to provide for my parents, who plodded and labored painfully, during my boyhood, to raise me above their own position in life, and to make me useful to my race. My efforts have failed; I have experienced a painful providence . . . I have walked the soil with sad remembrance that my parents were experiencing in extreme old age, a bitter pinching winter; and I their eldest son, here where there is no winter, pressed and straightened, and unable to do aught for them.

One solution that occurred to him was to publish a volume of his sermons "and therein in a preface, state the peculiar causes which forced me before the public." Another possibility was to solicit Jay's aid in collecting, by legal proceedings if necessary, nine hundred dollars back salary from the Church of the Messiah.[50]

His hostility towards his former congregation was provoked by an accusing letter from William Tyson, the chief vestryman, who had written him reporting that Crummell's parents hoped to come to Liberia. Boston Crummell had apparently applied to Rev. Dr. Tyng for support from the church missionary society so that on arriving in Liberia he might set up a farm. Crummell's mother had no desire to go to Africa, especially if it had to be done under the auspices of the American Colonization Society. Tyson wrote that if Crummell had made some provision for their passage, it might have "reflected a little more credit" on him. Tyson told him that perhaps he ought to sell the silver that had been given to him by his English friends and accused him of living in an "extravagant manner." He went on to accuse Crummell of having left behind a debt of thirty-two dollars when he departed for England, part of which he owed to Tyson.[51]

Crummell began to consider sailing for the United States, though what he hoped to accomplish by making such a voyage, he did not reveal. His financial needs were real. He denied living in luxury as his detractors claimed he did. The rumor stemmed, no doubt, from the fact that his wife had once, "with the pardonable weakness of a woman, displayed a dozen electro-plate forks, and about the same number of spoons on her table at dinner." These, in any case, had been lost in the fire. Why had this small display of refinement been blown out of proportion? "Some parties visiting out here so accustomed perhaps to Sambo in a miserable slave hut lose their sense of proportion at the sight of decent, respectable and educated black men." As for the harmonium that he had received as a gift for his son, what was he to do with such things but keep them and use them, "albeit they may be thought too good for me by some of our visitors out here."[52]

Once again, using Jay as a foil, he was really writing letters to himself— justifying himself to himself as well as to Jay. Jay apparently accused him of accepting or planning to accept the support of the American Colonization Society in the form of a professor's stipend at the proposed Liberia College. Crummell reminded Jay that the college was to be supported by a "Massachusetts education society." In view of the fact that so many clergymen in Liberia were forced into occupations unsuited to men of their calling, he felt that he should not be blamed for seeking to make a living by teaching, which was, in fact, a traditional occupation for the ministry. He responded to the charge that some white missionaries seemed to survive on less than he by reminding Jay that they lived in "heathen vicarages, where they get everything cheaper than in Liberia." Often they were unmarried or they had wives but no children. Their stay in the field did not average more than eighteen months. He remarked pointedly that his English friends, always "the kindest, most generous friends," were perhaps more understanding.[53]

In the middle of the month that Crummell wrote these thoughts to Jay, Bishop Payne visited Crummell. He found him and his "interesting family" living in "a modest cottage," which he had built. Payne reported that Crummell had proposed to take over a house at Cape Mesurado, near Monrovia, that was owned by the church. It was overgrown with weeds, the path to it unpassable. No one would live in it because of its lonely situation. The bishop had at one point engaged a caretaker, but he had proven unreliable. Payne now requested five hundred dollars to add a new wing to the house and make it a fit residence for the Crummells. The monies were to be diverted from the college building fund, for in time the building was to "of course constitute a part of the Institution, whatever it may be."[54] Crummell soon moved in. Within a few months, however, he was to abandon this house and return up the river to his farm, apparently without informing the bishop.[55]

In early October he wrote to P. P. Irving, threatening to resign his post as missionary in Monrovia. The salary of $850 per year was insufficient. Americans did not realize that the cost of living in Monrovia was higher than the cost of living in London or New York. He was aware that some missionaries were able to live on salaries of $700 or less, but many of them were known to supplement their salaries by becoming magistrates, legislators, army officers, traders, and merchants. The Board of Missions was, however, disinclined to increase his salary and apparently accepted his resignation without further correspondence. The Rev. Henry Carswell, secretary of the Church Missionary Society in England, after receiving a letter from Crummell, seemed convinced that the board had made its decision because it viewed Crummell as an inefficient missionary since he had failed to make headway against Stokes. There were of course other factors, such as the bishop's hostility to Crummell and Crummell's own irritability. But Carswell seems to have been convinced that Stokes had won support for having "taken up warmly the cause of African nationality, which makes him popular nonwithstanding his various defects."[56] The nationalism that Carswell alluded to was referred to by Bishop Payne, as well. The bishop felt that it was largely through the influence of Stokes that feeling against foreigners and whites, especially white Americans, had grown in Monrovia. Payne had witnessed such attitudes only in Monrovia; Stokes was advocating such attitudes in Monrovia, ergo Stokes was the cause.

But there were obviously other reasons why the bishop was not popular in Monrovia. He was a white man and a Southerner, and the Monrovians resented him. Monrovia was not a mission to indigenous Africans, as Cape Palmas was. The attitudes and skills required at the Cape were not necessarily the most useful in a settlement of Americo-Liberians with long memories of bitter experiences with whites. The Monrovian Episcopalians' dependence on the American church only tended to increase resentment and seemed to inspire irrationally contradictory assertions of independence. Stokes and his vestry clerk, a man named John B. Parton, were openly defiant of the bishop. Parton reminded him that he was an American, not a Liberian, saying "Go among your own people if you want to be Bishop." Stokes had allegedly said to Payne, "As Bishop elect of Liberia, I hereby forbid your coming into Liberia, without invitation . . . we do indeed consider you an intruder."[57]

Crummell apparently convinced Carswell that he had not wanted to break with the bishop, nor with the American church, and that this was the source of his unpopularity. And, as Carswell understood, Crummell suddenly became an object of high favor in the republic, as soon as his stipend was withdrawn. The fact that he was beginning to explore the possibility of leaving the American church and associating himself with the West Indian mission on the Poyas river, in Sierra Leone, under the bishop of Barbadoes, may also have contributed to his rise in popularity because of the Liberians' suspicion of Americans and admiration for the British. Carswell communicated this interpretation of the situation to the Board of Foreign Missions in America, saying that he thought it would be best for Crummell to remain in Liberia, but also saying that he would in all probability be accepted in the West Indian Mission in Sierra Leone.[58]

The rupture between Crummell and the board was apparently not complete, because he continued to serve the church in various capacities during the ensuing months. According to the report of the bishop and of local colleagues, including even Stokes, he continued to preach gratuitously and to devote the rest of his time to farming. A position in the Benson government did not materialize, and he found the other fiscal options inappropriate to his station and uncongenial. He could not abide the "incongruous mixture of the brawling priest and the noisy politician—of the missionary with the keen trader—resorted to sometimes even by white missionaries on the coast."[59]

In mid-summer 1857, he renewed his connection with the mission on a limited basis. The bishop employed him to preach and conduct Sunday services in the vicinity of his farm. Payne's heart was apparently softened by Crummell's straitened circumstances. He wrote to the board in New York asking that Crummell be given a salary for his months of service on the St. Paul's River settlements, beginning in August 1857, and continuing until the beginning of a new assignment at his old salary. This was to be a teaching position at the Mt. Vaughan High School in Cape Palmas, for the prospects of a college at Monrovia getting into operation seemed to the bishop "doubtful and remote." It was doubtful, in any case, that Crummell would have any connection with the college. The bishop seemed happy to appoint Crummell to the teaching position at Mt. Vaughan, where, associated with the Rev. C. C. Hoffmann, "he may do and receive much good." [60]

On July 10, 1858, Crummell arrived in Cape Palmas, where he remained through January 1861. During these two and a half years, his health apparently improved and he was happier, despite the belligerence of local tribes and the discomfort he felt associating with the white missionaries. A Mrs. M. B. Merriam, after a visit to the mission station, spoke of her meeting with "the eloquent and accomplished scholar, [who] spoke of England with affection and [whose] conversation on general subjects was very entertaining and instructive." The atmosphere seems to have been somewhat reminiscent of an English country parish:

> On a green knoll stands the little stone church. . . . It is comfortable and home-like, much like a rustic English church. It is built of gray stone which is found here in abundance; and the unavoidable roughness of the work adds to its interest by giving it the appearance of an older building. A boy was standing in the aisle, tugging at the bell rope, which descends into the church. The walls are plastered, and the pews are painted brown; the floor in the aisles is covered with matting. The paint is disagreeably sticky on touching the pews. Mr. Crummell who had entered said in reply to my inquiring look that it is a "specimen of the condition of the arts in Africa." Paint cannot be made proof against the climate. Mr. Crummell kindly led me to a seat near the reading desk. Presently the people entered in groups, forming a colored congregation such as may be seen in any of our cities. The children from the Orphan Asylum came in a procession. . . . The most interesting portion of the assembly consisted of the native converts who were neatly dressed. . . . There were eight or ten boys, who were members of the Christian school at Hoffman Station. The service was the morning prayer; the responses were made audibly, and the music, chanting included, was very pleasing, though entirely vocal. . . . I have seldom heard Jackson's *Te Deum* more beautifully rendered than by those African children.[61]

In the words of a visiting American naval surgeon, the high school at Mt. Vaughan was "ably presided over by the Rev. Mr. Crummell." Bishop Payne reported that he manifested "a deep interest in the agricultural as well as moral and intellectual advancement of the institution, and a marked improvement [had] characterized both departments" since his arrival. It is not surprising that Crummell showed such interest in the practical as well as the literary development of his charges. During his own education at the Oneida Institute of Beriah Green, it was required that every student devote three hours a day to manual labor. His attitudes on the importance of such training were no doubt reinforced by his own farming in Clay-Ashland; he had stated his opinions forcefully enough in a speech in Monrovia:

> Our youth must be trained to be active, and useful, and enterprising. For what use, I ask, will they be to the heathen, with all their Latin and Greek and Science

and history, if they come up into life and society with hands of baby softness, be-booted and be-strapped, be-muffled and be-scented—so delicate and gentlemanly that they cannot handle a hoe or wield an axe, if needed, and with no heart, if they become missionaries or commissioners, to build a hut in the bush, to cook with their own delicate hands, a meal of victuals. Out upon such creatures, I say, in a land like this! They are men-milliners, popinjays, ladies' maids.[62]

The most promising boys from the various missionary stations in the area were sent to Mt. Vaughan and there trained for work as missionaries. Some of the boys were also trained as soldiers to guard the Cape Palmas settlement against the local natives, who had burned the church and the mission buildings on Christmas Day, 1856. Life at Cape Palmas was thus not entirely so idyllic as Mrs. Merriam portrayed it. Among his students were a group of "recaptives," taken from the slaveship *Echo* around 1859. Having become citizens of the Republic, they were "enrolled among her soldiers" and could soon "perform their duties with as much precision as the others." There was nothing, Crummell hazarded to assert, "which does so much for civilizing a man as putting a gun into his hands. It makes a savage into a man directly."[63]

During his years at Cape Palmas, he continued to develop his ideas on the relationship between religion and an aggressive nationalism, but he also expressed himself on matters almost purely pietistic. His addresses "Laying the Cornerstone at St. Mark's Hospital" and "The Fitness of the Gospel for Its Own Work" are examples of the less political sermons preserved from that time. They offer insight into characteristics of mind that determined the content of more secular outpourings. The St. Mark's address, for example, with its commitment to the doctrine of the importance of good works, was, of course, consistent with ideas expressed in the political sermons. Like all Christians, he was strongly committed to the idea that salvation was by grace of God, merited by the vicarious atonement of Jesus Christ. He would not budge, however, on the necessity of working for one's own salvation. "The believer is under the rule of law as a rule of life," he wrote, "it is his duty to act as Christ Jesus acted." Works of mercy were manifestations of grace, but they were also acts of obedience to divine law. 'Blessed are the merciful, for they shall obtain mercy." Such biblical passages offered sufficient evidence "that God in his word approves . . . efforts, which are designed to lessen the miseries of earth." Thus it was "a mere mockery of the spirit of Christ, which, while pretending solicitude for the spirit of man, is at the same time indifferent to his temporal state."[64]

The more pietistic sermons that have been preserved from the late 1850s have the characteristic weaknesses of his homiletic style—ethnocentrism, begging the question, a failure to anticipate worthy counterarguments. For these very reasons the sermons are of great importance for what they reveal of the biases of new-world black intellectuals coming into contact with African cultures and societies in the nineteenth century. It is interesting to observe Crummell's struggles with the question of piety versus moralism, that is to say, the faith versus works controversy. On the one hand, his early education and youthful conversion experience had brought him under the influence of evangelical Protestantism, the narrowness of which he could never escape. Such religion, in Emerson's words, "dwelt . . . with noxious exaggeration about the person of Jesus." On the other hand, he was a product of the tradition that had produced David Walker's *Appeal,* a religion that was at once transcendentalist and tough-minded. His no-nonsense, practical nature made him susceptible to Arminian influences, and thus he preached that at the Last Judgement one must truly be washed in the blood of the Lamb, one must be prepared to be judged on one's deeds. One must work out one's salvation through constant daily effort and rigorous good works.[65]

Nonetheless—and he saw no contradiction here—he could preach a sermon on justification by faith, which was almost antinomian. He argued that the Christian was not bound by the law of the Bible. Although the law was the Christian's rule of life, "We are not bound by it; it is not the ground of our justification . . . but we are bound to manifest that we are servants of the Lord Jesus Christ." Of course an extreme antinomianism would have argued that with true faith one would effortlessly act righteously. But Crummell believed that even the truly faithful must struggle to perform works. In the sermon "The Fitness of the Gospel," we see that his pietistic biases and evangelical subjectivism, which made "the heart more important than the head," relieved him at times from the responsibility of thinking. If, as Burke had claimed, it was more important to feel inwardly than to know rationally that religion (i.e., Christianity) was the basis of all that was good in society, then it was not necessary to cultivate tolerances for African culture, based as it was on superstition. There was in his view no road to personal salvation or to national progress apart from Jesus Christ.[66]

The idea of progress that motivated Crummell in Liberia and ever afterward was based on a belief in Christianity as a historical force. The idea was rooted in his "common sense," that is to say, it was the result of his Christian biases, which he took to be universal principles of sound social order. The cultural relativism that would constitute the basis of Afro-American ideology two generations later was beyond Crummell's powers of imagination. The idea that the culture of every nation developed in response to peculiar historical circumstances might be accepted in theory, but its practical applications to heathen Africa were not perceived. Nor was it readily apprehended by most Victorian reformers that a philosophy of uplift must somehow evolve in conjunction with the culture that seeks to employ it. Crummell's problems in coming to grips with such problems was not simply the result of religious indoctrination. Hardened and embittered by a lifetime of disappointment and abuse, he had become rigid and dogmatic. There was no room in his philosophy to blend Christian with pagan wisdom, unless the pagan wisdom was safely embalmed in the works of classical authors. When forced to confront the question of how Socrates managed to be a man of superior morality although he was not a Christian, he simply begged the question. Socrates was moral, therefore he obviously had been guided by the Holy Spirit.[67]

By rejecting the concept of European culture and replacing it with the idea of Christian civilization, he could argue that black people need not feel inferior when confronting more advanced societies. Civilization was neither the creation nor the property of the white nations, but simply the result of Christian enlightenment. The gospel was singularly appropriate for the uplift of mankind, precisely because it did not address the local needs of "particular nations, and hemispheres" but carried a message that was "world wide in its adaptedness and universal in its efficacy." Many questions were obviously left unasked and unanswered in such a sermon, and it does not provide the most impressive picture of Crummell's intellectual powers. His points were merely asserted, not argued; he provided no evidence that Christianity is the cause of civilization's advancement, nor did he offer any systematic argument that Christians were morally superior. The evidence of his senses offered sufficient proof. Europe was more powerful, efficient, and orderly than Africa, and Christianity was all too hastily perceived as the reason for the existing gap. Crummell saw the world, as most of us do, from the perspective of his own experience. His own intellectual progress was the result of Christian influences and had occurred simultaneously with the growth of pious habits. It is not surprising that the two were related in his mind.

It is lamentable that Crummell could not adapt his doctrines to the Africans as Paul had adapted his to the Gentiles. It may be that Paul had a simpler mission. He did not have the additional burden of being cultural ambassador or technical emissary to an underdeveloped people. Crummell had to combine his Christian message with a secular one. He was painfully aware of African "backwardness," a backwardness in technology and commerce that seemed to be the direct manifestation of moral and spiritual backwardness. Christianity had a civilizing message for Africa in the broadest sense; its moral message was a social message and therefore a prescription for material as well as spiritual progress. Its heritage was:

> The bravery of Arms; the security of freedom; the order of states; the manliness
> of nationality; the purity and excellence of woman; the expansion of colonies; the
> beauty of art; the assiduities of philanthropy: what are these but the gracious fruits
> of Christianity? Aye and wherever Christianity goes she produces these fruits.

Crummell's missionary philosophy attempted to reconcile the humanitarian concerns of the Gospel with the otherworldly pietism of the Epistles. As a Protestant, he was obliged to accept the doctrine of justification by faith, but in his heart he considered that an easy doctrine. Despite lengthy protests to the contrary, he believed that salvation came from the triumph of the will over sin. The dangers of enthusiasm and antinomianism, of too great an emphasis on the conversion experience, were readily apparent among the ignorant and venal preachers, who pandered to the sensuality of untutored exslaves. This same personalism, subjectivism, and egotism that he found so deplorable among the unwashed immigrants troubled him in his reading of St. Paul. It seems to have been difficult for him to reconcile his own practical conception of religion with the otherworldly, anti-intellectual Christocentrism of Pauline doctrines.

The main concern of the Christian should be *"the Gospel of Christ in its adaptation to the needs of men."* The Gospel was made to meet the needs of the material world. It was obviously an agency of progress. In the historical experience of the modern world, the civilization of barbarians had always been contemporary with the dissemination of the Gospel. It was easy enough, given his biases, to attribute the "progress of barbarians" to the spread of Christianity. Like most of his black nationalist contemporaries, he chose to overlook the fact that contact with missions was invariably the first step to the eventual subordination and or extinction of tribes, who were seldom any better off after the coming of the Christians with their "liquor and lust and lies."

At Cape Palmas, Crummell was obviously under pressure from Payne and the other white missionaries to emphasize missionary preaching rather than civil and political sermonizing. He was under the bishop's constant supervision in a white-controlled mission, rather than a black-controlled nationalistic milieu. The experience could not have been satisfying, for he had to hold his peace and submit to the criticism and discipline of the whites, who observed him critically. His financial accounts were supervised by a Mr. Rambo.[68] Nonetheless, he was quite successful and received good reports for his work with the native catechumens, who reportedly listened with unusual attentiveness to his preaching.[69] But Crummell had not abandoned his secular interests and still yearned for activities of a more statesmanlike nature. He wanted to be a social teacher and a shaper of national policy, and he saw himself as a "First Father" of a new republic. In 1859 Martin Delany's West Africa exploring party visited him on its way to Nigeria to negotiate for a new black American colony. Shortly thereafter, he wrote "The Relations and Duty of Free Colored Men in America to Africa." With the shift in attitudes of black Americans and the outbreak of the Civil War, he felt that now was a good time to visit the United States. He was to leave on a speaking tour, publish a book of his sermons, and attempt to generate funds for the support of Liberia College. He had proven his willingness to submit to ecclesiastical authority. Now was perhaps the time to ask for the fulfillment of promises that he was to be a college professor, a civil leader, and a Liberian nation builder.

# 7

## Changing Attitudes in America and a Visit Home (1853–1863)

On July 7, 1853, a week and a day before Crummell's arrival in West Africa, the Colored National Convention, meeting in Rochester, New York, was hearing a report on colonization that compared the Americo-Liberians to the most brutal white settlers that had ever set foot on the continent. The "Report on Colonization" that was published in the convention proceedings directly compared the colonization of West Africa by blacks to the colonization of South Africa by whites. It argued that Liberia was not really an independent republic, "because the COLONIZATION PARTY in this country, several of the slave States, and pro-slavery individuals, still exert a controlling influence over its territory . . . . The British in the South and North, the French in the Southeast and the Americans in the West, speculating in lands, cheating and warring afford little promise of a political millennium in the land of Ham." Liberians, the report went on to assert, were pursuing "precisely the same policy that other colonizers have for the last hundred years in Africa." They made discriminatory laws against the natives. They "justified and connived at all the encroachments of the white foreigners, even to the damage of their own dignity." They were never heard to utter a word of remonstrance when the colonial "native whippers" destroyed towns and deposed kings. "The reason [was] obvious, men who live in glass houses cannot afford to throw stones." Indeed President Roberts himself had "acted deceitfully and cowardly in sending for King Boombo to meet him on the beach, as if to hold a palaver, thus inducing him to come unarmed, when he himself was armed to the very teeth." Prompted by his African-hating American backers, the report continued, Roberts had violated the protocol of diplomatic conduct, thrown King Boombo in jail, and fined him the impossible sum of fifty thousand dollars. The Liberians had "insulted the pride of the native kings of Africa . . . . The idea that the ancient

119

Kings of Africa owe allegiance to [this] petty government of yesterday is perfectly ridiculous."[1]

Attitudes towards emigration and colonization were changing, however, and shifting attitudes were nowhere more glaring than in the career of Martin R. Delany, whose self-help and separatist attitudes had been evident for some years. He was a very dark man, and like Crummell and Garnet claimed to be a pure, unadulterated African, descended from a royal line. Delany had apparently been exposed to some classical education and, more important, had developed an interest in the sciences, especially medicine.[2] Douglass made an interesting comment on his nationalistic sentiments when he remarked, "I thank God for making me a man, simply, but Delany always thanks him for making him a black man."[3] During the early 1860s Delany was known to appear on the podium in African ceremonial robes.[4]

Like Crummell, Delany became involved early in the competitive emulation of bourgeois whites. In 1833 he began a three-year study of medicine with Andrew McDowell, a white physician, and at the age of twenty-four he set up practice as a leecher and bleeder. In 1850, when Delany decided that he must resume his study of medicine more formally, the racism he encountered no doubt greatly contributed to his nationalistic tendencies. In the fall of 1850, the Harvard Medical School admitted Delany and two other black Americans. By the end of the first term, however, the officers of that institution, yielding to pressure from a group of medical students who had petitioned for the expulsion of the Afro-Americans, peremptorily expelled all three. It was around this time that nationalistic and emigrationist tendencies, as well as temperamental independence and egotism, seem to have won out in Delany. Like Crummell, he apparently became a black nationalist not from any desire to escape from whites, whom he liked and admired, but because his intelligence and ambition were hemmed in by white society, and because he intended to parallel and rival white institutions in a society of his own.[5]

The passage of the Fugitive Slave Law was another influence on Delany, though in his case it had the atypical effect of an immediate impulse to nationalism. Furthermore, its passage created a climate of opinion in which other blacks were less likely to shout down emigrationist proposals. Embittered by his ouster from Harvard Medical School, he spent the next year investigating prospects for migrating to Canada and attended a convention in Toronto. In the spring of 1852, he published *The Condition, Elevation, Emigration, and Destiny of the Colored People of the United States*, which signaled Delany's movement into the forefront of the nationalist-emigrationist movement. To those who had known him all along, there could have been nothing surprising about this. It was no sudden transformation, but the logical outcome of years of commitment to independent enterprise and ethnic boosterism. His position was the understandable reaction of a superiorly gifted black man whose high expectations were constantly thwarted. For Frederick Douglass, life's greatest battle, the struggle for freedom, had already been won. For Garnet, Delany, and Crummell, there had been no "great gettin' up morning." The struggle for the rights of citizenship was just as bitter as it had ever been, and, during the fifties, it seemed that life was getting worse, not better.

In an appendix to *The Condition of the Colored People,* Delany sketched out a plan for African development, including a plan for a trans-African railway. It would run from the Red Sea to the Atlantic and would constitute "the GREAT THOROUGHFARE for all the trade with the East Indies and Eastern Coast of Africa, and the continent of America." Although Delany rejected Liberian colonization, he shared with Crummell and the Liberian nationals certain black nationalist ideals. He believed that the free blacks had a duty to elevate themselves as speedily as possible, because "the redemption of the bondman depends entirely on the elevation of the freeman." This was the very idea that Crummell articulated at the British and Foreign Anti-Slavery Society convention to the apparent surprise of some listeners. Like Crummell, Delany insisted that "every people should be the originators of their own designs, the projector of their own schemes, and the creators of the events that led to their destiny— the consummation of their desires."

When Delany sent a copy of *The Condition of the Colored People* to Frederick Douglass in May 1852, he hoped it would be reviewed by his old journalist colleague, who was now editing *Frederick Douglass's Paper.* In the following month Delany complained that the book still had not been mentioned. It had not taken him long to decide that Douglass had little sympathy for his emigrationist position. He was right, for Douglass had become involved during 1851 and 1852 in a personal crusade against colonization. He had decided that colonizationists were among the worst enemies of black people and that colonization under any name could only mean the extermination of the black American population. During the early months of 1852, he became involved in a feud with Horace Greeley and the *New York Tribune,* attacking Greeley for his advocacy of African colonization. When the journalist responded that he would be equally happy to see black people colonizing a township in Southern Jersey or Nebraska in order to vindicate their capacity for productive enterprise, Douglass was far from appeased. He saw no reason why black people should "colonize," as the *Tribune* put it, even in this country. He offered the advice to "be a man where you are; neither a 'township in Southern Jersey' nor 'county in Nebraska' can serve you. You must be a man here, and force your way to intelligence, wealth, and respectability. If you can't do that here; you can't do it there."[6]

On March 8, 1853, shortly before Crummell's departure for Liberia, Douglass called on the men of ability who lived in exile, "the Russwurms—the Garnetts—the Wards—the Crummells and others—all men of superior ability and attainments," to return to the United States, where their simple presence could do much to remove the clouds of prejudice and doubt about the native ability of black people.[7] This was a sentiment that he would express often during the pre-Civil War decade. It is interesting to observe how he used the rhetoric of racial pride and responsibility (a favorite device of black nationalists) to undermine the arguments of separatists and emigrationists. "Our elevation as a race is almost wholly dependent upon our own exertions," he wrote. "The history of other oppressed nations will confirm us in this assertion." Here was a good example of how identical perceptions of a situation do not always lead to the same perception of what that situation implies. The nationalists like Crummell and Delany assumed that the need for self-elevation required the establishment of a black nation in which black people would be able to act independently and according to their own lights. To Douglass, it meant that black people had a duty to remain in the United States to take control of the abolition movement and assume responsibility for unshackling the enslaved nation. It meant wresting the control of the abolition movement from the hands of whites who felt that blacks were incapable of leading the antislavery movement. Those blacks who abandoned the field to white abolitionists, whether calling themselves expatriates in Europe, emigrationists in Haiti, or colonizationists under the American Colonization Society, were equally guilty of failing to work for the elevation of the nation.

When in 1849 Douglass praised Crummell for "doing battle" in England against the "subtile foe," Reverend John Miller, he still viewed Crummell's work in England as useful. Douglass began to have doubts about Crummell's effectiveness as his stay in England lengthened. In 1851, he wrote to Gerritt Smith, expressing his "fear that some whose presence in this country is necessary to the elevation of the colored people will leave us, while the degraded and worthless will remain to help bind us to our present debasement."[8] In later statements he named Crummell specifically as one of those whose talents were needed at home and called for his return to the United States. "We want such men as Ward and Garnet and Crummell at home," he wrote. "They must come and help us."[9] In this way Douglass was able to argue that those who searched for a black national homeland overseas were actually abandoning the nation already in existence. If they could accuse him of ignoring his national duty by staying in America, he could accuse them of ignoring theirs by staying away. What was even more clever was his lumping the proud nationalists together with expatriates who had gone to Europe simply to escape from the unpleasantness of life in America. Garnet would have some fun at Douglass's expense in 1859 after Douglass's departure for England in the wake of John Brown's raid.[10]

Douglass often used the word "nation" when referring to black people in America. The nation consisted of the brothers and sisters in bondage, rather than some present or future colony of free blacks in Africa. He maintained in a letter to Benjamin Coates, a Philadelphia wool merchant and colonizationist, that colonization had "a direct tendency to divert attention from the great and paramount duty of abolition" and that it furnished "an apology for delaying emancipation until the whole four millions can be sent to Africa."[11] If he must leave the country, proclaimed Douglass, he would at least remain in the Western hemisphere, perhaps in the islands of the Caribbean. Caribbean emigration was not without its adherents. Among the most notable was another black Episcopalian, James T. Holly, who eventually became bishop of Haiti.[12] At the time of the firing on Fort Sumter, Douglass claimed to have been preparing for a voyage to investigate conditions in Haiti, but in reality Douglass considered all schemes for resettlement unattractive, even projects for black communities in North America. This he had made quite clear in the response to Horace Greeley.

It is not surprising that Douglass clashed with Delany and Garnet as they continued to explore prospects of African colonization during the 1850s. As Delany had in 1852, Garnet found Douglass disinclined to give support through his newspaper to the general philosophy of the Civilization Society or to any of its specific aims. Garnet's well-known letter of February 1859 received a detailed editorial response from Douglass, who recalled that he had already made a detailed response to Benjamin Coates, "the real but not the ostensible head of the African Civilization movement." [13] He went on to list a number of points which prevented his cooperation, among other things his belief that the most important obstacle to the progress of Christianity and civilization in Africa was the slave trade. Abolition was a prerequisite for African civilization, albeit the Civilization Society would have it the other way around.

Although Delany was willing to consider emigration with all seriousness, he was in total agreement with Douglass on the Liberian question; his position was perhaps even more hostile. In the first half of the decade he never passed up an opportunity to malign Liberia and showed no hesitancy in endorsing the most negative diatribes, or delivering them himself. He wrote the preface for William Nesbit's *Four Months in Liberia, or African Colonization Exposed* (1855), giving it his hearty endorsement and, asserting the truthfulness of its contents, although it would be five years before he investigated their actuality. In this fanciful exegesis, he imaginatively adumbrated Nesbit's furious contentions, asserting, for example, that "the *whole country* of Liberia is daily over-flooded—the face of the earth completely *covered* by the *tide water* from the ocean." Many of the Liberians were former slaves, long corrupted by contact with slave-holding whites, and they had "acquired all of the folly and vices of their former wicked and unprincipled masters, considering themselves their equals, the more nearly they ape them." Thus in slavish adherence to the customs of their former owners, the Liberians had become slaveholders themselves. Delany launched into a heated digression on slave-holding heritage of the "pure white race," Circasians of Eurasia, "the women of whom stand continually in the public places and bazaars, offering their daughters as slaves to the passers by." Whether this was meant to illustrate the universality of slavery, or the hereditary propensities of whites, Delany did not say. But certainly there could be no customs among black Africans any worse than those of this unadulterated white stock of the Caucasus. Delany's logic would almost seem to suggest that there would never have been any slavery in Africa if the Americo-Liberians had not imported it. [14]

Delany reiterated his contention that Liberia was nothing more than "a slave-holder's hoax, perpetrated upon simple-minded and servile Negroes by a hypocritical puppet government. The so-called missionary operations of the region were nothing but scouting parties which were to be followed by military operations once the most congenial spots for European settlements had been designated. Nothing could "palliate the villainy" of Joseph Jenkins Roberts and his menials, who "knowingly are instrumental in entrapping their brethren in the trammels of their hell-originated scheme."[15]

It has been said that legal and political developments of the 1850s increased the willingness of free blacks to discuss possible emigrationist schemes.[16] But the shift of opinion was neither sudden nor dramatic, and Crummell's moving into the colonization camp was certainly viewed as a matter of grave consequence by the majority of the literate Afro-Americans who knew him. It would be several years before the emigration ideal regained respectability. Even Delany entertained African emigration only as an afterthought—in an appendix to his *Condition of the Colored People* (1852). The Fugitive Slave Law of 1850 did not have the immediate effect of turning large numbers of Afro-Americans into emigrationists or expatriates.

Although Crummell was somewhat isolated from Afro-American political and intellectual main currents at the time of his departure for Africa, he would soon witness changes in attitudes. With the passage of time, emigrationists began to enjoy a respectability they had not had since the death of Paul Cuffe. During the 1850s their ranks began to increase with the likes of Rev. Henry Highland Garnet, a militant abolitionist of impeccable credentials, but nonetheless a separatist. As Garnet's beliefs moved steadily in the direction of emigration, it became increasingly difficult for the anticolonizationists to defend the view that one was *either* an abolitionist *or* a colonizationist. Indeed the distinction between assimilationist and separatist was often difficult to make out, as when Garnet stood before the Female Benevolent Society of Troy, New York, and gave a very sarcastic speech on the inevitability of racial amalgamation in America, then digressed midway through into a celebration of the African past and a prediction of the heroic destiny of the black race.

The terms "African nationality," "emigration," and "colonization" were being tossed about in highly emotional ways, and Henry Highland Garnet was as capable as anyone of playing on emotions. By the end of the 1850s, he was involved in his well-known debate with Frederick Douglass over the purposes of the African Civilization Society and the validity of voluntary separatism—especially in the form of migration to Africa.[17] Garnet's position was always a complex one, undergoing shifting emphases over the decade, rather than reversals of opinion. He obviously saw the advantages of keeping his options open. Events of the 1850s such as the passage of the Fugitive Slave Law and the Dred Scott decision certainly had their effect on formerly stalwart opponents of African emigration. As Joel Schor has argued, rising nationalism in Europe, and the celebrated tour of Louis Kossuth, the Hungarian nationalist, may also have contributed to the resuscitation of quiescent black nationalism. By 1858, Garnet, with his excitable personality, was doing much to rekindle interest in African civilization. What Garnet and his cohort supported was described in the constitution of the African Civilization Society as "the civilization and Christianization of Africa and of the descendants of African ancestors in any portion of the earth, wherever dispersed." African resettlement, even in limited numbers, was not the ostensible goal of the society, although economic development and commercial ties with Africa were among its aims. It also stood for the abolition of the slave trade and of slavery. This was a major difference between the African Civilization Society and the American Colonization Society, because the latter organization had long sought to avoid the "delicate question" of general emancipation.[18]

Despite Garnet's claim that the African Civilization Society had nothing to do with the American Colonization Society, there was some overlap between the two organizations. Liberal colonizationists, who really did see themselves as favoring a two-stage process of abolition, thought to promote the emancipation of black people by the elevation of those who were already free. They believed that the arguments of black inequality and incapacity for self-government could best be countered by the living proof of an independent African republic.[19] Garnet resented the charge that the Civilization Society, of which he was president, encouraged free blacks to migrate en masse, leaving the slaves to worry about their own deliverance. He insisted that his organization would "strike the death blow" to American slavery, by creating a "grand center for Negro nationality." This need not be in Africa; the American South seemed a strategic spot, given its proximity to the West Indies, for these too were to be incorporated into the black nation. The idea of a Caribbean slave revolt as the basis of a black empire had been a theme of Martin Delany's novel, *Blake*. Garnet was already known for his call for a slave revolt in 1843. With such personalities associated with its work, the African Civilization Society could hardly be seen as a front for white proslavery conspirators.

On August 1, 1859, black Garrisonians engineered a mass meeting to denounce the civilizationists.[20] Later that month Garnet came to Boston and gave a lively defense of the society's position. He was introduced by J. Sella Martin, another of the society's spokesmen, who warmed up the crowd by castigating Boston leaders who had denied Garnet the use of their church buildings for the rally. Garnet, taking the stand, continued to harp on the same theme, characterizing his opposition as the opponents of black associations and independent efforts who supposed that black folk did not need to help themselves in the fight for liberty, "especially as people of color." This faction spoke as if black people had no special interests, as if they were not a "peculiar people," as if they were afraid to be identified as speaking for themselves. But only after black people had accomplished something for themselves would they be respected, only then would they be able to come together with other men and women as "members of the great American family." That day must be prepared for before it could be enjoyed. Now was not the time for dreamy talk about "universal rights and universal liberty." If black people knew what was good for them, they would come together in their own conventions, to "consider the interests of the colored people of this country."

Garnet questioned the common sense of the Garrisonian blacks and their commitment to the interests of black people. A meeting they had held in Boston earlier that month had been concerned mainly with attacking him and misrepresenting his views. Its only other object was to provide an occasion for the ladies of Boston to present George T. Downing with a bouquet. Downing, a vociferous opponent of the Civilization Society, had been a pupil at the African Free School along with Crummell, Garnet, and James McCune Smith. Although Downing's education was very sound, he did not enjoy the scholarly reputation of his three classmates. Tradition has it that he was known for great physical courage and for persistent opposition to segregation and discrimination.[21] Hostilities between Garnet and Downing were pronounced during the late fifties and early sixties. Downing insisted that Garnet was a colonizationist, which Garnet denied, saying anyone who called him one was "an assassin and a coward." Before a clearly sympathetic audience, he asserted his hatred for the Colonization Society and its slave-holding leaders. The colonizationists said that America was not the home of the Afro-American people. "I say it is the home of the colored man," proclaimed Garnet to the applauding crowd, "and it is my home." He believed that the condition of the colored people could be elevated in America, but only through the spirit of self-help. The African Civilization Society encouraged this, and the Garrisonians did not. Too long had the black people depended on white abolitionists, who were themselves guilty of racial prejudice. He did not deny that white supporters had their place in God's plan. They could help the blacks to achieve enfranchisement and other blessings of freedom. They might also begin to employ black workers in their places of business. But the task of raising black people to positions of economic status and political power in Africa, America, and throughout the world must be accomplished by black people themselves.

He ridiculed black leaders who opposed the Civilization Society simply because one of its goals was shared by the colonizationists. Those who would not go to Africa if a white man suggested they should, quipped Garnet, would probably not go to heaven if a white man said they should. Garnet reminded the Bostonians that thousands of white men were currently involved in trading on the coast of Africa. When, eager to learn from the experience of others, he had written to a certain English entrepreneur engaged in African commerce, asking about prospects for Afro-American traders on the coast, the trader replied, "We are not in favor of colored people going there in small companies, for this reason: If they do *they will interrupt the trade already established between Africa and England.*"

> That opened our eyes. If that trade was of so much value that English manufacturers were anxious to preserve it to themselves, we thought that was the very reason we should go and take advantage of it.[22]

While some whites were urging blacks to go to Africa, others were more concerned with equipping their own vessels, sailing off to Africa to fill their pockets, laughing at the foolish blacks who sat in conventions and quarreled among themselves. A dozen ships sailing out of Boston and keeping up an

African trade would do more for black dignity "than fifty thousand lectures of the most eloquent men in this land." The wall of prejudice would only be broken down "when we shall come up and stand by the side of other men, and in every department of cultivated life show that we are their equals in every respect." And so it was that advocates of African settlement and trade came to restate the arguments that had been advanced forty years earlier by James Forten and Paul Cuffe.[23]

Militant abolitionists were no more impressed by Garnet's line than their grandfathers had been by Cuffe's. William Wells Brown, William Cooper Nell, and George T. Downing denounced the Civilization Society, and Frederick Douglass used his newspaper to express fears that the civilizationists' efforts would give comfort and encouragement to those who denied the rights of colored citizens. Like Downing, Douglass refused to acknowledge a distinction between the goals of the Civilization Society and the colonizationists. He maintained that he had no hostility to the Christianization and civilization of Africa, but neither was he prepared to board the next ship. William Wells Brown, Frederick Douglass, and some others would develop a tentative interest in Haitian migration before the end of the decade. One scholar has suggested that it was the heating up of the political climate in the wake of John Brown's raid that led almost every major abolitionist to convert to the migration position by the end of the 1850s. This is probably true, but a prior disposition to separate black institutions and a radical stance on abolitionism seem to have been additional factors in Garnet's case.[24]

When Douglass, Brown, and a few other late converts expressed some grudging interest in Haiti on the eve of the Civil War, they lacked the conviction of a James T. Holly. The latter, who, like Crummell, was an Episcopal priest, had gone to Haiti expressing considerable enthusiasm for a Caribbean variety of nationalism. He had used his own adaptation of American Manifest Destiny myths (but not the Whitman variety) to argue that it was fruitless to return to Africa. The nation must follow the course of civilization, which was moving across the Western hemisphere. Representatives of the Haitian emigration movement writing in *The Weekly Anglo-African* readily accepted the idea of Garnet's African Civilization Society that such a Caribbean empire would be effectively situated to offer assistance to the enslaved masses of the southern states. The Haitian movement never achieved the importance of the African movement and seems to have thrived only during the years between John Brown's raid and the Emancipation Proclamation. Much of the support for the movement was nonideological and sporadic, and it was often the product of such circumstances as Lincoln's advocacy of colonization.[25]

African civilizationism, on the other hand, attracted an impressive array of supporters, whose passion for emigration mounted steadily throughout the 1850s. By the end of that decade Crummell must have felt that he had been vindicated by the shift of attitudes among militant abolitionists in the United States. Highly literate, enterprising, impatient men like Garnet and Delany, who had been free since early childhood, were unimpressed by the proposals of the exslave Douglass, who understandably gave such priority to the liberation of the slaves that he viewed emigrationism as a betrayal. The civilizationists began to question the feasibility of digging in for the seemingly interminable fight against American prejudice. Their nationalism was immediatist; their antislavery was implicitly gradualist, linked as it was to the rhetoric of African civilizationism. The Delanys, the Garnets, and the Crummells believed that only by putting first things first could the black race vindicate its claims to equality, and force the proud Anglo-Saxons to acknowledge its rights. They came to view Douglass's antislavery approach as utopian. Their first priority was to establish a black national power, which must serve as the necessary base for the struggle against slavery and prejudice. It is therefore not surprising that when Martin Delany came to Africa in 1859, he made it his business to spend some time with Alexander Crummell, who was now clearly in the vanguard of the movement.

On July 10, 1859, Martin Delany had his first glimpse of the land whose progress and prospects he had for so long disparaged. The bark *Mendi,* on which he arrived in West Africa, had been chartered by black entrepreneurs, Charles B. Dunbar, a physician, John D. Johnson, and Joseph Turpin, a tailor. They had sailed under the Liberian flag and had brought along thirty-three emigrants, sponsored by the American Colonization Society. Johnson had already become a Liberian, and Dunbar and Turpin apparently intended to follow in his footsteps. Garnet had expressed his regard for Dunbar, Johnson, and Turpin in his speech in Boston during the enthusiastic rally of the preceding summer. But their expedition had only the most tenuous relationship to the African Civilization Society. Delany actually traveled on behalf of his own splinter organization, the African Civilization Society of Canada, which, like Garnet's, had little in the way of practical apparatus. A simultaneous and nominally cooperative venture was indeed underway, sponsored by the African Civilization Society and headed up by Robert Campbell. Both parties, however, were funded by white colonizationists. The suspicions of Frederick Douglass and other antiemigrationists thus seemed to have been confirmed. If the African Civilization Society was not an adjunct of the American Colonization Society, its emissary to Africa was certainly a fellow traveler.[26]

The party disembarked "amid the joyous acclamations of the numerous natives," and Delany was welcomed ashore by a number of Liberians, among them Samuel Williams, who in his 1857 publication *Four Years in Liberia* gave a measured and balanced response to Delany's vituperations, which had appeared in the preface to William Nesbit's diatribe.[27] The reception was apparently more than cordial, and, after spending a night back on board the vessel, Delany took lodgings on shore. Determined to brazen it out, he wrote immediately to President Benson, announcing that he had "arrived . . . near your Government" and requesting "an interview with your Excellency, either privately or in Cabinet Council, or with any other gentlemen that the occasion may suggest." The president responded with assurances of "deep interest . . .

in your very laudable enterprise" but expressed his regret that he was "on the very eve of leaving [the] city on an official visit to the leeward counties." But Delany's arrival hardly went unregarded. He received on the following day, July 13, a letter from a group of Liberians welcoming him on behalf of the community. They recognized him as an "ardent and devoted lover of the African race" and acknowledged his efforts to elevate "our downtrodden race," though those efforts were not infrequently directed against Liberia. They respectfully requested that he "favor the citizens with a lecture to-morrow evening or on any other evening you may choose to appoint . . . ., on any subject you may choose to select." Delany cavalierly responded that the gentlemen were "mistaken" in "supposing" that he had "ever spoken directly against Liberia." He even made peace with former President Roberts, whom he had once called a parrot of the American Colonization Society. On July 19, when he addressed a crowd in the Methodist Episcopal Church, it was Roberts who introduced him "and in a short speech, in the name of the Liberians, welcomed [him] to Africa."[28]

After three weeks in Monrovia, he continued down the coast in the bark *Mendi* till he arrived at Cape Palmas on August 20. The white missionary C. C. Hoffman called on him within a half hour of his arrival, and not much later in the day he "was honored by a visit . . . from the Rev. Alexander Crummell, Principal of Mount Vaughan High School, where . . . I took up my residence during a month's stay in this part of Liberia." It was apparently Crummell who drafted a letter of invitation from a group of Maryland County citizens asking Delany for a public lecture and acknowledging his "reputation, talents, and noble mission." During the month he made an exploratory journey up the Cavalla River, accompanied by Crummell, whom he thanked "for making my task an easy one." They paddled up the "fine broad flowing river," with its spectacular scenery, through "a rich and populous country." There was "grand mountain scenery in the distance . . . . , visions of ravishing beauty." Crummell, who had made the journey at least once before, wrote that they were "everywhere . . . most cordially received, hospitably entertained," and, as it was a missionary expedition, Crummell proselytized. "My teachings," he wrote, were "eagerly listened to, by whole towns and villages, who invariably turned out in a body to hear the preacher."[29]

Delany was not the only guest that Crummell entertained that summer. He had earlier been visited by Robert Campbell, who represented Garnet's wing of the African Civilization Society and apparently hoped to usurp Delany's position as leader of Afro-American forces. Campbell had only been able to spend three hours at Cape Palmas, he was so eager to reach Lagos before Delany. Campbell did mention meeting the Reverend Alex Crummell, who conducted him "to the two or three places of interest which could be visited in that time" and showed him the church in which he sometimes officiated. He was "gratified to witness more than one hundred natives, including an old chief, listening with deep attention to the word of God." He did not have time to visit the high school at Mt. Vaughan, for on receiving intelligence of the arrival of the bark *Mendi* at Monrovia, he abruptly decamped, setting off for the Gold Coast and on to Nigeria.[30]

The arrival of the *Mendi* was no earthshaking event, but it provided the occasion for Crummell's systematic presentation of the case for emigration in *The Relations and Duty of Free Colored Men in America to Africa.* The essay took the form of a letter to Charles B. Dunbar, one of the charterers of the *Mendi,* although, as Crummell freely admitted, it was written in the hope that it might prove interesting to "many of our old friends and schoolmates in New York."[31] It was also intended as an address to the "Free Colored Men of America," and what applied to them should apply in equal degree to "our West Indian, Haytian, and eventually our Brazilian brethren." He wrote "with doubt and diffidence . . . , and only after having been encouraged to do so by Dunbar, Campbell, and Delany." Furthermore, he was not deaf to the argument so often put forth by black American leaders that it was "unjust to disturb their residence in the land of their birth by a continual call to go to Africa." The claims of Afro-Americans to all the benefits of American life were valid on three accounts: firstly, by virtue of three centuries' residency on the land; secondly, by virtue of the economic contributions that blacks had made; thirdly, by virtue of their Christianity. One would have to find "some new page and appendage to the Bible to get the warrant for Christians to repel and expatriate Christians on account of blood or race, or culture." He insisted that he intended no endorsement of such actions by his letter. He claimed to be advocating only a selective emigration—not colonization. He insisted that he did not intend "to vex any of our brethren by the iteration of the falsehood that America is not their home."

> I would not insult the intellect and conscience of any colored man who thinks it his duty to labor for his race on American soil, by telling him to come to Africa. If he is educated up to the ideas of responsibility and obligation, he knows his duty better than I do. And, indeed, generally, it is best to leave individuals to themselves as to the *details* of obligation and responsibility.

Crummell tried to frame his appeal in terms of humanitarian as well as racial duty. His concern was the spreading of a cosmopolitan civilization, rather than the nurturing of a cultural nationalism or separatism. All the world seemed to be focusing on Africa, "the maimed and crippled arm of humanity . . . the victim of heterogeneous idolatries," a dark continent, "wasting away beneath the accretions of civil and moral miseries."[32] The principle of self-love demanded that black people begin to take the same pride in the old world roots that Anglo-Americans supposedly felt. The "abject state of Africa" presented a "touching appeal to any heart for sympathy and aid." This appeal should come "with a double force to every civilized man who has negro blood flowing in his veins." But the great civilizing enterprises of the age seemed to be arising among the whites of Europe and America. The free blacks had not yet begun to assume the burdens of philanthropy. Africa thus remained a dark continent, her great powers wasted, her miseries so manifold that it "would take a volume to detail and enumerate them."

> Darkness covers the land, and gross darkness the people. Great social evils universally prevail. Confidence and security are destroyed. Licentiousness abounds everywhere. Moloch rules and reigns throughout the whole continent, and by the ordeal of Sassywood, Fethiches, human sacrifices, and devil worship, is devouring men, women, and little children. They have not the Gospel. They are living without God.

The appeal was not, however, a purely missionary one; Crummell addressed practical concerns. As did Dunbar, Delany, and Campbell, he stressed Africa's need for "skill, enterprise, energy, *worldly* talent, to raise her." The self-love, which would spur men on to self-advantage and self-aggrandizement, would work to the advantage of Africa. "That class of sentiments in the human heart which creates a thirst for wealth, position, honor and power [would] advance the material growth of Africa." The enterprising spirit would "prove the handmaid of religion, and . . . serve the great purposes of civilization and enlightenment." The treasures of Africa, the manifest gift of Providence to the African race, were in foreign hands, the "sons of Africa in foreign lands, inane and blinded, suffer the adventurous foreigner with greed and glut to jostle them aside, and "to seize with skill and effect upon their own rightful inheritance." [33]

For several pages he listed the economic products of Africa, describing the natural wealth and the products of cultivation awaiting exploitation by a class of African entrepreneurs. He conceived the future of Africa in terms of American history, applying manifest destiny myths to the great African undertaking. He foresaw the opening up of the continent to commerce and enlightenment as an inevitable historical process, which would in many ways recapitulate the history of North America.[34] He pointed to the fact, as Garnet had done, that Englishmen were already reaping the benefits of African trade. Was it not appropriate that blacks should have at least a share? Blacks in North America did not lack the necessary capital; it was simply that their wealth was unproductive. Black people had been "victimized in a pecuniary point of view as well as morally and politically." There was consequently an "almost universal dread of intrusting our moneys in the hands of capitalists, and trading companies, and stock." He focused respectfully on the capacity of the religious bodies to acquire capital, building brick edifices and taking up large collections. This was a demonstration of black people's capacity to work together toward economic goals.

The development of black trading companies would serve as an inspiration to West Africans. "The kings and tribesmen of Africa, having the *demonstration* of negro capacity before them, would hail the presence of their black kinsmen from America, and would be stimulated to a generous emulation." Crummell had already heard reports that such had been Delany's experience "at Lagos and other places." The result of such efforts would be the speedy formation of "leagues and combinations" between the native Africans and the men of commerce. Before long, "civilization, enlightenment, and Christianity would be carried to every state, town, and village of interior Africa." Here was a program on which men of diverse opinion such as Douglass and Delany could stand. "Hence those men whose feelings are the most averse to any thing like colonization cannot object to the promotion of trade and the acquisition of wealth." Crummell insisted that his concern in this essay was not with Liberia alone, but with African enterprise in general, and with the development of the continent as a whole.

Of course it would be only natural for many in the United States to think of his proposals in connection with the Liberian Republic, and he thought it would be "wise and judicious for them to do so." Like Samuel Williams, he refused to make extravagant claims for Liberia, but he claimed that the settlers were "laying good foundations," and he denied ever having "been disappointed in anything moral, social, or political" that he had met with. He had come to Liberia "expecting all the peculiarities of struggling colonial life." He knew that God had "married pain, and suffering, and death to the fresh beginnings of all new nationalities." When one considered that Liberia had the additional burden of "imported habits, tinctured with the deterioration, the indifference, the unthriftiness, which are gendered by any servile system," one could not be too sanguine in one's expectations. Nonetheless, he found much to admire among the Liberians, who showed an enterprising spirit. "The acquisitive principle manifests itself, the great principles of industry, of thrift, and expansion are daily taking root deeper in the soil." Of course Liberia had her corrupt and venal citizens, as every nation must, but these were "by no means the *representative* men of the land." Most were people with a sense of mission who were committed to "the expansion and compacting of this youthful republic, to save bleeding, benighted Africa, and to help redeem the continent."[35]

The retardation of Africa did not necessarily imply an incapacity to generate worthwhile indigenous institutions. Crummell saw his African ancestors as having "a history not of ignominy and disgrace, but of heathenism and benightedness." He referred to the British as living proof that the civilized world was "now magnanimous enough to recognize such traits." In addition, the Africans had in some instances created respectable political institutions. Indeed, it seemed a "manifest Providence" that Christianity was to be "engrafted upon such strong states as Dahomey and Ashantee." Their *"governmental* basis," if no other aspect of their manners and customs, ought to be allowed to endure, for it seemed to Crummell that it would not serve the interests of African civilization "to revolutionize or disturb" the old political order.[36] But the essence of Crummell's position, like that of most other black nationalists, was "civilizationist," based on the idea that Africa was backward and benighted, unenlightened and degraded, with little to offer the world. The continent must be redeemed through the agencies of "Commerce, Christianity, and Civilization.

This opinion was hardly a novel one. "Civilizationist" attitudes were clearly endorsed in the constitution of the society, which was founded to effect the "Civilization and Christianization of Africa, and of the descendants of African ancestors in any portion of the earth, wherever dispersed." Crummell, like Garnet, and presumably all members of the society, believed that the "intention of the Divine Mind towards Africa" was to use the free Negroes of the United States as agents of redemption. Crummell's letter, coming in the wake of the Delany expedition and addressed to Dunbar, a member of the same African civilizationist circle, advocated many of the Society's principles, focusing, for example, on the familiar proposal for "the destruction of the African Slave-trade, by the introduction of lawful commerce and trade into Africa: the promotion of the growth of cotton and other products there, whereby the natives may become industrious producers as well as consumers of articles of commerce."

The assumption behind such thinking is obvious. Neither Garnet nor Delany saw African cultures as having much to offer to the world, in part because of the same Christian bias that infected Crummell's thinking. All three were fond of quoting the prophecy of Psalms 63:31, "Princes shall come out of Egypt; Ethiopia shall soon stretch forth her hands unto God," which was murky enough to allow for boundless exegetical extravagance. What it usually meant to the "civilizationists" was that Africa was soon to be redeemed from the darkness of heathenism and barbarism. Delany sailed for Africa "with fullest reliance on this blessed promise." According to Garnet's interpretation, which Delany cited in the *Official Report of the Niger Exploring Party,* the word "soon" in the scriptural passage referred to "the period ensuing from the time of the beginning." In other words, African redemption would be a speedy process, once the work was begun. "The disease has long been known," wrote Delany of Africa's supposed spiritual and cultural retardation. The cure was now to be applied by Afro-Americans in the form of Christianity, Commerce, and Civilization.[37]

"Christianity certainly is the most advanced civilization that man ever attained to," wrote Delany. His bias was clearly in favor of Protestantism, however, for as far as he was concerned slavery seemed everywhere "the legitimate successor of Roman Catholicism."[38] Wherever Protestant missionaries were found, on the other hand, there were visible evidences of a purer and higher civilization. The influence of the Protestant religion was "against Slavery and in favor of civilization." The Protestant religion, wrote Crummell, "with its characteristic tendencies to freedom, progress, and human well-being," tended to encourage the development of republican institutions. An African civilization without a Protestant base was unthinkable to Crummell and other civilizationists. Haiti was an example of a black nation that might have experienced greater progress were it not for "the incubus of Romanism." Fortunately, the civilizationist spirit was spreading even into the Caribbean, for Haiti desperately needed "a PROTESTANT, Anglo-Saxon element of the stamp Mr. Holly will give her." Happily, Liberia was not held back by the deleterious effects of Romanism. The civilization of Africa would go hand in hand with mission work, for Christianity was not only an aid to civilization, it was absolutely indispensable to it. And naturally, as a Protestant missionary, Crummell saw the planting of the Protestant faith in West Africa as an end in itself.[39]

Crummell's letter to Dunbar was written toward the end of his first extended African tour. It was only one of the many treatises on African regeneration and Liberian prospects to be published during the decade. It should be viewed as one of the documents of reconciliation between the African Civilization Society and the Liberian colonizationists. It marked cloture on a debate that had been raging from the beginnings of the 1850s over whether or not the emigrationists and the colonizationists could work together. In 1853, the year of Crummell's resettlement and Nesbit and Williams's arrival, many emigrationists were doing everything conceivable to disassociate themselves from Liberia. By the time the *Mendi* sailed in 1859, attitudes among emigrationists had changed considerably. Here was a chance for Crummell and other Liberian nationalists to associate themselves with a group of black men respected for their spirit of practicality, enterprise, and assertiveness. Crummell would link his own aims with those of the African Civilization Society, quoting from its constitution in his essay. His thinking was in no way inconsistent with goals of all right-thinking black people—"The Evangelization and Civilization of Africa and the descendants of African ancestors, *wherever dispersed.*"[40] The duty of the hour for "enterprising spirits" must be to bring to the peoples of Africa "the culture and enlightenment that have raised [Europeans] from rudeness and degradation." It was their duty to induce the Africans, "to throw aside the exclusiveness of paganism, and the repulsiveness of barbarism . . . . To wrest a continent from ruin, to bless and animate millions of torpid and benighted souls; to destroy the power of the devil in his strongholds, and to usher therein light, knowledge, blessedness, inspiring hope, holy faith and abiding glory."[41]

Given such obvious enthusiasm for African redemption, it is understandable that he might wish to make a journey to the United States to proselytize for African emigration. There was certainly a great deal to be done from the American side to further the African Civilization Movement. Possibly Delany's and Campbell's visits awakened a desire for the companionship of others who shared his enthusiasms, and he naturally must have been curious about the Civil War and its effects on the lives of blacks in the North. He still had friends and family in New York, and he had been promising himself for some time that he would come to America to alleviate his aging parents' financial distress. In America he could investigate the prospects for publishing a book of sermons which would be a legitimate way of raising money. He also seems to have planned from the beginning to solicit funds and other support for Liberia College. He does not seem to have intended anything other than a brief visit, and toward the end he expressed annoyance at the delays that kept him in the United States for several months longer than he had planned.

Crummell and his family returned to the United States in the spring of 1861 aboard the *Mary Caroline Stevens*. Mrs. Crummell's health, according to the report of a fellow missionary, was very poor.[42] Crummell felt, and with perfect justification, that he was entitled to a leave from missionary duties at Cape Palmas. Such a leave had recently been granted to Bishop Payne and to C. C. Hoffman, who had just returned to Cape Palmas on the same ship that was to carry Crummell and his family to the United States. The *Mary Caroline Stevens* arrived at Cape Palmas on January 4, 1861, and left on January 18, with the Crummells on board. It stopped over in Monrovia for several weeks, and a day or two after Crummell's forty-second birthday sailed again. On April 4, 1861, after a passage of thirty days, the vessel arrived in Baltimore.[43]

It is sometimes reported that Crummell traveled to the United States under a commission from the Liberian government. Crummell's letters and other sources indicate that he came with the support of the Protestant Episcopal church, and that he received some support from the Massachusetts Colonization Society and from Pennsylvania colonizationists during that time. As a matter of fact, the letter appointing him a commissioner, as printed in *African Repository,* was written on March 8, 1862, a year after his departure from Monrovia; Crummell thus served as commissioner only during the last months of his sojourn.[44] Shortly after his arrival, the Rev. John Orcutt persuaded Crummell to speak on behalf of the American Colonization Society in New England and the mid-Atlantic states.[45] He was soon launched on this venture and in April made a triumphant return to New York. His friends prepared a reception for him at the A.M.E. Church at Bridge Street in Brooklyn. A banner representing Crummell instructing African children hung over the pulpit, and the crowd of around two hundred included Bishop Daniel A. Payne and Henry Highland Garnet. Payne, whose position on emigration was exceedingly difficult to pin down, was a member of the African Civilization Society, founded by Garnet, who had, of course, become one of the major voices for African emigration. Garnet honored his old school friend not only for his missionary work, but for laying the foundation for Africa's material progress. Another speaker, Professor J. W. Wilson, spoke of the signal importance of the black population who had been instrumental in bringing about the present national crisis of civil war. Crummell responded by reminding the audience of his early political activities in New York and assuring them that during his years abroad he had closely watched the progress of black Americans. He praised the black American population, not only for its powers of endurance, but for its ability to affect the course of American national life. "We have taken hold of the pillars of the country," he said, "and shaken them to their foundation."[46]

When early the following month he delivered a speech at the annual meeting of the New York State Colonization Society, and three weeks later at the Massachusetts Colonization Society delivered another, there could no longer be any doubt that Crummell had taken up with the colonizationists.[47] He reiterated the usual claims of the movement that the Liberian republic was to be the principal means whereby Africa, "the withered arm of humanity," was to be redeemed from the darkness of heathenism. But he spoke with a conviction born of resentment, derived from experience, when he raised the question of whether Africa could be successfully evangelized by white missionaries. Had not God chosen Greeks to evangelize Greece, and Romans to carry out his work in Rome? Why then it must also be the divine plan to bring about the conversion of Africa through the influence of Africans themselves. Although in its early days Liberia had suffered from "disorder, sickness, and uncertainty," the people, feeling that God had placed them there for a purpose, began to gain confidence and were now engaged in commerce. Coffee, cotton, gold, ivory, palm oil, and camwood were becoming items of export. Although in the early days there were indeed many colonists who did not know the meaning of work, it could now be seen that the Negro was not lazy. "Give the negro some incentive to labor, and there is not a more plodding or industrious man in the world than the African."[48]

It was a known fact that slavery was indigenous to African soil, but Liberia had become a beacon of liberty. Crummell testified that he had shielded fugitive slaves in his own home, and that when their master had come to reclaim them, the case had been taken before a magistrate, who proclaimed, "Our soil is sacred, and no fugitive coming from slavery can be returned." Crummell was obviously trying to show that going to Liberia did not mean abandoning the cause of black emancipation. He meant to show that he, in his own way, was just as committed as those who worked in the Underground Railroad. The civilizing mission of Liberia was indeed to exterminate the slave trade, destroying it at its African source. Since the courts and the public policy of Liberia were committed to ending the custom, it seemed that one could be just as good an abolitionist across the Atlantic as in Boston. He boasted that whole tribes of Africans had migrated from the interior seeking protection from slavery under the Liberian flag and spoke of the progress made in educating the tribes: "One day a naked savage came to my house and asked me for pen and paper. I inquired 'What do you want with them?' He replied, 'I want to write a letter.' The man, I have said, was a naked savage and the person to whom he sent it was another naked savage; yet, if there is one there are hundreds of savages who have been taught in our schools, and, after receiving some education, have returned to their homes." Crummell spoke of modern cities, with fine brick and stone houses, some of them "as fashionably furnished as the dwellings of the more respectable portion of the inhabitants of this country," and towns with streets "as clean as any in Boston." The inhabitants were fashionably dressed, usually adopting the style of dress in those parts of the United States from which they came. "They may be ostentatious, but they live better than people in the same circumstances—either white or colored—in this country. Perhaps at some future time more simplicity may be observed among them."[49]

The English language, he predicted, was destined to become dominant throughout West Africa. In the homes of Africa, one could find the classics of English literature and the outstanding authors of America. All the current newspapers and literary journals were readily available. The major religious denominations were well established, having built churches and high schools; a college was now "in course of erection." Recaptured natives, taken from the holds of slave ships, were placed with civilized Liberian families, where they demonstrated every disposition to rapidly become "civilized."

> Two years ago a large number of this class was recaptured in the slaver *Echo,* and brought to Liberia . . . . They are quiet, peaceable, industrious men. No vestiges of idolatry—such as fetishism, obeahism, or devil-worship—have been observed among them, and they have embraced the Christian faith. They have now become citizens of the Republic. They have been enrolled among her soldiers, and they can perform their duties with as much precision as the others. There is nothing which does so much for civilizing a man as putting a gun into his hands. It makes a savage into a man directly.[50]

The statement was followed by laughter and applause, but it was tough language for a Christian clergyman, and not a particularly enlightened example of humor. It may well be that neither speaker nor audience had any knowledge of the role firearms had played in the intertribal arms race and the West African slavery wars since the sixteenth century. Was he not aware that some village craftsmen were already making their own guns by the mid-nineteenth century? What could have caused such a lapse in his theory of civilization as to lead him (even jokingly) to assign a more prominent role to firearms than to literacy or Christianity as a civilizing agent? There was a ruthlessness in his personality, an intolerance, a tendency to see problems as solvable by force and authority. Perhaps this was only an opportunistic choice of phrase meant to impress the tough-minded Bostonians during wartime, which it apparently did. It may have been Crummell's way of speaking up for the use of black troops in support of the Union cause. Whatever the motivation, the statement was neither historically accurate, with respect to Africa, nor philosophically judicious.

He asserted that the tendency towards intermarriage and assimilation was strong, recounting the case of a Liberian woman who had married a fugitive slave. When he was missed by his former master, he was pursued and brought before a magistrate. When the master asserted that he was his apprentice, the woman replied, "But he's my husband!" The result of the trial was that "the lady was victorious, and carried off her husband in triumph."[51]

He then took up a theme that had appeared fourteen years earlier in "Ode on the Death of Thomas Clarkson" and that was to remain prominent in his oratory for many years to come. This was the "capability of endurance, and wonderful tenacity of life" that he believed black people to possess. In some quarters of the earth, the aboriginal races were known to "fade away and perish . . . at the approach of a civilizing power." The plastic nature of the African race allowed them to survive even the cruellest adversities. "By a kind of instinctive eclecticism, [the black Man] draws to himself good and advantages from the people whoever they may be to whom he is subjected, and among whom he lives; and assimilates himself to them, their habits, their political state, and their rules of life." As a result, black people had benefited from being in a Protestant country, despite the injustice of its laws. Black people had learned "the theory of free speech" and had participated somewhat in all the vast wealth, both religious and civil, of . . . Anglo-Saxon literature." Thus, in his Providence, God had severely tried the Afro-American, as he always put peoples through dread ordeals of pain and suffering, when he designed a people "to perform some signal service, to work out some larger and magnificent destiny." Through their severe training black Americans had become superior to many other peoples.

> The free American black man is the best in the world. He may be inferior in scholarship to the British black man, in refinement to the French black man. But in force of enterprise, and political capacity, he is superior to both. We have secured the sterling qualities of American Character, and we are what may be called "black Yankees."[52]

These statements were characteristic of Crummell's optimistic theological historicism and his pessimistic tendency to think of African culture as incapable of producing anything worthwhile.

History moved with a purpose; the pattern could be discerned. Providence was progressive and led to higher and higher forms of civilization, which ultimately were brought to fruition by the triumph of Christianity. The simultaneous Christianization and civilization of black Americans under Anglo-American auspices was clear evidence they were on the progressive road to a new stage in civilization. As for the ability of Africans to develop a culture on their own terms, he was indeed pessimistic, and indeed, like most conservative Christians, he had a pessimistic view of primitive humanity. All good in the world came from submission to Christian institutions, which must first have evolved up to a certain standard, namely modern Protestantism.

Crummell's conception of history was, of course, nothing new to Afro-American audiences. It had appeared in David Walker's *Appeal* of 1829, and Walker had himself drawn on an existing tradition of alluding to the rise and fall of civilizations and to the sacred destiny of black Americans as a chosen people. Many black writers before Crummell had seen history in this way. Walker in particular had viewed history as a series of covenants that God had made with consecutive civilizations—first with the biblical Hebrews, then with the Christianized Romans, and finally with Western Europe.[53] Each had violated its covenant, and as a result had been superseded by another race. Americans, the present beneficiaries of a sacred covenant, would likewise fall, unless they ceased to enslave and persecute the Africans in their midst. Any number of writers were, by Crummell's time, maintaining that a new order was soon to rise in Africa under Christianized blacks: F. Freeman, Hollis Read, Harriet Beecher Stowe, and contributors in the *African Repository* all spoke of a dawning day in Africa, predicting the rise of a civilization that would reflect the gentle traits that had led to the Negro's speedy adoption of Christianity and would be manifest in the African empire that was even now aborning.

Crummell delivered variations on this theme in speeches along the Northeastern coast over the next several months. On June 13, 1861, he spoke before

the New Hampshire Colonization Society. He spoke of "the benefit of affliction, which humbles a people and brings them where God can safely honor
them and make them great." He drew again on the lesson of the Jews, positing
his theory that Providence had foreordained a progression of civilizations, each
to be represented by a different race.

> Old civilizations are done away and new and higher orders of civilization are
> introduced. It is sometimes so in nature. The insect is imprisoned in the chrysalis
> before he can wear the gorgeous apparel of the butterfly. I believe that God is
> about to plant a new germ of civilization in Africa, and that we are fast rising to
> that lofty position designed by God for us.

In New Hampshire, and again in Maine the following month, colonization
meetings at which he spoke passed resolutions in support of renewed efforts
for African regeneration. The coming of war to America was seen as an "ad-
monishment" to the "vigorous prosecution of this work. It was an imperative
demanded of "true patriotism" as well as by pure philanthropy and religion.
The logic was a bit strained. Certainly it did not explore all possible readings
of the apocalyptic signs from heaven. In any case the Civil War did not immediately bring an end to the colonization plans of the truly committed. Frederick Douglass maintained that he had been on the eve of a departure for Haiti
to undertake a fact-finding mission, with an eye to possible Haitian colonization, but now he dropped the idea.[54] By contrast, New York's *Weekly Anglo-
African* continued to carry front-page stories on colonization. Articles on Haitian and Mexican emigration were given prominent play. On October 5, 1861,
Martin Delany proclaimed that he was still determined to migrate. "It is not
necessary for me to state that my destiny is fixed in Africa, where my family
and myself, by God's providence, will soon be happily situated."

Crummell's speeches over the next few months were exceedingly repetitious,
seeking to convince his audiences that Liberia was rapidly advancing towards
civilization and prosperity. When his first book, *The Future of Africa,* appeared
in 1862, it represented the more polished examples of Crummell's apologies
for Liberia. In a sense, this collection of essays may be seen as a contribution
to the debate which had begun in 1853, the year in which the *Isla de Cuba*
arrived in Liberia with its anti-Delany, procolonizationist passengers. Crummell, writing as a friend of the now-converted Delany, took the position of one
who had been vindicated by history, and, in some respects, he was right. Liberian colonization was no longer peremptorily dismissed as John Russwurm's
advocacy had been three decades earlier. The movement still had its enemies
however, the doubters and critics whose arguments *The Future of Africa* attempted to anticipate.

The review of *The Future of Africa,* written by Frederick Douglass for the
July 1862 issue of *Douglass' Monthly,* repeated much that he had said over the
past ten years. He had made many of the same points in exchanges with Martin
Delany and Henry Highland Garnet. He claimed to "accord all honor to Mr.
Crummell, and to men like him, who quit the shores of their native land, carry

away their learning, zeal and affections to Africa."[55] But this was hardly non-partisan phraseology, as Crummell was well aware; Douglass had long been calling on Crummell to return to the United States, where his talents were needed. He refused, at the same time, to accord to Crummell or anyone else "the right to charge even by implication those who see fit to stay here." Although he had never been to Africa, Douglass was ready enough to accept Crummell's judgement that "Darkness covereth Africa, and gross darkness the minds of her people."[56] But he was annoyed by the burden of the letter to Dunbar, which was reprinted in the volume, that anyone should make it his business to lecture on "The Relations and Duties of Free Colored Men in America to Africa." So while Douglass agreed with the civilizationists appraisal of Africa as a degraded continent, with unenlightened inhabitants, he saw no reason why black Americans should place its elevation above their own interests. There was work enough in America to command the attention of the missionary, and the argument that black Americans had special obligations to Africa did not impress him.

Douglass accused Crummell of delivering glowing reports of Liberia in New York that contradicted more critical statements made in speeches in Liberia. Crummell responded in a letter to the editor, taking exception to "the tacit charge of disingenuousness" in the review. He claimed that his critical statements about Liberia were made shortly after his arrival, while his speech "affirming progress, improvement, and growing wealth in Liberia" was made in 1861. He denied any contradictions or inconsistencies in his statements. "They are perfectly reasonable, because the contrast is history—but history crowded into a brief period of time. As Douglass reminded the reader, however, Crummell's critical statements simply did not fall into any such pattern, nor could his inconsistencies be readily explained away solely as a reflection of changing times and growing prosperity. Douglass correctly observed that he had recorded widely differing impressions of Liberian life as it "appeared to him . . . three days after his arrival." Douglass was, of course, in no position fully to appreciate the mixture of emotions that Crummell had experienced in Liberia, but, then, his arguments were not dependent on an intimate knowledge of Crummell's mind or on an accurate dating of his evolving opinions. He was on perfectly solid ground when he observed "that the condition of Liberia was capable of making two very opposite impressions even upon a mind already strongly prepossessed in favor of that country."

Crummell's statement made in Liberia referred to the ability of the country to be self-supporting in 1853; his later statement described the people's "manliness, thrift, energy," which quickened his hopes that the problem could be solved. The passages Douglass chose to cite in *Douglass' Monthly*, July 1862, and August 1862, support such an interpretation. While Douglass was not being entirely fair, it is also clear that Crummell's speeches present a very different picture than did the letters to Jay. Despite his well-known critical predisposition, however, Douglass was perfectly gracious about providing publicity for *The Future of Africa*, and Crummell was obliged to thank him for considerable publicity and serious treatment in *Douglass' Monthly.* In an adjoining column of that same issue of his newspaper, Douglass took another swing at Delany. Praising him for his courage and strength, and professing a heartfelt admiration for the man, Douglass was nonetheless a little hurt by Delany's constant emphasis on the superiority of the pure black to the Afro-American of mixed ancestry. And yet he wished Delany "health, long life, and success. . . . If we were going to Africa we should unhesitatingly enroll ourselves under his leadership for we should know, that the race would receive no detriment in his presence."[57]

Crummell continued to be plagued by financial problems. As a result of "the failure of funds of the Episcopal Mission Board," he turned to the Rev. William Tracy of Boston, the Rev. S. H. Tyng of New York, as well as other friends of colonization, to solicit support. *The Future of Africa* was originally sold by subscription at one dollar per copy.

> As it is published to help repair serious losses by fire in Africa, and to secure the education of his children, it will not be published until 400 subscribers are obtained.
>
> The aid of generous friends is requested, at an early day as possible, as the subscriber is anxious to return very soon to his duty in Africa.

But he was not to return to Africa until late in 1862, for on April 9 of that year, he discovered that the Liberian government had appointed him a "Commissioner to address colored people of this country on Emigration." In January 1863, some months after he had already left the United States, *African Repository* published a letter dated March 8, 1862, from President Benson, appointing Crummell, along with Edward Wilmot Blyden, and J. D. Johnson, commissioners of the "Government and people of Liberia." According to Crummell's letter to Rev. Tracy, dated April 10, 1862, this was news to him.

Crummell's fellow commissioner, Edward W. Blyden, was eventually to become the principal spokesman for Pan-Africanism in the nineteenth century. He was born in St. Thomas, Danish West Indies, in 1832, and emigrated to Liberia at the age of eighteen. A brilliant student at the Alexander High School in Monrovia, Blyden began to publish moral and political essays while still in his teens. By 1856 he had become editor of the *Liberia Herald,* at that time the nation's only newspaper. In 1858, he was ordained a Presbyterian minister, and his writings during the 1860s reflected, as did Crummell's, the Christian redemptionist bias characteristic of the African Civilization Movement. Blyden visited the United States in 1861 and again in 1862, and like Crummell he cultivated contacts with colonizationists in Massachusetts, who were interested in funding Liberia College.[58] His published lectures from this period show that he was inclined to share with Crummell a theory of Providence as the determinant of the evils in the history of the black race. "It cannot be denied," he wrote, "that some very important advantages have accrued to the black man from his deportation to this land, but it has been at the expense of his manhood." It was only by leaving the United States and returning to the Fatherland that black Americans could regain the lordly nature that had been theirs in ages past. By returning to Africa, they would place themselves in a position to carry out the divine plan for their rehabilitation. The signs that this was the aim of Providence were fourfold: First, God had permitted them to be placed in circumstances "fitting them for the work of civilizing and evangelizing the land." Second, he had allowed them to experience adversity in their American foster home. Third, he had caused the Liberian settlement to be established and to flourish. Fourth, he had kept "their fatherland in reserve for them in their absence."[59]

Not every black American was impressed by such arguments. Douglass, without mentioning any names, launched an attack on what he called "the colonization class of theologians" in the September 1862 issue of his newspaper. He spoke of "the satanic spirit of colonization, craftily veiling itself in the livery of Heaven, and speaking in the name of Divine Providence." He called the preachments of these ministers a "sanctimonious endorsement" of the spirit of mob rule and intolerance. Colonizationist theologians dealt in "history, philosophy, theology and treat[ed] all the base passions of one race towards another as the inevitable ordination of Divine Providence, not to be overcome by reason, justice, and humanity, but made the basis of political action for the separation of such races." Douglass, a true optimist, did not believe that such a spirit would ultimately triumph. In any case he recognized, correctly, that the war between the states must ultimately be a war over the issue not only of black freedom, but black equality.[60]

Immediately on receiving the commission from the Liberian government, Crummell and Johnson began a series of speeches in Washington, D.C. The Conference of the African Methodist Episcopal Church was meeting in Washington at the time, and Crummell was allowed to address the body, consisting of fifty ministers. He made a particularly strong impression on the young pastor of Israel Church, Henry McNeal Turner, who was later to become an A.M.E. bishop and was developing his own interest in colonization.[61] Leaving Washington, Crummell went to Maryland, where he was joined by Blyden, and addressed crowds in Baltimore that Crummell estimated in the thousands. Towards the end of July, Blyden headed for the West Indies and Crummell traveled alone through Philadelphia and Pittsburgh, Harrisburg, and Allegheny City. After a few speaking engagements in several cities in New York and New Jersey, he headed west, giving speeches twice in Toledo, twice in Oberlin, and at least once in Chicago. He traveled north to Michigan, speaking on "three occasions in Detroit and at Ann Arbor" and also in Chatham, Ontario. He had already visited the major towns of Maine, Massachusetts, Rhode Island, and Connecticut, before receiving his commission.[62]

During these months he developed stronger ties with white supporters of emigration like Benjamin Coates, the Philadelphia wool merchant, who had tried mightily to influence Garnet and Delany, and William Coppinger, secretary-treasurer of the American Colonization Society.[63] The period marked a shift in

Crummell's relationship to the American Colonization Society, which he had once abhorred and denounced. He was seeking to make himself less dependent on the Episcopal Mission, and he was thinking of ways to strengthen the economic basis of Liberian nationalism. He was now convinced that he would have to find some wider field of participation in Liberian life than the moral leadership. While there seems to be no evidence that he planned to give up the ministry, it is clear that he saw the need to lead by example in commerce. Coppinger and Coates encouraged him to think along these lines, although there was little that they were able or willing to do in concrete terms. Coates gave pep talks, and Coppinger solicited a number of articles for the *African Repository* emphasizing economic development through the cultivation of cotton and coffee.

Crummell's emigrationism does not seem to have been dampened either by the emancipation of slaves in the District of Columbia on April 16, 1862, or by the announcement of September 22, 1862, that all slaves in those states in rebellion against the Union would be emancipated on January 1, 1863. In fact, both events seem to have made him optimistic that he would soon find the capital he needed to begin his enterprises. On learning of emancipation in the District of Columbia he joined with J. D. Johnson in writing a letter to Caleb Smith, Secretary of the Interior. He inquired about the Emancipation Act's provision of a sum of $100,000, appropriated to assist emigrants from the District of Columbia. As Liberian commissioners for emigration, Crummell and Johnson had apparently been approached by several people who were interested in going to Liberia. The commissioners thus duly inquired "whether the Government of the United States [was] prepared, on application, to put the above appropriation to immediate use; and also to ascertain, if convenient, the terms and stipulations, on which it will be applied."[64]

Around the same time, Henry McNeal Turner sought an interview with the president, on his own initiative, about the emigration fund, which was now said to be $600,000. On August 10 a notice was read from the pulpits of several black churches in Washington that the president wanted to confer with a committee of the colored men of the city on a matter of importance. Subsequently a meeting was called at the Bethel Union Church by a Rev. J. Mitchell, a white man, acting as an agent of emigration for the government, and, for the record, seconded by Turner. Mitchell explained that it was the desire of the president to receive a delegation of black leaders in the White House to discuss the dispersal of the monies and to urge their support of colonization.[65] Lincoln's behavior was difficult to interpret. On the one hand, he was receiving black delegations in the White House, a gesture of novel symbolic significance. On the other hand, he was actively encouraging voluntary emigration, arguing that

> The aspiration of men is to enjoy equality with the best when free, but on this broad continent, not a single man of your race is made the equal of a single man of ours. Go where you are treated the best.[66]

Lincoln's behavior was interesting in another regard. He had chosen to consult the opinions of the Washington black community and to avoid, as much as possible, linking the colonization proposal with Liberia or the American Colonization Society. He had just been visited by Joseph J. Roberts, the former Liberian president, but he was still not prepared to endorse emigration to Liberia. He claimed to be thinking of a colony in Central America, where settlers would still be close to the United States and situated on "a great highway from the Atlantic or Caribbean Sea to the Pacific Ocean." Lincoln's support of colonization at this point, given his lack of enthusiasm for Roberts's visit or for Liberia in general, leads one to suspect that his colonization position in the summer of 1862 was not what it appeared to be. In fact, it was probably little more than an attempt to disarm anticipated criticism of the Emancipation Proclamation, which he had already decided to issue. The mind of Abraham Lincoln was known to few people, however. Daniel A. Payne, who had been with him on the day that the Proclamation of Emancipation in the District was signed, and who had been a vice president of Garnet's African Civilization Society, made a public statement that certainly was not without logical weight:

> Let us not forget that there is a vast difference between voluntary associations of men and the legally constituted authorities of a country; while the former may be held in utter contempt, the latter must always be respected. To do so is a moral and religious, as well as a political duty.
>
> The opinions of the government are based upon the ideas, that *white men and colored men cannot live together as equals in the same country* and that unless a voluntary and peaceable separation is effected *now,* the time *must come when there will be a war of extermination* between the two races.[67]

Whether or not they shared such views, the majority of black Americans do not seem to have interpreted them as Turner and Crummell did. They thought of colonization as a threat and made this clear in their response to Lincoln's proposal. Scholars have long observed that in many black communities meetings were called at which opposition to the president's views were expressed.[68] At the same time, many black Americans, Crummell among them, accepted as "common sense" the attitudes expressed in the *Colonization Herald:*

> We therefore say to our colored brethren in America, emigrate anywhere, and everywhere, until you find some country where you can be a free and great people. Liberia, with open arms, invites all Africa's children to come over and help build up a mighty nation; but if they will go elsewhere, then we wish them good speed.[69]

The Emancipation Proclamation was issued on September 22 and well publicized the following day, so it is extremely improbable that Crummell could have been unaware of it at least a week before his scheduled sailing date of October 4. By that time, however, his plans were set, and in any case Crummell realized that emancipation and colonization were not mutually exclusive. He had made preparations for his return home and was eager to get underway. America was still no land of opportunity for black people, and there was still good reason for skepticism about the immediate future of American race relations. But another reason for Crummell's return to Africa, and possibly a more important one, was that on January 23, 1862, Liberia College had been formally inaugurated. The main building had been completed, and all that was required for the opening of classes was Crummell's and Blyden's return. Thus, at the very moment when many black Americans perceived that the tide of American race relations was turning, Crummell stubbornly forged ahead and obstinately renewed his commitment to colonization.

# 8

# Liberia College
# and the Politics of Knowledge
# (1863–1867)

"I arrived home on the 25th of January," wrote Crummell on February 16, 1863. His time, during a stopover in England, had been "so fully occupied in travelling and preaching, that, in the end, I was glad to leave England in order to secure repose and quiet." During his months in the United States, Crummell had not only proselytized for Liberian colonization, he had busily collected materials for the library of Liberia College, some four thousand volumes, many of which he had personally catalogued. The college had been inaugurated on January 23, 1862, and he and Edward Wilmot Blyden had been elected to two of the three professorial posts. Classes could not begin immediately, of course, with two of the three professors still in the United States; it was a year later when Crummell finally arrived in Liberia to commence his duties. In the meantime, his old friend Eli Worthington Stokes resided in the college with his family and provided classical instruction to a few students. The college began its first term with eight freshmen, all males, in early February.[1]

Crummell's full title was Professor of Intellectual and Moral Philosophy and English Language and Literature and Instructor in Logic, Rhetoric, and History. He shared responsibility for mathematics and natural philosophy with Blyden, who was to be Professor of Greek Language and Latin Language and Literature and Instructor in Hebrew and French. Joseph Jenkins Roberts, former president of the republic, was to be president of the college, as well as Professor of International Law and Jurisprudence.[2]

The idea of a college in Liberia was, of course, not new. Bishop Payne had originally been in favor of a college and in 1848 had written to Simon Greenleaf, head of the Massachusetts Colonization Society, soliciting his aid in establishing a theological school at Cape Palmas. Greenleaf was convinced, however, that the needs of Liberia would be better met by a nonsectarian college in Monrovia than by a religious seminary at the Cape. He accordingly brought the subject to the attention of the Massachusetts Colonization Society, which then began to collect donations, and a cornerstone was laid on January 25, 1858. Political squabbles delayed any further progress for some time, however. It had originally been planned to locate the campus some fifteen miles from Monrovia in Clay-Ashland, but it was later decided to build on a lot of twenty acres on the southwestern slope of Cape Mesurado, within the municipal limits of Monrovia. The disappointed Clay-Ashland residents then initiated a series of legal actions, which caused some four years' delay in the building schedule. Crummell's lengthy stay in the United States also caused some delay, deferring classes for a year.[3]

In the months before sailing for America, Crummell had been developing his thoughts on the sort of higher education he would like to encourage in Liberia College. These he had set forth in a speech entitled "The English Language in Liberia," which was delivered during the summer of 1860 at Cape Palmas and again in Monrovia during the long stopover before the ship left for Baltimore. In his years as a professor of English he had ample opportunity to preach his doctrines on language and literature. This address gives us an idea of Crummell's educational philosophy, as well as of what he read and what he considered worth reading. It was, furthermore, his testament regarding the standards of culture that he considered worthy of emulation by Africans.

His attitudes on the desirability of promoting English culture were not uncommmon at that time, either among black Americans or coastal Africans. Crummell certainly articulated his ideas freely enough, and he seems never to have offended anyone by preaching the doctrine. As we have seen, he accepted the widely held view that a series of providential events had brought the slaves to America and then, after many centuries, replanted them in the ancestral home. In addition to Christianity (so obvious a blessing that its benefits required no demonstration), the exile and enslavement of Africans in America had endowed them with one noble item "of compensation, namely the Anglo-Saxon tongue." Possession of this language had put them "in a position none other on the globe could give." It was impossible to estimate too highly the advantages of being endowed with the "speech of Chaucer and Shakespeare, of Milton and Wordsworth, of Bacon and Burke, of Franklin and Webster."

He began with the observation that English was already widely spoken in Liberia. Not only was it encountered among the Americo-Liberians, whose very names and American antecedents were English, but among the natives. He recounted having met on the banks of the Cavalla River, remote from the capital city and fully eighty miles from the ocean, "a native trader, a man who presented all the signs of civilization, and who spoke with remarkable clearness, the English language." He recalled that he had had native boys working for him on the St. Paul's, "who when they wanted any thing, would write a note with as much exactness as I could." He recalled "one native man over the river, who is a leader in Devil-dances, and yet can read and write like a scholar." He told the story of a friend, who, traveling in the bush some two hundred miles from Monrovia, "stopped one night, exhausted, at the hut of a native man, who brought him his own Bible to read, but alas! it was accompanied by a decanter of rum!" Reflecting on these incongruities brought him a mixture of sorrow and of joy. "The moral of such facts I shall not enter upon," he wrote, and one can imagine why not. The facts were a challenge to his hypothesis, raising the question of whether the English language and European influences really did have such civilizing effects. He consistently stated his belief that hand in hand with the dissemination of the English language would come the manners and customs that had been responsible for the elevation of the British and the Americans. Was it not possible that evil could be imported as well?

The idea did impinge remotely on his consciousness, but if the Europeans brought rum with them, bad as that was, at least they were above "devil dancing." And there could be no questioning the inestimable superiority of English culture to anything that Africa had to offer. The "multitude of tribes and natives" grouped in the area between the Niger and the Senegal Rivers were divided by a variety of tongues and dialects. They had no doubt once had a common origin, but were now so diverse as to make communication impossible. Regardless of their differences, "definite marks of inferiority connected them all, which place[d] them at the widest distance from civilized languages." He dismissed all African languages with a quotation from one Dr. Leighton Wilson. They were "harsh, abrupt, energetic, indistinct in enunciation, meagre in point of words, abound[ing] with inarticulate nasal and guttural sounds, possess[ing] but few inflections and grammatical forms, and . . . withall exceedingly difficult of acquisition."[4]

Not only did Crummell accept this as correct, he went on to add that the languages were characterized by "lowness of ideas," for, as they were the languages of "rude barbarians," they must be "marked by brutal and vindictive sentiments" which showed "a predominance of the animal propensities." They lacked the capacity to express virtue and moral truth "and those distinctions of right and wrong with which we all our life long have been familiar." They were not capable of clearly expressing ideas of Law and Justice and human rights. And all truthful religious concepts were either entirely absent from West African languages, "or else exist and are expressed in an obscure and distorted manner."

The English language was by contrast "a language of unusual force and power." Dominated by short, crisp, one and two syllable words, it was "simple, terse, and forcible." Its vocabulary was derived in the main from the "old Saxon tongue," which gave it the "force, precision, directness, and boldness" that made it the most suitable vehicle for the man of common sense, integrity, and character. Essentially, the beauty of English, as well as its power to speak eloquently to the hearts of men, came from the Saxon element, although as a "composite language" it benefited as well from "other affluent streams, which contribute to its wealth."

The English language was the language of freedom, and in it were enshrined

*"those great charters of liberty which are essential elements of free govern-*
*ments, and the main guarantees of personal liberty."* Here Crummell skated
on thin ideological ice. He quoted from several authorities to the effect that
English people owed their political stability to "the original propensities of
race."

> A love of freedom rarely felt,
> Of freedom in her regal seat
> Of England; not the school-boy heat,
> The blind hysterics of the Celt.[5]

But then he seemed to be arguing at the same time that the qualities of the
English people were neither innate, nor peculiar to them, but transferable to
anyone who spoke their language.

> . . . We must
> Be free or die! who speak the language
> Shakespeare spake; the faith and morals hold
> Which Milton held![6]

There can be no denying that Crummell's thinking was confused here. He
wanted to attribute the strength of English culture to its Saxon origins, and yet
he wanted to argue that West Africans could take on the characteristics of the
English by acquiring their language. No doubt there was a bit of cultural La-
marckism in this belief. By stretching after the superior fruits of British culture,
the aspiring African would undergo a fundamental change after generations.
Indeed, the changes were probably already under way, because "Negro as we
are by blood and constitution, we have been as a people, for generations in the
habitual utterance of Anglo-Saxon speech . . . over 200 years."

The greatest blessings to be associated with the English language came from
its "peculiar identity with religion." There was an intrinsic relationship between the excellence of the English language and the diction of the English
Bible. Crummell did not go into any detail as to why English should be any
better suited to the expression of Christian truth than any other language, such
as Greek, for example. He simply rhapsodized over the beauties of the King
James text and credited it with having been "the prompting spirit of legal
statutes, constitutional compacts, and scientific ventures."

While dwelling as he did "with delight upon the massy treasures of this
English tongue" that Providence had bestowed on West Africa, Crummell did
not want to be misunderstood as lacking moral outrage over the effects of the
slave trade. He insisted that he had the normal "feelings of a man" at
the "loss that had accompanied all this gain," but he saw the acquisition of
the English language as, indeed, a noble acquisition. He wanted to illustrate
the ways in which Providence had favored the Anglicized blacks "and justify
the ways of God to man."[7] Thus it was not his purpose to make more than
passing allusion to the rape of Africa, to the "whole tribes of men . . . destroyed, and nations on the threshold of civilization reduced to barbarism."

Providence had already compensated for some of this evil and promised even more. The obvious destiny of the English language in West Africa was to endow its speakers with "its thought, its wisdom, its practicality, its enterprising spirit, its transforming power." [8]

As a college professor, he felt he was obliged, as were government officers, ministers, teachers, and parents, "to introduce among our youthful citizens a sound and elevating English Literature." To this end he provided a list of books that could be depended upon to cultivate in a youthful mind "thought and reflection . . . , judgment and reason . . . , [and] a chaste and wholesome imagination." "My catalogue," he said, "would include the following works":

| | |
|---|---|
| Locke on the Mind. | Life of Benjamin Franklin. |
| Bacon's Essays. | Life of James Watt. |
| Butler's Analogy. | Life of Mungo Park. |
| Paley's Natural Theology. | History of Rome. |
| Wayland's Moral Philosophy. | History of Greece. |
| Bunyan's Pilgrim's Progress. | History of England. |
| Robinson Crusoe. | Milton's Poems. |
| Alison on Taste. | Cowper's Poems. |
| Watts on the Mind. | Burder's Self-Discipline. |
| Channing's Self Culture. | Todd's Student's Manual. |

In fairness to Crummell it should be borne in mind that he intended this list for fifteen-year-old-boys as a preparation for higher education. Similarities to the readings that were standard at the Oneida Institute are to be noted. He made it clear that he was not offering a list of the greatest classics of the English language, "the brilliant Essayists . . . , the profound Historians . . . , [nor] the sagacious Moralists," but "another class of books, not less distinguished indeed, but more level to the common taste." [9] Neither Plato, Shakespeare, nor the Bible, which, needless to say, he considered to have more intellectual or literary merit than *Robinson Crusoe,* were listed.

He seemed to have no compunction about putting *Robinson Crusoe,* with its degraded conception of darker people, into the hands of young Liberians. Perhaps because he distinguished between the African and the Oceanic peoples, seeing the latter as inferior and decadent, he was not offended by Defoe's description of Friday's instinctive servility. Or it may simply be that Crummell believed that the untutored savage must of necessity be docile when confronted by the representative of a "superior civilization." But it seems likely that the same tendencies to Anglophilism and Christian ethnocentrism that made him speak pejoratively of African languages also blinded him to the attitudes of race supremacy in *Robinson Crusoe.*

We can be certain that he would have found certain histories of Rome unacceptable, and yet he listed no specific authors or editions. We know that he would have found Gibbon's theory of the decline of Rome antithetical to his own and a dangerous thing in the hands of a schoolboy. He probably had specific editions in mind, for he remarked that several of the works were abridged, but with characteristic nineteenth-century disregard for exact bibliographic details, he overlooked the importance of specific citations. In a small city like Monrovia, it would be simple enough for anyone who desired specific recommendations to contact him for details. Perhaps he felt it unnecessary to mention editions since only certain ones were readily available. The main point that he seemed to be making was that a basic library of worthwhile books was "within the reach of every intelligent boy in the country." At that time the entire list could "be purchased for less than three dollars." [10]

Literate culture was equally necessary for women and for men. Crummell held the standard Victorian view on this position, blandly accepting the facile doctrine that "women must become the true and equal companions of men, and not their victims." The influence of women on young minds "is deeper and more powerful than that of man." He was appalled at the state of education for women in nineteenth-century Liberia and at the "general frivolousness of the female mind in this country." He expressed amazement at the contrast between the "rugged aspects of existence in this young country" and the fact that Parisian millinery could "maintain such a tyrannous control, as it does, over the sex." But he did not blame women severely for that state of things since he regarded dress as "the *only* fine Art we have in Liberia." Higher disciplines must be cultivated. Every "respectable householder" had the obligation to introduce his wife to some thoughtful literary journal such as *Littell's Living Age* or *Chambers' Journal.* Influential people should form literary clubs. A "female seminary" should be founded. Crummell foresaw a growing danger that Liberian men, humble though their educational attainments were, would soon be far in advance of the women. Only by making a strenuous effort could the country avoid the "dangerous state" of "mental inequality." This would retard the progress of our children, and before long the nation would "lose the freshness and force of all our Anglo-Saxon antecedents."

Crummell was not like Blyden, who over the years was to develop a respect for indigenous culture and Muslim civilization. Blyden eventually introduced courses in Arabic into the curriculum of the college, but Crummell had no appreciation for anything that was not Christian and only limited admiration for what was not English. While Blyden never completely abandoned the Eurocentric and Christian biases of his youth, he recognized that it would be impossible to develop a West African civilization if one did not cultivate an appreciation for the indigenous languages and cultures. To this end, he busied himself with the study of African languages. As many as forty have been attributed to him. Like Crummell, though, he accepted the doctrine that African languages were "incapable of expressing the finer forms of thought." [11] It should never be assumed that either Blyden or Crummell could have been capable of the twentieth-century cultural relativism that would allow African culture to be judged completely on its own terms. The faculty of Liberia College, despite the ideological hostilities that eventually developed among them, were all biased in favor of European points of view. While they forcefully defended the innate natural abilities of Africans as a race, they nonetheless assumed the inferiority of African languages, cultures, and societies.

Both for the college and for the female seminary, Crummell recommended what he called "a good, sound, moral, English Education." He was aware that it was impossible to create a university comparable to Cambridge overnight, but he did hope to establish an elite institution. Knowing what we do of his personality, we can be certain that he was committed to a high standard, and we can make reasonable assumptions about the attitudes he would have brought to the undertaking. Crummell saw himself as the sober curator of a stately museum, where the treasures of civilization must be maintained in all their solemn splendor to inspire the nation's reverence for the universal truths that had stood the test of time.

Not only did he regard himself as a "founding father," but he attempted to get the students of the college to see themselves in this way. The young men of the country must come to understand "The Responsibility of the First Fathers of a Country for Its Future Life and Character." Liberia was a new society, lacking "the bonds of olden manners and ancient customs." It was a frontier society with a sparse population, where adulthood was often premature. The results were appalling:

> Laxity prevails, freedom is exaggerated, control is loose and relaxed, and the young, for the most part, desire to do as they please. Thus will and inclination prove more powerful than conviction and duty, and hence a disposition is gendered to turn liberty into license, and to make desire the criterion of law.
>
> Inasmuch, then, as we are in the very circumstances which naturally beget such results, I would fain exhort young men to practice self-government; to accustom themselves to self-restraint. *Do not use all the liberty you have. Fall back a little from the margin of your freedom. Do not be too hasty to be self-asserting men.* [12]

For self-government to succeed in any nation, the people must "cultivate a spirit of generous forbearance, and learn the lesson of self-restraint." Otherwise the people would be "trammelled, chained, handcuffed" by their own passions. The government of a truly free system must "proclaim the *duties* of citizens as well as their rights." A truly free system was one that "reverence[d] law in the person of rulers" and recognized "the authority of God in governers and magistrates." To those who truly hoped to become scholars, he extended the advice that "Greek and Latin and science, though valuable, are not education," that education was "prudence, common sense, judgement, discretion, practicality." It was possible to become educated without ever going to school. Learning must be leavened with experience and wisdom. "The period of youth [was] the period of study, the period of self-regulation, the period for mental acquisitions, the period for careful preparation." The young men would best serve their country "by standing quietly in [their] lot, as expectant but humble youth; and not by rushing into spheres unfitted to [their] years and unadapted to [their] untrained powers." Publicly expressing such sentiments does not invariably secure the good will of young people, but Crummell claimed to have the support of his students as he entered into a series of wars with the college administration.

"These young men understand fully the designs and desires of this miserable clique," he wrote, "who for years have given themselves to one single effort to crush and kill every intelligent and cultivated black man in the country." [13] The sources of his difficulties were complex. Several years earlier, it had been suggested by Bishop Payne, and generally understood by all concerned, that a college under Episcopalian auspices was to serve as the place of residence for at least some of the professors. On his arrival in Monrovia he was asked by the board of trustees to reside in the college building "and to discipline the institution." Such an offer might have been acceptable under conditions that reinforced his authority and facilitated discipline. Perhaps immediately after the fire of 1855, when he had been desperate for any sort of housing, lodging in the college might have been acceptable, but now he gave a list of reasons why it was impossible for him to live at the college. The road to College Hill was poor, and during the rainy season it flooded and became impassable. The rugged state of the road would have made the cost of moving prohibitive. He would have had to employ another servant to bring his provisions from the market, and his wife would have had "to be conveyed by bearers to church and to town on all occasions." The final reason was most important. In a young country such as Liberia, the customs were "as yet too unfixed for the securing of that obedience, subjugation and order among a number of young men such as would enable a resident professor to command that quiet and undisturbed regularity, so necessary for study, investigation, and instruction." [14]

In this and in subsequent letters, Crummell began to complain about his salary. "I expect my profession to support me," he wrote. Could not some Episcopal clergyman in America be found who would contribute some two or three hundred dollars annually with the understanding that Crummell would preach to a congregation on the St. Paul's River? He reminded the trustees that he had five children to support, three of them away at school. In addition to these financial difficulties, he began immediately to experience others. This was at least in part his own fault, for there can be no question of Crummell's "difficult personality." Here he was demanding of the trustees of donations that they give him a higher salary, while at the same time he refused to comply with the terms of employment set by the board of trustees. He preached to the students in the college on the necessity of submitting to authority and yet was unable to submit to the authority even of those who paid his salary. His livelihood, in this nominally black man's country, was still dependent on the good will of whites, because the professional services that he was able to offer were not sufficiently in demand among blacks for them to be willing to pay him a salary. And now, in the years from 1863 to 1865, Crummell found himself in the painfully familiar position of repeatedly entreating white American sources to meet his needs. His tone became accusatory, bitter, vituperative. Finally, the inevitable happened and Crummell's position at the college began to erode.

When Joseph Tracy received Crummell's letter of February 16, he responded as formally and coldly as might have been expected. He did not understand what the difficulties were regarding Crummell's salary. He was not certain of the basis of Crummell's complaints. He did correct him on the point of the amount of his salary, which was not $850, as Crummell had maintained. On inspecting the records, however, Tracy discovered that Blyden was to be paid $850 by the New York Colonization Society, and, since $850 was the standard salary paid by the Episcopal church to West African missionaries, he admitted the possibility of a misunderstanding and promised to look into the matter. In any event, it does not seem that Crummell was any better remunerated for his services as a teacher than as a missionary. The Episcopal Board of Missions paid Crummell a salary of $850 per year for the entire period of his services to them, with the exception of those times when in fits of pique he refused to accept any salary at all.[15]

Tracy admitted to some perplexity about Crummell's objection to living at the college. He cited the American tradition of a tutor residing in the building and assuming responsibility for overseeing the students. Perhaps it would be possible to find someone with "sufficient authority" to function as a steward and keep the boys in order, although if they were "very noisy, the presence of a Professor seem[ed] the more desirable." If a road to the college was needed, perhaps the city government could be persuaded to construct one. This would seem "a very proper business for them," wrote Tracy in the same letter. "I do not recollect that the City, as a corporation, had done anything for the college. When Cities and Towns in this country have colleges planned in them, they are commonly made to contribute liberally towards some such expenses."[16]

Tracy had, of course, identified the problem. Liberia was not yet able to support financially or culturally such an ambitious undertaking as a national institution of higher learning. A good high school would have been more appropriate, as Bishop Payne had long ago realized. On the Liberian side, no one involved, including Crummell, had a clear idea of the task of a small college. Lacking experience, and with only three professors and eight students, it must have been difficult to create the feeling of a community of scholars. It is also clear that the professors were overworked. Crummell was, by his own admission, not strong in mathematics, nor had he any real credentials in natural philosophy. He was unquestionably capable of being a first-rate student and teacher of literature, but the demands made of him during his years in Liberia hardly left time for the rigorous program of study that was necessary. He was asked to spread himself a bit too thin and to assume responsibility for nine different subjects. The establishment of this "college," with its lack of faculty, lack of student body, and lack of financial support, can only have been an act of irresponsibility on the part of the Liberians and of cynicism on the part of the Boston trustees, who would never have endorsed such a venture on the part of whites, and who were in any case not prepared to offer substantial financial backing.

Of Crummell, it must be said that he was the victim of a pride that forced him into a position in which he could not be successful. He must have realized that a respectable college could not be established with a faculty of three, especially when only one of them had any experience with a first-rate university. And even Crummell, despite the years in Cambridge, was in an impossible situation, as he was soon forced to realize. This was, after all, his first job, and he had no expertise in some of the fields he was to teach.

While Crummell's training in moral philosophy was solid, it suffered from the deficiencies of British philosophical training in the nineteenth century. Professors at Cambridge were not appointed directly by the faculties of the various disciplines, but by the individual colleges of the university. This meant that colleges selected professors on the basis of any number of criteria, but in any case, more in accord with the needs of the college than the mastery of the discipline in which they were to teach. Tremendous stress was placed on upholding the university's excellent reputation in natural sciences and mathematics. As a result, lectures on theology or philosophy were often given by mathematicians or natural scientists who were outstanding in their own field, but who were to make no lasting impression on the history of philosophy or theology. Cambridge and its membership were much impressed with their own seventeenth-century traditions, which meant that they tended to look into their own past for inspiration in shaping modern disciplines. This worked rather well for the scientists, who could have found no better inspiration than Sir Isaac Newton. In the case of philosophy, however, it had stifled development, for Cambridge moral philosophers like William Whewell were unaffected by lines of inquiry and traditions of thought that were developing elsewhere. They simply cultivated their own tidy little English garden. The Cambridge Platonists of the seventeenth century were quaint and charming, but they were little remembered outside England, and they were inadequate to the needs of nineteenth-century Liberia. Whewell's casuistry dwelt on the errors of Hobbes, while important developments in German philosophy and theology were virtually ignored. Thus Crummell was not much influenced by the German Romantics, who might have helped him to appreciate folk culture, nor by the German nationalist theology that might have assisted him in creating a truly Liberian theology.

Crummell made imaginative use of the moral philosophy and theology that he read, adapting it to the situation that he confronted, with a wisdom that was seldom equalled. But he was in no position to reshape the contours of Western philosophy. He had no sense of participating in an academic community, and he was deprived of the intellectual and moral support that he might have expected had he lived in a society more appreciative of letters and learning. It was indicative of the nation's cultural and intellectual impoverishment that Wilmot Blyden, professor of classics, had only a high school education. To be sure, his natural intellectual powers were remarkable (probably more impressive than Crummell's), but he was nonetheless entirely self-trained. Ironically, being self-trained did not free him from many of the same Eurocentric biases that British and American trained black intellectuals were victim to.

It was actually a poor excuse for a college, which ultimately explains Crummell's unhappiness there; the dream of being a college professor and making a living at his trade was unrealistic at that place and time. The economic, social, and political bases for a Liberian college did not yet exist. Americans, especially in the middle of the Civil War, could not be expected to finance the operation. In any case, they probably felt, in the months following the Emancipation Proclamation, that it was time for Liberians to become more self-sufficient. Crummell's bad–tempered and recurrent demands for assistance met with the same lack of sympathy that had greeted his complaints to the Episcopal Mission Board during the 1850s. His experience at the college ended in failure, for although the requirements he stated were perfectly legitimate, the people to whom he expressed them felt no obligation to meet his needs.

On March 8, 1865, he received word from his two daughters at Oberlin that they were in debt and wanted him to come there. It is interesting that he sent them to Oberlin and not to Wilberforce, a black institution run by the Methodist Episcopal church in Ohio. His reason may have been his growing distaste for mulattos, for Wilberforce had become a refuge for the natural children of Southern planters. It had also experienced considerable instability during the early 1860s. One daughter, Frances A. Crummell, was enrolled in the Preparatory Department of the College from 1863–1866. Where the other daughter was during those years is not certain, although it is possible she was enrolled in the Oberlin public schools.[17] He was certain that he could secure permission from the executive committee of the college to make the trip but assumed that during the leave of absence his salary was to be stopped. "Nevertheless I must go," he wrote, "for my daughters, girls 14 and 16 years old, must needs have their father with them to cross the ocean."[18]

The records of the Boston trustees reveal that some attempt was made to meet his needs, although the response was not particularly sensitive to emotional distress, aggravated by his frustrations in dealing with Roberts and the executive committee. While the trustees were not entirely unfeeling they decided that a leave of absence was neither necessary nor within their power to grant, but they tried to be helpful. They advised that the young ladies should remain at Oberlin until "opportunity could be found for their safe and respectable return to Liberia." In the meantime, the trustees were prepared if necessary to be responsible for the expenses of his daughters at Oberlin "to such amount as may be requested, not exceeding one hundred dollars each for one year."[19]

Despite their decision, during the spring of 1865 he returned for his daughters, which did not please the college administration. President Roberts felt that Crummell had "strange ideas" concerning "college government and privileges." When informed of the trustees' "very liberal proposition," he felt certain that Crummell would have realized that his trip was unnecessary. Unfortunately the letter of the trustees had reached Roberts on June 30 and Crummell had departed around May 17. Roberts' annoyance was certainly understandable. There were still only two teachers in the college, and a third professor, Martin H. Freeman, a graduate of Middlebury College, who had only recently been appointed and was "still laboring under the effects of acclimation." Thus, an undue burden has been placed on both the faculty and the students.[20]

Crummell's association with Liberia College lasted only three years, seven months of which he spent outside the country. There was perhaps sufficient justification for this absence, for his personal affairs were extremely trying. His father had died, and when Crummell returned to Liberia he brought not only his daughters, but his aged mother, all of them financially helpless.[21] But it was undeniable that he had inconvenienced his colleagues and aroused the resentment of the administration. Not surprisingly, his relations with the president and the executive committee of the college went from bad to worse. On April 20, 1866, the executive committee passed a set of resolutions accusing Crummell of failure to perform his teaching and other duties at the college. Crummell responded in detail, as was his wont, insisting that he had done everything that could reasonably be expected and refusing to do more. He reminded the committee that the eighteen days he had missed during the first term were due to "re-acclimation; and then only at the remonstrance of [his] physician, who rebuked [his] persistent attendance to duty and at length declared that he would not be responsible for [his] life unless [he] ceased the performance of [his] College labours." The process of reacclimation had to be repeated after returning from his second trip abroad. Then his mother had been dangerously ill, which had caused him to lose another four days. He had been kept away on one occasion by a "violent storm," and on another by "court duties."[22]

He complained bitterly of President Roberts, whom he characterized as an "informer," describing him with characteristically bitter sarcasm.

> The President of the College is perched day by day on the Piazza of the College. He watches the approach of a Professor. He setteth in his book when he cometh to the College or when he is absent. . . . . If any Committee were to make a request of the kind upon the President of either Harvard, Yale, Columbia, or any other College in the U.S. he would reject it as a gross personal insult.

Observing that the rains were coming, he informed the committee that he would soon provide them with the opportunity to cut his salary. During the rainy season the roads were impassable, and, claiming that he and nearly everyone else in Monrovia was sick and enfeebled, he was resolved to stay at home.[23]

He insisted that he gave the students sufficient work to do and that they constantly complained of the work load. If he were to push the students as hard as the college rules formally required, they would be forced to spend seven and a half hours a day in "close and strenuous mental application." Not even a man, much less a boy, could be expected to exert himself to such an extent in a tropical climate. It "would only prepare the road for numerous graves or a lunatic asylum." He went on to speak, as professors are fond of doing, of the strenuous nature of his discipline, which was abstract, which required close mental application,which embraced subjects that "tax the brain and body of great men." He must prepare himself for every lecture, and he flatly maintained that he could not spend three or four hours a day in his study and then "lecture three full hours more at the College in this clime."[24]

He recalled the practices he had observed at Cambridge, where Dr. Whewell had lectured on moral philosophy twice a week. The same was true of "the great Dr. Blunt." He had never known a professor at Cambridge to deliver over one lecture a day, or more than twice or three times a week. To buttress his point, Crummell cited the schedules of classes of a number of American colleges, where the amount of lecturing commonly required was "less than one half of what I have done in this College of Liberia; in this tropical clime." He accused the committee of blindly and inexcusably attempting to "measure with my brain and my time as you would measure tape or twine." And how was one to go about retaining the attention of youth beyond thirty or fifty minutes? From his experiences as a preacher, he knew that it was silly to try to hold the attention of an audience beyond thirty minutes, even when one gave sermons twice a week. He was righteously indignant at the idea that he should be expected to give a competent daily lecture for sixty minutes in each of his subjects.

> I beg to say that even as I wouldn't preach from the pulpit, so I do not intend to lecture in the class room one second beyond 35 minutes at the farthest. My usual lecture is about thirty minutes and when I have finished my lectures, I expect to dismiss the students and retire.[25]

He observed in another communication that Professor Roberts had "never opened his mouth to deliver a lecture since the College was opened. He *listens* indeed to a young man who reads Blackstone to him an hour or less in the morning."[26]

On April 12, 1866, a meeting of the faculty was held at which Crummell and Blyden were allowed to put questions to certain students about the quality and rigor of the instruction being provided. According to the minutes, Blyden's questions were quite terse, but Crummell gave a sermon.

> Have you or have you not frequently complained of the amount of labor the Professor of mental and moral science has given you from the first term 1863 to the present? Have you or have you not complained of the incessant daily toil and as a general thing with only the loss of a day to which I have subjected you from the first term 1863? Have you or have you not frequently remonstrated with me for coming to the College when I have been sick and enfeebled and had to pause in my lecture on account of it?

The faculty meeting ended after passing a resolution, unanimously adopted by the professors, over the president's dissent, to the effect that the professors were doing as much as possible, due mainly to their spirit of self-sacrifice. They would continue to toil faithfully away, and in recognition of this they demanded the respect of the president and trustees of Liberia College. The resolution went on to state their refusal to submit to indignities offered by the president, the executive committee, or the Boston board. They declared that "as Negroes, they [were] determined to uphold the honor of the race against the efforts and intrigues of some who [had] no confidence in the African, and whose malignity [was] ever at work in Liberia to humble and disgrace *black men.*"[27]

This last was an open attack on President Roberts, whom Crummell and Blyden blamed for many of their problems—both inside and outside the college. Both of them were now openly expressing their hostility to a mulatto clique, headed by Roberts, which sought the humiliation of all true Negroes. Blyden arose at four o'clock in the morning, two days after the meeting, to pour out his feelings on the subject to Crummell. On the preceding evening, he had spoken with John H. Chavers, Secretary of the Treasury, a man known for his conservatism, who had predicted "a terrible conflict . . . between the blacks and the confounded bastards." Blyden entreated Crummell to inform the trustees of donations that there could never be harmony between Roberts and the rest of the faculty. The Roberts clique was harassing members of the faculty by delaying salary payments, if not withholding them. They must put the financial matters of the college in the hands of sympathetic managers. Timely action must be taken on this and on related matters, "which unless soon settled may bring upon this country the scenes that have been enacted in Haiti." "As you are aware," wrote Blyden, "all the students are with us, and all the *thinking* black men."[28]

In the meantime, Crummell had become involved in a fight over the admission of women to the college. He had applied to the faculty for the admission of his eldest daughter, and a majority of the faculty had voted to admit "girls of a proper age and aquirements." The executive committee, however, had not consented, remarking that the "state of the country made it doubtful whether it would work well." Crummell, of course repeated his old arguments about the necessity of women in a new country being well educated. The lack of educational facilities for women was leading to "ruin in the highest spheres of life, girls and married women, till the land is filled with iniquity and grossness." The reason was plain; men were spoiling their daughters, bringing them up "in laziness, and ignorance, and indulgence." The trustees of the college were just as guilty for wanting to abandon young women to "the ways of sin and mental blindness." While it was commendable of Crummell to think of educating his daughters and opening the doors of education in Liberia to young women, it is interesting to note that he had earlier refused to live in the college because it was not a fit place to bring his family.[29]

Even if the resources of the college and the soul of its president had been larger, they would have found it difficult to meet his demands. In any case, they were justified in suspecting that perhaps he had some unstated reasons for his trip to the United States. To some extent he was seeking to advance his personal ambitions. To be sure his loyalties were divided, and his sense of commitment had begun to erode. On the other side, the institution lacked the generosity of spirit that a stable and competent institution might have had. It did not have the resources to respond to the professional or personal problems of its three-member faculty.

The Boston trustees eventually decided that Crummell was more trouble than he was worth and decided to give Roberts a free hand in disciplining him. Crummell, for his part, went so far as to work for several months without salary, rather than humble himself to Roberts. He continued to appeal to the board, apparently unaware that their sympathy was irretrievably lost. In his mind the issue was clearly a matter of mulatto caste-hostility toward him and other blacks. Indeed he was certain he knew what they were saying of him in private conversations: "Push the nigger thru!" "Take him down!" "Humble the dog!" How did he know this? He had heard "just the same remarks for three years concerning the late Stephen A. Benson, whose great misfortune was that he was a *black man*." He appealed to the trustees of donations to pay him directly, to take the responsibility "out of the hands of these wretched unscrupulous men," who were "as Negro hating as the voters of Memphis."[30] He attributed to one of the members of the executive committee the statement, "Your true black man is inferior, and can't do anything." The mulattos had been determined from the beginning to make things difficult for Blyden and Crummell. Blyden had said to him at the time they were hired that Roberts and his set would never allow them "to remain in [the] College as men."[31] He complained increasingly of being subjected to gross insult in the land where he had come to dispense religion and civilization "within a day's journey of the very spot whence my father was stolen in his boyhood." Even here, in this land which ought to be his own, he was pursued by "a filthy class . . . who hate the Negro more intensely than any slave-dealer at the South ever did.—men whose whole life has been spent crushing out black men."[32] He sent exactly the sort of letter that Blyden, at daybreak, on April 14, had requested of him, unveiling the ugly color conflicts that seemed to be central to the life of the college. "Through skill and by cunning, Liberia [had] been turned into a great Plantation. Colonizationists in the U.S.A. were, although unaware, employing two lazy overseers to exercise control over black men. At the risk of causing pain and displeasure, he felt constrained to set forth the plain facts. He did it, so he claimed, to fight against "one of the most wicked consipiracies and virulent principles of caste." The situation was even worse than that in the West Indies, Where the "half caste [was] more virulent than the prejudiced white man." There, at least, the mulatto often had the benefit of being sent to Europe by his white father for an education; in Liberia, the "brains, strong thought, the large mental capacity have been and are now, the Negro's."[33]

Blyden reports that Crummell eventually delivered an ultimatum; the board must either get rid of Roberts or accept his resignation. On July 11, 1866 the trustees decided to let Crummell go. Blyden was retained, partly because his salary was not paid out of Boston but by the New York Colonization Society. Apparently Roberts had spoken up for him too, saying that he would be more difficult to replace than Crummell since he was "unquestionably the best linguist in the country,and a good teacher of languages.'' Furthermore, he was more conciliatory. On January 28, 1867, he wrote to Roberts, ''I confess I was wrong. I most deeply regret it and hope that the executive Committee will accept my earnest apology.'' Thus, although Blyden was a less than tractable employee, he was by no means as temperamental, vituperative, or insubordinate as Crummell.[34]

Crummell loftily kept up the pretense that he still had some control over the situation. On October 10, he wrote to the trustees of donations to offer his resignation but changed his mind before finishing the letter. He insisted that the executive committee of the college had illegally deprived him of a portion of his salary. Five days later, he wrote again to Boston to say that the students in the college had called upon him and requested that he conclude his course of lectures on ''Intellectual Philosophy and Paley's Evidences.'' He had in consequence decided to withhold his resignation until late November, ''which will be within the sixty days prescribed by you.'' He requested that the committee have his salary paid to him in full at an early date.[35]

# 9

# Last Battles with the Bishop
## (1867–1870)

The years of humiliation and abuse were taking their toll on Alex Crummell. He had become defensive, irascible, and quick to take umbrage at the slightest offense. His sense of humor had suffered and he had lost the little toleration he had for human foolishness and frailty. Indicative of the hardening of his personality was an embarrassing exchange of accusatory letters with a neighbor who mistakenly believed him to have borrowed and then failed to return "a botanical work by Balfour." The neighbor hoped that their "present estrangement [would] not develop into an open rupture" but insisted that he must hold Crummell responsible and invoked the standards of "commonplace honor" in demanding the book's return. On the same day, apparently having discovered his mistake, he wrote to apologize, but Crummell's immediate response was to inform his accuser that he was "perfectly at liberty to run into an 'open rupture.' " Later in the day, after receiving the apology, Crummell wrote:

> Sir:
> I do not accept of yr. apology. Yr. note to me was couched in the language of a ruffian; and I beg to add that I am equally indifferent to yr. excusatory phrases as I was this noon to yr. rude and vulgar language.[1]

The exchange took place only three weeks before Crummell's departure for America to look after his daughters' welfare, and, perhaps his excessive reaction may be excused in view of his concern for their difficulties. The same righteous irritability was displayed in his reaction to a long-dead issue. He expended considerable emotional energy responding to a passing statement made in print by Bishop Payne that his services to the church from 1856 to 1858 had been irregular. He secured testimonials from a number of persons that he had performed the duties of pastor to the New York and Louisiana settlements out-

162

side Monrovia during those years. He continued to agitate for the formation of a black diocese in Liberia that would be administratively free of white control, although presumably entitled to financial support from the American church. Since returning to Liberia, he had continued his agitation, now thoroughly convinced that the bishop was determined to keep all power in his own hands at Cape Palmas and to prevent black men from gaining control of the church in Liberia. He continued to assert that Africa was to be evangelized by Africans, in which category he seemed to include himself.

Bishop Payne believed that Crummell's trip to the United States in 1865 had really been for the purpose of soliciting funds for the independent church.[2] Crummell had, in fact, taken advantage of his presence in the States to advocate his black separatist ecclesiastical views. His argument was systematic, if not completely logical, and based on three principles which he apparently held as axiomatic. First, it was clear that Africa could never be raised solely by her own efforts, for there was no record in history of any "rude, heathen people" who had raised themselves by their own spontaneous efforts from paganism to "spiritual superiority." Second, material economic efforts alone would never be sufficient for the elevation of Africa. The history of European commerce with West Africa had been nothing other than "a history of war, rapine, murder, and wide-spread devastation." It seemed obvious that material forces could not uplift Africa without the aid of spiritual ones. The economic redemption of Africa would require its spiritual redemption, thus the need for a missionary effort. This led to his third point, that missionary efforts had so far met with limited success; they had overlooked "the great principle which lies at the basis of all successful propagation of the Gospel, namely, the employment of all [sic] indigenous agency." He used the term indigenous with a cavalier comprehensiveness, blithely classifying all black people as Africans. He placed great value on the fact that there had been a migration of Barbadians into Liberia during the preceding two years. Only one week before he sailed for Liberia, a shipload of immigrants had arrived, and "most of these persons were Episcopalians."[3] Crummell presented the picture of "a steady, quiet, uninterrupted emigration of cultivated colored men, who are coming over from Jamaica, Antigua, Barbadoes, St. Kitts, St. Thomas, and Demarara" in large part due to an invitation extended by the Liberian president. The migrants were civilized, Christianized, many of them men who had "ate their teems" at the Inns of London, that was to say, products of the law schools, and others who had studied in British universities. He called on American Episcopalians to enter into the spirit represented by the Bishop of Barbadoes, the Baptist leadership in Virginia, and the Presbyterians of Jamaica in strongly supporting an "indigenous" ministry as the principal agent for the uplift of Africa.[4]

Crummell continued to agitate for an "indigenous" church administration during the years of his appointment at Liberia College. As he accepted the fact that the college was a travesty, he found more time to involve himself in church politics. He had not abandoned the idea of a career in education, and he wrote to William Coppinger, Secretary of the American Colonization Society, to express his continuing concerns. He had read in *African Repository* that a woman had left five thousand dollars for a High School for girls in Liberia, entrusted to the President of the American Colonization Society. Could Coppinger inform him if these funds were for an Episcopal school? Was it to be a missionary school or a school for the Liberians proper? Crummell also attempted to persuade the Colonization Society of the need for a theological seminary. It thus seems possible that as he became increasingly disappointed with the failings of Liberia College, he looked about for alternative ways of pursuing an academic career. But it also seems probable that when finally confronted with the demands of college teaching he decided that he had different interests.

He would rather be Bishop of Liberia than Professor of Moral Science. Much of his activity, according to Bishop Payne, was directed to that end. This was what lay behind his continual preaching on the need for an "indigenous ministry." He also angered the bishop by his failure to support him in the trial of Rev. Thomas J. Thompson, a black man. Payne wrote to Crummell in the spring of 1864, asking him to serve as a member of the court where Thompson was to be charged with sexual misconduct. The bishop gave credence to reports of Thompson's "carnality" with one Mrs. Minor, which he said were "universally" believed. In a letter to Thompson, he had accused him of having fathered a child with Mrs. Minor, "which all assert resembles you." He exhorted Thompson to make a confession, in which case he might hope for some sort of future connection with the mission. "But in case of trial and *deposition* from the *ministry* you could scarcely expect to be again employed."[5]

Crummell told the bishop that he and the other clergy were looking into the "sad case" of Rev. Thompson, and that Mr. John Dennis, Secretary of the Standing Committee of the Diocese, would forward full details. Crummell soon received from Thompson a copy of the bishop's letter of accusation, along with a cover letter in which Thompson neither confessed to nor denied the charges. In view of the fact that Crummell was making enemies all over Liberia at the time with his preaching against rum and sexual license, he was astonishingly quiet and tolerant when it came to the issue of Thompson. It is also interesting to note that Thompson was a political ally of Crummell, Stokes, and Gibson in the fight against Bishop Payne's attempt to define Liberia as a part of the Cape Palmas mission rather than as an independent diocese.[6]

Bishop Payne criticized him severely in his report of October 1864, complaining to the Board of Missions of the "hasty action of some of the Liberian clergy in . . . organizing the 'Diocese of Monrovia.' " The organization had been effected without the knowledge or consent of Payne, or the churches in Liberia, or the church in the United States. That Payne did not think much of the organization goes without saying. How could a diocese consist of but three clergymen, in this case Messrs. Stokes, Crummell, and Gibson? Indeed, at the time the report was written Stokes had gone abroad to solicit funds and Crummell was employed at Liberia College.[7]

In his report to the General Convention in the following year, and in correspondence with the Board of Missions, the bishop reiterated these points and added a few new ones. He presented a number of legal objections to the activities of the Monrovian clergy and objected further on the grounds that their principal concern was not with converting the heathen. In Payne's eyes, it was self-evident and practically indisputable that this ought to be the primary work of the church in West Africa. He lamented the fact that so many of the Liberian clergy followed secular occupations or accepted political offices. They gave the argument that they must do so in order to influence the institutions of their infant country, and Crummell had defended this evil doctrine in public addresses at home and abroad. This excessive secularity, which Crummell had supported, was the reason why they had so little time to work among the heathen. Thus the need for the continuing control of affairs by Bishop Payne, whose priorities were well-known. Matters could not be entrusted to such persons as Crummell, who was too obsessed with ungodly ambition to properly attend to his ministry.[8]

Crummell insisted that he had consistently performed priestly duties on a voluntary basis and out of a pure love of duty since returning to Liberia in 1863. He had, at that time, responded to a call from the people of Caldwell to become their rector. The church of St. Peter's had been under the nominal charge of Gibson, Stokes, and Russell at that time, with Gibson taking the greater part of the responsibility. Early in 1863, Gibson had presided at a vestry meeting during which Crummell was elected rector, Gibson gave up his charge, and a call was issued to Rev. Crummell. "From that time until '65, I served them in the dews and rains with rare intermission, and at my own expense."[9]

There were difficulties. The bishop reported to Denison that Mr. Russell was losing parishioners to Crummell's rival congregation. Russell soon found an ally in Crummell's senior warden, S. S. Powers. The man had given Crummell considerable difficulty, and he had been forced "to put him back from the communion table," for it was said "that he gave his wife up to pollution and lived off the gains of her sin." The man was widely reputed to be a most disgraceful womanizer, and when he drove his wife (who was also his adopted daughter) out of his house to take up with a new mistress, Crummell went to reprove him. "As was to be expected, he became bitter and indignant," but he was supported by Stokes and Russell and later by the bishop. Much of the hostility Crummell attributed to a sermon he had preached on divorce, which "aroused the ire of all the clerical as well as lay adulterers in this country." His enemies secured the services of "a drunken fighter" named Barnes and a "rum-seller" named Powers to threaten him physically if Crummell ever set foot in St. Peter's again. All the substantial people of the congregation had withdrawn with him, inspired by his sermons, which had brought about a minor awakening throughout the country and a tightening up of procedures in the divorce courts.[10]

When Russell failed to appear in the church after three or four weeks, Crummell and his congregation returned and attempted to hold a service. He had proceeded as far as the second lesson, when in came Barnes, Powers, and a third person named Blacklidge, who ordered him to leave the church. Barnes snatched the Bible from Crummell and threw it down on the floor, and Crummell "marched out of the church," his female members following. Mr. Russell meanwhile was "at the waterside, waiting intelligence of the result." Crummell enumerated the sins of his assailants:

> Powers: Rum-seller and adulterer
> Barnes: Drunken fighter, curser of heaven
> Blacklidge: charged to this day by a pure woman with *rape* . . .

He recalled that Hoffman had once said he "wouldn't touch Blacklidge with a ten foot pole," and he reminded the bishop of reports he had received on Russell's character.[11]

Crummell's friend, Rev. Mr. Gibson, who could always be counted on to transport rumors, informed him around this time that his enemies in the college were in collusion with his enemies in the church. Stokes had apparently been to see a man named Dr. F. McGill, a merchant and shipper of Monrovia, who was harassing him in the college, while Stokes and Russell badgered him in the church. "We'll root him out," Stokes was alleged to have said. Crummell was certain that McGill, on whom he depended for provisions, was in collusion with President Roberts. McGill had recently refused to honor his drafts and had then been heard to remark, "Now I have got him, and I'll hold him here!"[12]

Crummell's politics were Machiavellian as he plotted with Stokes to oppose the bishop; Stokes was no less devious, as he sided with Crummell against the bishop and with Russell against Crummell. In 1865 Crummell and Stokes, but not Russell, were among a group of Liberian clergymen who published a pamphlet attacking Payne. Payne responded with a lengthy letter to Bishops Burgess and Beddell, members of the Special Committee on Missions.[13] Payne insisted that Crummell was the author of the pamphlet and linked it with his well-known history of agitation on behalf of a black national church. Crummell had joined with E. W. Stokes, of all people, and Rev. T. J. Thompson to participate in "The General Councils of the Protestant Episcopal Church in Liberia," which Payne asserted had no legal status. Several years earlier, four clergymen, including Crummell, Stokes, Thompson, and G.W. Gibson, had taken over the general convocation. The four objected to the organization of the meetings, which they said concentrated all power in the bishop's hands. Stokes presided at the opening of the meeting and called it to order in the name of the clergy who were citizens of Liberia. Payne had known in advance that something was afoot, having been informed of it by Mr. Gibson in casual conversation. He had correctly interpreted this as a procedural move to exclude him on the basis of race, and had thought at first that he would not attend, but, after a sleepless night, Payne came anyway, feeling it was his right and duty to do so, regardless of the humiliation involved.[14]

Payne continued to press the point that he had made so often in the past. Cape Palmas was a missionary post. The duties of the Episcopalians in West Africa should be primarily missionary. The Liberian priests were not concerned with evangelizing the heathen. They pleaded instead "the necessity of giving their energies almost entirely to developing and promoting the interests, material and moral, of the Liberian population proper.'' Furthermore, the black Episcopalians were engaged in sundry political and commercial enterprises. They held political offices, engaged in business, became judges, and openly defended such conduct. Payne reported that ''Mr. Crummell, very soon after he came to Monrovia bought a farm, built a house on it, and soon after removed to it. He is now professor at Liberia College, and has a store in his house, kept by his son.'' Payne condemned such activities, claiming that it was because of their commercial and political involvements that the Liberian clergy had so little time for the heathen. By continuing to insist on the primacy of direct missionary work, and by emphasizing the fact that Liberians were preoccupied with other activities, Payne was able to justify his own presence in West Africa. The blacks were unwilling to perform the work which he considered most important of all, thus the need for a continuing white missionary presence under the jurisdiction of the Bishop of Cape Palmas and Parts Adjacent.[15]

Bishop Payne recounted the story of his relationship with Crummell, asserting that he had always handled him benevolently, even during the period of his estrangement from the Board of Missions in the mid-1850s. Crummell had been dismissed, not by the bishop, but by the Foreign Committee, ''because while receiving as much salary as any other missionary, he wrote that he could not live on his salary.'' The bishop had visited him on his farm and found him living in extreme poverty. On his own initiative he had made him principal of the high school at Cape Palmas, for it seemed at that time that the possibility of his being attached to the college was doubtful. On his arrival at Cape Palmas, the Bishop recalled, ''I gave him a favorite cow, which with other things given to his family by Mrs. Payne amounted to $30–40.'' He denied that anything discourteous or unpleasant had ever transpired between them. Although he had found Crummell ''blunt and dogmatical,'' he insisted that they had both always given and received the courtesies appropriate to their relationship, during this period.

But Crummell had never been able to live within his budget, and he had steadfastly refused to give an accounting of his finances to the acting treasurers of the diocese. Payne denied the charges made in a pamphlet published by the Liberian clergy that he had tried to keep them in a state of inferiority and subordinate tutelage. He reminded the committee that he was even now in the process of writing a series of articles for the *Cavalla Messenger* on the glories of ancient African kingdoms. This he offered as proof of his belief in the capacity of the African for civilization and self-government. Furthermore, the bishop cited instances when he had been received by the president of Liberia, entertained at large public banquets, and congratulated on the success of his mission. Clearly his contributions were appreciated by the Liberians, regardless of what the pamphlet said.

Payne went on to express his fears on the antiwhite feeling along the coast, in Monrovia, Sierra Leone, and Lagos. In Sierra Leone, a young native, believed to have been educated in the Church Missionary School, but lately returned from England, had caned a church missionary—Rev. Mr. Hindler—in the street, because he would not make way for him. On the whole, the nine churches of Sierra Leone were loyal to their English bishop, "yet there is at Sierra Leone, at Cape Coast Castle, and Lagos, a ceaseless war between the partially civilized native communities in those places and the English government as represented in its civil and military employees." Although it seemed clear that there was some resentment of whites among West Africans, Payne was convinced that "no Colony or Mission on the Coast can dispense with the active European and American influence for some time to come without a rapid retrograde succeeding."

Payne claimed that the principal cause of antiwhite sentiment among the Liberian clergy was to be found in "the character, antecedents, and principles of Alexander Crummell." Crummell was endowed with a vigorous mind; he was a good writer and preacher, "the mere composition and delivery considered." But the bishop feared that grace was wanting in Crummell's case, and that the many slights and insults he had experienced since his childhood in New York had filled his heart with indignation and hatred. He was "plucked" from his class, the bishop noted, apparently forgetting that he had earned a valid degree, albeit a very ordinary one. But the experiences in England had awakened desires in him that were impossible to fulfill, especially in a mission church in a politically undeveloped country. And he was inordinately ambitious, said the bishop. "From the time of his arrival, . . . he esteemed himself the proper Leader in all respects for the Church and Nation." The principle that seemed to guide his conduct was the belief "that the white man has no rights or mission in Africa." It mattered not how amiable the white man might be, Crummell was filled with the intensest hatred, a hatred that could only be disguised with difficulty. To illustrate this demonic aspect of his character, the bishop told the story of how Crummell once received an invitation to preach at St. Mark's for "my beloved brother Hoffman . . . grown gray in the service of Christ in Africa."

> He turned on his heel and said in the most angry manner, "Preach for him! I'll do no such thing!" But afterwards turned again with the most complacent smile and said, "I will preach," and he did . . .

Payne now blamed Crummell for almost every manifestation of racial hostility among the black Episcopalians. Ten years earlier, he had blamed everything on Stokes, but now Crummell was seen as the principal agitator, through whose influence the prejudice against whites in Monrovia had become as intense as the antiblack feeling in the United States.[16] The bishop had apparently forgotten that Crummell had once been his ally against Stokes. Now he recalled that shortly after Crummell's arrival he had heard disconcerting reports about his loyalty. Indeed he had heard from a reliable source that Crummell had labored to undermine his authority since his first day in Africa, and Crummell had himself practically confessed to a desire to circumvent his power by establishing a rival diocese in Liberia. His ego had been inflated by American churchmen, who had led him to aspire to the office. But in Africa, even the blacks, both clerical and lay, had spoken of his pride, called him a bad man, and in one case had even said that it would be better for Liberia if he had never come. The source of the discord could have been none other than Alexander Crummell. In the meantime Crummell was writing to the Foreign Committee to complain about Payne and the series of injurious reports filed against him during his twelve years of residence in Liberia. "For the missionaries who have come out here, especially the ladies, have told me of these reports and of their gratification at finding them false." [17]

The alliance between Crummell and Stokes was not fated to last. In January of 1866, Stokes visited Russell with reports of Crummell's machinations, which he feared would destroy the church. Crummell had drafted in his own hand "An Act for the Incorporation of Religious Societies." [18] Stokes rushed to Russell with tales of Crummell's political maneuvers. Russell described Stokes coming into the Senate chambers "with a most formidable 'bull' in shape of a protest against Crummell being made Bishop—said bull and charges being made formidable, and if true they leave brother C's soul in very bad health." Even with far superior documentation, it would be impossible to know all that happened in these secret political meetings, but it is clear that Crummell was prepared to use any means to gain control of the church in Liberia, and that he had no great reverence for the principle of separation of church and state.

Crummell continued to serve the congregation at Caldwell after his return to Liberia in 1865, except during September and October of 1866, when he was prevented from personally attending to the congregation by "a dangerous attack of liver complaint, superinduced by excessive labours during my connection, as professor, with Liberia College." He had been able to convert four Methodist families, one Baptist, and one Presbyterian. They constituted the basis for a new congregation, and so he had gathered St. Stephen's Church. His parishioners were mostly poor people, "most of the women" widows, living together like sisters and sharing their "slender portions of food." Native Africans and recaptured Congoes also attended all the services. Having already worked in the area before going to Cape Palmas in 1858, he was somewhat known there, and he expressed delight that there was still a strong desire for the Episcopal liturgy. "Generous Christian friends in the United States" were called on to send prayer books, a communion service, funds for the support of a resident schoolmaster, and a surplice. He noted in his letters that several members of the congregation could chant the *Gloria Patri* unassisted.

Amazingly resourceful at winning friends and influencing people when he wished to do so, Crummell was able to secure the aid of a prominent American clergyman, Rev. Dr. Stephen H. Tyng, Rector of St. George's Church in New York, to replace his frame building with a "neat brick chapel." During his trip to New York during 1865, he had described the need for a more substantial building to replace the old frame building which had been destroyed by tornadoes and the "bugabug." Dr. Tyng, who had already financed the building of Trinity Church in Monrovia, authorized him immediately to draw on him for funds, and Crummell hailed him as one who had labored most consistently "for the freedom of the black man on his own native soil." Apparently aware of the variety of criticism constantly lodged against the Americo-Liberian clergy by Bishop Payne, Crummell made certain that the missionary aspects of this event were advertised. The address on laying the cornerstone was published in the *Spirit of Missions*. Here he stressed the theme of "conquest and possession in the name of the Lord Jesus Christ of all this heathen country." He spoke of the duty to uplift the "abject and degraded population" from the tyranny of Satan and from "Paganism, Fetichism, Greegreeism, [and] Devilism." [19]

The bishop complained constantly that the Liberian clergy showed no interest in converting the heathen, but even his slanted tendentious letters acknowledge that Crummell could not be characterized as an Americo-Liberian elitist, seeking shelter in Monrovia from the rigors of frontier life. Missionary work along the river was, in fact, grueling and unglamorous. It was work among simple folk, and it involved considerable preaching to the heathen as well as to the inadequately instructed Christian settlers.

The settlement of New Georgia, where Crummell organized a congregation in May 1867, had a motley ethnic composition, which Crummell called "a mixed population, partly black American and partly recaptives . . . Eboes, Congoes, etc." Their religious teaching he described as the "worst character." The people had approached members of his Caldwell congregation, and through them invited him to visit their town, which he had done within a fortnight. "With a promptness and dispatch which surprised," they organized the Church of St. James, elected Crummell rector, and began to discuss the construction of a church. He described his new parishioners as "poor, uneducated, hard working." Not a man or woman at the organizational meeting wore shoes, "and yet they acted with the courtesy of the most polished gentle folk and with the generousness of the sincerest Christians." As a demonstration of this generosity, they provided lodging and board for their rector when he visited New Georgia, at the common expense. And yet for the most part the people were "indigent persons, who get their living by catching fish, cutting lumber, burning shells for lime, etc." A Sunday School was soon established, with a class made up of "natives, half-Americans, and Americo-Liberians." [20]

Crummell entreated American philanthropists on behalf of persons whom he thought were suited to assist him in his missionary work. There was a Mr. Paulus, "a most prudent and pious man, one of the noblest men I have seen on this coast." He had come from St. Thomas to the United States, with the purpose of migrating to Liberia, and had made the crossing with the Crummells when they returned in 1863. Although Crummell was inadequately supported himself, he nonetheless sought financial assistance for Paulus so that he could become a candidate for Orders. In the meantime, he had undertaken to provide this "sober grave man of a cheerful disposition [with] board, washing, and instruction in theology for at least six months," or until it was ascertained whether the board was prepared to give him support. [21]

He traveled up and down the river, to the settlements of Georgia, Virginia,

Caldwell, Lousiana, small, hot, humid towns, with none of the conveniences of modern life—no libraries, no witty intellectual discourse, no concerts or art galleries. The congregations were not large; there were a few baptisms per month, one or two marriages, a Sunday School class with perhaps two dozen scholars. Although small, the congregations were widely scattered and unreachable except by canoe or by hiking overland. This he found particularly difficult during the rainy season, when he was annually taken ill with "liver complaint and vertigo." He prayed that some "colored clergyman in the USA" would be willing to come over and take over the Virginian church. It was small but growing and there were "plenty of natives, Deys, Veys, Mandingoes, all around within two and three miles," as well as a large American population. He would have been glad to give it up and his doctor had advised him to take a holiday. But accepting the common superstition that work and sweat were a cure for "the fever," he decided that "the hoe would do as well as a voyage," and he would try to endure a little longer.[22]

The work was tiring and slow and was often interrupted by the many political and ecclesiastical disputes in which Crummell became involved. No matter how dismal his personal affairs, however, he always attempted to make positive statements with regard to his missionary charges, statements suitable for publication in *Spirit of Missions,* which would demonstrate the progress of the work. He discovered that some of the people were literate. In reading psalter at New Georgia he observed half a dozen men and a woman "who read as distinctly as though they had been always accustomed to our service." He remarked on the fact that the congregation at Caldwell was always attentive and devout. Their responses during services were "promptly rendered" and their chanting was "excellent." Family prayer and Sunday School teaching were on the increase, and he had been able to influence the parishioners through "private conversation and the distribution of tracts" to adopt the practice of "total abstinence from intoxicating drinks." In every respect the people of Caldwell seemed to be ripe for the missionary harvest, although they had as yet received little missionary attention. They had no school, although there were "swarms of children in the streets." It was the impression of the people of Caldwell that they had so far been neglected by all denominations of Christians because so many of them were recaptured Africans.[23]

At the end of 1867 Crummell could report that the junior warden of his parish in Virginia had begun a Sunday School for native boys of the Vai tribe, which now numbered sixteen. In the settlement at Caldwell, his eldest daughter, Fannie, taught without remuneration, and Crummell opened the school daily "with singing and Prayer, and the recitation of the Creed," then taught an hour of reading, arithmetic, and catechism. He was visiting the Congo towns, villages of recaptives, which were to be found "on every side," where he began to instruct them in reading and writing. "At first they were reluctant to begin . . . but I taught the grown-up men half the alphabet at one sitting, and they knew the whole of it after two other recitations." He ended this apparently successful year with a celebration in the parish and Sunday Schools. Hymns were sung, prayers were offered, and the parents and children marched in procession to the Crummell residence, where they "partook of a simple repast." Gifts were distributed, books donated by a kind lady of Philadelphia, and the children were dismissed.[24]

In the spring of 1868 he was worried about the future of the Liberian children in his vicinity. They must not be allowed to grow up in ignorance, for, alas, they were "learning all evil things from the heathen." Moreover there was near at hand "another danger than heathenism." The Roman Catholics threatened in a very brief time to appear in the midst of Liberia, "with large charities and profuse gifts of money." Simple black folk would be easy prey for them, for the religion of Negroes was "too generally one of excitement, and too often marred with the taint of corrupting antinomianism." All too often, they could give no reason or explanation for their professed faith, and there were very few who read their Bibles. It was such things that filled him with anxiety at the dreaded "approach of the Romanists." The Church must arm itself to preserve "our poor people from their delusions and errors and idolatries."[25]

The antinomian threat did not always come from Rome. Its Protestant manifestations were discussed in an unpublished letter to the Board of Missions, in which Crummell described one of the revivals that shook the country. "Of these converts are persons who have been converted two and three times over and back slidden." Some of them, he averred, were converted every quarterly meeting. How could it be otherwise? They were ignorant people, who never received any instruction from their church (the Methodist church). They were only fed from week to week with "exciting ditties." The meetings were characterized by waves of "excitement, and passionate intoxication, a wild hysteria, which none could escape nor resist." He doubted if he could have resisted it if he had attended, as some of the Presbyterian and even some Episcopalian clergy were doing. Women and children were being carried "alas beyond all decency and propriety!" Such was the work of the Methodists that "noise, hysterias, and shrieking" could be heard for two or three miles. Although his convictions kept him from attending, he had heard aplenty:

> The Bishop's son jumped out of the pulpit leaping, hallowing, gesticulating most violently; his father (the Bishop) clamoring into the pulpit; his wife crying to their son—"go to it Lewis!" "Go to it Lewis!" . . . Universal Antinomianism . . . Precisely the same thing I see in your reports from the South. Godliness and grossness; religion and lust! Alas! Alas! What shall we do?[26]

He had nothing against religious emotion, and he described touching scenes of candidates for baptism, "wonderfully wrought up," or elderly people on their deathbeds, finding consolation in meditation and prayer. But sedate emotion was one thing, impropriety another.[27] Crummell maintained that his congregation remained quietly and prayerfully steadfast in the midst of the revivalist storm. He struggled along with his faithful few and his two eldest children, who donated their services to the mission. He mentioned Fannie's contributions in 1867 and reported the following year that Sidney had introduced courses in Latin and algebra. Crummell requested that the readers of missionary magazines provide the mission with the means to compensate his teachers, especially Sidney, for their labors.[28]

At great personal sacrifice, Crummell had sent Sidney to school in England between the years 1862 and 1864. The son had returned to Liberia in January 1864, "prepared and anxious to enter into business" at the age of eighteen. Since his father considered him too young to be exposed to the temptations of the area's worst districts, he opened a small shop for him in the family home. This would "give him a chance to do a little trading and mercantile business." Sidney soon fell in with bad company, and his father fearing that his influence was so pernicious he was "leading [the] girls to ruin," had to drive him from the house. After a period of estrangement, the prodigal returned, professed repentance, and threw himself on his father's mercy, He wanted to come home, work on the farm, and contribute to his father's work. Crummell forgave him, allowed him to teach in the school, and they began to read theology together.[29]

Early in 1867, Rev. Eli Worthington Stokes died suddenly, and Crummell was appointed to take over his work.[30] Russell described Stokes's passing as a sort of martyrdom, saying that it was brought on more by want of the "necessaries of life" than by sickness. On the eve of his death, according to Russell, "he was dividing his morsels of food among the poor, crippled and unable to do manual labor." Crummell, however, was unforgiving, and would have had it believed that the circumstances were extraordinary, even providential. It was "a painful case of a Godless minister on a Godless errand." Crummell maintained that Stokes had been journeying from his home in Careysburg to Crozierville to hold a meeting at which Crummell was to be "driven from the Episcopal ministry." On his way he had stayed at the home of a married man who kept a native mistress, then, proceeding on his journey, he had "in some mysterious manner, wandered off a road, clear and plain and daily travelled as any street in New York, [and] lost his way. There he remained all night, cold, hungry, frightened at the noise of wild beasts! The next day he was found speechless. In a week he was a corpse."[31]

The story of Crummell's interaction with Stokes, Russell, Thompson, and Gibson, is a curious one. At times he would cooperate with Stokes, whom he despised, because Stokes shared his interest in an independent church and was ever ready to challenge the authority of the bishop. He cooperated with Thompson, whose morals were suspect, for the same reason. Stokes, for his part, had cooperated with Crummell in attacking the bishop, and with Russell in attacking Crummell. Russell, although he usually supported the bishop, worked with Stokes to undermine Crummell's position. Gibson was a bearer of tales, sometimes informing the bishop of insubordination, sometimes revealing to Crummell the schemes of his enemies. The petty conspiracies of the Liberian clergy were, of course, matched by the plottings of the bishop. All of them suffered constantly from the sickness and the heat, and their misery was increased by the necessity of working together. For these reasons they were constantly involved in political squabbles and character assassinations.

Crummell was dealt a singularly painful blow in 1869. It came like a "thunderbolt" on a Saturday in late June while Crummell was at home with his wife and daughters. A constable came to the door to summon Sarah Crummell and her eldest daughter to appear in Monrovia on the following Monday, as a result of charges made against Crummell that he had maltreated his wife and failed to supply his family with food and clothing. Mrs. Crummell refused to go, and Crummell claimed that he found it impossible to get her to go, but he did prevail on his daughter to answer the summons. The case came before the grand jury, and it happened that the foreman was Robert R. Johnson, a merchant and trader who supplied the Crummells with rice. Several of the other jurymen came from Caldwell, and, wrote Crummell, "the jury threw the indictment out at once with indignation." The cause of the attack, as he learned shortly, was his "wicked, ruined, son," Sidney. He had been used by Russell, the bishop, and others to defame the reputation of his father.[32]

Sidney's influence in Caldwell, in the school, and among the young men was for a time "most wholesome," Crummell later recalled. "But alas, my enemies, lewd and drunken men, tracked him." He began drinking again and, with the aid of his mother, was able to keep the truth hidden. Crummell was the last to know, but the neighbors were aware of how he had gone from place to place drinking, sometimes lying out of doors all night intoxicated. It was even rumored that he gave liquor to the schoolchildren. Finally, when he had caught him drunk on more than one occasion, Crummell dismissed him from the school. Sidney then turned upon him "for the first time, like a tiger, . . . abused [him] most shamefully, and declared he would do everything he could to injure" his father. After spending several days going from house to house in attempts to break up the school, he moved to Bassa, "where people do not drink water, rum is so abundant."[33]

On May 15, 1869, Sidney had written a letter to Bishop Payne charging that his father ran his household like a tyrant. In the name of family government, he insisted that his wife and daughters submit to his supreme authority. Provisions were doled out by the pound and quart. The family members were allegedly forced to dress in rags and were often left at home for three or four days with a bare larder. He had humiliated the eldest daughter publicly more than once, Sidney claimed:

> She was insulted before her scholars in the Day School,—and [he] once whipped her before them all because she had forgotten to carry the School Books. Another time she was publicly whipped through the streets of Caldwell. I, at the instigation of my father, prevailed on her to come home again, he promising her better treatment: but the same state of affairs.[34]

Sidney never charged his father with striking his wife, but since Crummell had not seen the letter, he was shaken by the rumor that the accusation had been made. He denied ever having struck his wife, even playfully, in twenty-five years of marriage. He claimed that his wife had asserted the same to "a number of most respectable and pious persons." Strangely, she does not seem to have taken it upon herself to defend her husband, neither before the grand jury, nor in a letter to the Board of Missions. With respect to Sidney's actual charge that he had beaten his daughter, Crummell did not respond. He may even have been unaware of the charge. Whether or not he doled out corporal punishment to his children and, if so, until what age, is not known. It is not unlikely that he accepted the stern attitudes towards childrearing that prevailed at the time. Sidney's word alone, however, is not a basis for intelligent conjecture. As to the other charges, a committee of neighbors and business associates came to his defense with a signed document attesting to his responsibility in providing for his family's material needs. It named the stores at which he shopped, the merchants from whom he bought, and the provisions that he regularly laid in. It also spoke of Fannie's having appeared before the grand jury in Monrovia to testify to the falsehood of the charges. As for Sidney's role in the affair, the document stated:

> When he was sober, virtuous and Godly he would not suffer any one to say a word against his father and he defended him through thick and thin and maintained that he was the only minister, with few exceptions, that nothing could be said about, and one of the best of fathers, but so soon as his father dismisses him from the school for improper conduct, drinking &cet., he begins to ruin his father. What shall we do? Shall we believe him when he is sober, or trust him when he is in liquor and half crazy?[35]

The way in which he chose to defend himself reveals much about the man. His bitterness and hypersensitivity were readily apparent. He admitted having had great difficulties in his family and stated that he always kept silent in the face of insult. Among his family, he admitted, "I say almost nothing: I try to keep silence even from good words." He maintained that he had never in his life descended to low quarreling, which he considered gross and tasteless. This may have been literally true, but we know that he had many disputes with his associates, and, although he may never have raised his voice, he was capable of rancor, displayed in his often vitriolic correspondence. He had a remarkable capacity for holding a grudge. His course of conduct during family disputes was, at the very least, sulky and uncommunicative. "In trying circumstances," he wrote, "although I have not turned the cheek for a second slap, I have always dropt my hands, put on my hat, and walked into the street."[36]

Given the three sources of disappointment that arose in Crummell's life after his return from America in 1863—church, university, and family—it is not surprising that he was of somewhat irascible temper. He found the physical and moral climate of Liberia uncomfortable, and to his amazement he was witnessing a dramatic change in the circumstances of black people in the United States. The material well-being of free blacks was undeniably improving, and he was stranded in a small African town with an (understandably) ungrateful family and a hostile circle of church associates. He complained once again to his ecclesiastical superiors about the inadequacy of his salary, which had remained the same for sixteen years, although shrinking in real value. Since 1865, and until the recent death of his mother, he had been responsible for the support of eight persons, including four daughters, his wife, his mother, himself, and Sidney. He could not provide his family with frills and luxuries and fine clothing after the manner of "merchants or foolish ministers of Liberia."

Liberia was "a land of great lewdness and drunkenness, and hence of great boldness and brazenness for evil." His son had brought into his very home much of the local sinfulness that Crummell attempted to avoid. He had introduced one of his sisters to one of his "drunken licentious companions," the product of one of the "fast families." With his mother's collaboration, they had become engaged, and Crummell, though doing everything in his power to break it up in order to save the girl, feared that everything was against him. He blamed his difficulty on the surroundings. In a land that lacked intellectual pursuits for women, wives must be mentally inferior and lacking in judgement, so that it seemed "impossible for them to restrain themselves from intrigue and cunning and artifice in the most delicate and dangerous matter of marrying daughters." In civilized nations, Crummell believed, such decisions should be in the hands of the father.[37]

With respect to Sidney, he had tried in vain to convince his "poor child of his sin," but he was "crazed." Crummell could think of no other word to describe him. He had become a liar, and when he could not escape by lying, he failed to show remorse. He was now worse off than he had been before his temporary reform; he had "rushed again into gross sin." This time Crummell feared he was "utterly unreclaimable." By "singular coincidence" he happened at that time to be reading Bateman's life of Bishop Wilson of Calcutta, which related the "depraved life of the Bishop's second son." He took consolation from the words of the bishop: "I believe this visitation is intended among others to teach me the fall of man more deeply; the doctrine of special grace; the vanity of creatures' expectations; the bankruptcy of domestic as well as of every other source of human joy."

The chief villain in the entire affair, as far as Crummell was concerned, was Bishop Payne, who had put Sidney's letter in the hands of his enemy, A. F. Russell. It was only a week before he received Sidney's letter, Crummell claimed, that he had informed the bishop that Sidney was ruined, and that he had "given up all hopes of him." Payne might at least have taken steps to investigate the matter privately, or he could have sent a letter of inquiry to Mrs. Crummell. But instead he had placed the communication in the hands of Russell, a man whose hostility to Crummell was universally known. Crummell had the gravest suspicions about Russell's sexual morality, listened with relish to every rumor concerning it, and attributed both Russell's vices and the bishop's strange tolerance of them to Russell's mulatto heritage.[38]

He asserted, however, that his reputation had not been destroyed by the bishop's "unwarrantable assaults." All Monrovia knew that the charges were untrue. His wife and his daughter had denied them repeatedly; Sidney had tearfully repented. Even the hardened sinner Barnes, who had once invaded his church, torn the Bible from his hands, and driven him from the pulpit, had come "limping into my study—still lame and miserable from the gross lewdness which I reproved—exclaiming, 'Mr. Crummell, don't mind this! Don't mind it! See how God has taken care of you in greater troubles.' " A few days later, he was called on by his neighbors in Caldwell to address them on July 26, the national anniversary. He was added to the program at the last moment, the principal orator having already been selected, and was "received in a most flattering manner." [39] He had endured the bishop's unfriendliness for seventeen years until he felt he was "obliged to speak or suffer the loss of all manliness." He had "swallowed offense in silence" for so long, because he was "aware of the imputation of oversensitiveness on the part of black men." [40]

From his own point of view, Crummell had tried to work with the bishop, but he felt that he had been justified in seeking a fully independent Liberian diocese, rather than remaining the subordinate to a mission run by a great white father. The American church did not encourage black ministers to remain in the United States. Almost all of those ordained before the Civil War were sent out to foreign missions. In view of the fact that the Episcopal church was not willing to welcome Crummell into an American diocese or support his claim to all the responsibilities and rights normally shared and enjoyed by members of the priesthood, Crummell thought it only fair that they should establish a truly independent, black-controlled church in Liberia. This, however, they were not prepared to do. They were paying the bill for the African mission and thus felt that they had the right to set the rules for its administration. The church was guilty of a double standard, and Crummell must either accept unequal treatment in the American church, or submit to a white bishop on African soil.

Bishop Payne returned to the United States in 1870 on one of his periodic visits for reasons of health. According to all reports, he was on the verge of physical collapse, and in October the Board of Missions accepted his resignation from the African post. There can be no denying the sincerity of his commitment to African civilization, and even Crummell never attacked his piety, but Crummell's characterization of him as having "an irascible temperament" was not without foundation. Like William Lloyd Garrison, he demanded an excess of gratitude and loyalty from the black people he chose to help, and he was suspicious of any manifestations of independent spirit. These flaws of personality notwithstanding, John Payne had demonstrated far greater willingness than most white people to work with black people on some semblance of an equal basis, to take them seriously, and to treat them as individuals.

Nonetheless, he believed that Crummell was guilty of base ingratitude. In his 1865 letter to Burgess and Bedell, Payne had recounted at length the many favors that he had done for Crummell, whom he characterized as spoiled, prideful, and ambitious. The bishop saw himself as a generous and charitable man, and would have been happy to play the role of Crummell's benefactor, but Crummell did not want his charity. He saw the bishop as a rival, and resented the fact that he had been forced to call on him for assistance during hard times. The bishop seemed to expect unquestioning submission in payment for his generosity. He understood all too well that gratitude can never be the basis of a relationship between equals, and thus hoped to keep Crummell constantly dependent and indebted. Strangely, he never understood Crummell's dislike for him, and he was not only mystified but genuinely hurt by his animosity.

Payne's departure did not mark the end of Crummell's political conflicts. Nor did it increase his chances of being appointed bishop of Liberia. New difficulties impended, more serious than any he had yet experienced. Crummell was on the verge of his most severe trials and disappointments, and he was to remain in Liberia for only another eighteen months after Payne's resignation.

# 10

# Missionary Work and Final Disillusionment (1870–1872)

Crummell kept up his missionary work along the river, sometimes dispatching the most glowingly optimistic reports, but in private communications with the Board of Foreign Missions frequently expressing pessimistic, even alarmist, sentiments. On one occasion, he wrote to the retired senior missionary, Dr. Thomas Savage, describing his progress in the most optimistic terms.

> Every rum shop is now closed. Every rum-seller has departed. The men who had stray women living with them have since married or since left town. One of the very men who helped drive me out of the church has since repented; given up his licentious life and his kept mistress, lives quietly with his wife, and regularly attends my church . . .

But this stood in marked contrast to what he wrote on the same day to the Secretary to the Committee on Foreign Missions:

> Iniquity runs riot, Licentiousness abounds, Drunkenness [sweeps] the land. Rum is sold by the worldly churchmen and ministers. For my part I feel a painful isolation.

Although there may have been some specific reason for this dramatic shift of mood within a few hours it is more likely that the two letters simply reflected the necessity of dealing with two conflicting interpretations of reality, and, as a consequence, two contradictory sets of beliefs. Each letter was a reflection of truth, and each was an honest expression of his feelings. Like most people, Crummell was capable of both optimism and pessimism, but in the years that remained of his African tour, the pessimistic strain prevailed.[1] Like most people, he was capable of some dishonesty, which perhaps stemmed from an attempt at optimism.

179

Crummell remained in Liberia for another eighteen months after the bishop's departure. Still committed to the idea of training an "indigenous ministry," he thought to set up a theological academy. He had long been committed to education that included manual labor. This had been the practice at Oneida Institute and the high school at Mt. Vaughan. What he proposed was a modest faculty of three, including himself as principal and teacher of Greek and theology for a salary of $1000. He left it to the board to decide how much the teacher of Latin and algebra should be paid and to choose the third member of the proposed faculty, who would teach English and catechism.[2]

In addition to requesting that missionary donors help him with salaries, he mentioned the school's need of farming utensils, for he felt he "must insist upon making the institution a manual labor school." It was necessary that students be taught the value of labor, since so many of them were infected with the customs of the Southern states, where it was held that to be a gentleman was not to work. At least two hours of work a day would "train and inure the students to self-dependency and secure health." They could grow their own cabbages, plantains, and rice, which would reduce operating expenses. And if they were to plant four or five acres of coffee, they would have a cash crop that could be sold to support the school.

Crummell had long been interested in cultivating coffee. He was among a group of citizens who printed a petition to the Liberian Senate and House of Representatives in support of the project of one Edward S. Morris, who proposed "to introduce into the Republic of Liberia labor saving machines to facilitate the hulling of coffee, but useful also in hulling rice." Morris had visited the Republic to promote his enterprise and had impressed numerous leading citizens as having the interests of Liberia at heart. Crummell, during his visit to the United States in 1865, had entered into an agreement to take charge of Morris's coffee-hulling machines in Liberia and he was to keep twenty-five percent of the coffee milled. Crummell's involvement in this enterprise drew sarcastic criticism from Bishop Payne, who referred to him as "a professor of Liberia College with a store under his house." He accused Crummell of using his son as a front for his own "extensive plan of coffee cultivation." But the Rev. C. C. Hoffman, whom the bishop regarded as a living saint, waxed enthusiastic at the prospects of coffee cultivation, proclaiming that "a new era" was now opening in Liberia, and with it was opening before the Africans "a source of wealth not exceeded by the gold mines of California." Was not "the hand of the Almighty in all this?" Coffee and sugar would "doubtless become the great staples of Liberia."[3]

The plan was not given financial support from the Mission Board, but Crummell went ahead, nonetheless, with his plans. He reported that a number of youths had come to him asking that he train them for the ministry, and in 1870 he had six such students under his tutelage. His rules required three hours of work daily; visits to neighboring towns to teach the Gospel; and preaching on Sundays. He commenced building a "pole house," twelve by eighteen feet, as a dormitory. The course of study, which was to last three years, included "sacred languages, systematic divinity, evidences, sermonizing, minor mathematics."[4]

Now that he had developed an immediate interest in "evangelizing the heathen," Crummell claimed that he was "constantly receiving applications" from chiefs of the local tribes. Ten miles distant was a town where numerous tribes met to trade. Its chief was building a schoolroom and asked if Crummell could send him a teacher to instruct his children. He received a similar request from another town, where the chief was eager to send girls as well as boys to school.[5]

Crummell lived an active life in the upriver settlements, traveling widely and having small adventures. Shortly before his fifty-first birthday, he was invited to lay the cornerstone at the church of St. Andrew's in the coastal town of Buchanan. "Failing to secure a direct conveyance by sea," he decided to make the trek overland and by canoe, which took him through an interesting series of settlements in Bassa County. He also had to travel through the bush, "the region of the alligator, the baboon, and the rhinoceros." He started on a Saturday, and made the first leg of the journey by canoe, eighteen miles up the Mesurado River to its head. His party spent the night at Ruebensville, a small trading town, where Crummell knew one of the villagers. He had been sexton of Trinity Church in Monrovia at the time that Crummell had organized that congregation, and he expressed a desire to see a mission established in his present location. The next morning, they arose before dawn and crossed the "Old Field," a four-mile stretch of swamp that separated the Mesurado from the Junk river. The country was "intersected on every side by tiny creeds [and] standing pools with the rankest vegetation." "The most luxuriant forms" of vegetation shot up, even from the middle of streams; "the bamboo, the palm, and other tropical trees, overshadow[ed] the streams giving, indeed, continuous shade, but shutting out every particle of air, and intensifying the mephitic odors, and the deadly malaria of the swamp land." After another stretch of canoe travel they came to the house of a friend, who allowed them to hold a religious service.[6]

Crummell rebuked an elderly man, a Baptist, who had failed to attend the service on account of his clothes. Crummell used his opportunity to remonstrate with him for such a flimsy excuse and instructed him in his duty to assemble the local folk for weekly prayer meetings. "He acknowledged his error, and promised that in the future he would do his best on the Lord's day." He slept that evening only till midnight and then traveled by the light of the moon through scenery that was "exceedingly wild." The area was "exceedingly disagreeable from the lack of air, the unsightly banks of mud, and the deadly odors." He spent the night with a "hospitable headman," who promised to help him along his way in the morning. After enjoying a delicious meal of boiled rice, boiled eggs, "and chicken *fried* in palm oil, which," he said, "tasted to me better than any fowl I ever ate in my life," he slept soundly. But when he rose to start for Bassa in the morning, he found that his host had vanished. He had paid him in advance to bear him by hammock to Bassa, but now he was forced to continue his journey on foot, "although quite lame." He finally reached the beach and limped along in the burning sun the remaining six miles to Little Bassa, "tired, faint, almost exhausted." [7]

Little Bassa was "something of an oasis," he discovered. The chief was a Christian, who lived in a commodious frame house. Crummell, exceedingly weary, "staggered up the hill with no little difficulty" and encountered "an active stirring little woman, with the brightest eyes, and the cheeriest good looks." This turned out to be Mrs. Crocker, the wife of the chief. She directed him to her husband, who was in the next building, a blacksmith shop, and there Crummell found him, "a short but rather stout man, who addressed [him] in a most courteous manner, in the plainest English, and invited [him] to his house." As it turned out, Crocker had been a pupil of the Rev. Dr. Savage many years before at Mt. Vaughan. He had later become a Baptist, married Mrs. Crocker, a native of Massachusetts, and returned to his native section of the coast. Since he was a chief, he exercised considerable authority, and he was able to bring many people into the church.

Crocker provided Crummell with four robust hammock bearers, "fine, strapping fellows, who ran all the distance down—say twenty-seven miles—in six hours." They traveled by night and in the morning reached the port of Edina, where Crummell secured a boat from a "devoted layman" and thus was able to reach his destination, the town of Buchanan, where he was to lay the cornerstone of St. Andrew's Church. The site of the ceremony was the spot where an important battle had taken place, and the cornerstone was laid "in the very identical place where, in the same battle, Taplin's head, the man who led the heathen hosts, was cut off during the fight by an American settler."

After breaking ground for the new church, Crummell gave an address to "vindicate" the people of Caldwell for their decision to found an Episcopal church in Buchanan. More important, he sought to vindicate his own view that the "special needs of the people of Liberia" could be met particularly well by the Episcopalians. Like all Christian denominations, the Episcopal church taught the gospel and the message of vicarious atonement. But the special mission of the Episcopalians seemed to be the stressing of an educated ministry. They offered a dignified form of worship and a stable, unchanging liturgy. The African church, as was well known, was far too inclined to a "warm, emotional, and impulsive energy, which was both its failing and its virtue." This universal, and undeniable "race peculiarity" required a "strong corrective, or, otherwise, the flame of religious life, however intense for a time [would] blaze with unhealthy violence, or else soon burn itself out." The ultimate result might be some sort of heresy or, worse yet, a reversion to heathenism." Most important, the Episcopal church ever conserved a high standard of morals. She did this by insisting that the Christian must accept the Old as well as the New Testament. True though it was that grace and truth came from Jesus Christ, it was nonetheless important to know the law that was given by Moses. By constantly reminding her members of the "validity of the law, as a rule of life," the Episcopal church guarded against antinomianism. He was "thankful for the authority" that his church gave her ministers "to wage a ceaseless warfare against all lewdness, grossness, irreverence, Sabbath desecration, and dishonesty."[8]

He stayed in the settlement for ten days, and on Sunday he preached to both the Episcopalian and the Methodist congregations. He traveled somewhat in the area, preaching again at St. Andrew's and visiting some of the local river settlements. On asking after some of his former students from Mt. Vaughan High School, he located one who had become a district attorney, and another who was now a merchant. Seventeen years had passed since he had first arrived in Liberia, and, although he had experienced many failures, he had not failed to learn. He had discovered, for example, that work outside Monrovia could be interesting and satisfying. It seems that he was beginning to recognize that work among the settlers and efforts among the natives were not mutually exclusive tasks. He was pleased to discover "not a few civilized natives, living Christian lives" in Bassa County. A few were married to Liberian women. The boundary between native and settler seemed to be disappearing in the frontier settlements. There were signs of hope that the Liberians would soon become one united Christian people.

To accomplish the goal of amalgamation, however, missionary work had to be pursued with vigor. He was now prepared to allow that the work need not be confined to coastal enclaves and river settlements; it must be carried into remote heathen strongholds. Recently a promising field had opened up in the country of the Barline people, 120 miles to the interior, which had been ceded to the Republic. The inhabitants had submitted to the Liberian authority cordially and with "the utmost willingness," for they saw it as an opportunity for greater contact with coastal ports. Crummell described the territory as "a lofty, cool, mountainous country, containing a large and crowded population, numerous towns, unusual and superior civil regulations, and distinguished withal, by great industrial energies." The capital city was reputedly large and surrounded by a stone wall. It was an important market town, where thousands of people came to trade. It was the site of important manufactures, where the people made their own "warlike and agricultural instruments, cultivat[ed] and cured their own tobacco," produced their own cloth, and prepared their own salt. But he had also heard that the people were "heathen and cannibals . . . , imbruted by all the grossness and ferocity of deadly superstition." Their territory, he wrote, is "a part of that vast interior land, which I believe to be the darkest place on earth." It has been isolated for ages from all contact with the outer world, a land" where Christian or Mohammedan never trod."[9]

Bishop Payne believed that Islam was a threat in the region. Among the Vai people, for example, Islam was beginning to spread, and their intelligent neighbors, the Mandingo, and other Muslim peoples were "fast converting them to their false faith." If possible, Episcopalian missionaries to the interior should be able to speak Arabic. Crummell agreed that the Muslim threat must be met, but as usual he disagreed with the bishop about how that end was to be achieved. The bishop felt that the best way to meet the threat would be to set up a new missionary jurisdiction, well-supplied with Arabic-speaking missionaries. Crummell did not feel that the Islamic threat was so immediate as to justify the bishop's recommendations for drastic reorganization of the West Coast missions. The Muslims were not present in Liberia in large numbers. "The native mind [had] not yet been perverted and poisoned by his duplicity, his insincerity, his hypocrisy, his deceit, his lying and his mischief." The important thing was to establish missionary influence as quickly as possible. As for the Muslim, "the governmental authority of Liberia will keep in check forever his eagerness for rule and domination."[10]

A few months later he "undertook a journey through the Dey and Vey countries, preaching from village to village." There may have been no connection between this trip and the bishop's assertion that the Liberian clergy had neither the aptitude nor inclination to work with these two tribes. Be that as it may, Crummell reported that he had been "sent for by the two chiefs, or kings, to talk with them about schools and missions." He went through the Dey country first, and there he was impressed by the people of the numerous towns, "active with energetic labour." He found the people willing to listen to the Word, but he admitted that "the truth [had] not penetrated deep." What he encountered was mainly intellectual desire. Villagers pursed him relentlessly with the request that he send them teachers.[11]

At the town of Pau, he encountered one of the two kings who had sent for him. This "tall, spare, fine-looking, man," who received Crummell cordially, had once been a servant to the governor of Buchanan. He was having a plank house constructed, because, as he said, he wanted "to live like Americans." But there was apparently something other than vanity at work, since he was also offering to have a schoolhouse and a mission house built "and to give us *all the children* in his various towns if we will take them, clothe, feed, and instruct them." He called in his headmen, "who readily acquiesced."

Crummell "pressed on three days through the wilderness," passing through a region that was sparsely inhabited, but where "the elephant abounds. . . . We saw their tracks on every side, where they had passed through only the night before." The general wildness of the surroundings was enchanced by what Crummell called "evidences of gross superstition."

> I have never seen so many "Greegrees" since I have been in Africa: in the towns on the highway, in the valleys, on tops of hills remote from any town, in the rice and cassada fields, Greegrees; a tall gallows, with a huge rock slung to the crossbar; or a stump covered by a cap made of bark; or a square reed box hung from a tree in the middle of the path.

Finally he reached Little Cape Mount River, whence they traveled upriver by canoe for eight miles to the town of King Bomba, a prince of the Vai people. He found them an industrious people and was much impressed by the appearance of the women, who were "beautiful as well in face as in figure." As for the town itself, he found it the finest, but not the largest, town he had seen in Liberia, and he was struck by "the completeness and finish of the huts." Walking through the town he came across two couples working at their looms, and found the sight "so singular and unique" that he "could not resist taking a sketch of the interesting sight." His interview with the king went well, and, after partaking of a dinner of "rice and palaver sauce," Crummell discussed with him first the Gospel and then schools. He was "a little man, about five feet five inches in height," with a "courteous and affable manner," who seemed "to live in great love and friendship with a large number of wives and a host of children." At the end of the discussion, the king said: "I am too old for all these things; but look at these children; take them all; put them in your schools, and train them as you please. I will build you a school, and a house for your Missionary, and give as much land as you please."

Crummell seemed to have learned how to give the Mission Board, the bishop, and the readers of *Spirit of Missions* what they desired. He found that he could work among the natives to a limited extent without abandoning his principles, and, more important, he was finally willing to accept advice given to him by the Foreign Committee years ago. He was willing to appeal to an interest in the exotic on the part of missionary magazine readers. He had indeed become more flexible, and seemed to be adjusting to the life of a missionary much better than he had to that of a scholarly divine or a theocratic statesman.

It is also interesting to note the apparent tolerance with which he greeted the manners and customs of King Bomba. Although we may be certain that he had no tolerance for polygamy, it is worth remarking that the unhappily married Crummell could admire the "love and friendship" that existed in the king's household. For, while on the one hand he felt most keenly "the deep degradation of heathenism," he was clearly enchanted by much of what he saw during the two days he spent with King Bomba. He praised the hospitality of the king's wives, who provided him "with everything pleasant and agreeable," preparing fire for him in his house "and a warm bath at night." Mornings he sat in the town, regarding the tall, slender Vai women, high cheekboned and keen featured. He admired the "childish laughter and glee of the young ones, and observed their artless ways," as they dressed themselves with their hand mirrors, applying the traditional clay paint that marriageable women used to keep the skin clear and smooth.

Crummell was happy to report that there was no Mohammedan influence in the Dey territory. There had been no "Mandingo wars" in the region. The people lived comfortable, industrious lives, "without the bloodshed which the Moslems have carried through a wide region further north." Even among the Vai, he found the bishop's fears to be unjustified. True enough, he had encountered one Mandingo in his travels, and, yes, he had been in King Bomba's town, "a keen, lively, talkative fellow," who was thought to be a spy, sent to find out the resources of the country. But he did not describe anything resembling a Moslem threat. The people were mostly heathen, but he saw "very clear evidences" of natural religion beneath the "thin incrustation" of their superstition. Beneath that "thin surface," one found "the ideas of God, his Providence, a sense of duty, consciousness of the sin of theft, and such like."

Furthermore the people had sufficient contact with Liberians that the name "the Lord Jesus Christ" was not unknown to them. They were warmly desirous for civilization, and "in almost every town the cry was for schools and teachers."

Aside from these concerns with the natives, there was, of course, plenty to keep him busy among the settlers. He passed through one of their villages on his way back to the coast. Isolated as they were from the larger outposts, they had not seen a preacher for months, and "their joy and gratitude was almost too much . . . to bear." In Caldwell itself he was developing a genuine interest in working among the poorest class of settlers, as well as with the Congoes and the indigenous peoples. There were problems with the Board of Missions, which did not approve of his setting up a "school fund". They had made no appropriations for any such thing, but they did not flatly refuse him appropriations for the purpose. He was able to erect a brick schoolhouse with contributions from Rev. Tyng in New York, who had contributed the money for his church. It was a small building, only sixteen by twenty-two feet, with the attic "fitted up for a dormitory for candidates and students." He also received donations of a church bell, an organ, "Greek and Hebrew study books, Testaments, and works in Sacred History and Divinity, for the use of students."[12] Perhaps he was truly optimistic, but more likely he was once again merely keeping up a public posture. As we have seen, his private correspondence usually revealed a greater awareness of the distance to be traveled than of the progress already made.

Crummell had been changed by Africa. Although he was just as intolerant, volatile, and authoritarian as he had ever been, he was aware of having made numerous mistakes, and he attempted to adjust and enlarge his philosophy accordingly. His statements, both published and unpublished, during his last two years in Africa reveal a somewhat different set of aims than those he arrived with in 1853 when he had dreamed of becoming a university don and civil religionist. At that time he had maintained that his primary commitment to working among the colonists precluded evangelization of the heathen. The latter project must be postponed until the first task had been completed. But now he was willing to allow that he and all Liberians were "guilty of a neglect, which has carried with it harm to the aborigines; and at the same time, visited grievous wrong upon ourselves."[13]

Once converted to the idea of directly evangelizing the native, he developed a martyrlike obsession with the idea. Conversion of the heathen was now to become central to his Liberian philosophy and basic to his criticism of the Liberian government. At first, and in the public forum, he accused the people of Liberia of acting without "malignant will." Later, and in private correspondence, the same anger that had dominated his statements on other issues began to appear in his tirades against the government, which he accused of antinative policies.[14] He expressed disappointment with Liberian developmental policy on Liberian Independence Day, June 26, 1867, in an address delivered at Virginia settlement. As he later informed William Coppinger, he had spoken on "Our National Mistakes and Their Remedy."[15] Although the address had not yet been published, he still hoped it would be; he delivered it again in Monrovia on July 26, 1870.

He began by speaking in general of the fact that "man beats toward the truth. We fall into an error, and then retrace our steps." We learn from painful and embarrassing experience, he confessed, quoting from the poet Young:

> At thirty, man suspects himself a fool,
> Knows it at forty, and reforms his plan.

Crummell, now well past forty, had certainly experienced considerable pain and embarrassment—in his church, in his university, and in his family. It was difficult for him to come around to the position that Bishop Payne and the Mission had maintained all along, that the work of evangelizing the native population must begin at once. Now he realized that this work, which was encouraged by the mother church in the Untied States, did indeed coincide with the needs of the Liberians. The problem was to make the government in Monrovia understand this. His own tardiness in coming to see the truth was a concrete instance of widespread national error. Once converted, he spoke with the passion and conviction of a convert.

In his address "Our National Mistakes and the Remedy for Them," he attributed to the Liberians in general the benefits of his own experience, attributing to them the circumspection that he had presumably acquired through his numerous embarrassments. Crummell believed that the Americo-Liberians, "ferried over in a month, or little more, from a state of degradation to a position of independence and superiority," were too conscious of their power over the natives. "In a little more than a monthly change of the moon, we were metamorphosed from the position of underlings to one of mastery." He did not question for a moment that "the heathen around us" were backward, but he felt that the Americo-Liberians, by constantly contrasting their relative "civilization" to the primitiveness of their "degraded subjects" had acquired an exaggerated view of their own capacities. He critcized his own Americo-Liberian group for failing to send their native boys to school, to teach them to read, or to accustom them "to proper habits of dress."

There is no question that Crummell was what social anthropologists have come to call "ethnocentric," but through his own alienation from the ruling elite, and because he had been forced to eat the dust of poverty and humiliation, he had a feeling for the problems of the underclasses that many other Americo-Liberians did not share. He spoke out forthrightly on problems that would plague Liberia for generations to come, and, although his solutions would be unacceptable today, one must admit that he had a commitment to uplifting the masses of black people that was not universally shared. Furthermore, although Crummell's opinions were ethnocentric, he did not accept the racist views of African ability that were common to so many of his contemporaries, black and white alike. The Africans had the makings of a civilized people. Even now, the typical African was a worker, "notwithstanding all that Mr. Carlyle and all his brother anthropologists may say to the contrary."[16]

The criterion of industry is, if I mistake not, this, that is—*"do a people work up to the level of their necessities and their cultivation?"* If they do, then they are industrious, if not, not!

The native African *does* work, and that most gladly, up to the level of his cultivation and his needs; not, indeed, I grant you, up to the civilized man's needs; for he is a barbarian. He does not work for a brick house, for carpets and chairs, for books and pictures. He has not reached that point of civilization, which requires such things. Neither did Mr. Carlyle's grandfathers when Caesar came to Britain. These things are not the native man's needs. His needs are rice, cassada, palm oil, and a hut; not awry, dirty, and ready to fall, like a thriftless Italian's or a rude Irishman's, but perfect and complete. . . .

They are industrious according to their habits and training; we must teach them ours.

Crummell could still repeat the standard arguments about the primitivism of ancient Britain, which had imported its civilization from Rome. He was capable of defending the African race according to the standard of the times. He was capable of comparing the African native favorably to the crude or decadent European. He was not, however, capable of entertaining the idea that Africans might have something to teach black Americans. He did not see the coming of the new civilization as a blending of the two cultures. It must come about through the transmission of Anglo-Saxon values from the black Americans to the native population. The fault was with the colonists, not with the natives, that the potential value of native labor was as yet unrealized. The colonists had never taken the pains "either by skillful increase of [the native's] wants, or by a generous mode of interesting them in the profits of labor, to avail themselves of their powers and fitness for wide and productive use." [17]

In response to the objection that perhaps the Liberians had no right to press their own forms of government and their attitudes toward industry on the natives, Crummell responded:

All historic fact shows that force, that is authority, *must* be used in the exercise of guardianship over heathen tribes. Mere theories of democracy are trivial in this case, and can never nullify this necessity. You cannot apply them to a rude people, incapable of perceiving their own place in the moral scale, nor of understanding the social and political obligations which belong to responsible humanity. "Force and right," says a brilliant writer, "are the governors of this world; *force till right is ready* * * * * And till right is ready, force, the existing order of things, is justified, is the legitimate ruler." [18]

Crummell looked on the indigenous population as children who had not yet attained the capacity to desire or even to recognize what is right. They must, therefore, remain under the tutelage of civilized people until they were prepared for self-government. He spoke of the "stern necessity of assuming the nonage—the childhood of the natives; and, consequently, our responsibility of guardianship over them." This did not imply that the natives had no moral rights, only that "barbarians" were entitled to "no rights as a nation." In support of these ideas he cited the authority of John Stuart Mill, who had said,

"Barbarians have no rights as a *nation,* except a right to such treatment as may, at the earliest possible period, fit them for being one." [19]

He did not question the legitimacy of using "force over blinded heathens," but he considered "despicable" any nation that used force only to retaliate "for real or supposed injuries." It was unjust to engage in sporadic, retaliatory warfare with the natives, or to implement the policies of expulsion and extermination that some Liberians advised. Crummell advocated what he called *"the force of restoration and progress,"* which should impose a lasting peace, introduce schools and training, and uproot "gross heathen domesticity by elevating woman and introducing the idea of family and home." Everything in Crummell's theory of development was based on the idea that non-Westernized peoples lived in "ignorance and superstition." The view expressed in this address denied even that they had a family life; they had only a "gross heathen domesticity." The statement must be contrasted to the views he expressed in the report on his travels to Vai territory, with its almost tolerant description of the hospitality of the king's wives.

Although he may strike the present reader as appallingly intolerant, Crummell was, in contrast to many of his Americo-Liberian contemporaries, a paragon of liberalism. He described one faction as "always ready for a war against the tribes: but on the other hand they [would] do nothing nor suffer anyone to do anything for the heathen." Their policies, he asserted, were driving the indigenous peoples further and further into the interior. He reported that one of the spokesmen for this group had stood up "at a missionary meeting and boldly declared that the heathen could never be converted until we put them to the sword." Crummell was not, of course, the only citizen who held enlightened opinions. Edward Wilmot Blyden, for example, had far greater tolerance for African traditions and customs than Crummell could ever muster. He learned numerous African languages, introduced the study of Arabic at Liberia College, and, through his studies, came to have considerable respect for Islamic thought. Blyden reasoned that Islam would prepare the way for Christianity in Africa, just as Ishmael had historically preceded Isaac. But Crummell discounted any incidental good that Islam might do, saying "While they may furnish a small modicum of enlightenment, they flood the continent everywhere with oceans of disaster, ruin, and bloodshed." [20]

Despite his early coolness to the idea of missionary work with the indigenous people, Crummell had always approved the political policy of blending the native tribes into the national fabric. Crummell had seen President Benson, who also supported such policies, as "a great man." He rejoiced when in January 1870 his friend Edward James Roye was inaugurated as the fifth president of the Republic of Liberia. In his address, Roye called on black people from all over the world to help Liberia to "gain a position of respectability for the entire race, by hastening to these shores and teaching Christianity, energy and industry to the millions of their benighted relatives." [21] He dedicated his administration to "the improvement and incorporation of the native tribes contiguous to us." He referred to them as "aborigines," but also as "our brethren,'' saying that "they should be entwined with our affections" and brought with all possible speed into the fullest participation in the national life. Indeed, he said, "We cannot have a permanent and efficient nationality without them." At the end of his address, in appropriating the well-known phrase of John Winthrop to declare that God had "set Liberia, as it were upon a Hill," Roye illustrated the derivative nature of black nationalism in the latter years of the nineteenth century. The Liberian idea of national destiny owed a great deal to its American antecedent.[22]

The dependency on the United States for a conception of national destiny had an ironic twist. In Crummell's case it was paralleled by a desire to return to the days of economic and military dependency. Just as the Liberians had a duty to uplift the tribes, Crummell argued that the United States had a moral duty to help Liberia along the road to progress. He did not propose that Liberia return to colonial status, but he felt that it had been untimely for Liberia to be thrust out on her own, and that America owed the citizens of Liberia a debt. Liberia needed help, and there was nothing inglorious in making such an admission. He proposed nothing less than that the United States "extend to this nascent state the many advantages of a colony without its disadvantages." What he had in mind was financial and military support, which would theoretically allow the Liberians to concentrate their efforts on internal improvements. One of his examples of "the compatibility of national life with a foreign protectorate" was the Sandwich Islands. What had he learned then? Certainly he had not yet accepted the fact that dependency on the United States was no way to get Liberia on a secure footing. What he was proposing was simply more of the same sort of dependency that he had found so personally disagreeable in the church and at the college. The fact was that Liberians had been appealing individually and collectively to the Untied States for years. Experience, if nothing else, should have taught the Liberians that no foreign capital would be coming to Liberia unless it could be shown that the investor could expect a handsome and certain profit.

A complicated venture involving the quest for foreign capital led ultimately to the downfall of the Roye government, and brought about the days of violence and despair that led to Crummell's hasty departure in 1871. President Roye had traveled to London in 1871, where he arranged a $500,000 loan under terms that were so disadvantageous as to be degrading. Although Crummell approved of the arrangements, there were many Liberians, including the faction led by Roberts, who did not. For Crummell and Roye the justification of the move outweighed the costs, for they were convinced that the program of internal improvements—building roads, setting up common schools, and opening up the interior—must begin at once. A storm of controversy arose, and while the loan agreement was awaiting approval by the legislature, national elections occurred. As if the confusion were not already great enough, Roye's True Whig party proposed as a platform plank that the constitution be amended to increase the length of presidential terms. Roye's party won the election, but the opposition Republican Party contested the constitutional amendment lengthening the presidential term.

In the meantime, the London bankers had worked out an arrangement whereby they could immediately discount a portion of the loan, deduct three years' interest in advance on the remainder, and hold the bulk of what was left to the credit of the government. What Liberia got from all of this was an initial payment in goods, some worthless notes, and an increase in the national debt. The anger of Roye's political opponents was hardly without justification, although the tactics they used to discredit him were probably unfair. They circulated rumors among the populace that the money had disappeared into Roye's pockets, whereas in reality it had been lost in the paper-shuffling of unscrupulous bankers, invulnerable in their London offices.

The summer following Roye's reelection, Crummell made a short trip to Liberia's northern neighbor, Sierra Leone. He had gone "at the advice of friends" and "owing to illness." As it happened, he had also been sent for by the bishop of Sierra Leone: "and knowing I could find the best advice there, I went to Freetown, and spent a fortnight in very pleasant interviews with Dr. Cheetham, who is an old university acquaintance of mine." He did not reveal the nature of the advice he had been seeking. Perhaps he was considering moving to Sierra Leone, but, if so, he did not mention it in his letters to the foreign secretary. He did, however, speak with considerable enthusiasm of the settlement, which he called, "a depot of catechists, teachers, and ministers, a Protestant propaganda." He was impressed by the large bookstore in Freetown, through which cheap copies made their way into "every urchin's hands." There were barefoot native African boys "talking in the streets of Dante and Longfellow," and there was poetry "dropping from the lips of schoolboys!"[23]

On returning to Liberia, he threw himself back into his work. Things seemed to be going well. Crummell was by no means inclined to paint a rosy picture in his letters to the Mission Board, but even here he gave the impression of optimism. He was delighted with his new church bell and the organ that a kind donor in America had provided. The continuing interest of Rev. Dr. Tyng in New York made him hopeful about the prospect of his manual labor school. He hoped to be able to expand so that he could work with a hundred students instead of only fifteen. In Monrovia, however, the political situation was reaching a crisis. Violent emotions were seething, and on August 21, 1871, Crummell wrote of an experience that "entirely unfits me for anything."[24]

That morning, while he was putting on his surplice and preparing for morning service, a young man came to his door with the news that Samuel Finley, the postmaster, had been shot and killed in Monrovia the night before. Moments later, the victim's father, W. W. Finley, who was Crummell's senior warden, burst into the house armed with a musket and announced that he was on his way to Monrovia. Crummell persuaded the man to lay down his weapon and agreed to accompany him to Monrovia. As they paddled down the river by canoe, the old man gave himself up to tears, and he resigned himself, in accordance with Crummell's pleadings, to the workings of Providence. They found the city in turmoil; it was believed that the assassination was political. Crummell did all he could "to restrain the president, the relatives of the deceased, and others from extreme measures of vengeance." [25]

But reason was rapidly losing all footing in Monrovia, and the remainder of the year saw the breakdown of law and order in Liberia. Blyden had already decamped for London, after receiving "brutal treatment at the hands of a drunken mob." Crummell and Blyden had had a falling-out over Blyden's belief that Crummell had told Bishop Cheetham during his visit to Sierra Leone the preceding month that President Roye had accused Blyden of committing adultery with his wife. Blyden saw this as an act of betrayal, calling it "the sorest trial I have had to undergo . . . that Rev. Mr. Crummell, with whom I labored and fought side by side in Liberia College . . . a man whom under great persecutions and trials, I defended and assisted," should be motivated by envy to convey rumors spread by common enemies. A common friend, Professor Martin H. Freeman, agreed that Crummell had treated Blyden badly but imputed his behavior "to his foolish ambition to be the greatest Negro in West Africa, and not to malice *per se.*" And he added, cryptically enough, "Do not retaliate. He has not injured you, do not injure him." [26]

Since the accusations of adultery were made by Roye himself, and Crummell was a friend of Roye's, it is possible that Crummell may have believed them, at least initially.[27] But what actually happened, and what Crummell believed, may never be established. We do know that Crummell was morally inflexible, even when dealing with his loved ones. If he truly believed that his friend Roye had been betrayed by Blyden, he might have felt troubled enough to have discussed Roye's public accusations with his old friend Cheetham, who was after all a senior clergyman of the same faith. Blyden, for his part, dramatized this as one of those events which "in all ages and in all history [occasion] the mournful retort, Et tu Brute." Blyden, however, later wrote to Rev. Henry Venn that Roye "has been convinced that he has grossly represented myself and his wife. He has not for two or three years been of sound mind." Later in the same letter he wrote that Roye had deliberately deceived the public. It is possible that Crummell was among the deceived.[28]

In any case, the wheels of the gods were grinding slowly away. Blyden was soon able to remark that "the same mob that attacked me before I left attacked and beat Mr. Crummell's son shamefully." [29] Roye was attacked by a mob, which fired a cannon shot into his home and led him off to the jail. What happened thereafter has never been established. He managed to escape from the jailhouse, apparently with the aid of the jailor, who was his own appointee. He secured a canoe and made for a ship in the harbor, but the canoe capsized. Some accounts say that he was dragged ashore, beaten in the street, and left to die in prison, others that he drowned while trying to make his escape. The government was then taken over by a three-man junta, which included Charles Benedict Dunbar, the very man to whom Crummell had eleven years before addressed his letter "The Relations and Duties of Free Colored Men in America to Africa."

"The times just now are terrible," Crummell wrote. Although it might be supposed by people in America that this was a political upheaval, it was in actuality something worse. It was a revolt of the ignorant against "newspapers, Colleges, improvement, civilization." It was a movement to "get rid of every man of letters in the land, and all the higher modes of instruction, and of all attempts to elevate the native." He felt that he and Professor Freeman were particularly under attack. There had been cries of "burn the College down." Missions were attacked as humbug by those who felt that nothing could ever be done with the native. Crummell maintained that many of the problems could be solved if the Episcopalians had a bishop "on the spot"; then, at least, the Episcopal clergy would be forced to desist from demagoguery. The presence of Bishop Auer at the Cape seemed to have had such a sobering effect. He and Gibson, and at least one other clergyman, were "refusing to have anything to do with the scene of violence; save to inculcate those principles which everywhere characterize the Episcopal Church, viz. submission to authority, respect for rules, quietness and order."[30]

Crummell's last letters from Liberia understandably displayed varying degrees of pessimism, for he was living through a reign of terror. Mr. Findley, Senior Warden of his congregation, had been condemned to hang. False witnesses had sworn that he was guilty of the "crime" of procuring guards for the president. Sidney, who had been acting secretary of state, was condemned by the testimony of the same two witnesses to two and a half years imprisonment and to work on the chain gang. Sidney had gone out one night to appraise President Roye of an assassination plot and was, according to Crummell's report, "shot at by a number of persons. He was hunted in Monrovia like a wild animal, but never struck a man, nor fired a shot, nor carried a weapon." Crummell repeated what he had said in an earlier letter. This was no "political occurrence"; it was "an uprising of persons who are opposed to culture, improvement, and native elevation." American philanthropists must not be deceived by their pious platitudes concerning native education, those who lived in Monrovia must "hear them cry against everything that is good and pure [and observe] their inebriate mode of life and mark the facility of their divorces, and listen to their utterances that nothing but the sword can convert the heathen, and notice their contempt for the native."[31]

He had despaired of the Americo-Liberian population's ever amounting to anything. They knew nothing of liberty, only of license, and rum-drinking, and swaggering. Unsigned letters to the editor of the *African Times* painted a distressing picture of a society in chaos. There were reports of "starvation and immorality" and sexual delinquency alongside and within the churches.

> Amid all the public wickedness, a great religious revival is going on, and scores of people are said to be getting conversion every night. These frenzied meetings are kept up all night until daybreak, while numbers of men and women are com-

mitting the grossest sins around and alongside the chapels in which the revivals are carried on.—Such alas is Liberia.[32]

Two months later, another letter in the *African Times* announced that President Roye was "deposed, imprisoned, tried, it is said, and condemned for high treason." It repeated the rumor that he had drowned. The letter went on to advise that "What Liberia wants is Spartan simplicity—Spartan virtues—hard work—self-denial; and not the corrupting influence of the luxurious excesses of our highly developed wealth and civilization." With godlessness, and laziness, and ignorance, they were doomed, if left to themselves, to "early, ultimate obliteration." These were sentiments that Crummell shared; indeed, the author may have been Crummell.[33]

As had Gibson and Freeman, Crummell had been assaulted on the streets and received assassination threats. His church had been broken into and the new organ destroyed. His neighbors had warned him again and again that he would have a bullet put through his head. Claiming poor health, Crummell left hurriedly for Sierra Leone. His deeds and other important papers were "left in a box [in] a safe and secure place." The only consolation of his last days in Liberia was his reconciliation with his son Sidney, who somehow had managed to avoid going to prison for two years and had found a job with an English house in the coastal town of Bassa. Crummell saw his son two weeks before he left, entrusting him with the personal effects and papers that he had to leave behind in his haste. From Freetown, he wrote on March 29, 1872, that he was on the eve of sailing for Boston. "In the present sanguinary state of Liberia," he was unable to do anything. No one's life was safe, and "all decent and intelligent people [were] preparing to leave." The *Spirit of Missions* reported that he "arrived in New York about the middle of May."[34]

When Crummell wrote of his African years in *Shades and Lights,* he made many statements that stand in marked contrast to what one discovers in his letters and official reports concerning his health, the length of his stay, and the constant optimism he professed. In the short autobiographical address, Crummell says that he enjoyed excellent health, with the exception of a short acclimation period at the beginning. We know that this is not true. On each of his arrivals in Africa, he spoke of severe difficulties with "acclimation." He spoke constantly of the difficulties that he experienced with "liver complaint" during the rainy season, which was always a bad time for him. He also spoke of the difficulty he had getting around without stretcher bearers, probably because of the varicose veins of which he began to complain while in England. Even the official journal *Spirit of Missions* attributed his departure from Africa to reasons of health.[35]

With respect to the length of his stay, it was closer to sixteen than to the twenty years usually attributed to him. He was away from Liberia for almost two years, from February 1861 to February 1863, and again for eight months, from April to November, in 1865. His final departure was another four months before the nineteenth anniversary of his arrival, so he was actually some thirty-six months short of nineteen years in Liberia.

With respect to his optimism, perhaps it prevailed in the end, but at the time of his departure from Liberia he was anything but optimistic. He hoped till the end for some Providence whereby either the United States or England would assume control over matters. But this hope was akin to despair, for it implied that he did not believe that the Americo-Liberians had thus far demonstrated the capacity of black people for effective self-government. And he seemed even more pessimistic when he predicted: "We shall pass away; I see every indication of it. Families are becoming extinct. Villages are going to decay." He could point to "scores of sites, where nothing but bush [was] growing."

For twenty years he had focused his activities on Liberia, and during the entire time he had been dependent on whites. He had come to the black man's country and found white men in control. They had controlled the church and missionary societies; they had controlled the university; they had controlled the purse strings of the government; and, although he had raged and protested every step of the way, they had controlled him.

# 11

## Reconsidering the Destiny
## of Black Americans
## (1872–1882)

Crummell was never completely candid about his reasons for returning to America. In his communications with church authorities he gave the impression that he would soon be resuming his African work, but he was meanwhile surveying the new social landscape and wondering if it might not be time for a prudent reconsideration of his long-cherished views. He was certainly conscious of the fact that there were hitherto undreamed of opportunities for a man of his abilities in America. Within a month of his return he had begun to explore the possibility of establishing himself in an American parish, and, as he relates in one of his rare personal reminiscences, he soon found employment in a missionary church "in the upper part of the city of New York." William H. Ferris reported that it was St. Philip's, but this is doubtful. Crummell mentioned his services to St. Philip's Church, of which he was quite proud, in *Shades of Lights* but did not mention any postbellum connection with it. Several of Crummell's sermons in the Schomburg contain notations to the effect that they were delivered in New York at the Church of the Messiah during 1873, and it is possible that he may have attempted to revive his work with that mission. For a while there seemed to be some possibility of his being called to St. Thomas Church in Philadelphia, but this hope disappeared when the vestry voiced their preference for another candidate, a young white man recently graduated from the seminary. They had considered Crummell but had judged him too old for the position, although he was only fifty-three. In any case, it was known that his health was poor.[1]

The opportunity that emerged was in Washington, where he eventually established himself among the more influential, if not always the most politically visible, post-Reconstruction leaders. He later claimed that he had not wished to leave New York and spoke of his move to the capital as having been determined entirely by Providence. It is clear, however, that he was exploring the possibility of taking a post in Washington almost immediately on his return from Liberia. Within a month of his arrival in the United States, he secured a long interview with Rev. John Vaughan Lewis, a moderately liberal clergyman of Washington, D.C., who was known for his charitable work, particularly among black Americans. Lewis had founded St. Mary's Chapel in Washington, which was supposed to serve all members of the community, regardless of race. The deacon who was at that time in charge Lewis considered to be marginally qualified. Crummell seemed "willing and even desirous of working in Washington for six months," although he expressed uncertainty whether or not he would remain in the United States for more than a year.

Lewis proposed that Crummell be given six months to prove himself at St. Mary's, a parish that had been "neglected by the whites and despised by the colored aristocracy." The problem was that St. Mary's had "never had a chance" because it had always been served by lay readers and deacons, "not our bright ones." Well-trained and experienced leadership was needed, and he thought that "an old presbyter like Crummell [would] be more likely to succeed in the work than a novice in the church, however able."[2] The present minister of St. Mary's, a Mr. John A. Graves, did not seem to be the man for the job. He was "a valuable man and an earnest man," and at deacon's work in the parish he was very good. As rector for a potentially thriving Washington congregation, however, he was unacceptable because his voice was "rasping and harsh."[3]

Whether or not he actively sought a position in Washington, Crummell's memory seems accurate on the point that he was earnestly entreated to take the position at St. Mary's. He received several letters from John Thomas Johnson, one of the most respected members of the vestry, urging him to accept the appointment.[4] He was also encouraged by Bishop Hobart of New York, who signed his letter dimissory assigning him to the new pastorate. He apparently found congenial the thought of working under his new bishop, William Robinson Whittingham, who had been in charge of the General Theological Seminary at New York at the time of his application. Whittingham, it will be recalled, had wanted to admit Crummell, but Bishop Onderdonk had taken the matter out of his hand. In later years, Crummell credited Whittingham with having preached the sermon that led to his conversion.

In the years following Crummell's return to America, there was some discussion among Episcopalians of the possibility of appointing a suffragan bishop for the freedmen. It seems that his name was discussed but that there was little willingness to vote for him. His name was also discussed in connection with the missionary bishopric in West Africa, an idea that also failed to gain support. If Crummell still had any desire to become an Episcopal bishop, he was not to realize this ambition. By 1876, he had in any case associated himself with the position that it was "pernicious and unscriptural" to establish separate churches, conventions, or diocese for black people.[5]

At the time of Crummell's appointment, St. Mary's Chapel might have been interpreted as a symbol of philanthropy or of racism, depending on one's point of view. It was a foster child of the fashionable St. John's parish, and, according to tradition, was the church of servants of wealthy Washington Episcopalians. Crummell knew how to make use of such parishioners, but he also aimed to reach a larger population. In those days, Washington was the cultural capital of black America and possessed intellectual and social advantages exceeding those of New York, which had not yet achieved its preeminence as the black metropolis. Crummell was well aware of the city's reputation as "the Mecca of the colored people" and felt the importance of making a "powerful impression" on the emergent black leadership class. Washington's black population, which he understood to be 43,000, included the black senators and congressional representatives, government clerks and other federal employees, and numerous professionals, among them doctors, lawyers, and some seventy-five schoolteachers. Finally, there was Howard University with its three hundred undergraduates.

> The common schools of the District, now twelve years in existence, have raised up a generation of colored youths, who have outgrown the crude and tumultuous religious systems of a former day. It is nothing but an act of mercy for the Church to step in front now, with her chaste, sober, yet warm and elevating system, to meet the needs and to satisfy the stimulated cravings of these trained and anxious minds.[6]

While developing his plans for a more impressive church, Crummell was effective in multiplying the size of the congregation at St. Mary's. There were only fourteen families and some forty-eight communicants in the parish when he arrived. Within four years, he had increased the number of communicants to ninety, the number of families to seventy, and the total number of persons associated with the cure to three hundred.

At the time of Crummell's arrival, the church of St. Mary's was a sixteen-year-old frame building located on Twenty-third Street between G and H Streets. The lot had been donated by a Mrs. Parsons, a parishioner of St. John's and a frame building had been erected by the former secretary of war, Edward M. Stanton. Crummell, of course, had plans for something more impressive. A stately edifice had always meant a great deal to him, and he set out immediately to plan a capacious new building, for, as he said,

> We *must* build a church that will hold a thousand or more persons; or otherwise the work will be perpetually a feeble, unhelpful, begging and beggarly scheme; unable to stand by itself, or to help others. Build us a large church, and then with God's blessing we shall sustain ourselves; and also become an arm of strength to the Diocese.

Within two years of his arrival at St. Mary's a cornerstone had been laid at the corner of Fifteenth and Sampson for a new church capable of seating over five hundred. The solid stone structure, modeled after the English church at Stratford-upon-Avon, was known as St. Luke's.[7] By May of 1879, *The People's Advocate,* edited by Crummell's friend John W. Cromwell, was reporting on the progress of St. Luke's. The first service was held in St. Luke's on Thanksgiving Day, 1879; by 1883, it was well established, with 125 families, amounting to 210 communicants and a total of 525 individuals in the parish. Although Crummell's relationship with the congregation was to prove tempestuous, the experience was no repetition of the Providence fiasco of the 1840s. The church membership was stable and substantial, and by the time of Crummell's retirement there were 135 families and a total of 600 souls associated with St. Luke's Church.[8]

St. Luke's was located at 1514 Fifteenth Street, N.W., which placed it within a few blocks of the White House and also in proximity to some of Washington's most dismal alley life. During the last quarter of the nineteenth century, Washington's black population was scattered throughout the city in what one recent demographer has called "mini-ghettoes." Some were literally within a stone's throw of such impressive residences as the presidential mansion. In such a milieu as late nineteenth century Washington provided, it was impossible for any black person to be unaware of the conditions under which the mass of black Americans lived.

If Crummell had been inclined to forget, he would have been quickly reminded by his old friend and loyal parishioner, Maria Stewart. This able author of declamatory essays and abolitionist tracts was born in Hartford, Connecticut, in 1803, and orphaned at the age of five. She had little education other than what she had been able to pick up in Sabbath Schools. She was widowed at the age of twenty and moved to New York, where Crummell met her shortly after returning from his studies at Oneida. At the time, she had only six weeks' schooling, and, according to Crummell's testimony, to publish her first book of meditations and prayers, "she had to get a little ten year old to write every word." She received basic instruction in reading, writing, and arithmetic from young women in New York and soon became a member of the Female Literary Society. In 1852, she migrated to Baltimore, where she worked as a teacher. During the Civil War she taught in Washington, and settled thereafter in the city, where she was known for her lectures, teaching, and various philanthropic activities. Crummell had been particularly moved by her activities on behalf of the "daughter of a respectable family, who had strayed from home and taken up her abode in a house of prostitution."

> The community was shocked, and the parents recoiled from any idea of reclaiming their daughter, but Mrs. Stewart went to the house in which the young woman was staying. Her request to see her was refused—in fact the mistress denied that the party sought for was there and shut the door in the face of the late Mrs. Stewart: but Mrs. S. on bended knees made an appeal to heaven for mercy in behalf of the erring one. The mistress relented, bade the erring one depart from her house, and in company with Mrs. Stewart, the child of sorrow soon found herself again at home. She was welcomed, and today lives in Baltimore, an honored member of Society.[9]

The kingdom of heaven could hardly be estranged from the practical affairs of the mundane world, or of Reconstruction Washington, and Crummell, of course, had no inclination to avoid taking stands on public issues. It was not possible to forget the presence of national power when many of one's parishoners were beneficiaries of the Republican Party and the "spoils system," and others were intimate confidants and family retainers of senators, congressmen, and other government workers. The fact that he was in Washington made it inevitable that he would participate in all sorts of political controversies. This pattern had been set back in the days of the Dorr War, when he had used his influence as a churchman to lobby for the voting rights of Rhode Island blacks. It had been evident throughout his career in Liberia, where he had tried to wield influence in the areas of economic development, internal improvements, and educational policy. When he returned to the United States, he continued to impress his values on political life, and, although he was not much involved in the practical side of politics, he often attempted to influence public policy and government ideology.

Partly because of its association with the prestigious St. John's, partly because of the abilities of its pastor, St. Mary's often attracted influential whites to its services. One church historian could recall seeing distinguished members of the Washington community attending services at St. Mary's "on other than special occasions." Among the distinguished occasional visitors at Crummell's Washington services were President Chester A. Arthur, William W. Corcoran, the banker, Senator George F. Hoar, and a Dr. Chickering. One early biographer of Crummell reported that around the time of the Hayes–Tilden compromise, Congressman Julius Seelye of Massachusetts was "a frequent worshipper" at St. Mary's Chapel; he recalled seeing Crummell and the congressman leaving the church at the close of services and walking "side by side through the streets arm in arm, chatting as if they had been comrades from boyhood days."[10]

Like many black Americans, he was upset by backroom politics following the presidential election of 1876. In the Hayes–Tilden compromise, the Democratic Party had contested the outcome of the election and conceded victory to the Republican candidate, Rutherford B. Hayes, in exchange for an agreement that the few remaining federal troops would be withdrawn from the South. This concession, along with the others, which effectively marked the end of Reconstruction, was naturally seen by black Americans as an issue of enormous consequence. Southern violence against black people was a matter of constant concern to the Washington intelligentsia, many of whom viewed the withdrawal of the troops as too steep a price for a Republican victory.[11]

Early in 1877, Douglass had been appointed by President Hayes to the office of Marshall of the District of Columbia. When Hayes agreed to the withdrawal of federal troops from the South, Douglass voiced no protest, and many of his critics felt that he had been overwhelmed by the honor. Crummell wrote to John W. Cromwell to express his disgust at the "Machiavellian policy of our leaders." He also criticized Hayes, because "putting *one* black man *forward* (the Honorable F. Douglass) does not compensate for his putting *back* a half million black men in the South and giving supremacy and domination to the old power-holding body.''[12] Still Crummell declined to comment on his "high character, the purity of his motives, [or] his real interest in the black man." He was alarmed, indeed, by the tone and language of some of the responses to the Hayes-Tilden compromise, and claimed to have as much faith in the president as he had in Garrison or Wendell Philips. Still this exercise in political expediency gave him some anxiety, and he cited the words of Edmund Burke, "Refinement of policy never has succeeded in the history of man, and never will to the end of the world."

He was certain that it could be generalized from history that "after slavery comes a state of feudality." It was perfectly normal that the Southern leadership should attempt to create such a system. He called this "a natural desire" at which black leaders should not be angered. Rather they should be attempting "to rob history of this consecutive link, and by organization, money, power, and culture to lift up our people to the level of ordinary American manly, social and political life." Thus the matter of real importance was not politics so much as uplift. The necessity at hand was "to organize and upbuild our people."[13]

Unfortunately, Alex Crummell, upbuilder of the race, advocate of ethnic pride, racial loyalty, and group solidarity, was constantly embroiled in internecine political squabbles, and often had to call on whites to support him in his battles against other blacks. His inability to function within black institutions without the intercession of whites was a pattern that became evident early in his career. It persisted throughout the years in Africa and continued into his pastoral life at St. Luke's. One early biographer felt that the difficulty was due to the inability of black people at that time to accept the leadership of one of their own number, but even this sympathetic observer admitted that Crummell's inflexible personality contributed to the atmosphere of strife. In any case, it is a fact that Crummell's authority was constantly being challenged, and he often strengthened the position of his opponents because of his inability to disarm them through diplomacy.

"Scandals, grossness, abominations" had been rare in his congregation, Crummell insisted in later years when he reflected on his experiences in Washington. During the period of his Washington ministry, he had not had to discipline more than a half dozen persons for "gross sins." "So far as abominations were concerned," Crummell could thankfully say, his church had been "almost spotless." It was, nonetheless, a sad fact that there had been troubles and difficulties, which had come from "men utterly rotten in character," who had fomented "anxieties and divers complications." Some of these "wretched souls" consistently opposed Crummell, from around the time of St. Luke's completion.[14]

The first public flare-up, a fight between Crummell and his choir, was, according to one informant, one of several embarrassingly noisy conflicts "of which the general public, not always interested, were always posted through both the daily and the weekly papers."[15] One reason for the church's high visibility was the richness of its musical offerings, thus it should not be surprising that when Crummell became embroiled in a feud with his choir, the fight attracted the attention of the entire city and was aired, not only in the black weekly, but in the white daily papers. Crummell accused his enemies even of bringing in newspaper editors from outside the state to wage war against him.[16]

Why it was that the business of a black church choir should have created such a stir among the population of Washington is difficult to understand, unless one remembers the importance generally attached to black music during the 1870s in the United States. The Fisk Jubilee Singers were at the height of their fame, having made triumphal tours of the United States, England, and the European continent. In 1873, the Colored American Opera Company had made a distinct impression on Washington and Philadelphia, for, as one newspaper reported,

> We all know that the colored race are *natural* musicians; and that they are susceptible of a high degree of cultivation is evinced by their rendition of the opera on the occasion of which I speak.
>
> As for the chorus, it is not saying any thing extravagant when I make the assertion, that it has never been excelled by that of any of the professional opera-troupes which have visited this city.[17]

On March 5, 1879, members of the opera company gave a concert at Lincoln Hall for the benefit of the new St. Luke's Church. A large number of workmen were meanwhile at work on the edifice, and the building was rapidly pushing towards completion. The company was led by Christian A. Fleetwood, a mercurial but intelligent and articulate local figure, who had held the rank of sergeant major during the Civil War and was thus referred to as "Major" Fleetwood.[18] Several performances of *H.M.S. Pinafore* were given around Washington during the next few months, adding to the choir's reputation. When St. Luke's opened, a select choir of fourteen voices under the directorship of Christian A. Fleetwood performed. Thus, although the church did not yet have an organ, and the windows were filled with canvas, its musical program was already well under way. A week after the opening of the church, an organization known as the Washington Church Choir gave another benefit performance of Gilbert and Sullivan's *H.M.S. Pinafore,* with Lena Miller, a member of the Colored American Opera Company, in the role of Josephine. Some of the impassioned responses in the press to Lena Miller and Mattie Laurence, her successor in the role, were reminiscent of the partisanship for favored divas in Milan.[19]

This sort of flamboyance must certainly have alarmed the easily ruffled Crummell. From the beginning he had disliked the choirmaster, who had been appointed during Crummell's absence on a fund-raising tour. Crummell maintained that "in order to prevent strife" he had "suffered this intrusion without a word." But shortly thereafter, and to his great dismay, Crummell discovered that the "Gloria in Excelsis" had been introduced into the Morning Service after the Psalter. Despite Crummell's repeated remonstrances, Fleetwood persisted "ever afterward," declaring "that he had always been accustomed to it.'' As early as December of 1879, it became necessary for the bishop to send a letter to the vestry lamenting ''the disquiet in your midst'' and reminding them that the music to be played in church was placed by the law of the church ''wholly in the hands of the Rector.'' He admonished them to ''work in sweet accord'' with their ''rector of great ability.'' Crummell's passion smouldered quietly during the winter months, but a week before Easter, the hostilities between rector and choir flared up violently. From Crummell's perspective, it must have seemed as if his church were being taken over by an opera company, with the full cooperation of his vestry. Not only did this violate what Crummell called ''the rules of church governance,'' it was a case of insubordination and a departure from common sense.[20]

Shortly before Easter of 1880, Crummell forbade the performance of a Magnificat that had been composed and rehearsed for the Easter service. Crummell's objections to the composition were twofold. First of all the Magnificat was traditionally a Christmas anthem; it was not appropriate for Easter and therefore ''utterly unfit for use.'' Moreover, this particular composition was ''more like a dance than a sacred anthem.''[21] Fleetwood and his choristers were indignant; they protested that they did not have time to rehearse an alternate piece and Crummell ''thereupon, as they understood, dismissed them.'' Some members of the congregation felt that the conduct of the rector had been arbitrary, and ''attendance at the church rapidly diminished.'' A notice that appeared in *The People's Advocate* on March 18 had described the music as ''highly attractive.'' Nonetheless, Cromwell, its publisher and a member of the choir, was loyal to Crummell and tried to persuade Fleetwood that he had no right to dictate the music to be sung at services. Fleetwood was obdurate, however, and refused to take part in the services at all. Crummell insisted that he had received a letter from the vestry in which they had refused to participate in the Easter service and that he was not guilty of having dismissed them from their task.[22]

Suddenly he was being attacked in the daily papers. On March 24, 1880, an article appeared in the *Washington Post* with the headline,''ST. LUKE'S CHOIR DISBANDED. The Rector of a Well-Known Episcopal Church Causes Trouble.''

> The choir of St. Luke's Protestant Episcopal church is famous for the musical skill of its members. Under the able direction of Mr. C. A. Fleetwood it was attracting immense audiences every Sunday to that church, and the extensive preparations made by it to celebrate Easter with appropriate music would probably have made the day a marked one in the annals of St. Luke's when yesterday it was announced that the choir had left the church, and hence their services at Easter would not be available.[23]

The article went on to describe an interview with Fleetwood, conducted in his home, in which Fleetwood rendered his account of the disagreement and its origins. Fleetwood insisted that he had informed Crummell of his plans to perform Millard's Magnificat six weeks before the flare-up and maintained that

Crummell's rejection of the music had been not only abrupt, but tardy. Under the circumstances, Fleetwood asserted, it would have been unfair to the choir to ask that they prepare another selection. Great things were expected of them, and it was anticipated that a large congregation would be attending the Easter services to hear the choir.

> From Mr. Fleetwood's THE POST proceeded to interview Miss Mattie Lawrence, the leading soprano, a very handsome and accomplished young lady, whose success as *Josephine* in the church choir *Pinafore* at Lincoln Hall last fall attracted much attention. Said Miss Laurence, "The choir will not yield, and the Doctor is said to be very determined. The result would seem to be that St. Luke's will have no choir for at least some time to come. I understand the doctor wants a choir composed entirely of little boys."
> "Going to Rome, eh?"
> "Ritualistic, at any rate."
> "What do the people say and think about the matter?
> "It is gratifying to us of the choir to know that the people are very sorry to think we shall leave, and that they wish the doctor would yield in the matter. But I think that as he desires to control the choir, he will not give in."

In response, a short editorial was published in *The People's Advocate,* which also printed some of the correspondence between Crummell and Fleetwood. It may be assumed that, as a member of the choir, Cromwell had some knowledge of the matters at issue. His succinct and dispassionate narrative placed part of the blame on Fleetwood for not having consulted Crummell before preparing the piece, and part of the blame on the choir for refusing to sing at all. Cromwell admitted that the choir had selected the piece "having more regard, mainly, if not exclusively to the rhythm of the score than to the words." He did not, however, absolve Crummell entirely of blame, maintaining that he might have "shown better diplomacy, and exercised more self-restraint as to his manner and temper."[24]

Around this time, Jerome Hopkins, "an eminent musical performer" and son of Bishop Hopkins, happened to be in Washington and read of the problems in the choir. He wrote to Crummell to say that he had been quite right to deny a performance of the Magnificat by Mr. Millard. The latter's works were unfit for the church, "not one of them grammatical or ecclesiastical."[25] Crummell accepted Hopkins's offer to come to St. Luke's and rehearse a group of singers for the Easter service. The choir for that occasion was mixed, made up of "several white gentlemen and ladies" who along with "a few of my people" performed music such as the church had never had "before or since."

That St. Luke's had received some recognition in the larger society as a musical showplace and an architectural symbol of black bourgeois culture had mixed effects. On the one hand this recognition made the black population of Washington feel that their cultural progress since the war was being acknowledged by the rich, the powerful, and the refined classes of whites. On the other hand, it opened up their private institutional affairs to public scrutiny in ways that did not always show them off to best advantage. The appearance of white men and women in St. Luke's choir led to further indiscreet discussion in the press. On September 11, 1880, several months after the Easter music controversy, *The People's Advocate* reported that Crummell was "preparing to introduce a choir in St. Luke's Church composed of a number of white ladies and gentlemen, said to be excellent amateur vocalists." On September 25, however, the *Advocate* printed a retraction, saying that there was "not a word of truth" in its earlier report.

> The item was furnished by a member of our staff and in type before it was discovered. Dr. Crummell is not reduced to the necessity of introducing a choir of white vocalists to furnish his congregation with acceptable music.

The report in question had been furnished by J. A. Johnson, the news editor of the *Advocate*. Johnson turned to the letters column of another newspaper, *The Sentinel,* to insist on the truth of his statement, but Cromwell's *Advocate* maintained that both *The Sentinel* and the *Christian Recorder* of the A.M.E. church had presented the information furnished by Johnson in a way injurious to Crummell. Cromwell clearly valued Crummell's good graces far more than Johnson's and his editorial gave up all credence of objectivity to insist that Crummell was not responsible for selecting the singers in his church, while at the same time presenting Crummell's claim that he had "repeatedly . . . spurned the advice of white clergymen to secure the permanent services of white vocalists." The choir was only partially white, *The People's Advocate* pointed out, and there was, in any case, nothing particularly odious about white vocalists in a church where the presence of white visitors seemed often to be "such a cause for exultation." [26]

Troubles continued throughout the following year, when the vestry charged Crummell with "secularity" for allowing a concert and a series of lectures in the church as a means of "monetary relief." As Crummell informed the bishop, nothing was to be sung save what was "sacred and religious." The bishop responded that, as the church was not yet consecrated, and as the program was to be devoted to sacred music, he had "nothing to say." But perhaps it would be better if in the future the church were used only for the purpose of worship. Throughout the year, the vestry remained at odds with Crummell, or, as he put it, they continued to "give themselves up to strife." [27]

In 1882 began a concerted effort to have Crummell removed from his rectorship. The bishop was delivered a petition. A committee of the vestry of St. Luke's, claiming to represent the sentiments of the vestry and the congregation, had resolved "that the best interests of said church demand the termination of the present pastoral relations therewith of Revd. Alexander Crummell." For anyone acquainted with Alexander Crummell, the charges would not have been difficult to believe. He had become alienated from at least a part of the congregation, who accused him of maintaining "a cold and forbidding manner." His expressions had become "contemptuous," his manners had become "offensive," and he had made charges "gross and unbecoming." One recalls Bishop Payne's portrayal of him as a brooding and sardonic man—the repressed anger,

and the cold smile as he said, ''Yes, I shall preach for Reverend Hoffman.''
One recalls the accusations of the Providence vestrymen, forty years earlier, of
frosty formality and cool aloofness. His son, Sidney, had made similar accusations, and Crummell himself admitted that those who ran afoul of him were
often treated to a silence colder than the ice of indifference.[28]

The vestry passed a series of resolutions calling for the suspension of Crummell's salary and the freezing of funds for the payment of an organist. They
voted to forbid the use of the organ during services and charged Fleetwood
write to the owner of the organ, calling for him ''to remove it at once from the
church.'' They raised the registration fee to $2.50 per year, making it impos-
sible for several of the poorer parishioners to retain voting rights ''and keeping
the voting power, in the Vestry elections, in the hands of a clique, who are
clerks and messengers in Departments.''[29] The petitioners maintained that
Crummell had accused the vestry of standing in the way of church harmony,
as a result of which they voluntarily retired at Easter 1881 and a new vestry
was elected.[30]

In this instance, Crummell felt compelled to respond with one of his lengthy
letters of self-justification, which included documentation in the form of correspondence exchanged with the choirmaster, C. A. Fleetwood, some of which
had already been published in *The People's Advocate* some years before. The
debate, so far as he was willing to say, had only to do with his unassailable
right to make decisions concerning the music and the liturgy in his own church.
He hinted at other issues, however, issues of class and culture. His opponents,
he asserted, were from the fashionable set and interested in the church only as
a stylish social gathering place. Crummell maintained that his support came
from the poorer people, ''many of them servants.'' These people, ardent and
devoted, were opposed to the clique and to Fleetwood, who was known
throughout the city for ''gross licentiousness.'' Indeed, Crummell maintained
that he often met expressions of surprise when it was mentioned that this man
with his ''universal reputation'' was vestryman of a church.

Crummell denied all but one of the charges, and that was the accusation of
contempt for the vestry. He claimed, in fact, to be surprised by the tameness
of the wording, for ''contempt'' was hardly the word to describe his passion.
''These men,'' he snorted, did ''not know how to use the English language,''
for he had indeed nothing short of ''disgust and indignation of the men.'' One
of them, Henry Johnson, had been accused of ''carrying colored school teachers to houses of prostitution, and debauching them.'' Another, William Cole,
had debauched a young girl, ''taking her for a long time to a house of infamy.''
He had been forced to marry her at gunpoint. He had subsequently been arrested in a house of ill-fame with a schoolteacher. The mother of the young
woman, driven to distraction had gone to the Pension Office, ''called him out,
and beat him in the public streets.'' It had been widely reported that Fleetwood
was in the house at the same time. Crummell claimed that one of them had
come to church drunk and noisy. Another had interrupted the sermon of a

venerable guest preacher with the exclamation, "Damn that minister, is he going to preach all day?"

There were at least two petitions of support for Crummell—one with fifty-seven signatures, and one with eighteen—but a committee of church superiors, convening on May 2, 1882, advised, nonetheless, that some way be found of removing Crummell from the rectorship of St. Luke's without doing damage to his reputation. Crummell was supported by Bishop Pinkney and retained in office. Needless to say, this constant turmoil had the effect of diminishing the influence that Crummell was able to have in the city. Even John Cromwell, who remained a loyal supporter in the church, described him as "tenacious of his rights and prerogatives," even when by a display of tact he might have avoided many conflicts and open ruptures.[31]

> In nearly *all* of these struggles the rector, though seemingly alone, came out more than victorious. In the early days of his ministration Bishops Whittingham and Pinkney were the friends and supporters of Dr. Crummell against the carping critics, but in Bishop Paret his enemies found one who would lend a listening ear.[32]

In defense of Crummell it should be said that his problems could not be attributed solely to the rigidity of his personality; many of them stemmed from the time and place in which he found himself. This was a period of breathless social advancement for black people, but periods of rapid upward mobility can be as traumatic as they are exhilarating for those who are caught in the updraft. Reconstruction Washington was as disconcerting as it was stimulating for black people. Although black Washingtonians were experiencing a dizzying elevation in social status, they were made aware of the precariousness of their new position by the constant, petty slights and insults of a society that viewed them either as pathetic wards or threatening upstarts. Prejudice, segregation, discrimination, and economic uncertainty were an ever-present threat to the black population. Jealousy, mistrust, and petty carping were products of a black psychology that had long developed under slavery and the caste system. Even among those who had never been slaves, there was much of what might be called a "slave mentality." It was thus astonishing that the people to whom Crummell ministered exhibited as much of a longing for culture and refinement as they did. It was remarkable that Crummell and his contemporaries were able to accomplish as much as they did during the 1870s.

The 1870s marked a dramatic shift in Crummell's political ideology. With remarkable blandness, he dug up old speeches that had been written in support of Liberian nationalism and recast them as American loyalist manifestos. While he remained true to his concept of group solidarity, racial destiny, African civilizationism, and even black nationalism, he abandoned, at least to all appearances, the idea that black Americans should work for a nation-state. One of the more forceful statements of his commitment to an American destiny for black Americans was made in a speech adapted from one of his old nationalistic sermons. It was on the American Thanksgiving Day of November 25, 1875, that he delivered his sermon "The Social Principle Among a People," which symbolized an acceptance of his identity as a black American and a sense of loyalty to the country's government, president, and traditions.

One scholar has discovered that portions of the address were from a sermon Crummell delivered in Liberia on the Liberian Thanksgiving Day, 1859—an observation that was perceptive enough. One recognizes, however, that a totally different view of the destiny of black Americans is expressed in the 1875 version. The latter was not a typical black nationalist celebration of self-help, solidarity, and racial pride as ends in themselves. Its central concern was cultural and political assimilation, which Crummell had come to view as a "simple point of practicality." [33]

While the continuity in Crummell's thinking cannot be denied, neither can the development and adaptation. The sermon cannot be reduced to a repetition of themes that dominated his thinking in Liberia. Its concerns are overwhelmingly American. The principal concern of the sermon is preparing oneself, getting ready, making oneself the model citizen who could be welcomed into the American society. This is no celebration of separatism, and no glorification of solidarity as a panacea for racial advancement. Solidarity and self-help are advocated, however, as essential means to a more important end: the same end that David Walker had long ago advocated, of making black and white Americans one "united and happy people." [34]

"The Social Principle Among a People" revealed some confusion about what exactly it meant to be a black American, but at the same time it offered a very clear idea of what Crummell hoped black Americans would become. "The destiny of the colored race of America" was "manifest." Black Americans were irreversibly on the road to becoming fully participating and accepted members of American society, but they would remain racially distinct.

> We are living in this country, a part of its population, and yet, in divers respects, we are as foreign to its inhabitants as though we were living in the Sandwich Islands. It is this our actual separation from the real life of the nation, which constitutes us "a nation within a nation."

Crummell had apparently disassociated himself from his earlier version of black nationalism, in which he advocated the establishment of a nation-state, the formation of a government, the possession of land, and the pursuit of a separate destiny. And yet, strangely, here was this reference to black Americans as de facto a nation. Throughout the address, he showed considerable inconsistency and confusion in his use of the terms "people," "race," and "nation." [35]

He held consistently to the idea, often articulated during the Liberian years, that there were universal laws of human progress, that these laws were very slow in their working, and that black people were not exempt from them. Civilization was a universal process; its rules applied uniformly all over the globe. He repeated the broad historical themes that he and William Wells Brown and Samuel Ringgold Ward had invoked during the antebellum years. He spoke of a period when England's "rude inhabitants lived in caves and huts, when they fed on bark and roots, when their dress was the skins of animals." They had once been "wild and bloody savages," and it had taken ten centuries to change them. Black people must accept the rules of historical progress; they must not be discouraged, nor believe themselves inferior, nor must they seek to circumvent the rules governing the process of civilization.

> The great general laws of growth and superiority are unchangeable. The Almighty neither relaxes not alters them for the convenience of any people.[36]

Just as he had once told the Liberians that their nation would succeed only through an understanding of the civilizational process, and by acknowledging that they were not yet a superior civilization, so too did he tell black Americans that they must undergo at least a century of development before they could hope to command the respect of whites. The success of their advancement within such a relatively short period of time could be achieved only by building strong cultural institutions.

Crummell cautioned against the dangerous philosophy that one should try to forget that one was black. In any case, the nature of segregation, barring black people from public accommodations, public carriers of the first class, and even from churches and schools, made that an impossibility. "Turn madmen, and go into a lunatic asylum, and then, perchance, you can forget it." But the attempt was not only folly, it was "socially destructive." It discouraged black people from taking advantage of the few social structures that might provide mutual aid. Black people were "shut out . . . from the cultivated social life of the superior classes of this country." The only opportunity for any of the mutual enlightenment that black people might enjoy was in black associations.

Black associations were to be viewed as a "temporary but needed expedient for the ultimate extinction of caste and all race distinctions." This was not black nationalism, but social integrationism, and it was now to be coupled to the cultural assimilationism that had been present in Crummell's ideology all along. But cultural assimilation must come first for social integration to be effected. To enter into warfare for acceptance, to engage in constant agitation, would in no way change the nature of American society. Agitation could destroy injustice, and it was capable of overcoming oppression, but it would have no effect on social acceptance.

Crummell did not, of course, use such terms as "cultural assimilation" or "social integration." One uses them here only to express clearly a distinction that must be made in order to understand his program. He posited that there were two barriers to black progress in America. One of these was color prejudice, pure and simple; the other was the fact that large masses of black people were "ignorant, unkempt, dirty, animal-like, repulsive, and half-heathen—brutal, and degraded." There was nothing that could be done directly to destroy the color prejudice of whites. The only thing to be done was to become one's brother's keeper and adopt the motto of lifting while we climb. In the meantime, one ought "not blink at the charge of inferiority." It was not a peculiarity of the black race and it could be rectified, for it was not innate. Black Americans must "rise to such elevation that the *people of the land* be forced to forget all the facts and theories of race, when they behold our thorough equality with them in all the lines of activity and attainment of culture and moral grandeur."

Here Crummell seemed to be momentarily forgetting that the ordinary white American, who lived under peasant conditions or industrial servitude, was neither culturally nor morally superior to the black freedman and had very little regard for concepts such as "culture and moral grandeur." White workers in the growing industrial cities certainly provided no high standard for black workers to measure up to and were no more inclined to recognize black social progress than were their Southern agrarian counterparts. The typical American had a certain sullen admiration for the "cultured classes," and behaved with grudging respect or resentful obeisance towards them, but it was not to be assumed that he or she truly valued or understood the manners and morals of the wealthy aristocrats, who dictated standards of culture and taste. Even less was it to be assumed that black people who attained such levels of education and refinement would automatically command the same deference. What Crummell seems to have hoped was that with the passage of time and the gradual cultural elevation of all lower-class Americans, there would be an evening out of social values and ethical ideals at a high level. This eventually would make it possible for currently degraded classes of Americans to recognize their commonality of taste, values, and interests. Before that could happen, however, there would have to be mass changes in the mentality of the black American masses.

It was obvious that progress could be made by the group only if it were also made on an individual level. It was therefore of utmost importance to cultivate personal character "as evidenced in high moral and intellectual attainments . . . general probity, honor, honesty, and self-restraint." Once these qualities became the rule among colored people, the problems of "caste" would fade away. Racial prejudice was, however, the problem of white men and women. Black people were not responsible for its creation, nor was it the responsibility of black people "to leave our camp and to go over, as it were, among the Philistines, and to destroy their idols." The concern of black people, both individually and collectively, should be to put their own house in order. Most of the political agitation in the country was "but wind and vanity," he declared. *"What this race needs in this country is* POWER." And the power of which he spoke would come only from the individual's development of character, religion, and virtue. These, alas, were "FORCES WHICH WE DO NOT POSSESS." Once the colored people laid hold of them, however, they would "take such root in this American soil, that only the convulsive upheaving of the Judgment Day [could] throw them out."[37]

Because Crummell laid such stress on the idea of collective destiny, it is easy to overlook the fact that he constantly emphasized the importance of individual character and personal responsibility, believing that nothing would be achieved collectively if the individual black man and woman did not develop the building blocks of personal character. Individuals, no less than races, must

work out their own salvation. He urged black Americans to rededicate themselves to the stoic principles that he associated with republican greatness. Such
dedication would inevitably lead to their emergence as the superior race in the
midst of a decomposing white world. Black Christianity did not wait for the
twentieth century to develop a "Decline of the West" theme. Even during
Crummell's youth the idea had dominated the writings of such literary outpourings as David Walker's *Appeal*. Crummell was one of those writers who
kept alive the tradition of emphasizing moral uprightness as the basis of racial
greatness throughout the nineteenth century and passed it along to such literary
heirs as W.E.B. Du Bois.

Crummell, with his emphasis on personal morality and hostility to "enthusiastic" religion, was what the Episcopalians called a "strict churchman." His
theology placed him closer to the Oxford Movement than to the American
evangelical mainstream, where many Episcopalians thrived. Evangelical protestantism often accommodated a seemingly contradictory social perfectionism,
however, and Crummell's religion allowed for such an accommodation. Thus
he could preach that works and deeds were the ultimate standard by which
every man and woman must be judged, without abandoning the idea that grace
was the ultimate justifying force. He had made this belief clear in his sermons
on the Last Judgment. In another sermon, "The Fitness of the Gospel for its
Own Work," he had struggled to reconcile the discipline, rationalism, and
social concerns of the gospel with the subjectivism and otherworldliness of St.
Paul.

He attacked the "excitable and hysterical pietists, people who think that
godliness consists in emotion and manifests itself in feeling." Such attitudes
were "a repudiation of moral obligation." At times Crummell may have seemed
to be teetering on the brink of Romanist doctrine, with his emphasis on works
and his repudiation of revivals and enthusiastic conversion. He always kept his
Protestant ideological balance, however, and made clear his belief that grace
rather than works was the source of salvation. Christian perfectionism and civil
religion were obviously at home within the American evangelical tradition.
Crummell's theology fell within the framework of the "Arminianized Calvinism" that permeated the thinking of many nineteenth-century Episcopalians.[38]

Some of Crummell's theological writings revealed an almost classical Arminianism. Simply put, he believed that grace was resistible, which implied
that salvation originated in an act of the will, not purely in the passive reaction
to grace. The idea that the Christian had to perform an act of will to accept
Christ's salvation seemed to imply that the Christian was responsible for his
own salvation. If this was heresy, Crummell seemed to believe that it could be
imbibed by black folk without grave danger. Arminianism seemed a lesser evil
than the immediate problems of antinomianism and otherworldliness that he
identified in black religion. Arminian ideas were openly expressed in his sermon "The Rejection of Christ."[39] It required an act of will to accept Jesus
and his redeeming grace. And even after accepting grace, Christians must "work
out their own salvation." Christ's atonement for sin did not mean that the

struggle would become easy as soon as one accepted Christ. Caught up in the classical problem of Christian theology, the problem of whether to emphasize works or faith, Crummell oscillated between emphasizing vicarious atonement and emphasizing the efforts that Christians must make for their own salvation. On the one hand, he stated that one was saved by grace alone, on the other, that the basis of Christ's judgement would be one's deeds. On one occasion, after his return to the United States, this even led to an apparently conscious distortion of St. Paul. Extreme evangelicals would certainly have seen it that way. In many cases they seemed to believe that Christians participated in their salvation only to the extent of deciding to accept the friendship of Jesus. Once befriended, Jesus would provide them with the grace to live lives of effortless virtue. For those who accepted this brand of evangelical Christianity, perennially popular in America, salvation was indeed an easy and simple thing, provided one was saved and had submitted to Jesus. Crummell believed otherwise.

In wrestling with the problem posed by the teachings of St. Paul of whether or not Christians were bound by the law, Crummell hedged. He averred that Christians were not bound by the law of Moses, but that they were nonetheless obliged to make the Ten Commandments their "rule of life." He warned of the dangers of falling back upon the assurance of the conversion experience. It was not enough to examine and search oneself to see if one were in the faith; one must strive to persevere. Among black people, it was particularly important to work against the "one sided and disproportionate" emphasis on the conversion experience. Black religion too often "substituted rhapsody and hallucinations for spiritual service and moral obligation." He spoke of the role of the black priest as "revolutionary," in that it was to correct the endemic fallacies of plantation religion. The black priest often found that he must "uproot . . . the roots of religious extravagance and enthusiasm." He must subject the pietistic tendencies of his race to the discipline of moralism, emphasizing works and deeds as well as faith.[40]

> God had thrown personal responsibility upon every man to achieve his own salvation. "Work out your own salvation, etc." We are not saved passively in a state of effortless inertia. We ourselves have got to ward our spirits from the power of Satan, to shield them from the poison of sin. And this is an arduous work; *not* the light easy effort which many suppose it to be.[41]

Crummell substituted an "etc." for the second half of verse 2:12 from Paul's Epistle to the Phillipians, which some would have interpreted as anything but an exhortation to self-reliance, and hardly a decisive affirmation of the doctrine of works. Crummell did not quote the passage in its entirety because it was really not appropriate to the doctrine he wished to expound. In context, the verse might have seemed like an argument against his point. For it was, in fact, a typical Pauline admonition: a reminder to the Christian of his utter dependency on God, and a warning that the will to do good was simply an effect of grace. Crummell was ready enough to cite Paul in support of his strenuous puritanical ethic of work, achievement, and constant moral effort. He was, however, ready to cut off a verse in midsentence to protect against the danger of antinomian misinterpretations. He was certainly not above time-honored exegetical tricks of judicious quotation to make the Bible say just what he wanted it to say. Not that he was afraid to quote the passage in its entirety. He was fully convinced that the Bible supported his extreme Arminianism—his doctrine that the will must be constantly exercised to maintain law, order, and civilization. "Struggle," he insisted, "is one of the prime conditions of existence."[42]

> In order to become saintly, we must do something ourselves. The Holy Ghost will never carry us to heaven without our own wills, and our own holy actions. To be saints we must "work out our own salvation with fear and trembling," relying upon God to work "within us to will and to do His good pleasure."[43]

More traditional American evangelicals would have found Crummell's doctrine—that to "walk worthy of the Lord," the Christian must accept responsibility for his own salvation—tinged with Arminian heresy. While he insisted, as most Christians do, that morality was the outward sign of piety, he would often lapse into revealing statements bordering on the heterodox, as when he enjoined his congregation, in a sermon on "Affluence and Receptivity,"

> Lay the foundations of your piety deep in the purest morals. Settle it as an axiom in religion that there is no such thing possible as true godliness without morality.[44]

He seemed, in this instance, to be implying that piety was a by-product of morality. This was a doctrine that might have been acceptable to some Roman Catholic theologians, who accepted the doctrine that salvation was possible without direct, conscious knowledge of Christ, but Protestant evangelicals were not often sympathetic to such doctrines. Crummell, teetering on the brink of this Romanist heresy, came very close to accepting the doctrine of justification by works. Piety was generated by acts of the will and by good works. He saw moral living as both an effect and a cause of piety; it was both a sign of piety and an agency that strengthened pious habits. Piety was a virtue that must be strengthened by constant effort. The road to salvation was an arduous path.

> And yet there are many who think it is the easiest simplest of all things to save their souls. The earnest constant labour which is demanded, they can't understand. The ceaseless watchfulness which is required, they esteem fanatical. The announcement that the way is straight and narrow, they disbelieve. . . .
>
> There are tares to be rooted up from the human heart. Can this be done without labour? The soil of unbelief is to be broken up. Is this a playful pastime? There are passions to be repressed, worldliness to be consumed, lust to be annihilated, gross desires to be quenched. Is all this easy achievement? Can all this giant effort be performed without sweatful toil, without anxious watchfulness?[45]

In his sermon "The Greatness of Christ," the evangelical impulse and the doctrine of vicarious atonement won out over the doctrine of works that was asserted in other sermons. Here, Christ was not only the source of salvation, but the root cause of civilization and worldly, material progress. An extreme Christocentrism and reliance on "the personality of Christ" dominated his thinking in this sermon. It was not the church as a temporal institution, nor the men and ministers who composed it, who were responsible for the progress seen in the modern world. "No system, of itself produces results," he wrote. "There is a personality behind every organized institution." "Christianity . . . does not work itself. . . . It is a result that is produced by Jesus Christ, present in this world by the power of the Holy Ghost."[46]

Crummell's theory of social change was grounded not only in Christian morality, but in Christian teleology. His works were informed by theological historicism, and he rejected the idea that God had "made the universe once for all" and then withdrawn into the grandeur of heaven, allowing the world carelessly to "spin round his finger." Neither in this world nor in the next could a nation or race escape the consequences of its behavior. Nor would individuals be allowed to act without responsibility or obligation. He believed that God made his presence felt not only in heaven but in history, in which the most important fact was the personality of Jesus Christ, whose mission was social and material as well as spiritual.

History was the story of progress, and Christ's incarnation on Earth had greatly accelerated the mechanisms governing progress. The growth of philanthropy since the dawn of the nineteenth century demonstrated the progression of history and, furthermore, that society as it progressed was being brought into closer accord with the laws of God. Progress could be witnessed in science, in technology, in the evolution of human morals, and in the arts. Crummell recalled his visit to the World's Exposition in London in 1851 and how he had reflected on what he perceived as the facts of moral progress. Here progress was evident in the arts, as well as in the miracles of physical and mechanical science. And from the arts one could deduce progress in the history of morals. It was a known fact that the art of the ancient Romans was so debased that no modern civilized man would allow his wife and daughters to see it. Were there not rooms in the museums of the Roman church that no woman was allowed to enter? But the power of Christ's personality in history had endowed mankind with the chaste representations of Victorian art—aesthetically inspiring and morally elevating.[47]

Theological historicism was the basis of Crummell's progressive theory,[48] which derived from his belief in the inexorable working of Providence; but, while his teleology was optimistic, he did not find it unsuitable to give his addresses all the possible force of rationalism and modern social theory. Although he was not a professional historian in an age of increasing professionalization of the social sciences, he was certainly not ignorant of the major figures and theoreticians of historical writing, and he was clever enough to find authoritative support for his theory of historical progress in the writings of François Guizot. It may be that Crummell cited Guizot because of some deep and abiding influence that the French historian's writings had worked on him. While this is not impossible, it seems more likely that he simply used the widely read and respected author to buttress his own theories. He cited Guizot in each of his three books, because he found useful the French author's insistence on the principle of Providence as a historical force.[49]

Guizot's theory of history was essentially mystical, and so was Crummell's.[50] Both based their ideas on faith rather than reason and seized on a teleology that almost seemed to justify the obstinacy of social evils with the rationalization that, although the laws of civilization moved inexorably, they were gradual in their working. The elevation of the black race was certain to occur but subject to the same laws of gradual progress that had required centuries to bring Europe to its still imperfect but nonetheless advanced state. More than once he quoted the French historian on the ways of God, whose Providence would not hurry "to display to-day the consequences of the principle that he yesterday laid down." God would draw out his plan "in the lapse of ages when the hour is come." The patterns of past events and present developments could be discerned by anyone with the willingness to see them. The orderly sequence of historical patterns would not suddenly be confounded by some chaotic, meaningless course of future events. Crummell read the march of historical progress as slow but steady—majestic, inexorable, and irreversible.

Crummell's religious historicism, like Guizot's, was intertwined with an incurable ethnic chauvinism. While both authors were Anglophiles, each was nonetheless convinced of the superiority of his own race. Both of them were convinced that the course of history that had led to the triumph of nineteenth-century Europe represented the mainstream of civilized progress, but each believed in the special role of his own group within the pageant of history. Guizot, albeit he had great admiration for the British system of law and government, believed nonetheless in the superiority of French culture. Crummell, with his Anglophilism, was no less a chauvinist for the black race; he believed, however, that the great days of his people were yet to come. This idea was celebrated in his sermon "The Destined Superiority of the Negro."

Portions of the address had been printed many years earlier in *African Repository,* and even before that the idea had made recurrent appearances in his essays. The theme had dominated the "Eulogy on Thomas Clarkson," and, for those who knew Crummell and his contemporaries, there was certainly nothing new about the idea that Providence had some special destiny for the black race, as it did for all peoples whom it subjected to testing and tempering in the fires of oppression. The idea that chosen peoples were always singled out for suffering was nothing new in the Judeo-Christian tradition. Here was a perfect example of one of Crummell's early ideological statements, formulated during his black nationalist phase in Liberia and easily maintained after his return to America. No major alterations were required to adapt it to the conditions under which black Americans lived, because African Civilizationist rhetoric had never been inflexibly committed to the Back to Africa Movement. This was spiritual Pan-Africanism, the expression of an optimistic teleology that could be equally inspiring to black people, regardless of where they happened to live.[51]

Although Crummell had dramatically revised his concept of black American destiny after his return to the United States, other areas of his philosophy remained consistent. These old religious dogmas continued to be important throughout his life. He maintained his belief in civil religion, so powerful that it overstepped the boundaries between church and state. He easily carried his antebellum Christian perfectionism into the era of the "social gospel." As a black pastor, he had a duty to provide practical guidance for his flock. He must lead them in the great social movement for the uplift of the race, which was clearly in accord with God's historical plan. He maintained his long-standing commitment to heirarchial relationship and to the Episcopalian principles of "submission to authority, respect for rules, quietness and order." There was never any wavering on Christianity, the centrality of Jesus Christ, or the doctrine of vicarious atonement. Therefore, he naturally denounced the Unitarianism of Theodore Parker and William Ellery Channing, whom he saw as rejecting the essential Christian doctrine.[52]

Social religion was based on the idea that man was by nature a social being and that all social order must be maintained in accordance with the laws of God. The idea that social morality was instinctual was a well-established theological idea, which had appeared in the writings of Henry More, the Cambridge Platonist. The moral basis of his teaching on the social principle among a people was universal. In some respects, however, the condition of Africans and Afro-Americans was peculiarly the same. He had spoken of native Africans as "the withered arm of humanity," and in later years he spoke of the freedmen in America as "an immense population who have been crippled, alike in body and in soul."[53] It seems likely that at times in his later years Crummell entertained the idea that black people could eventually come to be accepted by white Americans on an individual level. Certainly he spoke of black Americans' obligation to contribute to the mental and material wealth of the United States. Such ideas would, of course, conflict with his often expressed hope for a distinct racial destiny and Negro supremacy, which persisted from his Liberian nationalist years.

It is clear, however, that he trusted in a Providence that would bring black people through a process of regeneration and lead them to play an important role as a leavening agent in a society that was inclined to extremes of liberal permissiveness. Black Americans were undergoing a providential toughening process that would make them better suited to give the American nation moral backbone. This was a new theme for Crummell, whose message in the past had always been concerned with what black people could do for themselves. Now, he spoke to the question of what they could do for America in general. It was in a sense a preview of the doctrine that Booker T. Washington was to preach, and it seems to have been designed to convince white people of the usefulness of the black American. Indeed it is conceivable that Crummell made use of his opportunity to impress this message on the white congressmen who sometimes sat with his congregation.

Perhaps because St. Luke's parish was so near to the sordid temptations of Washington alley life, Crummell felt it necessary to warn constantly against the sins of the flesh. It was a tough doctrine that he preached, a gospel of self-restraint and repression. As a child of black New York's Five Points district, he had been exposed to much of the sexual vice and intemperance of the city's most sordid quarter. He had early rejected the street-corner morality and earthy sexuality of black ghetto boys and accepted the perfectionst and puritanical values of his abolitionist educators. Thus, he associated upward social mobility with bourgeois morality, sober behavior, and temperance. He preached a rigid sexual ethic and advised complete abstinence from strong drink. He preached with passion, sometimes throwing in bad grammar to good effect:

> I commend, then, abstinence on the grounds of personal safety. Every man, we may assume, loves himself . . . [and] what does self love tell us? Don't it tell us to take care of ourselves? Don't it urge us to look after our best interest, to be careful of our comfort? to have an eye to our advantage? . . . You all know the fact of the inheritance of physical qualities from our parents or our ancestors. . . . Ain't there something fearful in this?[54]

Crummell was bothered by the question of whether the use of wine in the communion service was an argument in facor of intoxicants. The question turned on the translation of certain Hebrew words, and the question of whether the prohibition of leavened bread could be extended to wine as well. In a letter to the black Presbyterian minister Francis J. Grimké, he referred to the works of biblical scholar Moses Stuart, who had taken a strong stand against fermented wine. Crummell confessed that he was "at sea" on the question and awaited more light. But whatever case might be made for fermented communion wine, he had no tolerance for what he called "social inebriation."[55]

Some of his most impassioned sermons were on marital sexual relations and duties. He knew that even under the best of circumstances the flesh was weak and gross, and he believed that circumstances had made the black race in America particularly susceptible to temptations of the flesh. The African race had been endowed by nature with emotional and aesthetic tendencies, but the experience of slavery had all too often perverted these tendencies in the direction of lust and sensuality. The spirit of the race, therefore, must be guarded against the dangers of concupiscence, from the temptations of lascivious literature, epicureanism, disproportion. Daughters and sons must be raised to know their duties. Frivolousness, tastelessness, the love of wine parties and gaudy ornamentation, were all to be discouraged. The necessity of self-restraint was endlessly stressed. Young men no less than young women must be instructed in social purity. Black parents must teach their sons to treat the daughters of others as they would wish to have their own daughters treated.

Crummell's sexual ethics were designed to strengthen black family life; he considered it idle to speak of other kinds of institutional development without addressing the problem of improving black American family life. The fundamental social institution was the nuclear family, and so long as the black family bore the marks of slavery, all institutions would reflect the consequences of the harm that had been done to it. Crummell wrote of the black family in several contexts during his later years. The theme that ran throughout these writings may be stated succinctly. The family was an institution of divine origin, most excellently suited to the natural needs of man, and essential to the evolution of all higher culture. But the catastrophe of slavery had left the black family in a degraded state. The strength or weakness of a race would be determined by its family life.

> Take the sanctity of marriage, the facility of divorce, the chastity of woman, the shame, modesty and bashfulness of girlhood, the abhorrence of illegitimacy; and there is no people in this land who, in these regards, have received such deadly thrusts as this race of ours. And these qualities are the grandest qualities of all superior people.[56]

For Crummell it was self-evident that the uplift of the black race in America must begin with the reconstruction of the black family. The tendency of a future generation of social scientists to romanticize or sentimentalize the slave family as an institution would have filled him with astonishment and anger. Crummell viewed the Victorian ideal of the middle-class nuclear family as "the basis of all human progress and of all civilization," for it nurtured "the gentle refinement, the pure speech, and the godly anxieties of womanhood; all the endurance, the courage and the hardy toil of men."[57]

The maintenance of the nuclear family as the basic social institution, then, was perhaps the most important issue facing black America in Crummell's opinion, since there could be no hope for black people in America unless the traditional family structure and traditional sexual roles and obligations could be institutionalized among the black population. Later writers, including W.E.B. Du Bois, Robert E. Park, E. Franklin Frazier, and Daniel Patrick Moynihan, would all repeat Crummell's observations: primitive Africans were backward but not debased. It was slavery that had destroyed the positive virtues black Americans had brought with them from Africa. The problem of improving black life in America was essentially the problem of eradicating the vicious habits acquired by black people under slavery.

Crummell accepted without question the same ideals that were sentimentalized, but so unevenly maintained, by the Anglo-American bourgeoisie. His views of family life were based on then standard conceptions of the characteristics of the sexes and the natural relationship between them. Thus we see him referring to "the shame, modesty and bashfulness of girlhood" in one address and to "the instinct of chastity" in another. These were natural traits of young women, which should at all costs be nurtured by social institutions. Crummell passionately voiced the opinion that there were many virtuous young colored women in Washington, but that they had little in the way of restraining, elevating, or encouraging influences to sustain them in their virtuous resolve, and many influences of the opposite sort.[58] He believed that women in highly civilized society would naturally aspire to their rightful condition—strong, clean, and angelic. The grossness of African paganism had prevented African women from attaining their natural state of refinement, and centuries of slavery had catastrophically debased the black woman even further. Bearing this in mind, it was the duty of the black leadership class to create a setting in which she might be able to realize "the delicate tenderness of her sex."[59]

He professed a belief in the equality of man and woman, which ought to be typified in the relationship between man and wife. Marriage was "the primal society of human beings," and a family was a government in which "the father and the mother are the joint heads. . . . But in this united authority, the man by the sanction of nature and revelation, by law and custom, by reason and instance, has the precedency." Thus, although he spoke of sexual equality, he maintained a conservative view of family life and the nature of sex roles. His views in this regard reflected the biases of the classes of British and American aristocrats with whom he identified. They were not dissimilar to the views that black women's groups were to take up in the ensuing quarter century.[60]

The principles on which Crummell's marital and sexual ethics are based have passed into oblivion. At the time of his death, however, the values that he promoted were conservative but not reactionary. He believed that intellectually gifted women should be educated on the same terms as intellectually gifted men and in the same institutions. Young girls of the peasant class should be provided with industrial training in boarding schools of the Tuskegee type. His formula for the uplift of the black woman of the South did not differ from that of such spokeswomen as Mary Church Terrell, or Margaret Murray Washington.[61]

Every major black thinker for the next seventy-five years accepted Crummell's belief that black Americans would either rise or fall depending on their ability to realize in practice the American family dream. He in no way anticipated the Harlem Renaissance tradition, which would romanticize a supposed African sexual abandon. His attitudes on this issue presaged those of Malcolm X, who was to portray the primal African culture as a world unmarred by Western sexual licentiousness. Crummell portrayed precolonial Africa as having a healthily restrained sexual climate. The catastrophe of slavery had destroyed what Du Bois would later call "ancient African chastity."

The appropriate relation between man and wife had been ordained by God in the Garden of Eden. Marriage was not only an honorable state, it was the only truly natural state of mankind. Every man should ideally be a warrior and a provider; every woman, a tender of the hearth and a mother. Everyone had a duty to be married, except for the "maimed, diseased, disabled, and unnatural cases among men who are shut out of consideration." Normal individuals all had the "reproductive faculty and instinct," the desire for fatherhood and motherhood. He spoke with loathing of those "unnatural mothers [who] resist the commands of nature and . . . turn their own bodies into the graves of their unborn infants."

Infanticide has been, we know, the practice of heathen mothers from immemorial times; but always, be it remembered, through ignorance, or superstition, or the demands of a false religion. But it has been left to our times for Christian women, through the demands of fashion or the love of ease, to turn back the tide of nature; to choose death in the place of life; and by deliberate murder to deny themselves the tender offices of the breast, and to deafen their ears to the sweet prattlings of infancy. . . . No Argument is needed to prove that all this is cruel and unnatural.[62]

Crummell's ideas on such issues deviated in no way from the doctrines of such groups as the National Federation of Afro-American Women.[63] Some black women were beginning to express modern feminist attitudes in their writings, but one searches in vain for anything that runs counter to the positions taken by Crummell on sexual morality. Anna J. Cooper, one of the more feminist black women writers of her time, spoke of his essay "The Black Woman of the South" with the highest respect. While influenced by feminist thought, black women writers like Mrs. N. F. Mossell and Josephine St. Pierre Ruffin did not aggressively question orthodox conceptions of women's role in society. Generally speaking, middle-class black Americans were no more inclined than their white counterparts to question patriarchal traditions. Black Americans with a strong sense of racial feeling tended, if anything, to be even more conservative than whites on questions of sexual morality. Among the more notable obsessions of classic black nationalism were the creation of a black patriarchy and the maintenance of bourgeois sexual and marital ideals.

One witnesses the survival of Crummell's patriarchal attitudes in more recent forms of twentieth-century black nationalism. Indeed, Crummell was the link between earlier nineteenth-century traditions and twentieth-century black messianism. His messianic conception of black American destiny was to reappear in Garvey and in Malcolm X. He was exposed as a youth to the chosen people rhetoric of David Walker and was aware very early of the apocalyptic interpretation of the Nat Turner revolt. Revolutionary religion was an ever-present force in his father's home; it was the salt with which his mother baked her bread. Crummell's sermons for the rest of his life spoke of the "destined superiority of the Negro" and of "Ethiopia stretching forth her hand unto God." His religious thought provided the bridge between the generation of David Walker and that of Marcus Garvey.

Even more important, Crummell's theology of self-help provided an important corrective to the excessive emphasis on the conversion experience that characterized black religion in the nineteenth century. Neither individuals nor races could be saved simply through frenzy or possession by the spirit. They must be saved by disciplined effort. The problem of the salvation of the black race was similar to the problem of saving the individual soul. Forces from without could help. God and Jesus could help. Laws and governments could help. Ultimately, however, the crucial force for salvation must be iron strength of character.

> There are passions to be repressed . . . , worldliness to be consumed, lust to be annihilated, gross desires to be quenched. Is this an easy achievement? Can all this giant effort be performed without anxious watchfulness?[64]

What was true for individual black people in the United States was also true of the group. Self-help was crucial. Self-help referred, of course, to the necessity of relying on their own efforts rather than on appeals to white morality. It meant that the black group, like the black individual, must learn to work for its own salvation. One did not get to heaven simply by knowing Jesus; one attained heaven by the same means that one attained success on this earth. One kept one's hand on the plough, and held it with an unfaltering grasp.

One of Crummell's contributions to American religious thought was, as Gayraud Wilmore has observed, "to question the *agape* doctrine of orthodox Christianity, by expounding self-love as a Christian principle which the oppressed Black race must espouse if it is to cast off the chains of oppression and rise to equality with the white nations of the world." He advocated, indeed, a religion of black power. But to this I would add that racial power was always seen as arising from the inculcation of individualism and character-building. Crummell did, indeed, strike a blow against the "pietistic religion of the northern missionaries and subservient Black preachers, who taught Negroes to humble themselves under the yoke of the meek and gentle Jesus." He saw the dangers of a religion that placed far too much emphasis on "waiting patiently upon the Lord," either for salvation or for worldly deliverance.[65]

# 12

# A Man of Mark
# (1882–1894)

Crummell was hardly an invisible man in 1882, the year that *The Greatness of Christ* was published. His intelligence, his mental vigor, his abilities in the pulpit, his reputation as a brilliant conversationalist, made him "a distinguished man in any social gathering." He was "tall, erect, majestic and noble in his carriage," said John Wesley Cromwell. "On the public highway, his natural stride, and his commanding appearance gave him a most striking individuality." "A true African in color," as another associate described him, and still very handsome as he entered his early sixties, Crummell was white-haired, white-bearded, "very neat and trim." He dressed in the most sober priestly fashion, wore dignified wire-rimmed spectacles, and affected the conservative clerical collar. His friends described him as having a "retiring disposition"; critics viewed him as "cold and contemptuous." His bearing was, indeed, formidable, his manner sometimes imperious and often sarcastic. There were some, however, who saw in him not only this commanding presence but also "a kindly demeanor." [1]

Rev. Matthew Anderson, a man he befriended in his later years, spoke of his "humor, wit, repartee, and even playfulness" and remembered him as a man of agreeable disposition, whose home was a congenial and happy place.[2] W. C. Bolivar recalled an occasion in the home of Rev. William Henry Josephus:

> There was gathered at his board, Richard T. Greener, George W. Williams, the author Dr. E. C. Howard. . . . Dr. Howard began to play an air on the piano. The attention was indeed rapt, and after the conclusion of the number some one asked Dr. Crummell to tell the message the music brought. In a burst of eloquence, he entranced those present in a manner that denoted the artist, the poet, the scholar, the music itself was delightful, but the thoughts of that great mind

were made infinitely more so by the way in which they were clothed by this gifted man.[3]

William Wells Brown, who had known Crummell for many years, contributed to the more widely held view of his character, however. While acknowledging that he was "a gentleman by nature," who "could not be anything else if he should try," he criticized him as "rather too sensitive, and somewhat punctilious."[4] Thus, even his admirers lent credence to the unflattering picture painted by old adversaries.

> He was a born ruler and could not brook opposition. This he showed in his whole manner and conversation. Dealing with a people who have not yet learned to submit gracefully to authority, when exerted by one of their own race, this trait of character in Dr. Crummell often militated against his immediate usefulness.[5]

He was now referred to as "Dr. Crummell," having received an honorary Doctor of Divinity degree from Lincoln University shortly after his return to the United States, although it was reputed that he did not put much stock in the degree. Nor was he entirely forgotten in Liberia, where the university awarded him an honorary Doctor of Laws degree in 1882. He was a grand old man, one of the few survivors of the heroic age of abolitionist agitation and, by 1885 one of the few remaining representatives of the Pan-African movement of the sixties.[6]

Sarah Crummell died in the summer of 1878, at the age of fifty-seven, of Bright's disease after a five months' illness. She was living in New York, where, according to the death certificate, she had been residing for ten years. Why she was living in New York and not with her husband in Washington at the time of her death has not yet been discovered. Their marriage had not been a happy one. She had endured at least seven difficult pregnancies, some of them during periods of very poor health and depression, and could hardly be accused of having failed her husband in terms of the biblical injunction of marriage. She had indeed been fruitful. They had disagreed about matters related to rearing the children, however, and it seems likely that Crummell often went without speaking to Sarah. As he put it, "I say almost nothing: I try to keep silence even from good words."[7]

We know that she was still living with her husband in Liberia as late as October 1867. Crummell described her as "a complete invalid" and listed her as a member of his household. Concerning Sidney's charges that year, she had been strangely silent; there is no record of her having written to the bishops in defense of her husband, although, as the Caldwell grand jury reported, she had been willing to testify in court that Crummell had never struck her. There is a cryptic note in Whittingham's journal of 1874 that discreetly refers to some undated and unspecified charges brought against Crummell and to a letter from Sarah Crummell. It reads as follows:

> Committed the investigation of charges against Rev. A. Crummell to the Rt. Rev. Dr. Pinkney, by verbal commission and delivery of Mrs. Crummell's letter.[8]

Crummell once said that the absence of love vitiated a marriage, but "we dare not say that this revokes the contract." The only grounds for divorce that Crummell accepted as legitimate was infidelity on the part of the wife. Whether or not the Crummells fell out of love, it is evident that there was much bitterness between them. Family life for the Crummells was a far cry from the forms idealized in Crummell's sermons on marriage. Nonetheless, Crummell once proclaimed from the pulpit, "By God's blessing and my mother's teaching, I can say that I never wronged a woman in my life!"[9]

He had married early, most likely with an eye to the Pauline caveat, "It is better to marry than to burn."[10] Whatever his feelings toward his first wife, they were very privately kept. It may be that he loved her to the end, but nothing has so far been found in the correspondence that mourns, or even mentions, her passing. Financial difficulties had plagued their life together. Their firstborn child had died as a result of their poverty, their second, as the result of a tragic accident. The daughters had resented the restrictions their father had placed on them. Although his views on the education of women were progressive, he resented any attempts they made to act independently. Sidney, the only surviving son, had often been a source of anguish and continued to be a source of embarrassment even as he entered full manhood. At twenty-seven, when he returned to the United States in 1873, he was apparently financially dependent, even at this age, not only on Crummell but on other members of the family, who found him something of a nuisance. Crummell's nephew, William A. Elston, wrote from New York in the summer of 1873 to report that Sidney had called on him the previous evening to borrow $3.00.

> I did not let him have it, besides the $20.00 you sent him, I gave him $10.00 on Sunday and $10.00 Monday evening, now he is without a cent now this you know is getting rid of Money just a little too fast for me and did not think it would be doing him any good to let him have it, I undertook to explain things to him, but he did not seem to understand my way of thinking. I think the sooner you send for him the better.[11]

Crummell was married for the second time on September 23, 1880, in St. Philip's Church of New York to Jennie Simpson. She was described by William J. Simmons as "refined and ladylike" and by a social columnist in *The People's Advocate* as "his handsome bride." On October 4, the couple was visited by a number of friends, who presented them with "a handsome silver pitcher and salver, a silver goblet, lined with gold, and a walnut stand." This was an occasion for Crummell to speak "very feelingly" to a group of those in the church, including John W. Cromwell, who had always supported him. "Dear friends," he said, "I feel very much encouraged by your kindness."[12]

His second marriage was undoubtedly happier than his first. References to his second wife are common in his letters, where he spoke of their companionship, as they read together in the evenings and she accompanied him on his travels. He once remarked in a letter to a friend that his wife had urged him to travel to Newport alone. His eyesight was failing, and he needed the rest, but he was hesitant to "obey." Not only did he consider it selfish to vacation without her, but he felt that he would miss her company. "How glad I am," he wrote to John Bruce, "that I am a married man,—a married priest in the church of God." It was important for priests to be married, because priests were leaders, and if leaders were untouched by the hand of woman, social disaster would result. How fortunate that priests in the Episcopal church were not placed under the Romish strictures of celibacy. For women, in the main, were better than men, and their influences went to make men better.[13]

Failing eyesight was a source of much anxiety to Crummell during the eighties and nineties. He wrote of it as if it were a mere annoyance, but he reported to Frank Grimké in 1886 that he was forced to employ an amanuensis. At that time, his doctor had told him that there was nothing that could be done for his degenerating vision, so, as he wrote to Grimké, he must "stand and wait."[14] His letters even before his return to the United States were written in very heavy broad black pen, in contrast to the finer and neater penmanship of his early letters and sermons. From around 1890 to 1897 he was blind in one eye, but, shortly before his fourth trip to England in the fall of 1897, the cataract was removed and he regained the use of both eyes. The temporary blindness must have been a burden to a man who was so visually oriented.[15] Not only was he an avid reader, but he took particular joy in the beauty of the human face. He would comment on handsome men and beautiful women in his writing, and he delighted in the physical beauty of the various African peoples he encountered.[16]

Crummell's letters often contain digressions on the beauties of nature. He also enjoyed art museums and made it a point to visit art galleries on his trips to England. He commented enthusiastically on the magnificence of the British metropole, its "palatial residences and fine equipages, its grand Cathedrals and noble churches." He greatly appreciated architecture and always placed great value on a fine church edifice. He spoke of having done architectural drawings and at least one sketch of a West African native village.[17]

Crummell was now frequently invited to lecture on ceremonial occasions that required a man of his dignity and presence. For, while he could not function amicably among his everyday associates, there was a fortunate contrast between his local ministerial life and the stature that he had achieved nationally. He could be counted on as an edifying occasional speaker. In 1882, while embroiled in his difficulties with the vestry of St. Luke's, he was invited by the Union Literary and Historical Association of Washington, D.C., to deliver the eulogy for Henry Highland Garnet. Shortly before his death, Garnet had accepted the position of Minister Resident to the Republic of Liberia, which made him the highest official of the United States in that country. Crummell recalled that Garnet had been in the habit of taking leave of friends with the salutation "Africa forever!"[18]

On the eve of Garnet's departure, Crummell had hosted a dinner in his honor during which a mutual friend overheard Garnet say, "Oh Alexander if I can just reach the land of my forefathers and with my feet press her soil, I shall be content to die.'' He died within two months of his arrival in Liberia and was given a state funeral that was attended by the president and his cabinet and the entire military garrison of Monrovia. After a funeral sermon preached by Blyden, he was buried in the Palm Grove Cemetery of Monrovia. The eulogy was delivered in the 19th Street Baptist Church, "before a packed house." Also on the platform were "some of the most distinguished men of the race," including Frederick Douglass and Henry McNeal Turner, who also spoke briefly, but the principal tribute was given by Crummell, "whose scholarship and eloquence, whose intimacy and sympathies made him the best qualified living human being for the discharge of this sad duty."[19]

Martin Delany died three years later in 1885. He had continued to advocate colonization long after Crummell's return, and in 1878 he had even supported a new Back to Africa Movement. In this he was joined by Henry McNeal Turner, a bishop of the A.M.E. church. As a young minister he had been inspired by one of Crummell's colonization sermons preached during his American tour of 1862; he later claimed that it was this sermon that converted him to the colonization cause. When Edward Wilmot Blyden visited the United States in 1882, Bishop Turner hosted a dinner for him in his home. Delany was there, and so was Frank Grimké, who is reported to have said that he would "join the Doctor himself in his great African work at some future time, perhaps." The movement had involved the emigration of 206 settlers, but it had not sparked a general enthusiasm for colonization, nor had it attracted the support that the earlier movement had in literary and intellectual circles.[20]

Frederick Douglass was alive and well and living in Washington. Crummell and he had a lively confrontation in 1885 at Harper's Ferry, where they both were speakers at the commencement exercises of Storer College. Douglass took exception to some of Crummell's remarks in his speech, "The Need of New Ideas and New Aims for a New Era," as Crummell later explained.

> It happened that my distinguished neighbor, Hon. Frederick Douglass, was one of the audience on that occasion. The leading thought of the address—the shifting of general thought from past servitude, to duty and service, in the present;—met with his emphatic and most earnest protest. He took occasion on the instant to urge his hearers to a constant recollection of the slavery of their race and of the wrongs it had brought upon them.[21]

Crummell had launched an attack on what he perceived as a common problem among black people, the tendency "to dwell morbidly and absorbingly upon the servile past." It was bad enough that for two hundred years the mind of the black race had been confined in the prison of bondage, but by dwelling on the past they ran the risk of falling into the state of "arrested development." Of course it was impossible to forget slavery, and it would be undesirable to do so. Slavery was the cause of many present difficulties and the source of the social and economic backwardness of black people. It was also true that the memory of slavery was capable of serving as a "stimulant to high endeavor." What Crummell proposed to guard against was not the memory of slavery, but the constant recollection of it.

Douglass, however, had understandable difficulty chewing on the idea of someone who had never been a slave calling on black people to forget slavery. This was an emotional subject for Douglass. The half-white former slave was well aware of Crummell's black chauvinism and could never pass up an opportunity to demonstrate that despite his stain of mulatto bastardy he was much more the man of the people. It was he, not Crummell, who had shared the slavery experience of the black masses.

The clash at Storer College arose from differences in experience and temperament as much as from a disparity in ideology. Douglass was no less egotistical than Crummell and loved to display his extraordinary rhetorical genius, as he had demonstrated in his debates with Crummell, Delany, and Garnet during the 1850s. In most respects, the substance of "The Need for New Ideas and New Aims for a New Era" did not conflict with well-known policy statements Douglass had made around the same time. The speech emphasized personal character and individual responsibility, just as Douglass's speeches of the 1880s did. Crummell and Douglass, like many self-made men, were advocates of the "bootstraps philosophy." They were in agreement that "self-help" was more important than the political agitation of racial issues. Both men believed that every individual had the personal responsibility to work out his own salvation. Although protest had been Douglass's stock in trade and the basis of his public identity in the early years, the aging abolitionist had lately begun to discourage the constant protest against racial injustice. He shared Crummell's belief that black folk should now work hard to reap the benefits of new opportunities freedom had brought.

Douglass would not have agreed with at least one ideological position in Crummell's speech: Crummell's emphasis on a collective racial effort. Douglass had always been hostile to the "Negro Improvement" position that black people required some sort of special preparation for freedom. He had argued in *Douglass' Monthly* of January 1862, that all that was required as a solution to the racial problem was to "free the slaves and leave them alone." Crummell, dwelling on the heathenness of Africans and the degradation of slaves, referred to black people as the "withered arm of humanity." Douglass insisted "there is nothing the matter with the Negro whatever; he is all right. Learned or ignorant, he is all right." [22] While Douglass acknowledged in a speech before the Bethel Literary Society in 1889 that prejudice had not yet disappeared, he clung to his theory that racism would inevitably decline. Douglass continued to oppose the idea that special educational efforts were required to bring black people up to the level of white America. He believed, as he asserted in the *North American Review* of July 1884, that the "religion and civilization" of the Negro were already "in harmony with those of the people among whom he lives." If black people would simply avoid calling attention to themselves by huddling together in ghettos, and if they would make individual efforts to make themselves useful to society, they would eventually blend into the rest of the population.

Douglass found Crummell's emphasis on "the social principle among a people'' and his constant references to racial pride irksome. During the 1880s Douglass came to the position that the sentiment of race pride was a pernicious idea. Douglass dramatically demonstrated his belief that ''social equality'' was ''a matter between individuals'' when, in 1884, he shocked many of his admirers by marrying Helen Pitts, a white woman in her mid-thirties. To many observers this symbolized his utter rejection of the idea of racial pride. Crummell believed that the collective social principle was necessary to bring about harmony between the races. Gifted and well-trained individuals must uplift the ignorant and degraded masses before any black person could expect to be happy in the society at large. It is therefore likely that it was the emphasis on racial pride, ethnic institutions, and group solidarity in Crummell's speech at Harper's Ferry that upset Douglass.[23]

Crummell did not, of course, question the value of individualism, since he numbered personal character and individual responsibility among the foremost values of American civilization. Both institutional and individual development were essential in his plan for black progress, and he saw the two as mutually dependent. Yet Crummell's plan for black progress had always included the ingredients of ethnic pride and collective effort, two of Douglass's pet peeves. Douglass had always been uneasy with the idea of racial pride, and he now referred to the ''error that union among ourselves is an essential element of success in our relations to the white race.''[24]

Douglass's program was for black people to remember slavery and to forget that they were black. Crummell's was for them to remember that they were black and forget slavery. Douglass's reform panacea was to rely on individual exertion and cleave to the Republican party. Crummell certainly did not disagree with this strategy, but he insisted, as Douglass did not, on the need for some sort of collective response. The slackening rate of progress in American race relations was evidence that America was experiencing a period of white backlash, and, as one young scholar was to put it, ''The nation was a little ashamed of having bestowed so much sentiment on Negroes.''[25] Crummell believed that black people were fated, at least for the immediate future, to rely on their own internal resources for uplift.[26]

Despite obvious differences in moral priorities and life experiences, the two men held one another in mutually high regard. This became increasingly evident toward the end of their lives. In a letter to Cromwell, Crummell grumbled privately about Douglass's political stance at the time of the Hayes–Tilden compromise, but did not question Douglass's ethics, although he felt strongly that Douglass was allowing himself to be used. He had decided that he would steer clear of public controversy on that issue. It was better to avoid political activity altogether, if possible.

Crummell's interest in political ideology, as opposed to political practice, remained strong. His politics were predictably Republican, and he continued to express his hostility to the Jacksonian conception of democracy.[27] He interpreted President Garfield's assassination as an illustration of the evils of the democratic ideology. A week after the shooting, and several weeks before the president's death, Crummell preached a sermon in which he passionately reiterated some of the ideas that he had articulated in letters written nine years earlier, after President Roye's assassination. The Roye episode, accompanied as it was by mob rule, anarchy, and government lawlessness, had hardened his opposition to what he considered excesses of democracy and consequent plebian disorder. Garfield's assassination he viewed as the result of false American values and prevailing heresies regarding government and authority. Ambition, the race for wealth, crass materialism, and a lack of regard for art, science, and philosophy were also in part to blame. The root cause of this shattering occurrence was, however, in the American political system. By its very nature it was designed to have "intoxicating and demoralizing effects." American "political agitations" seemed "designed . . . to produce widespread and convulsive upheavals." He described the "vast political assemblages" in terms of "burning blasts . . . tempests . . . paroxysms . . . tornadoes and blasting hurricanes." The basic trait of the American national character was "dislike of rule and authority." The attitude was nurtured in churches, schools, and families, with the result that men and women and even children "at a very early age, chafe under rule, reject authority, and spurn control." Liberty was perverted into license, and, as the people began to "eschew the principle of rule and authority," they ran the risk of "rapidly verging toward anarchy, toward speedy and certain ruin." [28]

Americans were inclined to forget that "the nation is a creation and manifestation of God." They did not understand "the duty of subjection to and reverence for constituted authority." Thus Crummell saw a painful Providence in the suffering of the dying president, which was to teach the nation the folly of its drift towards "lawless freedom." The problem was endemic. It had originated with the Declaration of Independence:

> When Thomas Jefferson declared that "governments derive their just powers from the consent of the governed," and left his dogma crudely at that point, he shut out a limitation which the pride and self-assertion of degenerate humanity is always relutant to yield, and too tardy to supply.
>
> The theory of the Declaration is incomplete and misleading. Governments, my brethren, derive their just authority, *first* of all, from the will of God, and then *next* from the consent of the governed. . . . Your president is as much a ruler, he is as truly a potentate as the Emperor of Russia or the Queen of Great Britain. He is your ruler and great magistrate and mine. [29]

The Providence of God had been made manifest "through the pistol shot of an assasin." Now the whole nation could recognize "the sin of its cheap estimate of the presidential office." Through the assassination, God had spoken to a nation that had failed to honor "the dignity, the reserve, the sanctity of national sovereignty" and had come to regard their president as "the biggest servant in the land."

> That great political prophet, Alexander Hamilton, predicted not a few of the evils I have pointed out, although he did not live to see them. [30]

Now that he had decided to be an American, Crummell worried much about the tendencies in American life that he considered dangerous. He approached politics in general with the same dogmatism that he directed towards black culture. While he declined to endorse political candidates, he did not remain innocent of strong political engagement. For Crummell, however, the practical workings of politics were always less interesting than the sober and reflective formulation of political ideology. The antidemocratic strain in Crummell's thought continued to assert itself; his political counsel was to avoid "the extreme of wild and thoughtless democratic opinion" and see "the danger of mistaking license for liberty." He was anxious that black Americans would ever be numbered among the "conservative elements" in America and counted among the "firmest upholders of law and authority." The assassination was unquestionably a "Providence," and black Americans, by observing folly and misrule among the whites, were to be better schooled for the inevitable day when their full political rights were obtained. In this way they would avoid the dangers of falling into plots and conspiracies and would forsee and avoid the dangers of "revolutions, communism, and revolt." [31]

Crummell viewed black Americans as a source of "conservative power" for the nation. They would be a "corrective influence . . . , a strong sturdy element to save [the nation] from destructive agencies working at its vitals. The promise of American freedom had attracted "crazed brains from every quarter of the globe." They had come to America, "wild, frenzied, insensate, mad, withal, on account of past restraint and hindrance; eager for license in the future; determined to make this soil the seed-bed of the most destructive political heresies." [32] This was a theme that Booker T. Washington, Josephine St. Pierre Ruffin, Archibald Grimké, and other younger thinkers would attempt to exploit during the final decade of the century. They would try to convince national policymakers that black Americans were intrinsically more useful to the country than the more recent immigrants from Europe. The nation needed a "patient, plodding, hard handed and industrious population, for its material interests." Black people had demonstrated such traits for two hundred years. The nation needed black people with their characteristically religious nature and spiritual insight. Where else could America derive these needed qualities?

> Not from the crazed Bohemian with his criminal propensities and his animal instincts! Not from the German with his godless speculations and his wild theories! Not from the superstitious Italian, ignorant of the simplest alphabet of freedom and paralyzed in every faculty by the stolidness of priestcraft! Not from the angry Irishman, with his "blind hysterics" and his schoolboy heat! Not even from the Anglo-Saxon; who is always preaching submission to oppressed people; yet himself ever shrieking "Liberty or death!" at a disagreeable tax, or an imaginary encroachment! [33]

Crummell had no sympathy for white socialists, Marxists, anarchists, or other revolutionaries. He marked as a "disturbing element of American society . . . the angry antagonism which has sprung up between labor and capital." For while it was universally true that capital was selfish and grasping, and labor was always exploited and underpaid, he found it purely astonishing that any large class of whites in America could think of themselves as victims of tyranny. Such a view approached "very nigh to the borders of fable, and reach[ed] to the outer limits of fiction." If black labor were to make such claims, it would be "easily understandable," and he "could at once proffer [his] warmest sympathies."[34]

Crummell was wracked with pain when he reflected on the exploitation of black labor. But while on the one hand he criticized what he referred to as "the selfish instinct of capital," he was not sympathetic to the more radical socialistic formulations of writers like T. Thomas Fortune. His attitudes on black labor were based on the same values as Thomas Carlyle's conservative anticapitalism, with its patronizing and sentimental view of the agricultural worker.[35] Furthermore, he viewed work as social therapy for the atrophied muscles of the black masses.

> Not until a people are able by their own activities and skill, to raise themselves above want, and to meet the daily needs of home and family, can they take the next great step to the higher cultivation which comes by letters, refinement, and religion; and which lifts them up to civility and power. The kernel of this higher cultivation is labour.

Crummell did not come tardily to this position. The dignity of labor had always been at the center of his theory of civilization, and he had always held that common labor was important to the building of character. He would find himself in later years fighting against what he saw as the oversimplification of this doctrine with the rise of Booker T. Washington, who said, "Not much religion can exist in a one-room log cabin or on an empty stomach."[36] Crummell could not accept the economic determination and materialism implicit in such a position, although he had come close to it with his pronouncement that labor was the foundation of religion.

Like Washington, however, he had come to the position that since black Americans were in America to stay, they should make every effort to be model citizens. They must contribute to the national life and character. Their interests were bound up with the interests of America and its citizenry, thus self-love and Christian duty argued that black Americans should serve the state. The state was defined as "that great organic instrument established by the Almighty for the continuance and development of humanity through all the ages . . . next to Christianity, the one great agent for the civilization of man."[37] His preference for a strong and conservative political order, and his abhorrence of even the whisper of anarchy, was obviously strengthened by his experience in Liberia, but it originated in his consistently authoritarian, formalistic temperament.

Crummell's commitment to the pragmatic values of late nineteenth-century America in economics and labor relations was as strong as his commitment to genteel manners and moral values. He could be a crusading Victorian liberal, with a righteous sense of outrage respecting the position of black labor. The problems of black workers were, after all, only one instance of the universal problems of unskilled and ignorant labor. Black workers had known drudgery under slavery but had never experienced the enlightenment that led to the "mingling of active brain with strained exertion." The newly emancipated black worker lagged behind civilization and thus might be compared to "the wild Indian of the West."

> [He] hunts, day by day, for a few skins of animals. He sells them to a Trader for a simple gew-gaw, or a jug of rum; but the Trader brings them East, and sells them for a sum which would have been a fortune to the whole tribe of simple Indians.[38]

The history of servitude and drudgery had left black people ignorant of the value of their labor and had burdened them pyschologically. Two centuries of slavery had bred into many black people the idea that servitude was their natural condition and that "they themselves were inferior because they were black." It had also "bred the notion in another larger class, that labour is degrading; that superior people ought not to work." One false lesson of the plantation school was that "all the glory and beauty of life [were] associated with ease, luxury and mastery." The other false lesson was that "all the toil, the drudgery, the ignorance and the suffering [were] allied to the Negro." "What sort of school was this," he angrily asked, "in which to learn the dignity of labour?"

Despite everything that had been done to them, black Americans had not become indolent. The historical record was clear on that. It was also clear that an appreciable number of black workers were highly skilled, but black labor "in the mass" was "rude, untutored, and debased." The prejudice of the land kept the masses of black workers in "defenseless abjectness." He went on to speak of the sharecropper system, which drove "hundreds and thousands of our people into theft and reckless indifference, and many thousands more into despair and premature graves!" He called on the young, educated blacks of America to apply their intellectual muscle to black labor problems. While he admitted "in all candor" that he was not able to supply an answer, he was certain of one thing, that the problem would not be solved through the application of external forces. "The emancipation of the black race in [America] from the injustice and grinding tyranny of their labor servitude" would be effected mainly through the development of "thrift, energy, and manliness."

Labor was related to education, then, and Crummell's continuing interest in industrial education came to the fore in a discussion relating to the so-called "Bounty Bill," which came before the House Committee on Education and Labor in 1880. The bill (H.R. 2571) was "to encourage and aid the education of the colored people in the several States and Territories by the appropriation of the unclaimed bounties and pay of the colored soldiers." The amount in question was over $500,000 and still accruing, and Crummell appeared before the committee on January 10, 1880, to advocate that the monies be used to support training in the skilled trades.[39] He had adapted his philosophy to changing times. In the 1850s he had advocated the establishment of colleges and universities for black people, because he recognized that opportunities for study or teaching in the arts and sciences were practically nonexistent. In 1872, however, he argued that colleges and universities had now opened their doors to black students, and that any number of institutions for black people had already been founded. The situation was different than it had been before the war in that respect, but the labor market had not changed. Young black men with college degrees still found it impossible to find labor except in the menial trades. Crummell then told a story that came back to haunt him some years later:

> I went, in 1872, in the city of New York, into the kitchen of the Union League Club, and there I saw a young man with a copy of Euripides and Tactius, in the originals, sitting there with his apron upon him awaiting his turn, as a servant, to stand as a waiter behind the table. I have seen young men who have graduated from college as lawyers and doctors, who have been forced at last to gain a livelihood as servants.

It is almost certain that Booker T. Washington borrowed this anecdote from Crummell, adding a few touches of his own, when he said:

> In fact, one of the saddest things I saw during the month of travel which I have described was a young man, who had attended some high-school, sitting down in a one-room cabin, with grease on his clothing, filth all around him, and weeds in the yard and garden, engaged in studying a French grammar.

Crummell's anecdote was also reminiscent of a statement he had made in 1861. He had spoken then of his unwillingness, as an educated man, to make his living by opening oysters as his father had done. At that time the lesson he had drawn was that educated black folk should go to Liberia, where a scholar supposedly had a chance to be something better than an oysterman. Now, however, the point was that education ought to focus on the acquisition of practical skills.[40] Although his testimony foreshadowed doctrines of Booker T. Washington, in one respect there was a significant difference, and that was the difference in tone. Crummell articulated his position before the House Committee with vigor and force. He roundly condemned the racism that had made his position necessary and denounced the "Combinations" that existed in every state, city, and village to keep black youth from learning trades. He asserted, however, that, regardless of how determined the whites were to keep the blacks down, it would be impossible for them to do so. The entire tone of his delivery was assertive, even defiant. The tone of Booker T. Washington's discourse in the following decade was to contrast markedly with that of Crummell.

Frank Grimké, in a letter to *The People's Advocate,* pointed out the fallacy of the position. Black people trained as mechanics, agriculturalists, and engineers would still be dependent for employment on whites, the very race that was determined to keep them in menial positions. What was there, asked Grimké, in the mere fact of their being mechanics that was destined to break down prejudice? The argument against appropriating the money for colleges and universities weighed equally against spending it according to Crummell's specifications.

> There is nothing in the nature of the mechanic arts more than there is in the higher training that is calculated to break down this bitter prejudice. And this, experience corroborates. There are colored mechanics in many parts of the country who find it exceedingly difficult, and in many cases impossible, to make a living. White employers are unwilling to give them work, and white workmen refuse to work with them.[41]

Crummell's response was predictably lengthy; the gist of it was that the congressional hearings had not allowed him to present his ideas in all their complexity and that Grimké had incorrectly paraphrased his arguments. Crummell made it quite clear that he was as much in favor of higher education as he had ever been. It was only that higher education alone would not be sufficient to bring about "the grand consummation." Crummell did argue, however, that, even if whites would not give them employment, the training of black mechanics would be beneficial. If only by working among their own people, they would be able to meet the needs of their own communities. Furthermore, they would become an "example of industry and demonstration of capacity." In any case, he could provide examples of cases in which black men and women were currently working in such skilled occupations as iron-working and dressmaking. He concluded his argument with the following ringing pronouncement:

> If the black man is not trained in skilled labor, he will be perpetually, "a hewer of wood and a drawer of water." AND HE MUST SPEEDILY GO TO THE WALL! [42]

He met with several other prominent black Washingtonians, who had also testified before the House Committee, to draw up an alternative bill advocating the establishment of a National Mechanical and Industrial Institute at Harper's Ferry.[43] The alternative bill named as incorporators of the institute a number of well-known black leaders, including his boyhood friend from New York, Charles L. Reason; James Trotter, the father of William Monroe Trotter; Robert Purvis; Frederick Douglass; John W. Cromwell; Richard R. Wright; James T. Rapier; and Crummell himself.

Crummell's 1886 essay "Common Sense in Common Schooling" was a more systematic treatment of his philosophy of education. In this essay, he found it necessary to criticize the almost superstitious respect that the masses of black people had for education. He recognized that this adulation for the education that could magically transmute the unsophisticated freedman or freedwoman into a gentleman or a lady could be a disappointing trap. Thus he counseled the parents of St. Luke's and of the nation to carefully appraise their children's aptitudes and chances in life before deciding to have them enrolled in classical high schools and academies. Crummell was never a narrow industrial educationalist, and it is misleading to think of him as having "practically reversed himself" in later years to become an advocate of the liberal arts. He always supported the idea of two streams of education, both of which should contain elements of the practical and of the theoretical. But he never believed that the same elements should be stressed in all students' education.[44]

While he had no intention of denying others the classical education that he had enjoyed, he shared the view of Washington and Du Bois that the emerging civil service elite were a class of drones. He described himself as "exceedingly anxious" for the "higher culture." He saw the need for "a class of trained and superior men and women."

> Moreover we need, and in our blood, the great molders and fashioners of thought among us. To delegate the thinking of the race to any other people would be to introduce intellectual stagnation in the race; and when thought declines then a people are sure to fall and fade away.[45]

He could not help but be aware of the supposed emotional and aesthetic propensity that some nineteenth-century authors were attributing to the African races. He warned, therefore, of what he called the "false and artificial tendency which is ruining colored society almost everywhere in the United States." He referred to a tendency among black people to harbor unrealistic expectations. It was not possible for every member of any race to enter the higher professions. Nor was it possible for a people to "get their living and build themselves up by refined style and glittering fashion or indulgence in bellettres." He warned of that "proneness to spontaneity, which though easy and agreeable to inclination, makes us rather the creatures of propensity; instead of giving us self-control." He believed that the very strength of black people, their natural love of "that which is pleasing, polished, and adorning," threatened to betray them.

> The mind of our people seems to be a hot-bed of rich, precocious, gorgeous and withal genuine plants:—and, if I mistake not, I discover in it all, that permanent *tropical* element which characterizes all the peoples whose ancestral homes were in the southern latitudes and who may be called "children of the sun" . . . [but] I see, nowhere, any counterbalance of the hardier studies, and more tasking scholarship, which serve to give vigor, hardihood and robustness to a race.[46]

Crummell contributed, as Du Bois later would, to the myth of black aestheticism, the idea that the greatest blessing of the African race was also its greatest curse. Crummell saw "addiction to aesthetical culture as a special vocation of the race." He saw this as a feminine quality, and he believed that it was essential to the potential greatness of black people. This feminine quality had been possessed by Henry Highland Garnet and was the source of his sensitivity and compassion. After two hundred years in the northern hemisphere black people were still "a tropical people." They had an aboriginal quality which made itself felt in their love of harmonies and colors. But only through discipline could this tendency be raised to the level of "taste and elegance."[47]

The same themes were addressed in "Right Mindedness," a speech delivered before the Garnet Lyceum, a group of young gentlemen at Lincoln University, a black college in Pennsylvania. He made on this occasion a number of biting, tough-minded observations, some of which must have irritated a part of his audience. He began by congratulating the young men who had assembled in Lincoln University ''for the purposes of study.'' He was certain that it was neither pride nor ambition that had brought them to Lincoln, but ''personal desire for knowledge.'' Was there intentional sarcasm in this opening statement? He was certainly well aware that the impulse that was drawing many blacks to colleges in those days was anything but ''enthusiasm for letters.'' What was the expression on his face, and what was the tone of his voice when he spoke of this ''enthusiasm for letters, which is a characteristic of your period of life?'' Perhaps he was remembering his own youthful enthusiasm for letters, but he also had some painful recollections of the youthful enthusiasms of his son Sidney. He suffered from no delusions when it came to the vagaries of young men.[48]

The need for discipline in attaining true manhood had been a subject of his sermons since the Liberia College days. The exercise of intellect over emotion and the ability to submit to authority were basic needs. So was the ability to fight, but even fighting must be carried out with discipline. Nature had not ordained that black people should manifest only the passive virtues. He criticized Blyden for suggesting in one of his speeches that blacks were by nature submissive, and he admired John W. Cromwell's essay on Nat Turner in which the younger man spoke of Turner as a hero. He praised the military contributions of black soldiers and sailors in every American war, and he encouraged military mindedness and martial arts in young men.[49]

Perhaps he remembered his own youthful excitability, as he and his friend Henry Highland Garnet had dreamed of going into the South to lead a revolt of the slaves. Knowing well what it was to allow emotion to get the better of judgement, he preached to the young men of the need to approach life's struggles with discipline, recounting an anecdote to illustrate his point:

> I remember an incident that took place once in London. A young sprig of fashion from the West End, tall, slender, almost boyish in his build, was insulted by a great burly coal-heaver,—a man over 6 feet in height; weighing more than 200 lbs. and carrying a fist as big as an ox's hoof. The young dandy put the reins of his horse into his servant's hands; jumped from his Gig, and pitched into the giant. Everyone thought the gentleman would have been killed. If the coal-heaver could have closed in with him, he would have eaten him up in a moment. But in as brief time as I have been telling the story, the gentleman had smashed the fellow's face to pieces, and left him sprawling on the ground. I believe you young gentlemen call that sort of thing *science*.[50]

Crummell gave vent to his own combative impulses through literary devices. In 1882, Dr. J. L. Tucker, a white clergyman of Jackson, Mississippi, read a paper at the Protestant Episcopal Church Congress, ''On the Relations of the Church to the Colored Race.'' The paper had been published as a pamphlet, which Crummell had read ''with very much care and attention.'' He had found it to be "one of the most unjust and injurious statements that [he] had ever met with." Crummell responded to Tucker with a pamphlet of his own, which, according to Crummell's supporters, completely silenced Tucker on all subjects for all time. The pamphlet was predictably strong in its defense of black Americans, but in its treatment of the native African it was widely at variance with statements Crummell had made earlier in his career. For perhaps the first time Crummell spoke of the native African in glowing terms and blamed all the deficiencies of the black American on America. This was a far cry from the "darkness covers the land" rhetoric of his open letter to Charles Dunbar in 1860.[51]

He was developing a new racial rhetoric. When convenient, he could now assert the nobility of savages, rather than their deficiencies. To be sure, the noble savage had been around in European and American thought for some time, but this was something different. Noble African savages had not played an important role in the racial mythologies of black nationalists and abolitionists. In the mid-nineteenth century, black abolitionist historiography had usually assumed the backwardness and degradation of African peoples, but had compared their shortcomings to those of the inhabitants of pre-Roman Europe. Crummell's later writings began to reflect a trend in late nineteenth-century black ethnology of seeing in both black Africans and early Europeans a barbarian vigor that was not to be found among civilized peoples.

> I have lived nigh twenty years in West Africa. I have come in contact with peoples of not less than forty tribes, and I aver, from personal knowledge and acquaintance, that the picture drawn by Dr. Tucker is a caricature. I am speaking of the *native* Negro. *(a.)* All along the West Coast of Africa the family tie and the mariage bond are as strong as among any other *primitive* people. The very words in which Cicero and Tacitus describe the homes and families of the Germanic tribes can as truly be ascribed to the people the West Coast of Africa. *(b.)* Their maidenly virtue, the instinct to chastity, is a marvel. I have no hesitation in the generalization that, in West Africa, every female is a virgin to the day of her marriage. The harlot class is unknown in all their tribes. I venture the assertion that any one walking through Pall Mall, London, or Broadway, New York, for a week would see more indecency in look and act than he could discover in an African town in a dozen years.[52]

The convention of comparing hearty barbarian cultures to decadent civilizations made more than one appearance in Crummell's later writings. At Storer College, in 1885, he ironically observed,

> You have perchance strengthened your powers with the robustness of Tactius; and you may remember how he refers, in plaintive, melancholy tones, to the once virile power of Roman manhood, and chaste beauty and excellence of its womanhood, and mourns their sad decline. And, doubtless, you have felt the deepest interest in the simple but ingenious testimony he bears to the primitive virtues of the Germanic tribes, pagan though they were, and which have proven the historic basis of their eminence and unfailing grandeur.[53]

Crummell's later writings contain many convenient descriptions of the noble Africans, who, despite the curse of heathenism, were known for their honesty, their industriousness, and the rigidity of their law. Everywhere, the spirit of commerce was alive and the continent was a veritable beehive of commercial activity.[54] All that was required to convert the acquisitive instincts of the natives into civilized commerce was to erase the heritage of heathenism.

Crummell had resuscitated the arguments he had known in his boyhood, the trusty rhetoric of David Walker, who had lamented his people's "wretchedness in consequence of the preachers of the religion of Jesus Christ." Crummell would take Dr. Tucker at his word and concede that black religion in the South was only "an outward form of Christianity with an inward substance of full license given to all desires and passions." The inference to be drawn from this was that the church in the South had neglected the missionary field at its doorstep. Black religion was therefore devoid of any rational discipline or relationship to sound social living. The slave preachers were usually unlettered, and "large numbers of them were unscrupulous and lecherous scoundrels."

> This was a large characteristic of "plantation religion," cropping out even to the present, in the extravagances and wildness of many of their religious practices!
>
> Their religion, both of preachers and people, was a religion without the Bible—a crude medley of scraps of Scripture, fervid imaginations, dreams, and superstitions. . . . The Ten Commandments were as foreign from their minds and memories as the Vedas of India or the moral precepts of Confucius. Ignorance of the MORAL LAW was the main characteristic of "PLANTATION RELIGION!"[55]

Slavery was a licentious and demoralizing system. In Crummell's estimation, "the prime functions of the race under slavery were 1st LUST, and 2d UNREQUITED LABOR." Slaveholders, with few exceptions, were greedy and tyrannical, carnal and unscrupulous. They herded their slaves together like animals and bred them like cattle. They separated families heartlessly and sold children away from parents.

Although black people had far to go in constructing a strong communal life, they had already come far. He introduced "proof from vital statistics" to demonstrate that blacks had progressed markedly since Emancipation. He cited the population growth, the increase in the literacy rate, the rise of educational institutions. He showed how black people had acquired 2,680,800 acres, "a territory equal in extent to the size of the STATE OF CONNECTICUT." Comparing statistics for the years 1857 to 1861 to those of 1878 to 1882, he demonstrated that the freedmen had produced one third more cotton in the most recent years of freedom than they had in all the last five years of slavery.

Tucker's solution to the "Negro problem" was to call on the Northern churches to send funds to the South. These were to be placed in the hands of the Southern churches, ostensibly for the benefit of black people. Tucker's argument was that the North had freed the slaves and left them on the Southerner's hands; now they should compensate the Southerners for the work of training them.

But only Southern whites should be entrusted with this work, because they were the only ones who truly knew what the task was all about. Crummell had no illusions about the Northern whites; they certainly had their own history of abuses to the black race. He would, however, defend them of the charge of not knowing how to work for the intellectual and spiritual elevation of black people. They had shown a willingness to undertake the task by abolishing slavery on their own soil and opening up their religious and educational institutions to the freedmen.

But the principal agency for the uplift of black Americans could in the long run be neither Northern nor Southern whites. Southern blacks must be uplifted by indigenous leadership. If white people sought to be the leaders of black people they would find the masses resisting all inducements. The leaders of a race must be men of that race. Any attempt to ignore this principle in the missionary field would fail, because the "racial impulse" would lead black folk to follow any rival standard lifted by a black man rather than subject themselves to white leadership.

Crummell's response to Dr. Tucker was an early exercise in the sociology of slavery. It anticipated much that would be written on the subject by progressive black historians in the twentieth century. The slave system had trained its victims for generations in "gross carnality" and had been destructive of family life. True enough, Crummell had never personally experienced slavery, but he had a great deal of experience with ex-slaves. He viewed the social disabilities of black people as the direct result of slavery, and in this he was typical of his contemporaries. There were no black nineteenth-century leaders who spent much time discussing the positive aspects of slavery, and many years would pass before it would become fashionable to promote the mythology of a healthy slave community.

In his essays "The Social Principle among a People" and "A Defence of the Negro Race," Crummell, although apparently reconciled to the fact that black people were in America to stay, still referred to them as a nation.[56] By 1888, he seemed willing to distinguish between the concept of nation and race and to address the problem of "various races of men in the same national community." This was the concern of his address that year on "The Race Problem in America."[57] Defining a race as "a compact, homogeneous population of one blood, ancestry, and lineage," he sought to discover the "laws of population" by which one might predict the future of American race relations. He was forced to admit, however, that there was no "fixed law" or historical axiom "by which to determine the probabilities of the race-problem in the United States." Some peoples forced into proximity had a history of antagonism and bloodshed; others lived comfortably side by side. Some contacts resulted in amalgamation, some in extermination or expulsion. The study of history would reveal no patterns that had predictive value for black Americans.

But Crummell, who was never squeamish about hazarding a guess, asserted that there were tendencies in the two hundred year history of black Americans that might suggest their racial destiny. It seemed fairly certain that the likelihood of racial amalgamation between white and black Americans was dying out. Race mixing had occurred in the past only because of the helplessness of the black woman, but since Emancipation the black woman had "gained possession of her own person." This spelled the end to "the base process of intermixture." The desire for racial self-preservation was instinctive, in his opinion, and, while racial antagonism was neither necessary nor desirable, racial feeling was of divine origin.

> Races, like families, are the organisms and the ordinance of God; and race feeling, like the family feeling, is of divine origin. The extinction of race feeling is just as possible as the extinction of family feeling. Indeed a race is a family. The principle of continuity is as masterful in races as it is in families—as it is in nations.[58]

White folk need not fear the amalgamation of their race with the black. It was an impossibility; the solution to the race problem in America was essentially a moral one, not merely a matter of physically mingling breeds and bloods. It was entirely a matter of ideas and principles. "Race-life" was to be "a permanent element" of the American system. The races would live together in amity only if the Christian ideals of human brotherhood and the American ideal of democracy could triumph.

Crummell's attitude to democracy, here, seemed strikingly different than that expressed in the eulogy on Garfield. He still rejected the hypocrisy of Jeffersonian, and the leveling tendencies of Jacksonian democracy, but he now seemed willing to consider that the best ideals of American democracy could, if properly applied, provide some hope for black Americans. He was still opposed to "that spurious, blustering, self-sufficient spirit, which derides God and authority on the one hand, and crushes the weak and helpless on the other."[59] But he recognized that the American democratic ideal at its best stood for the doctrine of human rights and turned to "the State as the means and agency for the unlimited progress of humanity." The idea of democracy had been much "distorted and exaggerated" in America, "but the democratic principle in its essence is from God."

Within the tradition of Christian idealism, all ideas originate with God, and it is only in this fallen world that good ideas, like democracy, become distorted. But it could not be denied that the spirit of democracy had led to the expansion of political rights and the rights of labor. It had demanded the abolition of slavery and got it, and now the principle of democracy was demanding the equality of all people, which was the ultimate solution of the race problem. Crummell believed that America's ability to solve her race problem would be the ultimate test of American democracy, the proof of whether it was the true Christian democracy that existed in the mind of God, or a false spirit of rabble-rousing mob rule and tyranny of the majority.

In calling for a realization of the American democratic ideal, Crummell reclaimed a theme that had recurred in black American writing since the beginning of the nineteenth century. It was a theme adapted from Thomas Jefferson, who trembled for America when he reflected that God was just:

> If this nation is not truly democratic then she must die! Nothing is more destructive than an organic falsehood! This nation cannot live—this nation does not deserve to live—on the basis of a lie!
>
> Her fundamental idea is democracy; and if this nation will not submit herself to the domination of this idea—if she refuses to live in the spirit of this creed—then she is already doomed, and she will certainly be damned.

Jefferson's jeremiadic rhetoric was to inspire many an impassioned outpouring in the coming century. Black American leaders like Washington, Du Bois, and the Grimkés would continue to argue that the treatment of its black population was the test of America's democracy—an assertion that was to become common during the Civil Rights Movement as it resurfaced in the speeches of Martin Luther King and Malcolm X.[60]

Crummell became more willing to accept the possibility of America's steady progress towards the realization of her democratic ideals, and he became more accustomed to thinking of himself as an American. He hedged his bets, however, continuing to think of black people as a nation within a nation and continuing to emphasize the importance of black people making a distinctive group contribution to America and to the world. While calling on America to demonstrate the sincerity of its democratic commitment, he never deviated from the principle that individually and collectively black people bore the responsibility for working out their own salvation.

# 13

# Pastor Emeritus
# (1894–1896)

Crummell was continuously under attack from the hostile faction in his congregation from 1879 until his retirement in 1894. But in nearly all of his struggles, a friendly insider reported, he seemed to emerge "more than victorious" even when he was "seemingly alone." The bishop of his diocese during the early days was the venerable William R. Whittingham, who remembered something of Crummell's very real grievances over the years and seemed willing to atone for them to some extent. Both he and Bishop Pinkney had been his "friends and supporters . . . against the carping critics, but in Bishop Paret his enemies found one who would lend a listening ear."[1]

Perhaps it was the reputed sympathy of Bishop Paret that emboldened his old enemy J. W. Cole, one of the signers of the 1882 petition against him, to come to his home on September 16, 1893, to ask for his resignation. It was a Saturday, and the seventy-four-year-old rector was sitting in his study when the buggy stopped at his door and Cole emerged. He had come to the house, Crummell claimed, with alcohol on his breath, claiming that he did not speak for himself alone, but for a number of wealthy and influential presbyters, black and white. If Crummell would not resign, they would form a new congregation in Washington and lead off the majority of his parishioners. The following morning, Crummell kept the congregation after the sermon and the benediction to recount the incident and denounce the "wretched and disorganized creature." He would not speak the name of the "depraved Moses," who proposed to "lead the saints of God in this City," this man "noted at all times for his drunken bouts; famous for his filthy amours and his gross blasphemies in the streets of Washington," but he published his remarks in the form of a neat, four-page flyer.[2]

Once again, the personality traits that had so often worked to his disadvantage had come to the surface. Crummell's overreaction to the importunities of Cole must certainly have given strength to the accusations of his foes. If, indeed, Cole did have the support of "wealthy and influential presbyters," Crummell's action would have been of doubtful usefulness in sidestepping their offensive. Indeed, by allowing himself to be provoked in such a way, he would have added fuel to the fires. Whether or not Cole's announcement was the opening shot of some covert and ultimately successful offensive is not known, but, in any event, Crummell announced his retirement some fifteen months later.

In the summer of 1894, he was enjoying "good health for a man in his seventy-sixth year," as he wrote to George Frazier Miller. His one good eye had been giving him trouble of late, but he underwent a cataract operation in the spring of 1894 which "soon set me right." This was the first of two cataract operations; the second would be performed in 1897. In his letters that summer to Miller, he complained of "time serving priests [who] let the people go to the devil, and live in peace and money-getting comfort." He invited him to come to Washington for the celebration of the fiftieth anniversary of his ordination, saying, "I expect to resign my rectorship on 2nd Sunday in December or 1st January, '95. I shall celebrate the 50th anniversary of my ordination to the priesthood."[3]

The celebration was something of a success. Crummell obviously commanded considerable respect in both the church and the larger community, although he went into retirement with reluctance. St. Luke's was filled with well-wishers from every denomination, including Frederick Douglass, a Methodist, and Francis J. Grimké, leader of the major black Presbyterian congregation. Crummell was presented with a purse of gold and known thereafter as "pastor emeritus." The women's organization of St. Luke's held a public church reception for him on the evening of December 10. Anna J. Cooper, the much respected educator, who had been an early black graduate of Oberlin college, was the speaker for the occasion. Her remarks seemed to be an acknowledgment of the fact that the old pastor had often been treated unjustly. On behalf of the congregation, she apologized for "not having lent more constantly the reinforcement of our sympathy and support during the struggle." She reminded him that "few men can appreciate an altitude above their own plane of activity."

> For one I have always thought St. Luke's too narrow a field to contain you. "The Black Woman of the South," whom you have so nobly defended; the black man of the South, groping despairingly amid the darkness and coldness of his unfriendly world, needs sorely your counsel and kindly touch.
>
> We cannot afford to let you retire for many, many years yet. We need you now more than ever; and your relief from the engrossments of your congregation, is only to give you to the larger work of the country.[4]

At the time of Crummell's retirement, a new pastor for St. Luke's had not yet been selected. There was no one even to write the annual parish report to the diocese. Crummell had wanted the position to go to George Frazier Miller, who had been ordained in 1892 and was serving a congregation in New York. Miller was not chosen, however, and Crummell accused the vestry and the church officials of wanting "putty, not a man."[5]

Crummell did not go willingly into retirement, and he does not seem to have had time on his hands. Although he complained to friends of failing strength, he continued to work and travel during 1895 and 1896. He claimed to be reading voraciously, despite his failing eyesight, and maintained that he was "up to my eyelids in work: not parochial indeed, but somewhat clerical and literary."[6] "My changed condition has left me like a fish out of water," he wrote to Miller, "for by *temperament* I am disposed to active duty; and added to this is the lifelong *conviction* that to work is to live."[7]

Since he no longer had the tumultuous affairs of St. Luke's to occupy him, he had to find other ways of keeping up an active routine. One of these was serving as president of a group of black clergymen, the Ministers' Union of Washington, D.C., which met in the upstairs study of Crummell's home at 1522 O Street. Francis J. Grimké credited Crummell with having founded the interdenominational association and remembered Crummell as a man entirely lacking in bigotry, or in the feeling that his church was the only church. Crummell had, of course, often displayed certain types of religious intolerance, but Grimké shared so many of Crummell's fundamental biases that he probably would not have recognized them, no matter how pronounced. Despite the denominational difference between them, the two men were of remarkably similar temperament. Grimké, too, was a black puritan, and, like Crummell, had little patience with extreme evangelical emotionalism. It is clear, however, that Crummell was capable of working with members of other denominations, so long as their doctrines did not neglect present social needs, and so long as their services were not too disorderly.[8]

Crummell also belonged to interracial groups, such as the Conference of Church Workers among Colored People, of which he was a founder. He turned down an invitation to address the conference in 1894, however, and refused even to attend, saying, "I can't see anything to praise in the history of our church pertaining to our race." As he explained to Miller, with whom he was sometimes quite open on church-related matters, to speak before the group would be "the most awkward and unnatural thing in my life," for the church had been "a cold and repulsive stepmother to us colored men."

> This church don't intend to be disturbed about the negro question. She pities the negro: she will never do any effective work for him until she learns to love the negro. But when love will come is a problematical question. It may arrive at the same time as the ingathering of the Jews![9]

Apparently well-provided for in his old age and freed from pastoral responsibilities, Crummell continued to employ the title "Member of the Commission on Work among the Colored People." The commission was made up of five bishops, five presbyters, and five laymen. The commission's work was largely missionary, and much of it was at the South. Although charges of rigidity and ritualism had sometimes been directed at him, Crummell used the pages of *Spirit of Missions* to call for "more elasticity in our system of spiritual culture." The church could make good use of educated lay readers in areas where ordained priests could not be found. The church should also modify certain of its "religious customs and routines." The black people of the South were, for the most part,

> brought up under religious customs and routines widely divergent from ours. Their training has been largely that of the "class system" and the "prayer meeting." Is not the sudden change from such a system too violent a wrench? Is it wise thus to repudiate entirely the spiritual habits of any people? Accustomed to free prayer and free speech, is not the change to absolutely fixed services at first likely to chill and repel them?

As a commissioner, Crummell received a salary, and he was expected to speak and to travel. He planned a speaking tour through the southern and midwestern states for the spring of 1895. In the month before his departure, however, Frederick Douglass died suddenly, and Crummell was called to offer a prayer at his funeral on February 25, 1895. In later years, the two had gotten along rather well, and, although Douglass was not Episcopalian, Crummell had used him as a character reference in one of his disputes with his vestry.[10] In his pamphlet *The Lesson of the Hour,* published only a few months before his death, Douglass had used Crummell to illustrate a very important point, although he made an unfortunate invidious comparison in passing.

> When a black man's language is quoted, in order to belittle and degrade him, his ideas are often put in the most grotesque and unreadable English, while the utterances of Negro scholars and authors are ignored. To-day, Sojourner Truth is more readily quoted than Alexander Crummell or Dr. James McCune Smith. A hundred white men will attend a concert of counterfeit Negro minstrels, with faces blackened with burnt cork, to no one who will attend a lecture by an intelligent Negro.[11]

Douglass's allusion to Sojourner Truth was unkind and, of course, untrue. He knew that Sojourner Truth had much of value to say and that well-educated black speakers could get the attention of whites, as, in fact, Douglass had. Nonetheless, he made a valid point about the reasons why Crummell never became what was called in those days "a popular preacher." He was astute enough and honest enough to see Crummell's worth as an intellectual and a man of letters, although they differed fundamentally on such issues as intermarriage.

In the funeral oration, Crummell chose to reflect not on ideology, but on the heroism that Douglass's life represented, "for his resistance to the audacity of slavery; for his defiance of the pagan caste spirit of our sinful country." He spoke of Douglass's "constant apprehension of truth [and the] moral elevation of his persistent life," calling him a "great preacher and prophet of justice and freedom." Crummell had come to accept many of the ideas that had divided him from Douglass in earlier years, and, most important, he had, like Douglass, come to think of America as "our country," sinful though it might be.

Shortly after the funeral, he embarked on his planned speaking tour. It lasted five months and took him over a large section of the eastern United States. During the course of his travels, he delivered three baccalaureate sermons, two of them at Normal Colleges in Alabama, and the other at Wilberforce University in Ohio. Crummell mentioned to Miller a working title for his discourse at Wilberforce, "The Solution of Problems: The Function of Humanity." It was a variation on a popular theme of that era, one that permeated much American writing of the 1890s (for example, Theodore Roosevelt's later and more famous prolusion, "The Strenuous Life"). The title of the sermon introduced a matter of concern to the reluctant retiree, "The Solution of Problems: The Duty and Destiny of Man." [12]

The problems that Crummell suggested his young hearers confront were of a practical nature, but the solutions were to be found in the philosophical idealism that always characterized his thought. When confronting issues raised by Marxist and other forms of revolutionism that were pervading the United States, he asked the question, "Is the laborer to be a freeman, exercising his own will, and using his own powers? Or is he to be a slave, both will and powers at the command of others?"

> You, yourselves, have seen the crowds of frenzied and insensate men, antagonizing capital, resisting authority, ready on the instant, to sling abroad flame and incindiarism. . . .
>
> What have been the fundamental causes of these disturbances? You tell me, perchance, that they were generally the outcome of friction in matters of sustenance and housing; that they were simply the unrest concerning the gross material condition of the masses.
>
> Nothing can be more shallow than such a judgment. The material aspect is only the surface aspect. . . . There has rarely, if ever, been a strike, a labor riot, an industrial disturbance, an Agrarian outbreak, in all the history of man, but what has had underlying, some absorbing moral problem which agitated the souls of men. . . .
>
> Man never passes beyond the boundary lines of dull content into the arena of strife or agitation, unless some deep moral conviction first circles his brain and fires his blood or tinges his imagination.

Predictably, Plato won out over Marx in the Wilberforce address, but it was more than a conventional presentation of Christian platitudes; it was a statement of his own defiant and almost heretical theology. It was grounded in his theology of discontent, and dominated by tensions that still remained questions of debate, despite his commitment to Christian doctrine. Clearly, he still wrestled with such problems as free will and the nature of man, and he invited students to debate the questions, "What is mind? The nature of mind? Is it a product of our physical nature, or a finer and more subtle essence?"

He closed with a statement that seemed to express his defiant refusal to accept retirement. He expressed the remarkable belief that there really was no place for leisure in the divine plan. Heaven would *not* be an everlasting sabbatical. The special blessing of the righteous would be never to experience rest. Heaven would be a place of eternal struggle, he wrote, for "men and angels are created for the unending, the everlasting ventures and anxieties of their spirits in the deep things of God."

The twenty-seven-year-old W.E.B. Du Bois was teaching Greek and Latin at Wilberforce at the time of Crummell's visit, and he recorded his first impressions of him in *The Souls of Black Folk.*

> Tall, frail, and black he stood, with simple dignity and an unmistakable air of good breeding. I talked with him apart, where the storming of the lusty young orators could not harm us. I spoke to him politely, then curiously, then eagerly, as I began to feel the fineness of his character,—his calm courtesy, the sweetness of his strength, and his fair blending of the hope and truth of life. Instinctively I bowed before this man, as one bows before the prophets of the world. Some seer he seemed, that came not from the crimson Past nor the gray To-come, but from the pulsing Now.[13]

Du Bois's short biography of Crummell promises much but leaves a great deal to the imagination. The life is sketchily presented, and the character is sentimentalized. Du Bois seems to have been unaware of Crummell's interaction with his grandfather, Alexander Du Bois, and perhaps it was only later that he came into possession of his grandfather's "Records of Donations for the Benefit of Alexander Crummell." Du Bois's handling of Crummell was filiopietistic, but in all his published writings, although he occasionally mentions and even quotes him, Du Bois records no conversations with Crummell, no anecdotes concerning his administration of the American Negro Academy, no observations on his interactions with peers. He does not even let us know his reaction to the speech at Wilberforce in the spring of 1895. Du Bois somehow missed the opportunity to link the biographical with the autobiographical and to analyze in detail the relationship between his ideas and those of Crummell.[14]

There was certainly a meeting of minds between Crummell and Du Bois. Both of them were educated abroad; both believed that the black masses ought to be guided by an educated elite. Much of Crummell's later writing, and much of Du Bois's early writing and speechmaking, was addressed to the importance of a "talented tenth," who would be responsible for the cultural uplift and spiritual guidance of the masses. The smoldering hostility between Crummell and Booker T. Washington foreshadowed the debate between Washington and Du Bois that was to dominate many discussions of black education and culture in the coming century.[15]

Continuing on his travels, he paid a visit to his boyhood friend George Downing, who now lived in Newport, Rhode Island. Crummell had been his house guest on at least one previous occasion, in 1879.[16] The old conflict that had divided them during the 1860s had been laid to rest, since Crummell was no longer in favor of emigration. While he was in New England, he took a notion to revisit Canaan, New Hampshire. He also made a stopover in Boston, where he made the acquaintance of George W. Forbes, a newspaperman, who recalled his holding forth on the value of classical studies and was fascinated by Crummell's ability to quote lengthy passages by heart. At an all-night symposium, at which several young Boston men were present, Crummell declared his preference for ancient writers, although the German absolutists also ranked high in his estimation. He found Plato more to his taste than Aristotle, holding that the minute observations and diligence of the latter could in no way compensate for the poetic vision and splendid generalizations of Plato.

> "Cold indeed must have been the age," said he, "and dead to every generous sentiment that could have led mankind for a moment to prefer the dry . . . syllogistic empiricisms of the Stagirite to lounging with Protagoras, Prodicus, and Hippias upon their couches while elevating with high discourses even the philosophic throng above its sphere, or to hearing lofty readings beside Ilissus, or lively symposia giving occasion to high discourses about love." [17]

Forbes's rhapsodies on Crummell's Platonism portray him in a way that is only partially believable, for it is difficult to imagine Alexander Crummell lounging on the couch with Alcibiades, engaged in "high discourses about love." His fondness for Plato was well known, however, and Forbes records that he called himself a direct descendant of the bee that lighted on the infant Plato's lips to taste "the latent sweetness" there. Theophilus G. Steward, an associate of Crummell's in his later years, probably came closer to understanding the nature of Crummell's Platonism. It was related to his elitist notions of leadership and to his absolutism, which Steward asserted was both idealistic and subjective. This was what made him, in Steward's interpretation, a follower of Socrates and Plato, and this, he maintained, was the source of Crummell's opposition to the objective and practical philosophy of Booker T. Washington, whom he identified as "a disciple of Aristotle." [18]

Crummell's growing opposition to the educational philosophy of Washington certainly had other sources than those Steward suggests and Steward's description of Washington as a disciple of Aristotle does not merit serious discussion. The key to Washington was not to be found in philosophical discipleship so much as in practical experience. Washington had been educated at Hampton Institute in Virginia, an industrial college founded by a former Civil War general, Samuel Chapman Armstrong, who based an educational theory on his own puritanical brand of Christian soldierism. After graduating from Hampton, Washington founded Tuskegee Institute and, in his speeches at the Tuskegee Chapel, practically canonized the general. Both institutions were rigidly administered and were seen as having a civilizing mission. They would convert a presumably languid and hyperemotional people into fit citizens of a modern industrial society—clean, efficient, and progressive.

Washington was an immensely practical man, far more interested in controlling ideas than in generating them. He had been born in slavery in 1856, and, although he had been emancipated at the end of the Civil War, while he was still a small child, he traded on the fact of his rise from humble conditions. Like Douglass, he brilliantly exploited the "log cabin" rhetoric that was then so effective in American political life. He had struggled mightily to achieve an education and to overcome the limitations of his impoverished cultural background. He was shrewd. He was perceptive. He grasped instinctively the spirit of his times. He assimiliated the thought, speech, and spirit of "triumphant capitalism," and he hoped to mold the character of the black masses into conformity with the great American industrial machine. The extraordinary powers of concentration, the singleness of purpose, that had made it possible for him to engineer his rise from the squalor of his boyhood to his position as a consultant to presidents and kings was also his great shortcoming. W.E.B. Du Bois observed, "It is as though Nature must needs make men narrow in order to give them force." [19]

In his testimony before the House Committee on Education in 1880, Crummell had argued that the immediate educational needs of black people could best be met by trade schools. He was irritated no end, however, by Washington's oversimplification of trade school arguments from the pre-Civil War years. Like Douglass and other abolitionists, he had advocated training the free black population, and later the freedmen, in basic industrial crafts. He was not so impractical as to ignore the material necessities of life, but he felt that purely mechanical education could never provide the necessary mental habits for racial progress. Education in philosophy, history, literature, and the classics provided discipline and toughness, no less than industrial education. Of course literary education could be perverted by the frivolous or lazy, but this did not diminish its intrinsic worth. Washington, however, mocked classical education in general. He pretended that trade schools were a new idea, and he presented industrial education as a panacea for all racial problems in America.

There was another even more important issue. In Crummell's view, Washington was contributing to the harmful view that slavery had been a school. Although Washington acknowledged the moral wrongness of slavery, he maintained that it had some salutary side effects. "We went into slavery in this country pagans; we came out Christians," said Washington. "We went into slavery without a language; we came out speaking the proud Anglo-Saxon tongue." "If in the providence of God the Negro got any good out of slavery, he got the habit of work." [20]

Although this position superficially resembled Crummell's own theory of the providential nature of the history of slavery, it was, to his way of thinking, not the same thing at all. In fact, Crummell was exceedingly impatient with such views and vehemently rejected the Washingtonian preachment that slavery had been a school. There were two kinds of knowledge, said Crummell; one was crude and mechanical, the other, spiritual and intellectual. There could be no educative value in labor when the worker was reduced to the level of an unthinking, servile drudge. [21] Labor was a necessity of life, "just like eating and drinking. . . . And the Negro has had it for centuries, but it has never given him manhood." Black people had been in the 'school of labor' under slavery for fully two hundred and fifty years; and everyone knows that it . . . never produced his civilization."[22] Contact with the Anglo-Saxon had some providential benefits, it was true, but the effects of slavery had been overwhelmingly evil. The slaveholders had sought to effect "a deeper paganizing of their serfs than the original paganism that these had brought with them from Africa." They had made the slaves worse, in some respects, than their barbarian forebears, leaving them with an ungrammatical and illiterate mockery of English, and a religion scarcely discernible from supersitition.[23]

There was one point, however, on which Crummell and Washington were in agreement. Neither had much tolerance for the gaudy world of make-believe generated by the fashionable set of Washington, D.C. Crummell was as hostile as Washington ever was to the venality, the conspicuous consumption, and the escapism that was beginning to characterize the life of the black bourgeoisie. Rightly or wrongly, he blamed the members of this set for the troubles in his church. The type was treated not only in Washington's *Up From Slavery,* but also in W.E.B. Du Bois's *The Quest of the Silver Fleece.* These were the precursors of what E. Franklin Frazier would later call the "Black Bourgeoisie."[24]

Crummell's observations on the class of petty clerks and minor office-seekers paralleled those made later by Booker T. Washington, who arrived in Washington in 1878 to study at the Wayland Seminary. Washington compared Wayland, which lacked industrial training, to Hampton Institute, where he had received his prior education. He was convinced that the Hampton method was superior, because the effort required to support oneself as a student had the effect of building character. Washington's experience at Hampton was similar to Crummell's at Oneida, and, like Crummell, he came to be critical of certain aspects of social life in Washington. Both men expressed contempt for this class of colored people who "had been drawn to Washington because they felt that they could lead a life of ease there," or who had come "in the hope of securing Federal positions." All of this was linked in Washington's mind to the miseducation of black people, many of whom had learned nothing other than to despise working with their hands.[25]

Crummell's theory of education derived from a rare complexity of experience, both as a student and as a teacher. His youthful experience at Beriah Greene's "Manual Labor Seminary" had stood him in good stead during his first years in Africa, when he was called on to administer the Mt. Vaughan High School at Cape Palmas. The military/industrial conception of education adopted at Tuskegee had already been endorsed by Crummell during the 1850s. As he had watched his students going about their martial exercises, he had thought of himself as sowing the seeds for an army of spiritual Myrmidons. The ideal Liberian scholar was to be a Cincinnatus, tilling the soil, cultivating the military virtues, accepting the call of civic duty. This should not be seen as in any way inconsistent with mastering the Greek Testament. Washington was perhaps not aware of Crummell's experiences with "industrial education." Neither Washington nor Crummell seemed willing to admit that on some aspects of educational philosophy they were in agreement. In any case, neither man ever publicly revealed any awareness of the similarity between their experiences.

Washington consolidated his power in the fall of 1895 at the Atlanta and Cotton States Exposition, which he orchestrated through his able friend I. Garland Penn. It was at the Atlanta Exposition that Washington gave his famous speech disavowing any ambition on his part to agitate militantly for social integration and calling on white Americans to rely on black industrial workers rather than immigrant labor. Washington was not the only black person to make a speech in Atlanta that fall. The Exposition was the site of the First Colored Women's Congress, and it was also the occasion for a Congress on Africa, organized by lieutenants of the Tuskegee Machine.

Due to his expertise on Africa, Crummell was invited to speak at the Congress, although he had fully accepted the fact that the future of black Americans was to be in the United States. African Civilization and the unity of African peoples remained important themes in his writing, but he had abandoned the classical Pan-Africanism that he had been instrumental in creating. He had become increasingly hostile to emigrationism and had increasingly identified with the opinion that African tribes were better off under European colonialism than under the rule of American repatriates.

Crummell's position on Africa during the past two decades had been procolonialist. He had made this position clear in an address before the American Geographical Society, "The King of Belgium's Congo State." Leopold was providing what Africa really needed, "some grand master influences" to forestall the Muslim threat and other evils. She required "an authoritative force . . . , a grand POLICE FORCE all over the continent." With the founding of the International African Association, the king of the Belgians had demonstrated that he recognized his Christian duty, and Crummell had "the largest expectations of good and beneficence from its operations." He predicted that there were "people of this present generation" who would witness the realization of Leopold's "noble imagination." By 1895, as we shall see, Crummell was to modify his optimism concerning European missionaries considerably.

A similar shift of opinions was evident in the thinking of other black intellectuals. George Washington Williams, who would later emerge as one of the leaders in the movement for reform in the Belgian Congo, seemed to be full of admiration for King Leopold, whom he called "one of the noblest sovereigns in the world." That was on the eve of his departure for the Congo in 1890. He returned with his eyes wide open, of course, and immediately published a strongly worded open letter to King Leopold, blaming him for the violence that characterized the affairs of his agents, for his inattention to education and uplift, and for his degradation of the people by encouraging superstition, brutality, and drunkenness.[26]

Blyden held similar opinions, for, despite his interest in African languages and customs, he did not romanticize African cultures, nor did he have much confidence in their ability to make the leap into the twentieth century unaided.

He therefore encouraged external influences of every sort, including Christianity, Zionism, colonialism, and Islam. Although Crummell and Blyden disagreed on whether or not Islam paved the way for Christianity, they agreed on the role of outside agencies in the promotion of Progress and Civilization. Blyden also admired King Leopold as late as 1884, when, at the Congress of Berlin, he was perceived as a philanthropist. Blyden praised him, saying that "with more than regal munificence, [he had] lavished a vast fortune in the Congo country with a view to the extinction of Slavery and the introduction of a select civilization among the aborigines." [27]

Crummell's admiration for British colonial adminstration was no secret. He found England blameworthy only in one respect; she had sometimes passed up opportunities to extend her rule in Africa. She had recently ignored the dictates of Providence by failing to march across the continent from the Kingdom of Ashanti to Abyssinia and to extend a band of civilization from the Atlantic to the Indian coast. The slave trade could have been suppressed, legitimate commerce encouraged, and with it the spread of Christianity, leading to the elimination of "the grand disturbing element, the malign and destructive influence of the Moslems."

These ideas did not mean that Crummell, Blyden, or Williams ever questioned for a moment the principle of "Africa for the Africans." They did mean, at least in Crummell's case, that he would no longer speak of the special duties of black Americans to return to Africa as missionaries. In the address he delivered on "The Absolute Need of an Indigenous Missionary Agency for the Evangelization of Africa," he argued that the continent could be redeemed only by her own native peoples. He no longer spoke from the extreme Pan-Africanist position that insisted that all black people were fundamentally the same. Now he was prepared to say that the missionary from without, whether white or black, was widely distanced from the heathen population. The foreigner had no knowledge of the "master convictions which rule their being," no understanding of the "unnatural inherited ideas of heathen life." The missionary from Europe or America must encounter three special hindrances: "First the bar of settled custom and the prejudice which follows; second the formidable barrier of language; and third, the natural repugnance to divine truth." Native converts would have easier access to the minds of their own people.

In another address at the Congress on Africa, Crummell spoke on "Civilization as a Collateral and Indispensable Instrumentality in Planting the Christian Church in Africa." Here, he advocated ideas that were, in some respects, congruent with Washington's. Crummell's belief that the missionary had an obligation to work for the material welfare of those whom he evangelized was certainly supported by the worldly Tuskegeean. He had long held that progress and material development would accompany the arrival of the Christian message in Africa. He had asserted that the personaility of Jesus Christ was the major historical force for promoting progress and reform. Now, however, he seemed to be stating a more materialistic ideology. Civilization must be seen as "a collateral and indispensable instrumentality in planting the Christian church in Africa.'' He did not say that civilization must precede Christianity, but even to describe it as ''indispensable and collateral'' was to make a very strong statement. It was in no way a contradiction of anything he had ever believed about practical Christianity, nor was it surprising, given the practical concerns he had demonstrated during his own missionary venture. It did, however, amount to a restatement of his position, which separated him quite distinctly from the otherworldly churchmen for whom Booker T. Washington expressed contempt.

In this speech Crummell used the term ''civilization'' to denote material as well as intellectual and spiritual forces. It meant ''the clarity of mind from the dominion of false heathen ideas'' and the implantation of cultural values such as ''individualism and personal responsibility.'' It involved the acceptance of Victorian bourgeois concepts of womanhood and family. It was tied to the late nineteenth-century dogma of ''social progress,'' as well as material progress, which meant ''an elevated use of material things and a higher range of common industrial activities.'' The missionary, according to Crummell, had no right to allow the native convert to remain in a degraded material condition; he had an obligation ''to put judicious but positive discontent into his soul.'' ''Progress, not passivity [was] the law of all evangelization.'' He was certain that he could see this principle at work wherever Christian missionaries had set foot in modern times. He attributed the industrial progress which seemed to be occurring among South African Zulus to the effects of evangelization. He even predicted that Japan's rapid modernization and progress would inevitably be accompanied by the triumph of the Christian religion.[28]

Crummell's shift on the issue of the Back to Africa Movement led him into conflict with another of the speakers at the Congress on Africa, Bishop Henry McNeal Turner of the A.M.E. church. Turner, who was born in 1834, was sixty-one years old at the time of the Atlanta Exposition, at the height of his formidable powers, and an enthusiast for African emigration. Robust, hearty, gregarious, excitable, the bishop was the very personification of the nineteenth-century race man. He was a mulatto and seemed compelled to demonstrate that in his heart and soul he was more African than anyone else. Even before the Civil War he had begun to favor emigration, but by 1866 he was actively voicing the opinion that ''the better class of colored men in this country will go to Africa and build up a mighty nation, while the riff-raffs of the race will remain here.'' Turner claimed to have been inspired by Crummell in his youth, when he heard him speak in Israel Church, Washington, D.C. on May 6, 1862. Crummell's ''eloquent, logical, scholarly, and magnetizing speech had made [him] a convert to African emigration,'' and Turner averred that Crummell's past arguments were no less logical in 1895.[29]

Turner's speech at the Atlanta Congress on Africa argued passionately for colonization. He made interesting readjustments in the old rhetoric that had been around for over a century, giving it the distinct imprint of his own personality. Slavery was no mistake, but a part of the divine plan. It was a ''divinely sanctioned manual laboring school'' that God had set up to bring a benighted people into contact with ''the mightiest race that ever trod the globe.''

Afro-Americans had been sold by the "superior African" to the white man, who had been allowed to keep them in slavery,

> so long as it was necessary to learn that a God who is a spirit made the world and controls it and that that Supreme being could be found by the exercise of faith in His only begotten Son. Slavery then went down, and the colored man was thrown upon his own responsibility, and here he is today, in the Providence of God, cultivating self reliance. . . . I believe that the Negroid race has been free long enough now to begin to think for himself and plan for better conditions than he can lay claim to in this country or ever will. *There is no manhood future in the United States for the Negro.*

Turner denied the reasonableness of Booker T. Washington's position that two races could live side by side contributing to one another's progress without interacting socially. He climaxed his address with observations recalling Martin Delany's fifty years earlier, accusing the black man, "with few honorable exceptions," of folding his arms and waiting "for the white man to propose, project, erect, invent, discover, combine, plan and execute everything connected with civilization." The shiftless, no good Negro would remain in America content to exist at the sufferance of the whites; intelligent and enterprising men and women would realize that the only way to attain self-respect was through independence and self-assertion in a land of their own.

Crummell would have no part of this. His thinking had gone through at least three major shifts. During his Liberian phase, he had spoken of the importance of American emigration as a civilizing agency in West Africa. During his period of disillusionment, he had called on England, the United States, and Belgium to assume a missionary role in Africa. In Atlanta in 1895, however, Crummell argued that only an indigenous missionary agency would be up to the work of African evangelization. The natives themselves, "so far as possible," were to be the agency for bringing the new truths to their fellows. Where, exactly, the role of the European backer was to end and that of the indigenous missionary to begin was not clear in the Atlanta speech.

Turner was right, therefore; Crummell had indeed reversed his opinion on "the relations and duties" of black people in America towards Africa. Several months before the Atlanta Congress, he had accused Crummell of inconsistency, challenging his assertion that "the colonization of Africa by the Negro is absurd," an opinion he found inconsistent with the position which Crummell still maintained, that "an African civilization society should be organized by the people of this country." Turner would never convince Crummell that he was sincere in his commitment to the black race. In a letter to John E. Bruce, written shortly before leaving for Atlanta, he referred to the bishop as "that truculent, screeching and screaming creature."[30]

Turner was apparently far more successful in his dealings with Blyden, who came to have great respect for Turner's movement and the Pan-African sentiments he expressed. In 1883, Turner had given a "quiet and elegant dinner" for Blyden in his Washington home, which the *Christian Recorder* described in the following manner:

Bishops Brown and Ward, Major Delany, Rev. Messers. Handy and Grimké and F. L. Cardozo were the guests of the Bishop to meet Dr. Blyden. All were present except Bishop Ward, who was unavoidably detained. After the choice things provided by the Bishop's excellent lady had received full justice from the guests, Bishop Turner . . . gave a toast—though no wines or liquor of any kind was served. Dr. Blyden—the scholar, philosopher, statesman, philanthropist, explorer, and Christian missionary—an honor to his race. Rev. Mr. Grimké was then called upon and spoke in the highest terms of his personal friend, Dr. Blyden, and the deep interest he had in the Doctor's work in Africa, and said that he would join the Doctor himself in his great African work at some future time, perhaps.[31]

If Crummell had been invited, he did not choose to go, perhaps because of his declining faith in the Back to Africa Movement, or perhaps for other reasons of a more personal nature. Blyden claimed that as late as 1880 Crummell "had not given up the idea of returning to Liberia, but it is clear that by the end of the decade Crummell had become involved in a reenactment of the emigration debate of the 1860s. This time it was Crummell who took the anticolonizationist position, even reviving arguments that Douglass had once used against him. There was a difference, however. Crummell spoke from experience when he said that the climate in Africa was as much against black people as against whites. And at the very core of his repugnance for Turner's doctrines was Crummell's experience with the Liberian settler elite, whose policies he considered genocidal. In his opinion, Turner was guilty of "despising the Negro" and yet ambitious of a high place in black affairs and "anxious to mount to official power on the backs of Negroes." He characterized Turner as a hater of black people who sneered "at what he calls the good for nothing Negroes."[32]

Turner had indeed referred to opponents of colonization as "the good for nothing Negroes," but he was exceedingly clear on the issue of black versus mulatto conflicts. He asserted that all black people, regardless of white admixture, were Negroes pure and simple. He accused Crummell of being a secret hater of black people, calling attention to Crummell's opinion that "the lynching of the negroes in the South occurs because they as a class are degraded." Crummell had certainly made statements to that effect, by which he meant that black people were victims of oppression because they were powerless and unsophisticated. Turner claimed that it was "a fearful charge to present to the world against us here in the South" that the Negro was degraded. He was willing to admit that black people now suffered under a recent degrading decision of the Supreme Court. Indeed, blacks would always be sufferers under whatever degradation whites chose to impose upon them. The only solution for black people was to make a mass exodus from the United States.[33]

Crummell voiced his antimulatto sentiments to Bruce, a staunch "race man" and a sympathetic listener. Bruce fervently opposed race-mixing, the integration of black institutions, and the pollution of the racial stock. He would eventually become an active member of Marcus Garvey's movement, as would William H. Ferris, another Crummell protégé. Bruce often communicated with Crummell concerning the mulatto conspiracy, and Crummell responded vigorously, denouncing the "fanatical and conceited junto, more malignant than white men, pushing themselves forward as leaders and aristocrats of the race, and at the same time repudiating the race! And what is the basis of their superiority? Bastardy!''

Again and again, Crummell's letters to Bruce returned to the theme of the "Jesuitical snares" of the deluded mulattos, who sought to set up a new caste system in America, just as white racial prejudice seemed to be dying out. Like Blyden, Crummell took offense at the term Afro-American, which was becoming popular with some prominent mulattos, especially T. Thomas Fortune and Victoria Earle Matthews. It was finding its way into the names of such racial associations as the National Federation of Afro-American Women and the Afro-American League. Crummell believed that the term symbolized the bastardy of which, in his opinion, all mulattos were covertly or overtly proud. He saw it as a bare-faced acknowledgment of the stain of bastardy, the unholy stigmata of those who were ashamed to be known as Negroes.[34]

Crummell believed he saw developing in the United States a repetition of the pattern in Liberia, where a mulatto clique led by Joseph Jenkins Roberts had ruled on behalf of whites in the United States. Blyden always insisted that Crummell had left Liberia because he despaired of ever defeating the "Roberts clique." Crummell's disgust would have been practically limitless when in 1883 the one-time ally of Bishop Payne, Rev. Alfred F. Russell, for whom Crummell had nothing but contempt, became president of Liberia and Blyden became his speechwriter.[35]

The fact that Booker T. Washington was a mulatto and enjoyed a special relationship to agencies through which upper-class whites funded black colleges probably contributed to Crummell's growing dislike for him. Frank Grimké, one of the several mulattos who were exempt from Crummell's bias, had once written to Booker T. Washington suggesting that he recommend Crummell for a position with the John F. Slater Fund for Negro Education. Since Grimké was well aware of Crummell's testimony before the House Committee on Education, he had every reason to suppose Crummell would be sympathetic to Tuskegee's interests, but there is no record of Washington's response to the suggestion.[36]

Never one to avoid a fight, Crummell headed for his last battle—confrontation with the Tuskegee Machine. Crummell obviously had not gone gently into the golden years of retirement. He had found plenty to keep him occupied and for the first time in many years had no vestry squabbles to distract him. For once in his life he was not saddled with the brick and mortar issues of church building. He was free to follow the advice of Annie Cooper and take his struggles into the wider world. The United States was searching for a new order as it changed from an agrarian economy into a new industrial commonwealth. Booker T. Washington spoke for the "New Negro," who hoped to find a place in the industrial democracy by stealing a march on the rest of the world and adapting more efficiently than anyone else to the age of industrialism. Crummell opposed such ideas. For him the issue was not how well black people could adapt to the new order, but what ideas they could bring to the shaping of it. Civilization must be conceived of as an organic process of growth towards an ideal form, not as a mechanical process.

# 14

# Tuskegee Under Fire:
# The American Negro Academy
# (1896–1898)

In October 1896, Crummell mentioned in a letter to John E. Bruce that he had a project in mind that he hoped would serve the "coalescence of superior powers among us as a people, and in which I desire very much your presence and assistance." During the months following the Atlanta Exhibition, he had complained in letters to Bruce that "ephemeral upstarts" were "constantly pushing themselves to the front and are called 'Leaders,' when in fact they are only 'Leaders for Revenue.' " He began to search for a way to castigate these self-appointed spokesmen, who aspired to lead black people while "writing and publishing the most outrageous and degrading descriptions of them." On December 5, he expressed his desire to somehow effect "a complete setback for the demagogic "Leaders (so-called) who are 'Leaders for Revenue,' pure and simple," his reason being:

> The primal need of the Negro, for some years to come, is absorption in civilization, in all its several lines, as a preparation for civil functions, and the use of political power. Just now he is the puppet and the tool of white demagogues and black sycophants.[1]

"Wretchedness in Consequence of Ignorance" had been a theme in black writing since the publication of David Walker's *Appeal* in 1829. All antebellum black nationalists, including Crummell, had insisted with brutal frankness that black Americans had serious cultural deficiencies to overcome and that they must do so largely by themselves. They viewed the world as an arena of competition where the various races were locked in a life and death struggle. The desire of the white race for superiority was perfectly natural, and the black race had only itself to blame if it were crushed under the wheels of fate. The battle could not be won without knowledge. Black people must create an intellectual elite who, like Plato's philosopher-kings or France's enlightened despots, would guide the masses for their own good. It was probably the idea of so-called "enlightened despotism," rightly or wrongly attributed to the French Academic tradition, that ultimately inspired the American Negro Academy.

On December 18, 1896, a meeting was called in the library of John W. Cromwell, a Howard Law School graduate, who by superior performance on a series of competitive examinations had secured an appointment and subsequent promotions in the Treasury Department.[2] In attendance were Walter B. Hayson, Kelly Miller, Paul Laurence Dunbar, and, of course, Crummell, who had come with clear ideas of what he intended to accomplish. Cromwell, in a handwritten record of the proceedings, reported that "the object of the meeting having been fully stated by Dr. Alex Crummell who acted as president of the meeting, a series of resolutions was adopted and a plan of organization agreed on." Although Crummell had intended to call it the African Academy, Dunbar suggested the name American Negro Academy, which was eventually accepted. In all other respects, however, Crummell seems to have had his way. The group agreed that this meeting would be seen as "the initial, the primary organization of the Academy, and that we hereby accept the Constitution presented to us for the same, and enroll our names as its members." Cromwell's manuscript record leaves no doubt that Crummell had organized the meeting, set its goals, decided on a name, and presented a constitution he had drawn up in advance of the meeting. Invitations that were sent to prospective members described an association whose specific purposes had already been defined.[3]

In a description of the December 18 meeting published in the *African Times and Orient Review* of November/December 1913, Cromwell attributed its origins to two Southern educators, Richard R. Wright and William H. Crogman, who were not actually in attendance. Crogman had written to Crummell and to Booker T. Washington late in 1893 to solicit their support for a national organization of black intellectuals who were to have the task of defending the race from attacks by white intellectuals and working out solutions for problems that confronted black America. Since Crummell and Washington were known to believe in racial solidarity and self-help, Crogman and Wright probably thought it reasonable enough to expect their support. Washington, however, displayed no interest, and Crummell was reported by Cromwell, his close friend and a cofounder of the Academy, to have dismissed the idea as "entirely impracticable."

Crogman, however, told a story that was significantly different. Crogman wrote to Frank Grimké on September 24, 1894, describing Crummell as "pleased with the idea" despite the fact that he did anticipate some serious difficulty. Crogman transcribed a portion of a letter that Crummell had written to him, but complied with Crummell's wish that it not be made public. Perhaps that was why Cromwell did not have a clear picture of Crummell's feelings. Crummell had some reservations about the problem of securing and keeping members, a fear that proved to be well-founded, but Crogman's verbatim transcription, the only surviving portion of the letter, can hardly be interpreted as the response of a man who found the idea "entirely impracticable."[4]

> He would like to see an "African Institute be composed of say fifty colored scholars the best we have; devoted to literary, statistical, ethnographical, folk-lore investigation, pertaining wholly and entirely to Africa and to the world wide Negro race. It should be both inclusive and exclusive; inclusive of all real thoughtful reading men who have done something; exclusive of all mere talkers and scream-ers. Its work should be so real and thorough that it would be an object of ambition to secure membership; so thorough that it would command the respect of the scholarly element outside. I think we have a few ministers, college professors, teachers, artists, writers, fitted for such an organization; many of whom would be glad to undertake the great work."

Cromwell reported Crummell's response years later, presumably not having seen the secret letter to Crogman. Crogman's report that "the old gentleman was pleased with the idea" seems to have been more accurate. It is difficult to understand why Crummell would have dismissed as *"entirely"* impracticable an idea with which he had been associated for many years. The fact is, he took the trouble to suggest areas of scholarship and even proposed that the group resurrect the name of his moribund "African Society." The black writers and thinkers of Washington moved constantly in and out of literary and intellectual clubs, with kaleidoscopically changing memberships and names. Crummell, Grimké, Cromwell, and others never ceased to be involved in activities of the sort that Crogman and Wright had urged, as Alfred Moss and Adelaide Cromwell-Gulliver have shown.[5]

The Negro American Society had been founded in Cromwell's home on December 15, 1877. He and Crummell became fast friends, but the Association passed out of existence after only eight meetings. Why the Negro American Society was unsuccessful is not known, but the fact that one such organization had failed in 1877 could hardly have been the reason for Crummell's oposition to founding another sixteen years later. He had, in fact, witnessed the growth of another and far more more successful black intellectual group not long after the collapse of the Negro American Society. The Bethel Literary Association, founded in 1881 by Daniel Alexander Payne, senior bishop of the African Methodist Episcopal church, was thriving. Crummell had addressed the group, socialized with its members, and participated enthusiastically in its activities. It was before this society that he eulogized Henry Highland Garnet. Perhaps Crummell felt more comfortable with the idea of promoting a group of his own after Payne's death in 1894.[6]

In January 1894, only nine months before receiving Crogman's letter, Crummell had proposed organizing an "African Society in Washington" in a letter to the *Southern Workman.*

> I wished last year [1893] to enlist two or three friends of mine in the attempt to organize an "African Society" for the preservation of traditions, folk-lore, an-

cestral remembrances, etc., which may have come down from ancestral sources. But nothing came of it. The truth of it is the dinning of the "colonization" cause into the ears of the colored people, the reiteration of the idle dogma that Africa is THE home of the black race in this land, has served to prejudice the race against the very name of Africa.[7]

Alfred Moss suggests that Crummell's original coolness towards Crogman and Wright's proposal was because of the failure of these previous associations and that he later changed his mind when, after his retirement, he found himself with time on his hands. This is certainly a possibility, but it is also likely that Crummell saw from the outset that it would be "impracticable" to get the cooperation of persons like Booker T. Washington, who would have opposed an organization dedicated to "intellectual enterprise." He must also have had some doubts about Frederick Douglass, who was still alive at the time, and who thought that black organizations would do well "to say less about race and race recognition." But with the death of Douglass in 1895, and the rise of Booker T. Washington later that year, the composition of black American leadership was clearly changing. Crummell's shifting position was in response to the shifting balance of power among black leaders and his increasing hostility to Booker T. Washington. Crummell's hidden agenda for the American Negro Academy was to formally oppose the rising power of Tuskegee.

It has been said that Crummell "in his last years practically reversed himself on the matter of industrial education and the gospel of wealth," but there is no evidence to support this view. The opinions he expressed in "Common Sense in Common Schooling" (1886) and his hesitancy in endorsing the proposal of Crogman and Wright are probably the sources of the opinion that he was a proto-Bookerite. But Crummell had been educated at Oneida by Beriah Greene, and he had advocated a system similar to that which had produced him—a mixture of classical and industrial education. He had never preached that those who worked with their hands must of necessity be innocent of letters. Having defended the worth of abstract intellectualism throughout his life, he did not need to reverse himself on educational theory. Crummell was an elitist who believed that higher education must by its very nature be rigorous and competitive and, thus, at some levels, beyond the reach of the ordinarily intelligent and industrious person. He was opposed to allowing fops and featherheads to masquerade as college students. Thus, the opinions he had expressed in "Common Sense in Common Schooling" were intended as a corrective to abuses and extremes. He made his continuing bias in favor of liberal education clear, however, in his essays "Right Mindedness" and "Excellence, an End of the Trained Intellect."[8]

He had maintained a remarkable consistency on black education theory for over fifty years. At the age of twenty-one, before a meeting of a black literary society called the Phoenixonian, he had held up the ideal of his departed young friend Thomas Sidney, who had been well-versed in the classics and at home with the works of Shakespeare, Milton, and Coleridge. Again, in 1844, speaking at the Hamilton Lyceum in New York, he had alluded to Cicero and Burke,

Haydn and Mozart, Rubens and Raphael, Galileo and Kepler, as representing the standard of cultural attainment to which black people should aspire. His philosophy of education had been consistently elitist and cosmopolitan. Thus his Academy represented the culmination of his philosophy—not a reversal of position.[9]

On March 5, 1897, the one hundred twenty-seventh anniversary of the Boston Massacre, "immortalizing Crispus Attucks as one of the first martyrs of the American Revolution," eighteen founders assembled for the first organizational meeting of the Academy. Booker T. Washington had been invited but chose not to attend. He would not have found the meeting much to his liking, for it was not his style to involve himself in open debate with other men. He clearly felt he had nothing to gain from sitting among equals to discuss an association "for the promotion of letters, science, and art." He preferred to influence organizations from behind the scenes, working through agents who could be depended on to do his bidding. In addition, Washington was well aware that the goals of such an organization must eventually work at cross purposes to his own.

Although there are no surviving copies of the constitution of the Academy, there can be no doubt regarding its ideological biases. Crummell called the meeting to order and gave a statement of the organization's purpose. This was later referred to as his inaugural address, "Civilization, the Primal Need of the Race." Its title was reminiscent of the African Civilizationist rhetoric that he and Garnet and Delany had employed from 1858 through the Civil War years. It stressed a perceived need for black people to stand on their own feet and earn a place of respect in the world. They must make a group contribution to the development of American culture and world civilization. Personal achievement was essential but not sufficient for racial progress. One must be able to point to something distinctively "Negro." In this collective sense, the black race in America had "no art . . . no science . . . no philosophy . . . no scholarship." True, there were superior individuals in each of those endeavors, but "mere individuality cannot be recognized as the aggregation of a family, a nation, or a race; or as the interpretation of any of them."

Civilization was "the special race problem of the Negro in the United States." If the race could not "attain the role of civilization," if it could not produce some collective material and spiritual symbols of power, wealth, and refinement, it would forfeit its place "in the world of culture and enlightenment," and the forfeiture of that place would mean "despite, inferiority, repulsion, drudgery, poverty, and ultimate death." He never offered a systematic definition of this term "civilization," which he considered so important. But since he used it fifteen times in the course of his address, it is possible to infer some of his meanings.

> What I mean by civilization is the action of exalted forces, both of God and man. Civilization is the *secondary* word of God, given for the nourishment of humanity. For civilization is, in its origins, ideal; and hence in the loftiest men it bursts

forth, producing letters, literature, science, philosophy, poetry, sculpture, architecture, yea all the arts . . . and lays them in the lap of religion.

But civilization never seeks permanent abidance on the heights of Olympus. She is human and seeks all human needs. And so she descends, recreating new civilizations; uplifting the crudeness of laws, giving scientific precision to morals and religion, stimulating enterprise, extending commerce, creating manufactures, expanding mechanisms and mechanical inventions; producing revolutions and reforms; humanizing labor; meeting the minutest human needs, even to the manufacturing needles for the industry of seamstresses and for the commonest uses of human fingers. All these are the fruits of civilization.

Progress, Christianity, and civilization were virtually identical as historical forces in his thinking, as they were in the perfectionist doctrines and social gospel ideology of many nineteenth-century Christians. It required no great leap of the imagination to begin thinking of the process of civilization as the historical force through which Providence was manifested. This had been the burden of his sermon "The Greatness of Christ." In equating the idea of civilization with the Western concept of progress, Crummell directly anticipated the ideas of J. B. Bury, Robert E. Park, Spengler, Toynbee, and other twentieth-century thinkers. Unlike these later, secular thinkers, Crummell showed no interest in distinguishing between the concepts of culture and civilization. It is clear that he saw them as separate but related concepts. Culture was the personal attribute acquired by the educated man, which must be disseminated among the masses in order to bring them to the state of civilization. In an earlier essay, "The Prime Need of the Negro Race," he spoke of "higher culture" as the "grandest source" of civilization.

There was no question as to whose academy it was. Crummell had presided over a series of five preliminary meetings of the "resident members" of the Academy throughout the winter, and he was naturally called on to chair the meeting. William H. Ferris moved the nomination, saying that he had been "one of the leading spirits" of the organization, and Crummell was elected without opposition. When it came to electing a president, Crummell's name was presented by the nominating committee. He attempted to decline the nomination, saying

> I am an old man. I must decline the presidency of this organization. I have been going over this country for forty-five years; I am too old a man to be put at its head. I think the young men, who have enthusiasm and youth, ought to be at the head. I beg that you will excuse me.[10]

But John Albert Johnson, president of the Metropolitan A.M.E. Church, reminded the Doctor that he and many others had come to the meeting only because Crummell had insisted on their presence. Du Bois argued forcefully that Crummell ought to accept the position, because it should be an honor conferred only on the most distinguished men of the race. The assembly concurred that Crummell be elected by acclamation.

That evening, Du Bois presented a paper, "The Conservation of Races," that was carefully crafted to gratify the emotions of the Academy and its founder. Rather than attacking the materialism of Booker T. Washington, however, it presented a critique of the extreme integrationism with which Frederick Douglass had been identified. It had a kind of sinister, morbid beauty, with its fantastic celebration of authoritarian, antidemocratic, and ethnocentric values. It embodied Du Bois's own dark racial romanticism, which would always be at war with his liberal, proletarian, and egalitarian sentiments. His purpose was to argue for the importance of races rather than for the rights of individuals.

> Turning then to real history, there can be no doubt, first as to the widespread, nay, universal prevalence of the race idea, the race spirit, the race ideal, and as to its efficiency as the vastest and most ingenious invention for human progress.[11]

In this essay, Du Bois was clearly the intellectual heir of Crummell, Eurocentric yet Pan-Africanistic, chauvinistic yet cosmopolitan. The address declared "as Darwin himself said, that great as is the physical unlikeness of the various races of men their likenesses are greater, and upon this rests the whole scientific doctrine of human brotherhood." Du Bois wanted a scientific democracy, but the essay was an attack on bourgeois democratic liberalism. Black Americans, "reared and trained under the individualistic philosophy of the Declaration of Independence and laissez-faire philosophy of Adam Smith," had thus come to share the American bias against a "patent fact of human history."

> The history of the world is the history, not of individuals, but of groups, not of nations, but of races, and he who ignores or seeks to override the race idea in human history ignores and overrides the central thought of all history.

The essay, with its assertion that great men were no more than the representatives of racial ideals, showed the influences of the racial ideology and historical theories of Emerson and Hegel. The ideas presented were neither new nor imaginative, and, furthermore, Du Bois was certainly aware that these were the very ideas that were being used to keep the non-European races in subordinate positions. Du Bois was guilty of irresponsibly confusing the concepts of nation and race, and he was also guilty of confusing several definitions of race. His method of argument was bold assertion, rather than careful introduction of empirical evidence. Rhetorically, however, the speech was a smashing success. Du Bois knew the emotional needs of his audience, who rewarded the young man with "prolonged applause."

No sooner had the applause died down, however, than a lengthy discussion ensued. Several scholars praised the speech, but others began to question whether it made any sense at all. William H. Ferris began the animadversions with an implicit attack on the Hegelian theory that Du Bois had just presented. He argued that men were great, not because they represented their race or their age, but because they were able to rise above both. Ferris argued that what was needed was not so much an emphasis on the race as on the "ablest individual[s] in the race." What was needed was "not so much a race of men as that the race shall produce its greatest geniuses." There was considerable discussion of other aspects of Du Bois's paper, but particularly of its central idea, the importance of conserving races. William S. Scarborough said that he could not "conceive of two races, equal in every particular, living side by side, without intermingling." Crummell, however, took exception, asking Scarborough to demonstrate his assertion with specific examples from the histories of England, France, and Austria. Crummell rambled on at some length saying in sum that races, like families, were established by God and that races, like families, would always exist, because they were established by God. He concluded by saying, "We have just had a paper here tonight which is essentially a paper on the uses of races, and I think that it is essentially a good one."[12]

As Anthony Appiah has shown, the philosophy expressed in "The Conservation of Races" was one of reprehensible racialistic thinking. It left itself open to interpretation as a diatribe against race-mixing. Du Bois had written it with the biases of Crummell and the Academy in mind, almost as if he felt he must defer to those among his elders in the room who were known to identify as "race men."[13] Racial chauvinism and Negro Improvement rhetoric of the sort that he employed in "The Conservation of Races" were by no means alien to Du Bois. When T. Thomas Fortune declared in a newspaper article that Du Bois's address was proof of the antimulatto, problack sentiments of the Academy, John W. Cromwell observed that two of the Academy's blackest members had disputed the central theme of Du Bois's address and that two men of mixed race had warmly defended it. But Fortune only saw this as proof of the absurdity of the Academy's position; he observed that Du Bois himself was of mixed ancestry and was thus a living argument against his own thesis. Crummell's response to Fortune was vehement, and his letters to Bruce around this time lead one to believe that the antimulatto attitudes he had acquired in Liberia were still with him.[14]

Later that month, *Spirit of Missions* carried a series of essays on the missionary responsibility of the church toward black Americans. Booker T. Washington, as one of the contributors, naturally addressed the need for industrial education. Crummell's essay had to do with methods of church work among black Americans. He made a number of simple suggestions, including the idea that missions be organized simply, according to the customs of worship that were familiar to the people. He suggested that local clergymen select two or three pious men as advisors, but that they not be granted the full powers of vestrymen. Only at a later stage, after a church had been built and a congregation assembled, should a vestry be elected, "but not until the Bishop considers this advisable. At this point, speaking from experience, Crummell observed, "We hear often of clergymen who are called failures, but people forget that not infrequently it is the vestries who are the real failures."[15]

Of the several articles printed in that issue of *Spirit of Missions,* two, in addition to Booker T. Washington's, were devoted to industrial education, one by William A. Leonard, bishop of Ohio, and the second by H. B. Frissell, principal of Hampton Institute. Crummell's enemies were bearding the old lion in his den, but he was not yet toothless, as he would soon show.

That August, Crummell launched a more direct attack on the Tuskegee philosophy in an article in *The Independent* that assaulted the "temporary fad of doubting or purblind philanthropy" which attempted to make industrial education a substitute for "higher culture." The editors of *The Independent* seemed, at first, to endorse Crummell's position that "the prime need of the Negro race is not industrialism but civilization." Washington supporters interpreted this as a "covered inference" that their faction did not believe in 'Higher Culture.' " They were confident, however, that no one would dare to oppose Tuskegee openly. Washington, convinced that *The Independent* had "never fully appreciated what we are trying to do through industrial education," prepared a response and promptly received confirmation that he would be given more than ample space for rebuttal. In a two-part article on "Industrial Training for the Negro," Washington described an encounter with a colored minister who was

> preparing his Sunday sermon just as a New England minister prepares his sermon. But this colored minister was in a broken-down, leaky, rented log cabin, with weeds in the yard, surrounded by evidences of poverty, filth, and want of thrift. This minister had spent some time in school studying theology. How much better it would have been to have had this minister taught the dignity of labor, theoretical and practical farming in connection with his theology, so that he could have added to his meager salary, and set an example to his people in the matter of living in a decent house, and correct farming.[16]

It seems more than likely that Washington stole this anecdotal formula from Crummell's testimony before Congress in 1880. He was to use several versions of this story over the years to illustrate the folly of classical education. These were always variations on the theme of "the saddest sight I ever saw." In one version it was an improvident peasant boy in a dilapidated southern cabin; in another it was "a colored girl recently returned from college, sitting in a rented one-room log cabin attempting day by day to extract some music from a second-hand piano." Another version, which may have been a direct reference to Crummell's Liberian years, told the following story:

> A friend of mine who went to Liberia to study conditions once came upon a negro shut up with-in a hovel reading Cicero's orations. That was all right. The negro has as much right to read Cicero's orations in Africa as a white man does in America. But the trouble with the colored man was that he had on no pants. I want a tailor shop first so that the negro can sit down and read Cicero's orations like a gentleman with his pants on.[17]

Crummell's objection was to Washington's ridiculing tone, rather than to the content of his narrative. Over the years his own attitudes on native African culture were seldom positive, but, unlike Washington, he was not given to making fun of Africans. Washington's characteristic ridicule, his use of minstrel show techniques to win the attention of whites, was making him many enemies among blacks.

The American Negro Academy revealed just how American it was with all its talk of creating a new civilization "along Negro lines." Like white Americans who were constantly declaring their cultural and literary independence from the "courtly muses of Europe," they had only the vaguest idea of what the distinguishing qualities of a new civilization might be. While Crummell and his peers paid lip service to the preservation of black folklore, their cultural values were not located either in the rural South or in the African village. They were embodied in the pseudo-epics of Tennyson, rather than the homely images of Dunbar's dialect poems. The members of the Academy were Europhiles, more specifically, Anglophiles. Majestic government buildings, enduring archives, solid church edifices, and stately boulevards represented the cultural ideals of Western civilization that they cherished.

Crummell did not deny that he encouraged imitation; indeed, he cited Edmund Burke, one of his favorite authorities, to the effect that "imitation is the second passion belonging to society," and this passion, according to Burke, "arises from much the same cause as sympathy." The capacity for imitation, Crummell went on to say, was "one of the strongest links of society." It was the means by which "all civilization is carried down from generation to generation or handed over from the superior to the inferior." Thus imitation, or the "assimilative tendency," was one of the strong points of the black race. In his essay "The Destined Superiority of the Negro," Crummell asserted,

> This peculiarity of the Negro is often sneered at. It is decried as the simulation of a well-known and grotesque animal. But the traducers of the Negro forget that "the entire Grecian civilization is stratified with the elements of imitation; and that Roman culture is but a copy of a foreign and alien civilization." These great nations laid the whole world under contribution to gain superiority. They seized upon all the spoils of time. They became cosmopolitan thieves . . . In the Negro resides, though crudely, precisely the same eclectic quality.

"This quality of imitation," which black people undeniably possessed to such a marked degree, had been "the grand preservative" of the race throughout the years of slavery. It was likely to have some bearing on the race's "future distinction in Art."

Since he felt no embarassment whatever at the idea that he was imitative or assimilationistic, Crummell remained as much an Anglophile as ever. The civilization most worthy of imitation had obviously reached its most magnificent forms in England, and the city of London was to be singularly resplendent in the summer of 1897. Crummell hoped to witness "if possible, the magnificent pageant of the Queen's jubilee, which takes place on 23rd June." He and Jennie Crummell embarked for that purpose with a group of other Washingtonians and remained in England for almost six months.

They sailed from Philadelphia on May 8, 1897, at 2:00 p.m., and Crummell wrote to Cromwell on June 15, 1897, describing a pleasant passage "in the company of our fellow passengers.'' These were days spent in reading and conversation and enjoyment of the soporific effects of ''the ozone of the ocean.'' Fortunately there had been no seasickness, although Mrs. Crummell was taken quite ill shortly after their arrival. The ocean crossing was eight days to Liverpool, and they went up to London immediately, where they ''received a right cordial welcome from old friends.'' [18]

He remarked that a number of black Americans were in London at the time. One of his ''first finds'' was Paul Laurence Dunbar, who was experiencing financial difficulties, living in a garret, and finding the experience neither elevating nor romantic. Dunbar had been in London since the beginning of the year, working on his novel *The Uncalled,* which concerned the problems of a white youth whose life is made wretched by a puritanical aunt with the suggestive name of Hester Prime. Dunbar at once changed his quarters to the boarding house where the Crummells were staying. Crummell also mentioned a meeting with Hallie Q. Brown, a chief organizer of the Colored Women's Club Movement, and Sidney Woodward, ''the great tenor,'' who ''spent a night with Dunbar and breakfasted with us.'' Crummell also described a surprising encounter with H. F. Downing, who had been living in London for four years, married to ''a white girl from Massachusetts. She recognized me at once, for some years ago, while in Massachusetts, I went to Wheaton College and addressed the young ladies and she was then a girl-student there.'' One of Crummell's more interesting contacts during those weeks was with Henry Sylvester Williams, who soon thereafter organized the African Association of London and three years later collaborated with W.E.B. Du Bois, Henry F. Downing, and Anna J. Cooper in organizing the London Pan-African Conference. [19]

Crummell was apparently worried about Dunbar, who had decided that he must ''devote himself to Literature as his life-work.'' They had several ''long conversations upon the subject,'' and Crummell found the young poet ''much perplexed as to plans for working out his purpose.'' He suggested to Dunbar that he ought to move back to Washington, and to Cromwell that he should help establish a literary magazine under Dunbar's editorship ''for purely Negro Literature.'' There was, he reasoned, a large enough class of educated black people to make such an enterprise viable. If one hundred subscriptions could be solicited in the cities with large black populations, it would be possible to raise $500 to $1000 annually. He was confident that ''A 'Monthly Magazine,' purely and entirely literary, would command very wide patronage from especially our own people, and to no small degree from the whites.'' [20]

He was now seeing with two eyes again after some seven years of half blindness. Shortly before sailing, Crummell had the cataract removed from his right eye, ''then came blindfolding of both eyes, and slow sailing with my right, until almost the present.'' It was, as he said, ''a great boon to an old man.'' He could now more fully enjoy the ''grand Cathedrals and noble Churches'' of London, the cloisters, halls, chapels, and gardens of Oxford, the ''grand Church'' at Stratford, and the excursion to Warwick Castle. The months in London were active ones, during which he claimed to have ''continual daily, sometimes hourly, engagements; talking, speaking, and sight-seeing.'' He had journeyed to Lincolnshire in the east and to Somersetshire in the west and more than once to London. He mentioned ''the delight, which certainly in our case, English hospitality [had] given.''

During the weeks in England he wrote several times to John E. Bruce, mostly on topics relating to the Academy and the universal concerns of caste and color. On October 5, he mentioned having sent a copy of Kelly Miller's review article on Frederick L. Hoffman's *Race Traits* to Sir Edward Russel, editor of the Liverpool *Post,* formerly a member of Parliament. He sent a reporter around on the morning of the fifth, and Crummell visited him in the afternoon ''for a talk on the 'Academy' and the 'Negro Cause' in general.''

Despite these encouraging signs, it is obvious that the Academy would have been headed for stormy seas if Crummell had lived. The issue of ''color caste'' within the black community was emerging as a divisive issue. In his letters to Bruce, Crummell obviously felt comfortable spilling his feelings on the topic of color as he once had in letters to Blyden. The letters became particularly vitriolic whenever the names of Bishop Turner, Richard T. Greener, or T. Thomas Fortune came up. Terms such as ''bar-sinister'' and ''bastard'' made their appearance, and Crummell was certain that the mulattos wanted to wreck the Academy. On one occasion, he wrote to Bruce asking him to nominate one or two ''thinking, race-devoted members'' but cautioning him that ''they must be genuine fellows, simon pures.'' But Crummell insisted that distinguished men of mixed race were welcome, and he praised in the same letter W.E.B. Du Bois's ''The Conservation of Races,'' the second occasional paper, published in 1897. No paper delivered before the Academy in its early years adhered more loyally to the Crummell philosophy than that delivered by W.E.B. Du Bois, who did not happen to be one of the ''simon pures.''[21]

Crummell returned to the United States after five months, arriving in Philadelphia on October 24. He resumed his attack on Tuskegee the following December with a speech he had been writing while in England, and which was referred to as his first annual address before the Academy, ''The Attitude of the American Mind Towards the Negro Intellect.''

> It is not that the Negro does not need the hoe, the plane, the plough, and the anvil. It is the positive affirmation that the Negro needs the light of cultivation; needs it to be thrown in upon all his toil, upon his whole life and its environments.
>
> What he needs is CIVILIZATION. He needs the increase of his higher wants, of his mental and spiritual needs. . . .
>
> But the ''Gradgrinds,'' are in evidence on all sides, telling us that the colleges and scholarships given us since emancipation, are all a mistake; and that the whole system must be reversed. The conviction is widespread that the Negro has no right to the higher walks of scholarship.[22]

The academician who agreed most with Crummell's ''civilizationism'' was William H. Ferris, a graduate of Yale, with master's degrees from Yale and Harvard. Affected, prolix, idiosyncratic, a great name-dropper, Ferris nonetheless a hard worker and widely read. Ferris was a sort of black Prufrock, "at times, almost the fool," with his embarrassing Eurocentrism and delusions of grandeur. Although predictably committed to positions that Crummell found acceptable, he was not afraid to dissent. In the discussion following Du Bois's paper, he took exception to some of Crummell's most cherished views, arguing at length that men of genius made their mark not by expressing a race ideal, but by transcending race. The tragicomic quality of Ferris's life was summed up in the ironically accurate word "Negrosaxon," which he coined to describe the culturally anomalous condition of black Americans at the turn of the century.

The term Negro was "so loaded down and freighted with ignominy and contempt," he argued, "that the colored race can never hope to dignify and exalt the term." As long as they called themselves Negroes, "the loophole out of our political and civil ostracism is to call ourselves Negrosaxons or Colored people."

> One eminent Negro Divine said that the colored man who points with pride to the Anglo-Saxon blood in his veins is boasting of bastardy, and that the colored man is the only being who boasts of his bastardy. There is a large measure of truth in this. But in coining a new name to describe the colored people of mixed descent in America there is only one that is ethnologically true and that is Negrosaxon. . . . The Negrosaxons, even those of pure Negro descent, have forsaken their African heritage and absorbed and assimilated the political, social, moral and religious ideals and customs and usages of the Anglo-Saxon race. In fact, Alexander Crummell, who became metamorphosed into a cultured and polished Englishman, was a pure blooded Negro.[23]

Crummell, who was strongly partial to the term "Negro" and rejected hybrid terms such as Afro-American, would have found the designation "Negrosaxon" absolutely silly and totally objectionable. It is fortunate that death spared him the embarrassment of hearing his name associated with it. Ferris apparently abandoned the term himself by the time he became a vice president of Marcus Garvey's Universal Negro Improvement Association.

Although far more restrained than Ferris, William S. Scarborough, who taught classics at Wilberforce University, embodied the Academy's elitism and civilizationism. He agreed with Crummell's doctrine that the exclusive society of superior black intellectuals must exist for the benefit of the masses. They were to be like a Platonic ruling elite, or perhaps a college of cardinals. As *servi servorum dei,* they would head up an organic racial body, giving guidance to the hands and the feet, but in no way despising them. *"Ich dien,"* must be the motto of the educated black man, wrote William S. Scarborough, an Academy member, "I serve—a service by leading . . . This idea of service to the race is particularly the mission of the educated Negro." That was the Academy ideal exactly; it was the duty of the elite to diffuse knowledge among the many, so that the whole could rise together. As Scarborough put it, the purpose of the Academy was to rectify the fundamental problem of black people in America, and, bluntly stated, "the special race problem of the Negro in the United States [was] his civilization."[24]

American Negro Academy members also subscribed to Crummell's conception of military virtue. The best representative of this view was T. G. Steward, a retired army chaplain who advocated a militaristic ideology similar to that which had been more subtly conveyed by General Armstrong at Hampton Institute. His statements on the value of military training were almost an echo of Crummell's assertion of 1861 that nothing makes a savage into a man so quickly as putting a gun into his hand.

> I am persuaded that nothing will do for the Negro race in this land what the rifle will do for him. War will winnow out his chaff; war will steady his nerves; toughen his fibre, assure him his limitations, harden his virtue and lay the foundation for his character. Civilization has its foundation on the battle field. If we could get fifty-thousand, or one hundred thousand black Americans in arms and keep them in training for a quarter of a century, the race would be carried forward many centuries.[25]

This spirit of "civilizationism" was really not in conflict with the uplift philosophy of Booker T. Washington, and it presaged the "Negro Improvement" philosophy of Marcus Garvey. All three ideologies had one common strand, as several scholars have noted. They assumed that black people must be changed through some sort of program of organized reform that would rebuild the race into a fighting machine, capable of making a united effort to achieve a position of power in the modern world.

The African Civilization, or "Negro Improvement," ideology was doomed to failure, because its standards were essentially nineteenth-century ones. It was divorced from the culture of the peasant masses and did not anticipate the new forms of nationalism in the twentieth century, including popular culture and "folkish" themes. It resembled the old African Civilizationism of the 1850s. While the academicians were unquestionably altruistic in their rhetoric, they were nonetheless associated with a lofty, imperious, and authoritarian approach to culture, and they were, in the main, insensitive or even hostile to the cultural and demographic changes that were occurring among the masses of black Americans. Their conception of black unity could never appeal to the developing black middle class, whose American democratic reflexes were too spontaneous for them to have patience with such an elitist notion of leadership and culture.

It was men like Cromwell and Grimké who were most capable of appreciating Crummell. Cromwell, in particular, provided him with support—both moral and spiritual. At times when Crummell was in trouble with the vestry, his livelihood was provided by people like Cromwell, who disassociated themselves from the vestry to found the "Pastor's Relief Association." More important, Cromwell remained active in St. Luke's as one of Crummell's staunch defenders. Grimké, although a Presbyterian minister, also gave Crummell moral support. He was a close friend, and the fact that he had a white father did not prevent him from agreeing with Crummell on many race-related issues. Grimké, like Cromwell, belonged to that select inner circle who could publicly disagree with Crummell and still retain his friendship. He and Cromwell were almost certainly responsible for convincing Crummell of the dangers of his position on trade schools before the House Committee on Education.[26]

In his eulogy on the life of Crummell, Grimké spoke mostly about the Colored Ministers' Union, giving a sympathetic but objective portrayal of Crummell's role in that organization. One of Crummell's last activities in the Union before his death was to organize a banquet; it was his task to choose speakers and assign topics for a series of addresses. To the general consternation of the group, Crummell decided that every member would have to contribute "to the intellectual uplift of the occasion." Grimké recorded that there had been some "murmuring" against this policy, but the Doctor's will prevailed, and, after his last dinner with the group, Crummell rose from his place at the head of the table, "his face beaming with satisfaction, and after expressing his gratification at what he had heard, he said, with a twinkle in his eyes, and a glance at some of us who had been most pronounced in our opposition to general speech making, 'This splendid meeting that we have had is a fitting rebuke to those brethren who felt that we ought not to have after dinner speeches.' " This was the occasion on which Grimké heard the good-humored comment of another minister, "Why the Doctor is a perfect Tsar." Grimké felt that it was "a good thing to be under such a Tsar."

> I wish we had a great many more of them—people who will not let us rest in our indolence, who keep constantly before us high ideals, and who speak to us with authority, with a power, a force which compels obedience. Such an imperial force was the Doctor in our Union.[27]

In August of 1898, Crummell complied with the advice that he had given to Frazier Miller and left Washington for Point Pleasant, New Jersey, for his annual vacation. He had been invited to spend a few weeks at Berea Cottage, the summer home of Matthew Anderson, pastor of Berean Presbyterian Church in Philadelphia and one of the Academy members present at the organizational meeting. For the past two years he had been complaining to his friends that his strength was failing, but, as he wrote to Bruce, he was still trying to work six or seven hours a day at his desk. Some days, however, he had to "sit and do nothing, and wait upon the Lord." As usual, however, this was to be a working vacation, and, according to Anderson, who saw him daily, Crummell's mental condition was very active and alert. He had stopped off in New York along the way and was planning to return there after his visit. He was engaged in correspondence with Thomas Whittaker, publisher of *The Greatness of Christ and Other Sermons,* who was planning to bring out another volume of his writings. Toward the end of August, however, his physical strength rapidly deteriorated, and one day, on returning from duties in Philadelphia, Anderson found that he had taken to his bed. "Anderson, I think this is death," he said.

and insisted on making known his wishes concerning his funeral. Anderson gave him his promise to assist Jennie in managing the details.[28]

His last days were peaceful, although he continued to worry about black leadership, sharing with Anderson a week before his death his suspicions of the motives of those who disagreed with him, and revealing the trait of "unbending righteousness" with respect to his own views.

> Friend Anderson, I have no fear of the future of the American Negro, for he belongs to a prolific, hardy and imitative race, there is a glorious future before him; but I do dread his leaders, because most of them are unscrupulous, ambitious, and ungodly men, who care nothing for the race but to use it simply to secure their own selfish and ungodly ends.[29]

His conviction that the British meant well in Africa remained unshaken, and when he was told a few hours before his death that Khartoum had fallen, he raised his hands and exclaimed, "Thank God! That marks the downfall of slavery in Central Africa."[30] The morning of September 10, 1898, he took part in devotions, praying and singing with his wife and friends, and when asked how he was, he replied that he was feeling much better and hoped to get up soon. He was only a few hours from death, but he dictated a letter to Paul Laurence Dunbar "without a break in the connection, on the philosophy of poetry."[31] His last moments were devoted to prayer, conducted according to the rules of the Episcopal church. He died at 10:30 a.m., his wife holding his hand. The body was sent back to New York and buried from St. Philip's Episcopal Church.

Walter B. Hayson, who had rushed to Point Pleasant on hearing that Crummell's condition had declined, arrived on September 1 and served as Crummell's amanuensis during the final days. After accompanying Jennie Crummell to the funeral, he sent Cromwell the following letter, which was printed with slight modifications in the Washington *Bee:*[32]

> The day dawned bright and clear—heaven smiled and so did the Doctor as he lay in his casket of black cloth with its silver trimmings and silver plate bearing the simple inscription:
>
> Born March 3, 1819<br>Alex Crummell<br>Died September 10, 1898
>
> All day yesterday and today the public viewed the remains as they lay in state at St. Philip's, indicated by the crowd which would have thronged the church had the service been held on any than a work-day. However, a good audience was present today and the services were very impressive in their simplicity, especially to those who knew the Doctor's wishes.
>
> The music, which included Gounod's chorus "There is a green hill far away," was well rendered. Mr. Bishop, the pastor, was assisted by Mr. Mitchell of Washington, Mr. Tinnell of Washington and Mr. Frazier Miller of Brooklyn.
>
> At the grave, the resolutions of the Academy and the Union were read. Members of St. Philip's Church vestry were the pall-bearers. Mr. Charles Crummell

and Mr. Sidney Crummell's wife attended the funeral and followed Mrs. Dr. Crummell and me. Mr. George Downing and brother were present as also was Jno [illeg.] Ferris came up too late. But Rev. Anderson was here and Rev. Reeves of Philadelphia. Mr. Pellew sent a large wreath of ivy leaves so did the vestry of St. Philip's. These with a large bouquet of roses from myself were all the floral tribute.

These facts I think will satisfy you till we meet again.

Mrs. Crummell and I leave for Philadelphia tomorrow and will reach Washington Thursday night or Friday morning.

> Your's sincerely,
> Walt B. Hayson

Hayson's description of the funeral leads one to believe that Crummell's children were not present. Why Mrs. Sidney Crummell came without her husband remains unknown. Obituaries in the Washington *Bee* and the *Colored American* said that Crummell was survived by a widow, a son, and a daughter.[33] Sidney would obviously have been the son; the daughter may have been Frances, who visited him in Washington in April 1884. Sophia Elizabeth had died in the autumn of 1879. "A young lady of fine ability," her short obituary read, "having decided talent for allegorical and other figurative writing."[34] In his last will and testament "it was apparent that a home for the aged women of this parish and diocese was a thought near his heart. What with long years of self-denial he placed on the altar as a faithful offering his entire fortune, which was supplemented by a similar bequest of his wife."[35]

Du Bois's eulogy on Crummell, sentimental and dreamy, recalled those traits that would have been most impressive to him as a somewhat fastidious and formal young man. He spoke of Crummell's "unmistakable air of good breeding," the "fineness of his character,—his calm courtesy." He portrayed him as a gentle martyr, constantly humiliated by white folk and persecuted just as cruelly by black people. Du Bois's essay on Crummell was dominated by melancholy words, images, and phrases, such as "grave shadow," "vain rebel," "wingless and alone." Crummell was portrayed as moving "beneath a dark despair" and as "haunting the streets." He described Crummell's life as the "weird pilgrimage" of a "vain rebel." More commonly, the obituaries of Crummell portrayed him as a forceful, tough-minded, shrewd, and stubborn man, not the "frail" "soul in search of itself" Du Bois depicted.

The eulogy of the Rev. Sterling Brown of Park Temple Church was a better characterization:

> He had but little sentimentalism. He keenly felt and boldly denounced the evil of ignorant and merely strong-languaged preachers. . . .
>
> He was bold and daring and powerful in his convictions. He asked no quarter of the enemy and yielded no principle of right. His moral character made him a target for the evil-minded, but they . . . never dared to be open or aggressive. He did, however, have enemies among this class of people. The success of Dr. Crummell can never be measured by the clamor and demonstration of the populace. He was not what is usually termed by colored people a popular preacher.

Crummell's idealism was not dreamy or impractical, although it was based on a belief in universal moral values that could not be altered by ephemeral mundane circumstances. This philosophical idealism was not to be confused with otherworldliness. It was something more than the commitment to nonmaterial values that one expects from a Christian clergyman, and it may have had something to do with his exposure to William Whewell's attempts to revive Cambridge Platonism. His classical training and his Platonic absolutism were linked to both his political and his religious thought. He decried as a half-truth the philosophy that black people would rise insofar as they acquired money and property. It was Crummell's idealism that led him to the statement that "the Negro problem in the U.S. [was] a problem of ideas," despite the "present but fleeting movement to give it the aspect of materialism." He warned of the dangerous tendency among modern thinkers towards "dogmatizing theories of sense and matter." But, at the same time, there was a decidedly tough-minded quality to his Christianity.[36]

In his later years Crummell expressed the belief that if black people became civilized enough, white Americans would eventually find them acceptable as fellow Americans. Racial antagonisms would then die out. At a meeting of the Bethel Literary Society on January 14, 1884, he was reported to have said that "as the colored race rose from plane to plane of superiority the prejudices of race would be forgotten." In order to carry the race forward toward this goal, he set almost impossibly high standards for himself, living a life characterized by mental toughness and moral self-castigation. He developed an ideology of black advancement based on self-improvement rather than agitation, which inspired an entire generation of black nationalists and Pan-Africanists, especially those academicians who found their way into the Garvey Movement.

But Alexander Crummell's perpetual discontent stemmed from his having adjusted far too well to the values of "civilization." He accomplished everything that could be asked in order to meet the cultural demands of the Anglo-American bourgeoisie, but this was not enough. The prejudices of whites were not simply a matter of ethnocentrism. They were based on color, not culture. The white racism that he encountered at every turn had nothing to do with how black people behaved or what they accomplished, nor with whether they could acquire polish and refinement. It had nothing to do with their ability to understand Greek syntax or the binomial theorem. Crummell's life proved that a black man in nineteenth-century America might actually exceed most whites in cultural and intellectual originality and still be ignored, purely and simply because it was assumed that a black thinker had nothing to say that could be of any usefulness to white people.

# 15

# Crummell's Universality
# and Significance

Every philosophy begins with an act of will, a decision as to what one perceives as real or true. Crummell's decision was to premise all his thinking on the idea that there is an objective and absolute reality, entirely separate from any individual observer. One discovered the truth by relying on the senses, the conscience, and reason. The senses were not perfect, and the "sense" of conscience was no more perfect than the sense of sight. Individual observations could be flawed and relativistic; they often varied from observer to observer. Thus conscience like the other senses must be strengthened, and morality must be reinforced by disciplining the senses and the mind.[1]

For the existence of conscience, Crummell accepted arguments provided by the standard canon of works in casuistry and "moral science." He contemplated the definitions of conscience provided by the Cambridge Platonists, by Bishop Butler, and by William Whewell. Conscience was more than a conditioned reflex; it was the response of the soul to absolute moral truths. Like the aesthetic sense, it was inborn. In fact, Crummell, like Archibald Alison, saw not only a similarity but a direct relationship between the moral and the aesthetic senses. Both senses provided the individual with a direct approach to absolute, objective reality. But the perceptions of conscience could be distorted: personal depravity, atheism, heathenism, slavery, ignorance, and superstition had all hampered the human conscience in this imperfect world.[2]

That was what made law necessary. Law, which in Christian societies must always be based on the law of Moses, had the function of reinforcing the moral absolutes. Even the laws and traditions of heathen societies gave evidence, although imperfect, of the universality of the law of Moses. There was universal evidence that conscience could function only imperfectly in a world confused by sin and by Satan. Conscience could also be distorted because human nature was depraved; therefore, one must live according to Mosaic law, as well as according to faith. The Ten Commandments must be the Christian's guide to life. "Knowing Jesus" was simply not enough.

In Crummell's view, American evangelical extremism too often put conscience above law, and seemed to favor enthusiasm over discipline. Adherents of enthusiastic religion often advanced presumptuous claims of personal revelation. Their doctrine of justification through antirational inspiration might easily lead to contempt for law, order, and institutions. Crummell, who was much enamored of Burke, saw Burke's linkage of radical Protestantism and American democratic extremism as valid. On the other hand, Jeffersonian rationalism was as dangerous as evangelical irrationalism, for Jeffersonianism, with its seeming endorsement of radical democracy, encouraged political antinomianism and nurtured that depravity of conscience that had allowed a Christian democratic republic to deprive black Americans of the rights of citizenship. In a depraved world, laws could, of course, be as perverse as the consciences that framed them. Thus, it was necessary for lawmakers to be guided by Scripture to create a true democracy. Without the guidance of the Mosaic law, the rule of conscience could be a prescription for anarchy. Without the guidance of the Gospels, law could become a mockery of justice.

## Formative Experiences and the Quest for Civilization

Crummell's childhood environment, although admittedly humble, provided much better opportunities than those most black children encountered in North America in 1819. Crummell took pride in the assertion that both of his parents were full-blooded "Negroes" and that his father was an African who had never known Southern slavery. The Crummells' aspirations for themselves and their children were clearly bourgeois, and they exposed their gifted son to the class of black New Yorkers who could be described as black Yankees and Puritans, people who were literate, enterprising, and committed to a severe puritanical ethic.

Crummell was convinced at an early age that he could help to overcome prejudice by intellectual achievement, and he made the most of every opportunity to educate himself—no mean task in a society where black education was greeted with hostility and outright violence from white and black alike. He eventually learned that becoming a gentleman did not automatically make a black man more acceptable to whites. A gentlemanly, well-mannered, soft-spoken black man might arouse even greater hostility than one who conformed to the minstrel stereotypes that were becoming popular at the time. Crummell's life was often a one-man fight against such stereotypes, and the constant struggle to prove himself, no doubt, contributed to the punctiliousness attributed to him. His pursuit of education was part of the struggle against slavery and the "caste spirit," for he intended to demonstrate by his own life that black people were capable of excellence in the literary disciplines. More important, he would become an "apostle of Negro culture," a civilizing missionary to the black masses, and by his accomplishments inspire them to achievements in the "higher culture."[3]

Early intellectual influences included abolitionism and black nationalism. He knew Samuel Cornish and was well acquainted with his bitter politics, his sense of outrage, and his anticolonization sentiments. He was much closer, however, to Peter Williams, who had been an apologist for Paul Cuffe, John Russwurm, and other colonizationists.[4] The child probably could not remember a time when he was unaware of the antislavery struggle. Like most black schoolboys, he heard at an early age the myth that God was on the side of black people, who were destined to rule the world some day; Ethiopia would soon stretch forth her hands unto God. Since David Walker's supposed assassination was household rumor in Crummell's circles, he would have known of David Walker's *Appeal* just as he knew of Nat Turner's slave revolt, and he tells us that he and his school comrades wove splendid fantasies of the day when they would lead a revolt of the slaves. Ethiopianism persisted in his rhetoric for the rest of his life and was the basis of his later homilies on black nationalism and his belief in the "destined superiority of the Negro."

Just as important as Ethiopianism in Crummell's youth was Civilizationism, an idea that was to be known in the twentieth century as Negro Improvement. He came into contact with it through black and white abolitionists, who supported his early interest in letters. Abolitionists were responsible for the existence of the African Free School, where he received his early education. Elizur Wright, Secretary of the New York Anti-Slavery Society, provided Crummell with employment in the Society's New York office. This certainly stimulated his intellect in ways that would not have been possible if he had gone early into the New York City streets to pursue the sorts of menial jobs open to black boys. The atypical experience of having continuous contact with people who believed in his abilities and encouraged their development gave him a confidence in white folk that many black people did not share. The fact that much of this support came from upper-class whites, like the Jays, led him to identify with the upper classes and to adopt many of their elitist attitudes. He was thus inclined to accept upper-class notions concerning the importance of tradition, law, and order.

The aristocrats did not, of course, treat him as their social equal; they did not invite him into their families or their private social life. The support he received from the white upper classes was often condescending, and there was always a line that he could not cross. But if the upper classes were aloof, they did not present the same sort of overt threat to life and limb that black people often encountered from the sunburned and the sweaty. Black people had little reason to identify with the white proletariat, and neither the Jeffersonian, nor the Jacksonian, brand of democracy held much appeal for Crummell.

Thus he arrived in Liberia with little respect for the rhetoric of democracy—anarchy, he called it. He found Liberia a situation in which political antinomianism prevailed. Since he viewed the Liberian masses as falling into two general categories—pagans and slaves—he saw them either as children or as victims of depravity and degradation. He came to argue for the necessity of using force and authority in governing childlike indigenes and former slaves. While in Liberia, he spoke of the "stern necessity of assuming the nonage—the childhood of the natives." He took the same view of the Afro-American people after returning to the United States. Yet "civilization," the "primal need of the race," had been discovered by whites, not invented by them; Western Europeans were merely participants in civilization, not its creators. Black people were destined to achieve superiority in the inexorable sweep of Providence.

## Autobiographical Writings and the Experience of Discontent

There is almost no self-analysis in Crummell's sparse autobiographical writings, the most important of which is the anniversary sermon *Jubilate: The Shades and Lights of a Fifty Years' Ministry*. This document, a mere twenty-five pages, not including Anna Cooper's epilogue, is a dim and unrevealing piece, containing several inaccuracies and some misrepresentations. It is a matter of some significance that Crummell says nothing in this short piece about his parents or his siblings, and nothing of his marriages or his children. It is a telling point that the most complete sources for any information on Crummell's youth are found in the eulogia on his childhood friends, Garnet and Sidney. His "Eulogium on Henry Highland Garnet" and the "Eulogium on Thomas Sipkins Sidney" provide most of the information that we have on Crummell's early years. These orations are not, however, reflective or confessional. Crummell reconstructed or glossed over some of his more significant experiences. He presented himself as a victim or a martyr, he confessed no sins, and he boasted of his faults. His response to the accusation of rigidity was to say,

> I am proud of this criticism. It is evidence that I tolerated no iniquity, and that I rebuked depravity. I told the people of Liberia, the naked truth, on all occasions, without flattery, and as a censor of great faults. All peoples, on their first passage from slavery to freedom, need moral rigidity.[5]

But moral rigidity is often accompanied by a lack of humility or self-awareness. Crummell's appraisal of his own morality was at times embarrassingly vain and at times bordered on the hypocritical. Once in the middle of a sermon he asserted that he had never in his life wronged a woman, but members of his immediate family saw things differently. As a father he had a strong sense of his Christian duty, but he was also intolerant and tyrannical. We know very little of his treatment of his daughters, except for the reports of Sidney, who was not always an objective source. As for Sidney, it is abundantly clear that Crummell loved his son. He forgave him his sins more than once and continued to have high hopes for him, at least until Sidney reached the age of thirty. Still, there is validity in the point made by Luckson Ejofodomi that many of Sidney's problems must be attributed to the rigidity of his father.[6]

There is nothing in Crummell's autobiographical writings about his marriages. There are none of the gushing, sentimental Victorian clichés praising the dutiful, steadfast helpmeet, which occur so often in nineteenth-century literature. Nor do the friends who wrote his early biographies mention his marriages. Among his surviving letters there is nothing from his first wife. It is difficult to believe that she never wrote him, or that he simply tossed her letters away. Crummell began saving his correspondence at the age of eighteen and did a remarkable job of keeping up with his papers, considering the amount of moving around he did. Either Crummell, or someone else who had access to his papers, seems to have made certain that there would be no record of his relationship with his first wife in the correspondence.

Autobiographies, as a rule, are somewhat disingenuous, and the twenty-five pages of *Shades and Lights* are likely to raise more questions than they answer in the mind of a judicious reader. Crummell was sensitive about certain aspects of his biography and was not willing to share many of its details with posterity. The pamphlet makes no mention of the time its author spent at Yale, nor does it go into any detail concerning his private studies in Boston or Providence. It does not treat the years spent in Providence or Philadelphia with any sort of frankness, and it makes no mention of Crummell's early political activities. The document reveals nothing concerning the music he enjoyed, the books he read, the ideas that influenced him, or his personal pastimes. Not even his preferences with respect to church ritual and doctrine were addressed in *Shades and Lights*. Crummell gives us a very interesting narrative of his first arrival in Africa in the undated fragment "Africa and Her People."[7] The pamphlet says almost nothing about his reasons for going to Africa and is totally unrevealing about the reasons for his return.

Crummell often cited his health as the reason for his emigration and eventual collaboration with the despised American Colonization Society. In *Shades and Lights,* he maintained that, after his acclimation, he "entered into health, such as I never had before, and such as I have never had since." But careful examination of his correspondence reveals that he was not at all candid about the effects of the African climate on his health. Either Crummell suffered the usual problems of Americans who went to Africa in the nineteenth century, or else he was lying in his reports to the Mission Board when he blamed his occasional neglect of responsibilities on the effects of the African climate. On the other hand, when one considers that he had been reared in a temperate northern climate, and that he was not immune to African diseases, one must think that he bore up rather well, despite the insects, the heat, and the humidity. Crummell may have been something of a hypochondriac, or perhaps the difficulties he endured produced a set of psychosomatic symptoms. Nineteenth-century methods of diagnosis and treatment had remarkable potential for turning harmless ailments into chronic illnesses. Considering everything, Crummell seems to have been exceedingly energetic, even when he was complaining most about his health. He displayed remarkable powers of physical as well as intellectual and emotional endurance. He drove himself relentlessly and traveled constantly throughout his long and active life. If his constant claims of ill health were, after all, something other than hypochondria, then one must admire all the more the strength of will with which he constantly lashed himself onward.

Crummell often exaggerated the length of his stay in Africa, omitting the fact that he made two lengthy tours of the United States during the years of his Liberian experiment. He spent only sixteen years actually in Africa. This was, of course, a very substantial period, and the exaggeration a matter of little significance, since Crummell undeniably devoted the substantial period of twenty years to the African movement. Liberia was his prime commitment during that time, and he set sail for his second lengthy stay in that country after the Emancipation Proclamation had been published, which would seem to be very telling evidence of his sincerity. Among his contemporary American black nationalists, including Delany and Garnet, he was the only one who was willing to make such a deep and long-standing commitment to the idea of an African nationality.

While on the one hand it is clear that life provided Crummell with his full share of unearned difficulties, it is also clear that many of his problems originated in his inflexible temperament. He was constantly embroiled in personality conflicts and power struggles, and he displayed an extraordinary knack for brewing tempests in teapots. Crummell's major battles were not trivial, of course. He really did stand for principle, and he had great courage of his convictions. Still, it must be said that everyone who worked closely with him, even his most ardent admirers, commented on his inflexibility, a trait that was related to his religious beliefs and intellectual commitments.

## Episcopalian Traditionalism

The Episcopal church symbolized stability and endurance, important needs for a man who spent significant periods of his life on the threshold of economic and political chaos. Through identification with Episcopalianism and its traditions, he could surround himself with symbols of order, stability, and power. The church had dignified rituals and was far removed from the plantation culture that he identified with barbarism, depravity, and weakness. Episcopalianism, with its principles of "submission to authority, respect for rules, quietness, and order," was congenial to Crummell's conservative temperament. The American Episcopal church brought him into contact with Anglicanism and nurtured his sense of participating in the literary and intellectual traditions of England. The Anglican music and architecture appealed to him, as did the dignified liturgy. His religious sentiments were closely linked to aesthetic preferences that were uncommon among black Americans.

He was a moderately high churchman, accused at least once of "going to Rome," because he believed that humanity had a natural need for "forms, rules, and observances." During his attempts to organize an Episcopal church of Liberia, he consulted with British and Scottish authorities on ritual. During the 1880s he expressed admiration for the "remarkable revival" that had lifted up the Church of England "as by a tidal wave from the dead passivity of the last century." He praised "the wonderful power of the "Sisterhoods," whose recent growth he attributed to that special school of devoted men called 'Ritualists.' " Crummell was by no means an extremist, however. He expressed his opposition to ritualistic excesses, which he associated with the Irish, whose affinity for Romanism he attributed to their excitability and disquietude, their "singular love of ceremony and outward form." Crummell let it be understood that he preferred the American over the British liturgy, and he never got along with Eli W. Stokes, who professed himself a "high churchman." It was the "strict church" as opposed to the high church, that claimed Crummell's loyalty to Episcopalianism.

As a strict churchman, Crummell emphasized a moralistic rather than a pietistic theology. This theology was closely linked to his civilizational ideals; it emphasized the Law of Moses as a guide to life for all Christians, but particularly for black Christians, who must rise simultaneously from heathenism and barbarism. He was doctrinally attached to the "Arminianized Calvinism" that one scholar has sardonically attributed to almost all Protestant American churchmen of the period. But, however prevalent Arminianism may have been among Americans in general, it did not widely infect the masses of black freedmen in the South. They believed that grace was irresistible, and that conversion came dramatically, unexpectedly, in the midst of a fainting spell, or accompanied by radical exuberance. Crummell was put off by such behavior, and he was contemptuous of the waves of revivalism that swept through black American communities. The fact that his church put greater emphasis on its catechism and on adherence to a set of dogmas than on the emotionalism of the conversion experience isolated him from some of the more characteristic manifestations of religion among the black American masses. Black American religion, as Du Bois suspected, was to some extent a surviving African institution, "with a thin Calvinistic creed." It emphasized grace rather than works as the means to salvation and placed greater emphasis on "knowing Jesus" than on imitating Christ. Episcopalian theology had never rejected the medieval doctrine of works, stressing individual effort and self-help in the attainment of salvation. In temporal as well as in spiritual matters, Crummell's motto was "work out your own salvation."[8]

Although Crummell was never actually on the road to Rome, I suspect that he sometimes lingered doctrinally in the vicinity of Oxford. I hasten to add that I have so far found no formal endorsement of the Oxford movement among his papers. Nonetheless, Crummell's theology seemed at times more Anglo-Catholic than truly Protestant. This was apparent in his handling of the important issue of faith versus works. In his most succinct statement on Episcopalian doctrine, his sermon "The Episcopal Church in Liberia," he stated unequivocally his belief in "justification by faith." He also made it clear that Episcopalians placed greater emphasis than some other denominations on the Law of Moses as their "rule of life," clearly considering the conduct of life more important than the conversion experience. While he believed that Jesus Christ was a real presence in the world, he also believed that the power of the Holy Spirit could bring about virtue even in those who did not know Christ. Socrates and Plato were his examples. In practical terms, he gave little evidence of believing in the sufficiency of faith for salvation. In his sermon "The Second Coming" it was neither faith nor grace, but deeds that he stressed as the measure by which Christians would be judged, and this was a sermon that he gave more than once and in more than one version.

William H. Ferris, with his indefatigable talent for creating embarrassing terminology, once referred to Crummell as the "Newman of the Negro Pulpit." True, Ferris was alluding only to matters of literary style, but Crummell would have cringed. Unlike Newman, Crummell left behind no systematic *Apologia* for his life, and Crummell could never have considered repeating the course of Newman, who followed the logic of the Oxford movement to its natural conclusion by converting to Roman Catholicism, even though Roman Catholics, like most American denominations, had their black congregations. In Washington, D.C. the Catholic congregation that was identified with black people was St. Augustine's. *The People's Advocate* announced its dedication in June 1876 "with imposing ceremonies" and described it as "one of the finest places in the city." But Crummell, despite his liking for the magnificence of churchly architecture, would not have succumbed to the lure of bricks and mortar. First of all, Crummell found the idea of priestly celibacy monstrously repugnant. Secondly, when Crummell thought of Catholicism, he did not think of the doctrine of works in its purest sense, but rather of idolatry, superstition, mindless ritualism, and antinomianism. Finally, it would have been impossible for Crummell to maintain his black nationalist commitments in the Catholic church. Episcopalians actively supported black nationalism and colonization, although not from the purest motives. Catholics supported neither movement.[9]

In the minds of many black Americans, Episcopalianism was not much better than Roman Catholicism, however. As Kelly Miller put it, the "logical and inevitable tendency" in black churches at the time seemed to be "toward negro ecclesiastical autonomy." Crummell's position with respect to the black American churches was much the same as that of Cardinal Newman with respect to the national Church of England. Like Newman, Crummell had performed what many of his compatriots considered an act of apostasy by opting for a religion in which he had to sustain "a dependent and missionary relationship." Black Episcopalianism, unlike black Methodism, was not black controlled; although it had black congregations, its bishops were white.[10]

Ironically, although the Roman Catholic church in America was criticized for not staffing its parishes with black clergy, it placed black Americans in positions of authority earlier than did the Episcopalians. The Irish-American mulatto Patrick Healy was appointed to the presidency of Georgetown University around the time of Crummell's arrival in Washington, and James Healy, his brother, was elevated to the rank of bishop at around the time the Episcopalians denied Crummell that honor. Of course, the path taken by the Healys would have been absolutely impossible for Crummell. They had been brought up in close association with white relatives, who acknowledged them and indoctrinated them in the values of the Roman Catholic church from childhood. Crummell was of unadulterated African stock, and his childhood had been dominated by black institutions and the influence of an African-born father.[11]

The Episcopal church provided Crummell with an excellent moral compass and stable intellectual moorings, but it sometimes left him socially adrift. The Holy Catholic church is a temporal institution and subject to human weakness. Despite the nobility of its traditions and the stateliness of its rituals, its mundane operations and policies were subject to pettiness, and Crummell experienced much diurnal strife. Furthermore, the emphasis that Episcopalianism placed on hierarchy and apostolic succession meant that Crummell had to spend his life under the rule of white men. In a private letter to George Frazier Miller, a fellow black priest, he referred to her as a "cold and repulsive stepmother." Yet he could not bring himself to join any of the black controlled churches, and thus his religious convictions were often a source of pain.[12]

The Paynes, the Onderdonks, and even the most sympathetic members of the Episcopal hierarchy were sometimes hostile, sometimes paternalistic, but white bishops were not the most important source of his difficulties. Black vestries gave him far more trouble, and, as he had said in the pages of *Spirit of Missions,* "We often hear of clergymen who are called 'failures'; but people frequently forget that not infrequently it is the vestries who are the real failures." Crummell's early experiences in Providence and Philadelphia, like his later experiences in Washington, were unpleasant mainly because of the alienation of both Crummell and his church from black cultural expression. His enemies among black people often condemned Crummell's elitism, while at the same time harboring their own bourgeois elitist aspirations. Crummell's superior intellectual accomplishments were also the source of considerable jealousy among whites and blacks, as Du Bois well knew. A John Henry Newman could accomplish the miraculous task of retaining a place of honor in both Roman Catholic and English literary history. Jealousy was not powerful enough to outweigh respect for his excellent qualities of mind, or to remove him from his earned position as one of the brightest lights of English literature. Crummell's audience was regrettably lacking in the qualities needed to accord him a similar status in the history of black American letters.

## Literary Significance

John Greenleaf Whittier mentioned Crummell's *The Future of Africa* in a letter to Charlotte Forten, although he spoiled his offering with a well-meaning, but clumsy, remark:

> Its author is a churchman and conservative, but his writings are a noble refutation of the charge of the black man's inferiority. They are model discourses, clear, classic and chaste.[13]

Crummell's worth as a writer should be neither minimized nor exaggerated. He was, of course, an excellent expository writer, who handled his themes with originality and polish. His reports in the *Spirit of Missions* describing his errands into the African wilderness are colorful and interesting, but he never expanded them into anything comparable to *Walden*. He compares more favorably to writers like William Ellery Channing, Henry Ward Beecher, and Theodore Parker. Crummell's writing is occasionally ornate, but seldom exceedingly so. If he occasionally indulges in "purple" prose, it seems to be a deliberate response to his audience rather than a sign of naiveté. As a preacher, he had to compete with other preachers who were often known for their ability to stir the souls of ordinary folk. And, although Crummell was never a "popular preacher," he had an excellent understanding of popular style. He played with some success to the gallery, and even on some occasions to the groundlings. His sentences were often constructed with rhythm in mind, rather than originality. That he did not lack the common touch is shown in the closing lines of his oration "The Duty of a Rising Christian State":

> And so, from this point boldly jutting out into the glad free sea,—this spot, dedicated to nationality, consecrated to freedom, and sacred to religion,—from this spot shall be heard, through all the coming times, the full, clear tones of justice, the grateful symphonies of truth, the silvery voices of piety and virtue, mingling ever harmoniously with the choral echoes of the ocean!

The above may be compared to the following lines by Grandville B. Woodson, a former slave and an ordinary black preacher, inspired by the rhetoric of African redemption and black nationalism that pervaded his country.

> In my estimation, this is a good Country, taking all things in consideration, especialy for the colored Man or the Suns of Ham Who have been So Long bound Down beneath the penetration of the Gospel light . . . . Liberia is now spreading her rich perfume roun and about the big valleys of the World and introducing and calling out her suns and Daughters to rise and come up out of the Valley of ignorence and Hethenism.[14]

Although the author had not attained the literacy of a Garnet, a Delany, or a Crummell, it is clear that he had somewhere acquired a feel for the rhetoric of African redemptionism. This style of discourse permeated every level of society and had its impact on all classes, both lettered and rude. Did the Crummells learn this rhetoric from the Woodsons, or did they learn it from the Crummells? Obviously neither was the case; everyone threw something into the superheated cauldron in which black nationalism seethed.

In some elements of his ideology, which I will return to, Crummell resembled Emerson; stylistically, the difference was vast. He did not employ an aphoristic style, and—given his purposes—it was wiser for him not to have. Emerson's aphorisms are susceptible to being quoted out of context and may be freely interpreted by devils and angels alike. Crummell eschewed the aphorism, and it is practically impossible to quote him out of context. Every sentence is so meticulously woven into the steely grill of its paragraph that its meaning is practically unequivocal. Thus, it may be said that Crummell did not seek after ambiguity as a literary value.

Although he was conservative, there was nothing in Crummell's brand of conservatism that required Whittier's apology. His style was formal and crafts-manlike, never prissy or affected. His theory of art was neoclassical, to the extent that he accepted the idea of art imitating nature. Literature should teach by pleasing. He saw the artist not as a self-indulgent adolescent, but as a disciplined craftsman. There was, however, tremendous passion in his style, and his writing frequently showed "the spontaneous overflow of powerful feelings."

Classical and biblical languages and literatures were the major literary influences on Crummell, which was natural enough, given the nature of his education. He passed several examinations in classics at Cambridge, read the Greek Testament, and studied Plato, Aristotle, and Aristophanes. He was familiar with some contemporary issues in literary analysis. We can deduce this from his reference to the book of Job as a Greek tragedy.[15]

The modern authors he most prominently cited were Burke and Guizot, but Carlyle, Mill, and Thomas Arnold also made frequent appearances. Crummell's citations of other authors, classical and modern, went beyond mere learned allusion. He read with understanding, thought deeply about what he read, and sought to apply his learning to the situation of black people in Africa and in the Americas. He made use of Aristotle's writings on slavery to justify some of his own notions, but apparently he liked Plato better. Perhaps the emphasis placed on the seventeenth-century Cambridge Platonists in Whewell's lectures during Crummell's years in the university had something to do with this. St. Paul was the biblical writer to whom he most frequently alluded. He seems to have been attracted more by his toughness than by his emphasis on vicarious atonement.

Unfortunately, we know little of Crummell's formal theory of literature. The letter on poetic theory that he supposedly dictated to Dunbar on his deathbed has not been located. There are some bits and pieces from which a theory can be deduced, such as the high-flown remarks he made at the age of twenty-five, speaking before the Hamilton Lyceum of the City of New York. There he spoke of poetry in rhapsodic but insubstantial terms.

> But O! the sylvan groves, the shady alcoves of Poetry! What rich treasures, what glorious creations, do they ever offer, as an inexhaustible and sumptuous feast, to the beauteous soul. Here are the most verdant fields, the serenest skies. Sweet airs and gentle breezes float around. A melody almost too rare for mortals enraptures the soul. Ethereal shapes and fairy forms of surpassing excellence, clothed with garments of light, present themselves to the mind's eye, as the inhabitants of this celestial realm.[16]

There was a certain kind of honesty here; poetry probably did offer him an idealized world, an escape from his own bitter universe into an existence that was better than life. Fifty years later, however, when he spoke at Wilberforce University on "The Solution of Problems," he offered a sterner view.

> For Art and Culture are no more released from the enigmas of being than is Law or Divinity, than Politics or Philosophy. They all, in their respective developments are the reach of the soul not simply for delight, but really and truly for truth. Poetry, for instance, what is it save the lofty, but sometimes agonized straining of the heart of man to pierce the mystery of being, and to solve the inscrutable problems of existence. What is the burden of the Book of Job? What less the tragedies of Aeschylus, pagan though they be? What the anguish and the wail of Othello, but baffled endeavors after the solution of the mysterious Providence of our human condition, which at every stage stimulates inquiry and demands interpretation.

Although he had no systematic theory of literature, Crummell's ideas on the aesthetics of poetry are relatively clear. He believed that poetry, like other aspects of intellectual life, should deal with taxing and ambiguous issues. He recognized a relationship between art and the enigmatic, and he recognized that the essence of tragedy is not mishap, but the void of uncertainty that separates the human soul from truth. Crummell's reflections at Wilberforce show that if he was in any sense "typically Victorian" it was in the same sense as was Matthew Arnold, who dwelt so effectively on the anxieties and uncertainties of the modern world. Crummell would never have agreed with Arnold that the sea of faith was receding, but he was not unfamiliar with the meaning of spiritual uncertainty. Crummell was the quintessential Victorian if by that one means that he had superb faculties, skepticism, and a sense of irony that was never completely smoothed over by his religious orthodoxy. And he shared with Arnold a pre-Freudian awareness of anarchy lurking in the civilized human consciousness. He did not express his doubts as pessimistically as Arnold, but Crummell knew that "both angels and men are created for the unending, the everlasting ventures and anxieties in the deep things of God."

## Intellectual Heritage

Like Frederick Douglass, Crummell had less affinity to the American enlightenment, represented by Jefferson, than to what Isaiah Berlin has called the "counterenlightenment," represented by Edmund Burke. Crummell's intellectual affinities were to neither the French nor the American Revolution, but to the conservative reactions of Guizot and Carlyle. There were, of course, prominent eighteenth-century influences on his thinking. These derived from the cult of "sensibility," that genial, philanthropic mode of thought that argued that the natural passions could be the source of virtue and taste. One of the eighteenth-century writers who influenced him along those lines was Archibald Alison, whose work on taste he recommended to Liberian schoolboys. The enlightenment was dangerous, as were the excesses of the French Revolution, although both had functioned in the Providence of God to bring about progress.

Crummell recognized the cruelties of *laissez faire* economics, as did Carlyle, but Carlyle caused problems for Crummell, as he did for many black writers who agreed with his anti-Mammonism but were offended by his psychotic ravings on *The Nigger Question*. The British authors who influenced Crummell most were those who accepted the importance of tradition, authority, and religion as the bases of their attacks on slavery. Crummell shared with Edmund Burke the idea that a moral system could never be based on reason alone. Like the Victorian writers of the "sensibility cult," he was able to reconcile the idea of universal order with subjective inspiration. On discovering Burke's willingness to give precedence to feelings over reason, Crummell cited him with approval. "We know, and indeed, what is better, we feel inwardly that religion is the basis of all civil society, and the source of all good and of all comfort."[17]

Although he was passionate in his religion, Crummell was committed in principle to rationality and calm reflection. He was stubborn, but he had the ability to reconsider opinions, and he was amenable to persuasion on the basis of new evidence or changing material conditions. His capacity for sociological thinking was demonstrated in such essays as "Defence of the Negro Race" and "The Black Woman of the South," but, despite his respect for facts, statistics, and evidence, his mentality was fundamentally deductive and authoritative rather than inductive and empirical. He was perfectly capable of making rational and testworthy observations, as he often did, but his method of argument often lapsed into the citation of authority—and, for Crummell, the ultimate authority was the Bible, his final source of unquestionable truth. Once he had entered the world of the Bible, he was inclined to become subjective and self-indulgent. His interpretations of Scripture were usually presented dogmatically and with a cranky, impenetrable emotionalism.

The fact that he was "conservative" and dogmatic, should not, however, lead us to Professor Rigsby's assertion that "Crummell accepted uncritically the beliefs of his age."[18] First of all, it is not helpful to employ such terms as "the beliefs of his age." Crummell's age had no commonly agreed on set of beliefs; it was an age of anxiety, characterized by criticism and conflict. The intellectual world of the nineteenth century forced literate people to ponder their uncertainties and to attempt to reconcile conflicting and disturbing beliefs. One need only scan the pages of the popular British and American newspapers, black and white, to see the level of intellectual inquiry to which the typical Victorian was exposed. Furthermore, the essence of Crummell's personality was to be critical. His many-layered consciousness was typically complex for a nineteenth-century intellectual. In his final years, we find him grappling honestly with the challenges of Marx and Darwin and trying to reconcile his basic love of order with his understanding that revolution can bring about necessary changes.

According to August Meier, Crummell was "generally regarded as the leading nineteenth-century Negro intellectual." Since Crummell was all but forgotten at the time of Meier's assessment, Meier presumably meant that Crummell's contemporaries would have viewed him in that way. John E. Bruce and William H. Ferris certainly did, but Crummell's contemporaries could have suggested at least two other candidates for the honor. Blyden would have been a strong contender, as would Frederick Douglass, despite the fact that neither had university credentials. Crummell reserved the accolade for his former schoolmate James McCune Smith, who had been educated as a medical doctor at the University of Glasgow. George Washington Williams, who died in 1890 at the age of forty-one, produced an unequivocally "intellectual" body of writings, including his two-volume *History of the Negro Race in America* and his *History of the Negro Troops in the War of the Rebellion.*

It may reasonably be argued that Crummell expressed a wider range of intellectual interests in his writings than did either Blyden or Douglass. While Crummell's writings on black advancement were voluminous, racial concerns were the subject of only a portion of his thought and writing. As a minister, he was acquainted with and forced to address every aspect of human behavior. Douglass and Blyden, on the other hand, wrote almost exclusively on race-related subjects.

Crummell was an apt student of languages, but he did not have Blyden's spectacular abilities. He possessed neither Blyden's open-mindedness toward African cultures, nor his capacity for making appreciative judgements on African cultures. He shared Blyden's belief that the native Africans were worthy of assimilation into the emerging Liberian nation, but Crummell saw assimilation as a one-way street. Africans, like Afro-Americans, must become Europeanized. Blyden was no less the "Civilizationist," no less the "Europhile," than Crummell, but neither that, nor the fact that Blyden was an ordained Christian minister, prevented his recognizing the importance of Islamic or indigenous tribal culture to the future of Africa. Blyden's ideology was a step in the direction of the emerging African consciousness of a later generation, as represented in the writings of J. E. Casely Hayford, who paid tribute to him. Even today there are African intellectuals who would describe their ideology as "Blydenism." Crummell's hostility to African languages and cultures prevented his creating a brand of Pan-Africanism with the staying power of Blydenism, which was, as it turned out, the wave of the future. Blyden's staying power was largely due to his interest in African languages and his willingness to study them before passing judgement on their aesthetic features or philosophical depth. Furthermore, he understood that Christianity must adjust to Africa in order to survive there. For these reasons, he was successful in impressing his name and his ideology on succeeding generations of African leaders to an extent that Crummell was not.

## Frederick Douglass and Individualism

Crummell did not possess Frederick Douglass's brilliance as a literary stylist, but if he lacked Douglass's rhetorical abilities, he was more systematic in his thinking. Relations between the two became increasingly cordial with the passage of time, although ideologically they never saw eye to eye. Douglass, for example, was more than once accused of religious skepticism, while Crummell's emotions required a dogmatic Christian faith. Crummell had a remarkable degree of trust for Douglass, even citing him as a character reference during one of his vestry disputes. Douglass always spoke with admiration of Crummell, and it speaks well for the character of both men that they were able to demonstrate such high regard for one another's minds.

Crummell and Douglass were often apparently at odds on the question of individual rights and racial responsibilities. Douglass usually insisted on the right of the individual to transcend race; Crummell usually stressed the responsibility of the individual to the racial group. Crummell took the position that black Americans were, *de facto*, "a nation within a nation," while Douglass impatiently responded that "a nation within a nation is an anamoly." Crummell asserted that black Americans were most likely to prosper economically in communities where they constituted a large percentage of the population. Douglass urged black Americans not to cluster together, but to disperse themselves throughout society, where he felt they would be less likely to isolate themselves or to draw attention to their differences. In social policy, Douglass was a *laissez faire* liberal, and there was probably no piece of antebellum black writing that annoyed him more than Crummell's pamphlet *The Relations and Duty of Free Colored Men in America to Africa.* He did not allow Crummell, Garrison, or anyone else to instruct him as to his duty, but he did not mind instructing others on theirs. He employed the rhetoric of collectivism and racial duty when he instructed Crummell and other expatriates to return to the United States and rejoin the struggle for abolitionism and civil rights. But Douglass's instincts were individualistic, and he prized his own personal freedom above all things. Thus, while he admitted that group efforts for racial elevation might be tactically expedient, he never considered black institutions to be anything other than a necessary compromise, resulting from the passing phenomenon of racial prejudice.[19]

In terms of personal temperament Crummell was no less individualistic than Douglass. He was, in fact, insubordinate, hard-headed, and self-willed, but, at the same time, he had a remarkable reverence for tradition and authority. This contradiction in his personality was reflected by a contradiction in his social philosophy. His addresses consistently emphasized personal responsibility and individual achievement, and yet he insisted that individuals must cultivate a sense of racial pride and collective duty. Crummell was not the only leader who contradicted himself on such issues.

Crummell was hardly unaware of the pitfalls of racial collectivism. He recognized the entrepreneurial quality of black leadership, and he knew that the rhetoric of solidarity often camouflaged the ambitions of "little great men," hoping to exploit the racial pride of others. In Liberia and in America he condemned the elites, whose appeals to racial loyalty concealed cynical opportunism and the desire to reign as giants among pygmies. He insisted, nonetheless, on the importance of "the social principle among a people" and its indispensability to a program of uplift. Long before Booker T. Washington borrowed the idea, Crummell had insisted that there must be a collective and programmatic remedy for the damage done to black people by slavery. At the same time he agreed with Frederick Douglass that individualism must be encouraged and that personal character was the indispensable ingredient for racial advancement. This position grew out of Crummell's religious slogan "work out your own salvation." This was as true of temporal as it was of spiritual salvation. He put great emphasis on the Taylorist concept of self-love, recognizing that philanthropic ideals could be realized only by those who had developed strong personal character.

Crummell saw individualism and free will as fundamental values of Christian civilization, and as prerequisites for any concept of moral responsibility. Indeed, one of the essential elements in his definition of "civilization" was "the conscious impress of individualism and personal responsibility." During his African years he placed great stress on personal character as the crucial building block of national character, and, later, he stressed character development as a means to the ultimate end of social assimilation in America. But while individual responsibility was the key to racial greatness, individual achievement alone would never solve the problems of black people in the modern world. Collective struggle must also be encouraged, along with respect for institutions, starting with the family. While the individual was "in God's sight, a large being, the family, as an organism is a larger idea than he." In its turn, "society at large" was a greater and more important idea than the family, and the nation had "a vastness of importance . . . unequaled by either the individual, the family or society." Still, it must be remembered that the chain would never be any stronger than its weakest link, and the group would never advance unless individual black men and women saw the importance of cultivating the individual character.[20]

Crummell's life and writings demonstrated a fascination with the self-reliant, entrepreneurial values celebrated by Emerson. He was not committed to the transcendentalism of Emerson that rejected the personality of Jesus Christ, but both were caught up in the infectious individualistic rhetoric of late nineteenth-century America. In social or business life, as in spiritual life, every individual was responsible for achieving his own success through the principles of will-power, self-love, and moral strength. This theme dominated such essays as "Right Mindedness" and "Character, The Great Thing." Like Emerson, he sometimes contradicted himself, and, like Emerson and other American intellectuals, he could even dabble in the American pastime of anti-intellectualism. His proclamation, "Brains is the first knowledge; brains as a power, and instrument, *before* books," was similar to Emerson's laconic assertion, "Books are for the scholar's idle times." Emerson would certainly have agreed with Crummell's advice that every young person should develop a "consciousness of [the] power which was a real thing within him." It was impossible, said Crummell, to overvalue "this conviction and assurance" in a traditional salute to the values of self-trust and self-reliance that all Americans like to believe were singularly related to their heritage. The extreme self-reliance associated with transcendentalism could not be accommodated in Crummell's philosophy, however, nor could Crummell accept the iconoclasm that was becoming characteristic of American literary expression. He could endorse the confident, optimistic precepts of the Emersonian creed, so long as they did not lead to radical enthusiasm, or a mindless dependency on subjective inspiration. Personalism was dangerous, for it might lead to relativism, antinomianism, and apostasy. Solitary thought and reflection were worthy practices, but they must be tempered by discipline. The mind was a muscle that must be toughened and trained before its genius could be effective. He cited the aphorism of Thomas Arnold, "Discipline is superior to enthusiasm."[21]

## Booker T. Washington and His Civilizing Mission

The belief in the primacy of discipline was the basic ideological similarity between Crummell and Washington. Both believed that a period of tutelage would be necessary before black people could assume a place in American society. An important difference was that Washington believed that this period of tutelage had begun under slavery; Crummell did not. Nonetheless, they were both believers in "uplift," both believers in "African Civilization," and both were prophets of the "Negro Improvement" ideology. Washington attempted to portray himself as heir to the leadership mantle of Douglass, which was, to some degree, legitimate. Like Douglass, Washington was committed to industrial education and to the utilitarian philosophy that black people would advance in America insofar as they made themselves economically useful, but he was never the radical egalitarian that Douglass was. Ironically, most black leaders shared a belief that the black masses would be saved by a leadership elite, they only disagreed about what sort of people would constitute this cadre. For Crummell and Du Bois, it was the scholar, the philosopher, the classicist, the mathematician; for Washington and Douglass, it was the technocrat, the engineer, the agronomist, and the businessman.

Much has been said in these chapters concerning the friction between Crummell and Booker T. Washington, which foreshadowed the later friction between Washington and Du Bois. The surface issues had to do with education, but the real conflicts were much deeper; they originated in the clash between Washington's materialism and Crummell's idealism. Washington borrowed mercilessly from Crummell's anecdotal material, as he improvised on the story of the hotel waiter with a volume of Cicero in his hand. Crummell repeated rumors that the true friends of the Negro saw Washington as a "white man's nigger." As a matter of fact, both men were committed to cultivating upper-class whites and interacting with them on a personal level, each presenting himself as the true "voice of the Negro." Crummell and Washington both held the insupportable opinion that it would be possible for black people to remain in America and become increasingly like whites culturally, while remaining segregated.

Although the term "Negro Improvement" was coined by Marcus Garvey, it can easily be applied to the philosophies of Booker T. Washington, W.E.B. Du Bois, and Alexander Crummell as well. All four men were in a Pan-African Civilizationist tradition, whose goals were clearly stated in such documents as David Walker's "Our Wretchedness in Consequence of Ignorance" and Henry Highland Garnet's Constitution of the African Civilization Society, the central idea of "African Civilizationism" or "Negro Improvement" being that black people must "work out their own salvation" rather than relying on white philanthropy or constantly appealing to liberal guilt. Of equal importance was the idea that unity must be achieved under the leadership of one man or group of men, who in their superior wisdom would chart out a course for the rest of the race to follow. The grievances of a group could not be rectified by individual efforts alone. Personal character and individual efforts were essential to progress, but so too was collective effort.

## W.E.B. Du Bois and the Decline of the West

Du Bois's fascination with Crummell was more than sentimental esteem for a dignified-looking old man. Like Crummell, he was a "law and order" man, who had a distaste for leveling democracy and a belief in enlightened despotism. The puritanism, elitism, and reverence for "civilized" Western traditions that characterized Crummell's political philosophy were well-known characteristics of Du Bois. Du Bois placed great emphasis on Victorian middle-class gender roles and sexual morality in his early writings. In short, they both relished the manners and customs of the nineteenth-century bourgeoisie. Needless to say, this emphasis was present in Booker T. Washington's philosophy as well. Unlike Washington, however, Crummell and Du Bois couched their ideology of assimilation in the rhetoric of Pan-Africanism. Even half a century after Crummell's death, similarities to Crummellism were detectable in Du Bois's writing, as when Du Bois describes African cultures in terms of his cherished Victorian sexual ideal. Describing his first trip to West Africa, in *Dusk of Dawn,* Du Bois says, "I saw less of sex dalliance and appeal than I see daily on Fifth Avenue," recalling Crummell's assertion that "anyone walking through Pall Mall, London, or Broadway, New York, would see more indecency in look and act than he could discover in an African town in a dozen years."[22] The statements illustrate not only their respective authors' commitment to Victorian moral standards, however, but a relentless justice that judged Victorian civilization by its own standards. If the cultures of England and America were analogous to the civilization of Rome, then African tribes resembled the virile barbarians of Tacitus' *Germania*.

Crummell, like most other nineteenth-century black literary figures, had called attention to the barbarism of Europe at the time of the Roman conquest. Africans were also barbarians by comparison with the civilized Europeans, but a universal rotation of elites would eventually bring about the destined superiority of the Negro. Crummell developed this idea in terms of traditional theological historicism. Du Bois followed the pathway of Leninist historicism to the same end.

Du Bois, like Crummell, wrote in the teleological tradition inherited from such documents of nineteenth-century black nationalism as David Walker's *Appeal* and the preamble to the Constitution of the African Civilization Society. Crummell employed this teleology in "The Destined Superiority of the Negro" and in the several essays where he spoke of "Ethiopia stretching out her hands." Du Bois often wrote poetry and essays in the Ethiopianist tradition and also made allusions to the verse. Specific Ethiopian references appeared in such writings of Du Bois as his "Star of Ethiopia," and he employed the theological historicism of that tradition in such poems as "The Riddle of the Sphinx" and "Children of the Moon." Du Bois's inheritance from the black literary tradition endowed him with a particular receptiveness to the "decline of the West" theme when it began to appear in Anglo-American literature after the First World War. Augmenting his Crummellism with Spenglerism and Marxism, Du Bois converted the Christian mysticism of earlier black leaders into the anti-Westernism that is witnessed in these lines from one of his last poems:

> I lifted my last voice and cried
> I cried to heaven as I died
> O turn me to the Golden Horde
> Summon all western nations
> Toward the Rising Sun
>
> From reeking west whose day is done
> Who stink and stagger in their dung

Du Bois also shared Crummell's distrust of Jeffersonian principles. The anti-Jeffersonianism of Crummell and Du Bois did not stop at the vulgar level of merely pointing out that Jefferson had been a slaveholder. In fact, their attacks on Jefferson were not motivated entirely by his attitudes on race. Crummell feared the "unscrupulous and boisterous democracy" of America and felt that Jefferson had encouraged the political presumptions of the lawless and the illiterate. American ideology was fundamentally in error due to Jefferson's claim that governments derived their legitimacy from the consent of the governed. In his address on the Garfield assassination, he praised Alexander Hamilton as a "great political prophet" because he had foreseen the evils of "extreme wild and thoughtless democratic opinion." One of the reasons Crummell admired Du Bois's essay "The Conservation of Races" was its specific attack on "the individualistic philosophy of the Declaration of Independence."

The young Du Bois clearly respected tradition and supported elitism just as he opposed "red radicalism" and sudden empowerment of the masses. His antidemocratic, authoritarian, racial chauvinistic strain was always at war with his proletarian sentiments. His gravitation towards tsarlike figures, and his own tsarlike attributes, are elements of his personality that cannot be denied. In the end Du Bois was able to reconcile his proletarianism with his authoritarianism by embracing Stalinism. Du Bois called Stalin "a great man . . . simple, calm, and courageous,'' and, in his later years, advocated a Stalinist/Maoist brand of Pan-Africanism. Du Bois eventually went to Africa to join forces with Kwame Nkrumah, who some historians regard as an enlightened despot and others refer to as a ''Leninist Czar.'' Pan-Africanism and authoritarianism were constant themes in Du Bois's life. Du Bois's partnership with Nkrumah was consistent with and in many ways an echo of his partnership with Crummell in the 1890s.[23]

## Pan-Africanism and Garveyism

Crummell's black nationalism was marked by certain inconsistencies, but they derived from the inconsistencies and hypocrisy of American racism, rather than from any intellectual shortcomings on his part. It was impossible to create an ideology that responded rationally to an irrational system. Crummell's commitment to the search for a black nationality during his middle years is unquestionable. At the same time it cannot be denied that his positions on political and ecclesiastical independence during those same years were riddled with contradictions. He wanted political independence to go hand in hand with cultural assimilation. He wanted ecclesiastical independence to go hand in hand with at least a temporary economic dependency. Crummell eventually abandoned all activities on behalf of a black American nation-state and became downright abusive toward those who attempted to revitalize emigrationism after the end of Reconstruction. Nonetheless, he continued to employ a nationalist rhetoric, to refer to black people as ''a nation within a nation,'' and to speak of the destined superiority of the Negro.

Crummell's later writings were often adaptations of sermons and addresses he had written in Africa, but his concerns during the later years were predominantly American. Without denying ''the close affinity between Crummell's Liberian nationalism and his later advocacy of racial solidarity,'' one may find even more striking the distinctly American character of his discourse after he returned to the United States and began to doctor up his old sermons.[24] And as he rewrote his sermons and reconsidered his theories concerning the duties of black Americans, he found that the same laws of progress and civilization that had once seemed to dictate the necessity of African colonization now revealed a God-given destiny for the Negro people in America. Although he continued to think of black Americans as a nation within a nation, he had, by 1875, adapted his philosophy to suit the goal of full participation in American life. Of course he still considered the total biological assimilationism of Frederick Douglass not only irrational, but unnatural. Thus, Crummell obviously did not remain a black nationalist, although elements of black nationalism never entirely disappeared from his thinking.

At the same time that he discouraged black people from basing their struggle for a place in the sun purely on moral arguments or on appeals to white philanthropy, he nonetheless believed in philanthropy and the power of moral suasion. He believed that laws of moral progress had been placed at work within human destiny by the creator and that right must triumph over might. Early in his career, he had shocked the British and Foreign Anti-Slavery Society by expressing the opinion that enslaved people were always, to some extent, responsible for their own condition. He admired Nat Turner, and, while he opposed strikes and labor wars as represented by the spirit of "Haymarket," he believed that extremist claims might be justifiable in the case of black workers in the South. Despite the fact that he had had to depend on white benevolence to build every church he ever built, he discouraged black people from constantly throwing themselves on the mercy of white people and their charity. In midcareer essays, such as "The Destined Superiority of the Negro," and in his late position paper "Civilization, The Primal Need of the Race," he seemed uncertain whether he was advancing a "black power" ideology or a policy of continuing accommodation and cultural assimilation. He seemed always to adhere to David Walker's position that black wretchedness was at least partially due to the ignorance of black people themselves, and that this ignorance led to a slavish mentality. This was an idea that had been advanced by the conspirator Denmark Vesey. It was an idea that Marcus Garvey would later take up. If black people wanted to be respected, then they must stop blaming white people for slavery, colonialism, and racism. In Garvey's case, this led to the logical extreme of asserting that "in our material civilization, might is right." The alleviation of black suffering must ultimately be the business of black people. Black people must develop the military virtues. Alexander Crummell, T. G. Steward, and William H. Ferris, all of them black ministers, were prophets of Marcus Garvey's Warrior God. They believed in the workings of a moral law in history, but their God was, in the words of the old Negro spiritual, which Ferris reiterated, "A Man of War."[25]

The American Negro Academy embodied many of the inconsistencies in Crummell's position. Its goal was to build a black civilization, yet its domineering president was opposed to territorial separatism. Its purpose was to promote the unique racial contribution of black people to the progress and fulfilment of human destiny, yet it was hostile to the distinctive elements of culture that were found among the black masses and the indigenous Africans. The Academy was committed to cultural assimilation, but at the same time it called for a distinctive and collective contribution by black Americans to world civilization.

One of the great ironies of the American Negro Academy was the drift of some of its members in the direction of African emigrationism. Crummell's hostility to emigrationism centered in the end on his dislike for Henry McNeal Turner, but some of his disciples seem to have been willing to reconsider the subject of colonization. Orishatukeh Faduma, who had been inducted into the Academy with Crummell's support and over Du Bois's objection, eventually became a collaborator in Chief Alfred C. Sam's 1914 Back to Africa scheme, which Du Bois publicly denounced. Faduma's involvement with Sam undoubtedly confirmed Du Bois in his opinion that he had been right to oppose Faduma's candidacy. Within two years of Sam's and Faduma's departure for the Gold Coast, Marcus Garvey arrived in the United States.

In Garveyite propaganda, ironically, one sees little recognition of any linkage between the Universal Negro Improvement Association and its ideological forebears. Henry McNeal Turner, Alfred C. Sam, and Orishatukeh Faduma were the most significant African colonizationists at the turn of the century, but they do not seem to have been included in the UNIA hagiography. Neither were Blyden or Crummell, but the antiemigrationists Frederick Douglass and Booker T. Washington were accorded great reverence. This seems unforgivable when one recalls that two of Crummell's protégés, John E. Bruce and William H. Ferris, had interacted with Faduma in the American Negro Academy and would certainly have been aware of the similarities between Turner's movement and Garvey's Universal Negro Improvement Association. It was ironic, furthermore, that Bruce and Ferris should find themselves in company with T. Thomas Fortune in the UNIA. Crummell's loathing for both Turner and Fortune, and for the motives he attributed to them, had been mighty, and Bruce had seemed to share Crummell's revulsion. And yet, twenty years after Crummell's death, both Bruce and Ferris found themselves comrades of Fortune, working for goals similar to those of Bishop Turner.[26]

The ties of Garveyism to the network of black Episcopalians, especially those with a West Indian connection, are noteworthy. Indeed, the connection between black nationalism and Episcopalianism is, in itself, a topic worthy of extensive development by future researchers. Here it will be sufficient to note that James T. Holly, J. Robert Love, Sylvester Williams, and George Alexander McGuire were all Episcopalians within the West Indian nationalist tradition that produced Garvey. Sylvester Williams was an Episcopalian from Trinidad, and an acquaintance of Crummell's, who was early inducted into the Academy as a corresponding member. He was an organizer of the London Pan-African Conference in 1900. Bishop Holly we have encountered in an earlier chapter. George Alexander McGuire, an Episcopal priest and sometime chaplain to the Garvey Movement, eventually organized the African Orthodox Church. One of the indirect but nonetheless significant links to Marcus Garvey was a Jamaican nationalist, J. Robert Love, born in the Bahamas but educated in the United States, where he took a medical degree from the University of Buffalo. Garvey proclaimed that Love had been his mentor in Jamaica, and in 1914 Garvey's organization commemorated Love's death, citing him as an inspiration of the movement. Bruce was well-acquainted with Love's work, referred to him as "one of the blackest and most scholarly men in Jamaica," and praised him for glorying in his "beautiful black skin." Crummell considered him "remarkably clever." Love's newspaper, the *Jamaica Advocate,* was one of the few newspapers to report on the organizational meeting of the American Negro Academy.

If Garvey did not first become aware of the American Negro Academy through Love's influence, he would definitely have heard of it through Duse Mohamed

Ali, a London journalist and editor of the *African Times and Orient Review*. Duse Mohamed was inducted into the Academy as a corresponding member during Garvey's first residency in London (1912–14). Garvey was, in fact, working for Duse Mohamed when the *Review* published John W. Cromwell's article on the Academy, complete with pictures of Crummell and other members, and a full list of its membership, including its West Indian and African associates. Duse Mohamed later came to America and contributed articles on a regular basis to Garvey's newspaper, *Negro World*. Garvey was surrounded by Academy members, and Bruce even attempted to secure a speaking engagement for Garvey before the Academy, while Ferris attempted to justify the Garveyite position to Frank Grimké.[27]

## Sociological Writings

One should not be surprised that Crummell regarded the Bible as the indisputable final authority on every moral issue. In contrast to this, however, one notes the sophisticated use of empirical evidence in much of Crummell's mature writing. Crummell made several contributions to nineteenth-century black sociology that were empirically based, highly regarded by his contemporaries, and, in some cases, superior to the contributions being made by younger men. In his publication "The Relations and Duty of Free Colored Men in America to Africa," for example, the moral and ideological arguments are supplemented with statistics and economics. Crummell's liking for facts and statistics was revealed early in his career. He continued to swing back and forth between arguments that were based on biblical exegesis and arguments that were based on the systematic introduction of facts.

One document often praised by Crummell's contemporaries was his response to J. L. Tucker (discussed at length in an earlier chapter), "Defence of the Negro Race in America." It was an appeal to reason based on facts, rather than an appeal to common-sense morality. "The Black Woman of the South: Her Neglects and Her Needs" was Crummell's best-known essay of a sociological nature. It was printed in an edition of 500,000 copies and is said to have generated over one million dollars for the Freedman's Aid Society, the organization before which it originally had been delivered and which sponsored its publication.[28] Of all Crummell's efforts in the area of social policy, this pamphlet probably had the most far-reaching consequences. Its purpose was twofold. On the one hand it was to elevate the black woman above the level of a menial laborer and to assist her in becoming a class-conscious worker and a prudent and efficient homemaker. Even more important, it was to encourage among black women and men alike an appreciation for the Anglo-American, Victorian, bourgeois conception of gender roles. Woman must be a wife and mother, and man a warrior and provider.

Crummell consistently argued that slavery had corrupted the sexual morality of the masses of blacks. Black leadership in late nineteenth-century America, with its perfectionist ideals, viewed the deviation on the part of black Americans from middle-class cultural ideals as a matter of great seriousness. A case in point was Du Bois's *The Philadelphia Negro,* which revealed the author's prim disapproval of the sexual morality of the black working class. Black social thinkers and moral reformers, men and women alike, focused with painful scrutiny on the fact that only a relatively small proportion of their people had attained the economic and cultural foundation that made it possible for them to conform to Victorian bourgeois gender stereotypes and sexual ideals. Black organizations such as the American Negro Academy and the National Federation of Afro-American Women sought to strengthen the commitments of black institutions to such stereotypes and ideals. Later organizations, such as the Universal Negro Improvement Association, the Southern Christian Leadership Conference, and the Nation of Islam, also sought to strengthen the middle-class, male-headed, nuclear family in black America.[29]

Crummell's judgement that the basic building block of a healthy black society must be the male-headed nuclear family was hardly a radical idea in its time. Nonetheless, he described an ideal that, for better or for worse, was difficult to put into practice. Subsequent black leaders shared his judgement, however, as a matter of "common sense." Du Bois in his essay "The Damnation of Women" quoted at length from Crummell's celebrated pamphlet "The Black Woman of the South." E. Franklin Frazier, who knew the work of both Du Bois and Crummell, acknowledged a debt to Du Bois and his analysis of black family disorganization. Whether Frazier knew Crummell's essay on the black woman of the South directly is difficult to say. We may be certain he had seen the excerpt from it in Du Bois's *Darkwater.* The catastrophic interpretation of black family history that began in "The Black Woman of the South" was carried into the more recent literature by Frazier.

Seen within this context, the so-called "Moynihan Report" of 1965 was nothing more than the ill-timed culmination of tendencies in black sociology, finally articulated in public policy at a time when the progressive Christian bases of its assumptions had eroded. Moynihan's recommendations for the black family, if not his analysis, differed markedly from Crummell's, however. Crummell's solution focused on women. He sought to provide training in the skills that made for the model housewife; Moynihan's approach was to focus on males and their economic position. He argued that if the economic bases of the patriarchal nuclear family could be established in black America, the role of women within the family would naturally resolve itself in accord with the economic determinants of nuclear family stability. Nonetheless, for Moynihan, as for the black sociologists that preceded him, it was taken for granted that the nuclear family must be strengthened. This was the essence of Crummell's policy, and it was the core of programs for the improvement of black life that were articulated by Du Bois, Frazier, Martin Luther King, Elijah Muhammed, and Jesse Jackson.

## Restoring Alexander Crummell's Place in American Letters

While the efforts of several scholars in recent decades have guaranteed that Alexander Crummell can no longer be considered an obscure figure, his name has not yet become a household word. During the first forty years of this century, black authors were systematically ignored by the creators of American literary history. A figure like Crummell could easily have been accommodated within the tradition as it was defined by Perry Miller and F. O. Matthiessen, for he exemplified the sort of highly literate, elitist Northeasterner who was most accessible to the sort of method that they used. His literary corpus was ideally suited to the methods they developed.

Current trends in literary scholarship are no more helpful to Crummell than the old ones were. The most prominent recent attempts to include black authors in American literature have centered on folklore, slave culture, the birth of the blues, and the concepts of *Négritude* and "Africanity." Such approaches obviously cannot do full justice to Crummell. The folklore and folkways of the black masses did not fit well into his theory of racial progress, and he was not given to romanticizing them. His letter to the *Southern Workman,* cited in an earlier chapter, reveals that his interest in "folklore" was confined to what we would call "oral history." There is no evidence that he relished the sort of narrative that was popularized by Joel Chandler Harris, although the later efforts of the Works Progress Authority might have interested him. It does not seem likely that Crummell would have cared to have his sermons judged by the criteria of folk preaching. His literary concerns were seldom, if at all, related to mass culture, and his ideas on "slave culture" were made plain in letters to the Episcopal Board of Foreign Missions. He described immigrants, fresh from the plantations of the South, as "ignorant, benighted, and besotted." Slave culture was, in the opinion of this man, who had worked for many years on the Liberian frontier, totally divorced from, and inferior to, African culture. While he viewed the Africans as virile barbarians, he saw the black masses of the South as victims of a "history of moral degradation," and affirmed that they "would have been more blessed and far superior as pagans in Africa than slaves on the plantations of the South." [30]

Crummell's reformist attitudes in politics must be contrasted with his elitist notions of literature and the arts. He was, in fact, living proof of the principle that militant theories of political economy are not always accompanied by an appreciation for mass cultural expression. He defended the rights of the black masses as oppressed workers, but did not find in them a source of literary or intellectual values. He saw their economic and social problems as a reason to engage in political struggle, but not as a source of art. If Crummell's deathbed letter to Paul Laurence Dunbar has survived, it may offer some insight into Crummell's attitudes on folk art, dialect verse, and their relationship to the development of a black American aesthetic. We know that it was extremely rare for Crummell to make use of colloquialisms in his own discourse and that his literary contribution is ill served by any theory of art that gives primacy to vernacular, folkloristic, or popular modes of expression.

With respect to Africanity and Pan-Africanism, Sterling Stuckey and Gregory Rigsby have attempted to justify Crummell within the framework of the concerns implied by these terms. He may be called a pioneer of Pan-Africanism, *Négritude,* or Afrocentricity only in the political sense. He certainly believed in the redemption of Africa from the ravages of the slave trade and the eventual elevation of the continent to a position of economic and military power. He believed in the capacity of Africans to *achieve* "superiority," but it would come only in proportion to their ability to become cosmopolitan. He did not presage twentieth-century ideas of "Afrocentrism" or anticipate Cheikh Anta Diop or Molefe K. Asante on that topic. Stuckey has correctly identified him as one of those nineteenth-century black nationalists who failed to appreciate the rites and traditions associated with African value systems.[31]

It is pointless and futile to try to force Crummell into the framework of any of our recent Africanity models. He was not a forerunner of the modernism or relativism that have informed so much of twentieth-century black aesthetics and critical theory. He had visited the museums of London to survey the trophies that British warlords had carried home from the ruins of the ancient world. He had come to understand that the British Empire, like every other world power, had made its reputation by engaging in worldwide cultural theft. He viewed the British Empire in much the same way that he viewed the Greek and Roman Empires of classical times, which he described as "cosmopolitan thieves," observing, "They stole from every quarter." Black empire builders must be acquisitive, like the great civilizations of the past, who had "pounced, with eagle eye, upon excellence wherever discovered, and seized upon it with rapacity." The coming African civilization must build on the culture, literature, and civilization of Europe, just as Europe had built on the heritage of the ancient Mediterranean. He did not advocate constructing a self-contained black worldview on the foundations of a sub-Saharan culture.[32]

In our attempts to understand Alexander Crummell, it is best that we see him as a strong and unrelenting fighter for his individual interests and his own definition of self. True enough, he saw these issues as inextricably bound up with the interests of black people all over the world. That was why he expended so much energy in attempts to provide leadership, which were not always appreciated. He was convinced that "civilization" was the primary need of the African race, but, as Du Bois noted, he was guilty of an unbending righteousness that often limited his effectiveness. Western, Christian civilization, the very thing that he most valued, had burdened him with a brooding discontent and forced him into the role of a civilizing missionary. His greatest failing was linked with his most heroic struggle, the effort to reshape the African race in conformity with his own view of his life and times. We can pay Alexander Crummell the homage he is due by making the effort to judge him in terms of his dedication to those things for which he lived and labored—Christianity, civilization, law and order, and the destined triumph of the African race.

# Notes

## Chapter 1. Introduction

1. Douglass's flair for the dramatic is observed by Benjamin Quarles in *Frederick Douglass* (Washington: Associated Publishers, 1948); the most striking (although tragic) example is the description of Douglass's death (p. 348). William Wells Brown's tricksterish quality is revealed in his own autobiographical writings. See "Memoir of the Author," in William Wells Brown, *The Black Man: His Antecedents, His Genius and His Achievements* (New York: Thomas Hamilton, 1863). See the story of his tricking the Ku Klux Klan in William J. Simmons, *Men of Mark, Eminent, Progressive, and Rising* (Cleveland: George M. Rewell & Co., 1887). More recently, William H. Farrison reported on Brown's remarkable medical practices in his *William Wells Brown: Author and Reformer* (Chicago: University of Chicago Press, 1969), pp. 399–418.

2. For example, Benjamin Brawley recognizes Crummell's importance in *The Negro Genius* (New York: Dodd Mead & Co., 1937) and *A Social History of the American Negro* (New York: Macmillan, 1921). Carter G. Woodson recognizes him in several editions of his *The Negro in Our History* (Washington: Associated Publishers, 1922–47). See also W.E.B. Du Bois, *The Souls of Black Folk* (Chicago: McClurg, 1903), pp. 226–27.

3. Crummell's unmistakable sympathy with the elitism of the federalist tradition has also been observed by Otey M. Scruggs in "Two Black Patriarchs: Frederick Douglass and Alexander Crummell," in *Afro-Americans in New York Life and History* (January 1982), pp. 17–30. Crummell's sense of his responsibility as a "founding father" is discussed at length in later chapters.

4. Theodore Draper, in *The Rediscovery of Black Nationalism* (New York: Viking, 1970), makes no mention of Crummell. Alphonso Pinkney, in his *Red, Black and Green* (London: Cambridge University Press, 1976), devotes only one sentence to Crummell, identifying him as a supporter of the American Colonization Society. August Meier,

303

John H. Bracey, Jr., and Elliot Rudwick, editors of *Black Nationalism in America* (Indianapolis: Bobbs-Merrill, 1970), have recognized the significance of Crummell, as has Meier in his *Negro Thought in America, 1880–1915* (Ann Arbor: the University of Michigan Press, 1963). Particularly insightful is Otey M. Scruggs, *We the Children of Africa in this Land* (Washington, D.C.: Department of History, Howard University, 1972). There is much insightful material in William Toll, *The Resurgence of Race* (Philadelphia: Temple University Press, 1979) (see his index citations), and Alfred Moss, *The American Negro Academy: Voice of the Talented Tenth* (Baton Rouge: Louisiana State University Press, 1981). Also see Leonard I. Sweet, *Black Images of America, 1784–1870* (New York: Norton, 1976). Although there has never been a full-length biography, the present study benefits, of course, from several articles, obituaries, etc., mentioned in notes and bibliographic references.

5. The relation of Crummell's educational theories to Booker T. Washington's is discussed in a later chapter. Also see W. J. Moses, *Black Messiahs and Uncle Toms* (University Park: Pennsylvania State University Press, 1972), pp. 98–99.

6. Christopher Lasch, *The Culture of Narcissism* (New York: Norton, 1979). For another analysis of current intellectual fashions, see Russell Jacoby, *Social Amnesia* (Boston: Beacon, 1975). Both identify intellectual relativism and subjectivism as characteristic attitudes in contemporary American life. Crummell found such attitudes objectionable.

7. Definitions of modernism are many and contradictory. A treatment of modernism that is consistent with my own is fundamental to the work of A. James Arnold, *Modernism and Negritude: The Poetry and Poetics of Aimé Césaire* (Cambridge, Mass.: Harvard University Press, 1981).

8. Crummell's attack on political radicalism is in an untitled sermon in the Crummell Papers, Schomburg Collection, New York Public Library, MSC 315. Also see Crummell's *The Greatness of Christ and Other Sermons* (New York: Thomas Whittaker, 1882), pp. 318–21; *The Solution of Problems: The Duty and Destiny of Man. The Annual Sermon at the Commencement of Wilberforce University, June 16th, 1895* (Philadelphia: Recorder Press, n.d.), p. 6; and *Jubilate: 1844–1894, The Shades and Lights of a Fifty Years' Ministry* (Washington, D.C.: St. Luke's Church, 1894), p. 20.

9. In *The Golden Age of Black Nationalism* (Hamden, Conn.: Archon Books, 1978), pp. 15–31, I offer a fuller exposition of this thesis concerning nineteenth-century black writing.

10. Phyllis Wheatley, "On Being Brought from Africa to America," in G. Herbert Renfro, ed., *The Life and Words of Phyllis Wheatley* (Washington, D.C.: Robert L. Pendleton, 1916), p. 48.

11. Crummell to the Foreign Secretary of the Domestic and Foreign Missionary Society, 16 January 1872, Papers of the Domestic and Foreign Missionary Society, Archives of the Episcopal Church, Austin, Texas.

12. George Schuyler, *Black and Conservative: The Autobiography of George Schuyler* (New Rochelle, New York: Arlington House, 1966), p. 18. Schuyler mistakenly referred to Crummell as a bishop. The same mistake occurs in Emma Lou Thornbrough, *T. Thomas Fortune* (Chicago: University of Chicago Press, 1972), p. 229. It is interesting, although purely coincidental, that the black conservative Clarence Pendleton was once an altar boy at St. Luke's Episcopal Church in Washington, D.C., which Crummell founded.

13. John Blassingame writes in *The Slave Community: Plantation Life in the Antebellum South*, 2d. ed. (New York: Oxford University Press, 1979), p. 5, "Antebellum

black slaves created several unique cultural forms. . . . '' Eugene D. Genovese says in *Roll, Jordan, Roll: The World the Slaves Made* (New York: Vintage, 1976), p. xv, that "the slaves as an objective social class laid the foundations for a separate black national culture," a valid point, and one with which I agree. I think it well, however, to bear in mind Lawrence Levins's observation in *Black Culture and Black Consciousness: Afro-American Folk Thought from Slavery to Freedom* (New York: Oxford University Press, 1977), p. xiv, that "folk expression is only one part of a people's culture." Sterling Stuckey, *Slave Culture: Nationalist Theory and the Foundations of Black America,* (New York: Oxford University Press, 1987).

14. Moses, *The Golden Age of Black Nationalism;* Genovese, *Roll Jordan Roll;* Moses, *Black Messiahs and Uncle Toms.*

## Chapter 2. The Early Years

1. George W. Forbes, "Alexander Crummell," unpublished typescript, Forbes Papers, Boston Public Library, is the source of Crummell's birth date. Royal ancestry was attributed to Crummell by most of his early biographers. For example, see Simmons, *Men of Mark,* p. 530. Simmons, a minister of the A.M.E. church, knew Crummell personally, but his biographical sketch of Crummell contains a few minor errors.

2. Crummell, "Africa and her People," unpublished manuscript, Crummell Papers. Also see Crummell to Jay, June 29, 1849, where he refers to the "Timanee" as "my father's tribe," Jay Family Papers, Butler Library, Columbia University.

3. William H. Ferris, "Alexander Crummell, an Apostle of Negro Culture," *American Negro Academy Occasional Papers,* no. 20 (Washington D.C.: The American Negro Academy, 1920), p. 6.

4. *Harper's Weekly,* April 14, 1866, p. 238. There is an engraving of Crummell on p. 237, which was brought to my attention by Professor Anani Dzidzienyo.

5. Forbes, "Alexander Crummell," Forbes Papers, p. 11.

6. *The African Times,* January 23, 1866, reports Crummell's departure with his mother from Boston on November 22. Right Rev. Thomas Clark in his introduction to Crummell's *The Greatness of Christ,* p. v, mentions "his mother and her ancestors for several generations never having been subjected to servitude." Crummell's statement on his maternal ancestry is in his *The Future of Africa: Being Sermons and Addresses, Etc., Etc., Delivered in the Republic of Liberia* (New York: Charles Scribner, 1862), p. 21. Some information on Crummell's mother, but not her name, is given in "A Colored Professor," *African Repository* (August, 1866), pp. 242–43. The only mention of Charity Hicks by name is in Walter B. Hayson, "Eulogy," *The Church Standard,* 14 January 1899, pp. 355–56, cited in Gregory U. Rigsby, *Alexander Crummell: Pioneer in Nineteenth-Century Pan-African Thought* (Westport, Conn.: Greenwood Press, 1987), p. 3.

7. Nathaniel P. Rogers in *The Liberator,* July 25, 1835.

8. Lamont D. Thomas, *Rise To Be a People: A Biography of Paul Cuffe* (Urbana and Chicago: University of Illinois Press, 1986). Sheldon Harris, ed., *Paul Cuffe: Black America and the African Return* (New York: Simon and Schuster, 1972). Peter Williams, Jr., *A Discourse Delivered on the Death of Captain Paul Cuffe, Before the New York African Institution, in the African Methodist Episcopal Zion Church, October 21, 1817* (New York, 1817). Williams's discourse was originally printed in *Freedom's Journal,* beginning with the first issue on March 16, 1817.

9. Kenneth G. Wylie, *Political Kingdoms of the Temne: Temne Government in Sierra Leone, 1825–1910* (New York: Africana Publishing Co., 1977).

10. Thomas, *Rise To Be a People*, p. 12; Harris, *Paul Cuffe*, p. 30. Also see Wm. A. Tyson to Crummell, n.d., Bruce Papers, Schomburg Collection, New York Public Library.

11. Crummell to John Jay, December 1, 1848, Jay Papers.

12. Crummell was described in this way by Jacob Trusswell in a letter to the *Concord Patriot*, August 11, 1835. Quoted from *The Liberator*, September 5, 1835, in Forbes, "Alexander Crummell," Forbes Papers.

13. In a sermon of 1862, Crummell says, "My father was an oysterman in New York, but after I had been to college, I didn't want to use my Latin and Greek in opening oysters! Thomas Downing in New York is also a Oysterman," Crummell Papers, MSC 317. It seems reasonable to suppose that the senior Crummell kept an "oysterhouse," as did Downing. His apparently high status in the community and the relative prosperity that allowed him to hire tutors for his children allows for such an interpretation.

14. M. A. Harris, *A Negro History Tour of Manhattan* (New York: Greenwood Press, 1968), p. 42. In September 1833, a fire that started in the National Theatre at the corner of Leonard Street and Church Street destroyed several nearby buildings, among them the A.M.E. Zion Church at 156 Church Street. The Crummell home may have been destroyed in this or in another of the many fires that occurred in New York's Negro Quarter.

15. Joel Tyler Headley, *The Great Riots of New York, 1712–1873* (New York: E. B. Treat, 1873), pp. 78–96.

16. I. Garland Penn, *The Afro-American Press and Its Editors*, p. 27ff.

17. *Freedom's Journal*, March 16, 1827.

18. Dated, but nonetheless indispensable, P. J. Staudenraus, *The African Colonization Movement, 1816–1865* (New York: Columbia University Press, 1961), contains basic information on white colonizationists. It must be supplemented by Floyd J. Miller, *The Search for a Black Nationality* (Urbana: University of Illinois Press, 1975) for an understanding of black participation in the movement. There is also much useful information in John R. Bodo, *The Protestant Clergy and Public Issues, 1812–1848* (Princeton: Princeton University Press, 1954). On Forten's and Cuffe's vacillation, see Harris, *Paul Cuffe*. For Peter Williams's support of Russwurm, see his letter to the citizens of New York of July 14, 1834, in *African Repository*, vol. 10, pp. 186–88, reprinted in Carter G. Woodson, *The Mind of the Negro as Reflected in Letters Written During the Crisis, 1800–1860* (Washington, D.C.: Association for the Study of Negro Life and History, 1926), pp. 630–34, esp. p. 632. For Andrews's support of Russwurm, see Andrews to Gurley, June 28, 1828; November 6, 1828; January 9, 1829; Moore to Gurley, April 9, 1829; Russwurm to Gurley, July 24, 1829, American Colonization Society Papers, Library of Congress. Cited in Benjamin Quarles, *Black Abolitionists* (New York: Oxford University Press, 1969), pp. 12, 255. Russwurm's "betrayal" and the resultant "persecution" are also described in Quarles, p. 7.

19. John W. Cromwell, *The Negro in American History* (Washington: The American Negro Academy, 1914), p. 130.

20. Garnet eventually reissued *Walker's Appeal, with a Brief Sketch of his Life* and his own *Address to the Slaves of the United States of America* (Troy, New York, 1848; reprint New York: Arno, 1969). In his preface Garnet reported the rumor that Walker had been poisoned.

21. Quarles, *Black Abolitionists,* p. 102.

22. Dorothy Porter, ''The Organized Educational Activities of Negro Literary Societies, 1828–1846,'' *Journal of Negro Education* V (October, 1936), contains information on the Phoenix Society, as does Quarles, *Black Abolitionists,* p. 102. See also *Address and Constitution of the Phoenix Society of New York and of the Auxiliary Ward Association* (New York, 1833).

23. Howard H. Bell, ed., *Proceedings of the National Negro Conventions, 1830–1864,* contains a number of contemporary documents, including proceedings of the convention of 1831 and materials relating to the meetings of 1830. Boston Crummell was not an official delegate to the convention, but he is mentioned in the *Minutes and Proceedings of the First Annual Convention of the People of Color* (1831) as a member of a committee formed to solicit funds for a proposed trade school in New Haven.

24. *Minutes and Proceedings of the Second Annual Convention of the Free People of Color,* in Bell, ed., *Proceedings of the National Negro Conventions.* Robert A. Warner, *New Haven Negroes: A Social History* (New Haven: Yale University Press, 1940), pp. 54–60.

25. For Prudence Crandall, see Quarles, *Black Abolitionists,* and Edmund Fuller, *Prudence Crandall: An Incident of Racism in Nineteenth-Century Connecticut* (Middletown, Conn.: Wesleyan University Press, 1971).

26. Charles S. Andrews, *The History of the New York African Free Schools* (New York, 1830), pp. 1, 18, 23; Harris, *A Negro History Tour of Manhattan,* p. 49; Henry L. Phillips, *In Memoriam of the Late Rev. Alex Crummell, D.D.* (Philadelphia, 1899), p. 10.

27. Andrews, *History of the African Free Schools,* p. 65.

28. Ibid., p. 27.

29. Phillips, *In Memoriam,* p. 10; Clark, introduction to Crummell's *The Greatness of Christ.*

30. Crummell, ''Eulogium on Henry Highland Garnet, D.D.,'' in *Africa and America: Addresses and Discourses* (Springfield: Wiley & Son, 1891), p. 274.

31. Crummell, ''Eulogium on Garnet,'' in *Africa and America,* pp. 274–78.

32. There is an article on James McCune Smith in the *Dictionary of American Biography* (1935). Many of Smith's letters have been reproduced on microfilm in Carter and Ripley, eds., Black Abolitionist Papers, 1830–1865.

33. Simmons, *Men of Mark,* p. 1004.

34. David Walker, *An Appeal, in Four Articles, Together with a Preamble, to the Colored Citizens of the World, but in Particular and very Expressly to Those of the United States of America* (Boston, 1829). I have used the edition reprinted by Arno Press (New York, 1969). Although the Arno editions are accurate in that they are photographic reproductions, they are not scholarly in that full publication details are not given. Arno used the edition republished by Henry Highland Garnet (Troy, New York, 1848), p. 46.

35. Crummell, ''Eulogium on Garnet,'' in *Africa and America,* p. 277.

36. Little is known of Sidney. Crummell eulogized him shortly after his death, and two drafts of the eulogy are in the Crummell Papers. See MSC 25 (on microfilm, this would be in the letters reel), and the more complete version, MSC 392.

37. Crummell, ''Eulogy on Sidney,'' Crummell Papers, MSC 392, p. 7. That Sidney was born around 1846 can be deduced from the Cambridge census of 1851, which lists his age as 5.

38. The handiest descriptions of black New York in the nineteenth century are Har-

ris, *A Negro History Tour of Manhattan*, and Roi Ottley and William Weatherby, *The Negro in New York* (New York: The New York Public Library, 1967).

39. Karl Bernhard, *Travels Through North America*, I, pp. 126, 133. Reprinted in Bayrd Still, *Urban America: A History With Documents* (Boston: Little, Brown, 1974), p. 128.

40. Mrs. Frances Trollope, *Domestic Manners of the Americans*, reprinted in Still, *Urban America*, pp. 28–29.

41. Charles Dickens, *American Notes for General Circulation*. Also see Five Points Mission (by the Ladies of the Mission), *The Old Brewery and the New Mission House at Five Points* (New York: Stringer & Townsend, 1854).

42. Joel Tyler Headley, *The Great Riots of New York*, pp. 79–96.

43. Ottley and Weatherby, *The Negro in New York*, p. 102.

44. Crummell to Elizur Wright, June 22, 1837, Elizur Wright Papers, Library of Congress. Reprinted in Carter and Ripley, eds., *Black Abolitionist Papers*, and in Milton Sernett, ed., *Newsletter of the Afro-American History Group of the American Academy of Religion*, 1983.

45. Alexander Crummell, "The Attitude of the American Mind toward the Negro Intellect," in *American Negro Academy Occasional Papers*, no. 3 (Washington, D.C.: The American Negro Academy, 1898), p. 11. Cf. Crummell, "The Race Problem in America," in *Africa and America*, p. 55. William Allen Wallace, *The History of Canaan New Hampshire* (Concord, New Hampshire: The Rumford Press, 1910).

46. Crummell, "Eulogium on Garnet," in *Africa and America*, pp. 279–80.

47. Nathaniel P. Rogers, in *The Liberator*, July 25, 1835, cited in Forbes, "Alexander Crummell," p. 3 Also see Nathaniel P. Rogers, in *Herald of Freedom*, August 8, 1935, and August 22, 1935.

48. Letter of Jacob Truswell in *Concord Patriot*, August 11, 1835. cited in Forbes, "Alexander Crummell," p.3.

49. Crummell, "Eulogium on Garnet," in *Africa and America*, pp. 280–81.

50. *Catalogue of the Officers and Students in the Oneida Institute*, 1836 (Whitesborough: Oneida Institute, 1836). Also see circular describing Oneida Institute in Weld Papers, Library of Congress. I am indebted to Professor Milton Sernett for graciously sending me copies of these documents.

51. Ibid. In "Eulogy on Sidney," Crummell Papers, MSC 392, Crummell says he left for Oneida only eight days after returning from New York. Since, according to the catalogue, the school year ended in November and began in February, it seems likely that Crummell was able to use the final months of the 1835 school year to demonstrate a freshman level of competency.

52. Crummell, "Eulogy on Sidney," p. 28. Crummell Papers, MSC 392.

53. Crummell, "Eulogy on Sidney," Crummell Papers, MSC 392.

54. Crummell to Elizur Wright, June 22, 1837, Wright Papers, Library of Congress.

55. [John Jay], *A Tract for the Times*, Jay Papers, p. 2.

56. George Freeman Bragg, *History of the Afro-American Group of the Episcopal Church* (Baltimore: Church Advocate Press, 1922), pp. 59–62.

57. Ibid.

58. Ibid., pp. 81–82.

59. Williams's complex views on colonization are stated in his letter "To the Citizens of New York," reprinted in Woodson, ed., *The Mind of the Negro*, pp. 630–34.

60. Ibid.

61. Crummell, "Reply to Bishop Onderdonk," Jay Papers, p. 20.

62. Crummell, *Shades and Lights*, p. 7.

63. Crummell, "Reply to Bishop Onderdonk," Jay Papers, insert in Crummell's handwriting attached to p. 19.

64. Crummell, *Shades and Lights*, p. 6.

65. Garnet studied for the ministry with Amos G. Beman while living in Troy. See Crummell, *Africa and America*, p. 281.

66. Woodson, ed., *The History of the Negro Church* (Washington, D.C.: Associated Publishers, 1972), pp. 67–73 and 89–90.

67. [John Jay], *A Tract for the Times*, Jay Papers.

68. William H. Pease and Jane H. Pease, *They Who Would Be Free: Blacks' Search for Freedom, 1830–1861* (New York: Atheneum, 1974), p. 14.

69. Ibid. Also see Sarah and Angelina Grimké to Theodore Weld, November 30, 1837, and Theodore Weld to Sarah and Angelina Grimké, December 15, 1837, in Gilbert Hobbes Barnes and Dwight L. Dumond, eds., *Letters of Theodore Dwight Weld, Angelina Grimké Weld, and Sarah Grimké, 1872–1844* (New York: D. Appleton-Century Co., 1934), vol. 1, pp. 486–87.

70. See Rev. Matthew Anderson, "Introductory Address" in Phillips, *In Memoriam*, p. 6. Also see William Wells Brown, *The Rising Son* (Boston: A. G. Brown & Co., 1876), p. 456.

71. Woodson, *History of the Negro Church*, pp. 84–85.

72. Woodson, *History of the Negro Church*, pp. 62–73.

73. Crummell, *Shades and Lights*, p. 7

74. Extract from De Grasse's diary, reprinted in A Churchman [John Jay], *Caste and Slavery in the American Church* (New York: n.p., 1843), p. 15. The published edition, from which I quote, differs substantially from the manuscript in the Jay Papers entitled *A Tract for the Times*.

75. From De Grasse's diary, in A Churchman [John Jay], *Caste in the Church*.

76. De Grasse's complexion is described in Crummell, "Reply to Bishop Onderdonk," Jay Papers, p. 5.

77. From De Grasse's diary, in A Churchman [John Jay], *Caste in the Church*.

78. Crummell, "Reply to Bishop Onderdonk," Jay Papers, pp. 5, 21. William Jay, "Introductory Remarks to the Reproof of the American Church Contained in the *Recent History of the Protestant Episcopal Church in America* by the Bishop of Oxford" [1846], in *Miscellaneous Writings on Slavery* (New York: 1843), pp. 440–48. A Churchman [John Jay], *Caste in the Church*, pp. 16, 22–36.

79. [John Jay], *A Tract for the Times*, Jay Papers, p. 6.

80. Crummell, *Shades and Lights*, p. 8, and "Reply to Bishop Onderdonk," Jay Papers, p. 11.

81. Crummell to Jay, October 24, 1839, Jay Papers.

82. Crummell, *Shades and Lights*, p. 23.

83. William Jay, *An Inquiry into the Character and Tendency of the American Colonization Society and the American Anti-Slavery Societies*, in *Miscellaneous Writings on Slavery*, pp. 149–53.

84. William Jay, *Inquiry into the American Colonization Society*, pp. 68–69.

85. William Jay, *Inquiry into the American Colonization Society*, p. 148.

86. Crummell to Jay, October 24, 1839, Jay Papers.

87. See A Churchman [John Jay], *Caste in the Church*, and letters by A Churchman in *Anti-Slavery Standard*, July 13, 1843, and *Colored American* during the summer of 1839. Bishop Onderdonk's side of the story appeared in *The Churchman*.

88. William Jay, "Introductory Remarks to the Reproof of the American Church," in *Miscellaneous Writings on Slavery,* p. 448.

89. Crummell, "Reply to Bishop Onderdonk," Jay Papers.

90. Crummell, "Reply to Bishop Onderdonk," Jay Papers, pp. 22, 27; Crummell to Jay, October 24, 1839, Jay Papers. Benjamin Onderdonk was often referred to by his contemporaries as coarse, and he apparently had a habit of unconsciously touching people when he talked to them. The exact date when rumors of his "improper conduct" began to circulate is uncertain. One authority relates, "If, at a party, the gaslight failed, there was always some wag whose voice would be heard in the darkness, 'Ladies need not fear: the bishop is not present.' " See James Elliott Lindsley, *This Planted Vine: A Narrative History of the Episcopal Diocese of New York* (New York: Harper and Row, 1984), pp. 149–50.

91. The nature of Crummell's connection with Yale is as yet unclear. On January 29, 1986, Martha Lund Smalley, Archivist of the Yale Divinity School, wrote to inform me that there is "no evidence" that Crummell was a student at Yale. "The reference works that we have available do not list him as a graduate or a non-graduate." On February 20, 1986, Patricia Bodak Stark, Principal Reference Archivist of the Yale University Library wrote, "I have examined the college catalogues for the years 1834–50 but find no record of attendance for Alexander Crummell." In *African Repository,* August 1866, p. 242, a biographical sketch entitled, "A Colored Professor," says, "He went to New Haven to complete his theological studies at Yale, after which he was ordained deacon by Bishop Griswold in St. Paul's Church Boston." Similarly, *Harper's Weekly,* April 14, 1866, reported that "He went to New Haven to complete his studies at the Yale Theological Seminary." Crummell gave a New Haven address in his letter to John Jay, October 29, 1839. At the time of Sidney's death he was in New Haven. (See his letter to a friend, in which he eulogizes Sidney, June 22, 1840, Jay Papers, MSC 25.) He also mentions Yale College in a letter to the vestry of Christ Church, Providence, Rhode Island, June 13, 1842. Randall Burkett generously shared with me extracts from Harry Crosswell's diaries, which describe Crummell as "a candidate in the church . . . Pursuing his studies in the Yale Theo. Sem." (entry for Tues., June 23, 1840). Crosswell was rector of Trinity Church, New Haven. His diaries are in the Sterling Library, Yale University. Crummell mentions receiving a visit from Peter Williams in New Haven, "shortly before his death," in his "Reply to Bishop Onderdonk," Jay Papers. There are two copies of the manuscript, but only one is in Crummell's hand; it is dated Bath, England, April 1849.

92. See Warner, *New Haven Negroes.*

93. The notes are written in what appears to be Crummell's youthful hand and are identified with the brief notation "Dr. Taylor New Haven" in Crummell's mature handwriting.

94. Warner, *New Haven Negroes,* pp. 86–87. *Account of Money Contributed for the Benefit of Mr. Alexander Crummel* [sic.] (New Haven: Connecticut, 1840), manuscript in the W.E.B. Du Bois Papers, microfilm edition, reel 89, frames 94–97.

95. *The Dictionary of American Biography* describes Vinton (1807–1881) as a low churchman, prominent in the evangelical group. He was one of the leading preachers in the Episcopal church.

96. Crummell to John Jay, October 24, 1839, Jay Papers.

97. Pease and Pease, *They Who Would Be Free,* p. 151, and *Colored American,* May 18 and October 19, 1839, cited by Pease and Pease.

98. Crummell, "Eulogy on Sidney," Crummell Papers, MSC 392.

99. Crummell, *The Greatness of Christ,* p. 243.

100. Undated manuscript, Christ Church Vestry Minutes, Rhode Island Historical Society. Neither Crummell's name nor his wife's appears in the New York census of 1840, when he probably was not a New York householder in any case. The census of Cambridge, England for 1851 does list the members of the Crummell household, giving Mrs. Crummell's name as Sarah, age 30. The ship's log at the time of her arrival in the United States in 1862 gives her age as 37. The birth dates do not reconcile. I have not been able to locate an announcement of the wedding in the *Colored American* for the years 1840 or 1841. By the time of the 1850 census, the Crummells were in England. Marriage and baptismal records of St. Philip's Church for the relevant years contain no reference to the young couple or their children. City of New York marriage records in the New York Municipal Archives and Records Retention Center apparently do not go back any further than 1847, well after the Crummell's marriage date. Also see Crummell to Jay, December 29, 1843, and August 9, 1848, Jay Papers. The reference to Crummell as "a perfect Tsar" is in Carter G. Woodson, ed., *Works of Francis J. Grimké* (Washington, D.C.: Associated Publishers, 1942), vol. 1, p. 31.

101. Crummell reprinted the sonnet at least twice in publications of his own. See *The Future of Africa* (1862) and *Shades and Lights,* pp. 11–12.

102. The topic of Ethiopianism is discussed in Moses, *The Golden Age of Black Nationalism,* chapter 8, and in *Black Messiahs and Uncle Toms,* chapter 12.

103. Crummell, *Shades and Lights,* pp. 12–14.

104. Ibid.

## Chapter 3. The Struggles of a Young Priest

1. Crummell mentions the invitation in his letter to the vestry of Christ Church, Providence, Rhode Island. Copy in Rhode Island Historical Society, Christ Church Vestry Minutes. The congregation never numbered more than thirty or forty families, although it dwindled during Crummell's residency. Crummell was typical of most preachers and teachers in his tendency to exaggerate the size of his congregations. As a black Episcopalian in the 1840s he was doubly tempted, for congregations were often embarrassingly small. Christ Church eventually was absorbed into St. Stephen's Parish.

2. Crummell to Jay, October 24, 1838, Jay Papers.

3. Du Bois, *The Souls of Black Folk,* p. 226. Crummell, *Shades and Lights,* p. 21.

4. *The New Age and Constitutional Advocate,* October 22, 1842. Julian Rammelkamp, "The Providence Black Community," *Rhode Island History,* vol. 7, no. 1, January, 1948, pp. 20–33. Rammelkamp's footnotes do not provide documentation for Crummell's role. Crummell's name does not appear in the list of five black delegates printed in the Congressional Report. William J. Brown's autobiography, another source cited by Rammelkamp, mentions only five delegates to the suffragist convention. *The Life of William J. Brown of Providence, R. I.* (Providence, 1883), pp. 107–108. Cf. A. M. Mowry, *The Dorr War* (Providence: Preston & Rounds, 1901); also see *Burke's Congressional Report,* Rpt. no. 546, House of Representatives, 28th Congress, 1st Session, pp 111–13.

5. Rammelkamp, "The Providence Black Community," p. 33.

6. Crummell to Jay, 12 September 1851, Jay Papers.

7. Ibid.

8. Crummell to the Vestry of Christ Church, Providence, June 13, 1842. Christ Church Vestry Minutes, Rhode Island Historical Society.

9. Undated manuscript in Christ Church Vestry Minutes, Rhode Island Historical Society.

10. Christ Church Vestry Minutes, Rhode Island Historical Society.

11. Du Bois, *The Souls of Black Folk,* pp. 221–23.

12. Crummell's displeasure with typical black religiosity is expressed in "The Relations and Duties of Free Colored Men in America to Africa," in *The Future of Africa,* p. 274.

13. Randall K. Burkett, "A Profile of Black Episcopal Clergymen in Antebellum America." Working paper presented at the American Academy of Religion, November 9, 1980, Dallas, Texas.

14. Du Bois, *The Souls of Black Folk. Harper's Weekly,* April 14, 1866.

15. Crummell, *Shades and Lights,* p. 10.

16. Crummell to Jay, July 17, 1843, Jay Papers. William Jay, *Miscellaneous Writings on Slavery,* p. 144. Crummell, *Shades and Lights,* p. 9.

17. Crummell, *Shades and Lights,* p. 15.

18. Resolution of the Philadelphia Convention, 1848, reprinted in William Jay, *Miscellaneous Writings on Slavery,* pp. 446–47.

19. Bragg, *History of the Afro-American Group of the Episcopal Church,* pp. 61–68.

20. Crummell to Jay, July 24, 1843, Jay Papers.

21. Crummell to Jay, October 24, 1839, Jay Papers.

22. Crummell to Jay, July 17, 1843, Jay Papers. The Philadelphia priest who would seem to fit the description in terms of age and years in the ministry was William Douglass (1805–1862). See Burkett, "Profile of Black Episcopal Clergymen," presented at the American Academy of Religion, 1980. Also see Bragg, *History of the Afro-American Group of the Episcopal Church,* pp. 59–80.

23. Crummell to Jay, July 17, 1843, Jay Papers.

24. Ibid.

25. Crummell to Jay, August 9, 1848, Jay Papers.

26. Crummell to Jay, September 12, 1851, Jay Papers.

27. Quarles, *Black Abolitionists,* pp. 171–72, and *Colored American,* July 4, 1838; October 6, 1838; and August 17, 1839.

28. *Colored American,* August 26, 1837.

29. Williams, *A Discourse Delivered on the Death of Paul Cuffe.*

30. Crummell, "The Relations and Duties of Free Colored Men in America to Africa," in *Africa and America.*

31. Minutes of the Albany convention of 1840 were printed in *Colored American,* October 31, 1840, January 2, and 9, 1841. Reprinted in Philip S. Foner and George E. Walker, eds., *Proceedings of the Black State Conventions, 1840–1865* (Philadelphia: Temple University Press, 1979).

32. Samuel Cornish in *Rights of All,* September 18, 1829; *Colored American,* May 3, 1838; *The Liberator,* June 1, 1838. Also see Pease and Pease, *They Who Would Be Free,* pp. 12–13.

33. *Colored American,* January 2, 1841, reprinted in Sterling Stuckey, *The Ideological Origins of Black Nationalism* (Boston: Beacon, 1972), pp. 243–45.

34. Ibid.

35. *Colored American,* January 30, February 6, and February 20, 1841, reprinted in Stuckey, *Ideological Origins of Black Nationalism,* pp. 252–60.

36. *Colored American*, February 13, February 20, March 6, and March 13, 1841.

37. Crummell to Jay, August 9, 1848, Jay Papers.

38. Crummell, "Condition of the Black and Colored Population of the United States, *The Record*, June 5 [1848]; reprinted as a leaflet, Crummell Papers, MSC. 35. Also see Crummell's second anniversary sermon, Church of the Messiah, April 4, 1847, MSC. 74, Crummell Papers. Crummell, *Shades and Lights*, p. 10.

39. Crummell, *Shades and Lights*, pp. 10–11. *Journal of the Convention of the Diocese of New York*, 1846, pp. 77–79.

40. *Journal of the Convention of the Diocese of New York*, 1846, pp. 72–77.

41. *Proceedings of the National Convention of Colored People and Their Friends, Held in Troy, New York on the 6th, 7th, 8th, and 9th October, 1847*, p. 31. The Arno reprint edition does not contain Crummell's committee's report on education.

42. *Proceedings of the National Convention in Troy, 1847*, pp. 13, 17. *Minutes of the National Convention of Colored Citizens, Held in Buffalo, August, 1843*, p. 13.

43. *Proceedings of the National Convention in Troy, 1847*, pp. 18–21, 33–37.

44. The controversy concerning a black college is detailed in Pease and Pease, *They Who Would Be Free*, pp. 138–39. Also see *Proceedings of the National Convention in Troy, 1847*, p. 13.

45. Crummell, *Eulogium on the Life and Character of Thomas Clarkson*, reprinted in *Africa and America*, p. 201.

46. The revolutionary role of Charles Lyell in revising concepts of geological time has recently been questioned by Stephen Jay Gould in his *Time's Arrow: Time's Cycle* (Cambridge: Harvard University Press, 1987). In later years, Crummell seems to have accepted the idea that the universe dated from "vast epochs in the past" and that the process of creation had worked "through vast and endless eternities." See Crummell, "The Agencies to Saintly Sanctification," in *The Greatness of Christ*, p. 158. But he seems to have believed literally in the flood of Genesis, arguing that the bibilical account corresponded to accounts in the mythologies of numerous peoples, including the ancient Greeks, the American Indians, and the Polynesians. That Darwin himself accepted the Ussher chronology as late as 1861 has been documented by Bentley Blass, Oswei Temkin, and William L. Strauss, Jr., in their introduction to *Forerunners of Darwin: 1745–1859* (Baltimore: Johns Hopkins Press, 1959), pp. 356–414. Also see Francis Darwin and A.C. Seward, eds., *More Letters of Charles Darwin* (New York, 1903), vol. 2, pp. 30–31.

47. Jacques Barzun, *Darwin, Marx, and Wagner* (New York: Doubleday, 1958). Sidney Pollard, in *The Idea of Progress* (New York: Basic Books, 1969), traces social evolutionism to such figures as William Paley during the eighteenth century and Saint-Simon in the nineteenth, pp. 78, 105–106. The influences of Comte and Guizot on Crummell's social thought are recurrent themes, as observed in later chapters.

48. Crummell, *Eulogium on Thomas Clarkson*, in *Africa and America*, pp. 202–203.

49. Ibid., pp. 203, 264.

50. Arguing for universal suffrage, Douglass said, "It is said that we are ignorant; I admit it. But if we know enough to be hung, we know enough to vote. If [the Negro] knows as much when he is sober as an Irishman knows when he is drunk, he knows enough to vote on good American principles." "What the Black Man Wants" (1865), reprinted in Philip S. Foner, ed., *The Life and Writings of Frederick Douglass* (New York: International Publishers, 1955), vol. 4, p. 162.

51. See A. O. Lovejoy, *Great Chain of Being* (Cambridge: Harvard University Press, 1936). Crummell's interesting quote from Pope on the "Chain of Being" is in *Africa and America*, p. 53.

52. William E. Farrison describes Brown's facile entry into the medical profession, along with some of his dubious practices, in his *William Wells Brown: Author and Reformer* (Chicago: University of Chicago Press, 1969), pp. 399ff. Simmons describes Brown's tricksterish usage of the hypodermic needle and acetate of morphia in his *Men of Mark*, pp. 448–49.

53. The most convenient source for Douglass's attitude on trade schools is Foner, ed., *Life and Writings of Frederick Douglass*, vol. 2, which includes the following articles: "Learn Trades or Starve," from *Frederick Douglass's Paper*, March 4, 1853; "To Harriet Beecher Stowe," from *Proceedings of the Colored National Convention, Held in Rochester, July 6th, 7th, and 8th, 1853*, pp. 33–38; and "A Few More Words about Learning Trades," from *Frederick Douglass's Paper*, March 11, 1853.

54. Theodore Dwight Weld to Gerrit Smith, October 23, 1839, in Barnes and Dumond, eds., *Letters of Weld, Weld, and Grimké*, vol. 2, p. 812.

55. Crummell, in his "Reply to Bishop Onderdonk," Jay Papers, quotes this endorsement. See Thomas Fry to "Sir," July 15, 1845, Crummell Papers.

56. Frederick Douglass to William Lloyd Garrison, *The Liberator*, January 30, 1846.

57. In his celebrated address *The American Scholar*, Emerson called for an American declaration of literary independence, but in his essays on *English Traits* (1856) and in his well-known admiration for German transcendentalism, he demonstrated an unmistakable Europhilism. Hawthorne's assumption that the American writer must overcome the disadvantages of living in a land that lacked a feudal heritage is clear in the preface to *The Marble Faun*. The American sense of cultural inferiority is also a pronounced theme in the writings of Crummell's younger contemporaries Mark Twain, William Dean Howells, and Henry James.

## Chapter 4. Arrival in England

1. The best treatment of black expatriates in England during the years concerned is R. J. M. Blackett, *Building an Antislavery Wall: Black Americans in the Atlantic Antislavery Movement, 1830–1860* (Baton Rouge: Louisiana State University Press, 1983). Also see Quarles, *Black Abolitionists*, pp. 116–42. Crummell to Jay, September 12, 1851, Jay Papers. The ability of extraordinarily gifted and resourceful blacks to capitalize on the novelty of their presence in white society in exceptional instances was openly admitted even in the late twentieth century. See "Career Success in Technical Sales: An Interview With Xerox V.P. Kerney Laday" in *The Black Collegian* (January/February, 1985), pp. 78–79.

2. Garrison's denial of the debt is in his letter to Austin Steward, dated Boston, June 1856, reprinted in Woodson, ed., *The Mind of the Negro*. But Garrison had already acknowledged the debt in a letter to Lewis Tappan; see his letters dated December 17, 1835, and February 24, 1836, Lewis Tappan Papers, Library of Congress. Gilbert Hobbes Barnes quotes the following remark from the Tappan Papers: "It was exceedingly kind, and truly reasonable, in brother Paul to lend the money to me, so that I could return home without begging." See Gilbert Hobbes Barnes, *The Anti-Slavery Impulse, 1830–1844* (1933; reprint New York: Harcourt, Brace, and World, 1964), pp. 53, 221 n. 37.

3. Nathaniel Paul to William Lloyd Garrison, April 10, 1833, in Woodson, ed., *The Mind of the Negro*, p. 166.

4. Robert Purvis to William Lloyd Garrison, July 13, 1834, in Woodson, ed., *The Mind of the Negro*, p. 176.

5. C. Lennox Remond to C. B. Ray, June 30, 1840, in Woodson, ed., *The Mind of the Negro*, p. 297.

6. *The Liberator*, January 1, 1846, reprinted in Philip S. Foner, ed., *Life and Writings of Frederick Douglass*, vol. 1, p. 127.

7. William Craft to Mr. May, November 10, 1852, and Ellen Craft to *The British Anti-Slavery Advocate*, October 26, 1852. Both letters reprinted in Woodson, ed., *The Mind of the Negro*, pp. 262–65.

8. William Wells Brown to William Lloyd Garrison, October 12, 1849, in Woodson, ed., *The Mind of the Negro*, p. 359.

9. William G. Allen to William Lloyd Garrison, June 20, 1853, in Woodson, ed., *The Mind of the Negro*, pp. 285–86. Other observations on the situation in America by William G. Allen are in his *The American Prejudice Against Color. An Authentic Narrative Showing How Easily the Nation Got into an Uproar* (London, 1853) and *A Short Personal Narrative* (Dublin, 1860).

10. Samuel Ringgold Ward, *Autobiography of a Fugitive Negro: His Anti-Slavery Labours in the United States, Canada and England* (London, 1855).

11. Crummell to Jay, August 9, 1848, Jay Papers. Wilson A. Armistead in *A Tribute for the Negro*, p. 490, attributes the following to Crummell: "When I was in America, I THOUGHT I was a man;—in England I FEEL—I KNOW that I am."

12. Crummell, *Shades and Lights*, p. 16.

13. Venn, *Alumni Cantabrigiensis*.

14. Bragg, *History of the Afro-American Group of the Episcopal Church*, pp. 103–104. Also see *Journal of the Convention of the Protestant Episcopal Church of Rhode Island* (Newport, Printed for the Convention) 1847, p. 35; 1848, p. 27; 1849, pp. 16, 22; 1850, pp. 19, 37; 1851, p. 11; 1852, p. 29.

15. Crummell to Jay, July 14, 1848, Jay Papers.

16. *The Record*, June 5 [1848]; reprinted as a leaflet, "Condition of the Black and Colored Population of the United States." Crummell Papers, MSC 35.

17. Ibid.

18. Crummell, *Improvement of the Negro Race in the United States of America*, Crummell Papers. This circular, written to solicit funds for Crummell's education, contains a printed letter from Rev. Carswell, October 27, 1848, in which the author attests to Crummell's "love of learning and quickness of apprehension" and endorses the plan to send him to Cambridge.

19. Letter of Thomas Fry, July 15, 1848 [addressee unknown], Crummell Papers.

20. Crummell to Jay, December 1, 1848, Jay Papers.

21. Crummell to Jay [August 1848], Jay Papers.

22. *Bath and Cheltenham Gazette*, July 1848, p. 3; copy in British Library at Colindale. I am indebted to Professor R. J. M. Blackett for sharing with me this and other references to British newspapers.

23. *Anti-Slavery Reporter*, June 1, 1848, p. 101.

24. Ibid.

25. Cited in Armistead, *A Tribute for the Negro*, p. 481.

26. Crummell to Jay, August 9, 1848, Jay Papers.

27. Ibid.

28. Ibid.

29. Ibid.

30. Crummell, *Shades and Lights*, p. 23.

31. Crummell to Jay, August 9, 1848, Jay Papers.

32. Crummell to Jay, December 1, 1848, Jay Papers. Crummell sent Jay a circular describing the work of the committee to support him and his family.

33. Crummell mentioned his correspondence with Mr. Tyson and denied having attacked the church in his letter to Jay of December 1, 1848, Jay Papers.

34. Crummell to Jay, February 9, 1849, Jay Papers.

35. Ibid.

36. Ibid.

37. Du Bois, *The Souls of Black Folk*, pp. 221–22.

38. Crummell to Jay, February 9, 1849, Jay Papers.

39. *Midland County Herald*, April 12, 1849; copy in British Library at Colindale.

40. Crummell to Jay, December 1, 1848, Jay Papers.

41. Reprinted in *The Non-Slaveholder* (Philadelphia), Seventh Month, 2, 1849, p. 152.

42. Blackett, *Building an Antislavery Wall*, pp. 164–65. Also by Blackett, see *Beating Against the Barriers*, pp. 41–42. *Anti-Slavery Standard*, May 3, 1849; *Anti-Slavery Reporter*, May 1, 1849; *African Repository*, January 1850. For additional information, see John Blassingame, ed., *The Frederick Douglass Papers* (New Haven: Yale University Press, 1982), series 1, vol. 2, pp. 160–63, and Foner, ed., *Life and Writings of Frederick Douglass*, pp. 111–25 and 519–20.

43. Crummell to Jay, June 29, 1849, Jay Papers.

44. *Anti-Slavery Reporter*, June 1, 1849, p. 91.

45. *Anti-Slavery Reporter*, June 2, 1851, p. 86.

46. Ibid.

47. Ibid., p. 87.

48. Ibid.

## Chapter 5. Cambridge Influences

1. Crummell to Jay, April 1849, Jay Papers.

2. Crummell to Jay, June 29, 1849, Jay Papers. The 1851 Census of Cambridge contains the following information on the Crummell family: Alexander Crummell, age 32; Sarah M., age 30; Sidney G., age 5; Alexander, age 3; Frances A., age 2; Sophia H., age 2 weeks.

3. Crummell to Jay, August 2, 1850, Jay Papers.

4. Crummell to Jay, February 9, 1849, Jay Papers.

5. See J. H. Gray, *The Queens' College of St. Margaret and St. Bernard in the University of Cambridge* (London: F. E. Robinson, 1899), pp. 1–36.

6. Crummell to Jay, June 29, 1849, Jay Papers.

7. Physicians' statements concerning Crummell's health are in his letter to Jay of January 27, 1852, Jay Papers. Dr. Thomas Hodgkin was noted for his antislavery writings and his support of the American Colonization Society.

8. Crummell to Arthur Cleveland Coxe, September 30, 1852, Jay Papers. Also see Crummell to Jay, April 15, 1853.

9. Crummell mentions to Jay that his children are one and three years old in a letter of August 9, 1848, Jay Papers. The birth of a girl, Frances, is mentioned in a letter of June 29, 1849, Jay Papers. Crummell says she followed two boys in succession. The boy lost in Philadelphia is mentioned in a letter to Jay of January 27, 1852, Jay Papers. Alexander's death was reported in *Cambridge Chronicle and University Journal*, June

14, 1851, p. 4, as reported in C. R. Stockton "The Integration of Cambridge," in *Integrated Education*. Crummell mentions the death of the boy and the doctors' diagnosis of "incipient consumption" in a letter to Jay of September 12, 1851, Jay Papers. On February 18, 1852, Crummell wrote Jay a most painful letter mentioning the illness of his children. The birth of a daughter in 1853 is announced in a letter to Jay of April 15, 1853, Jay Papers. The name Dillwinna is not clearly written in the list of passengers of the ship the *Mary Caroline Stevens,* which landed the Crummell family in Baltimore on April 5, 1861. See records of arrivals in National Archives.

10. J. McCune Smith's statement and those of other physicians are mentioned in a letter to Jay of September 12, 1851, Jay Papers. Crummell to John Scoble, 28 May, 1851, British and Foreign Anti-Slavery Society Papers, Rhodes House Library, Oxford.

11. Crummell to Jay, September 12, 1851, Jay Papers.

12. I am indebted to Professor John Oldfield for bringing to my attention the diaries of Charles Clayton and Joseph Romilly and for sharing his references to them with me. Romilly's diaries are in the Rare Book Room of the Cambridge University Library; Charles Clayton's are in the Library of Caius College.

13. Crummell to Jay, August 9, 1848, Jay Papers.

14. This "previous examination" is described in the *Cambridge Chronicle,* March 15, 1851. The ordinary examination, which Crummell failed, is described in the Senate House Examination Papers, January 1853. The record of his attaining the degree is in *The Book of Matriculation and Degrees,* p. 149, and J. A. Venn, comp., *Alumni Cantabrigiensis* (Cambridge: Cambridge University Press, 1922–54), vol. 2, p. 193. The honors examination or *tripos* was given only in mathematics at the time of Crummell's matriculation. See Mathematical Tripos Lists, February 1853, in Cambridge University Archives. Romilly mentions Crummell's being "bumped," or failing his examinations, in his diary, January 28, 1853. The *Cambridge Chronicle,* February 12, 1853, p. 4, announces that Crummell was "examined approved" at the additional examination.

15. Forbes, "Alexander Crummell," Forbes Papers, pp. 10–13.

16. Crummell, *The Future of Africa,* pp. 196–97.

17. Crummell, "Civilization, the Primal Need of the Race," *American Negro Academy Occasional Papers,* no. 3 (Washington, D.C.: The American Negro Academy, 1898); Moss, *The American Negro Academy,* p. 124. In *Black Messiahs and Uncle Toms,* I discuss conflicts between Crummell and Booker T. Washington.

18. Crummell to Jay, September 12, 1852, Jay Papers.

19. Crummell to Peter Jones Bolton, May 28, 1851, Anti-Slavery Society Papers.

20. Crummell to Jay, September 12, 1851, Jay Papers.

21. Aristotle, *Politics.*

22. The statement traditionally attributed to Vesey is mentioned in Archibald Grimké, "Right on the Scaffold," *American Negro Academy Occasional Papers,* no. 7, (Washington D.C.: The American Negro Academy, 1901), p. 10.

23. *Anti-Slavery Reporter,* June 2, 1851, pp. 87–88, and Crummell to Jay, September 12, 1851, Jay Papers.

24. Allusions to Tacitus are in Crummell's *The Future of Africa,* p. 52, and *Africa and America,* pp. 32, 87, 364. Cf. Edward Wilmot Blyden, *Christianity, Islam, and the Negro Race* (London: W. B. Whittingham & Co., 1887), p. 59, who finds less admirable Germanic predelictions among Africans.

25. Information on Crummell's attendance at lectures was provided by the staff of the Cambridge University Archives, who guided me through documents relevant to him. The interpretations are my own. William Whewell, *Lectures on the History of Moral*

*Philosophy* (Cambridge, 1862), the essential feature of which is its assertion of the existence of a moral faculty, attacks the idea that sensationalism or materialism can serve as the basis of a moral system. Hobbes was the great villain of this treatise; Locke, Paley, Mill, and Bentham were viewed as equally in error, if somewhat less guilty of mischief.

26. Whewell, *Lectures*, p. 42.

27. Ibid., pp. 64–65.

28. Ibid., pp. 91–99.

29. Ibid., pp. 277–88.

30. Crummell, *The Future of Africa*, p. 42.

31. Crummell alluded to the feminine instinct of chastity in "The Black Woman of the South, Her Neglects and Her Needs," in *Africa and America*.

32. Crummell's homage to Wordsworth was mentioned in the preceding chapter. He boasted in *The Future of Africa* of the fact that the writings of Coleridge were available in Liberia, p. 12. Cowper appears in the list of required readings in *Future of Africa* p. 42.

33. Carl Stockton believes that Crummell heard Grote's lectures while at Cambridge, but according to the Cambridge archivist he was entitled to hear only those of Whewell. See C. R. Stockton, "The Integration of Cambridge: Alexander Crummell as Undergraduate, 1849–1853," *Integrated Education*, 15 March–April 1977).

34. Crummell in *Anti-Slavery Reporter*, June 1, 1849, p. 91.

35. Crummell, "Hope for Africa," in *The Future of Africa*.

36. See St. Clair Drake, *The Redemption of Africa and Black Religion* (Chicago: Third World Press, 1970), which offers an introduction to the concept of "Ethiopianism." Also see George Shepperson, "Ethiopianism and African Nationalism," *Phylon*, 14 (1953), pp. 9–18. Literary Ethiopianism is treated in my "The Poetics of Ethiopianism: W.E.B. Du Bois and Literary Black Nationalism," *American Literature*, 47 (1975), pp. 411–26.

37. Crummell, "The Negro Race Not Under a Curse," in *The Future of Africa*, pp. 327–54. Reprinted with corrections and additions from the *Christian Observer*, September [1850 or 1852].

38. "Mutability of Human Affairs" and "The Curse of Canaan," *Freedom's Journal*, April 6, 1827, and May 4, 1827. Also see "The Colored Race," *Colored American*, July 7, 1838, for the argument that all civilization comes from Egypt and Ethiopia. On the backwardness of the ancient Europeans, see "Early Britons," *Colored American*, July 27, 1839.

39. Ward, *Autobiography of a Fugitive Negro*, pp. 269–71. James W.C. Pennington, *A Textbook of the Origin and History, &c. &c. of the Colored People* (Hartford, 1841), is a very brief treatment of black history. Sensationalistic comparisons are made in Brown, *The Black Man*.

40. Crummell to Jay, September 12, 1851, Jay Papers.

41. Crummell to Jay, September 12, 1851, Jay Papers.

42. Ibid.

43. Crummell to Jay, January 27, 1852, Jay Papers.

44. Ibid.

45. Crummell quotes from the letter that Coxe wrote to Rev. H. Carswall in Crummell to Arthur Cleveland Coxe, September 30, 1852, Jay Papers.

46. Ibid.

47. The federalist comparison is made by Otey M. Scruggs in "Two Black Patriarchs," p. 22.

48. Stuckey, in the introduction to his *The Ideological Origins of Black Nationalism,* p. 11, asks, "Where else among black people can one find such gloomy and devastating, such stereotypical portraits of black humanity as among nationalists?" After noting the tendency in the writings of Henry Highland Garnet, Martin Delany, and David Walker, Stuckey says, "Perhaps such a view reached its grim consummation in the writings of Alexander Crummell."

49. *Anti-Slavery Reporter,* June 2, 1851.

50. On cultivating free blacks, see Crummell to Jay, September 12, 1851, Jay Papers.

51. Ibid.

52. I have found no correspondence between Crummell and Hodgkin dating from the 1840s or 1850s other than the letter describing Crummell's illness cited above, Crummell to Jay, 27 January 1852, Jay Papers. There are a few letters from Hodgkin to Crummell dating from the 1860s, but they simply reiterate old procolonization arguments. See, for example, Hodgkin to Crummell, April 22, 1865, Crummell Papers.

53. Randall Burkett has graciously shared with me the data he has compiled for his work in progress on nineteenth-century black Episcopalian ministers.

54. The quotation concerning Roberts's influence on Crummell occurs at the beginning of the pamphlet edition of *The Duty of a Rising Christian State to Contribute to the World's Well-Being and Civilization* (London: Werthheim & Macintosh 1856). A similar statement appears as a note at the beginning of the pamphlet edition of *The Relations and Duties of Free Colored Men in America to Africa* (Hartford: Case, Lockwood and Company, 1861).

55. Crummell to Arthur Cleveland Coxe, September 30, 1852, Jay Papers.

56. Ibid.

57. Crummell, "Hope for Africa," in *The Future of Africa,* p. 306.

58. The correspondence with Jay is summarized in the preceding chapter and its notes.

59. It was reported that John Jay was in 1852, "as the counsel of a Fugitive slave, brutally assaulted and struck in the face by the catching agent and counsel, Busteed," in *Proceedings of the National Emigration Convention of Colored People, 1854* (Pittsburgh: A. A. Anderson, Printer, 1854).

60. Crummell to Jay, August 1848, Jay Papers. From the tone of the correspondence it seems unlikely that any meeting took place—certainly none that could be interpreted as contact between social equals. Crummell does not, for example, ask to be remembered to Mrs. Jay in his letter of December 1, 1848, when he writes to express his happiness at their safe return home.

61. Crummell, "The Relations and Duties of Free Colored Men," in *Africa and America,* p. 280.


## Chapter 6. Adjustment to Africa

1. Crummell, "Africa and Her People," Crummell Papers, MSC 23.

2. Ibid.

3. Crummell to P. P. Irving, 8 August 1853, Papers of the Domestic and Foreign

Missionary Society. Alexander Payne, "Report of the Protestant Episcopal Mission in West Africa," in *Journal of the General Convention of the Protestant Episcopal Church in the United States Held in 1856,* appendix E, p. 287. *Spirit of Missions* (October, 1853), p. 368.

4. For examples of treatments for disease see the report of the colonial physician and U.S. agent in Liberia, J. W. Lugenbeel, *Sketches of Liberia: Comprising a Brief Account of the Geography, Climate, Productions, and Diseases, of the Republic of Liberia* (Washington: C. Alexander, 1850).

5. Crummell came to Liberia with two children in addition to an infant. See Crummell to P. P. Irving, 22 April 1853, Papers of the Domestic and Foreign Missionary Society. On the death of the infant see Crummell to P. P. Irving, 8 December 1853, Papers of the Domestic and Foreign Missionary Society. The Crummells were reported to have had four children as of July 10, 1858, according to extracts from C. C. Hoffman's journal published in *Spirit of Missions* (February, 1859). There is no reason to assume any were adopted. Four daughters in addition to the son are mentioned in Crummell's letters of September 7 and October 16, 1867, Papers of the Domestic and Foreign Missionary Society. References to Sarah Crummell's health are in Crummell's letters to the Domestic and Foreign Missionary Society of November 11, 1854; April 1855; and February 3, 1856. Also see *Spirit of Missions* (April 16, 1860), Bishop's Report, pp. 260–61. For the matter of the government appointment see Crummell to Jay, January 1856, Jay Papers.

6. Crummell's hopeful sermon of November 11, 1853 is in Carter and Ripley, eds., Black Abolitionist Papers, microfilm 08:475. Payne's report on Stokes's career is in *Journal of the Proceedings of the Bishops, Clergy, and Laity of the Protestant Episcopal Church in 1856* (Philadelphia: King & Baird, 1857), appendix E., pp. 287–88 and in the proceedings for 1862, appendix E, p. 247. Crummell's observations on Stokes are in Crummell's letters to P. P. Irving of 8 December 1853 and 10 January 1856, Papers of the Domestic and Foreign Missionary Society.

7. E. W. Stokes to William R. Whittingham, July 21, 1858, Whittingham Papers, Maryland Diocesan Archives, Maryland Historical Society.

8. Crummell to P. P. Irving, February 3, 1856, Papers of the Domestic and Foreign Missionary Society.

9. Crummell to P. P. Irving, 10 January 1856, Papers of the Domestic and Foreign Missionary Society.

10. Penelope Campbell, *Maryland in Africa: The Maryland State Colonization Society, 1831–1857* (Urbana: University of Illinois Press, 1971), p. 235.

11. Crummell to P. P. Irving, 16 August 1854, Papers of the Domestic and Foreign Missionary Society. Crummell, "God and the Nation," in *The Future of Africa,* pp. 150–51.

12. Crummell, "God and the Nation," in *The Future of Africa,* p. 153.

13. Ibid.

14. Ibid., pp. 154–59.

15. Ibid., pp. 157–63.

16. Carlyle's treatment of the question in *Heroes, Hero-worship, and the Heroic in History* (1841) is well known, as is Emerson's response in *Representative Men* (1850).

17. Crummell, "God and the Nation," in *The Future of Africa,* pp. 167–70.

18. For a more romantic appraisal of nineteenth-century black nationalism see Leopold Senghor, "Edward Wilmot Blyden, Precursor of Negritude," in Hollis R. Lynch, ed., *Selected Letters of Edward Wilmot Blyden* (New York: KTO Press, 1978), pp. xix–

xxii. But it is clear to other authors that a true appreciation of African culture did not emerge until the end of the nineteenth century; see, for example, Jacob Drachler, ed., *Black Homeland, Black Diaspora: Cross Currents of the African Relationship* (Port Washington, N.Y.: Kennikat Press, 1975), p. 6. Wilson J. Moses, "Cambridge Platonism in West Africa," *New England Journal of Black Studies,* no. 3 (1983), pp. 60–77.

19. *Journal of the Proceedings of the Protestant Episcopal Church, 1865* (Boston: William A. Hall, 1856), p. 313. Report of Bishop Payne, "Extension of the Mission to the Liberian Settlements," *Spirit of Missions* (November, 1853), p. 313.

20. *Spirit of Missions* (August, 1854), pp. 330–31; (November–December, 1854), pp. 529–30. Crummell to P. P. Irving, 4 October 1853, and 8 December 1853, Papers of the Domestic and Foreign Missionary Society, speaks of the need for funds to erect a suitable edifice. Also see Crummell's letter dated 7 November 1853, in *Spirit of Missions* (February, 1854), which reads, ". . . it is a matter of importance that our church here should be strong, substantial, capacious, chaste, and beautiful." In a letter to Irving of 27 November 1854, he writes that there are "families who say they are only awaiting the completion of our church edifice to become Episcopalians."

21. John Payne to Samuel D. Denison, August 7, 1855, Papers of the Domestic and Foreign Missionary Society.

22. "Extract from a letter of the Rev. Alex Crummell," dated Monrovia, November 11, 1854, in *Spirit of Missions* (March, 1855), p. 131. Payne to Crummell, Cavalla, December 8, 1854, Crummell Papers.

23. Crummell's complaint against Payne is in a letter to Coppinger of November 1, 1864, Papers of the American Colonization Society, vol. 13, no. 51, reel 160. Payne rebukes Crummell in his letters of December 8, 1854, and May 10, 1855, Crummell Papers.

24. Anna M. Scott's *Day Dawn in Africa, or Progress of the Prot. Epis. Mission at Cape Palmas, West Africa* (The Protestant Episcopal Society for the Promotion of Evangelical Knowledge, 1858) is a gushy little account of the community of white missionaries, written from an outsider's point of view. Most accounts of West African missions in *Spirit of Missions* focus on this community, a reflection of the bishop's interest. His priorities are clearly discernible in *Journal of the General Convention, 1865,* appendix C, p. 311.

25. The importance of black elites for the uplift of the masses appears throughout Crummell's writings. See his address to the British and Foreign Anti-Slavery Society in *Anti-Slavery Reporter,* June 2, 1851, p. 87. In this speech he called for the development of the leadership class in America and for the training of an indigenous ministry in Liberia. Crummell's ideas on civil religion are discussed above and in his address "God and the Nation," in *The Future of Africa.* Also see Robert Bellah, "Civil Religion in America," *Daedalus,* 96 (Winter, 1967).

26. Reverend Dr. Carswell, in a letter to Mr. Cox of April 15, 1857, Papers of the Domestic and Foreign Missionary Society, describes the interaction between Crummell, Payne, and Stokes and accepts Crummell's description of events, although there is no evidence that he ignored other possible sources. Payne's reaction to news of the convention is in Payne to Crummell, December 8, 1854, Crummell Papers. Also see *Extract Proceedings of the Christmas Convocation for 1854 of the Episcopal Church in Liberia, March 18, 1855;* copy in Papers of the Domestic and Foreign Missionary Society.

27. Payne to Denison, August 7, 1855, Papers of the Domestic and Foreign Missionary Society.

28. See Crummell to Denison, 29 November 1870, Papers of the Domestic and Foreign Missionary Society.

29. Payne to Denison, August 7, 1855, Papers of the Domestic and Foreign Missionary Society.

30. The bishop complained that Crummell had been given too much financial independence by the Board of Foreign Missions in his letter to Denison, September 13, 1855, Papers of Domestic and Foreign Missionary Society. Payne discusses his diversion of funds from Crummell to Russell in *Journal of the General Convention, 1865,* appendix C, p. 315. The bishop makes several appeals for the church in Monrovia, which is to be supported by the church in Virginia, in *Spirit of Missions* (November, 1853), p. 511; (February, 1854), pp. 56–57; (August, 1854), pp. 330–31. Crummell expresses his hostility to A. F. Russell in a letter to Denison, August 11, 1869, Papers of the Domestic and Foreign Missionary Society.

31. Crummell, "The Second Coming of the Lord", MSC 234, Crummell Papers. The meaning of the sign of Jonah is in Matthew 12:39. "For as Jonas was three days and three nights in the whale's belly; so shall the Son of man be three days and three nights in the heart of the earth."

32. Ibid. Crummell was not a heretic. He believed, as all Christians must, that the soul is saved by the grace of God, which was merited by the sacrifice of Jesus, but he placed great stress on the attainment of salvation through works. It was the individual man who achieved his own salvation. See undated manuscript, Crummell Papers, MSC 26.

33. Crummell Papers, MSC 26. The original twelfth-century text of the *Dies Irae* is attributed to Thomas of Celano, who borrowed its language from the Latin Vulgate Bible. It has many English translations; the one used here by Crummell is not among the most literal. For a brief introduction to the Oxford movement see Owen Chadwick, ed., *The Mind of the Oxford Movement* (Stanford: Stanford University Press, 1960). Any sympathies that Crummell might have had to the Oxford movement were purely coincidental. If they existed at all they were doctrinal, not political. He showed no inclination to drift into the Roman Catholic church. Indeed his hostility can be seen in his attributing Haiti's problems to "the incubus of Romanism." See *The Future of Africa,* p. 169.

34. Crummell, "The Second Coming," MSC 234, Crummell Papers.

35. Report of John Payne on the African mission, *Journal of the General Convention, 1865,* appendix C. Also see letters of Bishop Payne in *Spirit of Missions* (August, 1854), pp. 330–31; (November–December, 1854), pp. 529–530; (April, 1855), p. 131; (May, 1855), pp. 229–30. The editor of *Spirit of Missions* says in the May, 1855 issue that Payne's budget was to be cut by one third instead of increased. Crummell mentions the fire in a letter to P. P. Irving, May 11, 1855; also see *Spirit of Missions* (April, 1855), pp. 184–85. Crummell to Jay, January 1856, Jay Papers.

36. Payne to Irving, May 8, 1856, Papers of the Domestic and Foreign Missionary Society.

37. Report of the Missionary Bishop at Cape Palmas, *African Repository* (February, 1857), p. 45, written in January 1856 and addressed to the Board of Missions; originally published in *Spirit of Missions.* The bishop published two other reports during 1855. One appeared in *Spirit of Missions* (November–December, 1855); the other in *African Repository* (April, 1856), pp. 111–116. The account by Dr. James Hall appeared in *African Repository* (January, 1858), p. 25.

38. Payne to Denison, May 8, 1856, Papers of the Domestic and Foreign Missionary Society.

39. Payne advised Crummell in a letter of December 8, 1854, as follows: "Your female school should prosper, at least if you do not set the terms of admission too high. It is a matter worthy of consideration whether it is not more important to have the moral training of the many or the intellectual training of the very few." Cf. *African Repository* (February, 1857), p. 45, and *Spirit of Missions* (November–December, 1855), p. 619. The Benson address is in the *Liberia Herald,* December 3, 1856, p. 2, reprinted in *African Repository* (March, 1857), pp. 87–95. Benson's willingness to help Crummell is mentioned in Crummell's letter to Jay, January 1856. The donation for the library may have come from Benjamin Coates, to whom Crummell wrote in March 1856 asking for library funds. See Carter and Ripley, eds., Black Abolitionist Papers, microfilm 10:0259.

40. Crummell, "The Duty of a Rising Christian State," in *The Future of Africa,* pp. 57–102.

41. Crummell, *The Future of Africa,* p. 87; Crummell to Denison, 7 August 1856, Papers of the Domestic and Foreign Missionary Society.

42. Crummell, *The Future of Africa,* p. 74.

43. Crummell, *The Future of Africa,* p. 60. The sentence from Herder is quoted by Hans Kohn in his article on nationalism in *Dictionary of the History of Ideas* (New York: Charles Scribner's Sons, 1973) vol. 3, p. 326a. The translation is mine. Kohn also discusses in the same article the cosmopolitanism and internationalism of Herder and Rousseau, who were nonetheless "fathers of modern nationalism." In *The Golden Age of Black Nationalism,* I discuss parallels between German nationalist ideology and the nationalist ideologies of black Americans, as does Kohn, op. cit.

44. Crummell, *The Future of Africa,* p. 62.

45. Crummell, *The Future of Africa,* p. 63.

46. For theories of progressive evolutionism that were a part of the mid-nineteenth century world-picture, see Thomas A. Goudge, "Evolutionism" in *Dictionary of the History of Ideas* (New York: Charles Scribner's Sons, 1973) vol. 2, pp. 174–89; Samuel Butler, *Evolution Old and New, or the Theories of Buffon, Dr. Erasmus Darwin, and Lamarck, as compared with that of Charles Darwin* (New York: E. P. Dutton & Company, 1911); Bentley Glass, Oswei Temkin, and William L. Strauss, Jr., eds., *Forerunners of Darwin, 1745–1859* (Baltimore: The Johns Hopkins Press, 1959); and Stephen J. Gould, *Time's Arrow: Time's Cycle* (Cambridge, Mass.: Harvard University Press, 1987).

47. Crummell, *The Future of Africa,* pp. 62, 63–64.

48. Crummell, *The Future of Africa,* pp. 72–102, passim.

49. Crummell to Denison, January 1856; February 3, 1856; May, 1856, Papers of the Domestic and Foreign Missionary Society.

50. Crummell to Jay, January 1856, Jay Papers. Crummell to P. P. Irving, 11 November 1854; April 1855; 11 August 1856, Papers of the Domestic and Foreign Missionary Society. Crummell to Jay, May 1856, Jay Papers.

51. William A. Tyson to Crummell, n.d., Crummell Papers.

52. Crummell to Jay, May 1856; September 1857, Jay Papers.

53. Crummell to Jay, September 1857, in Carter and Ripley, eds., Black Abolitionist Papers.

54. Payne to Denison, May 27, 1856, Papers of the Domestic and Foreign Missionary Society.

55. Payne claimed to have heard of Crummell's departure from Monrovia in April 1857 from another missionary, R. Gibson. Payne to [Denison], April 23, 1857, Papers of the Domestic and Foreign Missionary Society.

56. Rev. Dr. Carswell to Mr. Cox, April 15, 1857, Papers of the Domestic and Foreign Missionary Society.

57. Payne to Denison, May 15, 1856, Papers of the Domestic and Foreign Missionary Society.

58. Henry Carswell to the Domestic and Foreign Missionary Society, April 1, 1857; Alonzo Potter to the Domestic and Foreign Missionary Society, May 6, 1857, Papers of the Domestic and Foreign Missionary Society.

59. The bishop's report for 1857, printed in *Spirit of Missions* (November–December, 1858), pp. 624–25, speaks of Crummell's removal to his farm "fifteen miles up the river and the consequent gradual withdrawal of his services from the [Monrovia] station." But it also tells of his officiating at the Clay-Ashland and Louisiana settlements on alternate Sundays. In late March and early April 1865 Crummell procured affidavits from Stokes and other witnesses attesting to this point. See Crummell letters, Bruce Papers. Also see Crummell to Jay, September 1857, Papers of the Domestic and Foreign Missionary Society.

60. Payne to Denison, May 11, 1858, Papers of the Domestic and Foreign Missionary Society.

61. Crummell's arrival in Cape Palmas was recorded in C. C. Hoffman's journal and printed in *Spirit of Missions* (February, 1859). See also *African Repository* (September, 1859). For Mrs. M. B. Merriam's account, see her *Home Life in Africa* (Boston: A. Williams, 1868), pp. 111, 113–14.

62. The report of D. Thornley, a naval surgeon, is in *African Repository* (August, 1860), p. 251. The bishop's report is in *Spirit of Missions* (November–December, 1859), p. 774. Crummell, "Duty of a Rising Christian State," in *The Future of Africa*, p, 79.

63. The drilling recaptives are mentioned in "Address of Rev. Alexander Crummell at the Anniversary Meeting of the Massachusetts Colonization Society, May 29, 1861," published in the society's annual report and in Crummell and Edward Wilmot Blyden, *Liberia: The Land of Promise to Free Colored Men,* (Washington: The American Colonization Society, 1861).

64. Crummell, sermon on Galatians 5:18, Crummell Papers, MSC 396. Crummell, *The Future of Africa,* pp. 195–96, 208.

65. See especially "The Fitness of the Gospel for Its Own Work," in *The Future of Africa.* Also see Crummell's sermons on Galatians 5:18 (microfilm 10:209, 210, 218–19, 220) and on Peter 1:27 (microfilm 11:272) in Carter and Ripley, eds., Black Abolitionist Papers. Emerson's criticism of extreme Christocentrism is in his address at the Harvard Divinity School, July 15, 1838.

66. Sermons on Galatians 5:18 and on Peter 1:27, in Carter and Ripley, eds., Black Abolitionist Papers, microfilm 10:209 and 11:272.

67. Sermon on Galatians 5:18, in Carter and Ripley, eds., Black Abolitionist Papers, microfilm 10:212–13.

68. Denison to Rev. J. Rambo, January 9, 1860; Denison to Crummell, January 11, 1860, Papers of the Domestic and Foreign Missionary Society.

69. Excerpts from Mr. Rambo's journal, printed in *Spirit of Missions* (September, 1860), p. 336.

## Chapter 7. Changing Attitudes in America

1. *Proceedings of the Colored National Convention Held in Rochester, July 6th, 7th, and 8th, 1853* (Rochester: Printed at the Office of *Frederick Douglass's Paper*, 1853), pp. 47–57.

2. See Victor Ullman, *Martin R. Delany: The Beginnings of Black Nationalism* (Boston: Beacon Press, 1971).

3. The only source for this quotation I have been able to locate is in Benjamin Quarles' introduction to Martin Delany, *The Condition, Elevation, Emigration, and Destiny of the Colored People of the United States* (Philadelphia, 1852; reprint New York: Arno, 1969).

4. *The Liberator*, May 1, 1863; reprinted in Philip S. Foner, ed., *The Voice of Black America*, (New York: Capricorn Books, 1973), pp. 288–92.

5. Delany's experience at Harvard is discussed in Miller, *Search for a Black Nationality*, and Ullman, *Martin R. Delany*.

6. *Frederick Douglass' Paper* (February 26, 1852), reprinted in Foner, ed., *The Life and Writings of Frederick Douglass*, vol. 2, pp. 172–73.

7. Frederick Douglass, "Letter to Harriet Beecher Stowe," printed in *Proceedings of the Colored National Convention Held in Rochester, July 6th, 7th, and 8th, 1853*, pp. 33–38.

8. Frederick Douglass to Gerritt Smith, January 21, 1851, in Foner, ed., *The Life and Writings of Frederick Douglass*, vol. 2, p. 51.

9. Frederick Douglass, "Self-Elevation—Rev. S. R. Ward," *Frederick Douglass' Paper* (April 13, 1855), reprinted in Foner, ed., *The Life and Writings of Frederick Douglass*, vol 2, p. 361. Douglass calls for Crummell's return in the issues of July 31, 1851 and November 27, 1851. Both are reprinted in Foner, ed., *The Life and Writings of Frederick Douglass*, vol. 5, pp. 199, 216–18.

10. See Joel Schor, *Henry Highland Garnet: A Voice of Black Radicalism in the Nineteenth Century* (Westport, Conn.: Greenwood Press, 1977), p. 163. Garnet's statement is in the *Weekly Anglo-African*, 7 April 1860.

11. Frederick Douglass to Benjamin Coates, April 17, 1856, William M. Coates Papers, Historical Society of Pennsylvania; reprinted in Foner, ed., *The Life and Writings of Frederick Douglass*, vol. 2, pp. 387–88.

12. James M. McPherson, *The Negro's Civil War* (New York: Vintage, 1965), chap. 6. Also see Howard H. Bell's introduction to Jas. Theo. Holly, *A Vindication of the Capacity of the Negro Race (1857)*, in Howard H. Bell, ed., *Black Separatism and the Caribbean, 1860* (Ann Arbor: University of Michigan Press, 1970).

13. Frederick Douglass, "African Civilization Society," *Douglass' Monthly* (February, 1859), reprinted in Foner, ed., *The Life and Writings of Frederick Douglass*, vol. 2, p. 443.

14. See Martin R. Delany's introduction to William Nesbit, *Four Months in Liberia, or African Colonization Exposed* (Pittsburgh: J. T. Shryock, 1855).

15. Ibid.

16. Benjamin Quarles, *The Negro in the Making of America* (New York: Collier Books, 1969), p. 95.

17. This debate is discussed in Moses, *The Golden Age of Black Nationalism;* Robert C. Dick, *Black Protest: Issues and Tactics* (Westport, Conn.: Greenwood Press, 1974); Pease and Pease, *They Who Would Be Free;* Miller, *Search for a Black Nationality;* Schor, *Henry Highland Garnet;* Earl Ofari, *Let Your Motto Be Resistance: The Life and*

*Thought of Henry Highland Garnet* (Boston: Beacon Press, 1972). The tone of the exchange between Douglass and Garnet is vividly preserved in Foner, ed., *The Life and Writings of Frederick Douglass,* vol 2, pp. 441–45.

18. Staudenraus, *The African Colonization Movement,* pp. 28–35. Schor, *Henry Highland Garnet,* p. 153.

19. Such opinions are consistently expressed in the writings of white colonizationists. See, for example, the enthusiastic speech of Robert J. Breckinridge before the Maryland Colonization Society, 2 February 1838, in *African Repository,* (1838), 141. Also see Rev. F. Freeman, *Africa's Redemption: The Salvation of Our Country* (New York: Fanshaw, 1852), and Rev. Hollis Read, *The Negro Problem Solved, or Africa as She Was, as She Is, and as She Shall Be. Her Curse and Her Cure* (New York: A. A. Constantine, 1864).

20. Schor, *Henry Highland Garnet,* pp. 159–70.

21. Simmons, *Men of Mark,* pp. 1003–1006.

22. Garnet's speech delivered in Boston was published in the *Weekly Anglo-African,* September 19, 1859.

23. See Harris, *Paul Cuffe,* pp. 243–45.

24. See Schor, *Henry Highland Garnet,* p. 150, on the shift of almost every black leader to a migrationist position. Schor sees George T. Downing as perhaps the most notable exception to this pattern.

25. The colonization question on the eve of the Civil War is well discussed in McPherson, *The Negro's Civil War,* which provides an interesting collection of documents. There has, as yet, been little discussion of the reasons for this sudden burst of colonization sentiment among blacks at a time when many leaders, Douglass and Downing, for instance, seemed to become more optimistic about the prospects for eventual integration.

26. Miller, *Search for a Black Nationality,* pp. 198–200. Howard Holman Bell, ed., *Search for a Place: Black Separatism and Africa, 1860* (Ann Arbor: University of Michigan Press, 1971), p. 47.

27. Samuel Williams, *Four Years in Liberia: A Sketch of the Life of the Reverend Samuel Williams* (Philadelphia: King and Baird, 1857), pp. 55–66.

28. Martin R. Delany, "Official Report of the Niger Valley Exploring Party," reprinted in Bell, ed., *Search for a Place,* pp. 47–50.

29. Delany, "Official Report," in Bell, ed., *Search for a Place,* pp. 51, 52, 61, 105. Crummell, "The Relations and Duties of Free Colored Men in America to Africa," in *The Future of Africa,* pp. 269–70.

30. Robert Campbell, "A Pilgrimage to My Motherland: An Account of a Journey among the Egbas and Yorubas of Central Africa in 1859–60," in Bell, ed., *Search for a Place,* pp. 158–59.

31. Crummell, "The Relations and Duties of Free Colored Men," in *The Future of Africa,* p. 215.

32. Ibid., p. 220.

33. Ibid., p. 222.

34. Crummell, "The Duty of a Rising Christian State," in *The Future of Africa,* p. 100. Liberia was frequently referred to as the African America; see, for example, *African Repository* (1854), pp. 147–345.

35. Crummell, "The Relations and Duties of Free Colored Men," in *The Future of Africa,* pp. 245–48.

36. Ibid., p. 250.

37. Delany, "Official Report," in Bell, ed., *Search for a Place,* p. 122.

38. Delany, "Official Report," in Bell, ed., *Search for a Place,* p. 103.

39. Crummell, "The Relations and Duties of Free Colored Men," in *The Future of Africa,* pp. 169, 278.

40. Ibid., p. 278.

41. Ibid., p. 280.

42. An excerpt from Mr. Rambo's journal, in *Spirit of Missions* (January 15, 1861), mentions Mrs. Crummell's health.

43. The movements of the *Mary Caroline Stevens* are reported in *African Repository,* (1861) vol. 37; pp. 117, 129, 134, 147. *List of Passengers Taken on Board of the Mary Caroline Stevens,* recorded April 5, 1861, Baltimore, Maryland. National Archives.

44. Howard Brotz makes this understandable mistake, due to the fact that *African Repository* (January, 1863) reprinted an article from the *Colonization Journal* (date not given), in which it said that Crummell came as commissioner, but the same issue of that journal printed the letter of commission, dated March 8, 1862.

45. *African Repository* (July, 1861), pp. 193, 196.

46. "A Hearty Welcome Home," reported for the *Weekly Anglo-African,* May 4, 1861.

47. "Tract No. 7: Speech of Rev. Alexander Crummell at the Colonization Anniversary, New York, May 9, 1861," Crummell Papers. An expanded version appears in *The Future of Africa.* Crummell's Massachusetts address was published in the annual report of the society and reprinted in the *African Repository* (September, 1861).

48. Crummell, *African Repository* (September, 1861), pp. 272–74.

49. Ibid., p. 275.

50. Ibid., p. 277.

51. Ibid.

52. Ibid., pp. 278–79. See Lydia Maria Child's essay, "The Black Saxons," in the *Weekly Anglo-African,* August 17, 1861. Also see William Cooper Nell, *Colored Patriots of the American Revolution* (Boston, 1855).

53. The tendencies described are to be seen in David Walker's *Appeal.* Numerous instances can be found in Dorothy Porter, ed., *Negro Protest Pamphlets* (New York: Arno, 1969). Harriet Beecher Stowe, whose ideas were well developed throughout the text of *Uncle Tom's Cabin,* is quoted and endorsed by Hollis Read, who holds similar opinions, in *The Negro Problem Solved,* pp. 387–88. In a similar vein, see Freeman, *Africa's Redemption.*

54. *Douglass' Monthly,* May, 1861.

55. *Douglass' Monthly,* July, 1862, p. 674. Also see Crummell's response, p. 695.

56. Crummell's actual words were, "Darkness covers the Land, and gross darkness the people." *The Future of Africa,* p. 220.

57. Notice in *Douglass' Monthly,* May through November, 1862. For Douglass on Delany, see issue of August 1862, p. 695.

58. See letters of Edward Wilmot Blyden to Rev. Joseph Tracy, dated Boston, August 7, 1861; Monrovia, November 1, 1861; New York, May 28, 1862, Records of the Trustees of Donations, Massachusetts Historical Society. Tracy was Secretary of the Trustees of Donations for Education in Liberia.

59. Edward Wilmot Blyden, *The Call of Providence to the Descendants of Africa in America* (New York, 1862); collected in *Liberia's Offering* (New York: John A. Gray, 1862).

60. *Douglass' Monthly,* September, 1862.

61. *African Repository* (May, 1863), pp. 140–42. Henry McNeal Turner in the *Washington Post,* February 2, 1895; reprinted in Edwin S. Redkey, ed., *Respect Black: The Writings and Speeches of Henry McNeal Turner* (New York: Arno, 1971), p. 162.

62. *African Repository* (May, 1863), pp. 140–143.

63. Frederick Douglass, "African Civilization Society," *Douglass' Monthly,* February, 1859, reprinted in Foner, ed., *The Life and Writings of Frederick Douglass,* vol. 2, p. 443. See Benjamin Coates to Crummell, January 13, 1862; February 2, 1862; February 3, 1862; April 14, 1862, Coates Papers.

64. Crummell and J. D. Johnson to Caleb B. Smith, May 1862. Letter in Crummell's hand, both signatures apparently by Crummell, National Archives, RG48, M160, Records of the Secretary of the Interior Relating to the Suppression of the African Slave Trade and Negro Colonization.

65. Lincoln's views on colonization are discussed in John Hope Franklin, *The Emancipation Proclamation* (Garden City, NY: Anchor, 1962), pp. 20, 31–32, 98–99, 107–108, 131–32. Also see Lawanda Cox, *Lincoln and Black Freedom* (Columbia, S.C.: University of South Carolina Press, 1981), pp. 22–23. For one variety of black reaction, see Herbert Aptheker, ed., *A Documentary History of the Negro People in the United States* (New York: The Citadel Press, 1971), vol. 1, pp. 471–76.

66. The committee consisted of Edward M. Thomas, John F. Cook, John T. Costin, Cornelius Clark, and Benjamin McCoy. See *Pacific Appeal,* September 20, 1862, in Carter and Ripley, eds., Black Abolitionist Papers, microfilm 14: 507. *The Collected Works of Abraham Lincoln,* ed. Roy Basler (New Brunswick: Rutgers University Press, 1953), vol. 5; pp. 370–75.

67. Daniel Alexander Payne, "To the Colored People of the United States," reprinted from the *Weekly-Anglo African,* William Wells Brown, *The Black Man* (Boston: Thomas Hamilton, 1863), p. 209.

68. Aptheker, ed., *A Documentary History of the Negro People,* vol. 1, pp. 471–76. Foner, ed., *The Life and Writings of Frederick Douglass,* vol. 3, pp. 24–25.

69. Editorial from the *Colonialization Herald,* reprinted in *African Repository* (May, 1963), p. 142.

## Chapter 8. Liberia College and the Politics of Knowledge

1. See "History of Liberia College," *African Repository* (September, 1865), p. 266. Crummell mentions his stopover in England in the *Colonialization Herald,* February 16, 1863. The letter was reprinted in *Anti-Slavery Reporter,* October 1, 1863.

2. Crummell's appointment was announced in *African Repository* (April, 1862), p. 127, but full duties and titles were not given. A more complete description was given in "History of Liberia College," *African Repository* (August, 1865), p. 230. There have been a number of variant or incomplete descriptions in the works of other scholars, but the Records of the Trustees of Donations contain a memo dated August 8, 1861 specifically listing faculty appointments. In letters to Tracy of November 1861, and 9 November, 1861 Records of the Trustees of Donations, Crummell mentions efforts to build a library collection. Crummell's letter to the trustees of February 16, 1863 explains his failure to collect funds in England. It also mentions that Blyden had examined and admitted "8 young men."

3. "History of Liberia College," *African Repository* (July, 1865), pp. 193–206, and (August, 1865), p. 230

4. Alexander Crummell, "The English Language of Liberia," in *Africa and America*, p. 19. Crummell derived his descriptions of African languages from John Leighton Wilson, *Western Africa: Its History, Condition and Prospects*. He did not identify his edition but cited page 416.

5. Tennyson, "In Memoriam."

6. Wordsworth, "It Is Not to Be Thought Of," l. 11

7. Milton's original line in *Paradise Lost*, I:22, reads, ". . . justify the ways of God to men." Crummell's substitution of the singular form (unlike A. E. Housman's in the same quotation) was probably inadvertent.

8. Crummell, "Progress of the English Language," in *The Future of Africa*, pp. 32–33.

9. Crummell, "Progress of the English Language, in *The Future of Africa*, p. 41.

10. In a footnote (p. 42) to the essay, Crummell acknowledged "the vast debt of obligation Liberian citizens owe Benjamin Coates, Esq., of Philadelphia. . . . The families are not a few, who, as in my own case, besides other books, have likewise their valuable Coates Library."

11. Blyden borrowed this idea from Professor Post of Syrian Protestant College, Beirut, whom he quoted from in his *Christianity, Islam, and the Negro Race* (London, 1887; reprint Edinburgh: Edinburgh University Press, 1967), p. 187. He felt that the singular providential function of Islam was to prepare the way for the acceptance of Christianity; see p. 24.

12. Crummell, "Responsibility of the First Fathers," in *Africa and America*, pp. 153–54.

13. Undated letter signed A. C., gathered with the minutes of the faculty of Liberia College, April 12, 1866, Records of the Trustees of Donations.

14. Crummell to Tracy, February 16, 1863, Records of the Trustees of Donations.

15. As was seen in an earlier chapter, he preached from 1856–1858 without compensation. He reopened discussion of this in 1865, as discussed below. Crummell's salary at Liberia College was eventually raised to one thousand dollars. See Crummell to Tracy, October 15, 1866, Records of the Trustees of Donations.

16. Tracy to Crummell, April 27, 1863, Crummell Papers.

17. Mr. W. E. Bigglestone, archivist at Oberlin, kindly provided me with information on Frances Crummell in his letter of March 13, 1981. Mr. Bigglestone also recalled coming across the name Bessie Crummell in public school records of 1864. This name does not appear on any other document referring to the children of Alexander and Sarah Crummell that I have been able to locate.

18. Crummell to the Trustees of Donations, March 8, 1865, Records of the Trustees of Donations.

19. Minutes for meeting of May 8, 1865, Records of the Trustees of Donations.

20. Roberts to Tracy, July 31, 1865, Records of the Trustees of Donations.

21. *African Times*, January 23, 1866, p. 71, reported that Crummell left Boston on November 22, 1865 in the *Thomas Pope* "with his daughters and aged mother."

22. Crummell to the Trustees of Donations, April 26, 1866, Records of the Trustees of Donations.

23. Ibid.

24. Ibid.

25. Crummell probably referred to John James Blunt (1794–1855), who was Lady Margaret Professor of Divinity at Cambridge during Crummell's years there. Crummell to Tracy, April 26, 1866, Records of the Trustees of Donations.

26. Crummell to Tracy, August 1, 1866, Records of the Trustees of Donations.

27. Minutes of the Faculty of Liberia College, April 12, 1866, Records of the Trustees of Donations.

28. Blyden to Crummell, April 14, 1866, Crummell Papers. Reprinted in Lynch, ed., *Selected Letters of Edward Wilmot Blyden,* p. 72.

29. Crummell to Tracy, 7 May 1866, Records of the Trustees of Donations.

30. Crummell to Tracy, August 24, 1866, Records of the Trustees of Donations.

31. Ibid.

32. Crummell to Tracy, August 1, 1866, Records of the Trustees of Donations.

33. Crummell to Tracy, August 24, 1866, Records of the Trustees of Donations.

34. This was one of those cases in which both employer and employee claimed to have severed the relationship. See interpretations of the rupture in Lynch, *Edward Wilmot Blyden,* also see Blyden to J. C. Braman, March 27, 1884, in Lynch, ed., *Selected Letters of Edward Wilmot Blyden,* p. 322, and Gardner W. Allen, *The Trustees of Donations for Education in Liberia* (Boston: Thomas Todd, 1923), p. 28.

35. Crummell to Tracy, October 10 and October 15, 1866, Records of the Trustees of Donations.

## Chapter 9. Last Battles with the Bishop

1. The catalogue of the Schomburg Collection describes the letter by "Maur or Naur" (the name is illegible) as written "in sharp terms." See the letters to Crummell dated April 20, 1865, Crummell Papers. Indeed some might consider it rude, but "vulgar" or "ruffianly" are perhaps rather strong descriptions of the language. See Crummell's responses of April 20, 1865, Crummell Papers.

2. See A. F. Russell to G. W. Gibson, June 28, 1863, Papers of the Domestic and Foreign Missionary Society, and the undated manuscript in Crummell's handwriting, "An Act to Provide for the Incorporation of Religious Societies so far as the Same Relates to Churches in Connection with the Protestant Episcopal Church Now Existing as a Mission Under the Direction of the Protestant Episcopal Church in the U.S.A.," Crummell Papers, MSC 51. See also Payne to Bishops Burgess and Bedell, March 22, 1865, Papers of the Domestic and Foreign Missionary Society.

3. See Crummell "The Regeneration of Africa," in *Africa and America,* esp. pp. 444–51.

4. It is to be noted that some thirty years later, when speaking on this same theme after his permanent resettlement in the United States, Crummell used the term "indigenous" to denote persons who were actually born in Africa. See his sermons in J.W.E. Bowen, ed., *Africa and the American Negro* (Atlanta: Franklin Publishing Co., 1896).

5. Payne to Crummell, May 13, 1864; Payne to Thompson, April 16, 1863, Crummell Papers.

6. Crummell to Payne, June 7, 1864; Thompson to Crummell, April 16, 1863, Crummell Papers. Payne to Bishops Burgess and Bedell, March 22, 1865, Papers of the Domestic and Foreign Missionary Society.

7. "Report of the African Mission," *Spirit of Missions* (1864), vol. 29.

8. "Report of the African Mission," *Journal of the General Convention of the Protestant Episcopal Church in the United States* (1865), appendix C5, pp. 310–20.

9. A letter from M. H. Freeman, Crummell's colleague at the college, in *African*

*Repository* (March, 1865), p. 88, discusses Crummell's self-sacrifice and the self-sacrifice of clergy of several denominations.

10. Crummell to Denison, 1 June 1867, Papers of the Domestic and Foreign Missionary Society.

11. The bishop admitted that Russell had once been dismissed from Liberian missionary work "chiefly on the acknowledgement in his own letters that he had beaten his wife." Payne found this inexcusable, although not unprovoked. Payne to Bishops Burgess and Bedell, March 22, 1865; also see Russell to Denison, May 30, 1861, Papers of the Domestic and Foreign Missionary Society.

12. Crummell to Denison, 1 August 1866, Papers of the Domestic and Foreign Missionary Society.

13. Payne to Burgess and Bedell, March 22, 1865, Papers of the Domestic and Foreign Missionary Society.

14. Ibid.

15. Ibid.

16. On October 21, 1856, Payne had written to Samuel Denison, Secretary of the Foreign Committee, blaming "the influence of Mr. Stokes" for the rising "feeling against foreigners," Papers of the Domestic and Foreign Missionary Society.

17. Crummell to Denison, 8 March 1865, Papers of the Domestic and Foreign Missionary Society.

18. Crummell, "An Act for the Incorporation of Religious Societies," MSC 51, Crummell Papers.

19. *Spirit of Missions* (1867), vol. 32, pp. 657–60.

20. *Spirit of Missions* (1867), vol. 32, pp. 670–71.

21. Ibid.

22. Crummell to Denison, 5 November 1869, Papers of the Domestic and Foreign Missionary Society. He apparently accepted the current medical opinion that "the fever" was preventable through "active employment." (See Martin R. Delany, *Official Report of the Niger Valley Exploring Party,* sections 6 and 17, for description of the stages of "fever and ague," their causes and their cures.)

23. Ibid.

24. *Spirit of Missions* (1868), vol. 33, pp. 62, 140, 300, 568.

25. Ibid., pp. 699–700.

26. Crummell to Denison, 1 February 1869, Papers of the Domestic and Foreign Missionary Society.

27. *Spirit of Missions* (1868), vol. 33, pp. 843–45.

28. In *Spirit of Missions* (1868), vol. 33, p. 62, Crummell drops a hint concerning Frannie's needs. In *Spirit of Missions* (1869) vol. 34, p. 348, Sidney's needs are mentioned specifically. Crummell speaks of Sidney's success as a Sunday School teacher in his letter to Denison, 1 February 1869, Papers of the Domestic and Foreign Missionary Society.

29. Crummell to Denison, 11 July 1869, Papers of the Domestic and Foreign Missionary Society. Crummell to Coppinger, 15 April 1864, American Colonization Society Papers.

30. Henry H. Morrell to Alexander Crummell, June 7, 1867, Crummell Papers.

31. A. F. Russell, February 24, 1867. Crummell to Denison, 1 June 1867. Both in Papers of the Domestic and Foreign Missionary Society.

32. Crummell to Denison, July 11, 1869, Papers of the Domestic and Foreign Missionary Society. But a letter from the grand jury from Virginia dated Caldwell, August

1869, signed by the foreman and several other citizens of Caldwell, attested that Sarah Crummell "was willing to go before a court and swear to" her husband's innocence of ever having struck her, Papers of the Domestic and Foreign Missionary Society.

33. Crummell to Denison, 10 June 1869; 19 May 1869, and 11 July 1869 Papers of the Domestic and Foreign Missionary Society.

34. Sidney Crummell to Bishop Payne, Papers of the Domestic and Foreign Missionary Society.

35. Letter replying to Sidney Crummell's charges signed by John Stokes, Charles Stokes, and others of Virginia Settlement, and R. R. Johnson, foreman of the grand jury and several citizens of Caldwell, dated Caldwell, August 1869; also see letter to Denison signed by Edward W. Blyden, E. J. Roye, G. W. Gibson, and othes, dated July 1, 1869, Papers of the Domestic and Foreign Missionary Society.

36. Crummell to Denison, July 11, 1869, Papers of the Domestic and Foreign Missionary Society.

37. W. F. Ferguson to Crummell, May 25, 1967, Crummell Papers. Crummell to Denison, 11 July 1869, Papers of the Domestic and Foreign Missionary Society.

38. Crummell to Payne, August 11, 1869, Papers of the Domestic and Foreign Missionary Society.

39. Crummell to Denison, August 11, 1869, Papers of the Domestic and Foreign Missionary Society. Sidney stated his repentance in a letter to Crummell of April 27, 1870, in which he speaks of "sleepless nights" and apologizes to his father, and in a letter to Mr. Francis Briggs, of April 27, 1870, in which he expresses remorse and claims that he loves his father. Crummell copied it and sent it to the Board of Foreign Missions. Both copies in Crummell's hand are gathered with Crummell to Denison, 10 June 1870, Papers of the Domestic and Foreign Missionary Society.

40. Denison to Crummell, March 17, 1870, and Crummell to Denison, 20 November 1870, Papers of the Domestic and Foreign Missionary Society.

## Chapter 10. Missionary Work and Final Disillusionment

1. The letters to Denison and Savage of 19 May 1869 are both in the Papers of the Domestic and Foreign Missionary Society.

2. A document entitled "Crummell Report 1868" is not in Crummell's own handwriting and seems rather to be a proposal for a manual labor school to support himself and Sidney, as well as (presumably) one of his daughters, who would have filled the position of "female cook" at $3.00 per month, Record Group 72–35, Papers of the Domestic and Foreign Missionary Society.

3. D. B. Warner and other petitioners to the Senate and House of Representatives of the Republic of Liberia, printed letter, undated, but probably 1863, Crummell Papers. Crummell and Edward S. Morris, agreement that Crummell will take charge of hulling machines, dated New York, 1865, Crummell Papers. Payne to Denison, March 13 and April 3, 1866, Papers of the Domestic and Foreign Missionary Society. C. C. Hoffman to Edward S. Morris, January 13, 1863, printed letter, Crummell Papers. Also see the exultant letter of Abraham Hanson, U.S. Commercial Agent to Edward S. Morris, February 17, 1863, Crummell papers. There are several other letters from Morris in the Crummell Papers, dated May 2, 1866; July 6, 1866; July 31, 1866; October 4, 1866; October 26, 1866.

4. Crummell to Denison, January 1870, Papers of the Domestic and Foreign Missionary Society.

5. *Spirit of Missions* (1868) vol. 34, p. 349.

6. *Spirit of Missions* (1870), vol. 35, p. 415.

7. Ibid., p. 417.

8. Crummell, *An Address Delivered at the Laying of the Corner Stone of St. Andrew's Church, Buchanan, Bassa County, Liberia, West Africa on the 24th of February, 1870* (Preston: Oakny Caxton House, Fishergate, 1870).

9. *Spirit of Missions* (1871), vol. 36, pp. 77–78.

10. Payne and Crummell are both quoted in *Spirit of Missions* (1871), vol. 36, pp. 77–79. Also see Crummell to Denison, 9 September 1870, Papers of the Domestic and Foreign Missionary Society.

11. "Report of Rev. A. Crummell," *Spirit of Missions* (1871), vol. 36, pp. 485–89.

12. Crummell, "Annual Report," *Spirit of Missions*, p. 235.

13. Crummell, "Our National Mistakes and the Remedy for Them," delivered before the Common Council and the Citizens of Monrovia, Liberia, July 26, 1870; reprinted in *Africa and America*, p. 170

14. Ibid., p. 169. This mild attack should be contrasted with that in Crummell to Secretary of Foreign Committee, Episcopal Board of Missions, January 31, 1872, Papers of the Domestic and Foreign Missionary Society.

15. Crummell to Coppinger, October 30, 1867, American Colonization Society Papers, reel 161, vol. 14, part 1, no. 112.

16. Crummell's footnoting was not painstaking. He identified his source on Carlyle simply as *Latter Day Tracts*. See Crummell, "Our National Mistakes," in *Africa and America*, p. 175.

17. Crummell's views of African labor were relatively advanced, unlike those of Booker T. Washington, for example, who believed that black people learned "the habit of work" under slavery. See his *Black Belt Diamonds: Gems From the Speeches, Addresses and Talks to Students of Booker T. Washington* (New York: Fortune and Scott, 1898), p. 10. Few Afro-American scholars have spoken of the importance of labor in West African cultures. An important early exception was Carter G. Woodson in *The African Background Outlined* (Washington, D.C.: Association for the Study of Negro Life and History, 1936), pp. 171–72.

18. Crummell, in "Our National Mistakes," *Africa and America*, p. 185, cited Matthew Arnold's *Essays in Criticism* as his source. The quotation comes from the essay "The Function of Criticism in the Present Time," in *Essays in Criticism: First Series* (Chicago: University of Chicago press, 1968), p. 14.

19. Crummell, in "Our National Mistakes," *Africa and America*, p. 185, quoted from John Stuart Mill's "A Few Words on Non-Intervention," in Mill, *Dissertations and Discussions*, vol. 3.

20. See Blyden, *Christianity, Islam, and the Negro Race*. Crummell's Episcopal colleague, G. W. Gibson, subscribed to this view as well. See *Spirit of Missions* (April, 1869). Crummell's dissenting view is in *The Future of Africa*, p. 319

21. Reprinted in C. Abayomi Casell, *Liberia: A History of the First African Republic* (New York: Fountainhead Publishers, 1970), p. 273.

22. See Denison to Crummell, March 17, 1856, Papers of the Domestic and Foreign Missionary Society. Also see "Speech of Robert J. Breckinridge Before the Maryland Colonization Society, 2 February 1838," in *African Repository*, vol. 14, p. 141.

23. Crummell to the Secretary, Board of Foreign Missions, 22 August 1871, Papers of the Domestic and Foreign Missionary Society.

24. The letters lead to some confusion as to when exactly the disturbing incident took place. He was highly wrought up in the letter dated August 21, and yet on August 22 he wrote calmly about his trip to Sierra Leone. It may be that in his highly agitated state he wrote the date August 21 on a letter that was actually written a day or two later. Crummell to Foreign Secretary, Episcopal Board of Missions, August 21, 1871, Papers of the Domestic and Foreign Missionary Society.

25. Ibid.

26. Blyden quoted the letter from Freeman in the following: Blyden to Venn, 2 August 1871, in Hollis R. Lynch, ed., *Selected Letters of Edward Wilmot Blyden*, p. 85, also contains Freeman to Blyden.

27. In an exchange of letters between Crummell and a friend in Sierra Leone, Crummell apparently denied having believed the gossip, and the friend confirmed Crummell's denial. See H. to Crummell, March 21, 1872, Crummell Papers.

28. Blyden to Venn, September 16, 1871, and November 15, 1871, in Hollis R. Lynch, ed., *Selected Letters of Edward Wilmot Blyden*, pp. 93–94, 99.

29. Blyden to Venn, September 16, 1871.

30. Crummell to Hare, 3 January 1872, and 16 January 1872, Papers of the Domestic and Foreign Missionary Society.

31. Crummell to [Hare?], 31 January 1872, Papers of the Domestic and Foreign Missionary Society.

32. *African Times,* August 23, 1871; January 23, 1872.

33. Unsigned letter to the editor, *African Times,* March 23, 1872.

34. Crummell to Hare, 29 March 1872, Papers of the Domestic and Foreign Missionary Society. *Spirit of Missions* (1872), vol. 37, p. 486.

35. *Spirit of Missions* (1872), vol. 37, p. 486.

## Chapter 11. Reconsidering the Destiny of Black Americans

1. See Crummell's personal reflections in his sermon on Pslam 48, MSC 39, Crummell Papers. Ferris was clearly uninformed as to both the date of Crummell's return and his activities during 1872. See Ferris, *Crummell: An Apostle of Negro Culture,* p. 6. Josephus to Alexander Crummell, September 20, 1872, Crummell Papers, reported the preference of the vestry for the young white man.

2. John Vaughan Lewis to Bishop William R. Whittingham, 12 June 1872, Maryland Diocesan Archives.

3. Lewis to Whittingham, July 18, 1872, Maryland Diocesan Archives.

4. John Thomas Johnson to Crummell, August 6, 1872; May 2, 1873; May 7, 1873; May 23, 1873, Crummell Papers.

5. Whittingham to Bishop John B. Kerfoot, May 27, 1872; Kerfoot to Whittingham, May 23, 1872; copy of a letter of Thomas Atkinson to Bishop Benjamin B. Smith, July 7, 1873, Maryland Diocesan Archives. Coppinger to Crummell, May 5, 1870 [or 1871], Crummell Papers. The statement opposing the establishment of separate colored churches and diocese is in article II of the "Constitution of the Society for the Promotion of Church Work Among Colored People"; copy in the Maryland Diocesan Archives. Crummell was on the executive committee of the society.

6. "St. Mary's Church, Washington D.C., (Colored People)," Leaflet published by

Alexander Crummell and a committee of churchmen [July 13, 1876]; copy in the Maryland Diocesan Archives.

7. A photograph of the church is to be found in I. Garland Penn, *The United Negro* (Atlanta: D. E. Luther Publishing Co., 1902; reprint, New York: Negro University Press, 1969), between pp. 526 and 527. *Historical Sketches of the Parishes and Missions in the Diocese of Washington,* compiled for the Washington Branch of the Women's Auxiliary to the National Council for the Committee on the Diocese, Washington, D.C., 1928. Also see *Inventory of Church Archives in the District of Columbia,* prepared by District of Columbia Historical Records Survey, Division of Professional and Service Projects, Works Progress Administration, 1940.

8. *Diocesan Convention of Maryland, Parochial Reports* (1873–95) contain annual tabulations of parish statistics.

9. *People's Advocate,* February 28, 1880.

10. Unsigned document, possibly by John W. Cromwell, in Woodson Collection, "Additional Manuscripts, 1807–1935, and Undated," and "Episcopal Church, Letters and Writings," container no. 9, reel no. 6, Manuscript Division, Library of Congress. Much of the writing is by John W. Cromwell, but specific identification is difficult, since the individual documents in these folders are not catalogued and are usually unsigned, untitled, and unpaginated.

11. John Hope Franklin, *Reconstruction After the Civil War* (Chicago: University of Chicago Press, 1961), pp. 211–18.

12. Crummell to Cromwell, 25 April 1877, Crummell Papers.

13. Ibid.

14. Crummell to Bishop William Pinkney, 22 April 1882, Maryland Diocesan Archives. Twentieth anniversary sermon on Mark 4:26–28, undated, MSC 38, Crummell Papers.

15. Unsigned document, Woodson Collection, "Episcopal Church, Letters and Writings."

16. Ibid. Crummell to Bishop William Pinkney, 22 April 1882, Maryland Diocesan Archives.

17. Quoted from the *Vineland Weekly,* February, 1873, in James M. Trotter, *Music and Some Highly Musical People* (Boston: Lee and Shephard, and New York: Charles T. Dillingham, 1881), pp. 250–51.

18. A few items relating to Fleetwood are in the Woodson Collection, and a substantial article appears in Rayford W. Logan and Michael R. Winston, *Dictionary of American Negro Biography* (New York: Norton, 1983).

19. *People's Advocate,* May 24, 1879, and December 18, 1879.

20. Copy of Bishop William Pinkney's letter to the Vestry of St. Mary's Church, Washington, D.C., contained in Bishop Whittingham's official journal, 1879, as continued by Bishop Pinkney, between pp. 136 and 137, Whittingham papers. Also see Crummell to Pinkney, 22 April 1882, Maryland Diocesan Archives.

21. Crummell to Pinkney, 22 April 1882, Maryland Diocesan Archives.

22. Committee of the Vestry to Bishop William Pinkney, March 28, 1882, signed by Francis Upsher, J.W. Cole, Solomon Johnson, Spencer Murray, Jr., Henry Johnson; Crummell to Pinkney, 22 April 1882, Maryland Diocesan Archives.

23. Crummell attributed the article to Henry W. Johnson, calling him "the leader of all the disturbance in the church, since 79." He also accused Johnson of sending an article to the *National Republican,* which was reprinted in the *People's Advocate* March 27, 1880. Crummell to Pinkney, 22 April 1882, Maryland Diocesan Archives.

24. *People's Advocate,* March 27, 1880.

25. Crummell to Pinkney, 22 April 1882, Maryland Diocesan Archives.

26. *People's Advocate,* September 11, 1880; September 25, 1880; October 16, 1880, Maryland Diocesan Archives.

27. *People's Advocate,* October 30, 1880. Crummell to Pinkney, 22 April 1882.

28. Committee of the Vestry to Bishop Pinkney, March 28, 1882, Maryland Diocesan Archives.

29. Crummell to Pinkney, 22 April 1882, Maryland Diocesan Archives.

30. Committee of the Vestry to Bishop Pinkney, March 28, 1882, Maryland Diocesan Archives.

31. The *People's Advocate* made frequent mention of Crummell's absences from the city. Many of his trips were probably for fund-raising, but they would hardly have been overlooked by hostile members of the congregation.

32. Unsigned manuscript, probably by John W. Cromwell, Woodson Collection, "Episcopal Church, Letters and Writings."

33. Crummell, "The Social Principle Among a People," in *The Greatness of Christ;* the earlier version is MSC 49, Crummell Papers.

34. August Meier, in *Negro Thought in America,* has correctly perceived the nationalist precedents for this speech but has overlooked its overwhelmingly Americanist emphasis. See Crummell, *The Greatness of Christ,* pp. 285–311, and David Walker's *Appeal,* p. 81.

35. Crummell, *The Greatness of Christ,* pp.. 290–91.

36. Ibid. p. 295.

37. Ibid. p. 310.

38. See William G. McLoughlin, *The American Evangelicals, 1800–1900* (New York: Harper Torchbooks, 1968), p. 10. Crummell's sermon on Ephesians 4:20, preached October 12, 1890, MSC 111, Crummell Papers.

39. Arminianism is a Protestant heresy, named for its originator Jacobus Arminius (1560–1609), who denied the strictly Calvinist interpretation of predestination and denied the irresistibility of God's grace. Crummell, "The Rejection of Christ," in *The Greatness of Christ,* pp. 116–33.

40. For law of Moses see MSC 338; for extravagance and enthusiasm see MSC 340, Crummell Papers. Both are undated but postdate 1872.

41. Sermon on Luke 9:62, undated, MSC 26, Crummell Papers. Crummell's commitment to the doctrine of works is documented in the two versions of this sermon on Matthew xxiv, "The Second Coming," discussed in an earlier chapter. For the 1854 version, see Carter and Ripley, eds., Black Abolitionist Papers, microfilm 09:0288, reproduced from MSC 234, Crummell Papers. There is also an 1873 version of this sermon, MSC 370, Crummell Papers.

42. Crummell, "The Solution of Problems: The Duty and Destiny of Man," *A.M.E. Church Review* (April, 1898).

43. Crummell, "The Agencies to Saintly Sanctification," May 1, 1881, MSC 8, Crummell Papers, reprinted in *The Greatness of Christ.*

44. Crummell, "Affluence and Receptivity," in *The Greatness of Christ,* p. 171.

45. Crummell, undated sermon on Luke 9:62, MSC 26, Crummell Papers.

46. Crummell, "The Greatness of Christ," in *The Greatness of Christ,* p. 3.

47. Ibid., pp. 11–12.

48. See, for example, comparisons between his theory of history and the theories of William Wells Brown and Samuel Ringgold Ward, discussed in chap. 2.

49. *The Future of Africa,* p. 104. Three passages are quoted from Guizot, *General History of Civilization,* but a full reference to the edition is not provided. Also see *Africa and America,* p. 447, and *The Greatness of Christ,* p. 14.

50. Douglas Johnson, *Guizot: Aspects of French History, 1787–1874* (London, 1963).

51. *African Repository* (September, 1867), pp. 257–63. Crummell, "The Destined Superiority of the Negro," in *The Greatness of Christ,* pp. 332–52.

52. Crummell, "The Lamb of God," in *The Greatness of Christ,* pp. 61–62.

53. Crummell, "Address at the Anniversary Meeting of the Massachusetts Colonization Society," *African Repository* (September, 1861), pp. 272–74. An even stronger statement on the same theme occurs in an address, circa 1888, inspired by the story of "Eddie the Cripple," in which Crummell says, "The case of the freedmen of the South is the case of Eddie the Cripple on a large scale." MSC 315, Crummell Papers.

54. Crummell, MSC 260, Crummell Papers.

55. Crummell to Francis J. Grimké, 30 June 1886, reprinted in Woodson, ed., *The Works of Francis J. Grimké,* p. 5.

56. Crummell, "The Need of New Ideas and New Aims for a New Era," in *Africa and America,* p. 32.

57. The departure from the catastrophic view of slavery represented in Crummell's writings is to be observed in Charles S. Johnson, *Shadow of the Plantation* (Chicago: University of Chicago Press, 1934) and Hortense Powdermaker, *After Freedom: A Cultural Study of the Deep South* (New York: Viking, 1939; reprint Atheneum, 1968). More recent studies which have benefited from the pioneering work of Johnson and Powdermaker are Herbert G. Gutman, *The Black Family in Slavery and Freedom* (New York: Vintage, 1976) and Robert William Fogel and Stanley L. Engerman, *Time on the Cross* (Boston: Little, Brown, 1974). While the work of the aforementioned scholars has done much to correct the excessively catastrophic view of black family life in the nineteenth century, Fogel, Engerman, and Gutman have perhaps gone to another extreme, with their claim that family life under slavery was characteristically healthy and wholesome.

58. E. M. Edson, *The Girl's Friendly Society of America* (Lowell, Mass.: St. Anne's Rectory, 1880); letter to the Lady Associates of the Society, printed as a leaflet, May 1880. The letter reports some of Crummell's opinions concerning the needs of young black women. For Crummell on bashfulness and on the "instinct to chastity," see *Africa and America,* pp. 32, 64, 87.

59. Crummell, "The Black Woman of the South: Her Neglects and Her Needs" (1882), in *The Future of Africa.*

60. Such views are well represented in *The Woman's Era,* a magazine published by Josephine St. Pierre Ruffin, which served for a short while as the official publication of the National Federation of Afro-American Women. There is some discussion of this periodical in Moses, *The Golden Age of Black Nationalism,* chap. 5.

61. See *A History of the Club Movement Among the Colored Women of The United States of America* (The National Association of Colored Women, 1902).

62. Crummell, "Marriage," in *The Greatness of Christ,* p. 47.

63. The stress laid on the inculcation of bourgeois morality can be seen in Mrs. N. F. Mossell, *The Work of the Afro-American Woman* (Philadelphia, 1894) and Mary Church Terrell, "Club Work of Colored Women," *Southern Workman* (August, 1901), pp. 435–38. Also see the essays in Penn, *The United Negro,* pp. 458–83. An additional series of essays, stressing domestic feminism, is in D. W. Culp, ed., *Twentieth Century Negro Literature,* pp. 167–86.

64. Crummell, sermon on Matthew xxiv, MSC 370, Crummell Papers.

65. Gayraud S. Wilmore, *Black Religion and Black Radicalism* (Garden City, New York: Doubleday, 1973), pp. 156–59. Wilmore is correct and might well have documented his contention regarding self-love by reference to MSC 260, discussed above in connection with abstinence. In "The Motives to Discipleship," *The Greatness of Christ,* p. 138, Crummell speaks of the virtue of self-love and cites the authority of Bishop Joseph Butler in support of his view.

## Chapter 12. A Man of Mark

1. See the descriptions in Simmons, *Men of Mark,* pp. 530–35, and Cromwell, *The Negro in American History,* pp. 130–38.

2. *In Memoriam of the Late Rev. Alex Crummell, D.D. of Washington, D.C. An Address Delivered before the American Negro Historical Society of Philadelphia, by Rev. Henry L. Phillips, November 1898, With an Introductory Address by Rev. Matthew Anderson, Pastor of the Berean Presbyterian Church* (Philadelphia: The Coleman Printery, 1899), p. 6.

3. M. C. Bolivar, *Philadelphia Tribune,* September 17, 1898. Copy in Cromwell scrapbook in the John W. Cromwell Papers in Dr. Adelaide Cromwell's possession. The evening that Bolivar recollects must have been before 1891, the year in which Williams died.

4. Brown, *The Rising Son,* p. 456.

5. Henry N. Philips, *In Memoriam,* p. 15.

6. Certificate for honorary Doctor of Laws degree from Liberia College is in Crummell Papers. Crummell's attitude towards the D.D. from Lincoln University is mentioned in Calbraith B. Perry to William Whittingham [1874], Whittingham Papers. Brown, *The Rising Son,* p. 456, reports that Avery College conferred an honorary D.D. on Crummell.

7. Certificate of Death, Health Department, City of Brooklyn, received at the Registrar's Office, August 4, 1878.

8. William Whittingham's journal, 1874, p. 231, Whittingham Papers.

9. Crummell, sermon on Genesis 2:18, delivered 30 October, 1892, Crummell Papers, MSC 259. His opinion on divorce was mentioned in the *People's Advocate,* January 29, 1881: "Dr. Crummell, in his sermon on Divorce last Sunday, said that the right which a man has to divorce his wife for adultery is not a reciprocal one, but she has instead the right of separation."

10. Corinthians 7:9. Crummell quoted the following in a sermon on marriage, MSC 259, Crummell Papers: "To avoid fornication, let every man have his own wife."

11. William A. Elston to Crummell, June 18, 1873, Crummell Papers.

12. See Certificate of Marriage, September 23, 1880, Letters, C.4, Bruce Papers. Simmons, *Men of Mark,* p. 535. Also see *People's Advocate,* October 16, 1880. Some years later, in a bitter attack on Crummell, T. Thomas Fortune asserted that Jennie Crummell was a "mulatto" woman, claiming that "it is very generally the case that those black men who clamor most loudly and persistently for the purity of the Negro blood have taken to themselves mulatto wives." *New York Sun,* May 2, 1897, sec. 3, p. 3. Crummell angrily denied to Bruce that his wife was a mulatto, in Crummell to Bruce, December 15, Bruce Papers.

13. Crummell to Grimké, June 30, 1886, in Woodson, ed., *The Works of Francis J. Grimké*, pp. 4–6. Crummell to Bruce, 17 January 1894, Bruce Papers.

14. Crummell did not call attention to this allusion to Milton's sonnet, "When I consider how my light is spent," but allusions to Milton were frequent in his writings.

15. Crummell describes his vision problems in a letter to George Frazier Miller, 19 June 1894, Bruce Papers. Also see Crummell to Bruce, 1 June 1897, Bruce Papers, and Crummell to Grimké, June 30, 1866, in Woodson, ed., *The Works of Francis J. Grimké*, vol. 4, pp. 4, 5.

16. See Crummell, "Africa and Her Peoples," Crummell Papers, MSC 23.

17. As mentioned in chapter 10, I have unfortunately not been able to discover any sketches by Crummell in the papers.

18. See Hanes Walton, Jr., et al., "Henry Highland Garnet Revisited," *Journal of Negro History* (Winter, 1983), pp. 80–92. Crummell to Bruce, 21 January 1898, Crummell Papers.

19. Cromwell, *The Negro in American History,* p. 129, and *History of the Bethel Literary and Historical Association* (Washington, D.C.: H. L. Pendleton, 1896), p. 9.

20. George B. Tindall, "The Liberian Exodus of 1878," *South Carolina Historical Magazine,* 3:3 (July, 1952), pp. 133–45. "Dinner to Dr. Blyden," *Christian Recorder* (March 29, 1883).

21. Crummell, preface to *Africa and America,* p. iv.

22. Crummell's withered arm analogy is in his "Address at the Anniversary Meeting of the Massachusetts Colonization Society," in Crummell and Blyden, *Liberia, The Land of Promise.* Douglass, "Why is the Negro Lynched?" in Foner, ed., *The Life and Writings of Frederick Douglass,* vol. 4, p. 518.

23. Frederick Douglass, *The Nation's Problem: A Speech Delivered at the Bethel Literary Society in Washington, D.C., April 16, 1889,* in Howard Brotz, ed., *Negro Social and Political Thought, 1850–1925: Representative Texts* (New York: Basic Books, 1966), pp. 311–28.

24. Frederick Douglass, *The Nation's Problem,* in Brotz, ed., *Negro Social and Political Thought,* p. 316.

25. Douglass was criticized in the *Indianapolis Freeman,* September 15, 1888, for his unswerving loyalty to the Republicans. Crummell, too, was a staunch Republican, describing his principles as "all Republican so far as party, is concerned." See Crummell to Bruce, Feruary 28, 1896, Bruce Papers. For collective response, see "The Disipline of Freedom," Crummell Papers, MSC 16. The young scholar was W. E. B. Du Bois in *The Souls of Black Folk,* p. 41.

26. Crummell's preachments on self-reliance are in "The Discipline of Freedom," Crummell Papers, MSC 16.

27. Crummell's political ideology and continuing suspicion of Jacksonian Democracy are evident in his address "The Discipline of Freedom," Crummell Papers, MSC 16. His commitment to the Republican party is declared in Crummell to Bruce, February 28, 1896, Bruce Papers.

28. Crummell preached "The Assassination of President Garfield" on July 10, 1881, one week after the shooting. Garfield did not die until September 19. The sermon was printed without substantial revision in *The Greatness of Christ,* where Crummell speaks of "this attempted assassination" (p. 319) as being the natural result of the problems in the American political system, which undermined respect for orderly rule and authority.

29. Crummell, "The Assassination of President Garfield," in *The Greatness of Christ,* p. 325.

30. Ibid., p. 328.

31. Crummell, "Address," MSC 315, Crummell Papers. The document is untitled and undated but was probably in the late 1880s. The list of manuscripts at the Schomburg Center lists the title of this sermon as "Negro as American Citizen Must Make Contributions to Its Life and Character." The source of this title is unknown.

32. Ibid.

33. Ibid.

34. Ibid.

35. Crummell quotes from Carlyle's *Sartor Resartus* in "The Dignity of Labor and Its Value to a New People," in *Africa and America*, pp. 392–94. Timothy Thomas Fortune, *Black and White: Land, Labor and Politics in the South* (New York, 1884).

36. Booker T. Washington, in Matthews, ed., *Black Belt Diamonds*, p. 32.

37. Crummell, "Address," MSC 315 ["Negro as American Citizen"], Crummell Papers.

38. Crummell, "The Dignity of Labour and Its Value to a New People," in *Africa and America*, pp. 379–404, was originally given as an address at the "Working Men's Club" in Philadelphia. The allusion to *Othello,* was probably intended.

39. I have made use of the most current and sophisticated finding aids to Congressional documents and have been unable to locate, either in the *Congressional Record* or in any other publication, any materials detailing the debates surrounding the "Bounty Bill." Crummell's testimony is printed in the *People's Advocate,* February 14, 1880. See also O. Ferris, Auditor of the Treasury Dept. on House Bill No. 878, 47th Congress, 1st session. 47th Congress, 1st session, H.R. 608 is substantially the same as H.R. 2571, 46th Congress. Also see *House Journal,* 2nd session, 46th Congress, p. 270. The amount was $478,000 at the time discussions began but increased rapidly to $504,435. At the time of Crummell's testimony, he and his associates reported to the *People's Advocate* that the amount was $510,000, but the same journal announced on February 14, 1880, that "Secretary Sherman has reported that only $200,000 of unclaimed bounty is available."

40. *People's Advocate,* February 14, 1880.

41. *People's Advocate,* February 21, 1880.

42. *People's Advocate,* February 28, 1880.

43. *People's Advocate,* February 14, 1880.

44. Meier asserts another view in *Negro Thought in America,* p. 222, but does not document it.

45. Crummell, "Civilization, the Primal Need of the Race," *American Negro Academy Occasional Papers,* no. 3 (Washington, D.C.: The American Negro Academy, 1898).

46. For a discussion of stereotyping see George Frederickson, *The Black Image in the White Mind* (New York: Harper and Row, 1971). Crummell, "Common Sense in Common Schooling," in *Africa and America,* pp. 333, 367.

47. Crummell, "The Need of New Ideas and New Aims," in *Africa and America,* p. 23, and "Eulogium on Henry Highland Garnet," in *Africa and America,* p. 284. Benjamin Brawley commented on Crummell's appraisal of black aestheticism in his *The Negro Genius,* pp. 101–105.

48. Crummell, "Right Mindedness," in *Africa and America,* pp. 355–78.

49. See Crummell, *A Thanksgiving Sermon* (Washington, D.C., 1895), pp. 10–11; Cromwell's typescript on Nat Turner with notes in Crummell's handwriting, Crummell Papers; and Crummell, "Right Mindedness" in *Africa and America,* p. 367.

50. Crummell, "Right Mindedness," in *Africa and America*, pp. 366–67.

51. See "The Relations and Duties of Free Colored Men in America to Africa," in *The Future of Africa*, p. 107. Cf. p. 220.

52. Crummell, "A Defence of the Negro Race," in *Africa and America*, p. 87.

53. Crummell, "The Need of New Ideas and New Aims," in *Africa and America*, p. 32. The title is cited differently on the title page. Crummell's references to Tacitus should be compared to those in Blyden, *Christianity, Islam, and the Negro Race*, p. 69.

54. Crummell, "A Defence of the Negro Race," p. 88. Cf.. Crummell's similar opinion in *Future of Africa*, pp. 316–20.

55. Ibid, p. 94.

56. "Here is a nation, for a population that runs up its numbers to six or seven millions is not merely a people—it is a nation." Crummell, "The Social Principle Among a People," in *The Greatness of Christ*, p. 290, and Crummell expressed the same opinion in "A Defence of the Negro Race," in *Africa and America*, p. 89.

57. Crummell, "The Race Problem in America," in *Africa and America*, pp. 37–57.

58. Ibid., p. 46.

59. Ibid., pp. 52, 54.

60. See Martin Luther King, *Stride Toward Freedom* (New York: Harper and Row, 1958), and Malcolm X, *The End of White World Supremacy: Four Speeches by Malcolm X*, edited with an introduction by Imam Benjamin Karim (New York: Seaver Books, 1971).

## Chapter 13. Pastor Emeritus

1. Unsigned manuscript, probably by John W. Cromwell, Woodson Collection.

2. Crummell, *Statement to the Congregation of St. Luke's Church, Washington, D.C., Sunday morning September 17th, 1893, by Alexander Crummell Rector*, copy in Bruce Papers. A handwritten note on page three of the flyer identifies the person in question as "J. W. Cole Clerk in Pension Office. Escapade with a female named Lena Amse [?] was cowhided and both parties arrested." See Crummell's accusation in Crummell to Pinkney, 22 April 1882, p. 22, Maryland Diocesan Archives.

3. Crummell to [George] Frazier Miller, 18 September 1894, Crummell Papers.

4. Mrs. Anna J. Cooper, "Address in Behalf of the Women of St. Luke's Church," appended to Crummell, *Shades and Lights*, p. 29.

5. Crummell to [George] Frazier Miller, 13 March, 1895. Bruce Papers.

6. Crummell to George Frazier Miller, 24 January 1895, and 13 March 1895, Bruce Papers.

7. His friend John E. Bruce urged him to take a more active part in politics, but Crummell responded that, while he entertained strong political opinions, he did not intend to change his long-standing policy. He had "never, in any way, taken part *publicly* in any political action." Crummell to Bruce, February 1896, Bruce Papers. Crummell to George Frazier Miller, 13 March 1895, Bruce Papers.

8. Francis J. Grimké, "Rev. Alexander Crummell," in Woodson, ed., *The Works of Francis J. Grimké*, pp. 28–34.

9. Crummell to G. Frazier Miller, 18 September 1894, Bruce Papers.

10. Crummell to Bishop William Pinkney, April 22, 1882, Maryland Diocesan Archives.

11. Frederic Douglass, *The Lesson of the Hour* (1894), in Foner, *The Life and Writings of Frederick Douglass,* vol. 4, p. 507. Douglass was seventy-seven when he made the statement. There had been some friction between Douglass and Truth long ago, because she had publicly called his religiosity into question.

12. Crummell wrote to John E. Bruce that he had delivered baccalaureate sermons "at the commencements of colleges; viz, the Normal Colleges at Petersburgh and Normal, in Huntsville Ala., and at Wilberforce University." Crummell to Bruce, 4 November 1895, Bruce Papers. The list of black institutions in A. M. Kletzing and W. H. Crogman, *Progress of a Race* (Atlanta: J. L. Nichols & Co., 1897), includes Central Alabama Academy in Huntsville and State Normal and Industrial School in Normal, Alabama. The sermon was printed in the *A.M.E. Review* of April, 1896 and reprinted in pamphlet form under the title, "The Solution of Problems: The Duty and Destiny of Man." Theodore Roosevelt, *The Strenuous Life: Essays and Addresses* (New York: Century, 1902).

13. Du Bois, *The Souls of Black Folk,* p. 216

14. For a fascinating interpretation of the psychological motivations behind Du Bois's autobiographical writings, see Allison Davis, *Leadership, Love, and Aggression* (New York: Harcourt, Brace, Jovanovich, 1983), chap. 2.

15. As August Meier has astutely observed, Washington nevertheless had strong support among the educated classes of black Americans. See his chapter on "Booker T. Washington and the Talented Tenth," in *Negro Thought in America.*

16. *People's Advocate,* August 30, 1879.

17. George Washington Forbes, "Alexander Crummell," typescript, Forbes Papers.

18. T. G. Steward, "Washington and Crummell," *Colored American,* November 19, 1898.

19. Du Bois, *The Souls of Black Folk,* p. 43.

20. Washington in Matthews, ed., *Black Belt Diamonds,* pp. 8, 9, 10.

21. Crummell, "The Dignity of Labour and Its Value to a New People," in *Africa and America,* p. 381.

22. Crummell was obviously proud of this pithy observation and made it in at least two different articles: "The Primal Need of the Negro Race," *The Independent,* August 19, 1897, pp. 1–2, 14, and "The Attitude of the American Mind Toward the Negro Intellect," *American Negro Academy Occasional Papers,* no. 3 (Washington, D.C.: The American Negro Academy, 1898), p. 15. The turn of phrase was associated with Crummell in the minds of his contemporaries; see Kletzing and Crogman, *Progress of a Race,* p. 161. Also see Nathaniel R. Richardson, *Liberia's Past and Present* (New York: Diplomatic Press and Publishing Company, 1959), pp. 77–78.

23. Crummell, "Defence of the Negro Race," in *Africa and America,* pp. 94–95. Crummell, "The Attitude of the American Mind Toward and Negro Intellect," p. 9.

24. Criticism of the moral, economic, and intellectual values of middle-class blacks is a common thread running through Afro-American thought. People of great ideological dissimilarity have often agreed on the assumed frivolity of much black educational experience. See, for example, Carter G. Woodson, *The Miseducation of the Negro* (Washington: Association for the Study of Afro-American Life and History, 1933). E. Franklin Frazier, "Education of the Black Bourgeoisie," in his *Black Bourgeoisie: The Rise of a New Middle Class in the United States* (New York: Free Press, 1957), does not acknowledge his ideas' affinity to the earlier observations of Washington or Woodson.

25. Louis R. Harlan, *Booker T. Washington: The Making of a Black Leader, 1856–1901* (New York: Oxford University Press, 1972), pp. 96–98. Booker T. Washington, *Up From Slavery,* reprinted in Louis R. Harlan, *The Booker T. Washington Papers* (Urbana: Illinois University Press, 1972–87), vol. 1, p. 260.

26. A copy of the letter is printed in John Hope Franklin, *George W. Williams: A Biography* (Chicago: University of Chicago Press, 1985), appendix 1. Leopold came to be viewed as one of the great villains of African history by the end of the century. See Mark Twain, *King Leopold's Soliloquy* (Boston: P. R. Warren, 1905).

27. See Blyden, *Christianity, Islam, and the Negro Race,* p. 24. Blyden, in a footnote to the work, cited Bishop Samuel Crowther, the Nigerian Methodist, for whom Crummell had consummate respect, as one of the notable Christians who shared the view that Islam was sympathetic to the Christian message and its missionaries. Blyden's invitation to the Jews is in his pamphlet *The Jewish Question* (Liverpool, 1898).

28. Bowen, ed., *Africa and the American Negro,* pp. 119–24.

29. Turner to William Coppinger, July 18, 1866, American Colonization Society Papers; reprinted in Redkey, ed., *Respect Black,* p. 13. Henry McNeal Turner, "The Question of Race," *Baltimore American,* May 12, 1884; reprinted in Redkey, ed., *Respect Black,* p. 73.

30. Crummell to Bruce, 26 November 1895, Bruce Papers (also in Crummell Papers, microfilm inside).

31. *Christian Recorder,* March 29, 1883.

32. Crummell to Bruce, 26 November 1895, Bruce Papers.

33. Turner did not specify in this essay which Supreme Court decision he referred to, but see his pamphlet *The Barbarous Decision of the Supreme Court* (Atlanta, 1896), reprinted in Redkey, ed., *Respect Black,* pp. 133–34. Also see Rayford W. Logan, *The Betrayal of the Negro: From Rutherford B. Hayes to Woodrow Wilson* (New York: Collier, 1965), chap. 6, "The Supreme Court and the Negro."

34. Crummell to Bruce, 4 November 1895, Bruce Papers.

35. Blyden's opinions on Crummell's reasons for leaving Liberia were often recorded in his letters. See Lynch, ed., *Selected Letters of Edward Wilmot Blyden,* pp. 196, 286, 290, 322, 340. Blyden admits he wrote speeches for Russell in a letter to Coppinger, 19 September 1883, American Colonization Society Papers.

36. Francis J. Grimké to Booker T. Washington, March 17, 1889, in Harlan, ed., *The Booker T. Washington Papers,* vol. 2, pp. 516–17.

## Chapter 14. Tuskegee Under Fire

1. Crummell to Bruce, 26 November 1895; 30 October 1896; 5 December 1896; and Bruce to Crummell, November 6, 1897, Bruce Papers.

2. Culp, *Twentieth Century Negro Literature,* opp. p. 291.

3. See John W. Cromwell's handwritten manuscript, "History of the American Negro Academy," p. 1, cited hereafter as Cromwell, *ANA History.* This document is bound together with Edward J. Beckham, *The Organization of the Academy for the Promotion of Intellectual Enterprise Among American Negroes,* cited hereafter as Beckham, "Organization of the Academy." They are in the possession of Cromwell's granddaughter, Dr. Adelaide Cromwell of the Afro-American Studies Program, Boston University, which also holds a microfilm of same. In the spring of 1986, Dr. Cromwell collegially allowed me to photocopy the entire document, and it has been deposited in

the Rockefeller Library of Brown University. John Wesley Cromwell, "The American Negro Academy," in the *African Times and Orient Review* (Nov.–Dec., 1913), pp. 243–44; Moss, *The American Negro Academy: Voice of the Talented Tenth.*

4. William H. Crogman to Francis J. Grimké, September 24, 1894, reprinted in Woodson, ed., *The Works of Francis J. Grimké,* vol. 4, pp. 34–35.

5. Adelaide Cromwell-Gulliver, "Minutes of the Negro American Society," *Journal of Negro History* vol. 44, no. 1, (Winter 1979), pp. 59–69. Moss, *The American Negro Academy: Voice of the Talented Tenth,* pp. 17–21.

6. John W. Cromwell, *History of the Bethel Literary and Historical Association, Being a Paper Read Before the Association on Founder's Day, February 24, 1896* (Washington, D.C.: H. L. Pendleton, 1896).

7. *Southern Workman,* January 1894, p. 5.

8. For another view, see Meier, *Negro Thought in America,* pp. 42–43.

9. Crummell, "Eulogium on the Life and Character of Thomas Sipkins Sidney, Delivered Before the Phoenixonian Society of the City of New York, July 4th, 1840," and "The Necessities and Advantages of Education Considered in Relation to Colored Men," MSC 392 and MSC 45, Crummell Papers.

10. Beckham, "Organization of the Academy," p. 9, Cromwell Papers.

11. Du Bois, "The Conservation of Races," *American Negro Academy Occasional Papers,* no. 2.

12. Beckham, "Organization of the Academy," p. 19, Cromwell Papers.

13. W.E.B. Du Bois, *The Philadelphia Negro* (Philadelphia, 1899; reprint New York: Schocken, 1967), pp. 385–97. Anthony Appiah, "The Uncomplemented Argument: Du Bois and the Illusion of Race," in *Race, Writing, and Difference,* ed., Henry Louis Gates, Jr. (Chicago: University of Chicago Press, 1986), pp. 21–37.

14. See Moss, *The American Negro Academy: Voice of the Talented Tenth,* pp. 54–55. T. Thomas Fortune, *New York Sun,* May 16, 1897, sec. 3, p. 3.

15. *Spirit of Missions* (1897), vol. 62, pp. 237–38.

16. *The Independent,* August 19, 1897, pp. 1, 2, 14; January 1898, pp. 105–106; and February 1898, pp. 145–46. These and related commentary are printed in Harlan, ed., *The Booker T. Washington Papers,* vol. 4, pp. 321–22, 353, and 366–74.

17. Booker T. Washington tells the story of the boy in the one-room cabin studying French in *Up From Slavery;* reprinted in Harlan, ed., *The Booker T. Washington Papers,* vol. 1, p. 280. Matthews, ed., *Black Belt Diamonds,* p. 25. The anecdote of the Liberian reading Cicero is cited in the entry for Oct. 20, 1897, *Indianapolis in the "Gay Nineties": High School Diaries of Claude G. Bowers,* ed. Holman Hamilton and Gayle Thornbrough (Indianapolis, 1964), p. 99; reprinted in Harlan, ed., *The Booker T. Washington Papers,* vol. 4, p. 331.

18. Crummell to Bruce, 1 June 1897, gives the departure date as May 8, 1897. Cf. Crummell to Cromwell, 8 August 1897, Cromwell Papers.

19. In *Oak and Ivy: A Biography of Paul Laurence Dunbar* (New York: Doubleday, 1971), p. 65, Addison Gayle says that Dunbar encountered Crummell in the British Museum, where Crummell was strolling with Hallie Q. Brown. According to Gayle, Crummell invited Dunbar to move into his quarters. Crummell wrote to Cromwell on 15 June 1897 that he had not seen Brown at the time that Dunbar moved into his rooming house, where Dunbar apparently occupied quarters of his own. Moss, *The American Negro Academy: Voice of the Talented Tenth,* p. 54. Owen C. Mathurin, *Henry Sylvester Williams and the Origins of the Pan-African Movement, 1869–1911* (Westport, Conn.: Greenwood Press, 1976).

20. Crummell to Cromwell, 15 June 1897, Bruce Papers.

21. Crummell to Bruce, 4 December 1897, Bruce Papers. These matters are easily traced through Crummell's letters to Bruce of 1 June 1897; August 1897; 27 September 1897; 21 January 1898; and Crummell to Cromwell, 5 October 1897, Crummell Papers.

22. The well-known definition of civilization as "the multiplication of our wants and the means of supplying them" had appeared in some American editions of Guizot's *History;* Crummell was clearly influenced by it in this address, as well as in his essay, "Our National Mistakes, and the Remedy for Them," *Africa and America,* pp. 175–76. Also see Booker T. Washington's critique of black education in Matthews, ed., *Black Belt Diamonds,* pp. 10–11.

23. William H. Ferris, *The African Abroad, or His Evolution in Western Civilization: Tracing His Development Under Caucasian Milieu* (New Haven: Tuttle, Morehouse and Taylor, 1913), vol 1., pp. 303, 304.

24. See William S. Scarborough, *The Educated Negro and His Mission, The American Negro Academy Occasional Papers,* no. 8 (Washington, D.C.: The American Negro Academy, 1903), p. 5.

25. T. G. Steward, "Washington and Crummell," *Colored American,* November 19, 1898. See "Address of Rev. Alexander Crummell at the Anniversary Meeting of the Massachusetts Colonization Society," May 29, 1861, published in the society's annual report; reprinted in Crummell and Blyden, *Liberia: Land of Promise.*

26. Document on Pastor's Relief Association, unsigned document, Woodson Collection.

27. Francis J. Grimké, "Rev. Alexander Crummell," in Woodson, ed., *The Works of Francis J. Grimké,* vol. 1, p. 31.

28. Crummell to Bruce, March 22, 1898, Bruce Papers; Matthew Anderson, *Introductory Address to Henry L. Phillips, in Memoriam of the Late Rev. Alex. Crummell, D.D.: An Address Delivered Before the American Negro Historical Society.* (Philadelphia: The Coleman Printery, 1898), p. 7.

29. Anderson, *Introductory Address* p, 7.

30. Phillips, *In Memoriam.*

31. Cromwell, *The Negro in American History,* p. 138, mentions the letter to Dunbar. Unfortunately, neither the Crummell nor the Dunbar Papers in the Schomburg Collection contains this letter. In a telephone interview with the staff of the Ohio State Historical Society I was informed that the catalogue of the Dunbar Papers in their possession contains no reference to this letter.

32. Walter B. Hayson to John Wesley Cromwell, September 17, 1898. *Washington Bee,* November 5, 1898.

33. Washington *Bee,* September 17, 1898; *Colored American,* September 17, 1898.

34. *People's Advocate,* October 4, 1879.

35. Unsigned manuscript, p. 20, Woodson Collection.

36. Crummell to Frazier Miller, 30 June 1898, Bruce Papers (also in Crummell Papers, microfilm). Crummell, "Character: The Great Thing," in Bragg, *History of the Afro-American Group of the Episcopal Church,* p. 264. Crummell, "Civilization, The Primal Need of the Race," *American Negro Academy Occasional Papers,* no. 3, p. 4.

## Chapter 15. Crummell's Universality and Significance

1. The following three books were recommended to schoolboys in Crummell's essay "The English Language in Liberia," reprinted in *The Future of Africa:* William E. Channing, "Self Culture" [in *Works of William Ellery Channing* (Boston: James Mun-

roe & Co., 1841), vol. 2, pp. 347–411]; Henry Foster Burder, *Mental Discipline* [(New York: Johnathan Leavitt, Boston: Crocker & Brewster, 1830)]; and Francis Wayland, *The Elements of Moral Science* [originally published in 1837, new edition with introduction by Joseph L. Blau (Cambridge: Harvard/Belknap, 1963)].

2. Alison, *Essays on the Nature and Principles of Taste.*

3. Robert C. Toll, in *Blacking Up: The Minstrel Show in Nineteenth Century America* (New York: Oxford University Press, 1974), says that "Minstrelsy swept the nation in the mid 1840's" and makes the astute observation that racism in entertainment accompanied "the emergence of a common man's culture."

4. See Williams' letter in Woodson, ed., *The Mind of the Negro.*

5. Crummell, *Shades and Lights,* pp. 20–21.

6. Luckson Ejofodomi, "The Missionary Career of Alexander Crummell in Liberia: 1853–1873," dissertation, Boston University, 1974, p. 192.

7. Crummell, MSC 23, "Africa and Her People," Crummell Papers.

8. Crummell's attitudes with respect to ritual are in his sermon on Galatians, 6:13, MSC 66, Crummell Papers.

9. Ferris, *Crummell, An Apostle,* p. 8. St. Augustine is mentioned in the *People's Advocate,* June 10, 1876.

10. Kelly Miller, *Out of the House of Bondage* (New York: Neale Publishing Company, 1914), pp. 204–206.

11. Albert S. Foley, S.J., *Bishop Healy: Beloved Outcast* (New York: Farrar, Straus and Young, 1954). Randall Burkett has shown that of the twenty-five black priests ordained in the Protestant Episcopal Church between 1802 and 1865, seventeen were sent out to Africa or the West Indies. Randall K. Burkett, "Afro-American Episcopal Clergyman to 1865," unpublished typescript, compiled August 1980.

12. Crummell to [George] Frazier Miller, in 18 September 1894, Crummell Papers.

13. John Greenleaf Whittier to Charlotte Forten [1862] in John B. Pickard, ed., *The Letters of John Greenleaf Whittier* (Cambridge: Harvard University Press, 1975), vol. 3, p. 35.

14. Bell I. Wiley, *Slaves No More* (Lexington: University Press of Kentucky, 1980), p. 162.

15. Crummell mentions Job in "The Solution of Problems: The Duty and Destiny of Man," n.p. n.d. Copy in Crummell Papers, New York Public Library, Schomberg Collection. Originally printed in *AME Church Review,* April 1896.

16. Crummell, "The Necessities and Advantages of Education, Considered in Relation to Colored Men," MSC 45, Crummell Papers.

17. Isaiah Berlin, "The Counter Enlightenment," in *Dictionary of the History of Ideas* (New York: Scribners, 1973), vol. 2, pp. 100–112. Crummell gave no source for the quotation from Burke, which appeared at the beginning of his essay "God and the Nation," in *The Future of Africa,* p. 50.

18. Gregory Rigsby, *Alexander Crummell: Pioneer in Nineteenth Century Pan-African Thought* (Westport, Conn.: Greenwood, 1986), p. 182.

19. Crummell, "The Social Principle Among a People," in *The Greatness of Christ,* p. 290. Douglass, "The Nation's Problem," reprinted in Brotz, *Negro Social and Political Thought,* pp. 311–28. Also see Crummell's debate with Grimké in the *People's Advocate,* February 28, 1880, as discussed above.

20. Crummell, "Character the Great Thing," in Bragg, *History of the Afro-American Group of the Episcopal Church* (Baltimore: Church Advocate Press, 1922), pp. 262–66.

21. Crummell, "Common Sense in Common Schooling" (1886) and "Right Mindedness," in *Africa and America,* pp. 362, 366.

22. W.E.B. Du Bois, *Dusk of Dawn: An Essay Toward an Autobiography of a Race Concept* (New York: Harcourt Brace, 1940; reprint Shocken, 1971), p. 128.

23. W.E.B. Du Bois, "He Knew the Common Man . . . Followed His Fate," *The Guardian* (March 16, 1953). See Ali Mazrui, "Kwame Nkrumah: The Leninist Czar," reprinted in S. Okechukwu Mezu and Ram Desai, eds., *Black Leaders of the Centuries* (Buffalo: Black Academy Press, 1970), pp. 185–202.

24. Meier has overstated the continuity in Crummell's thought in his nonetheless very sound *Negro Thought in America,* pp. 42–43.

25. Ferris, *The African Abroad,* vol. 1, p. 416. Marcus Garvey, *Philosophy and Opinions of Marcus Garvey* (New York: Universal Publishing House, 1923–25), vol. 1, p. 43.

26. Emma Lou Thornbrough, *T. Thomas Fortune: Militant Journalist* (Chicago: University of Chicago Press, 1972).

27. William H. Ferris to Francis J. Grimké, January 20, 1921, in Woodson, ed., *The Works of Francis J. Grimké,* pp. 297–98.

28. Cromwell, *The Negro in American History,* p. 133.

29. See Moses, *Golden Age of Black Nationalism,* pp. 183, 193, and chap. 5.

30. Crummell, "Defence of the Negro Race in America," in *Africa and America,* p. 92.

31. Sterling Stuckey, *Slave Culture: Nationalist Theory and the Foundations of Black America* (New York: Oxford University Press, 1987). Rigsby, *Alexander Crummell: Pioneer.* Molefe K. Asanti, *Afrocentricity: The Theory of Social Change* (Buffalo: Amulefi Publishing Company, 1980). Cheikh Anta Diop, *Black Africa: The Economic and Cultural Basis for a Federated State* (Westport, Conn.: Lawrence Hill, 1974).

32. Crummell, "The Destined Superiority of the Negro," in *The Greatness of Christ,* p. 347.

# Bibliography

## A Note on Sources

When I began working on the life of Alexander Crummell, I was advised to limit the scope of my project and to concentrate on a systematic exposition of Crummell's ideas. I found, however, that in order to write an "intellectual biography" I would first have to do some detective work. This had the desirable result of bringing to light much information on Crummell that had been inaccessible, if not entirely forgotten.

There has not been a great deal of biographical writing on nineteenth-century black Americans. The sources are exceedingly limited. Public lives are difficult enough to reconstruct, because middle-class black people were all but invisible in nineteenth-century America. They were usually ignored by newspapers, in much the same way that they were ignored socially and politically. As Leon Litwack has ably demonstrated, they were grossly misrepresented in the census. Antebellum black communities did little better than the white majority when it came to preserving records of black middle-class life. Black institutions, with rare and remarkable exceptions, have not understood what it means to record history or to preserve historical documents, and very rarely, if at all, have they had either the wealth or the sophistication required to recognize the value of maintaining archives and employing archivists. Private lives are even more difficult to uncover. There are no great treasure troves of personal correspondence, because black families have not enjoyed the sort of economic stability that ensures the preservation of bourgeois life styles over several generations. As a result, photographs, diaries, heirlooms, and letters have often been lost. In the case of Crummell, we are somewhat fortunate, because although very little of his intimate correspondence has survived, the record of his intellectual life is well preserved, particularly in the area where his religious and political concerns overlapped.

Crummell never wrote a true autobiography, although he did publish his jubilee sermon, delivered on the fiftieth anniversary of his ordination: *Jubilate: 1844–1894, The Shades and Lights of a Fifty Years' Ministry* (Washington, D.C.: St. Luke's Church,

1894). A number of sermons contain passing autobiographical references, the most important of which are his eulogies on Thomas Sipkins Sidney and Henry Highland Garnet. There is also considerable information in his correspondence in *Spirit of Missions.*

## Scholarly Biographies of Alexander Crummell

A number of dissertations treat Crummell's life: Luckson Ejofodomi, "The Missionary Career of Alexander Crummell in Liberia, 1853 to 1873" (Ph.D. diss., Boston University, 1974); Ronald Fox, "The Reverend Alexander Crummell: An Apostle of Black Culture" (Ph.D. diss., General Theological Seminary, 1969); and John Oldfield (Ph.D. diss., Cambridge University). Nearing completion is a biography by C. R. Stockton. Gregory U. Rigsby, *Alexander Crummell: Pioneer in Nineteenth-Century Pan-African Thought* (Westport, Conn.: Greenwood Press, 1987), is based mainly on the papers in the Arthur A. Schomburg Collection, New York Public Library, and on the Papers of the Domestic and Foreign Missionary Society.

There are several early short accounts of Crummell's life, three of the most fascinating of which are George W. Forbes, "Alexander Crummell" (Rare Books Room, Boston Public Library, Typescript); William H. Ferris, *Alexander Crummell, An Apostle of Negro Culture,* American Negro Academy Occasional Papers, no. 20 (Washington, D.C.: American Negro Academy, 1926); W.E.B. Du Bois, "Of Alexander Crummell," in *The Souls of Black Folk* (Chicago: McClurg, 1903).

The following scholarly articles are generally considered the most important: Kathleen O'Mara Wahle, "Alexander Crummell: Black Evangelist and Pan Negro Patriot," *Phylon* (1968); Otey M. Scruggs, "We the Children of Africa in this Land," in *Africa and the Afro-American Experience,* ed. Lorraine A. Williams (Washington, D.C.: Howard University Press, 1977); Wilson J. Moses, *The Golden Age of Black Nationalism* (Hamden, Conn.: Archon Books, 1978), which contains a chapter on Crummell, an earlier version of which appeared in the *Journal of Negro History* (April 1975); and M. B. Akpan, "Alexander Crummell and His African Race Work," *Historical Magazine of the Protestant Episcopal Church,* June 1976, pp. 177–99. Also see August Meier, *Negro Thought in America, 1880–1915: Racial Ideologies in the Era of Booker T. Washington* (Ann Arbor: University of Michigan Press, 1963), pp. 42–43; C. R. Stockton, "The Integration of Cambridge: Alexander Crummell as Undergraduate, 1849–1853," *Integrated Education* (March–April 1977); and Alfred A. Moss, Jr., *The American Negro Academy: Voice of the Talented Tenth* (Baton Rouge: Louisiana State University Press, 1981).

## Collections of Published and Unpublished Manuscripts

The compilation of a definitive Crummell bibliography would require years of research in widely scattered collections. Fortunately, the major collection of Crummell materials in the Schomburg Collection of the New York Public Library is available on microfilm. I made two visits to the Liberian National Archives, shortly before the 1980 coup, but documents were mysteriously disappearing at that point. Luckson Ejofodami made use of the "Minutes of St. Luke's Protestant Episcopal Church," for his 1974 Boston University dissertation, but Richard Hewlett, Archivist of the Episcopal Diocese of Washington, informed me that he could find no record of that document, and that it had probably been destroyed before his administration. Amalie M. Kass shared with me the one letter from the Thomas Hodgkin Papers, which she had located in her many years of research. British collections must certainly contain other uncatalogued items, as does the Library of Congress.

Professor Richard Blackett graciously brought to my attention the fact that the Columbia University Library has a substantial collection of Crummell materials in the Jay Family Papers. Some of these have been microfilmed in *The Black Abolitionist Papers, 1830–1865,* edited by George E. Carter and Peter Ripley, for the Microfilming Corporation of America. The Episcopal Seminary of the Southwest in Austin, Texas, has an essential collection of Crummell correspondence covering the African years. There is a good collection of Crummell letters in the American Colonization Society Papers at the Library of Congress. Professor John Oldfield kindly brought to my attention the material in the Cambridge University Archives and in the Caius College Archives, Cambridge.

## Manuscript and Archival Sources

British and Foreign Anti-Slavery Papers. Rhodes House Library, Oxford University.

John E. Bruce Papers. Arthur A. Schomburg Collection, New York Public Library, New York, New York.

Church Missionary Society Papers, Church Missionary Society Archives, London.

Charles Clayton Diary. Library of Caius College, Cambridge University, Cambridge, England.

William M. Coates Papers. Historical Society of Pennsylvania, Philadelphia, Pennsylvania.

John W. Cromwell Family Papers. Manuscript Division. The Moorland-Spingarn Research Center, Howard University, Washington, D.C.

John W. Cromwell Papers. In Possession of Dr. Adelaide Cromwell, Boston University, Boston, Massachusetts.

Alexander Crummell Papers. Arthur A. Schomburg Collection, New York Public Library, New York, New York.

W. E. B. Du Bois Papers. University of Massachusetts Library, Amherst, Massachusetts.

George W. Forbes Papers. Rare Books Room. Boston Public Library, Boston, Massachusetts.

Francis J. Grimké Papers. Manuscript Division. The Moorland-Spingarn Research Center, Howard University, Washington, D.C.

Jay Family Papers. Rare Book and Manuscript Room. Butler Library, Columbia University, New York, New York.

Some of the Crummell material in the Jay Family Papers is reproduced in George E. Carter and Peter Ripley, eds., *The Black Abolitionist Papers, 1830–1865.* New York: Microfilming Corporation of America, 1981.

Foreign Correspondence. Liberian National Archives, Monrovia, Liberia.

List of Passengers Taken on Board of the *Mary Caroline Stevens.* Recorded April 5, 1861, Baltimore, Maryland. National Archives, Washington, D.C.

The Maryland Diocesan Archives. Housed in the Maryland Historical Society, Baltimore, Maryland.

Papers of the American Colonization Society. Library of Congress, Washington, D.C.

Papers of the Domestic and Foreign Missionary Society. Protestant Episcopal Church of the United States. Archives of the Episcopal Church, Austin, Texas.

Records of the Trustees of Donations for Education in Liberia. Massachusetts Historical Society, Boston, Massachusetts.

Joseph Romilly Diaries. Rare Book Room. Cambridge University Library, Cambridge, England.

Weld Papers. Library of Congress, Washington, D.C.

William R. Whittingham Papers. Maryland Diocesan Archives. Maryland Historical Society, Baltimore, Maryland.

Carter G. Woodson Collection, "Additional Manuscripts, 1807–1935, and Undated," and "Episcopal Church, Letters and Writings." Manuscript Division. Library of Congress, Washington, D.C.

Elizur Wright Papers. Library of Congress, Washington, D.C.

## Newspapers and Serial Publications

*African Repository*
*African Times*
*African Times and Orient Review*
*A.M.E. Church Review*
*The Anglo-African Magazine*
*Anti-Slavery Reporter*
*Anti-Slavery Standard*
*Bath and Cheltenham Gazette*
*Bath Herald*
*British Banner*
*Burke's Congressional Report*
*Cheltenham Examiner*
*Christian Recorder*
*Colored American*
*Diocesan Convention of Maryland, Parochial Reports*
*Douglass' Monthly*
*Frederick Douglass' Paper*
*Freedom's Journal*
*The Independent*
*Indianapolis Freeman*
*Journal of the General Convention of the Protestant Episcopal Church*
*The Liberator*
*Liberia Herald*
*Midland County Herald*
*New York Age*
*The Non-Slaveholder*
*The North Star*
*The People's Advocate*
*The Slave*
*Southern Workman*
*Spirit of Missions*
*Vineland Weekly*
*The Voice of Missions*
Washington *Bee*

Washington Post
Weekly Anglo African
The Woman's Era

## Other Published Sources

Address and Constitution of the Phoenix Society of New York and of the Auxiliary Ward Association. New York, 1833.

Akpan, M. B. "Alexander Crummell and His African Race Work." Historical Magazine of the Protestant Episcopal Church, June 1976, pp. 177–99.

Alison, Archibald. Essays on the Nature and Principles of Taste. Edinburgh, 1811; Boston: Cummings and Hilliard, 1812.

Allen, Gardner W. The Trustees of Donations for Education in Liberia. Boston: Thomas Todd, 1923.

Allen, William G. The American Prejudice Against Color. An Authentic Narrative Showing How Easily the Nation Got into an Uproar. London: Cash, 1853.

Andrews, Charles S. The History of the New York African Free Schools, from the Time of Their Establishment in 1787, to the Present Time. New York: Mahlon Day, 1830.

Appiah, Anthony. "The Uncompleted Argument." In "Race," Writing, and Difference. Edited by Henry Louis Gates. Chicago: University of Chicago Press, 1986.

Aptheker, Herbert, ed. A Documentary History of the Negro People in the United States. New York: Citadel Press, 1971.

Armistead, Wilson A. A Tribute for the Negro: Being a Vindication of the Moral, Intellectual, and Religious Capabilities of the Coloured Portion of Mankind with Particular Reference to the African Race. New York and London: Wilson G. Armistead, 1848.

Arnold, A. James. Modernism and Negritude: The Poetry and Poetics of Aimé Césaire. Cambridge, Mass.: Harvard University Press, 1981.

Arnold, Matthew. Essays in Criticism. London: Macmillan, 1902.

———. Essays in Criticism, First Series. A Critical Edition. Edited by Sister Thomas Marion Hoctor, S.S.J. Chicago: University of Chicago Press, 1968.

Asante, Molefe K. Afrocentricity: The Theory of Social Change. Buffalo, N.Y.: Amulefi, 1980.

Barker, Ernest, ed. The Politics of Aristotle. Oxford: Clarendon Press, 1946.

Barnes, Gilbert Hobbes. The Anti-Slavery Impulse, 1830–1844. New York: Appleton-Century, 1933. Reprint, with introduction by William G. McLoughlin. New York: Harcourt, Brace & World, 1964.

Barnes, Gilbert Hobbes, and Dwight L. Dumond, eds. Letters of Theodore Dwight Weld, Angelina Grimké Weld, and Sarah Grimké, 1822–1844. New York: Appleton-Century, 1934.

Barzun, Jacques. Darwin, Marx, and Wagner: A Critique of a Heritage, rev. 2nd ed. New York: Doubleday, 1958.

Bastide, Roger. African Civilizations in the New World. New York: Harper & Row, 1971.

Bell, Howard Holman, ed. Black Separatism and the Caribbean, 1860. Ann Arbor: University of Michigan Press, 1970.

———. Proceedings of the National Negro Conventions, 1830–1864. New York: Arno Press, 1969.

————. *Search for a Place: Black Separatism and Africa, 1860.* Ann Arbor: University of Michigan Press, 1971.

Bellah, Robert. *The Broken Covenant: American Civil Religion in Time of Trial.* New York: Seabury Press, 1975.

Bittle, William E., and Gilbert Geis. *The Longest Way Home: Chief Alfred C. Sam's Back to Africa Movement.* Detroit: Wayne State University Press, 1964.

Blackett, R.J.M. *Beating Against the Barriers: Biographical Essays in Nineteenth-Century Afro-American History.* Baton Rouge: Louisiana State University Press, 1986.

————. *Building an Antislavery Wall: Black Americans in the Atlantic Antislavery Movement, 1830–1860.* Baton Rouge: Lousiana State University Press, 1983.

Blassingame, John W. *The Frederick Douglass Papers.* New Haven, Conn., and London: Yale University Press, 1979—.

————. *The Slave Community: Plantation Life in the Antebellum South.* 2nd ed. New York: Oxford University Press, 1979.

Blyden, Edward Wilmot. *Christianity, Islam, and the Negro Race.* London: Whittingham, 1887.

————. *Liberia's Offering.* New York: John A. Gray, 1862.

————. *Selected Letters of Edward Wilmot Blyden.* Edited by Hollis R. Lynch. Millwood, N.Y.: KTO Press, 1978.

Blyden, Edward Wilmot, and Alexander Crummell. *Liberia: The Land of Promise to Free Colored Men.* Washington, D.C.: American Colonization Society, 1861.

Bodo, John R. *The Protestant Clergy and Public Issues, 1812–1848.* Princeton, N.J.: Princeton University Press, 1954.

Bone, Robert. *The Negro Novel in America.* New Haven, Conn.: Yale University Press, 1958.

Bowen, J.W.E., ed. *Africa and the American Negro, Held Under the Auspices of the Stewart Missionary Foundation of Gammon Theological Seminary in Connection with the Cotton States and International Exposition, December 13–15, 1895.* Atlanta: Gammon Theological Seminary, 1896.

Bracey, John H., Jr., August Meier, and Elliot Rudwick, eds. *Black Nationalism in America.* Indianapolis: Bobbs-Merrill, 1970.

Bragg, George Freeman. *History of the Afro-American Group of the Episcopal Church.* Baltimore: Church Advocate Press, 1922.

Brawley, Benjamin. *The Negro Genius: A New Appraisal of the Achievement of the American Negro in Literature and the Fine Arts.* New York: Dodd, Mead, 1937.

————. *A Social History of the American Negro.* New York: Macmillan, 1921.

Brotz, Howard, ed. *Negro Social and Political Thought, 1850–1920: Representative Texts.* New York: Basic Books, 1966.

Brown, William J. *The Life of William J. Brown of Providence, R.I.* Providence, 1883.

Brown, William Wells. *The American Fugitive in Europe: Sketches of Places and People Abroad.* Boston: John P. Jewett, 1855.

————. *The Black Man: His Antecedents, His Genius, and His Achievements.* New York: Thomas Hamilton, 1863.

————. *My Southern Home: or the South and Its People.* Boston: Brown, 1880.

————. *The Rising Son, or The Antecedents and Advancement of the Colored Race.* Boston: Brown, 1874.

Burder, Henry Foster. *Mental Discipline.* New York: Johnathan Leavitt; Boston: Crocker & Brewster, 1830.

Burkett, Randall K. *Black Redemption: Churchmen Speak for the Garvey Movement.* Philadelphia: Temple University Press, 1978.

Butler, Joseph, bishop of Durham. *Analogy of Religion to the Constitution and Course of Nature, to Which are Added two Brief Dissertations.* London, 1736.

Butler, Samuel. *Evolution Old and New, or the Theories of Buffon, Dr. Erasmus Darwin, and Lamarck, as Compared With that of Charles Darwin.* New York: Dutton, 1911.

Campbell, Penelope. *Maryland in Africa: The Maryland State Colonization Society, 1831–1857.* Urbana: University of Illinois Press, 1971.

Campbell, Robert. *A Pilgrimage to My Motherland: An Account of a Journey Among the Egbas and Yorubas of Central Africa in 1859–60.* In *Search for a Place: Black Separatism and Africa, 1860.* Edited by Howard Holman Bell. Ann Arbor: University of Michigan Press, 1971.

Carlyle, Thomas. *On Heroes, Hero Worship, and the Heroic in History.* London: Chapman and Hall, 1870.

———. *Latter Day Pamphlets.* New York: Harper, 1850.

———. *Sartor Resartus.* Boston: James Munroe, 1836.

Cassell, C. Abayomi. *Liberia: A History of the First African Republic.* New York: Fountainhead, 1970.

*Catalogue of the Officers and Students of the Oneida Institute.* Whitesboro, N.Y.: Oneida Institute Theological Association, 1836.

Chadwick, Owen. *The Victorian Church.* 2 vols. London: Black, 1960, 1970.

———. ed. *The Mind of the Oxford Movement.* Stanford, Calif.: Stanford University Press, 1960.

Channing, William Ellery. *Works of William Ellery Channing.* 6 vols. Boston: James Munroe, 1841–43.

Cox, La Wanda. *Lincoln and Black Freedom: A Study in Presidential Leadership.* Columbia: University of South Carolina Press, 1981.

Cromwell, John W. *History of the Bethel Literary and Historical Association, Being a Paper Read Before the Association on Founder's Day, February 24, 1896.* Washington, D.C.: Pendleton, 1896.

———. *The Negro in American History.* Washington, D.C.: American Negro Academy, 1914.

Crummell, Alexander. "Address to the Albany Convention." In *A Documentary History of the Negro People in the United States.* Edited by Herbert Aptheker. New York: Citadel Press, 1971.

———. *An Address Delivered at the Laying of the Corner Stone of St. Andrew's Church, Buchanan, Bassa County, Liberia, West Africa on the 24th of February, 1870.* Preston, Eng.: Oakney Caxton House, Fishergate, 1870.

———. "Address of Rev. Alexander Crummell at the Anniversary Meeting of the Massachussetts Colonization Society." In *Liberia: The Land of Promise to Free Colored Men.* Edited by Edward Wilmot Blyden and Alexander Crummell. Washington, D.C.: American Colonization Society, 1861.

———. *Africa and America: Addresses and Discourses.* Springfield, Mass.: Willey, 1891.

———. *The Future of Africa: Being Addresses, Sermons, Etc., Etc., Delivered in the Republic of Liberia.* New York: Charles Scribner, 1862.

———. *The Greatness of Christ and Other Sermons.* New York: Thomas Whittaker, 1882.

———. *Jubilate: 1844–1894, The Shades and Lights of a Fifty Years' Ministry.* Washington, D.C.: St. Luke's Church, 1894.

————. *The Solution of Problems: The Duty and Destiny of Man. The Annual Sermon at the Commencement of Wilberforce University, June 16th, 1895*. Reprint, from *A.M.E. Church Review*, April 1898.

————. *Statement to the Congregation of St. Luke's Church, Washington, D.C., Sunday morning September 17th, 1893, by Alexander Crummell Rector*. n.p., n.d.

————. *A Thanksgiving Sermon*. Washington, D.C., 1895.

————. "Tract No. 7. Speech of the Rev. Alexander Crummell at the Colonization Anniversary of New York." *African Repository*, September 1861.

Culp, D. W., ed. *Twentieth Century Negro Literature: or A Cyclopedia of Thought on the Vital Topics Relating to the American Negro*. Naperville, Ill.: J. L. Nichols, 1902.

Curry, Leonard P. *The Free Black in Urban America, 1800–1850: The Shadow of the Dream*. Chicago: University of Chicago Press, 1981.

Davis, Allison. *Leadership, Love, and Aggression*. New York: Harcourt Brace Jovanovich, 1983.

Davis, Arthur P., and Saunders Redding, eds. *Cavalcade: Negro American Writing from 1760 to the Present*. Boston: Houghton Mifflin, 1971.

Delany, Martin R. *The Condition, Elevation, Emigration, and Destiny of the Colored People of the United States*. Philadelphia: The Author, 1852. Reprint. New York: Arno Press, 1969.

————. *Official Report of the Niger Valley Exploring Party*. New York: Thomas Hamilton, 1861.

Dick, Robert C. *Black Protest: Issues and Tactics*. Westport, Conn.: Greenwood Press, 1974.

Dickens, Charles. *American Notes for General Circulation*. New York: Harper and Brothers, 1842.

Diop, Cheikh Anta. *Black Africa: The Economic and Cultural Basis for a Federated State*. Westport, Conn.: Lawrence Hill, 1978.

Douglass, Frederick. *Why Is the Negro Lynched? The Lesson of the Hour* [1894]. In *The Life and Writings of Frederick Douglass*. 4 vols. Edited by Philip S. Foner. New York: International Publishers, 1955.

————. *The Life and Times of Frederick Douglass*. 1892. Reprint. London: Collier-Macmillan, 1962.

————. *The Nation's Problem: A Speech Delivered at the Bethel Literary Society in Washington, D.C., April 16, 1889*. Washington, D.C., 1889.

Drachler, Jacob, ed. *Black Homeland/Black Diaspora: Cross Currents of the African Relationship*. Port Washington, N.Y.: Kennikat Press, 1975.

Drake, St. Clair. *The Redemption of Africa and Black Religion*. Chicago: Third World Press, 1970.

Draper, Theodore. *The Rediscovery of Black Nationalism*. New York: Viking, 1970.

Du Bois, W.E.B. *The Conservation of Races*. American Negro Academy Occasional Papers, no. 2. Washington, D.C.: American Negro Academy, 1897.

————. *Dark Princess*. New York: Harcourt, Brace, 1928.

————. *Dusk of Dawn: An Essay Toward an Autobiography of a Race Concept*. New York: Harcourt, Brace & World, 1940. Reprint. New York: Schocken, 1971.

————. *The Philadelphia Negro*. Philadelphia: University of Pennsylvania Press, 1899. Reprint. New York: Schocken, 1967.

————. *The Quest of the Silver Fleece*. Chicago: McClurg, 1911.

————. *The Souls of Black Folk*. Chicago: McClurg, 1903.

————. "The Talented Tenth." In *The Negro Problem: A Series of Articles by Representative American Negroes.* Booker T. Washington et al. New York: James Pott, 1903.

Dunbar, Paul Laurence. *The Complete Poems of Paul Laurence Dunbar.* New York: Dodd, Mead, 1913.

Earl, Riggins Renal, Jr. *Toward a Black Christian Ethic: A Study of Alexander Crummell and Albert Cleage.* Ann Arbor: University Microfilms, 1978.

Ejofodomi, Luckson. *The Missionary Career of Alexander Crummell in Liberia: 1853 to 1873.* Ann Arbor, Mich.: University Microfilms, 1974.

Emerson, Ralph Waldo. *The Collected Works of Ralph Waldo Emerson.* Cambridge, Mass.: Harvard University Press, 1971—.

Faduma, Orishatukeh. "In Memoriam: The Centenary of Sierra Leone." *A.M.E. Church Review,* October 1889, pp. 239–40.

Farrison, William E. *William Wells Brown: Author and Reformer.* Chicago: University of Chicago Press, 1969.

Ferris, William H. *The African Abroad, or His Evolution in Western Civilization: Tracing His Development Under Caucasian Milieu.* 2 vols. New Haven, Conn.: Tuttle, Morehouse, and Taylor, 1913.

————. *Alexander Crummell, An Apostle of Negro Culture.* American Negro Academy Occasional Papers, no. 20. Washington, D.C.: American Negro Academy, 1920.

Five Points Mission (by the Ladies of the Mission). *The Old Brewery and the New Mission House at Five Points.* New York: Stringer & Townsend, 1854.

Fogel, Robert W., and Stanley L. Engerman. *Time on the Cross.* Boston: Little, Brown, 1974.

Foley, Albert S. *Bishop Healy: Beloved Outcast.* New York: Farrar, Straus and Young, 1954.

Foner, Philip S., ed. *The Life and Writings of Frederick Douglass.* 4 vols. New York: International Publishers, 1950—.

————. *The Voice of Black America: Major Speeches by Negroes in the United States, 1797–1973.* New York: Capricorn Books, 1973.

Foner, Philip S., and George E. Walker, eds. *Proceedings of the Black State Conventions, 1840–1865.* Philadelphia: Temple University Press, 1979.

Fortune, Timothy Thomas. *Black and White: Land, Labor and Politics in the South.* New York: Fords, Howard & Hulbert, 1884. Reprint. New York: Arno Press, 1969.

Franklin, John Hope. *The Emancipation Proclamation.* Garden City, N.Y.: Doubleday (Anchor Books), 1965.

————. *George Washington Williams: A Biography.* Chicago: University of Chicago Press, 1985.

————. *Reconstruction After the Civil War.* Chicago: University of Chicago Press, 1961.

Frazier, E. Franklin. *Black Bourgeoisie: The Rise of a New Middle Class in the United States.* New York: Free Press, 1957.

————. "La Bourgeoisie Noire." In *Anthology of American Negro Literature.* Edited by V. F. Calverton. New York: Modern Library, 1929.

————. *The Negro in the United States.* New York: Macmillan, 1949.

Frederickson, George. *The Black Image in the White Mind.* New York: Harper & Row, 1971.

Freeman, Frederick. *Africa's Redemption: The Salvation of Our Country.* New York: Fanshaw, 1852.

Fuller, Edmund. *Prudence Crandall: An Incident of Racism in Nineteenth-Century Connecticut.* Middletown, Conn.: Wesleyan University Press, 1971.

Fullinwider, S. P. *The Mind and Mood of Black America.* Homewood, Ill.: Dorsey Press, 1969.

Garnet, Henry Highland. *An Address to the Slaves of the United States.* Troy, N.Y., 1848.

Garvey, Marcus. *"Home to Harlem:* An Insult to the Race." *Negro World,* September 29, 1928.

————. *Philosophy and Opinions of Marcus Garvey.* 2 vols. Edited by Amy Jacques Garvey. New York: Universal Publishing House, 1923, 1925.

Gates, Henry Louis, ed. *"Race," Writing, and Difference.* Chicago: University of Chicago Press, 1986.

Gayle, Addison, Jr. *Oak and Ivy: A Biography of Paul Laurence Dunbar.* New York: Doubleday, 1971.

Geiss, Imanuel. *Panafrikanismus.* Frankfurt am Main: Europäische Verlagsanstalt, 1968.

Genovese, Eugene D. *Roll, Jordan, Roll: The World the Slaves Made.* New York: Vintage Books, 1976.

Gilbert, Peter, ed. *The Selected Writings of John E. Bruce.* New York: Arno Press/New York Times, 1971.

Gloster, Hugh. "Sutton Griggs: Novelist of the New Negro." *Phylon* 4, no. 4 (1943), pp. 335–45.

Gould, Stephen Jay. *Time's Arrow, Time's Cycle.* Cambridge, Mass.: Harvard University Press, 1987.

Gray, J. H. *The Queens' College of St. Margaret and St. Bernard in the University of Cambridge.* London: Robinson, 1899.

Green, Constance McLaughlin. *The Secret City.* Princeton, N.J.: Princeton University Press, 1967.

Griggs, Sutton. *Imperium in Imperio.* Cincinnati: Editor Publishing Company, 1899.

Grimké, Charlotte Forten. *The Journal of Charlotte Forten.* Edited by Ray Allen Billington. New York: Collier Books, 1961.

Grimké, Francis James. *Works of Francis James Grimké.* 4 vols. Edited by Carter G. Woodson. Washington D.C.: Associated Publishers, 1942.

Grote, John. *An Examination of the Utilitarian Philosophy.* London: Bell and Daldy, 1870.

Gulliver, Adelaide Cromwell. "Minutes of the Meetings of the Negro American Society." *Journal of Negro History* 44, no. 1 (Winter 1979), pp. 59–69.

Gutman, Herbert G. *The Black Family in Slavery and Freedom, 1750–1925.* New York: Vintage Books, 1976.

Harlan, Louis R. *Booker T. Washington: The Making of a Black Leader, 1856–1901.* New York: Oxford University Press, 1972.

————. *Booker T. Washington: The Wizard of Tuskegee, 1901–1915.* New York: Oxford University Press, 1983.

————. *The Booker T. Washington Papers.* 14 vols. Urbana: University of Illinois Press, 1972–87.

Harris, M. A. *A Negro History Tour of Manhattan.* New York: Greenwood Press, 1968.

Harris, H. Sheldon, ed. *Paul Cuffe: Black America and the African Return.* New York: Simon and Schuster, 1972.

Headley, Joel Tyler. *The Great Riots of New York, 1712–1873.* New York: Treat, 1873.

Hill, Robert A. "The First England Years and After, 1912–1916." In *Marcus Garvey and the Vision of Africa,* edited by John Henrik Clarke. New York: Vintage Books, 1974.

Holly, James Theodore. *A Vindication of the Capacity of the Negro Race for Self Government and Civilized Progress as Demonstrated by Historical Events of the Haytian Revolution.* New Haven, Conn.: Afric-American Printing Company, 1857.

Huggins, Nathan Irvin. "Afro-American Studies and American Studies." In *American Character and Culture in the 1980s: Pluralistic Perspectives.* University of Massachusetts/Boston Occasional Papers, no. 1. Boston: University of Massachusetts, 1982.

————. *Harlem Renaissance.* New York: Oxford University Press, 1971.

Hull, Gloria T., ed. *Give Us Each Day: The Diary of Alice Dunbar-Nelson.* New York: Norton, 1984.

*Inventory of Church Archives in the District of Columbia.* Washington, D.C.: District of Columbia Historical Records Survey, Division of Professional and Service Projects, Works Progress Administration, 1940.

Jacoby, Russell. *Social Amnesia.* Boston: Beacon Press, 1975.

[Jay, John]. *A Tract for the Times by a Churchman.* New York, 1843.

Jay, William. *An Inquiry into the Character and Tendency of the American Colonization Society and the American Antislavery Societies.* In William Jay, *Miscellaneous Writings on Slavery.* New York, 1853.

————. *Miscellaneous Writings on Slavery.* New York, 1853.

Johnson, Charles S. *Shadow of the Plantation.* Chicago: University of Chicago Press, 1934.

Johnson, Douglas. *Guizot: Aspects of French History, 1787–1874.* London: Routledge & Kegan Paul, 1963.

King, Martin Luther, Jr. *Stride Toward Freedom: The Montgomery Story.* New York: Harper & Row, 1958.

Kletzing, H. F., and W. H. Crogman. *Progress of a Race, or The Remarkable Achievement of the Afro-American.* Atlanta: Nichols, 1897.

Kornweibel, Theodore. *No Crystal Stair: Black Life and the Messenger, 1917–1928.* Westport, Conn.: Greenwood Press, 1975.

Lasch, Christopher. *The Culture of Narcissism: American Life in an Age of Diminishing Expectations.* New York: Norton, 1978.

Levine, Lawrence W. *Black Culture and Black Consciousness: Afro-American Folk Thought from Slavery to Freedom.* New York: Oxford University Press, 1977.

Lewis, David Levering. *When Harlem Was in Vogue.* New York: Vintage Books, 1982.

Lincoln, Abraham. *The Collected Works of Abraham Lincoln.* 9 vols. Edited by Roy Basler. New Brunswick, N.J.: Rutgers University Press, 1953.

Lindsley, James Elliott. *This Planted Vine: A Narrative History of the Episcopal Diocese of New York.* New York: Harper & Row, 1984.

Litwack, Leon F. *North of Slavery: The Negro in the Free States, 1790–1860.* Chicago: University of Chicago Press, 1961.

Livingston, Thomas W. *Education and Race: A Biography of Edward Wilmot Blyden.* San Francisco: Glendessary Press, 1975.

Locke, Alain. *The Negro and His Music.* Washington, D.C.: Associates in Negro Folk Education, 1936.

————, ed. *The New Negro: An Interpretation.* New York: Albert & Charles Boni, 1925.

Logan, Rayford W. *The Betrayal of the Negro: From Rutherford B. Hayes to Woodrow Wilson*. New York: Collier Books, 1965.

Logan, Rayford W., and Michael R. Winston. *Dictionary of American Negro Biography*. New York: Norton, 1982.

Lovejoy, Arthur O. "The Argument for Organic Evolution Before the *Origin of Species, 1830–1858.*" In *Forerunners of Darwin: 1745–1859*. Edited by Bentley Glass, Oswei Temkin, and William L. Straus, Jr. Baltimore: Johns Hopkins University Press, 1959.

————. *The Great Chain of Being: A Study of the History of an Idea*. Cambridge, Mass.: Harvard University Press, 1936.

Lugenbeel, J. W. *Sketches of Liberia: Comprising a Brief Account of the Geography, Climate, Productions, and Diseases, of the Republic of Liberia*. Washington, D.C.: Alexander, 1850.

Lynch, Hollis R. *Edward Wilmot Blyden: Pan-Negro Patriot, 1832–1912*. London: Oxford University Press, 1967.

————, ed. *Black Spokesman: Selected Published Writings of Edward Wilmot Blyden*. New York: Humanities Press, 1971.

————, ed. *Selected Letters of Edward Wilmot Blyden*. New York: KTO Press, 1978.

Lynn, Kenneth S. "Regressive Historians." *American Scholar* 47 (Autumn 1978), pp. 471–500.

Malcolm X. *The End of White World Supremacy: Four Speeches by Malcolm X*. Edited by Imam Benjamin Karim. New York: Seaver Books, 1971.

Mathurin, Owen Charles. *Henry Sylvester Williams and the Origins of the Pan-African Movement, 1869–1911*. Westport, Conn.: Greenwood Press, 1976.

Mazrui, Ali. "Kwame Nkrumah: The Leninist Czar." In *Black Leaders of the Centuries*. Edited by S. Okechukwu Mezu and Ram Desai. Buffalo, N.Y.: Black Academy Press, 1970.

McLoughlin, William G. *The American Evangelicals, 1800–1900*. New York: Harper & Row, 1968.

McPherson, James M. *The Negro's Civil War: How American Negroes Felt and Acted During the War for the Union*. New York: Vintage Books, 1965.

Meier, August. *Negro Thought in America, 1880–1915: Racial Ideologies in the Age of Booker T. Washington*. Ann Arbor: University of Michigan Press, 1963.

Merriam, Mary Bates. *Home Life in Africa: A New Glimpse into an Old Corner of the World, Written for the Young People, by One of Their Friends Who Went There*. Boston: Williams, 1868.

Mill, John Stuart. *Dissertations and Discussions*. 4 vols. London: Parker, 1859–75.

Miller, Floyd J. *The Search for a Black Nationality: Black Emigration and Colonization, 1787–1863*. Urbana: University of Illinois Press, 1975.

Miller, Kelly. *Out of the House of Bondage*. New York: Neale, 1914.

Moses, Wilson J. *Black Messiahs and Uncle Toms: Social and Literary Manipulations of a Religious Myth*. University Park: Pennsylvania State University Press, 1982.

————. "Cambridge Platonism in West Africa: Alexander Crummell's Theory of Development and Culture Transfer." *New England Journal of Black Studies*, no. 3 (1983), pp. 60–77.

————. "Civilizing Missionary: A Study of Alexander Crummell." *Journal of Negro History*, April 1975, pp. 229–51.

————. *The Golden Age of Black Nationalism, 1850–1925*. Hamden, Conn.: Archon Books, 1978.

————. "The Poetics of Ethiopianism." *American Literature* 47, no. 3 (November 1975), pp. 411–25.

Moss, Alfred A., Jr. *The American Negro Academy: Voice of the Talented Tenth.* Baton Rouge: Louisiana State University Press, 1981.

Mossell, N. F., Mrs. *The Work of the Afro-American Woman.* Philadelphia: G. S. Ferguson, 1894.

Mowry, Arthur May. *The Dorr War, or the Constitutional Struggle in Rhode Island.* Providence: Preston & Rounds, 1901.

Moynihan, Daniel Patrick. "The Negro Family: The Case for National Action." In *The Moynihan Report and the Politics of Controversy.* Edited by Lee Rainwater and William L. Yancey. Cambridge, Mass.: MIT Press, 1967.

National Association of Colored Women. *A History of the Club Movement Among the Colored Women of the United States of America.* n.p., 1902.

Nell, William Cooper. *Colored Patriots of the American Revolution. With Sketches of Several Distinguished Colored Persons: To Which Is Added a Brief Survey of the Conditions and Prospects of Colored Americans.* Boston: R. F. Wallcutt, 1855.

Nesbit, William. *Four Months in Liberia, or African Colonization Exposed.* Pittsburgh: J. T. Shryock, 1855.

Nielson, David Gordon. *Black Ethos: Northern Urban Negro Life and Thought, 1890–1930.* Westport, Conn.: Greenwood Press, 1977.

Nisbet, Robert A. *History of the Idea of Progress.* New York: Basic Books, 1980.

Ofari, Earl. *"Let Your Motto Be Resistance": The Life and Thought of Henry Highland Garnet.* Boston: Beacon Press, 1972.

Ottley, Roi, and William Weatherby. *The Negro in New York.* New York: New York Public Library, 1967.

Paley, William. *Natural Theology: or, Evidence of the Existence and Attributes of the Deity, Collected from the Appearances of Nature.* New York, 1814.

Pease, Jane H., and William H. Pease. *They Who Would Be Free: Blacks' Search for Freedom, 1830–1861.* New York: Atheneum, 1974.

Penn, I. Garland. *The Afro-American Press and Its Editors.* Springfield, Mass.: Willey, 1891.

————. *The United Negro.* Atlanta: Luther, 1902. Reprint. New York: Negro Universities Press, 1969.

Pennington, James W. C. *The Fugitive Blacksmith: or, Events in the History of James W. C. Pennington, Pastor of a Presbyterian Church in New York, Formerly a Slave in the State of Maryland.* 3rd ed. London: Charles Gilpin, 1850.

————. *A Text Book of the Origin and History, &c. &c. of the Colored People.* Hartford, Conn.: Skinner 1841.

Peplow, Michael W., and Arthur P. Davis, eds. *The New Negro Renaissance: An Anthology.* New York: Holt, Rinehart and Winston, 1975.

Phillips, Henry L. *In Memoriam of the Late Rev. Alex Crummell, D. D.: An Address Delivered Before the American Negro Historical Society.* Philadelphia: Coleman Printery, 1899.

Pickens, William. *The New Negro: His Political, Civil, and Mental Status, And Related Essays.* New York: Neale, 1916.

Pinkney, Alphonso. *Red, Black, and Green: Black Nationalism in the United States.* London: Cambridge University Press, 1976.

Pollard, Sidney. *The Idea of Progress: History and Society.* New York: Basic Books, 1969.

Porter, Dorothy. "The Organized Educational Activities of Negro Literary Societies, 1828–1846." *Journal of Negro Education,* October 1936, pp. 556–66.

———, ed. *Negro Protest Pamphlets.* New York: Arno Press/New York Times, 1969.

Powdermaker, Hortense. *After Freedom: A Cultural Study in the Deep South.* New York: Viking, 1939.

Quarles, Benjamin. *Black Abolitionists.* New York: Oxford University Press, 1969.

———. *Frederick Douglass.* Washington, D.C.: Associated Publishers, 1948.

———. *The Negro in the Civil War.* Boston: Little, Brown, 1953,

———. *The Negro in the Making of America.* New York: Collier Books, 1969.

Rammelkamp, Julian. "The Providence Black Community." *Rhode Island History,* January 1948, pp. 20–33.

Read, Hollis. *The Negro Problem Solved, or Africa as She Was, as She Is, and as She Shall Be. Her Curse and Her Cure.* New York: Constantine, 1864.

Redkey, Edwin S. *Black Exodus: Black Nationalist and Back-to-Africa Movements, 1890–1910.* New Haven, Conn.: Yale University Press, 1969.

———. "The Flowering of Black Nationalism: Henry McNeal Turner and Marcus Garvey." In *Marcus Garvey and the Vision of Africa.* Edited by John Henrik Clarke. New York: Vintage Books, 1974.

———, ed. *Respect Black: The Writings and Speeches of Henry McNeal Turner.* New York: Arno Press, 1971.

Reynolds, Charles H., with Riggins R. Earl, Jr. "Alexander Crummell's Transformation of Bishop Butler's Ethics." *JRE* 6, no. 2 (1978), pp. 221–39.

Richardson, Nathaniel R. *Liberia's Past and Present.* London: Diplomatic Press and Publishing Company, 1959.

Rigsby, Gregory U. *Alexander Crummell: Pioneer in Nineteenth-Century Pan-African Thought.* Westport, Conn.: Greenwood Press, 1987.

Roosevelt, Theodore. *The Strenuous Life: Essays and Addresses.* New York: Century, 1902.

Schor, Joel. *Henry Highland Garnet: A Voice of Black Radicalism in the Nineteenth Century.* Westport, Conn.: Greenwood Press, 1977.

Schuyler, George S. *Black and Conservative: The Autobiography of George S. Schuyler.* New Rochelle, N.Y.: Arlington House, 1966.

Scott, Anna M. *Day Dawn in Africa, or Progress of the Protestant Episcopal Mission at Cape Palmas, West Africa.* n.p.: Protestant Episcopal Society for the Promotion of Evangelical Knowledge, 1858.

Scruggs, Otey M. "Two Black Patriarchs: Frederick Douglass and Alexander Crummell." *Afro-Americans in New York Life and History,* January 1982, pp. 17–30.

Scruggs, Otey M. "We the Children of Africa in This Land." In *Africa and the Afro-American Experience.* Edited by Lorraine A. Williams. Washington, D.C.: Howard University Press, 1977.

Shepperson, George. "Ethiopianism and African Nationalism." *Phylon* 14, no. 1 (1953), pp. 9–18.

Simmons, William J. *Men of Mark: Eminent, Progressive, and Rising.* Cleveland: George M. Rewell, 1887. Reprint. New York: Arno Press, 1968.

Sochen, June. *The Unbridgeable Gap: Blacks and Their Quest for the American Dream, 1900–1930.* Chicago: Rand McNally, 1972.

Stanton, William R. *The Leopard's Spots: Scientific Attitudes Toward Race in America, 1815–1859.* Chicago: University of Chicago Press, 1960.

Staudenraus, P. J. *The African Colonization Movement.* New York: Columbia University Press, 1961.

Steward, Theophilous G. "Washington and Crummell." *The Colored American,* November 19, 1898.

Still, Bayrd. *Urban America: A History with Documents.* Boston: Little, Brown, 1974.

Stockton, C. R. "The Integration of Cambridge: Alexander Crummell as Undergraduate, 1849–1853." *Integrated Education* 15 (March–April 1977), pp. 15–19.

Stuckey, Sterling. *The Ideological Origins of Black Nationalism.* Boston: Beacon Press, 1972.

————. *Slave Culture: Nationalist Theory and the Foundations of Black America.* New York: Oxford University Press, 1987.

Thomas, Lamont D. *Rise to Be a People: A Biography of Paul Cuffe.* Urbana and Chicago: University of Illinois Press, 1986.

Thornbrough, Emma Lou. *T. Thomas Fortune: Miliant Journalist.* Chicago: University of Chicago Press, 1972.

Thorpe, Earl E. *The Mind of the Negro: An Intellectual History of Afro-Americans.* Westport, Conn.: Negro Universities Press, 1970.

Tindall, John B. "The Liberian Exodus of 1878." *South Carolina Historical Magazine,* July 1952, pp. 133–45.

Todd, John. *The Student's Manual Designed by Specific Directions, to Aid in Forming and Strengthening the Intellectual and Moral Character and Habits of the Student.* Northampton, Eng.: Butler, 1835.

Toll, Robert C. *Blacking Up: The Minstrel Show in Nineteenth-Century America.* New York: Oxford University Press, 1974.

Toll, William. *The Resurgence of Race: Black Social Theory from Reconstruction to the Pan-African Conferences.* Philadelphia: Temple University Press, 1979.

Trollope, Frances. *Domestic Manners of the Americans.* London: Whittaker, Treacher, 1832. Reprint, with introduction by Donald Smalley. New York: Knopf, 1949.

Trotter, James M. *Music and Some Highly Musical People.* Boston: Lee and Shepard; New York: Charles T. Dillingham, 1878.

Turner, Darwin T. "W.E.B. Du Bois and the Theory of a Black Aesthetic." *Studies in the Literary Imagination* 7, no. 2 (1974), pp. 1–21.

Twain, Mark. *King Leopold's Soliloquy.* Boston: Warren, 1905.

Ullman, Victor. *Martin R. Delany: The Beginings of Black Nationalism.* Boston: Beacon Press, 1971.

Venn, John, and J. A. Venn, comps. *Alumni Cantabrigiensis: A Biographical List of all Known Students, Graduates, and Holders of Office at the University of Cambridge, from the Earliest Times to 1900.* Cambridge: Cambridge University Press, 1922–54.

Wahle, Kathleen O'Mara. "Alexander Crummell: Black Evangelist and Pan-Negro Patriot." *Phylon* (1968), pp. 388–95.

Walker, David. *An Appeal in Four Articles, Together with a Preamble, to the Colored Citizens of the World, but in Particular and very Expressly to Those of the United States of America.* Boston: David Walker, 1830. Reprint. New York: Arno Press, 1969.

Wallace, William Allen. *The History of Canaan, New Hampshire.* Concord, N.H.: Rumford Press, 1910.

Walton, Haynes, Jr., et al. "Henry Highland Garnet Revisited." *Journal of Negro History* (Winter 1983), pp. 80–92.

Ward, Samuel Ringgold. *Autobiography of a Fugitive Negro: His Anti-Slavery Labours in the United States, Canada and England.* London: Snow, 1855.

Warner, Robert. *New Haven Negroes: A Social History.* New Haven, Conn.: Yale University Press, 1940.

Washington, Booker T. *Black-Belt Diamonds: Gems from the Speeches, Addresses and Talks to Students of Booker T. Washington.* Edited by Victoria Earle Matthews. New York: Fortune and Scott, 1898.

———. *A New Negro for a New Century.* Chicago: American Publishing House, 1900.

———. *Up from Slavery* [1901]. In *The Booker T. Washington Papers.* Edited by Louis R. Harlan, vol. 1. Urbana: University of Illinois Press, 1972.

Watts, Isaac. *The Improvement of the Mind of a Supplement to the Art of Logick: Containing a Variety of Remarks and Rules for the Attainment and Communication of Useful Knowledge, in Religion, in the Sciences, and in Common Life.* London: Brackstone, 1741.

Wayland, Francis. *The Elements of Moral Science.* New York: Cooke, 1835.

Weisenburger, Francis P. "William Sanders Scarborough: Early Life and Years at Wilberforce." *Ohio History,* October 1962, pp. 204–26, 287–89.

———. "William Sanders Scarborough: Scholarship, the Negro, Religion, and Politics." *Ohio History,* January 1963, pp. 25–50, 85–88.

Welch, Richard E., Jr. *George Frisbie Hoar and the Half-Breed Republicans.* Cambridge, Mass.: Harvard University Press, 1971.

Wheatley, Phyllis. *The Life and Works of Phyllis Wheatley.* Edited by G. Herbert Renfro. Washington, D.C.: Robert Pendleton, 1916.

Whewell, William. *Lectures on the History of Moral Philosophy.* Cambridge: Deighton, Bell, 1862.

Whittier, John Greenleaf. *The Letters of John Greenleaf Whittier.* Edited by John B. Pickard. Cambridge, Mass.: Harvard University Press, 1975.

Wiley, Bell I., ed. *Slaves No More: Letters from Liberia, 1833–1869.* Lexington: University Press of Kentucky, 1980.

Williams, Peter, Jr. *A Discourse Delivered on the Death of Paul Cuffe, Before the New York African Institution, in the African Methodist Episcopal Zion Church, October 21, 1817.* New York: Young, 1817.

Williams, Samuel. *Four Years in Liberia: A Sketch of the Life of the Rev. Samuel Williams. With Remarks on the Missions, Manners and Customs of the Natives of Western Africa. Together with an Answer to Nesbit's Book.* Philadelphia: King and Baird, 1857.

Wilmore, Gayraud S. *Black Religion and Black Radicalism: An Examination of the Black Experience in Religion.* Garden City, N.Y.: Doubleday, 1973.

Wilson, John Leighton. *Western Africa: Its History, Condition and Prospects.* 1856. Reprint. New York: Harper & Row, 1969.

Women's Auxiliary to the National Council for the Committee on the Diocese, Washington Branch. *Historical Sketches of the Parishes and Missions in the Diocese of Washington.* Washington, D.C.: Women's Auxiliary, 1928.

Woodson, Carter G. *The African Background Outlined.* Washington, D.C.: Association for the Study of Negro Life and History, 1936.

———. *A Century of Negro Migration.* Washington, D.C.: Associated Publishers, 1918.

————. *The History of the Negro Church.* Washington, D.C.: Associated Publishers, 1921.

————. *The Miseducation of the Negro.* Washington, D.C.: Association for the Study of Negro Life and History, 1933.

————, ed. *The Mind of the Negro as Reflected in Letters Written During the Crisis, 1800–1860.* Washington, D.C.: Association for the Study of Negro Life and History, 1926.

Wylie, Kenneth G. *The Political Kingdoms of the Temne: Temne Government in Sierra Leone, 1825–1900.* New York: Africana, 1977.

# Appendix
## Constitution and By-Laws
## of the American Negro Academy

This document, originally published as an undated, four-page leaflet, was recently located by Dr. Adelaide Cromwell, Professor Emerita of Sociology at Boston University, among the papers of John W. Cromwell in her possession. Aware of the common belief that no copies of it had survived, she generously donated a copy to the present author in March 1989. W.J.M.

### The American Negro Academy.

This Academy is an organization of Authors, Scholars, Artists, and those distinguished in other walks of life, men of African descent, for the promotion of Letters, Science, and Art; for the creation, as far as possible, of a form of intellectual taste; for the encouragement and assistance of youthful, but hesitant, scholarship; for the stimulation of inventive and artistic powers; and for the promotion of the publication of works of merit.

### *Article 1.*
The officers of the Academy, to be elected annually, shall be a President, four Vice-Presidents, a Corresponding Secretary, a Recording Secretary, a Treasurer, and an Executive Committee of five persons, who shall perform the usual duties of such offices.

When onerous duties are judged to demand it, the Secretaries may be salaried men.

### *Article 2.*
The membership of the Academy shall be limited to fifty persons.

### *Article 3.*
The conditions of membership shall be:

(a) Candidates shall be men of Science, Letters and Art, or those distinguished in other walks of life.
(b) Candidates must be recommended by six enrolled members, in a written application, through one of the Secretaries.
(c) Admission to membership shall be by ballot—by a two-thirds vote of all the membership, voting in person or by proxy—due notice having been given, two months before the balloting, to every member.

### *Article 4.*
The Academy shall endeavor with care and diligence:

365

(a) To promote the publication of scholarly works;

(b) To aid youths of genius in the attainment of the higher culture, at home or abroad;

(c) To gather into its Archives valuable data, and the works of Negro Authors.

(d) To aid, by publications, the dissemination of the truth and the vindication of the Negro race from vicious assaults.

(e) To publish, if possible, an "ANNUAL" designed to raise the standard of intellectual endeavor among American Negroes.

## Article 5.

The Academy may invite authors and writers, members and others, to submit their proposed publications to the criticism and judgment of the Academy; and if they shall receive its approval, such publications may be issued under the recommendation of the Academy.

## Article 6.

The Annual Meetings of the Academy shall take place in the City of Washington, which shall be its seat, in the month of December, when papers shall be read, and such other exercises be held as the Academy, from year to year, may order.

## Article 7.

The admission fee to the Academy shall be $5.00 (including the first annual fee), and members shall be assessed annually $2.00, failure in payment of which for two years shall cause membership to cease. Special assessments may be made for publications.

## Article 8.

In the publications of the Academy no titles of degrees shall be joined to the names of the members.

## By-Laws.

1. Special Meetings of the Academy may be held at the call of the Executive Committee, when and where they may decide.

2. All Meetings of the Academy shall be opened with prayer.

3. Abstracts of all papers to be read before the Academy must be submitted to the Executive Committee before reading, and their decision regarding such papers will be final.

4. Papers and other literary productions brought before the Academy shall be limited to thirty minutes, except in case of the Annual Address by the President, to which this By-Law shall not apply.

5. Publications of the Academy of whatever kind shall be made only under authorization of the Executive Committee.

6. Foreigners of great distinction may be elected corresponding members of the Academy by a two-thirds vote of the members in attendance upon any regular meeting of the Academy, on condition that such persons have been recommended by the Executive Committee.

7. Amendments to the Constitution and By-Laws may be made by a two-thirds vote of members at any regular meeting subsequent to that in which they have been proposed.

# Index